Nonfiction Reading and Writing Workshops

Letters and Journals

Teacher's Guide

Comprehension Strategy
Making Inferences

Writing Focus
Letters and Journals

Program Consultants

Stephanie Harvey

P. David Pearson

Picture Credits

Page 4 (left) courtesy Stephanie Harvey, courtesy P. David Pearson; page 7 © Breck P. Kent, (inset) David M. Schlessor/Photo Researchers, Inc.; page 9 (first row) Kevin Schafer/Getty Images, Michael Nichols/National Geographic Image Collection, (second row) © Gerry Ellis/Minden Pictures, Scotts Bluff National Monument, (third row) ANT Photo Library, Andrew Chapman Photography bigcheez@vicnet.net.au; page 11 (top left) Culver Pictures, NY; page 11 (bottom right) M & C. Denis Huot-Bios/Auscape; pages 15, 32-33, 39 Culver Pictures, NY; pages 29, 30 Maurice & Katia Krafft/Auscape; pages 34-35 © Museum of the City of New York; pages 36-37 Library of Congress.

Info Pal icon art by John Haslam.

Produced through the worldwide resources of the National Geographic Society, John M. Fahey, Jr., President and Chief Executive Officer; Gilbert M. Grosvenor, Chairman of the Board; Nina D. Hoffman, Executive Vice President and President, Books and Education Publishing Group.

Prepared by National Geographic School Publishing

Ericka Markman, Senior Vice President and President, Children's Books and Education Publishing Group; Steve Mico, Vice President, Editorial Director; Marianne Hiland, Executive Editor; Jim Hiscott, Design Manager; Kristin Hanneman, Illustrations Manager; Matt Wascavage, Manager of Publishing Services; Sean Philpotts, Production Manager.

Manufacturing and Quality Control

Christopher A. Liedel, Chief Financial Officer; Phillip L. Schlosser, Director; Clifton M. Brown, Manager

Program Consultants

Stephanie Harvey, National Educational Consultant, Colorado; P. David Pearson, Professor and Dean, University of California, Berkeley

English Language Learners Consultant

Josefina Tinajero, Assistant Dean, College of Education, University of Texas at El Paso

Program Development

Mary Anne Wengel

Book Development

Morrison BookWorks

Book Design

Steven Curtis Design

Copyright ©2004 National Geographic Society

Published by the National Geographic Society
1145 17th Street, N.W.
Washington, D.C. 20036-4688

ISBN: 0-7922-4528-8

Printed in Canada.

Contents

About the Program

Goals

Teachers everywhere agree: students need more support and practice in reading and writing nonfiction. The *Nonfiction Reading and Writing Workshops* make up a program designed to provide explicit instruction in the strategies students need to read and write different kinds of informational text. The program develops the skills and strategies students need to

- Use comprehension strategies proven effective, based on research studies
- Understand a variety of nonfiction forms and genres

- Use the text features found in nonfiction
- Use the writing process for nonfiction forms
- Connect reading and writing

Program Consultants

The *Nonfiction Reading and Writing Workshops* make up a research-based program that incorporates the best teaching and learning practices that have been proven effective through carefully designed educational research. The program has been developed in conjunction with Stephanie Harvey and P. David Pearson, two nationally recognized educators and researchers.

Stephanie Harvey

Stephanie Harvey is a consultant and staff developer for the Public Education and Business Coalition in Denver, Colorado. She works with educators around the country, leading workshops and conducting classroom demonstrations. *Nonfiction Matters* and *Strategies That Work: Teaching Comprehension to Enhance Understanding* are two of her recent books.

P. David Pearson, PhD

P. David Pearson, PhD, is the Dean of the Graduate School of Education at the University of California, Berkeley. He is a former co-director of the Center for the Study of Reading and president of the National Reading Conference and the National Conference of Research in English. His numerous publications include the *Handbook of Reading Research*, now in its third volume, and *Reading Difficulties: Instruction and Assessment*.

Research-Based Instruction

The findings from numerous research studies and from the National Reading Panel's comprehensive review of educational research conclude that

Comprehension can be improved by explicit instruction that helps readers use specific comprehension strategies.

The *Nonfiction Reading and Writing Workshops* provide this instruction. This research-based program incorporates best practices that have been proven effective in nonfiction literacy instruction.

Good readers are active and purposeful readers who use a range of comprehension strategies to make sense of text. These strategies can be taught through carefully designed instruction. Each Workshop in the *Nonfiction Reading and Writing Workshops* begins with an explicit explanation of a comprehension strategy that is modeled by the teacher and followed by opportunities for students to use the strategy in guided and independent practice. The program develops these six reading comprehension strategies.

Reading Comprehension Strategies
Making Connections taps into students' prior knowledge and helps them connect what they read to personal experiences, other texts they have read, and general world knowledge.
Asking Questions encourages students to generate their own questions as they read, look for answers that may or may not be in the text, and self-monitor their own comprehension.
Visualizing shows students how to create mental images of what they are reading.
Making Inferences guides students in filling in the missing information that the writer has not stated in the text. This strategy helps students move beyond literal comprehension.
Determining Importance helps students recognize the big ideas and critically evaluate the author's intent. Students develop the ability to sift interesting details from stated and unstated main ideas in text.
Synthesizing helps students summarize the important ideas so they can think about what the information means to them and develop opinions, perspectives, and new ideas.

Components

Student Books

- The fifteen *Nonfiction Reading and Writing Workshops* are organized into three levels, according to the difficulty of the reading selection and application of the strategy.

- Each Workshop focuses on a specific reading comprehension strategy, as well as characteristics of one kind of nonfiction writing.

Level A	Level B	Level C

Level A

Personal Narrative
- Comprehension Strategy
  Visualizing
- Writing Focus
  Personal Narrative

Compare-Contrast Article
- Comprehension Strategy
  Asking Questions
- Writing Focus
  Compare-Contrast Essay

Articles Using Sequence
- Comprehension Strategy
  Determining Importance
- Writing Focus
  How-to Report

Interview
- Comprehension Strategy
  Making Inferences
- Writing Focus
  Interview

Visual Information
- Comprehension Strategy
  Making Connections
- Creating Visuals
  Maps

Level B

Cause-Effect Article
- Comprehension Strategy
  Asking Questions
- Writing Focus
  Explanation

Description
- Comprehension Strategy
  Visualizing
- Writing Focus
  Description

Informational Article
- Comprehension Strategy
  Determining Importance
- Writing Focus
  Informational Article

Feature Story
- Comprehension Strategy
  Making Connections
- Writing Focus
  Feature Story

Visual Information
- Comprehension Strategy
  Making Inferences
- Creating Visuals
  Diagrams

Level C

Problem-Solution Article
- Comprehension Strategy
  Synthesizing
- Writing Focus
  Problem-Solution Essay

Letters and Journals
- Comprehension Strategy
  Making Inferences
- Writing Focus
  Letters and Journals

Biographical Sketch
- Comprehension Strategy
  Asking Questions
- Writing Focus
  Biographical Sketch

Informational Article
- Comprehension Strategy
  Making Connections
- Writing Focus
  Informational Article

Visual Information
- Comprehension Strategy
  Determining Importance
- Creating Visuals
  Graphs

Teacher's Guides

- Each Workshop has a separate Teacher's Guide.

- Teacher's Guides provide explicit instruction and sample modeling for reading comprehension and writing strategies.

- Additionally, Teacher's Guides provide mini-lessons, strategies and materials for meeting individual needs, graphic organizers, and more.

Reading Comprehension and Writing Transparencies

- A set of transparencies is available for modeling reading comprehension and writing strategies.

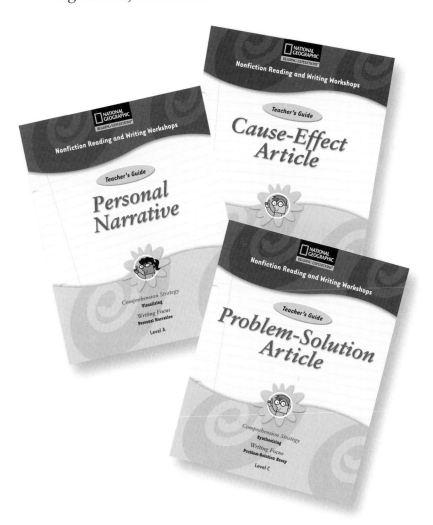

Managing Instruction

Flexibility

The *Nonfiction Reading and Writing Workshops* can easily become part of your regular reading and writing routines. You can use the Workshops in several ways.

- **Full Unit of Instruction** Use one of the Workshops as a 2–3 week reading and language arts unit of instruction. With this model, students might spend 4–5 days in the Reading Workshop before moving on to the Writing Workshop. Students can wrap up the unit by selecting from the "On Assignment" activities.

- **Reading Genre Study** Teach the Reading Workshop as a nonfiction genre study.

- **Writing Genre Study** Teach the Writing Workshop to focus on writing a specific nonfiction writing form. Help students prepare for formal writing tests.

- **Extend the Reading Workshops** Use the Reading Workshops to support students as they learn specific comprehension strategies. Provide additional strategy practice by using recommended titles from *Reading Expeditions*.

- **Supplement Core Instruction** Use the Workshops to supplement reading and writing skills and strategies introduced in core programs. The Workshops can be used in any order and can be easily integrated into your instructional sequence.

- **Center Work** Put copies of the Workshops in the Reading Center for students who need independent activities related to your reading and writing instruction.

Grouping Options

All students will benefit from your modeling of strategic reading, note-taking, responding, and following the steps of the writing process. Students learn best when they see what another reader and writer does. So, even if you plan to use the Workshops for independent work, set aside some time to model the strategies for students. Here is an instructional routine you might consider.

Introduce the Workshop to the Whole Group

- Teach the genre
- Model the reading strategy
- Model taking notes

Work with Individuals or Small Groups

- Guide practice
- Provide independent practice
- Use the mini-lessons for targeted instruction
- Use the easier selection for strategy practice

Bring the Whole Group Back Together

- Model using the graphic organizer to check understanding
- Pair students for sharing oral responses
- Model writing a response to the reading

Meeting Individual Needs

Nonfiction Reading and Writing Workshops are designed to support a wide range of students. You support students when you show them how to accomplish tasks, rather than just tell them. The *Nonfiction Reading and Writing Workshops* help you reach all students. The Teacher's Guides provide:

- Models for using reading and writing strategies

- Mini-lessons for extra support in reading comprehension strategies, using text features, and topics in writing

- An additional easier reading selection you can use with students who need more support

More Reading

The *Nonfiction Reading and Writing Workshops* include authentic reading selections from *Reading Expeditions, Windows on Literacy,* and *National Geographic Explorer* magazine. These can be ordered from National Geographic and can be used to support your teaching in reading and writing nonfiction. For more information, call 1-800-368-2728.

Assessment

The Reading and Writing Workshops help you to informally assess student progress.

- **Check Understanding** offers an opportunity to check whether students comprehended the important ideas and content presented in the reading selection. Sample answers shown on graphic organizers are provided on page 17 of the Teacher's Guide.

- **Write a Response** Use the criteria presented on page 18 of the Teacher's Guide to evaluate students' written responses to the reading selection.

- **Assess Writing** Use the rubric presented on page 24 of the Teacher's Guide to evaluate the writing products done in the Writing Workshops. The rubric uses the six writing traits as a basis for evaluation.

ELL Supporting English Language Learners

To be successful in mainstream academics, students acquiring English need to understand grade-level content as well as acquire the academic language to access that content. *Nonfiction Reading and Writing Workshops* help all students develop the skills and strategies they need to access and comprehend content-area reading. The program supports English Language Learners by

- Developing learning strategies that empower students to become more independent and self-directed in their learning

- Focusing on nonfiction text structures and features so that students see how to access the content in informational writing

- Using pictures and other visuals to provide comprehensible input

- Using graphic organizers as tools for understanding content and the connections among ideas

- Providing explicit instruction, modeling, and practice of key comprehension strategies

- Offering less challenging reading selections for initial strategy instruction

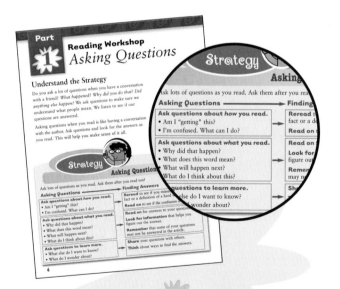

ELL Each Workshop provides explicit instruction and practice in a reading comprehension strategy. Students develop independent learning strategies.

ELL Building background at the start of each lesson taps into students' background and connects what they already know to what they are learning.

ELL Annotations support students in acquiring vocabulary and understanding how text features, such as titles and photographs, clarify content.

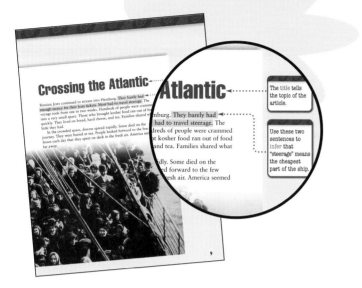

ELL Graphic organizers help students organize ideas and see ways concepts are related.

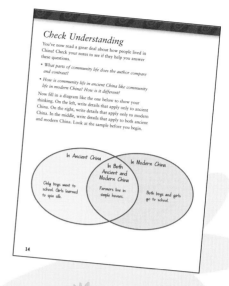

ELL Mini-lessons in the Teacher's Guide offer explicit instruction in a range of strategies that support English Language Learners.

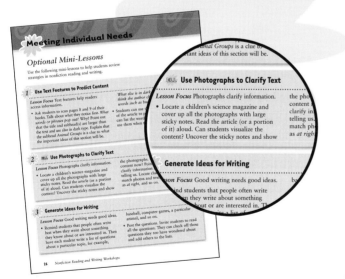

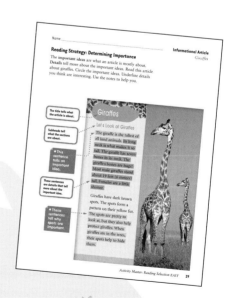

ELL Using an easier reading selection for initial reading strategy instruction allows students to develop grade-level skills.

Overview

Objectives

Reading Strategies

- Learn the strategy of **making inferences**
- Use **text features** to predict content: titles, subheads, historical photographs
- Use a **graphic organizer**
- Identify characteristics of **letters and journals**

Writing Strategies

- Use the **writing process** to write a letter or journal entry
- Use **prewriting** strategies
- Use **revising** strategies
- Use **traits** to evaluate writing
- Write in **response** to reading

Meeting Individual Needs

Reading and Writing Mini-Lessons

- Activate Prior Knowledge
- Understand Letter Form
- Writing for Your Audience

Using an Easier Reading Selection

- Learn the strategy of **making inferences**

Materials

Student Book

- Reading Workshop, "Making Inferences," pp. 6–15
- Writing Workshop, "Letters and Journals," pp. 16–21
- Extend, "On Assignment," pp. 22–24

Teacher's Guide Activity Masters

- Reading Selections
  EASY "On the Scene at Mount St. Helens," pp. 29–31
  AVERAGE "Crossing the Atlantic," pp. 32–37
- Graphic Organizer, p. 38
- Comprehension Model, p. 39
- Sample Draft, p. 40

Modeling Transparencies

- Comprehension Transparency C3
- Writing Transparency C4

More Books to Read

The following are other books that include letters and journal entries:

Reading Expeditions

Colonial Life
The Spirit of a New Nation
Our Journey West
Blue or Gray? A Family Divided

Windows on Literacy

Volcanoes

For more information about the Reading Expeditions and Windows on Literacy series, call 1-800-368-2728.

Before You Begin

Set the Stage

Collect some different examples of letters and journals for students to look through. Include invitations, e-mail, letters to the editor from newspapers, journals, and personal notes. Use them to provide examples of contemporary forms of communication.

Management Tips

• All students will benefit from teacher modeling of the comprehension strategies.

• Partner less experienced readers with proficient readers during guided practice of the strategies.

• Bring the whole group together to share responses.

• See pages 27 and 29–31 of this Teacher's Guide for a strategy lesson and a reading selection you can use for less experienced readers.

Introduction

 Student Book, page 4

 Activate Prior Knowledge

Show students a journal of yours (or use a volunteer's). Talk about the purpose of journals and how people use them. Ask:

Why do people keep journals?
How do you feel when you look back at something you have written?

Help students understand that a journal can be a way to record personal feelings.

Read aloud page 4 of the Student Book. Ask:

What is Sonya's great-grandmother writing about?
What clues tell you this journal was written about something that happened a long time ago?

If necessary, point out some of the clues, including the date of the entry and the fact that she is waiting for a letter, not a phone call.

 Student Book, page 5

Teach Letters and Journals

Introduce page 5 by explaining that letters and journals can be a window to the past because they offer a personal perspective on events. Read page 5 aloud. Point out that letters and journals can be used to write historical fiction. This is a genre in which factual information is used to create a fictional story.

With the class, generate a list of events they think people might want to know about their life and times 100 years from now. Ask:

How will people in the future learn about these events?
How might a letter or journal entry about one of these events be different from a news story about the same event?

Making Inferences

Understand the Strategy

Student Book, page 6

Introduce the Strategy

Remind students of Sonya's great-grandmother's journal. Ask:

Did Sonya's great-grandmother tell us everything we need to understand what exactly happened? How did we fill in the missing pieces?

Explain that we had to add information of our own: we had to know that many people immigrated to America. Talk about the strategy of making inferences. Read the steps of the strategy shown in the tinted box on page 6. As students preview, remind them to look carefully at the photographs since they can provide information about the time and place of the letters. (See also page 26 of this book for a mini-lesson on activating prior knowledge.)

Comprehension Transparency C3*

Model the Strategy

Before students read the letters and journals, use Transparency C3 to model the strategy

of making inferences. This transparency shows one page from *Our New Life in America*, the book from which the letters and journal entries are drawn.

Model the strategy: *Today we are going to learn about an event in history through letters and journals. I am going to show you how I make inferences when I read. As I read, I am going to stop and think aloud about the inferences I make.*

Read the transparency aloud. Use the Sample Think-Alouds to model making inferences. Review the key steps of the strategy as shown on page 6 of the Student Book:

- Read the words carefully.

- Study all the pictures.

- Ask questions about what you read.

- Use words, pictures, and what you already know.

- Look beyond the words and pictures to infer.

---

* Transparencies are available in a separate transparency package and also as Activity Masters at the end of this book. You may wish to create transparencies from these masters.

Making Inferences

> The date is a clue about *when* this journal entry was written. "

> From these words and the picture, I can infer that Emma's life is pretty hard. Maybe a war is going on. "

> From this, I can infer that they don't speak English. "

> From these phrases, I can infer that the trip is going to be dangerous. I think this family is risking a lot to come to America. I'm going to write that down. "

The family is planning a dangerous journey to escape Russia and come to America.

> The caption gives a clue that the *where* is Russia. "

Emma Markowitz

May 12, 1893

Father and Mother talked to us. We are leaving the Pale for America. I am scared and excited. Every day here seems worse. Soldiers are everywhere. Schools keep closing. Sometimes, I am frightened just to go to town. They say America is a land of opportunity. I do not believe, like others, that the streets are made of gold. But we would be free there.

Father says that I will have to work in America. I will also go to school. I will have to learn English. Nathan laughs when I talk about school. He says he doesn't miss it. He and his friends play in the forest all day. I read.

Father has made us all coats. Mine is not very pretty, but it is warm. Mother has sewn two gold pieces in her coat. It is most of our money. Father says the trip will cost a lot. We have to pay a guide to help us cross the Pale border. I hope we make it. I will miss my Bubbe. Who will laugh at her jokes? Not Grandfather. He is too serious, always reading.

Children selling strawberries at a rail station in Russia

from *Our New Life in America*

Think As You Read

Review the Reading Routine

Review with students the five steps of the reading routine on page 7 of their book. These steps provide a routine that good readers use. Students can use this routine before, during, and after they read anything.

Students need to read with a pencil in hand! See "Tools for Taking Notes" for note-taking options. Model how to use the tool of your choice.

Practice and Apply the Strategy

ELL Have Students Practice the Strategy

Guided Practice Ask students to read pages 8–11 of their books to make their own inferences about the trip, the people, and so on. Point out the annotations on pages 8–11 to students. Explain that these are hints to help them use the strategy. After reading, have volunteers share their notes. Ask:

> *What inferences did you make about the trip and the family?*

> *What other inferences did you make?*

Independent Practice Students can read pages 12–13 on their own. These pages do not provide strategy hints, so they can be used as independent practice.

Tools for Taking Notes

Choose one of these note-taking tools for your students to use as they read. Model using the tool for students.

 Use sticky notes

Provide students with sticky notes. They can write on them and place them in the margins. Suggest that they code their notes:

* = Words that help me visualize
? = I have a question
! = Remember this!

 Write in the margins

Provide students with a photocopy of the article on pages 8–13. Students can take their notes by writing in the margins, circling words and phrases, and so on. (See the Activity Masters on pages 32–37 of this Teacher's Guide.)

 Use a graphic organizer

Provide students with a photocopy of the Activity Master on page 38 of this Teacher's Guide. This Master is the same graphic organizer shown on page 7 of the Student Book. They can write facts and details in column 1 and anything they already know in column 2. They should write the inferences they make in column 3.

Check Understanding

Student Book, page 14

Activity Master, Teacher's Guide, page 38

Assess Content

Ask students to read the notes they took as they read "Crossing the Atlantic." Then provide a photocopy of the graphic organizer shown on page 38 of this Teacher's Guide. Students can write in the most important inferences they made and the information they used to make the inferences in columns 1 and 2. If students wrote in the margins or used sticky notes, model how to transfer their notes to the spaces on the graphic organizer. Sample answers are shown in the chart below.

Ask:

Will we all make the same inferences? Why or why not?

Point out that everyone brings his or her own knowledge and experience to a reading passage, and so the inferences they make may be different.

Review the Strategy

Talk with the class about how they used the strategy of making inferences. Write down their ideas. You might make a chart that shows their ideas and post it so students can refer to it when they read other nonfiction articles.

Here's a list of tips one class came up with.

ELL

What I Read	What I Infer
NATHAN • Nathan has a bad eye. • Sick people are rejected.	Nathan may not be able to stay in America.
EMMA • A doctor checked her for lice and she had her hair cut off.	There were probably lice in her long hair.
SASHA • The ship smells awful. • Sasha throws up a lot. • The ship is crowded.	The ship smells because everyone is sick in such a crowded place.
JACOB and SOPHIA • Jacob is a tailor. • Being a tailor is a good skill to have.	The family may be able to have a good life because he can get a job.

Activity Master 38

ELL

MAKING INFERENCES

- Read everything carefully.
- Check out the pictures. You can get information from the pictures that's not in the story.
- Ask questions to help you understand what you are reading.
- Think about what you know about the topic or how you might feel if you were in the situation.
- When you come to something weird, try to connect it to something you already know or something in the pictures.
- Sometimes reading on helps you figure things out.

Share and Respond

Have Students Share Responses

Ask students to read over the notes they took as they read. Have them think about their responses to the questions on page 15 of the Student Book:

What information was surprising or new?
What questions do you still have?

They can write some of their responses in column 3 of their graphic organizers.

Pair students so they can share their responses. Remind students that every reader brings his or her own interests and experiences to reading and that talking about our responses to what we read helps everyone learn more about a topic.

Write a Response

Have Students Write a Response

Ask each student to write a response to the article.

Student responses should include

Information from the article, for example,

- Jewish people fled Russia for America in the 1890s

- poor people traveled by steerage

- the journey was very difficult and many died on the way

Evidence the student used the strategy, for example,

- the student presents information inferred from reading the passage and some prior knowledge

- the student refers to pictures to make inferences

- the student asks questions about the content

Evidence of student thinking, for example,

- the student connects information in the passage to something he or she already knows

- the student states an opinion about what he or she has read

- the student makes a judgment about what he or she has read

2 Letters and Journals

Author's Chair

 Student Book, page 16

Share Writing Experiences

To introduce "Author's Chair" on page 16, ask students to think about and share some of their experiences as writers. Ask:

> *What have you written lately?*
> *How did you decide what to write about?*
> *What did you do to get information for your writing?*

Read the interview on page 16 with students to discover how Gare Thompson, the writer of *Our New Life in America,* works. Work with the class to create a list of possible interview questions, and write them on a chart. Then have students work with partners to write a list of questions about writing, for example, *How do you get good ideas to write about? What are you interested in? What do you know a lot about?* Have students share their questions, and add them to the chart paper. Each pair can then interview another pair of students, using their questions. Tell students the goal is to gather tips for writers.

After students have interviewed each other, collect the tips. Write them on the chart paper, and post them in the room for students to add to or refer to. Here are some tips one class listed. Leave space at the bottom so students can add additional tips. You can also use these tips as teaching opportunities to develop young writers.

ELL

TIPS FOR WRITERS

1. Start writing and see what happens.
2. Keep a journal of ideas.
3. Look at interesting books or websites to get new information.
4. Interview someone about something you want to know more about.
5. Have fun. Try to write as someone else.
6. Give your writing to someone to read.

Prewriting

Student Book, pages 17–18

Discuss Reading/Writing Connection

Have students read the first paragraph and the Reading/Writing Connection on page 17. Explain that the letter or journal entry they write should exhibit these features. Help students relate each feature to the list on page 5 of their books.

In this Writing Workshop, students have the option of writing a letter or journal entry about an event in their own lives or writing a letter or journal entry about an event in history, from the point of view of a person who experienced the event. The latter is a more sophisticated writing task. You may want to make the choice of writing about their own lives or as someone from history for students.

Discuss Writing as Yourself or as Someone from the Past

Remind students that letters and journals are personal. In a letter or journal, the writer describes an event as he or she sees it. Personal letters and journal entries also often include the writer's feelings about the event. Have students first discuss these questions in small groups. Then talk about their ideas as a class.

What is personal about the letters and journal entries on pages 10–11 of "Crossing the Atlantic"?
What kinds of information do you learn about the voyage by reading the letters and journals that you might not find in a history book?

Talking to Young Writers Tips for helping students select topics

Try the following to help students make decisions about what to write about.

- Encourage students to choose their own topics, even when the assignment has certain content requirements.
- Suggest that students keep lists of things they might like to write about. When you think of it, mention topics you'd like to write about too.
- Keep a class list on chart paper of possible writing topics. Let students add to it as they think of new topics.
- Read nonfiction books and magazines aloud to students. Point out personal reactions and

opinions that writers include when they write about real events.
- Encourage observation. Point out that it's the details that make reading about people and real events compelling. Ask students to begin watching people when they are at a ball game, running errands with family members, and such. Tell them to begin to notice the small things that people do. Not everyone does things in the same way.

Help students locate and point out phrases and descriptions from the letters and journal entries that tell about personal reactions, a personal perspective on factual events, and so on. Have students discuss the question in small groups then share their ideas as a class.

What are the most compelling parts of these letters and journal entries? (for example, the personal details, the description of the death of Pauline's sister, the conditions of the ship, and so on)

Think aloud about how you choose a topic. Write down topics, modeling for students how to choose a topic to write about. For example, *I am very interested in the Civil War. That is something I could write about. I'll put it on this topic list.* Talk through each topic, explaining how (or if) each could be compelling to a reader. See *Talking to Young Writers* for more tips.

Guide Pairing Facts and Feelings

Once students have chosen a topic, students should plan their writing. Using the graphic organizer on page 18 of the student book as an example, have students write the events they will write about in order. Create your own graphic organizer and model matching the facts of each event with possible feelings, using your own topic.

Students might also work together to pair facts and feelings. Have each student read the other's events. Students can then brainstorm ways people might feel. Students can ask each other questions, such as, *How do you think you would have felt? What specific words tell about how you felt?*

Have students record their responses on a graphic organizer like the one shown on page 18 to arrange their thoughts and feelings.

TOPIC LIST

the Civil War

the first moon landing

my grandparents

Talking to Young Writers Tips for helping students narrow their topics

Try the following to help students focus their writing.

- Tell students to focus on what interests them most about a topic.
- Ask students to name historical movies or books they have enjoyed. Ask: What was your favorite part? Why do you still remember it? What character did you find most compelling? Why? Then tell students to try to write with these ideas in mind.

- Tell students to focus on just one part of a big event. Writing about the day before a family's journey to a new land. This is more focused than the entire trip. Small topics are easier to write about and are more compelling to read about.
- Tell students to focus on a specific amount of time, such as a day or an hour.

Drafting

Student Book, page 19

Help Students Start Writing

Provide time for students to write. Assure them that there will be time to change and add to their selections, but that getting something down is important. Students can see a sample of a draft on page 19. This draft has punctuation errors, as well as errors of organization, clarity, word choice, and so on.

Take the time to model writing a letter or journal entry based on your own topic or one of the students' topics. Using the Writing Tip on page 19, check out the form of a letter and journal entry by looking back at "Crossing the Atlantic." Write quickly, getting ideas down. Then go back and think of ways to improve your writing. (See page 26 of this Teacher's Guide for mini-lessons on Understanding Letter Form and Writing for Your Audience.)

Revising and Editing

Student Book, pp. 20–21

Writing Transparency C4

Activity Master, Teacher's Guide, page 40

Model Revising the Draft

Writing Transparency C4 provides a copy of the student draft shown on page 19 of the Student Book. You can use the draft provided, or your own draft to model ways to revise and edit a draft. This draft is also shown here on the facing page. Using the

Revising Checklist (shown below and on page 20 of the Student Book), model for students how to begin revising and editing a draft. Use the Sample Think-Alouds as a starting point for your modeling. Students can practice revising and editing the draft on Activity Master 40.

Give students time to work on revising their own letters or journal entries. Ask: *Have you communicated your feelings along with the facts?* They may want to give their writing to a partner to evaluate and review. Together they can edit their drafts. Copy and distribute the Checklist for Letters and Journals (on the inside back cover of this Teacher's Guide) as a final review.

Revising Checklist

- Do I tell about a real event from one person's point of view?

- Do I include my own thoughts and feelings about the event?

- Have I used the words *I, you, me, mine, our,* and other pronouns?

- Does my writing sound like someone who is writing to a best friend?

- Do I use a heading, greeting, closing, and signature in a letter?

- Do I include the date and the place for a journal entry?

Sample Think-Alouds

Revising and Editing

❝ First, I'm going to check to see what the correct form is. It's a letter and all the parts are there. I'm going to correct the punctuation and capitalization in the date, place, and greeting. ❞

❝ I'm going to scan the letter to see what the event is. I think it's coming to Ellis Island, but I'm going to revise to make that clear. ❞

❝ If I change *We* and tell who *we* stands for, this sentence will be much clearer. ❞

❝ I think I want to include that people had medical exams here. That's a fact my reader might not know. ❞

April 25, 1896

New York city

Dear Maria, I will never forget today! We finally arrived at Ellis Island.
It was a long trip but we got there today. We were led off the   Papa,
                                                                     Mama,
ship and sent to stand in a long line in a huge building. I was excited—   and I
                                                grabbed
but also nervous, scared, and worried! I grabed Mama's warm hand.
                                             because I only speak Italian
I was confused by everyone speaking English. They spoke so fast,

asking questions and waiting for answers. I just stared at them as

they chattered.
                                                       immigrants
We had to get medical examinations.
    Papa said people in America are worried that we will bring eye
                                                              not sleeping.
diseases into the country. I knew I looked tired from the ship. I tried
         I didn't want to look like I had a disease.   puzzled
to look healthy. So there I was, waiting in line, puzzled by the language,

and worried about my eyes. But the worst was yet to come.
   A man
Some guy used a shoe hook to lift up my eyelid and look in my
                       the medical examination
eye—that really hurt! Then it was over, and my family moved into

another line.

Your friend from far away,

Rosaria Vitale

Sharing and Publishing

Student Book, page 21

Review with students the Sharing and Publishing options on page 21 of their books. Conference with groups and/or individuals regarding their publishing plans. Students might choose from the following ways to share their writing.

Print Media

- **Fast Facts** Students sharing facts uncovered in their research can use posters, charts, or time lines to illustrate how all the facts fit together.

Electronic Media

- **School Website** Students posting work on a school website can work together to find pictures to scan. Help students with other details, such as breaking pages, including folios, scanning in illustrations, creating boxes, and so on.

Performance

- **Oral History** Oral histories provide outgoing students with ways to share not only their writing, but also their feelings toward their subjects and research.

Assess Writing

The following rubric for letters and journal entries is based on a six-trait model of writing. It represents beginning, developing, and proficient performance.

Scoring Rubric

A well-written letter or journal entry

- Letter or journal format used correctly.
- Organized around facts and related impressions.
- Voice is natural and conversational. Voice used matches audience.
- Sentences are descriptive, balancing facts and feelings.
- Words are precise. Writing is easy to understand.
- Writing is free of mechanical errors.

An average letter or journal entry

- Letter or journal format used somewhat correctly.
- Organization is fairly clear. Not all impressions are based on facts.
- Does not have a natural sounding voice. Writing is sometimes inconsistent with audience.
- Sentences are fairly descriptive. Facts and feelings are not always matched.
- Some words are precise. Writing is relatively easy to understand.
- Writing has some mechanical errors.

A poorly written letter or journal entry

- Letter or journal format used incorrectly.
- Organization is not apparent. The letter or journal entry includes feelings, but few facts.
- Writing does not match audience. Voice is forced and not natural.
- Sentences are not descriptive. Facts and feelings are not presented or are not matched.
- Writing is vague and includes fragments. Only simple sentences are used.
- Writing has many mechanical errors.

Extend

On Assignment

 Student Book, pages 22–24

Review Concepts

Ask students to read "Look Back" on page 22 and to think about what they learned in this book. Prompt discussion with questions:

What strategy did you learn for reading?
Is anything still confusing?
How do you think you might use this information in the reading and writing you do?

Share responses to the question Sonya posed on page 4. (Students might say that using inferences can help people learn about other peoples' experiences.)

Discuss the Assignments

Read over the assignments on pages 22 and 23 with students. Note that the scope of these assignments is smaller than the Writing Workshop, but that each assignment requires students to read and write informational text.

Students might work in pairs or small groups to complete the activities. See the chart below for a brief summary of skills students will use while completing the assignment(s).

Direct students to the list of sources on page 24 of their books. Current Internet sites and books are listed. If possible, spend some time perusing these materials with the class.

Use this chart to help make assignments.

ELL Match Assignments and Students	Apply concepts	Research	Synthesize ideas	Use map skills	Use visuals to explain	Express ideas creatively
AVERAGE **Assignment 1:** Summarize a book for the class on immigration.	✓		✓			
EASY **Assignment 2:** Interview a recent immigrant.	✓		✓			
CHALLENGING **Assignment 3:** Draw a map showing immigration routes to the United States.	✓	✓	✓	✓	✓	
AVERAGE **Assignment 4:** Design a cut-away diagram of an Ellis Island building.	✓	✓	✓		✓	✓

Meeting Individual Needs

Optional Mini-Lessons

Use the following mini-lessons to help students become more proficient in reading and writing nonfiction.

1 ELL Activate Prior Knowledge

Lesson Focus Text features help readers activate prior knowledge.

- Write on the board *Things I Know*. Explain that prior knowledge is what we already know. Ask students to scan pages 8 and 9. Ask: *What do you already know about the picture or title?* List responses on the board.

- Students can continue with the rest of the article. They may need help with letter format but should be able to find bold heads and interpret photographs.

- Encourage students to ask questions about what they see. Sharing knowledge can help broaden individual students' knowledge base.

2 Understanding Letter Form

Lesson Focus Letter format helps readers understand content.

- Ask students to compare the letters on pages 10 and 12. Talk about their similarities. *What features are the same? Why do you think that is important?*

Explain that all letters are written with the same form. Ask: *Do you ever use this form?* (Students may use it with thank you cards.)

- Students can use text clues to infer other information about the letter—where it was written, who wrote it, who read it, and so on.

3 Writing for Your Audience

Lesson Focus Audience is who will read our writing.

- Explain that we act differently in different situations. Writing is the same way. We must remember whom we are writing to as we write. Ask: Do you speak differently to your grandmother than to your friends? How?

- Ask students to have an audience in mind as they write. Pair students up. Have one student play the writer and the other student play the person being written to. Students can create a "letter dialogue" between themselves.

Using an Easier Reading Selection

Activity Masters, Teacher's Guide pages 29–31, 38

Provide students who need an easier reading selection with copies of "On the Scene at Mount St. Helens," found on the Activity Masters on pages 29–31 of this Teacher's Guide.

Activate Prior Knowledge

Model previewing the article with students. Point out the title, the photographs, and the subheads. Ask:

> *What do you notice about the subheads?* (They each tell the time and date.)
> *What kind of article do you predict this will be, based on the title and the subheads?* (Help students understand that this is a journal excerpt.)
> *By looking at the pictures and the journal entries, what do you think the writer is describing?* (what it was like when Mount St. Helens erupted)

Model using the photographs and the subheads to predict the content of the article.

Model the Strategy

Show students how to use the strategy of **making inferences**. Think aloud as you read and take notes on all or a portion of "On the Scene at Mount St. Helens." Use the margin notes on the first page as a guide. (See strategy steps on page 14 of this Teacher's Guide.) Show students how to connect words and phrases to what you already know to make an inference.

Guide Practice

Guide students as they read and take notes. Students might circle two related things and write what they infer in the margins. You may want to read the article aloud first with students and then have them go back and use the strategy.

Assess

Ask students to share their notes. You might draw a chart like the one shown here on the board. (Or use Activity Master 38 to model in a small group.) Working with all the ideas students offer, help them make inferences using what they read and write the information in the appropriate places on the chart. Make sure students understand that they may have to use prior knowledge to make inferences.

Discuss the article with students. Ask:

> *What did you learn?*
> *What else do you want to know?*
> *What questions do you have for the author?*

Together, jot down responses in column 3. Share yours as well.

What I Read	What I Infer	Personal Responses and Questions

Activity Masters

Contents

Activity Master	Purpose
Activity Masters 29–31 Reading Selection *EASY* "On the Scene at Mount St. Helens" from *Volcanoes*	• Provides more practice in using the strategy • Provides strategy instruction for less experienced readers
Activity Masters 32–37 Reading Selection *AVERAGE* "Crossing the Atlantic" from *Our New Life in America*	• Provides a copy of the article in the Student's Book. With this copy, students can take notes right on the text.
Activity Master 38 Graphic Organizer	• Provides a tool students can use during reading
Activity Master 39 Comprehension Model	• Provides a copy of the transparency used to model the Comprehension Strategy. You can use this to make your own transparency, or you can provide a copy to students to follow along as you model the strategy.
Activity Master 40 Sample Draft	• Provides a copy of the transparency used to model Revising and Editing. You can use this to make your own transparency, or you can provide a copy to students to follow along as you model the strategy.

Reading Strategy: Making Inferences

Readers use clues in the writing and in pictures to **infer** what unfamiliar words mean and how to figure out puzzling events. Read these journal entries about Mount St. Helens. Circle words and phrases that help you make inferences. Then write your inferences in the margins. Use the notes to help you.

The title tells what the article is about.

The subhead tells the date of the journal entry. Remember: this article is made up of journal entries.

This word could help you infer that Mount St. Helens is a volcano.

These words could help you infer that the gas and ash turned the sky black.

Introduction

On the Scene at Mount St. Helens

Sunday Evening, May 18, 1980

I woke up to a beautiful Sunday. It was a bright, sunny day. I looked out my window. I could see Mount St. Helens in the distance. The snowcapped mountain shone in the sun. I could see the deep green forests covering its slopes. Below, a crystal clear lake sparkled.

Then, at 8:32 a.m., I heard a tremendous explosion. I was knocked off my feet. I rushed to the window. The volcano had blown! All I could see was a big cloud of gas, ash, and steam. The sky had turned black.

I learned later that the blast was so loud that people 200 miles (322 kilometers) away heard it. The sky was dark for more than 250 miles (402 kilometers).

Directions

Read this page. Take notes as you read. Circle words and phrases that help you infer and fill in the missing pieces. Write the inferences you make in the margins. Use the notes to help you.

> You can infer from this that Mount St. Helens is part of the Cascade Mountains.

> This subhead tells you this entry was written on a different day.

No one should have been surprised by this blast. Scientists knew it was coming. In March, the mountain began to send out a little steam and ash. Then, a bulge grew on one side of the mountain. The bulge grew bigger and bigger. By mid-May, it looked like a huge blister about to pop.

This isn't the first time that Mount St. Helens has exploded. Native Americans who have lived in the Cascade Mountains for a long time call Mount St. Helens "Fire Mountain." It has blown up five times in the last 280 years. The last time was in 1857.

► Monday Evening, May 19, 1980

I continued to watch the mountain send out red-hot rock and steaming mud. I saw rocks thrown high into the air. The hot ash and burning rocks melted the snow. I watched a boiling river of mud race down the mountain. It destroyed everything in its path.

▼ This car was buried under the ash that blew from Mount St. Helens.

Name ....

Letters and Journals

*On the Scene at
Mount St. Helens*

Directions

Read this page. Circle ideas related to what you already know.
Make inferences in the margin. Take other notes as you read.

Sunday Evening, May 25, 1980

Another smaller blast took place this morning. The sky was dark with ash and smoke again. The street lights came on in some places.

Gray ash covers everything. People are shoveling it out of the streets. Some towns are using snowplows to clear the ash away. The land looks like pictures of the moon. Will anything ever grow here again?

Think About What You Read

Do you have questions about what you read? Write down what you still wonder about the explosion of Mount St. Helens.

I wonder _____

_____

_____

_____

Practice and Apply the Strategy

Try out the strategy of making inferences as you read about one family's journey to America. Remember, read the selection one part at a time. The margin notes will help you get started.

Use this background information for previewing.

In the 1800s, many Jewish families were forced to flee Russia to escape the discrimination that Jewish people faced there. This story tells what life was like for the Markowitz family as they fled from Russia in 1893. The family includes the father Jacob; the mother Sofia; an older son Sasha, 16; a daughter Emma, 12; and a younger son Nathan, 9. They travel to Hamburg, Germany, to begin their long and difficult journey to the United States. Their letters and journal entries are based on real experiences.

Crossing the Atlantic

Russian Jews continued to stream into Hamburg. They barely had enough money for their boat tickets. Most had to travel steerage. The voyage took from one to two weeks. Hundreds of people were crammed into a very small space. Those who brought kosher food ran out of food quickly. They lived on bread, hard cheese, and tea. Families shared what little they had.

In the crowded space, disease spread rapidly. Some died on the journey. They were buried at sea. People looked forward to the few hours each day that they spent on deck in the fresh air. America seemed far away.

The title tells the topic of the article.

Use these two sentences to infer that "steerage" means the cheapest part of the ship.

Connect the photo and the text to infer that the ship was very crowded.

Practice and Apply the Strategy

Use the strategy to make inferences about this part of the selection. Look for clues that can help you. Then write down the inferences you make.

Use the first sentence and the heading to infer that the ship's name is the S.S. Nightingale.

Use these details to infer that life in steerage was pretty bad.

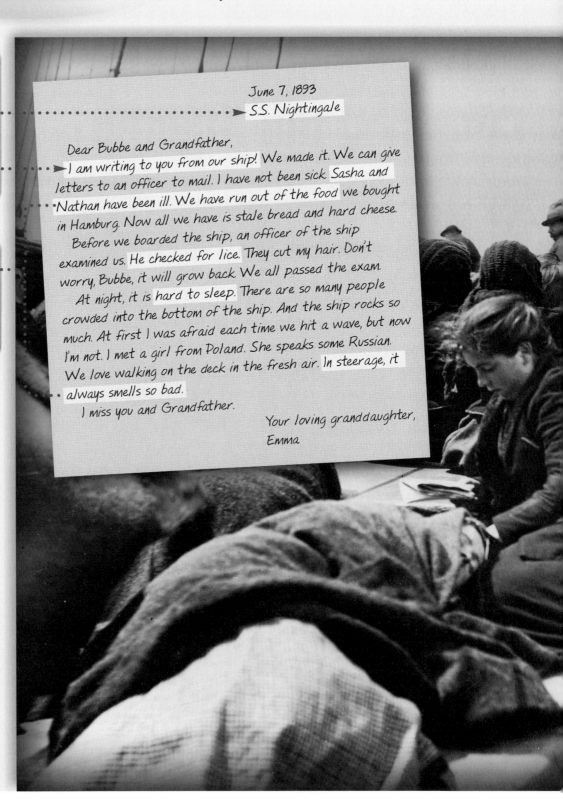

June 7, 1893
S.S. Nightingale

Dear Bubbe and Grandfather,
I am writing to you from our ship! We made it. We can give letters to an officer to mail. I have not been sick. Sasha and Nathan have been ill. We have run out of the food we bought in Hamburg. Now all we have is stale bread and hard cheese.
   Before we boarded the ship, an officer of the ship examined us. He checked for lice. They cut my hair. Don't worry, Bubbe, it will grow back. We all passed the exam.
   At night, it is hard to sleep. There are so many people crowded into the bottom of the ship. And the ship rocks so much. At first I was afraid each time we hit a wave, but now I'm not. I met a girl from Poland. She speaks some Russian. We love walking on the deck in the fresh air. In steerage, it always smells so bad.
   I miss you and Grandfather.

                                   Your loving granddaughter,
                                   Emma

Family member's name and date of journal entry

Sasha Markowitz

June 8, 1893

I hate this ship. It smells awful. This is worse than the army, but it is only for one week. Emma has not been sick. I have been sick almost every day. I spend all my time sleeping or throwing up. It is so crowded I sleep standing up. I can't sleep at night, so I count the bugs crawling up the wall. I want to scratch all the time. I think we will never get there.

Emma Markowitz

June 9, 1893

My friend Pauline's sister died last night. It was so sad. There was nothing we could do. Pauline's mother just held her. Today her parents buried her. It was horrible. They tied her body in a sheet. Then they put her overboard into the water. We said prayers, but it was not the same. Poor Pauline. All she does now is cry. I hope she does not get sick. Mother is worried about Nathan. His eyes are red and puffy.

Sasha Markowitz

June 10, 1893

At last, one day without being sick! Nathan is a little better, too. Only one eye now looks strange. I call him Cyclops, the one-eyed monster. We are allowed on the deck for short periods of time. The other people stare at us. I think I look like a scarecrow. Even the birds do not come near me. I want a bath and good food.

These personal reactions help you infer that Sasha is angry and depressed.

Use these details to infer that people who got sick sometimes died.

Use these details and reactions to infer how Sasha and Nathan look.

Using the photo, what can you infer about life on the ship?

Practice and Apply the Strategy

Use what you have learned about inferring to help you understand this part. Remember to use clues in the writing and in the pictures to help you make an inference. Read and take notes on your own.

Ellis Island

> These details help you infer that the statue is the Statue of Liberty.

June 13, 1893
S.S. Nightingale

Dear Bubbe and Grandfather,
We are almost there. I am on deck. It is sunny. That is a good sign. In the distance we can see a statue. It is tall. It looks like a lady with a torch. She is wearing a crown, too. I think I hear her calling us. It is just the birds. But she is an amazing sight.

When the ship docks, we will have to go to Ellis Island. There doctors will check us. We are worried about Nathan. One of his eyes is still pink. If he is sick, will Mother have to go back with him?

A man noticed Father's coat. He asked if Father was a tailor. The man said that being a tailor is a good job. Father can make lots of money. The man's cousin has three people who work for him! He must live in a fine house and be rich. I am learning English. "How do you do?"

Your loving granddaughter,

Emma

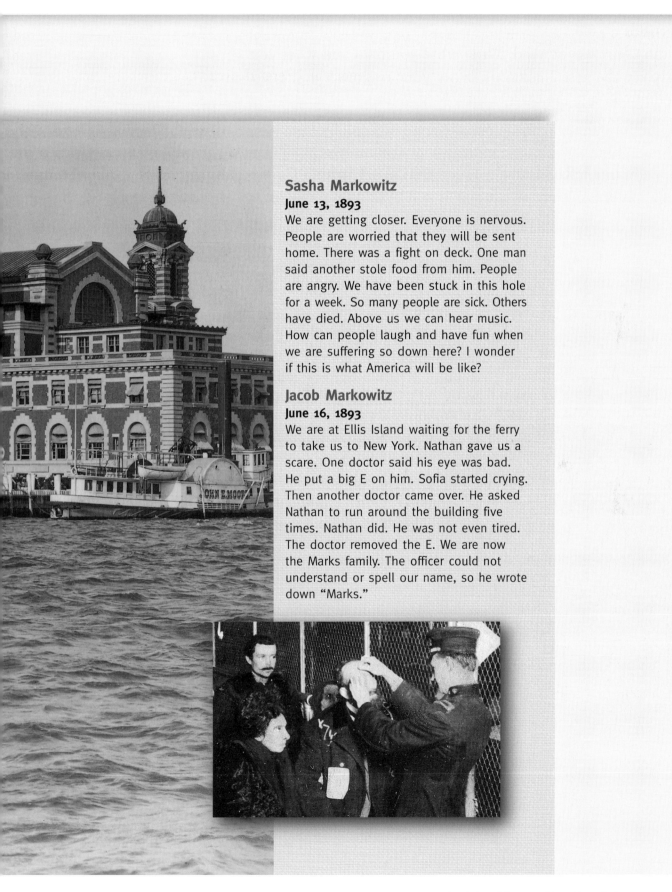

Sasha Markowitz
June 13, 1893
We are getting closer. Everyone is nervous. People are worried that they will be sent home. There was a fight on deck. One man said another stole food from him. People are angry. We have been stuck in this hole for a week. So many people are sick. Others have died. Above us we can hear music. How can people laugh and have fun when we are suffering so down here? I wonder if this is what America will be like?

Jacob Markowitz
June 16, 1893
We are at Ellis Island waiting for the ferry to take us to New York. Nathan gave us a scare. One doctor said his eye was bad. He put a big E on him. Sofia started crying. Then another doctor came over. He asked Nathan to run around the building five times. Nathan did. He was not even tired. The doctor removed the E. We are now the Marks family. The officer could not understand or spell our name, so he wrote down "Marks."

Taking Notes

Directions

Use this chart as you read. Write what you read and what you inferred in the first 2 columns. Write your responses and questions in column 3.

What I Read	What I Infer	Personal Responses and Questions

Name ....

Letters and Journals

Comprehension Model

Emma Markowitz
May 12, 1893

Father and Mother talked to us. We are leaving the Pale for America. I am scared and excited. Every day here seems worse. Soldiers are everywhere. Schools keep closing. Sometimes, I am frightened just to go to town. They say America is a land of opportunity. I do not believe, like others, that the streets are made of gold. But we would be free there.

Father says that I will have to work in America. I will also go to school. I will have to learn English. Nathan laughs when I talk about school. He says he doesn't miss it. He and his friends play in the forest all day. I read.

Father has made us all coats. Mine is not very pretty, but it is warm. Mother has sewn two gold pieces in her coat. It is most of our money. Father says the trip will cost a lot. We have to pay a guide to help us cross the Pale border. I hope we make it. I will miss my Bubbe. Who will laugh at her jokes? Not Grandfather. He is too serious, always reading.

Children selling strawberries at a rail station in Russia

Revising a Draft

Directions

Read this draft of a letter. Use the Revising Checklist on page 20 of the Student Book and make changes. Share your revising ideas with a partner.

April 25 1896

New York city

Dear Maria

It was a long trip but we got there today. We were led off the ship and sent to stand in a long line in a huge building. I was excited—but also nervous, scared, and worried! I grabed Mamas warm hand. I was confused by everyone speaking English. They spoke so fast, asking questions and waiting for answers. I just stared at them as they chattered.

Papa said people in America are worried that we will bring eye diseases into the country. I knew I looked tired from the ship. I tried to look healthy. So there I was, waiting in line, puzled by the language, and worried about my eyes. But the worst was yet to come. Some guy used a shoe hook to lift up my eyelid and look in my eye—that really hurt! Then it was over, and my family moved into another line.

Your friend from far away,

Rosaria Vitale

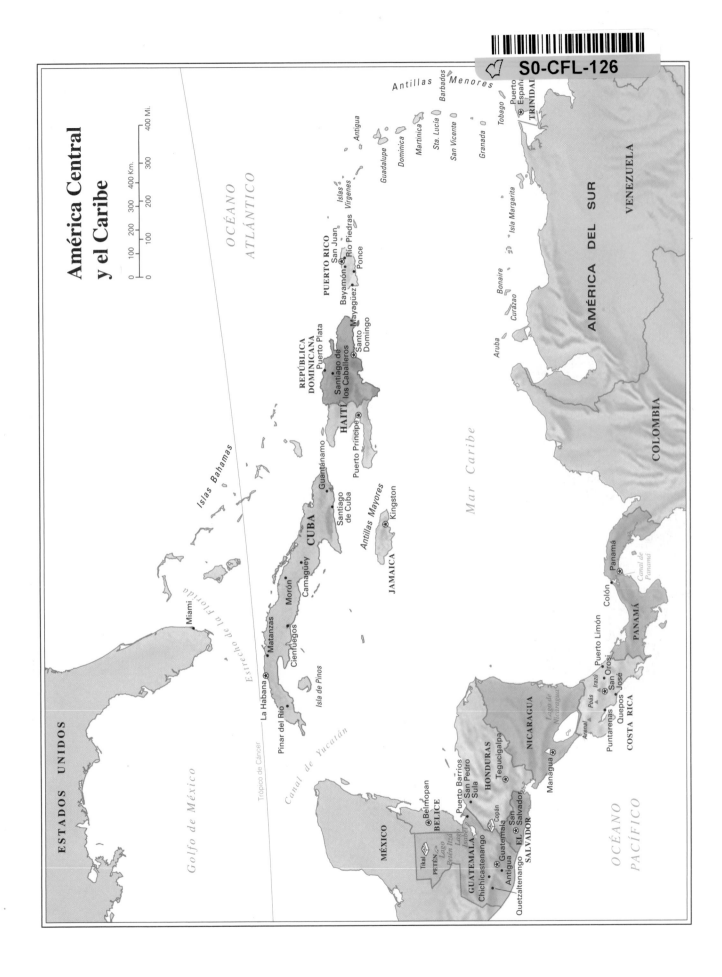

América Central y el Caribe

ESTADOS UNIDOS

Miami

Golfo de México

Trópico de Cáncer

MÉXICO

Canal de Yucatán

Estrecho de la Florida

OCÉANO ATLÁNTICO

0   100   200   300   400 Km.
0   100   200   300   400 Mi.

Islas Bahamas

La Habana ⊕
Pinar del Río
Matanzas
Cienfuegos
Morón
Camagüey
Isla de Pinos

CUBA

Santiago de Cuba
Guantánamo

Antillas Mayores

JAMAICA
Kingston

REPÚBLICA DOMINICANA
Puerto Plata
Santiago de los Caballeros
HAITÍ
Santo Domingo
Puerto Príncipe ⊕

PUERTO RICO
San Juan
Bayamón ● Río Piedras
Mayagüez ● Ponce

Islas Vírgenes

Antigua

Guadalupe

Dominica

Martinica

Sta. Lucía

San Vicente

Barbados

Granada

Antillas Menores

Tobago

Puerto España ⊕
TRINIDAD

Mar Caribe

Isla Margarita

Aruba
Curazao
Bonaire

VENEZUELA

AMÉRICA DEL SUR

COLOMBIA

Tikal
PETÉN
Lago Petén Itzá
Lago Izabal

Belmopan ⊕
BELICE

Puerto Barrios
San Pedro Sula

Copán

HONDURAS
Tegucigalpa ⊕

Guatemala ⊕
Antigua
GUATEMALA
Chichicastenango
Quetzaltenango
San Salvador ⊕
EL SALVADOR

Managua ⊕
NICARAGUA
Lago de Nicaragua

Arenal

Poás
Irazú ● San Orosi
Puntarenas ● San José
Quepos
COSTA RICA

Puerto Limón

Colón
PANAMÁ
Panamá
Canal de Panamá

OCÉANO PACÍFICO

SO-CFL-126

CAMINOS

THIRD EDITION
CAMINOS

JOY RENJILIAN-BURGY
Wellesley College

ANA BEATRIZ CHIQUITO
Massachusetts Institute of Technology
University of Bergen, Norway

SUSAN M. MRAZ
University of Massachusetts, Boston

HOUGHTON MIFFLIN COMPANY
Boston   New York

DEDICATORIA

- Para mi marido, Donísimo, el don de dones; a mis gemelos-hijos-jaguares-bostonianos Lucien y Sarkis; y a mi querida familia. Los quiero mucho. (JR-B)

- Para mi querida familia con todo amor, en especial para mis padres, Lucio y Ofelia, mi marido, Ivar, y mi hijo, Edvard. (ABC)

- A mi familia, con todo mi amor y cariño: a mi madre, Margie; a mi hermana, Mary Beth y a su familia, Buko, Angela, Charles, Malissa, Joe, Paul y Lillian Marie. También a mi hermosa perrita-hijita de peluche, Mitzi, que me hace reír y sonreír cada día. (SMM)

Un *abrazo* fuerte a nuestros estudiantes de quienes aprendemos tanto.

Publisher: Rolando Hernández
Senior Sponsoring Editor: Glenn A. Wilson
Executive Marketing Director: Eileen Bernadette Moran
Development Manager: Judith Bach
Development Editor: Kim Beuttler
Senior Project Editors: Amy Johnson and Carol Newman
Art and Design Manager: Jill Haber
Cover Design Director: Tony Saizon
Senior Photo Editor: Jennifer Meyer Dare
Composition Buyer: Chuck Dutton
New Title Project Manager: James Lonergan
Marketing Assistant: Lorreen Ruth Pelletier
Editorial Assistants: Erin Beasley/Emily Meyer/Paola Moll

Cover credit: © Randy Faris/CORBIS. El Faro del Comercio and the Cathedral of Monterrey, Monterrey Mexico.

Text credits: Page 487

Printed in the U.S.A.

Instructor's exam copy:
ISBN 13: 978-0-618-87027-1
ISBN 10: 0-618-87027-X

For orders, use student text ISBNs:
ISBN 13: 978-0-618-81684-2
ISBN 10: 0-618-81684-4

Library of Congress Catalog Card Number: 2007926714

23456789–VH—11 10 09 08 07

Preface

Welcome to *Caminos,* and congratulations for choosing to learn Spanish. Perhaps you want to travel to learn more about other cultures; or possibly you will use Spanish in your chosen profession; or maybe you just need to fulfill a language requirement at your institution. Whatever your reason for studying Spanish, one thing is certain: you will in the future most likely find yourself in a real-life situation where your knowledge of Spanish will help you to better communicate at work, at home, or in your community.

Spanish is spoken by a diverse population of almost 500 million people world-wide and is second only to Mandarin Chinese. In the United States alone, 12.5% of the population is Spanish-speaking (Bureau of the Census 2000), making Hispanics the largest minority, numbering over 39 million. It also makes the United States the third largest Spanish-speaking country in the world. Wherever you live, as you begin to learn Spanish, look for opportunities to benefit from the Spanish being spoken around you—on television, in newspapers, at the movies, or in your community.

By studying with *Caminos* not only will you learn how to speak Spanish, but you also will have the opportunity to explore the numerous cultures that make up the ethnic tapestry of the twenty-one Spanish-speaking countries of the world. Our hope is that by discovering their diversity and vitality you will make learning Spanish a passionate, life-long pursuit.

—Joy Renjilian-Burgy
Ana Beatriz Chiquito
Susan M. Mraz

Overview of Your Textbook's Main Features

U N I D A D

5
Vacaciones en la playa

VOCABULARIO Y LENGUA

▶ Checking into a hotel
▶ Using direct object pronouns
▶ Talking about the beach and leisure activities
▶ Narrating events in the past: Preterite of verbs with spelling changes: *ir, ser, dar*

▶ Discussing vacations
▶ Using double object pronouns
▶ Narrating events in the past: Preterite of stem-changing *-ir* verbs
▶ Narrating events in the past: Preterite of irregular verbs

CAMINOS DEL JAGUAR

▶ Volibol y amor en la playa
▶ Dos espías

LECTURA

▶ Vamos al Caribe hispano: Cuba, Puerto Rico y la República Dominicana

NOTAS CULTURALES

▶ El turismo en el Caribe hispano
▶ Los parques nacionales

ESTRATEGIAS

▶ Reading: How to use the dictionary
▶ Writing: Using a dictionary

ciento sesenta y ocho

Caminos sets the stage for learning by outlining each color-coded section of the unit so that the architecture of the unit is apparent.

Each unit of *Caminos* contains two *pasos*. The *Primer paso's Vocabulario y lengua* section starts with a visual and related text to contextualize the presentation. Vocabulary sections present cognates and thematic vocabulary and expressions visually.

Luis Germán Cajiga, *Flamboyán entre palmeras*

Preguntas del tema

▶ ¿Adónde te gusta ir de vacaciones?
▶ ¿Qué actividades te gusta hacer?
▶ ¿Con quién/es vas de vacaciones?
▶ ¿Cuál es tu hotel favorito?

Primer paso • ciento sesenta y nueve 169

Más palabras y expresiones

Cognados
el (mini) bar	el/la recepcionista
confirmar	la reservación
la recepción	reservar

Sustantivos
el alojamiento	*lodging, accommodations*
el botones	*bellhop*
el buzón	*mailbox*
el cajero automático	*automated teller machine (ATM)*
el cambio de dinero / moneda	*money exchange*
el cheque de viajero	*traveler's check*
el/la conserje	*concierge*
el (dinero en) efectivo	*cash*
el estacionamiento / aparcamiento	*parking lot*
el equipaje	*luggage*
la habitación	*room*
la maleta	*suitcase*
el salón (la sala) de conferencias	*conference room*
la tarifa	*rate, fare, tariff*
la tarjeta de crédito / débito	*credit / debit card*

Verbos

PRIMER PASO

Vocabulario y lengua

CHECKING INTO A HOTEL

HOTEL NACIONAL, HABANA, CUBA

Inaugurado el 30 de diciembre de 1930, El Nacional es uno de los hoteles más clásicos de La Habana. Su *lujo*, *elegancia*, distinción y servicios de *primera clase*, se mantienen intactos después de seis décadas en la *industria hotelera* cubana. *Rodeado* por hermosos jardines, el hotel ocupa un lugar privilegiado cerca del Malecón habanero, ofreciendo una de las *vistas* más bellas de la ciudad. Sus *huéspedes* pueden disfrutar de *habitaciones* espléndidas y cómodas.

luxury
first class
hotel industry / surrounded

views
guests
rooms

FACILIDADES DE LAS HABITACIONES
TV satélite	Aire acondicionado
Minibar	Baño privado
Radio despertador	Radio
Teléfono	Refrigerador

alarm clock

FACILIDADES DEL HOTEL
Bar	Buró de turismo
Centro de negocios	Caja de seguridad
Elevador / Ascensor	Jardín
Estacionamiento	Piscina
Restaurante	Sala de conferencias
Sala de ejercicios	Servicio de habitación
Servicios médicos	Tenis

Online Study Center
For additional practice with this unit's vocabulary and grammar, visit the *Caminos* website at http://college.hmco.com/languages/spanish/renjilian/caminos/3e/student_home.html. You can also review audio flashcards, quiz yourself, and explore related Spanish-language sites.

Primer paso • ciento setenta y uno 171

ciento setenta • Unidad 5

Questions related to the theme of the unit prepare you for the material to come.

The vocabulary presentation is immediately reinforced with listening and comprehension activities, role-plays, and other pair and group activities.

Actividades

🎧 **1** **Hotel Real de Minas.** Listen to the description of a hotel in Guanajuato, México, then determine whether the statements are **verdadero (V)** or **falso (F).** Correct the false statements.

1. _____ Guanajuato es una ciudad bonita.
2. _____ El Hotel Real de Minas es un hotel económico.
3. _____ Hay 12 restaurantes en el hotel.
4. _____ Hay 175 habitaciones en el hotel.
5. _____ Veinte suites tienen aire acondicionado.
6. _____ No hay estacionamiento.
7. _____ Hay un bar cerca de la alberca.
8. _____ Su número de teléfono es el 63-215-80.

2 **¿Qué es?** Write the correct word that matches each definition.

1. Cuando viajas, pones mucha ropa (*clothing*) allí.
2. Es una forma de pagar el hotel si no tienes dinero en efectivo.
3. Se usa para abrir una puerta.
4. Allí descansas en el hotel.
5. Allí los turistas reciben la llave de la habitación.
6. Es un aparato para ir al piso doce.
7. Es la persona que ayuda a los huéspedes a encontrar sitios turísticos.
8. Es un lugar donde guardar el coche.

3 **Símbolos internacionales.** Match the international hotel symbols on the right with their meanings on the left.

_____ piscina (alberca)
_____ dos camas sencillas
_____ tarjetas de crédito
_____ cama sencilla
_____ cambio de moneda
_____ restaurante
_____ salón de conferencias
_____ teléfono
_____ ascensor
_____ bar
_____ estacionamiento
_____ cama doble
_____ televisión
_____ perros no
_____ minibar

4 **¿Qué necesitas?** State what hotel amenities you will need in the following situations. Follow the model.

» **MODELO:** Tienes hambre.
  Necesito un restaurante.

1. No tienes dinero.
2. Debes llamar a tu madre.
3. Tus maletas son muy grandes.
4. Tu habitación está en el piso veinticuatro.
5. Tienes sed.
6. Quieres hacer ejercicio.
7. Tienes hambre a medianoche y el restaurante está cerrado (*closed*).
8. Llegas al hotel en coche.

ciento setenta y dos » Unidad 5

---

5 **En el hotel.** Complete the following conversation between a guest and the receptionist at a hotel using the vocabulary from the word bank below.

con vista al mar	¿En qué le puedo servir?	tarjeta de crédito
reservar	¡Que disfruten de su estadía!	habitación
sencilla	¿A nombre de quién?	

—Buenas tardes. _____
—Buenas tardes. Quisiéramos _____ una habitación para esta noche.

—De los Señores Guzmán.
—¿Por cuántas noches?
—Por dos, por favor.
—¿Qué tipo de _____ prefiere Ud.?
—Nos gustaría una habitación _____
—¿Con cama _____ o doble?
—Con una cama doble. ¿Cuánto cuesta?
—La habitación cuesta $132 por noche.
—Muy bien. ¿Se puede pagar con _____?
—Claro que sí.

6 **Entre nosotros.** Role-play the following situation with a partner.

Turista:	**Recepcionista:**
You are traveling through Spain by bicycle. After a difficult day, you arrive at your hotel very tired. When you arrive, the receptionist tells you that he or she doesn't have your reservation. You have a copy of your confirmation. Do whatever you can to get a room for the night.	A young bicyclist arrives at your hotel, but you can't find his or her reservation in the computer. There's a medical conference (**congreso**) in the hotel and there are no rooms left. Do your best to solve this dilemma.

USING DIRECT OBJECT PRONOUNS

Preparando el viaje

Amanda No encuentro mi bolsa azul. **La** necesito para empacar mis cosas.
Arturo Yo **la** tengo. Aquí está la bolsa. También tengo los boletos de avión.
Amanda **Los** tienes también. ¡Qué bien! Mil gracias.

Primer paso » ciento setenta y tres

Charts highlight key material such as verb or pronoun forms, while examples illustrate the explanations.

Amanda ¿Y el dinero?
Arturo También **lo** tengo aquí. Supongo que llamaste a la embajada norteamericana y sacaste las visas, ¿verdad?
Amanda ¿Las visas? Claro, ayer hablé con la embajada para pedir**las.**
Arturo Es importante tener**las.**
Amanda Tienes razón. Sin visas no podemos viajar.

A direct object is the person or thing that directly receives the action of the verb. In the first sentence on page 173, **mi bolsa azul** is a direct object. Once the object is stated, it is often replaced by a direct object pronoun to avoid redundancy: *La necesito para empacar mis cosas.*

In the dialog above, can you identify the direct object nouns that correspond to the direct object pronouns in boldface? Note that third person direct object pronouns agree in number and gender with the nouns that they replace.

Direct object pronouns			
me	*me*	**nos**	*us*
te	*you*	**os**	*you*
lo, la	*him, her, you, it*	**los, las**	*them, you*

The direct object **lo** is often used to express a previously mentioned idea as in, *Sí lo sé.* (Yes, I know it.).

Direct object pronouns precede the conjugated verb.

—¿Y **los boletos?** —*And the tickets?*
—**Los** recogemos en Madrid. —*We'll pick them up in Madrid.*

When the direct object pronoun is used with a conjugated verb and an infinitive (**tengo que comprar, voy a hacer, acabo de escribir,** etc.) the pronoun can go either before the conjugated verb or attached to the end of the infinitive.

Quiero pedir **una habitación** *I want to ask for a larger room.*
  más grande.
La quiero pedir. *I want to ask for it.*
Quiero pedir**la.**

Direct object pronouns are attached to the end of the infinitive when the infinitive is used with expressions such as **es importante / bueno / necesario,** etc., or in prepositional expressions such as **para recibirlas, de visitarla.**

—Me gusta tener un **buen mapa.** —*I like to have a good map.*
—Sí, es bueno tener**lo.** —*Yes, it's good to have it.*

When the direct object pronoun is used with progressive forms (**estar** + present participle), the pronoun can go either before the conjugated form of **estar** or attached to the end of the participle. When attached to the participle, you must add a written accent.

—¿Estás escribiendo **la tarjeta postal?** —*Are you writing the postcard?*
—Sí, **la** estoy escribiendo. —*Yes, I'm writing it.*
—Sí, estoy escribiéndo**la.**

Actividades

1 **Sin repeticiones.** Write sentences replacing the direct object nouns with direct object pronouns. Follow the model.

» **MODELO:** Miranda compra los pasajes. *Miranda buys the tickets.*
  Miranda los compra. *Miranda buys them.*

ciento setenta y cuatro » Unidad 5

Grammar explanations have been revised, and topics have been resequenced throughout the program to decrease the breadth of topics and increase the depth of coverage. Grammar points are introduced by language modeling texts, often in the form of a dialogue. They are then followed by grammar explanations and activities that progress from mechanical to open-ended.

Each *paso* presents an installment of the all-new ***Caminos del jaguar*** graphic novel, which parallels the award-winning ***Caminos del jaguar*** video. The graphic novel tells the story in easy-to-understand Spanish that you can read on your own or as an advance organizer for the video. The mystery-adventure story also provides a fascinating view into Mayan culture, supports further learning, and reinforces topics presented in the textbook.

As with the *Primer paso*'s *Vocabulario y lengua* section, the *Segundo paso*'s *Vocabulario y lengua* starts with a drawing and related text to contextualize the presentation.

The contextualized presentation of the vocabulary emphasizes its use in real life and reinforces learning.

To support greater understanding of the material, comprehension questions and a role-play and writing activity accompany each installment.

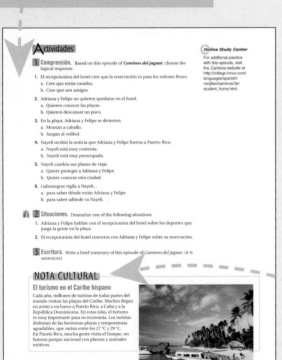

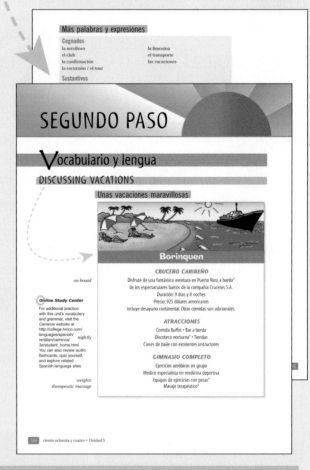

Notas culturales on the regions featured in ***Caminos del jaguar*** provide you with a context in which to learn about Hispanic cultures and make cross-cultural comparisons. These cultural notes include information on the traditions, pastimes, and geography throughout the Spanish-speaking world.

The *Lectura* section offers authentic works and author-generated passages thematically related to the active vocabulary and culture notes of the unit.

Reading strategies provide you with various techniques for approaching diverse texts. A variety of pre- and post-reading exercises, including comprehension checks, personalized questions, and expansion activities, supporting skill development.

Lectura

Online Study Center
For further reading practice online, visit the *Caminos* website at http://college.hmco.com/languages/spanish/renjilian/caminos/3e/student_home.html.

Reading Strategy

How to use the dictionary

When reading a text in Spanish, go through it several times, checking for words you already know as well as for cognates, which you have studied in earlier chapters. You should also try to guess the meaning of words you do not know through the context of the sentence and the text. Once you have applied this strategy, use the dictionary to confirm your guesses. The dictionary may give you several different meanings for a word. It is important to determine the grammatical form of the word because that can affect its meaning. Note the following facts about Spanish dictionaries.

▸ Verbs (**verbos**) appear in the infinitive form. If you are looking up a conjugated form of a verb, you will have to determine its infinitive before you start your search.
▸ Masculine and feminine forms of nouns (**sustantivos**) are listed and marked *m.* or *f.* The meaning of a noun may change depending on its form.
▸ Only the masculine singular form of an adjective (**adjetivo**) is usually listed and marked *adj.*
▸ Idiomatic expressions (**expresiones idiomáticas**) are listed by their most important word. Sometimes you need several attempts to determine the main word.
▸ The letter **ñ** is listed as a separate letter after **n**. In older dictionaries, the letter combinations **ll** (as in **llover**) and and **ch** are listed as separate letters, after **l** and **c** respectively.

Vamos al Caribe hispano: Cuba, Puerto Rico y la República Dominicana

Las tres islas caribeñas de habla española, Cuba, Puerto Rico y la República Dominicana, tienen una herencia[1] tricultural común: la indígena[2] de cada región, la española y la africana. Esta mezcla[3] étnica les da gran riqueza a sus tradiciones, a su música, a su literatura y a su vida diaria, pero cada isla tiene también su identidad propia. Las islas tienen bellas playas y hermosa arquitectura colonial. Estas islas del Caribe comparten aspectos de su cultura, herencia y tradiciones con otras regiones hispanas como las costas caribeñas de Costa Rica, Panamá, Colombia y Venezuela.

[1]heritage; [2]indigenous; [3]mix

198 ciento noventa y ocho ▸ Unidad 5

La Playa de Varadero, La Habana, Cuba

Pareja dominicana en la playa

Cuba

Cuba es la más grande de las tres islas caribeñas. Fue el segundo lugar[a] al que llegó Cristóbal Colón[b]. Los españoles llevaron esclavos africanos para trabajar en las plantaciones de azúcar[c]. Al azúcar lo llamaban "el oro blanco" por su valor económico en esa época. Con el tiempo, se mezclaron los africanos con los españoles para producir la rica mezcla racial que hoy existe en la isla. En 1959 Fidel Castro lideró una revolución en Cuba y por más de treinta años, hasta 1990, Cuba estuvo bajo el socialismo de la Unión Soviética. Actualmente[d] la isla está en transición económica. Tiene más de once millones de habitantes.

Puerto Rico

Puerto Rico es la más pequeña de las tres islas hispanas y es un Estado Libre Asociado[e] de los Estados Unidos. Los puertorriqueños pueden viajar libremente entre la isla y los EE. UU.[f] La población indígena de la isla de Puerto Rico, los taínos o arauacos, tenía[g] una sociedad bastante avanzada en esta isla de 175 kilómetros de largo[h] y 56 kilómetros de ancho[i]. La población hoy en día[j] es de casi cuatro millones de habitantes.

La República Dominicana

La República Dominicana comparte[k] la misma isla que la República de Haití. Éste país fue el primer centro administrativo español en América y sus

habitantes indígenas, los taínos, la llamaban "Quisqueya". La población de la isla tiene también herencia europea y africana debido a[l] los esclavos que llevaron a trabajar allí. Actualmente es un gran centro turístico en la región caribeña, aunque también sufre de mucha pobreza económica y desigualdad social. Tiene casi[m] ocho millones de habitantes.

Un arrecife de coral en el Mar Caribe

[a]place; [b]Christopher Columbus; [c]sugar; [d]Today; [e]free associated state; [f]U.S.; [g]had; [h]in length; [i]in width; [j]today; [k]shares; [l]because of; [m]almost.

Segundo paso ▸ ciento noventa y nueve 199

Actividades

1 ¿Verdadero o falso? Write **V** if the following ideas are **verdaderas** or **F** if they are **falsas**. Correct the false sentences.

1. _____ El azúcar fue importante para la economía de Cuba.
2. _____ Cuba es la más pequeña de las islas de habla española.
3. _____ Los taínos llamaban (called) "Quisqueya" a Puerto Rico.
4. _____ En las islas caribeñas de habla española hay una mezcla étnica de influencia indígena, española y africana.
5. _____ Puerto Rico es un Estado Libre Asociado de los Estados Unidos.
6. _____ Haití y Cuba comparten la misma isla.
7. _____ Puerto Rico tiene ocho millones de habitantes.

2 Cómo buscar palabras en el diccionario. Keep a list of the words that you needed to look up in the dictionary for this reading and compare them with that of a friend. Are there any that you could have guessed without looking them up? Which ones?

3 Compara y contrasta. Compare and contrast the different characteristics of Cuba, the Dominican Republic, and Puerto Rico. Which island do you find the most interesting? Why? Work with a partner.

	Cuba	Puerto Rico	La República Dominicana
Población			
Etnicidad			
Sistema político			
Productos económicos			
Otros aspectos			

4 Conversaciones cortas. Work with a partner to answer the following questions.

1. ¿Qué islas hay en tu región? ¿Cómo son? ¿Tienen playas?
2. ¿A qué isla del mundo quieres viajar? ¿Dónde está? ¿Cómo es?
3. ¿Qué influencia étnica hay en tu región o estado?
4. ¿A qué grupo étnico pertenecen los padres y los abuelos de tu compañero/a de cuarto?
5. ¿Qué idiomas hablan en tu país actualmente? ¿Y en tu familia?

200 doscientos ▸ Unidad 5

Writing Strategy

Using a dictionary

Review the reading strategy prior to reading this strategy. To use a dictionary effectively, be sure to keep the following in mind.

There are many translations for some words. Look for the definition that best suits your needs. Once you have selected a word in the English-Spanish section, cross check its meaning in the Spanish-English section of the dictionary to assure accuracy, and be sure to read any grammar notes that will tell you about irregular forms, different translations, and so on. Always review the guide to using a particular dictionary to understand important symbols and abbreviations. Below are some common abbreviations and sample dictionary entries.

Workshop

f.	femenino	*adv.*	adverbio	*adj.*	adjetivo
m.	masculino	*s.*	sustantivo (*noun*)		

fan[1] (fan) I. s. (*paper*) abanico; (*electric*) ventilador *m*; AGR. aventadora II. tr. **fanned, fan-ning** (*to cool*) abanicar; FIG. (*to stir up*) avivar, excitar; AGR. aventar —intr. • **to f. out** abrirse en abanico
fan[2] (fan) s. FAM. (*enthusiast*) aficionado, hincha *m*.
support (se-port´) I. tr. (*weight*) aguantar, sostener, corroborar; (*a spouse, child*) mantener; (*a cause, theory*) sostener, respaldar; (*with money*) ayudar • **to s. oneself** (*to earn one's living*) ganarse la vida; (*to learn*) apoyarse II. s. (*act*) apoyo; (*maintenance*) mantenimiento; ARQ., TEC. soporte *m*.

Strategy in Action

For additional practice using a dictionary, complete the exercises below and in the *Escritura I* section of your Student Activities Manual for *Unidad 5*.

1 **Usando el diccionario.** Refer to the dictionary entries above to translate the italicized words. Be sure to use the appropriate form of the word or phrase. Work in groups.

1. Can I count on your *support*?
2. I can't *support* myself on this salary.
3. My psychology instructor *supports* the Freudian school of thought.
4. The house has good *support* beams.
5. I'm a sports *fan*.
6. It's hot outside and you need to *fan* yourself to keep cool.
7. Turn on the *fan*! It's hot in here.

2 **Querido/a amigo/a.** You are on vacation. Write a postcard to your best friend, telling about your trip. Describe the hotel, its amenities, what there is to do, and what you like and don't like about the hotel. Then narrate a sequence of events to tell your friend what you did on your first day there. Be sure to use the preterite tense to talk about the things you did.

3 **Mi primer día del trabajo.** Congratulations! You just landed your dream job. Your first day on the job, however, was not what you expected. By the end of the day you are very frustrated and decide to write an email to your best friend to tell him / her all about your bad day. Describe your day to your friend, and don't forget to include all the details. Remember to use the preterite.

Online Study Center
For further writing practice, visit the *Caminos* website at http://college.hmco.com/languages/spanish/renjilian/caminos/3e/student_home.html.

Segundo paso • doscientos uno 201

The new *Artes y letras* section introduces you to the music, art, and literature of the Spanish-speaking world. Appearing after every even-numbered unit, this section includes an overview of well-known personalities as well as short pieces on art and music specific to the featured region.

Caminos also takes a process approach to writing. Each writing section includes a writing strategy to ease you into the activities that follow and culminates in the writing of some type of prose.

The end-of-unit *Resumen de vocabulario* lists include thematically and functionally grouped active vocabulary presented in the unit for easy review and reference.

Resumen de vocabulario

PRIMER PASO

CHECKING INTO A HOTEL

Sustantivos

el alojamiento	lodging, accommodations
el ascensor/elevador	elevator
el botones	porter
el buzón	mailbox
el cajero automático	automated teller machine (ATM)
el cambio de dinero/moneda	money exchange
el cheque de viajero	traveler's check
el/la conserje	concierge
el despertador	alarm clock
el (dinero en) efectivo	cash
la elegancia	elegance
el equipaje	luggage
el estacionamiento	parking lot
la habitación	room
el/la huésped	guest
el lujo	luxury
la maleta	suitcase
el (mini) bar	(mini)bar
la primera/segunda clase	first / second class
la recepción	reception
el/la recepcionista	receptionist
la reservación	reservation
el salón (la sala) de conferencias	conference room
la tarifa	rate, fare, tariff
la tarjeta de crédito	credit card
la vista	view

Verbos

alojar(se)	to stay (in a hotel)
atender (ie)	to attend to, wait on
confirmar	to confirm
hacer una llamada (de larga distancia / por cobrar)	to make a (long distance / collect) phone call
registrar	to register
reservar	to reserve

Adjetivos

cómodo/a	comfortable
doble	double
lujoso/a (de lujo)	luxurious
sencillo/a	single (room or bed)

Otras expresiones

¿A nombre de quién?	In whose name?
¿En qué le(s) puedo servir?	How can I help you?
con desayuno	with breakfast
con media pensión	with two meals
con vista al mar	with an ocean view
¿Cuánto cuesta...?	How much does . . . cost?
¿Dónde puedo cambiar el dinero?	Where can I exchange money?
Lo siento.	I'm sorry.
por supuesto	of course
¡Que disfrute/n de su estadía/estancia!	Enjoy your stay!

TALKING ABOUT THE BEACH

Sustantivos

el balón	(beach) ball
las gafas de sol	sunglasses
la novela	novel
el picnic	picnic
la playa	beach
el protector/bronceador solar	sunscreen
el/la radio	radio
la sandalia	sandal
el sombrero	hat
la sombrilla	parasol / beach umbrella
la toalla	towel
el traje de baño	bathing suit

Verbos

broncearse	to get a tan
bucear	to go skindiving, snorkeling
buscar conchas	to look for shells

203 doscientos dos • Unidad 5

ARTES Y LETRAS

Artes y letras

FLORIDA
La Habana
CUBA
Isla de Pinos
Guantánamo
JAMAICA
HAITÍ
REPÚBLICA
DOMINICANA
San Juan
PUERTO RICO
OCÉANO ATLÁNTICO
Mar Caribe
0   150   300 Kilómetros
0   150   300 Millas

EL CARIBE

Online Study Center
To learn more about the people featured in this section, visit the *Caminos* website at http://college.hmco.com/languages/spanish/renjilian/caminos/3e/student_home.html.

PERSONALIDADES

Hay muchas personalidades importantes en las artes de las islas del Mar Caribe. Las influencias en muchas de sus creaciones de arte, música y literatura son de origen africano, indígena y europeo. Entre los artistas cubanos están Wilfredo Lam, pintor surrealista y Yamilys Brito, que incluye imágenes con palabras en algunas de sus obras artísticas. Entre los artistas importantes de Puerto Rico hay dos que crean carteles de acontecimientos en la isla: José Alicea y Lyzette Rosado. En la República Dominicana dos artistas famosos son Enriquillo Rodríguez y Clara Ledesma.

Muchos caribeños recibieron un Grammy Latino en 2005. De Puerto Rico ganaron Marc Anthony por el Mejor Álbum de Salsa; Elvis Crespo por el Mejor Álbum de Merengue y Mejor Álbum de Rock Vocal; y Obie Bermúdez, por el Mejor Vocal Pop Masculino. También el dominicano Juan Luis Guerra ganó en dos categorías: el Mejor Álbum Cristiano en español y la Mejor Canción Tropical del año. Entre los cubanos, Bebo Valdés ganó por el Mejor Álbum de Jazz Latino; Israel "Cachao" López por el Mejor Álbum Tropical Tradicional y la cantante Lila Downs, que nació en Cuba, recibió el Grammy Latino por el Mejor Álbum Folklórico de 2005.

Hay muchos escritores caribeños de importancia en las épocas recientes. La puertorriqueña Esmeralda Santiago, la dominicana Julia Álvarez y la cubana Cristina García son tres novelistas que viven en Estados Unidos y escriben sobre la condición humana de los caribeños. Visita el sitio web de *Caminos* para leer más en español sobre estas personalidades y otros caribeños influyentes.

"Crecer no tiene que ver con ser famoso, crecer está dentro de ti. Y llevar la música de mi pueblo es lo que me ha hecho crecer". —Carlos Vives (Colombia)

Comprensión
Trabajando en parejas, háganse las preguntas.
1. ¿Qué influencias hay sobre el arte, la música y la literatura del Caribe? ¿Conoces alguna obra de los artistas mencionados?
2. ¿En qué categorías ganaron los cantantes los Grammy Latinos? ¿Cuál prefieres escuchar tú? ¿Por qué?

ARTE

AIMÉE GARCÍA
Aimée García es una artista cubana que nació en 1972 en la ciudad de Matanzas. Su arte apareció en muchas exhibiciones en Cuba, México, Corea del Sur y Estados Unidos. En el año 1999 pintó *La guía*, pintura que es una combinación de óleo en lienzo, con hilo y madera.

guide

La guía

oil on canvas
string / wood

Comprensión
Trabajando en parejas, estudien esta pintura y contesten las preguntas.
1. La artista está pintando una escena con árboles". ¿Qué colores usa para pintar la escena? En tu opinión, ¿qué hora del día es?
2. Describe a la artista en la pintura. ¿De qué color es su vestido? ¿Cuántos años crees que tiene ella? ¿Cuántos años tiene la artista Aimée García?
3. ¿Qué función tiene la jirafa"? ¿Hay otro animal posible?
4. ¿De qué colores es la jirafa? En tu opinión, ¿qué efecto produce en la pintura? ¿cómico? ¿absurdo? ¿interesante? ... ? ¿Por qué?
5. ¿Qué relación hay entre la fotografía de la artista y la artista en la pintura? ¿Son dos mujeres diferentes o es la misma persona?
6. ¿Te gusta o no te gusta esta pintura? ¿Por qué?

trees

giraffe

Poems, quotes, and literary excerpts by writers of the region help further develop reading and critical thinking skills.

"...tengo el gusto de andar por mi país, dueño de cuanto hay en él".
—Nicolás Guillén (Cuba), "Tengo"

"Estatuas"
Las estatuas mueren también, si nadie las mira.

Comprensión
En parejas, contesten las preguntas.
1. ¿Es el poema sobre las personas, los lugares o las cosas?
2. En la opinión del poeta, ¿cuándo mueren las estatuas?
3. El poeta indica que las estatuas son como personas. ¿Qué opinas tú?
4. Describe una estatua famosa de tu región: ¿De qué color es? ¿Dónde está? ¿Es grande o pequeña? ¿De qué o de quién es? ¿Por qué es importante? ¿Por qué (no) te gusta?

"Apuntes" para el poema
Hice apuntes para escribir un poema a la primavera, y de tanto (re)escribirlo, sólo quedó de las flores, el recuerdo de su aroma, y mi asombro ante tanto verdor".

Notes

memory
amazement / greenness

Comprensión
Trabajando en parejas, contesten las preguntas.
1. Antes de crear el poema, ¿qué escribió el poeta?
2. ¿A qué estación del año le escribió el poema?
3. ¿Qué quedó de las flores que el poeta puso en el poema?
4. Al final del poema, ¿qué color asocia el poeta con la primavera?
5. ¿De qué color es tu flor favorita? ¿Tiene un aroma delicado o fuerte?
6. ¿Te gustan más las flores de la primavera o del verano? En tu región, ¿hay flores también en el otoño o en el invierno?

MÚSICA

OLGA TAÑÓN
La artista musical, Olga Tañón, es puertorriqueña. Ganó un Grammy Latino de la Mejor Interpretación Vocal Femenina de 2003 por su álbum, "Sobrevivir". Ella canta diversos estilos musicales como merengue y balada pop. Tañón incluye en su nuevo álbum, "A puro fuego", sus discos más celebrados de los diez años pasados de su carrera.

Survive

Pure Fire

Comprensión
Trabajen en parejas para contestar las preguntas.
1. ¿De dónde es Olga Tañón?
2. Según la lectura, ¿qué tipo de música canta? ¿Qué premio ganó?
3. ¿Cómo se llaman dos de sus álbumes musicales? ¿Qué emociones despiertan los títulos?
4. ¿A qué otro/a cantante hispánico/a conoces? ¿De dónde es? ¿Qué canta?

LITERATURA

NORBERTO JAMES RAWLINGS
El autor Norberto James Rawlings nació en la República Dominicana en 1945. Este poeta dominicano es también profesor de español. Se graduó de la Universidad de La Habana y, en 1992, recibió su doctorado en lengua y literatura hispánica de Boston University. Los poemas aquí son de su nuevo libro, *La urdimbre del silencio* (The Weaving of Silence), que se publicó en 2000 en La República Dominicana.

Comprehension activities reinforce linguistic practice of the themes presented through the art, music, and literature.

Student Components

STUDENT TEXTBOOK

This textbook is your primary resource for learning Spanish. It contains cultural information, vocabulary and grammar presentations and practice, and activities to help you develop listening, speaking, reading, and writing skills in Spanish.

IN-TEXT AUDIO CD

Packaged with your textbook, the audio CD contains recordings that correlate to activities in the *Vocabulario y lengua* sections of the units. There are generally two listening activities in each unit, designed to develop your listening skills.

STUDENT ACTIVITIES MANUAL (SAM)

The Student Activities Manual contains workbook, lab, and video activities that provide important additional practice of topics in your text. The Workbook section, which parallels the organization of the units in your text, includes activities to reinforce the vocabulary and grammar that you learn in class as well as practice to help develop your reading and writing skills. The Lab section contains a variety of listening activities for each unit to build your ability to comprehend spoken Spanish. The Video section of the SAM provides pre- and post-viewing activities that correspond to each episode of the ***Caminos del jaguar*** video.

SAM AUDIO CD PROGRAM

The SAM Audio CDs contain the recorded material that coordinates with the lab activities in the Student Activities Manual.

CAMINOS DEL JAGUAR VIDEO

Available in DVD format as well as on the ***Caminos*** Online Study Center, this award-winning video features an exciting, action-packed mystery that incorporates myth, folklore, and local regional culture. Filmed on location in Mexico, Spain, Costa Rica, Puerto Rico, Ecuador, and the United States, the video's twenty-four segments are divided into two 7- to 12-minute segments per unit. The graphic novel episodes in the textbook parallel and summarize each video episode to prepare you for viewing, and video activities in the SAM help focus your viewing and check your understanding of the episodes.

e-SAM POWERED BY QUIA

This online version of the Student Activities Manual contains the same content as the print version, plus the material recorded on the SAM Audio CDs, in an interactive environment that provides immediate feedback for many activities so you can monitor your progress. It also includes links to the video and to verb charts and Spanish-English and English-Spanish vocabularies from the textbook.

e-SAM

The Blackboard/Web CT Premium Access Code Card allows access to the SAM on the Blackboard or Web CT platform. These platforms also include links to verb charts and Spanish-English and English-Spanish vocabularies from the textbook.

e-BOOK + e-SAM

A completely interactive experience, the e-Book provides the entire text online, integrated with links to a wide variety of resources that are accessible with the click of a mouse. Each resource expands on the content of the text and allows you to practice and reinforce what you have learned. Each link is located at the point of relevance in the text. A synchronous voice chat feature also allows you to collaborate with other students and your instructor on pair and group activities. In addition, audio pronunciations of each chapter's active vocabulary and grammar terms are included.

ONLINE STUDY CENTER

The *Caminos* web site includes a variety of activities and resources to help you practice vocabulary and grammar, review for quizzes and exams, and explore Spanish-language web sites. The **Improve Your Grade** section includes MP3 files of the in-text audio; the video transcript; flashcards; web search activities; interactive multimedia activities (drag-and-drop, matching, multiple choice, fill-in, games, and more) that practice unit vocabulary and grammar and reinforce understanding of the *Caminos del jaguar* video through video-based activities. **Ace the Test** offers ACE practice tests designed to check your progress with unit vocabulary and grammar, as well as video comprehension. **Resources** provides web links to cultural sites (attractions, cuisine, geography, etc.), maps, and academic resources. The Online Study Center is accessible at **http://college.hmco.com/languages/ spanish/renjilian/caminos/3e/student_home.html.**

SMARTHINKING ONLINE TUTORING

Access online tutorial support using chat technology, feedback tools, and virtual whiteboards. SMARTHINKING lets you work one-on-one with trained Spanish tutors in live sessions during your usual homework hours. If a question arises outside of a tutorial session, you can submit it to a tutor any time and receive a reply within 24 hours or access around-the-clock independent study resources. You can learn more about SMARTHINKING at **http://college.hmco.com/languages/ spanish/renjilian/caminos/3e/student_home.html.**

Scope and Sequence

Acknowledgments

We would like to thank the World Languages group of Houghton Mifflin's College Division for supporting us throughout the different stages of development and production of *Caminos.* To Rolando Hernández, Glenn Wilson, Kim Beuttler, Sandy Guadano, Beth Wellington, Eileen Bernadette Moran, Amy Johnson, Carol Newman, Emily Meyer, Paola Moll, and Shirley Webster, we appreciate your helpful insights and guidance. To Mary-Anne Vetterling, we express our deepest thanks for all your contributions to this project.

My deepest gratitude to Wellesley College and the Spanish Department for your enduring love and professional support on all my *caminos;* to the Knapp Media and Technology Center, for your continued assistance; to the Education Department, for your partnership in so many educational endeavors; and to Natalie Drorbaugh, María García, Kerry Renjilian-Gough, and Hillary Hurst for your constant contributions and assistance.

—*Joy Renjilian-Burgy*

Special thanks to Senior Lecturer Douglas Morgenstern, Professor Steven Lerman, and all my colleagues at MIT for their inspiration and support.

—*Ana Beatriz Chiquito*

I would like to thank the members of the Department of Hispanic Studies, University of Massachusetts, Boston, for creating such a collegial atmosphere in which to teach and learn. A very special thanks to Reyes Coll-Tellechea, Clara Estow, Esther Torrego, and Peggy Fitzgerald for your support and encouragement. I also thank our students and language instructors for your inspiration and collaboration.

—*Susan M. Mraz*

We would like to gratefully acknowledge our reviewers, focus group participants, and special contributors:

Estíbaliz Alonso, *University of Iowa*
Francisco Álvarez, *Miracosta Community College – Oceanside Campus*
María Amores
Brenda Barceló, *University of California – Santa Cruz*
Rebeca Bataller, *University of Iowa*
Robert Baum, *Arkansas State University*
Patricia Bazán-Figueras, *Fairleigh Dickinson University*
Rosamel S. Benavides, *Humboldt State University*
Raquel Blázquez-Domingo, *University of South Carolina – Columbia*
Christine Bridges-Esser, *Lamar University*
Alan Bruflat
Obdulia Castro, *University of Colorado*
Clara Chávez Burchardt, *Rose State College*
Susan Cheuvront, *University of Iowa*
Alicia Cipria, *University of Alabama*
Guillermo "Memo" Cisco, *Oakland Community College – Auburn Hills Campus*
Felice Coles, *University of Mississippi*
Purificación Crowe, *University of South Carolina – Columbia*
José Cruz, *Fayatteville Technical Community College*
Lee Daniel, *Texas Christian University*
Mary Doerfeld, *University of Iowa*
María Dorantes, *University of Michigan*
Gene DuBois, *University of North Dakota*

Héctor Enríquez, *University of Texas – El Paso*
Toni Esposito, *University of Pennsylvania*
Ana Esther Fernández, *University of Iowa*
Ken Fleak, *University of South Carolina – Columbia*
Yolanda Flores, *University of Vermont*
Donald B. Gibbs, *Creighton University*
Mark Goldin, *George Mason University*
Juan Gómez-Canseco, *Santa Fe Community College*
Ana González, *University of North Carolina – Charlotte*
Yolanda L. González, *Valencia Community College – East Campus*
María Grana, *Houston Community College*
Lisa Hall López, *Trident Technical College*
D. Carlton Hawley
Nancy Hayes, *University of Iowa*
Ellen Haynes, *University of Colorado – Boulder*
Margarita Hodge, *Northern Virginia Community College – Alexandria Campus*
Cathy House, *Miracosta Community College – San Elijo Campus*
April Howell, *Coastal Carolina Community College*
Paloma Lapuerta, *Central Connecticut State University*
Susan Larson
Luis E. Latoja, *Columbus State Community College*
Miguel Lechuga
Roxana Levin, *St. Petersburg Jr. College – Tarpon Campus*
Margarita Lezcano
Judith Liskin Gasparro, *University of Iowa*
Rosa M. López Cañete, *The College of William and Mary*
Constance Marina, *Regis College*
William Martínez, Jr., *California Polytechnic State University*
James C. Michnowicz, *The University of Virginia's College at Wise*
Montserrat Mir, *Illinois State University*
Stephen C. Mohler, *University of Tennessee at Martin*
Holly Monheimer, *University of Pennsylvania*
Paula Moore, *North Arkansas College*
Patricia Moore-Martínez, *Temple University*
Rachelle Morea, *Norfolk State University*
Glen Morocco, *La Salle University*
Janet B. Norden, *Baylor University*
Ana Oscoz, *University of Iowa*
Federico Perez-Piñeda, *University of South Alabama*
Inmaculada Pertusa, *University of Kentucky*
Margarita Pillado-Miller, *Grinnell College*
Anne Pomerantz, *University of Pennsylvania*
Oralia Preble-Niemi, *University of Tennesse – Chattanooga*
Gunther F. Puschendorf, *College of Alameda*
Celia Ramírez, *Big Bend Community College*
Herlinda Ramírez Barradas, *Purdue University Calumet*
Cheryl Reagan, *Sussex County Community College*
April Reyes, *University of South Dakota*
Victoria Robertson, *California State University - Hayward*
Karen L. Robinson, *University of Nebraska at Omaha*
Beatriz Rosado, *Virginia State University*
Benita Sampedro, *Hofstra University*
Amanda Samuelson, *University of Iowa*
Joy Saunders, *Texas Tech University*
Virginia Shen, *Chicago State University*
Wayne Steely
Suzanne Stewart, *Daytona Beach Community College*

Octavio de la Suaree, *William Paterson University*
Nancy Taylor Mínguez, *Old Dominion University*
Veronica Tempone, *Indian River Community College*
George Thatcher, *Treasure Valley Community College*
Dulce Tienda-Martagón, *University of South Carolina – Columbia*
Jacquelyn Torres, *University of Iowa*
Vicky L. Trylong, *Olivet Nazarene University*
Beverly Turner, *Truckee Meadows Community College*
John H. Turner, *Bowdoin College*
Mayela Vallejos-Ramírez
Helen Webb, *University of Pennsylvania*
Joseph Weyers, *College of Charleston*
Helen Wilson, *Towson University*

CAMINOS

preliminar

Sylvia Laks
Casitas 1

▶ Greetings
▶ Introductions
▶ The Spanish Alphabet

▶ Hispanics in the United States
▶ Nationalities
▶ Myth and Mystery: Who's Who in *Caminos del jaguar*

SALUDOS (GREETINGS)

Buenos días

—Buenos días. ¿Qué tal?
—Muy bien, gracias, ¿y tú?
—Bastante bien, gracias.

—*Good morning. How's it going?*
—*Very well, thank you, and you?*
—*Quite fine, thanks.*

Buenas tardes

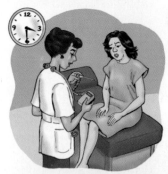

Paciente	Buenas tardes, doctora. ¿Qué hay de nuevo?	*Good afternoon, doctor. What's new?*
Doctora	Nada en particular. ¿Cómo está usted?	*Nothing special. How are you?*
Paciente	Muy mal, bastante mal.	*Very bad, quite bad.*
Doctora	¿Verdad? Lo siento.	*Really? I'm sorry.*

Buenas noches

—Buenas noches.
—Buenas noches. Hasta mañana.
—Adiós. Hasta pronto.
—Chao.

—*Good night.*
—*Good night. See you tomorrow.*
—*Good-bye. See you soon.*
—*Bye.*

Note: **Buenos días** is normally used from sunrise to noon; **buenas tardes** from noon through approximately suppertime; and **buenas noches** after the evening meal.

Actividades

Online Study Center

For additional practice with this unit's vocabulary and grammar, visit the *Caminos* website at http://college.hmco.com/languages/spanish/renjilian/caminos/3e/student_home.html. You can also review audio flashcards, quiz yourself, and explore related Spanish-language sites.

1 ¿Día, tarde o noche? Indicate whether you would say **"Buenos días,"** **"Buenas tardes,"** or **"Buenas noches"** in each of the following situations.

1. You see a friend at an afternoon matinée.
2. You run into a classmate at an after-dinner theater.
3. Your mom calls you before breakfast.
4. You have a doctor's appointment after a late lunch.
5. You talk with your roommate before going to bed.

2 Conversación. You run into your Spanish professor in the hallway and have a brief conversation. Number the following lines from 1–6 to put the conversation in a logical order. Then read the conversation with a partner.

_____ Buenos días. ¿Qué hay de nuevo?
_____ Chao.
_____ Buenos días.
_____ Adiós. Hasta mañana.
_____ Nada en particular. ¿Cómo está usted?
_____ Bastante bien, gracias.

3 Saludos. Recombine expressions from the conversations above to create a conversation around the theme of greetings. Work with a partner.

PRESENTACIONES (INTRODUCTIONS)

En la cafetería

Sara	Hola. ¿Cómo te llamas?	*Hello. What's your name?*
Pablo	Me llamo Pablo. ¿Y tú?	*My name is Pablo. And you?*
Sara	Me llamo Sara.	*My name is Sara.*
Pablo	Mucho gusto.	*Pleased to meet you.*
Sara	Igualmente.	*Likewise.*

En la oficina

Rafael	Hola. ¿Cómo se llama usted?	*Hello. What's your name?*
Mirta	Me llamo Mirta Pérez. ¿Y usted?	*My name is Mirta Pérez. And you?*
Rafael	Me llamo Rafael Ramírez.	*My name is Rafael Ramírez.*
Mirta	Mucho gusto.	*Pleased to meet you.*
Rafael	El gusto es mío.	*The pleasure is mine.*

En la sala de clase

—Buenos días, profesora.	*—Good morning, professor.*
—Buenos días. ¿Cómo te llamas?	*—Good morning. What's your name?*
—Me llamo David Romero Solar. ¿Y usted?	*—My name is David Romero Solar. And you?*
—Me llamo Susana Alegría Ramírez.	*—My name is Susana Alegría Ramírez.*
—Mucho gusto, profesora.	*—It's a pleasure, professor.*
—El gusto es mío. ¡Bienvenido, David!	*—The pleasure is mine. Welcome, David!*

Actividades

1 El gusto es mío. Look at the conversations above. With whom would you use the following phrases?

1. ¿Cómo te llamas? / ¿Y tú? _____
2. ¿Cómo se llama usted? / ¿Y usted? _____

2 ¿Cómo te llamas? Practice introducing yourself to three classmates. Use the conversation between Sara and Pablo as a model.

3 ¿Cómo se llama usted? Using the conversations above as models, role-play with different classmates using formal introductions as: (a) head of your school, (b) president of your country, or (c) a famous celebrity.

EL ALFABETO ESPAÑOL (*THE SPANISH ALPHABET*)

As your instructor pronounces the 27 letters of the Spanish alphabet with their corresponding names, repeat each one, noting some of the differences compared with the English alphabet (which has only 26 letters).

La letra	El nombre	La letra	El nombre	La letra	El nombre
a	*a*	j	*jota*	r	*ere*
b	*be, be grande*	k	*ka*	s	*ese*
c	*ce*	l	*ele*	t	*te*
d	*de*	m	*eme*	u	*u*
e	*e*	n	*ene*	v	*uve, ve chica*
f	*efe*	ñ	*eñe*	w	*doble ve, doble u*
g	*ge*	o	*o*	x	*equis*
h	*hache*	p	*pe*	y	*i griega*
i	*i*	q	*cu*	z	*zeta*

Note: In older dictionaries you will find the letters **ch** (*che*) and **ll** (*elle, doble ele*); these were removed from the Spanish alphabet in 1994. Also, **rr** (*erre*) is now considered a sound, not a letter.

Las consonantes (*Consonants*)

The letters **b** and **v** have the same pronunciation as *b* at the beginning of words. These letters have the same pronunciation as *v* between two vowels.	bien, victoria uva, sabe
The **c** of **ca, co, cu** is pronounced like the *c* in *cot*.	cama, coco, cubo
The **c** of **ce, ci** is pronounced like the *c* in *center* in Latin America, and with a *th* sound in Spain.	cerebro, cierto
The **g** of **ga, go, gu** is pronounced like *go*.	gato, gorro, guante
The **g** of **ge, gi** is pronounced like *helium*.	gente, gira
The letter **h** is always silent.	hotel, hospital
The letter **j** is pronounced like the *h* in *heavy*.	jaguar
The letters **k** and **w** are usually found in words borrowed from other languages.	kilogramo, *windsurf*
The letter combination **ll** is pronounced like the *y* in the word *you* or like the *s* in the word *measure*.	lluvia, calle
The letter combination **que** is always pronounced like *kay* in the word *okay*.	queso, quetzal
The letter combination **qui** is always pronounced like the word *key*.	Quijote, arquitecto
The letter **r** at the beginning of a word is trilled just like the *rr* sound in Spanish.	Rita, rosa
The letter **r** between two vowels is pronounced like a double *d* or *t*, as in *ladder* or *butter*.	para, cura
The letter **z** is pronounced like *s* in Latin America and like *th* in Spain.	lápiz, zona

Las vocales (*Vowels*)

Because vowels are critical in Spanish pronunciation, it is important to master their sounds. Repeat the following words after your instructor. Be sure to pay close attention to your instructor's face as you listen to the words.

La vocal	La pronunciación	El vocabulario	El inglés
a	*as in the word "palm"*	casa	*house*
		fama	*fame*
		cama	*bed*
e	*as in the word "very"*	lento	*slow*
		verde	*green*
		mes	*month*
i	*as in the word "elite"*	mitad	*half*
		primo	*cousin*
		vino	*wine*
o	*as in the word "oh"*	no	*no*
		oso	*bear*
		todo	*all*
u	*as in the word "lunar"*	luna	*moon*
		uno	*one*
		cuna	*crib*

Acentuación (*Stress*)

A few basic guidelines will help you learn which syllable to stress when pronouncing words in Spanish. By carefully studying these rules, you will listen, speak, read, and write with greater ease.

1. Spanish words ending in a vowel (**a, e, i, o, u), n** or **s** carry the spoken stress on the second to last syllable. No written accent is necessary.

ofi**ci**na	*office*	**chi**cos	*boys*	**ha**blan	*you / they speak*
clase	*class*	pro**gra**ma	*program*	estudi**an**tes	*students*

2. Words ending in a consonant other than **n** or **s** carry the spoken stress on the last syllable. No written accent is necessary.

liber**tad**	*liberty*	pa**pel**	*paper*	ha**blar**	*to speak*
re**loj**	*watch*	escri**bir**	*to write*	profe**sor**	*professor*

3. Words that are exceptions to the previous two rules carry written accents to indicate which syllable carries the stress.

in**glés**	*English*	sim**pá**tico	*nice*
página	*page*	televi**sión**	*television*

4. Written accents in words ending in **-ión** are not needed in the plural:

composic**ión**   composic**ion**es   lecc**ión**   lecc**ion**es

5. The following words, when used as *interrogatives*, always carry accents:

¿cómo?	*how?*	¿qué?	*what?*
¿cuándo?	*when?*	¿quién/es?	*who?*
¿dónde?	*where?*	¿por qué?	*why?*
¿cuánto/a/s?	*how much?, how many?*	¿cuál/es?	*which?, what?*

6. Although their pronunciation remains the same, certain words carry accents to distinguish their meaning:

el	*the*	él	*he*
como	*as, like*	¿cómo?	*how?*
tu	*your*	tú	*you*
si	*if*	sí	*yes*

Actividades

1 Pronunciemos. With a classmate, pronounce the following words. Then ask each other how to spell each one in Spanish. Use the letter and pronunciation charts above for reference. Note that if a word carries an accent, add the phrase **con acento** to the name of the letter. Follow the model.

▶ **MODELO:** —*¿Cómo se deletrea **lápiz** en español?*
—*ele, a con acento, pe, i, zeta*

1. amigo
2. igualmente
3. rápido
4. página
5. bien
6. gemelo
7. códice
8. televisión
9. gusto
10. español
11. sí
12. jaguar
13. lápiz
14. profesora
15. universidad
16. hola

2 Los acentos. Add the missing accent to each word, if needed.

1. señora
2. aguila
3. papel
4. television
5. programas
6. lapices
7. luz
8. dificil

Hispanics in the United States

Today, almost 500 million people worldwide speak Spanish! Spanish is spoken by approximately 350 million people in 21 countries (Mexico: 98 million; Spain: 39 million; United States: 39 million; Argentina: 35 million; Colombia: 36 million; Venezuela: 22 million; Peru: 20 million). Spanish is the world's third most spoken language, after Mandarin Chinese and English, and ranks second in terms of native speakers.

The U.S. Census Bureau reports that the nation's Hispanic population is expected to jump to 59.7 million by 2020. The 40 million Hispanics currently living in the United States make up 14% of the total population. This population growth has increased demand for Spanish language media: radio, television, newspapers, and magazines.

Hispanics contribute to all aspects of life in the United States; from the foods we eat, to the music we enjoy; they are political leaders, athletes, news anchors, entertainers, scientists, teachers, and students. Their ethnic diversity is also noteworthy and reflects the cultural richness of the Spanish-speaking world.

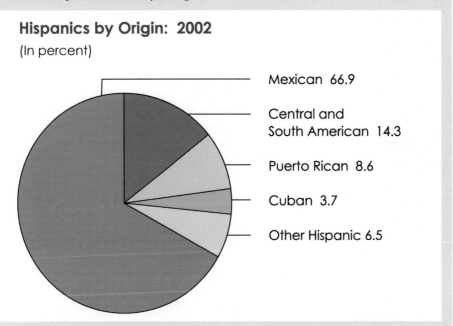

Hispanics by Origin: 2002
(In percent)

Mexican 66.9

Central and South American 14.3

Puerto Rican 8.6

Cuban 3.7

Other Hispanic 6.5

Source: U.S. Census Bureau, Annual Demographic Supplement to the March 2002 Current Population Survey.

Discusión en grupos

1. Why are you studying Spanish? How do you think this course will be useful for you in the near or distant future?
2. Is there a large Hispanic population in your community? If so, where are they from? If not, what are the ethnic backgrounds of the people in your community?
3. Look at the map of Hispanics in the United States at the front of your textbook. Which states have the largest Hispanic population? Which states have the smallest? How does your state compare to other states on the map? Why do you think certain states have larger Hispanic populations than others?
4. Discuss which states might have a large percentage of people from these countries: México, Puerto Rico, Cuba, and Guatemala. Why do you think this is so?

NACIONALIDADES / IDENTIDADES (NATIONALITIES / IDENTITIES)

Caela	¿De dónde eres?	Where are you from?
Aída	Soy de La Paz. Soy boliviana. ¿Y tú?	I am from La Paz. I am Bolivian. And you?
Caela	Soy hondureña. Soy de Tegucigalpa.	I'm Honduran. I am from Tegucigalpa.
Aída	Mucho gusto.	It's a pleasure.
Caela	El gusto es mío.	The pleasure is mine.

Nacionalidades / Identidades

Country / Island	For females	For males	English
África + Estados Unidos	afroamericana	afroamericano	African American
Alemania	alemana	alemán	German
Argentina	argentina	argentino	Argentine
Asia + Estados Unidos	asiáticoamericana	asiáticoamericano	Asian American
Bolivia	boliviana	boliviano	Bolivian
Brasil	brasileña	brasileño	Brazilian
Canadá	canadiense	canadiense	Canadian
Chile	chilena	chileno	Chilean
China	china	chino	Chinese
Colombia	colombiana	colombiano	Colombian
Corea	coreana	coreano	Korean
Corea + Estados Unidos	coreanoamericana	coreanoamericano	Korean American
Costa Rica	costarricense	costarricense	Costa Rican
Cuba	cubana	cubano	Cuban
Cuba + Estados Unidos	cubanoamericana	cubanoamericano	Cuban American
Ecuador	ecuatoriana	ecuatoriano	Ecuadorian
El Salvador	salvadoreña	salvadoreño	Salvadoran
España	española	español	Spanish
Estados Unidos	estadounidense	estadounidense	from the U.S.
Europa	europea	europeo	European
Francia	francesa	francés	French
Guatemala	guatemalteca	guatemalteco	Guatemalan
Haití	haitiana	haitiano	Haitian
Honduras	hondureña	hondureño	Honduran
Inglaterra	inglesa	inglés	English
Irlanda	irlandesa	irlandés	Irish
Italia	italiana	italiano	Italian
Japón	japonesa	japonés	Japanese
México	mexicana	mexicano	Mexican
México + Estados Unidos	mexicanoamericana	mexicanoamericano	Mexican American
Nicaragua	nicaragüense	nicaragüense	Nicaraguan
Panamá	panameña	panameño	Panamanian
Paraguay	paraguaya	paraguayo	Paraguayan
Perú	peruana	peruano	Peruvian
Portugal	portuguesa	portugués	Portuguese
Puerto Rico	puertorriqueña	puertorriqueño	Puerto Rican
República Dominicana	dominicana	dominicano	Dominican
Rusia	rusa	ruso	Russian
Uruguay	uruguaya	uruguayo	Uruguayan
Venezuela	venezolana	venezolano	Venezuelan

Actividades

👥 **1 Nacionalidades.** Below are some of the characters you will meet in ***Caminos del jaguar.*** Read where they are from and, using the Nacionalidades / Identidades chart, identify their nationalities. Work in groups.

Me llamo Luis Ortiz López.

Soy de Puerto Rico.

Soy _____

Me llamo Patricia.

Soy de San Antonio, Texas.

Soy _____

Me llamo Gerardo Covarrubias.

Soy de España.

Soy _____

Me llamo Zulaya Piscomayo Curihual.

Soy de Ecuador.

Soy _____

Me llamo Esperanza.

Soy de México.

Soy _____

2 Orígenes. How many of these people do you recognize? Identify their nationalities. Refer to the nationality chart on page 8. Be sure to use the nationality that corresponds to a female or a male.

1. Penélope Cruz
2. Hideki Matsui
3. Audrey Tatou
4. Gloria Estefan
5. Luciano Pavarotti

6. Shakira
7. Vladimir Putin
8. David Ortiz
9. Prince William
10. Carlos Santana

👥 **3 ¡Hola!** In pairs, role-play two of the characters from ***Actividad 2.*** Use the information about their names and nationalities to create a conversation in which you practice greetings, introductions, and expressions of courtesy.

CAMINOS DEL JAGUAR

Myth and Mystery

The *Popol Vuh*, the sacred book of the Mayans, reveals the story of the Mayan Hero Twins (**Los héroes gemelos**) **Yax-Balam** (YASH-BA-LAM) and **Hun-Ahau** (U-NA-HOW). They are twin figures from Mayan lore who symbolize the triumph of good over evil. The Jaguar Twins have mythical powers and are the central figures in this exciting mystery.

According to the Mayans, the universe is divided into three worlds: the sky (**el cielo**), the earth (**la tierra**), and the underworld (**Xibalbá**)—a parallel world beneath the earth, full of plants, animals, and people. In the *Popol Vuh*, the Jaguar Hero Twins overpowered the Lords of Xibalbá.

The Mayans played a ball game similar to modern-day soccer. The hero twins Yax-Balam and Hun-Ahau were the best ball players on earth, but the noise they made while playing the game infuriated the Lords of Xibalbá. The Lords invited the Jaguar Twins to play ball in Xibalbá and designed a series of challenges to make the twins fail. However, the Hero Twins won the game as well as the challenges and became gods themselves.

The story in **Caminos del jaguar** is based on this myth of the Jaguar Twins. In our video, archaeology professor Nayeli Paz Ocotlán, of the University of Puebla, has just published her book, *Los héroes gemelos de Xibalbá*, which narrates the history of Yax-Balam and Hun-Ahau.

These representations of the Jaguar Twins were created to accompany the great Mayan King Pacal to Xibalbá when he died on August 31. Centuries later, thieves stole these artifacts from the grave site and sold them for riches.

Join us and two archaeology students, Adriana and Felipe, who take a journey down an unexpected path where the forces of good and evil (**los buenos y los malos**) battle over the fate of the Jaguar Hero Twins. Will the missing Jaguar Twins find their way back to Mexico or will they fall into the wrong hands forever?

NAYELI PAZ OCOTLÁN

Born to a Mexican mother and a Spanish father, Nayeli was raised in New York City and later studied at the Universidad Autónoma de México (UNAM). She is now a well-known professor of archaeology at the Universidad de Puebla, where she is dedicated to locating Mexican artifacts and preserving them. She is an expert on the story of the Jaguar Twins and has recently published the book, *Los héroes gemelos de Xibalbá*. Hernán, her husband, died in the Mexican earthquake of 1985. Nayeli feels responsible for his death.

GAFASNEGRAS

Born and raised in Mexico City, she was one of Nayeli's first archaeology students in Puebla and has always been jealous of her. Her nickname is Gafasnegras because she wears sunglasses. (**gafas**=*glasses*, **negras**=*dark*). Her real name is Mariluz Gorrostiaga Hinojosa.

ADRIANA REYES TEPOLE

Born in San Antonio, Adriana Reyes Tepole grew up in Guayaquil, Ecuador, where her father worked on a United Nations project. When she was twelve, the family then returned to Texas, the birthplace of her father. Her mother is from Puebla, Mexico. Adriana recently studied at the Universidad de Puebla and lived with her maternal grandparents. Currently a graduate student in archaeology at the University of Texas at San Antonio, she was awarded a summer fellowship to go on an excavation with Nayeli.

FELIPE LUNA VELILLA

For many years, Felipe lived with his Venezuelan father in Caracas before returning to Miami to live with his Cuban mother and stepfather. He completed his undergraduate studies in archaeology at the University of Miami and is doing graduate work at the University of Texas at San Antonio. He also has been awarded a summer fellowship to go on a dig with Nayeli.

ARMANDO DE LANDA CHÁVEZ

Armando is a Mexican entrepreneur who helps fund Adriana and Felipe's summer travels.

LA ABUELITA (*GRANDMOTHER*)

Nayeli's grandmother lived in Puebla all her life and Nayeli was her favorite grandchild. She has passed away but visits Nayeli often in vivid dreams. Nayeli adores her grandmother.

MYSTERIOUS RING-FINGERED MAN

Friend or foe? You decide.

DOÑA CARMEN QUESADA ARAYA

Doña Carmen, an art collector, lives on a ranch outside of San José, Costa Rica. Nayeli is her godchild, and the two have been very close for years. Nayeli's mother and doña Carmen were art history majors and best friends in college. After Nayeli's mother died, doña Carmen funded Nayeli's college studies.

Adiós.	*Good-bye.*
Bastante bien, gracias.	*Pretty well, thanks.*
¡Bienvenido!	*Welcome!*
Buenas noches.	*Good evening. / Good night.*
Buenas tardes.	*Good afternoon.*
Buenos días.	*Good morning.*
Chao.	*Bye.*
¿cómo?	*how?*
¿Cómo está usted? / ¿Cómo estás tú?	*How are you?*
¿Cómo se llama usted ? / ¿Cómo te llamas?	*What's your name?*
¿cuál/es?	*which?, what?*
¿cuándo?	*when?*
¿cuánto/a/s?	*how much?, how many?*
¿dónde?	*where?*
El gusto es mío.	*The pleasure is mine.*
está / están	*is, are*
Hasta mañana.	*See you tomorrow.*
Igualmente.	*Likewise.*
Lo siento.	*I'm sorry.*
Me llamo...	*My name is . . .*
Mucho gusto.	*Pleased to meet you.*
Muy bien, gracias.	*Very well, thank you.*
Muy mal, bastante mal.	*Very bad, quite bad.*
Nada en particular.	*Nothing special.*
¿por qué?	*why?*
porque	*because*
¿qué?	*what?*
¿Qué hay de nuevo?	*What's new?*
¿Qué tal?	*How's it going?*
¿quién/es?	*who?*
¿Verdad?	*Really?*
¿Y usted? / ¿Y tú?	*And you?*

MÁS PALABRAS Y EXPRESIONES

Abre (tú) / Abran (ustedes) el libro a la página...	*Open your book to page...*
la actividad	*activity*
el/la alumno/a	*student*
el/la amigo/a	*friend*
el/la chico/a	*boy, girl*
la clase	*class*
¿Cómo se dice... ?	*How do you say . . . ?*
el/la compañero de clase (de cuarto)	*classmate (roommate)*
Con permiso.	*Excuse me.*
contesta (tú) / contesten (ustedes)	*answer (verb)*
De nada.	*You're welcome.*
el/la doctor/a (Dr. / Dra.)	*doctor*
don (D.)	*male title of respect, used with first name*
doña (Dña.)	*female title of respect, used with first name*
en grupos	*in groups*
en parejas	*in pairs*
escucha (tú) / escuchen (ustedes)	*listen*
el/la estudiante	*student*
habla (tú) / hablen (ustedes)	*speak*
Hasta la vista.	*Until we meet again.*
Hasta luego / mañana.	*See you later / tomorrow.*
más despacio	*more slowly*
No sé.	*I don't know.*
¡Ojo!	*Be careful!*
la página	*page*
Perdón.	*Pardon. / Excuse me.*
por favor	*please*
la pregunta	*question*
pregunta (tú) / pregunten (ustedes)	*ask*
el/la profesor/a	*professor*
¿Qué quiere decir... ?	*What does . . . mean?*
la regla	*rule*
regular	*OK*
repite (tú) / repitan (ustedes)	*repeat*
señor (Sr.)	*Mr.*
señora (Sra.)	*Mrs.*
señorita (Srta.)	*Miss*
Sí, cómo no.	*Of course.*
también	*also*
la unidad	*unit*
¡Vamos! / ¡Vámonos!	*Let's go!*

En la universidad

VOCABULARIO Y LENGUA

- ▶ Describing things in a room
- ▶ Using articles and nouns
- ▶ Identifying colors (Noun and adjective agreement)
- ▶ Counting from 0 to 199

- ▶ Discussing academic schedules and subjects
- ▶ Telling time
- ▶ Describing people and things using **ser**
- ▶ Using adjectives

CAMINOS DEL JAGUAR

- ▶ ¿Arqueóloga o criminal?
- ▶ El destino llama

LECTURA

- ▶ Estudiantes talentosos

NOTAS CULTURALES

- ▶ Los héroes gemelos
- ▶ Los mayas de México

ESTRATEGIAS

- ▶ **Reading:** Identifying cognates and prefixes
- ▶ **Writing:** Creating a cluster diagram

Miguel Suárez-Pierra, *Girasol*

Preguntas del tema

▶ ¿Cómo es la universidad? ¿enorme? ¿moderna? ¿excelente?

▶ ¿Son fascinantes las clases?

▶ ¿Cuál es una clase popular? ¿historia? ¿matemáticas? ¿biología?

▶ ¿Hay estudiantes interesantes en la universidad?

PRIMER PASO

Vocabulario y lengua

DESCRIBING THINGS IN A ROOM

¿Qué hay en el cuarto? (*What is in the room?*)

Cognates (**cognados**) are words that have similar spellings and meanings in both Spanish and English. How many of these cognates can you match with items in the drawing below?

un teléfono	una televisión	un calendario	una lámpara
una calculadora	un/a computador/a	un mapa	una rosa
una oficina	una universidad	un/a radio	

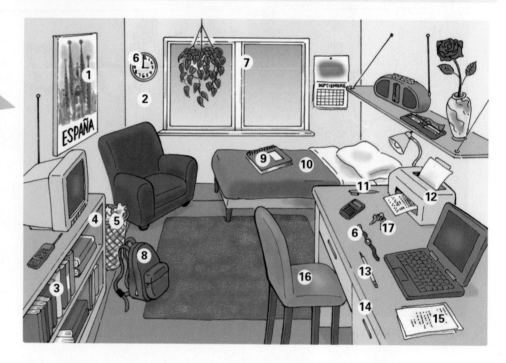

1. un cartel
2. una pared
3. unos libros
4. un estante
5. un basurero
6. un reloj
7. una ventana
8. una mochila
9. un cuaderno
10. una cama
11. un bolígrafo / una pluma
12. una impresora
13. un lápiz
14. un escritorio
15. unos papeles
16. una silla
17. unas llaves

Más palabras y expresiones

Sustantivos

un borrador	*a blackboard eraser*	una puerta	*a door*
una carpeta	*a folder*	un pupitre	*a writing desk*
un dormitorio	*a bedroom*	una residencia	*a dormitory*
una mesa	*a table*	una sala de clase	*a classroom*
una pizarra	*a blackboard*	una tiza	*a piece of chalk*

Otras expresiones

de	*of, from*
en	*in, on, at*
(no) hay	*there is (not); there are (not)*
y	*and*

Actividades

1 ¿Qué hay en el cuarto? Listen to the description of Ernesto's room. Number the items in the order that you hear them. Not all items will be mentioned.

 _____    _____    _____

 _____   _____    _____

 _____    _____   _____

 _____   _____

2 **Asociaciones.** Match each word in the left-hand column with the most closely associated word in the right-hand column.

_____ **1.** papel	a. estante
_____ **2.** pizarra	b. tiza
_____ **3.** silla	c. bolígrafo
_____ **4.** cartel	d. impresora
_____ **5.** libro	e. residencia
_____ **6.** cuaderno	f. escritorio
_____ **7.** universidad	g. mochila
_____ **8.** lápiz	h. pared

3 **En la sala de clase.** Work with a partner to list as many things in your classroom as you can.

▶ MODELO: —¿Qué hay en la sala de clase?   —*What is in the classroom?*
—Hay una pizarra.   —*There is a chalkboard.*

4 **En el cuarto.** List three things in your bedroom and three things *not* in your bedroom. Play "twenty questions" with your partner to guess what is on each other's lists. Follow the model.

▶ MODELO: —¿Hay una computadora?   —*Is there a computer?*
—Sí, hay una computadora.   —*Yes, there is a computer.*
or   *or*
—No, no hay una computadora.   —*No, there isn't a computer.*

USING ARTICLES AND NOUNS

Indefinite articles: *a, an, some*

un alumno

unos alumnos

una alumna

unos alumnos

unas alumnas

The indefinite article has four forms.

	Masculine	Feminine
Singular	un	una
Plural	unos	unas

Definite articles: *the*

el libro

los libros

la silla

las sillas

The definite article has four forms.

	Masculine	Feminine
Singular	el	la
Plural	los	las

Masculine and feminine nouns

Nouns in Spanish are either masculine or feminine. Usually, nouns that refer to males are masculine and nouns that refer to females are feminine.

Masculine	Feminine	
el alumno	**la** alumna	*the student*
el amigo	**la** amiga	*the friend*
el chico	**la** chica	*the boy, the girl*
el compañero de clase	**la** compañera de clase	*the classmate*
el profesor	**la** profesora	*the teacher*
el señor	**la** señora	*Mr., Mrs.*

Nouns ending in -**ista** or -**e** that refer to people can be either masculine or feminine. The context or the article will indicate the gender.

Masculine	Feminine	
el art**ista**	**la** art**ista**	*artist*
el dent**ista**	**la** dent**ista**	*dentist*
el estudiant**e**	**la** estudiant**e**	*student*
el pacient**e**	**la** pacient**e**	*patient*

In some cases, the nouns for people are different for men and women.

Masculine		Feminine	
el hombre	*man*	**la** mujer	*woman*
el padre	*father*	**la** madre	*mother*

Most nouns that refer to things and end in -**o** are masculine while most feminine nouns end in -**a.**

Masculine		Feminine	
el calendari**o**	*calendar*	**la** pintur**a**	*painting*
el basurer**o**	*garbage can*	**la** calculador**a**	*calculator*
el libr**o**	*book*	**la** impresor**a**	*printer*

There are nouns whose gender is not obvious just by looking at the endings. But certain endings may give you a clue about a noun's gender.
Nouns ending in -**ión, -dad,** and -**tad** are usually feminine.

la lecc**ión**	*lesson*	**la** activi**dad**	*activity*	**la** liber**tad**	*liberty*
la composic**ión**	*composition*	**la** ciu**dad**	*city*	**la** mi**tad**	*half*

Certain nouns ending in **-ma** are masculine. These are exceptions. Here are some that are used frequently.

el cli**ma**	*climate*	**el** idio**ma**	*language*
el siste**ma**	*system*	**el** proble**ma**	*problem*
el te**ma**	*theme*	**el** progra**ma**	*program*

Nouns ending in **-e** may be masculine or feminine.

la clas**e**	*class*	**el** puent**e**	*bridge*
la gent**e**	*people*	**el** cin**e**	*movie theater*

Whenever a feminine word begins with a stressed **a** (with or without a written accent), the definite article **el** is used to avoid combining two stressed sounds.

el agua	*water*	**el** águila	*eagle*	**el** alma	*soul*

Here are three common words that are exceptions to the rules above:

el día	*day*	**la** mano	*hand*	**el** mapa	*map*

When talking *about* people with titles such as **señor, señora, señorita, doctor** and **doctora,** the definite article is used. When talking *to* them directly, the definite article is not used.

El señor Medina es doctor.	*Mr. Medina is a doctor.*
Doctor Medina, ¿cómo está usted?	*Doctor Medina, how are you?*

Plural of nouns

Nouns ending in a vowel generally add **-s** to form the plural.

el alumn**o**	los alumn**os**
la chic**a**	las chic**as**
la clas**e**	las clas**es**

Nouns ending in a consonant add **–es** to form the plural.

el pape**l**	los papel**es**
el relo**j**	los reloj**es**

When pluralizing nouns ending in **–z**, the **–z** changes to **–c** before **–es.**

el lápi**z**	los lápi**ces**

Nouns typically keep their gender in both singular and plural forms. One common exception is:

el arte *art*	**las** art**es** *the arts*

Actividades

1 **Los artículos indefinidos.** Identify the correct indefinite article for these words.

1. _____ actividades
2. _____ ciudades
3. _____ carteles
4. _____ cuartos
5. _____ compañeras
6. _____ estudiantes
7. _____ impresoras
8. _____ televisiones

2 **Los artículos definidos.** For each noun, give the correct definite article. Then, give the plural form of the noun and article.

1. _____ cuaderno

   _____

2. _____ día

   _____

3. _____ lápiz
_____

4. _____ mano
_____

5. _____ papel
_____

6. _____ reloj
_____

7. _____ silla
_____

8. _____ teléfono
_____

3 Práctica. Work with a partner. Replace the indefinite article **un** or **una** with the definite article **el** or **la.** Then make each word plural. Follow the model.

▶ **MODELO:** Student 1: _un libro_   Student 1: _unos libros_
               Student 2: _el libro_   Student 2: _los libros_

1. un señor
2. una estudiante
3. una calculadora
4. un basurero
5. una composición
6. un tema
7. una compañera de clase
8. una mano

4 ¿Qué es? Work with a partner. Indicate whether each noun is masculine, feminine, or both, by writing the definite article **el, la,** or both articles in front of each noun. Then say the words aloud.

1. _____ puente
2. _____ artista
3. _____ bolsa
4. _____ calendario
5. _____ dentista
6. _____ cine
7. _____ clase
8. _____ día
9. _____ idioma
10. _____ impresora
11. _____ estudiante
12. _____ mapa
13. _____ oportunidad
14. _____ papel
15. _____ profesor
16. _____ señora

5 Hombres y mujeres. Work with a partner. Read aloud a word from the list and your partner will give its equivalent in the opposite gender. Be careful to use the correct definite or indefinite article.

▶ **MODELO:** Student 1: _un hombre_   Student 2: _una mujer_

1. un profesor
2. el chico
3. un señor
4. una estudiante
5. la mujer
6. una alumna
7. un amigo
8. el artista

IDENTIFYING COLORS
(NOUN AND ADJECTIVE AGREEMENT)

¿De qué color es? (*What color is it?*)

rosado   negro   café   morado   rojo   azul   blanco   amarillo   verde   anaranjado   gris

Both Spanish and English use **adjectives** to describe the color of an object. In Spanish, adjectives usually modify nouns and must agree in *gender* (masculine or feminine) and *number* (singular or plural) with the nouns they modify. Adjectives that end in **-o** or **-a** have corresponding plural forms ending in **-os** and **-as.** The ending needed depends on the gender of the noun.

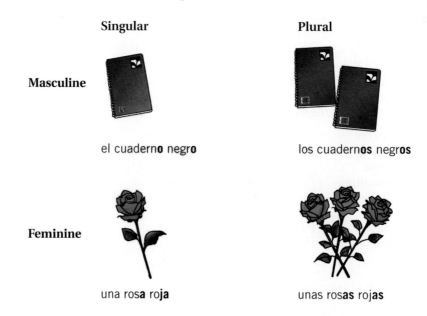

	Singular	**Plural**
Masculine	el cuader**no** neg**ro**	los cuader**nos** neg**ros**
Feminine	una ros**a** ro**ja**	unas ros**as** ro**jas**

Adjectives that end in any letter other than **-o** or **-a** have only two forms, singular and plural.

	Singular		**Plural**	
Masculine	el libro interesant**e**	*the interesting book*	los libros interesant**es**	*the interesting books*
Feminine	la clase interesant**e**	*the interesting class*	las clases interesant**es**	*the interesting classes*

To describe a noun with more than one adjective, connect the adjectives with the conjunction **y** (*and*).

el libro blanco y rojo.   *the white and red book*

Actividades

1 **Los colores.** Name the colors of the items in the picture on page 18. Make the color agree with the item and add the correct definite article. Work with a partner. Follow the model.

> **MODELO:** _____ mochila _____
> <u>la</u> mochila <u>roja</u>

1. _____ basurero _____
2. _____ cama _____
3. _____ papeles _____
4. _____ pared _____
5. _____ rosa _____
6. _____ teléfono _____
7. _____ cuaderno _____
8. _____ lámpara _____

2 **Adjetivos.** Add the correct definite article to each noun in Column A. Ask your partner to select an adjective from Column B and make it agree with that noun. Take turns. Follow the model.

> **MODELO:** Student A   Student B
> _los libros_   _verdes_

A	**B**
1. libros	a. blanco
2. silla	b. rojo
3. alfombras	c. interesante
4. mochila	d. gris
5. papel	e. amarillo
6. lápices	f. verde
7. foto	g. azul
8. mapa	h. negro

3 **Cosas y colores.** Work in pairs to describe the objects and their colors in the drawing.

> **MODELO:** —¿Qué hay en la oficina?   —_What is in the office?_
> —Hay unos lápices   —_There are some_
> amarillos.   _yellow pencils._

Los números del 0 al 199

0	cero	10	diez	20	veinte	30	treinta
1	uno	11	once	21	veintiuno	40	cuarenta
2	dos	12	doce	22	veintidós	50	cincuenta
3	tres	13	trece	23	veintitrés	60	sesenta
4	cuatro	14	catorce	24	veinticuatro	70	setenta
5	cinco	15	quince	25	veinticinco	80	ochenta
6	seis	16	dieciséis	26	veintiséis	90	noventa
7	siete	17	diecisiete	27	veintisiete	100	cien
8	ocho	18	dieciocho	28	veintiocho	101	ciento uno
9	nueve	19	diecinueve	29	veintinueve	199	ciento noventa y nueve

Number notes

uno / una	**Uno** changes to **una** in front of a feminine noun: *41 computers* = cuarenta y **una** computadoras **Uno** changes to **un** in front of a masculine noun: *31 telephones* = treinta y **un** teléfonos
veinte +	**Veinte +** is usually written as one word: *23* = **veintitrés** *25* = **veinticinco**
treinta + *to* **noventa+**	The numbers from 31–39; 41–49 etc. are always written as three separate words: *37* = **treinta y siete** *98* = **noventa y ocho** Note that **"y"** appears only between the "tens" and "ones" place.
cien	**Cien** is used when the number is *exactly* 100: *100 students* = **cien alumnos** *100 books* = **cien libros**
ciento	**Ciento** is used in the numbers **101** to **199;** it doesn't change its form: *103 computers* = En la universidad hay **ciento tres** computadoras.

Actividades

1 La clase de matemáticas.
In pairs, practice these mathematical problems in Spanish. Follow the model.

▶ **MODELO:** 5 + 33 = __38__.
Cinco más treinta y tres son treinta y ocho.
33 − 5 = __28__.
Treinta y tres menos cinco son veintiocho.

1. 85 + 11 = _____.
2. 73 − 27 = _____.
3. 15 + 67 = _____.
4. 24 − 13 = _____.
5. 101 + 36 = _____.

6. 99 − 12 = _____.
7. 183 + 14 = _____.
8. 199 − 94 = _____.
9. 75 + 111 = _____.
10. 43 − 10 = _____.

2 Las páginas amarillas panameñas.
In pairs, practice saying the phone numbers taken from the Panamanian Yellow Pages. Follow the model.

▶ **MODELO:** ¿Cuál es el número de teléfono de la Universidad Interamericana de Panamá?
Es el cinco, cero, siete; dos, sesenta y tres; setenta y siete, ochenta y siete

UNIVERSIDAD INTERAMERICANA DE PANAMÁ
Av Manuel Espinosa Batista, Pmá
PANAMÁ – Panamá, Panamá
Teléfono: (507) 263-7787
Fax: (507) 263-3688

LA CASA DEL MÚSICO
Vía Rdo J Alfaro, L-15
PANAMÁ – Panamá, Panamá
Teléfono: (507) 260-9715

INFOTUR
Vía España Perejil, Pmá
PANAMÁ – Panamá, Panamá
Teléfono: (507) 227-3729

UNIVERSIDAD LATINA
Vía Rdo J Alfaro
PANAMÁ – Panamá, Panamá
Teléfono: (507) 230-8600
Fax: (507) 230-8686

COLEGIO INTERNACIONAL OXFORD
Av Fdco Boyd, Pmá
PANAMÁ – Panamá, Panamá
Teléfono: (507) 265-6422
Fax: (507) 265-7446

UNIVERSIDAD AMERICANA
Cl Rdo Arias y Av 3 Sur, Área Bancaria
PANAMÁ – Panamá, Panamá
Teléfonos: (507) 213-1967
(507) 213-1214

3 Números importantes.
You need to make up a class list of phone numbers for five of your classmates. Interview your classmates and complete the following chart with this information. Follow the model.

▶ **MODELO:**
—¿Cómo te llamas?
—Me llamo Marcos.
—¿Cuál es tu número de teléfono?
—Es el seis, noventa y nueve; cinco, veinticuatro; cuarenta y nueve, setenta y seis.

—What's your name?
—My name is Marcos.
—What is your phone number?
—It's six, ninety-nine; five, twenty-four, forty-nine, seventy-six

	Nombre	Teléfono
Modelo:	Marcos	699-524-4976
1.		
2.		
3.		
4.		
5.		

¿Arqueóloga o criminal?

Actividades

Online Study Center

For additional practice with this episode, visit the *Caminos* website at http://college.hmco.com/languages/spanish/renjilian/caminos/3e/student_home.html.

1 Comprensión. Based on this episode of *Caminos del jaguar,* choose the logical response.

1. Adriana y Felipe están en...
   a. la cancha de fútbol.
   b. la cancha de béisbol.

2. Felipe es...
   a. delgado y guapo.
   b. gordo y guapo.

3. ¿Dónde es la excavación?
   a. en Puebla
   b. en San Antonio

4. La excavación es...
   a. una oportunidad terrible.
   b. una oportunidad increíble.

5. Adriana es...
   a. organizada.
   b. desorganizada.

6. El viaje a Puebla...
   a. es muy largo.
   b. no es muy largo.

2 Situaciones. Role-play one of these situations with a classmate.

1. Adriana asks three persons whether they are Felipe´s friends.
2. Felipe and Adriana talk about the excavation and their trip to Puebla.

3 Escritura. Write a brief description of Felipe and Adriana (4–6 sentences).

NOTA CULTURAL

Los héroes gemelos

The story of Yax Balam and Hun-Ahau, the Jaguar Twins and heroes of the Mayan mythology is told in the sacred book of the Mayans, the **Popol Vuh.** The twins were two very clever young Mayan ball players who liked to challenge others with their unusually good skills at the ball game. This game was a difficult one and would often cost players their lives. When the gods of the Mayan underworld, Xibalbá, realized that the twins seemed to be invincible, they decided to set up a trap to kill them and invited the boys to play a ball game with them. The Mayan Jaguar Twins accepted the challenge. Once in Xibalbá, they had to overcome incredible challenges and defeated the evil gods. After their victory in Xibalbá, the Jaguar Hero Twins became two bright stars in the sky.

SEGUNDO PASO

Vocabulario y lengua

DISCUSSING ACADEMIC SCHEDULES AND SUBJECTS

Una semana típica (*A typical week*)

Adela Esquivel

LUNES — historia, arqueología
MARTES — arte, química
MIÉRCOLES — historia, arqueología
JUEVES — música, química
VIERNES — historia, arqueología
SÁBADO — volibol, cine
DOMINGO — tenis, concierto

In many Spanish-speaking countries, the calendar week begins on Monday. Some countries, however, use calendars that start with Sunday, as in the United States. In Spanish, the days of the week are masculine and are not capitalized.

el lunes	(*on*) *Monday*
los lunes	(*on*) *Mondays*

To talk about the days of the week, use the following models.

¿Qué día es hoy?	*What day is today?*
Hoy es martes.	*Today is Tuesday.*
¿Qué día es mañana?	*What day is tomorrow?*
Mañana es miércoles.	*Tomorrow is Wednesday.*

To talk about what someone studies and on which day(s), use the following models.

Adela **estudia** música los jueves.	*Adela studies music on Thursdays.*
Adela **no estudia** los domingos.	*Adela doesn't study on Sundays.*

Actividades

1 ¿Qué estudia? (*What does she study?*) Answer these questions according to Adela's schedule.

1. ¿Qué estudia los lunes?
2. ¿Estudia historia? ¿Cuándo?
3. ¿Qué estudia los jueves?
4. ¿Cuándo estudia química?
5. ¿Qué estudia los viernes?
6. ¿Qué estudia los martes?
7. ¿Estudia los sábados y los domingos?

2 El horario de Luis. (*Luis's schedule.*) Work with a partner to complete Luis's schedule with the information given.

1. Estudia música los martes y jueves.
2. Estudia historia los lunes.
3. Estudia español los jueves.
4. Estudia arqueología los viernes.
5. Estudia química los lunes, miércoles y viernes.
6. No estudia los sábados.

¿Qué fecha es hoy? (*What is today's date?*)

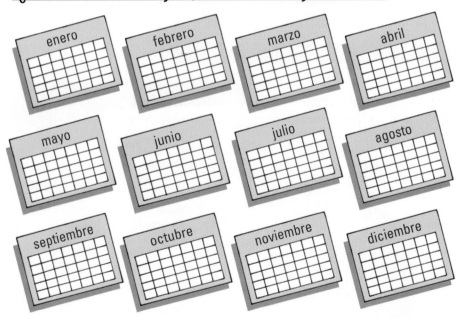

To talk about dates, use these models.

¿Qué fecha es hoy?   *What is today's date?*
¿Cuál es la fecha de hoy?   *What is today's date?*
Hoy es el veintitrés de septiembre. *Today is September 23.*

As with the names of days, months are not capitalized in Spanish. In Latin America, the first day of the month is **el primero.**

Hoy es el **primero** de abril.   *Today is April first.*

For dates in Spanish, the day of the month always comes first: **9/12 = el nueve de diciembre.** This is different from the United States, where the the month precedes the day.

Actividades

1 ¿Qué fecha es? Say the following dates in Spanish.

1. December 9
2. October 15
3. July 4
4. April 19

5. January 1
6. March 13
7. May 31
8. February 22

2 Fechas importantes. Write the dates in Spanish for these occasions. Then practice them with a classmate.

▶ **MODELO:** Independence Day (USA)
el cuatro de julio *the fourth of July*

1. Valentine's Day
2. Thanksgiving Day this year
3. April Fool's Day
4. New Year's Eve
5. Your birthday
6. Your sister or brother's birthday
7. The first day of classes this term
8. The last day of classes this term

En la universidad (*At the university*)

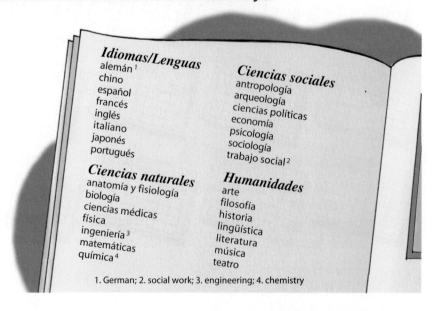

Idiomas/Lenguas
alemán [1]
chino
español
francés
inglés
italiano
japonés
portugués

Ciencias sociales
antropología
arqueología
ciencias políticas
economía
psicología
sociología
trabajo social [2]

Ciencias naturales
anatomía y fisiología
biología
ciencias médicas
física
ingeniería [3]
matemáticas
química [4]

Humanidades
arte
filosofía
historia
lingüística
literatura
música
teatro

1. German; 2. social work; 3. engineering; 4. chemistry

A false cognate (**cognado falso**), sometimes called **amigo falso,** is a word in Spanish that looks like a word in English but has a different meaning. Below are some examples you may encounter when talking about academic subjects.

► To ask what someone's major is, you say **¿Cuál es tu** *(your)* **especialización?** The word **mayor** means *older.*
► The faculty of a university is **el profesorado. La facultad** means *school,* as in **La facultad de humanidades,** *The School of Humanities.*
► An academic subject is **la materia. El sujeto** often refers to the grammatical subject of a sentence.

Actividades

1 Asociaciones. What subject areas do you associate with these words? Use your knowledge of cognates.

1. el átomo
2. el cadáver
3. el laboratorio
4. el oxígeno
5. la composición
6. las elecciones
7. la fórmula
8. la infección
9. los números
10. la psicosis
11. la sociedad
12. la trompeta

 2 ¿Qué enseña? *(What does s/he teach?)* Work with a partner to determine in which academic department you would find the following people.

1. Sigmund Freud
2. Isaac Newton
3. Stephen King
4. Abraham Lincoln
5. Florence Nightingale
6. Jane Goodall
7. Aristotle
8. Malcolm X
9. Pablo Picasso
10. Carlos Santana

 3 ¿Qué estudias? Ask three of your classmates to name a subject they are studying other than Spanish. Then, based on their answer, guess what other subject they might be studying. Write the subjects next to the **materia** categories below. Conduct your interview according to the model.

► MODELO: —¿Qué estudias?   —*What do you study?*
          —Estudio matemáticas.   —*I study mathematics.*
          —¿Estudias química?   —*Do you study chemistry?*
          —No, no estudio química, —*No, I don't study chemistry,*
            estudio psicología.   *I study psychology*

	Estudiante 1	Estudiante 2	Estudiante 3
Materia 1	_____	_____	_____
Materia 2	_____	_____	_____

DESCRIBING PEOPLE AND THINGS USING *SER*

Subject pronouns

In Spanish, subject pronouns are used to clarify or emphasize a subject. In most cases they are optional because you can tell what the subject is by looking at the verb ending.

Subject pronouns					
	Singular		**Plural**		
1st person	yo	*I*	nosotros / nosotras	*we*	
2nd person	tú	*you (fam.)*	vosotros / vosotras	*you (Spain)*	
3rd person	usted (Ud.)	*you (formal)*	ustedes (Uds.)	*you*	
	él / ella	*he / she*	ellos / ellas	*they*	

Tú
Used when addressing familiar people in an informal, friendly situation. (Normally used with friends, family, and co-workers.)

Usted (Ud.)
Used when speaking in formal situations with unfamiliar people or when you need to show respect for someone (grandparents, colleagues, certain professionals).

Ustedes (Uds.)
Latin America distinguishes between formal and informal situations only in the singular form. This distinction does not exist when speaking to more than one person; therefore **ustedes** is the form used in the plural in both formal and informal situations.

Vosotros/as

Spain distinguishes between informal and formal forms in the plural. In an informal situation, **vosotros/as** is used. For formal situations, **ustedes** is used.

Nosotras, vosotras, ellas

Used only when referring to all-female groups.

The verb *ser* (*to be*)

Ser is one of the most common verbs in Spanish and has irregular conjugation forms.

ser (*to be*)					
	Singular			**Plural**	
1st person	yo	**soy**	*I am*	nosotros / nosotras	**somos**	*we are*
2nd person	tú	**eres**	*you are*	vosotros / vosotras	**sois**	*you are*
3rd person	usted él / ella	**es**	*you are he /she is*	ustedes ellos / ellas	**son**	*you are they are*

Ser has many uses. This list summarizes some of them. (Note that the first letter of each usage type spells POTIONS. This mnemonic device can help you remember the uses of the verb.)

Ser is used to describe:

P eople	Arturo **es** inteligente.	*Arturo is intelligent.*
O ccupations	Ellos **son** estudiantes.	*They are students.*
T hings / Time*	La silla **es** negra.	*The chair is black.*
	Son las tres.	*It's three o'clock.*
I dentity	**Soy** Roberto.	*I am Roberto.*
O rigin	**Somos** de México.	*We are from Mexico.*
N ationality	Ellos **son** mexicanos.	*They are Mexican.*
S ubstance: What things are made of	El libro **es** de papel.	*The book is made of paper.*

_____

*You will learn how to use **ser** to tell time on page 40.

When using **ser** to describe someone's occupation or nationality, the indefinite article is omitted unless an adjective follows the description.

Carmen es artista.	*Carmen is an artist.*
Carmen es cubanoamericana.	*Carmen is Cuban-American.*
Carmen es **una** artista cubanoamericana.	*Carmen is a Cuban-American artist.*
Carmen es **una** artista talentosa.	*Carmen is a talented artist.*

Remember to connect adjectives with the conjunction **y** (*and*) when describing someone or something with more than one adjective.

Enrique es alto **y** guapo.　　　*Enrique is tall and handsome.*

Before a word that starts with **i-** or **hi-,** **y** changes to **e.**

La profesora es simpática **e** inteligente.	*The professor is friendly and intelligent.*
Hay clases de inglés **e** historia.	*There are English and history classes.*

To place emphasis on an adjective, use **muy** + *adjective.*

El libro es **muy** interesante.	*The book is very interesting.*
Los estudiantes son **muy** inteligentes.	*The students are very intelligent.*

Negation

Simple negation is formed by adding **no** before the verb.

Nosotros **no** somos de México.	*We are not from Mexico.*
El libro **no** es amarillo.	*The book is not yellow.*

To answer a question negatively, start the sentence with **no,** in addition to adding **no** before the verb.

—¿La ventana es blanca?	*—Is the window white?*
—**No,** la ventana **no** es blanca.	*—No, the window is not white.*
—¿Eres de España?	*—Are you from Spain?*
—**No, no** soy de España.	*—No, I'm not from Spain.*

Actividades

1 ¿Quién eres? Work with a partner to complete the dialog with the correct forms of **ser.** Take turns answering the questions affirmatively or negatively. If answering negatively, do not forget to add **no** before the verb.

1. ¿Tú _____ estudiante de español? Sí / No, yo _____ estudiante de español.
2. ¿Tú _____ de los Estados Unidos? Sí / No, yo _____ de los Estados Unidos.
3. ¿El / La profesor/a _____ de México? Sí / No, él / ella _____ de México.
4. ¿La pared _____ azul? Sí / No, la pared _____ azul.
5. ¿Nosotros/as _____ amigos/as? Sí / No, nosotros/as _____ amigos/as.

2 Isabel. Complete Isabel's description of her classroom and life at school with the correct forms of **ser.**

Me llamo Isabel. Yo (**1**) _____ estudiante de español. Mis compañeros de clase también (*also*) (**2**) _____ estudiantes de español. La profesora (**3**) _____ muy inteligente y simpática. ¡La clase de español (**4**) _____ muy interesante! En la sala de clase hay mesas, sillas, computadoras y libros. Las computadoras (**5**) _____ excelentes y modernas y las mesas (**6**) _____ de Puerto Rico. En las mochilas de los estudiantes hay libros, calculadoras y papeles. Los libros (**7**) _____ interesantes y las calculadoras (**8**) _____ muy prácticas. Las actividades de deportes (*sports*) (**9**) _____ muy divertidas (*fun*). Hay golf, volibol y básquetbol. Nosotros (**10**) _____ estudiantes muy afortunados.

3 ¿De dónde son? Working with a partner, state where these people are from and their nationalities. Be sure to review the vocabulary for nationalities on page 8.

▶ MODELO: Gabriela Sabatini

Gabriela Sabatini <u>es</u> de Buenos Aires. <u>Es argentina</u>.	*Gabriela Sabatini is from Buenos Aires. She's Argentinean.*

1. Juan Luis Guerra _____ de Santo Domingo. _____.
2. Cameron Díaz y su familia _____ de California. _____.

3. Arantxa Sánchez _____ de Barcelona. _____.
4. Rigoberta Menchú _____ de Chimel, Guatemala. _____.
5. Laura Esquivel _____ de México. _____.
6. Isabel Allende _____ de Santiago. _____.
7. Yo _____ de _____. _____.
8. Mi compañero/a de cuarto _____ de _____. _____.

USING ADJECTIVES

¿Cómo son? (*What are they like?*)

El diablo es malo.

Sara es trabajadora.

Pedro es amable.

El ángel es bueno.

Carlos es perezoso.

Raquel es tímida.

Rosa

David

alta   bajo

Luisa

Daniel

Graciela

rubia   moreno   pelirroja

Don Diego

Beatriz

joven   viejo, mayor

GATO   PERRO

gordo   delgado

Elvira

Antonio

fea   guapo

In some countries it is more polite to say **mayor** (*older*) or **grande** instead of **viejo/a** (*old*) to describe someone's age. Also **gordito/a** (*fat*) is used instead of **gordo/a** as a term of affection in some countries.

 La computadora es nueva.

 La computadora es vieja.

 La mesa es grande.

 La mesa es pequeña.

 El coche es rápido.

 El coche es lento.

 El lápiz es largo.

 El lápiz es corto.

Más palabras y expresiones

Cognados

atractivo/a	fascinante	organizado/a	romántico/a
cómico/a	inteligente	pesimista	serio/a
excepcional	optimista	popular	tímido/a

Adjetivos

agradable	*pleasant*
amable	*friendly*
antipático/a	*unfriendly*
bueno/a	*good*
desagradable	*unpleasant*
difícil	*difficult*
envidioso/a	*envious*
fácil	*easy*
hermoso/a, bonito/a, lindo/a	*beautiful, pretty, lovely*
listo/a	*smart, clever*
malo/a	*bad*
perezoso/a, flojo/a	*lazy*
simpático/a	*nice, friendly*
trabajador/a	*hard-working*

Actividades

1 **¿Cómo son?** Working with a partner, ask and answer questions about the people or animals in the drawings on page 37. Follow the model.

▶ **MODELO:** Sara
—¿Cómo es Sara?   —*What is Sara like?*
— Sara es trabajadora.   — *Sara is hard-working.*

1. Graciela
2. el gato
3. Beatriz
4. el ángel
5. Don Diego

6. David
7. Luisa
8. Raquel
9. Elvira
10. Carlos

11. Antonio
12. el diablo
13. Rosa
14. Daniel
15. el perro

2 **Futuros arqueólogos.** Listen to the description of the main characters in *Caminos del jaguar,* and fill in the blanks with the missing words.

Adriana y Felipe son (**1**) _____ de arqueología en los Estados Unidos.
(**2**) _____ es morena. Ella es (**3**) _____, amable y atractiva. Felipe es
(**4**) _____. Es (**5**) _____, muy simpático y (**6**) _____.

3 **La oficina.** Here is a list of items in Alberto's design office. Find the objects, state how many there are, and describe their appearance.

▶ **MODELO:** —¿Cuantos basureros   —*How many trash cans*
hay en la oficina?   *are there in the office?*
—Hay un basurero.   —*There is one trash can.*
—¿Cómo es?   —*What does it look like?*
—Es grande y anaranjado.   —*It's big and orange.*

radio
reloj
papel
ventana
basurero
teléfono
computadora
lámpara
carpeta
estante
lápiz
escritorio
cartel
silla
libro

4 **Personalidades.** Describe the following people. Include both physical and personality traits.

1. Shakira
2. Carlos Santana
3. Antonio Banderas

4. Andy García
5. Rosie Pérez
6. Christina Aguilera

7. Enrique Iglesias
8. Rafael Nadal
9. ¿...?

5 Así es. Write a brief description of one of your classmates on a piece of paper. Be sure to include details such as hair color, type of clothing, etc. Your instructor will collect these descriptions and hand them out at random for students to read. Try to guess each person being described.

TELLING TIME

¿Qué hora es? (*What time is it?*)

Time is expressed with the verb **ser**. Use **¿Qué hora es?** to ask what time it is. When giving the time, **es** is used only with times that begin with **una** (*one*); otherwise use **son.**

Son las once.	*It's eleven o'clock.*
Es la una.	*It's one o'clock.*

Son las dos de la tarde.

The exact time of day can be expressed by adding **de la mañana / tarde / noche.**

Son las cinco **de la mañana.**	*It's five A.M. (in the morning)*
Es la una **de la tarde.**	*It's one P.M. (in the afternoon)*
Son las ocho **de la noche.**	*It's eight P.M. (in the evening)*

Es la una y media de la mañana.

Son las cuatro y veinte de la tarde.

Time *after* the hour is expressed using **y** + *minutes* (or + **cuarto / media**).

Son las siete **y** veinte (de la noche).	*It's seven twenty (P.M.).*
Es la una **y cuarto.**	*It's quarter past one (one-fifteen).*
Son las seis **y media.**	*It's six-thirty.*

Son las once menos cuarto de la mañana.

Time *before* the hour is expressed using **menos** + *minutes* (or + **cuarto**).

Son las cinco **menos** veinte.	*It's twenty minutes to five.*
Es la una **menos cuarto.**	*It's a quarter to one.*

Es mediodía.   **Es medianoche.**

To express noon and midnight you can say for either one

Son las doce.	*It's twelve o'clock.*

or use the expressions **mediodía** and **medianoche** as shown on the clocks.

To express "at" what time an event occurs, use **a + la/s** + *hour*.

—¿Es la clase **a las** dos de la tarde? —*Is the class at two P.M.?*
—No, es **a la** una de la tarde. —*No, it's at one P.M.*

General time periods are expressed using **por la mañana / tarde / noche.**

—¿Estudia Juan **por la mañana**? —*Does Juan study in the morning?*
—No, Juan estudia **por la tarde** y —*No, Juan studies in the afternoon and*
por la noche. *in the evening (at night).*

Actividades

1 ¿Qué hora es? With a partner take turns telling the time on each clock below.

5:30

10:40

4:15

12:00

7:55

9:45

2 La hora en el mundo. You have friends all over the world and to keep in touch with them, you need to know what time it is where they live. Use the clocks in different time zones to figure out what time it is in each location for each time indicated. Complete the chart and practice telling time with a partner.

Tokyo, Japón   Anchorage, AL   Los Ángeles, CA   Nueva York, NY   Madrid, España

1. _____   _____   _____   _____   2:30 A.M.
2. _____   3:00 P.M.   _____   _____
3. _____   _____   4:45 P.M.   _____
4. _____   _____   1:16 P.M.   _____   _____
5. 10:48 A.M.   _____   _____   _____

El destino llama

San Antonio. En el apartamento de Adriana.

Dos boletos de autobús para Puebla, el viernes.

Adriana, ¡tú y Felipe en Puebla! ¡Qué romántico!

No, Patricia, la arqueología es muy seria.

No, la arqueología no. ¡Felipe! ¿Cómo es Felipe?

En el apartamento de Felipe.

Adriana es muy agradable,... muy simpática.

Adriana es muy trabajadora.

No, Adriana no. ¿Cómo es la excavación?

¡Felipe! ¿Cómo es la excavación?

¿Cómo es Felipe? ¿Es simpático?

No es desagradable.

¿Y es listo?

Sí, es inteligente.

¿Y de dónde es?

Es de Miami. La familia es cubana.

La arqueología es fascinante.

Adriana también es fascinante.

Arturo, la excavación no es un romance. La arqueología es seria.

Tú eres muy romántico.

El viaje a Puebla no es un viaje romántico. La arqueología es importante.

Ah... ¿Y cuándo es el viaje a Puebla?

A las once, el viernes.

¿Felipe? ¡Hola!

¿Cuándo es el viaje?

El viernes.

¡El destino llama!

¡Y yo contesto!

¿Aló? ¡Adriana! ... Ah, sí, en la estación a las diez y media.

San Antonio. En la estación de autobuses.

¿Qué pasa?

El autobús no está aquí. Va a llegar pronto.

Ah...

¿Qué libro es?

Es el libro de Nayeli: "Los héroes gemelos de Xibalbá".

La historia es muy interesante.

Sí, los héroes gemelos siempre triunfan sobre los malos espíritus.

¡Y nosotros también!

En la calle, cerca del apartamento de Nayeli.

En la estación de buses de Laredo:

¿Adónde vamos?

Al aeropuerto, por favor.

¡Dos tiquetes para Puebla, por favor!

Actividades

Online Study Center

For additional practice with this episode, visit the *Caminos* website at http://college.hmco.com/ languages/spanish/ renjilian/caminos/3e/ student_home.html.

1 Comprensión. Based on this episode of *Caminos del jaguar,* choose the logical response.

1. Adriana reserva *(reserves)* dos boletos para...
   a. San Antonio.   b. Puebla.

2. El viaje es...
   a. el lunes.   b. el viernes.

3. La arqueología es...
   a. muy seria.   b. muy fácil.

4. Adriana opina que Felipe es...
   a. inteligente.   b. desagradable.

5. Felipe opina que Adriana es...
   a. trabajadora.   b. cubana.

6. La familia de Felipe es...
   a. de Miami.   b. de Cuba.

7. Arturo opina que Felipe es...
   a. fascinante.   b. romántico.

8. Nayeli viaja *(travels)* en...
   a. taxi.   b. autobús.

2 Situaciones. With a classmate, dramatize one of the situations below.

1. Adriana and Felipe talk about Nayeli's book.
2. Felipe and Arturo talk about Adriana and the excavation.
3. Adriana and Patricia talk about Felipe and the excavation.

3 Escritura. Describe one of the places listed below (4–6 sentences).

1. El apartamento de Felipe
2. El apartamento de Adriana
3. La estación de autobuses

NOTA CULTURAL

Los mayas de México

The Mayan civilization is one of the great civilizations of Central America. Long before the Spaniards arrived in the region, they lived in what is today southern Mexico, Guatemala, western Honduras, El Salvador, and northern Belize. Their descendents comprise a large ethnic group that still speaks the ancient Mayan language and keeps many of the Mayan traditions alive. The Mayans had advanced knowledge of astronomy and mathematics, and developed their own hieroglyphical writing, a numerical system, and an elaborate calendar. They were also skilled architects and built pyramids and palaces in stone, many of which we can admire today in Tikal, Copán, and Palenque. As artists, they created beautiful pottery and textiles and developed important trade routes with several other ethnic groups in Central America. Their mythology is depicted in old graphic books, or **códices,** representing the beliefs of the Mayan religion and views of the world and the afterlife.

Lectura

Online Study Center

For further reading practice online, visit the *Caminos* website at http://college .hmco.com/languages/ spanish/renjilian/caminos/ 3e/student_home.html.

PRELECTURA

In the reading that follows, you will practice recognizing *cognates*, a valuable skill that will help you learn Spanish. Cognates, or **cognados,** are words that have similar spellings and meanings in two languages. The strategies that follow will help you identify cognates in a text.

Reading Strategy

Recognizing Cognates

Knowing cognates can help you increase your Spanish vocabulary tremendously. The following is a list of adjectives that can be used to describe people, places, and things. Listen to your instructor and pronounce these words to hear how they compare to similar words in English. What are the comparable endings for these groups of words in English?

arrogante	importante	pesimista
egoísta	increíble	profesional
elegante	interesante	realista
emocional	internacional	sentimental
evidente	nacional	terrible
excelente	natural	tradicional
final	optimista	transparente
horrible	original	tropical
idealista	persistente	virtual

Actividades

1 ¿Qué quiere decir? What do the words in the cognates list mean?

2 Categorías. The cognates you've learned fall into four categories according to their endings. List them in the following chart. The first one is done for you.

-nte	-ista	-al	-ible
arrogante	_____	_____	_____
_____	_____	_____	_____

Reading Strategy

Identifying Prefixes

By adding prefixes to some cognates you can expand your Spanish vocabulary even further. The prefix **in-** means "not," and is very common in both English and Spanish. Note that in Spanish **in-** is spelled **im-** before **b** and **p.**

3 Opuestos. With a partner, take turns saying aloud the opposites of the given words.

▶ **MODELO:** conveniente   *inconveniente*
perfecto   *imperfecto*

in-	im-
dependiente	probable
estable	personal
flexible	posible
formal	paciente
tolerante	popular

4 ¿Positivo o negativo? From the cognates you've learned, which adjectives have positive meanings? Which are negative? Which can be both? Work in pairs and write down the adjectives that fit into each of these categories.

Positivo	Negativo	Positivo y negativo

Now, describe yourself to a classmate, using one positive and one negative characteristic. Begin with **Soy...** *(I am . . .)*.

5 Persona a persona. Working in pairs, ask each other these questions that include cognates.

1. ¿De dónde eres? ¿Y tu familia?
2. Y tu compañero/a de cuarto, ¿de dónde es?
3. ¿Es enorme tu universidad?
4. En tu opinion, ¿qué especialización es difícil? ¿Cuál es interesante?
5. ¿Qué día es tu favorito en la universidad?
6. ¿Qué materias son fáciles, en tu opinión?

6 Personalización. Complete each sentence below with the most appropriate cognate.

personal   elegante   popular
favorita   inteligente   optimistas

1. Las relaciones internacionales es una especialización _____.
2. Soy una estudiante excelente. Soy _____.
3. Me llamo Jennifer López y soy _____.
4. Mis amigos y yo somos muy _____.
5. El problema es _____ no académico.
6. ¿Es el arte mexicano o colombiano tu materia _____?

Estudiantes talentosos

Mi nombre es Rosa Fernández y soy de la República Dominicana. Mis idiomas son el inglés y el español. Soy estudiante universitaria en la ciudad de Nueva York, con una especialización en la historia y cultura de Latinoamérica. Soy poeta bilingüe y actriz. Las telenovelas[1] son mis programas preferidos en la televisión. También soy bailarina[2] de danzas afrocaribeñas. El autobús es mi transporte público favorito. En el futuro mi plan es ser profesora de historia y cultura latinoamericanas. Soy tradicional y realista.

Me llamo Cuahtémoc Villagrán. Soy guatemalteco, de la ciudad de Chichicastenango. Soy estudiante de doctorado[3] de psicología clínica. Tengo[4] clase los lunes, miércoles y viernes. Los martes y jueves, soy investigador[5] en un laboratorio de biología. Mi intención es ser psicólogo en una clínica internacional, en la capital, para las personas con serios problemas emocionales. Soy una persona flexible y optimista. Los sábados, el fútbol es una parte importante de mi vida, que es simplemente fantástica.

¡Hola! Me llamo Elena Vera y soy una española alta y rubia. Mi apartamento en Madrid, que es una ciudad enorme con millones de personas, es espectacular y muy decorado. Mi motocicleta es una máquina rápida y conveniente para la ciudad. Soy creativa, especialmente en componer[6] música original contemporánea. Los viernes y sábados, soy guitarrista en las discotecas, con un grupo de amigos universitarios. La antropología es mi especialización en la Universidad Complutense de Madrid. En el futuro, mi idea es ser antropóloga internacional en Asia, África y las Américas. Soy una persona natural, independiente y sentimental.

---

[1]soap operas; [2]dancer; [3]Ph.D.; [4]I have; [5]researcher; [6]in composing.

POSTLECTURA

 1 Cognados en acción. Re-read the profiles of the three talented university students. Make a list of the cognates that you recognize. In class, compare your list with a partner.

 2 Estudiantes fascinantes. Answer the following questions with a classmate.

1. ¿De dónde es Rosa? ¿Cuál es su especialización? ¿En dónde?
2. ¿De dónde es Cuahtémoc? ¿En qué laboratorio es investigador?
3. ¿De dónde es Elena? ¿Qué transporte es su preferencia?
4. Es la intención de Cuahtémoc de ser psicólogo en el futuro. ¿En dónde? ¿Quiénes van a ser (will be) sus pacientes?
5. ¿Cuáles son las intenciones de Elena y Rosa en el futuro?
6. En tu opinion, ¿quién de los tres estudiantes es muy interesante? ¿Por qué?

 3 Personalidades famosas. Using as many cognates as possible, write a description in Spanish of three famous people. Read your descriptions and have your classmates guess who is being described. Work in groups of four.

Escritura

When beginning to write in a new language, it is a good idea to use strategies that help you organize your thoughts. Although you might be tempted to write in English and then translate your writing into Spanish, you can become a better writer if you apply some of the suggestions provided in this textbook. At the end of each segment in your Student Activities Manual, you will also practice these strategies in a section called *Escritura*.

Online Study Center

For further writing practice online, visit the *Caminos* website at http://college.hmco .com/languages/spanish/ renjilian/caminos/3e/ student_home.html.

Writing Strategy

Creating a Cluster Diagram

A cluster diagram is a commonly used visual organizer. It allows you to see the connection between main topics and details and helps you find the words that you need to write in Spanish.

Workshop

1. Choose your topic and write it in the center of a piece of paper. Circle it.
2. Focus on the main ideas for your topic. Write them down, circle them, and connect them to your topic.
3. Think about these main ideas and write any related words around them until you have a diagram that looks like this one.

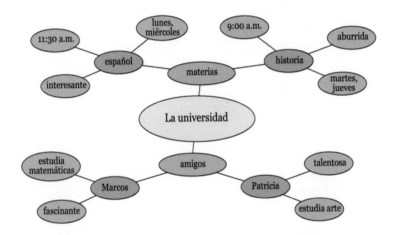

Strategy in Action

For additional practice with the strategy of creating a cluster diagram, turn to the *Escritura* section of your Student Activities Manual.

La vida universitaria. You are homesick and decide to send your best friend a letter describing your university. Include a description of your classes and new friends. Using the cluster diagram above as a guide, create your own diagram to organize your thoughts before writing the letter.

Resumen de vocabulario

PRIMER PASO

¿QUÉ HAY EN EL CUARTO?

Sustantivos (Nouns)

el basurero	*garbage can*
el bolígrafo	*pen*
el borrador	*blackboard eraser*
la calculadora	*calculator*
el calendario	*calendar*
la cama	*bed*
la carpeta	*folder*
el cartel	*poster*
el/la computador/a	*computer*
el cuaderno	*notebook*
el dormitorio	*bedroom*
el escritorio	*desk*
el estante	*bookshelf*
la impresora	*printer*
la lámpara	*lamp*
el lápiz	*pencil*
el libro	*book*
la llave	*key*
el mapa	*map*
la mesa	*table*
la mochila	*backpack*
la oficina	*office*
el papel	*paper*
la pared	*wall*
la pizarra	*blackboard*
la pluma	*pen*
la puerta	*door*
el pupitre	*writing desk*
el/la radio	*radio*
el reloj	*watch, clock*
la residencia	*dormitory*
la rosa	*rose*
la sala de clase	*classroom*
la silla	*chair*
el teléfono	*telephone*
la televisión	*television*
la tiza	*a piece of chalk*
la universidad	*university*
la ventana	*window*

OTRAS EXPRESIONES

de	*of, from*
en	*in, on, at*
(no) hay	*there is (not); there are (not)*
y	*and*

USING ARTICLES AND NOUNS

Sustantivos

el/la artista	*artist*
la composición	*composition*
el hombre	*man*
la lección	*lesson*
la madre	*mother*
la mitad	*half*
la mujer	*woman*
la noche	*night*
el padre	*father*
la pintura	*painting*
el problema	*problem*
el sistema	*system*
la tarde	*afternoon*
el tema	*theme*

COLORES

amarillo	*yellow*
anaranjado	*orange*
azul	*blue*
blanco	*white*
café	*brown*
gris	*grey*
morado	*purple*
negro	*black*
rojo	*red*
rosado	*pink*
verde	*green*

LOS NÚMEROS DEL 0 AL 199

0	cero	20	veinte
1	uno	21	veintiuno
2	dos	22	veintidós
3	tres	23	veintitrés
4	cuatro	24	veinticuatro
5	cinco	25	veinticinco
6	seis	26	veintiséis
7	siete	27	veintisiete
8	ocho	28	veintiocho
9	nueve	29	veintinueve
10	diez	30	treinta
11	once	40	cuarenta
12	doce	50	cincuenta
13	trece	60	sesenta
14	catorce	70	setenta
15	quince	80	ochenta
16	dieciséis	90	noventa
17	diecisiete	100	cien
18	dieciocho	101	ciento uno
19	diecinueve	199	ciento noventa y nueve

SEGUNDO PASO

Los días de la semana

el lunes	*Monday*
el martes	*Tuesday*
el miércoles	*Wednesday*
el jueves	*Thursday*
el viernes	*Friday*
el sábado	*Saturday*
el domingo	*Sunday*

Otras expresiones

el día	*day*
estudia	*he / she studies / you (formal) study*
la fecha	*date*
el horario	*schedule*
hoy	*today*
mañana	*tomorrow*
el primero	*first*

Los meses del año

enero	*January*
febrero	*February*
marzo	*March*
abril	*April*
mayo	*May*
junio	*June*
julio	*July*
agosto	*August*
septiembre	*September*
octubre	*October*
noviembre	*November*
diciembre	*December*

EN LA UNIVERSIDAD

Sustantivos

el alemán	German
la anatomía	anatomy
la antropología	anthropology
la arqueología	archaeology
el arte	art
la biología	biology
el chino	Chinese
las ciencias médicas	medical sciences
las ciencias naturales	natural sciences
las ciencias políticas	political science
las ciencias sociales	social sciences
la economía	economics
el español	Spanish
la especialización	major
la facultad	school (as in School of Humanities)
la filosofía	philosophy
la física	physics
la fisiología	physiology
el francés	French
la historia	history
las humanidades	humanities
el idioma	language
la ingeniería	engineering
el inglés	English
el italiano	Italian
el japonés	Japanese
la lingüística	linguistics
la literatura	literature
las matemáticas	mathematics
la materia	subject (in school)
la música	music
el portugués	Portuguese
el profesorado	faculty
la psicología	psychology
la química	chemistry
la sociología	sociology
el sujeto	subject (part of speech)
el teatro	theater
el trabajo social	social work

Otras expresiones

estudias	you study
estudio	I study

DESCRIBING PEOPLE AND THINGS

Adjetivos

agradable	pleasant
alto/a	tall
amable	friendly
antipático/a	unfriendly
atractivo/a	attractive
bajo/a	short (height)
bonito/a	pretty
bueno/a	good
cómico/a	funny, comical
corto/a	short (length)
delgado/a	thin
desagradable	unpleasant
difícil	difficult
envidioso/a	envious
excepcional	exceptional
fácil	easy
fascinante	fascinating
feo/a	ugly
flojo/a	lazy
gordo/a	fat
grande	big, large
guapo/a	handsome, good-looking
hermoso/a	beautiful
inteligente	intelligent
joven	young
largo/a	long
lento/a	slow
lindo/a	lovely
listo/a	smart, clever
malo/a	bad
mayor	older
moreno/a	dark-haired
nuevo/a	new
optimista	optimistic
organizado/a	organized
pelirrojo/a	redhead
pequeño/a	small

perezoso/a	*lazy*	**Verbo**	
pesimista	*pessimistic*	ser	*to be*
popular	*popular*		

LA HORA

perezoso/a	*lazy*
pesimista	*pessimistic*
popular	*popular*
rápido/a	*fast*
romántico/a	*romantic*
rubio/a	*blonde*
serio/a	*serious*
simpático/a	*nice, friendly*
tímido/a	*shy / timid*
trabajador/a	*hard-working*
viejo/a	*old*

Subject pronouns

yo	*I*
tú	*you (fam.)*
usted (Ud.)	*you (formal)*
él / ella	*he / she*
nosotros / nosotras	*we*
vosotros / vosotras	*you (Spain)*
ustedes (Uds.)	*you*
ellos / ellas	*they*

Otras expresiones

muy	*very*

Verbo

ser	*to be*

LA HORA

Sustantivos

cuarto	*quarter (ex: It's quarter past two.)*
el mediodía	*noon*
media	*half (thirty); (ex: It's two thirty.)*
la medianoche	*midnight*

Otras expresiones

de la mañana / tarde / noche	*in the morning / afternoon / evening (for specific time periods)*
menos	*minus*
por la mañana / tarde / noche	*in the morning / afternoon / night (for general time periods)*
¿Qué hora es?	*What time is it?*

En la ciudad

VOCABULARIO Y LENGUA

- ▶ Describing an apartment
- ▶ Expressing possession
- ▶ Identifying furnishings and household chores
- ▶ Describing actions in the present: Regular verbs

- ▶ Indicating likes and dislikes
- ▶ Expressing location and emotion with *estar*
- ▶ Talking about places in a city
- ▶ Describing present actions in progress

CAMINOS DEL JAGUAR

- ▶ Malas noticias
- ▶ Jaguares gemelos

LECTURA

- ▶ Bienvenidos a Puebla: Ciudad de ángeles

NOTAS CULTURALES

- ▶ La universidad de las Américas
- ▶ Los códices mayas

ESTRATEGIAS

- ▶ **Reading:** Asking questions
- ▶ **Writing:** Brainstorming ideas

Joan Miró, *Prades, the Village*

Preguntas del tema

► ¿Es grande o pequeña tu casa? ¿Cuántos cuartos hay en la casa?

► ¿Hay restaurantes internacionales en tu ciudad?

► ¿Hay un museo famoso?

► ¿Hay un parque central?

PRIMER PASO

Vocabulario y lengua

DESCRIBING AN APARTMENT

Un apartamento en la Colonia[1] Villareal

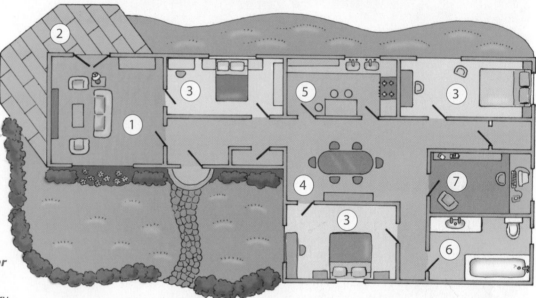

Online Study Center

For additional practice with the unit's vocabulary and grammar, visit the *Caminos* website at http://college.hmco.com/languages/spanish/renjilian/caminos/3e/student_home.html. You can also review audio flashcards, quiz yourself, and explore related Spanish-language sites.

1. la sala	**4.** el comedor	**6.** el (cuarto de) baño
2. la terraza	**5.** la cocina	**7.** la oficina
3. el dormitorio		

Más palabras y expresiones

Cognados

el balcón	completo/a	moderno/a
el clóset	el garaje	privado/a

---

[1]In Mexico, a **colonia** is similar to a town district.

Sustantivos

el alquiler, la renta	*rent*
la bañera, la tina	*bathtub*
la casa	*house*
la ducha	*shower*
el/la dueño/a	*owner*
el piso	*floor; apartment (Spain)*
el/la inquilino/a	*tenant*
el jardín	*garden, yard*
la piscina, la alberca	*swimming pool*

Otras expresiones

amplio/a	*spacious*
barato/a	*inexpensive*
con	*with*
caro/a	*expensive*
pequeño/a	*small*
pero	*but*

Actividades

1 El apartamento ideal. You have found the perfect apartment. Work with a partner to discuss the floor plan. Follow the model.

▶ MODELO: —¿Cuántos dormitorios hay?   —*How many bedrooms are there?*
—Hay dos dormitorios.   —*There are two bedrooms.*
—¿Hay una piscina?   —*Is there a swimming pool?*
—No, pero hay un jardín.   —*No, but there is a garden.*

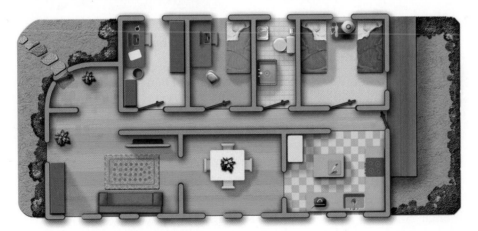

2 ¿Qué cuarto es? Think of one room in the apartment shown in *Actividad 1*. Have a partner guess which room you've chosen, then switch roles.

> **MODELO:** —¿Hay una computadora?
> —Sí, hay una computadora.
> —¿Es el dormitorio pequeño?
> —Sí, es el dormitorio pequeño.

3 Necesito compañero/a. You decide that it would be more economical to look for an apartment with a roommate. Write down the five most important things that you need in an apartment. Then find a classmate whose list matches yours with at least 3 of the items. Once you have found a match, present your roommate to the class and describe what you have in common.

EXPRESSING POSSESSION

There are many ways to express possession. Look at the conversations above and find these expressions in Spanish.

Álvaro's car	María and Benito's house
his house	my car
our house	your dog

In English the words *my, your, his, her, our,* and *their* are called possessive adjectives.

Possessive Adjectives

English	Singular	Plural
my	mi	mis
your (fam., sing.)	tu	tus
your (formal, sing.), his, her, its	su	sus
our	nuestro, nuestra	nuestros, nuestras
your (fam. plural, Spain)	vuestro, vuestra	vuestros, vuestras
your (formal, plural), their	su	sus

Your (formal singular), *his, her, its, your* (plural), and *their* all use the same possessive adjective in the singular, **su,** and in the plural, **sus.**

1. In Spanish, a possessive adjective must agree in number (singular/plural) with the noun it modifies.

mi auto	*my car*	su perro	*(his, her, their, your) dog*
tu**s** auto**s**	*your cars*	su**s** perro**s**	*(his, her, their, your) dogs*

2. In addition to agreeing in number, **nuestro/a** and **vuestro/a** also agree in gender.

nuestr**o** apartament**o**	*our apartment*	nuestr**a** cas**a**	*our house*
nuestr**os** apartament**os**	*our apartments*	nuestr**as** cas**as**	*our houses*

3. The preposition **de** is also used to express possession before names or pronouns.

El auto **de Álvaro** es grande. —*Álvaro's car (the car of Álvaro) is big.*

¡El perro **de él** es maravilloso también! —*His dog is marvelous too!*

When the preposition **de** precedes the article **el,** the two words contract to form **del.** There is no contraction with the pronoun **él.**

—El perro es **del** chico, ¿verdad? —*The dog is the boy´s, isn´t it?*
—Sí, el perro es **de él.** —*Yes, its his.*

4. Use **de quién** to ask who owns something. (Note that the verb **ser** agrees with the item possessed, not with **quién.**) When asking about ownership of more than one thing, and you suspect that there is also more than one owner, you may use **de quiénes.**

—**¿De quién es** la casa grande? —*Whose large house is it?*
—Es de Pablo. —*It belongs to Pablo. (singular)*
—Es de María y Benito. —*It belongs to María and Benito. (plural)*
—**¿De quiénes son** las plumas? —*Whose pens are they?*
—Son de los estudiantes. —*They belong to the students. (plural)*

Actividades

1 Práctica. Replace the English word in parentheses with the appropriate Spanish possessive adjective. Then create a sentence with the phrase.

▶ **MODELO:** mochila *(my)*
   Mi mochila es verde y negra.

1. computadoras *(his)*
2. auto *(our)*
3. ducha *(their)*
4. compañero/a de cuarto *(my)*
5. jardín *(our)*
6. apartamento *(her)*
7. balcón *(your, familiar)*
8. clases *(our)*
9. oficina *(their)*
10. dormitorio *(your, formal)*

2 Posesión. Create sentences using **ser** and the correct possessive adjective.

▶ MODELO: el libro / de Paco
Es su libro.

1. la clase / de nosotros
2. las llaves / de Uds.
3. la televisión / de Rosalita
4. el apartamento / de los Gómez
5. el estéreo / de ellos
6. los cuadernos / de la profesora
7. el teléfono / de papá
8. la computadora / de ella

3 Preguntas. Answer the questions. Work with a partner.

▶ MODELO: —¿De quién es la televisión? (la Sra. Pérez)
—*La televisión es de la Sra. Pérez.*

1. ¿De quién es el auto? (nosotros)
2. ¿De quién es el estéreo? (mi compañero/a de cuarto)
3. ¿De quiénes son las impresoras? (él y ella)
4. ¿De quién es el teléfono celular? (los señores Vera)
5. ¿De quién son los papeles? (la estudiante de español)
6. ¿De quiénes son las mochilas? (ellos)

4 ¿De quién es? Ask and answer who owns each of the items listed in the chart below.

▶ MODELO: —¿De quién es la televisión?
—*La televisión es de Alicia.*

Alicia	Roberto	Mis amigos	Ella	Nosotros	Ellos
televisión	auto	estéreo	impresoras	papeles	teléfonos
sillas casa	llaves	llaves	calculadora	mesita	mochilas

5 ¿Qué hay aquí? Make a list of six things in the classroom or at home. Then take turns asking a partner who owns them.

▶ MODELO: —*En la clase hay muchos cuadernos.*
—*¿De quiénes son?*
—*Son de los estudiantes.*

Los muebles y quehaceres de la casa (*Furniture and household chores*)

Los muebles

1. el espejo
2. la cómoda
3. el ropero,
   el armario
4. la alfombra
5. el sillón
6. la mesita
   de noche
7. el lavabo,
   el lavamanos
8. el/la secador/a
   de pelo
9. la escoba
10. el inodoro
11. las escaleras
12. la mesita
13. el sofá
14. la aspiradora
15. el/la refrigerador/a
16. la estufa

Los quehaceres
(*Household chores*)

17. aspirar, pasar
    la aspiradora
    (por la alfombra)
18. barrer (el piso)
19. arreglar (la cama)
20. lavar (los platos)
21. sacar (la basura)
22. sacudir (los muebles),
    sacar el polvo de
    (los muebles) (*Spain*)

Otros quehaceres

cocinar	*to cook*
limpiar / ordenar (el cuarto)	*to clean / tidy (the room)*
planchar (la ropa)	*to iron (clothes)*
secar (los platos, la ropa)	*to dry (the dishes, clothes)*

Actividades

1 El apartamento de Elena Make a diagram of Elena's apartment. Begin by drawing a large rectangle; then add the following rooms, labeled in Spanish: bedroom, living room, bathroom, and kitchen and dining room. Then, as she describes the apartment, draw and label all of the items found in each room.

2 ¿Recuerdas? Work with a partner to review the names of the rooms and furniture that appear in the drawing of the house on page 59. Take turns pointing to items and naming each one. Try to use as many vocabulary terms from *Unidad 1* as you can.

3 Los quehaceres. Match the drawings with the chores.

1. _____ planchar la ropa
2. _____ ordenar el cuarto
3. _____ aspirar la alfombra
4. _____ barrer el piso
5. _____ sacudir los muebles

6. _____ lavar los platos
7. _____ cocinar
8. _____ secar los platos
9. _____ hacer la cama
10. _____ sacar la basura

a.

b.

c.

d.

e.

f.

g.

h.

i.

j.

4 **El apartamento perfecto.** You are a real estate agent and have some furnished apartments you need to rent. Which apartment would you suggest for each the following clients? Work in groups.

Clientes	Apartamentos
1. **La familia Rodríguez:** 2 adultos, 3 hijos (*children*) muy activos, 2 autos.	**Apartamento a:** Un dormitorio amplio, cocina con comedor, balcón, sala, jardin y garaje.
2. **La familia Iglesias:** 2 adultos, 1 auto, 1 perro (*dog*).	**Apartamento b:** Un jardín grande, un dormitorio grande y un dormitorio pequeño, cocina amplia con comedor, jardín y balcón.
3. **El Sr. Roberts:** 1 adulto muy activo, 2 perros, 1 auto.	**Apartamento c:** 3–4 dormitorios grandes, 2 baños, cocina amplia, comedor y garaje.
4. **La familia Castillo:** 1 adulto, 1 hijo pequeño.	**Apartamento d:** Un dormitorio amplio, una oficina grande, garaje, jardín y piscina.

5 **Soy creativo/a.** Draw one of the apartments above complete with furnishings labeled in Spanish. Share your apartment design with a classmate.

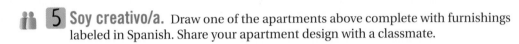

DESCRIBING ACTIONS IN THE PRESENT: REGULAR VERBS

Present indicative of regular *-ar*, *-er*, and *-ir* verbs

Él canta.   Ellos corren.   Ella sube la escalera.

A verb is made up of two parts: the *stem* and the *ending*. The stem defines the word's meaning. The ending indicates the subject and tense.

estudiar *(to study)*		
estudi stem	**o** ending (1st person, singular = I)	*I study*
estudi stem	**an** ending (3rd person, plural = they, you)	*they, you (plural) study*

Spanish verbs are categorized by their infinitive form (<u>to</u> sing, <u>to</u> run, <u>to</u> climb, etc.). There are three main categories: infinitives ending in **-ar (cant<u>ar</u>), -er (corr<u>er</u>),** or **-ir (sub<u>ir</u>).**

Regular verbs are conjugated by replacing the **-ar, -er,** or **-ir** infinitive ending with an ending that reflects both tense and person. The present indicative tense of regular verbs is formed as follows.

Present Indicative Tense of Regular Verbs

		-ar verbs		-er verbs		-ir verbs	
		cantar	*to sing*	**correr**	*to run*	**subir**	*to climb*
Singular							
1st	yo	cant**o**	*I sing*	corr**o**	*I run*	sub**o**	*I climb*
2nd	tú	cant**as**	*you sing*	corr**es**	*you run*	sub**es**	*you climb*
3rd	usted	cant**a**	*you sing*	corr**e**	*you run*	sub**e**	*you climb*
	él / ella		*he / she sings*		*he / she runs*		*he / she climbs*
Plural							
1st	nosotros/ nosotras	cant**amos**	*we sing*	corr**emos**	*we run*	sub**imos**	*we climb*
2nd	vosotros/ vosotras	cant**áis**	*you sing*	corr**éis**	*you run*	sub**ís**	*you climb*
3rd	ustedes ellos / ellas	cant**an**	*you sing they sing*	corr**en**	*you run they run*	sub**en**	*you climb they climb*

The present indicative tense describes actions that happen in the present.

Yo **estudio** arqueología.	*I study / am studying archaeology.*
Celina **habla** inglés.	*Celina speaks / is speaking English.*
Nosotros **bebemos** leche.	*We drink / are drinking milk.*

Common Regular Verbs

-ar verbs

acabar	*to finish*	hablar	*to speak*
acabar de + (infinitive)	*to have just (done something)*	investigar	*to research*
alquilar	*to rent*	lavar	*to wash*
andar	*to walk, move*	llamar	*to call*
bailar	*to dance*	llegar	*to arrive*
buscar	*to look for*	llevar	*to bring*
caminar	*to walk*	mandar	*to send*
comprar	*to buy*	mirar	*to look at*
desear	*to wish for*	necesitar	*to need*
escuchar	*to listen*		

pasar	*to happen; pass*
practicar	*to practice*
preguntar	*to ask*
tomar	*to take*
trabajar	*to work*
terminar	*to finish*
usar	*to use*
viajar	*to travel*
visitar	*to visit*

-er verbs

aprender	*to learn*
beber	*to drink*
comer	*to eat*
comprender	*to understand*
creer	*to believe*
leer	*to read*
responder	*to answer*

-ir verbs

abrir	*to open*
compartir	*to share*
decidir	*to decide*
describir	*to describe*
escribir	*to write*
recibir	*to receive*
vivir	*to live*

To express actions that have just happened, use **acabar de** + infinitive.

¿**Acabas de** llegar?	*Have you just arrived?*
Sí, **acabo de** llegar.	*Yes, I have just arrived.*

Actividades

1 Actividades estudiantiles. Complete the following activities using the correct present indicative tense form of the verb in parentheses.

1. Yo _____ (comprar) una mochila.
2. Elena _____ (hablar) tres idiomas.
3. Juan y Pepe _____ (trabajar) en la oficina.
4. Isabel _____ (viajar) a México.
5. Carmen y yo _____ (estudiar) arqueología.
6. Nosotros _____ (comer) en el comedor.
7. Alicia _____ (vivir) en una casa grande.
8. Yo _____ (abrir) las ventanas.
9. Rosita _____ (alquilar) un apartamento moderno.

2 La vida en la universidad. Paloma is on the phone telling her sister about a few of her academic activities for this week. What does she say? Imagine that you are Paloma and create sentences from the phrases below using the **yo** form (1st person singular).

1. estudiar para un examen
2. escribir una composición en inglés
3. visitar el museo de arte
4. investigar en el laboratorio de química
5. mirar un video de antropología
6. practicar el español

3 Preguntas personales. In pairs, ask each other the following questions. Then share three interesting pieces of information that you have learned about each other with another pair.

1. ¿Estudias español?
2. ¿Escribes cartas o correo electrónico (*e-mail*)?
3. ¿Lees libros?
4. ¿Hablas mucho por teléfono?
5. ¿Necesitas dinero (*money*)?
6. ¿Usas bolígrafo? ¿lápiz?
7. ¿Miras televisión?
8. ¿Vives en una residencia, un apartamento o una casa?

4 Actividades recientes. With a partner, pretend that you are talking with your roommate about the activities that you and your friends have just finished. Use **acabar de** + infinitive to describe the activities.

▶ MODELO: Enrique (comer) sopa.
Enrique acaba de comer sopa.

1. Patricio (escuchar) música
2. Paco y Graciela (comprar) pizza
3. Elvira (escribir) una carta
4. Las chicas (mirar) un video
5. Rodrigo y yo (lavar) el auto
6. Mario (recibir) un cheque
7. Yo (practicar) deportes

5 Querido/a amigo/a. Write a postcard to a friend describing your dormitory, apartment or house and what you do there. Use as many different verbs as possible.

Malas noticias

Actividades

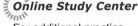
Online Study Center

For additional practice with this episode, visit the *Caminos* website at http://college.hmco.com/ languages/spanish/ renjilian/caminos/3e/ student_home.html.

1 Comprensión. Based on this episode of *Caminos del jaguar*, choose the logical response.

1. Adriana y Felipe buscan a...
   a. Nayeli.
   b. Armando.

2. Hay una nota en...
   a. la oficina de Nayeli.
   b. la oficina de Armando.

3. Armando es amigo de...
   a. Adriana y Felipe.
   b. Nayeli.

4. La nota en la puerta es...
   a. para Armando.
   b. para Adriana y Felipe.

5. Esperanza trabaja en...
   a. la casa de Nayeli.
   b. la oficina de Nayeli.

6. La policía cree que...
   a. Nayeli es inocente.
   b. Nayeli no es inocente.

2 Situaciones. Role-play one of the following situations.

1. Armando, Felipe and Adriana introduce themselves to each other.
2. The detectives discuss what Nayeli does with the Jaguar Twin.

3 Escritura. Write a brief summary of this episode of *Caminos del jaguar* in Spanish. (4–6 sentences)

NOTA CULTURAL

La Universidad de las Américas

This university is located in San Andrés de Cholula, five kilometers outside of the city of Puebla and 120 kilometers (about one hour by car) from Mexico City, in an area where pre-Hispanic, colonial, and modern Mexico converge. On a clear day the university offers a magnificent view of four of the tallest volcanoes in Mexico: Orizaba, Popocatépetl, Iztaccíhuatl, and La Malinche.

SEGUNDO PASO

Vocabulario y lengua

INDICATING LIKES AND DISLIKES

¿Qué te gusta hacer? (*What do you like to do?*)

1. caminar
2. escribir cartas
3. tocar la guitarra
4. escuchar música
5. pintar
6. jugar al volibol
7. leer libros
8. hablar con amigos

Más palabras y expresiones

Verbos

alquilar videos	*to rent videos*
dar un paseo	*to take a walk*
hacer ejercicio	*to exercise*
mirar una película	*to watch a movie*
navegar por Internet (la Red / la web)	*to surf the Internet (Web)*
practicar deportes	*to play sports*
ver televisión	*to watch television*

Otras expresiones

mucho	*a lot, very much*
(un) poco	*(a) little*
también	*also, too*

Using *gustar* (*to like*)

To say that you . . .	use this structure:	
like to do one activity or a series of activities,	**me / te gusta** + *infinitive*	
	Me gusta pintar.	*I like to paint.*
	Te gusta estudiar y comer.	*You like to study and to eat.*
like one specific thing,	**me / te gusta** + *singular noun*	
	Me gusta mucho la clase de español.	*I like Spanish class a lot.*
	Te gusta el fútbol.	*You like soccer.*
like many things or a series of things,	**me / te gustan** + *plural noun*	
	Me gustan las clases de idiomas.	*I like language classes.*
	Te gustan el fútbol y el volibol.	*You like soccer and volleyball.*
do not like any of the above,	add **no** before the structure.	
	No me gusta pintar.	*I don't like to paint.*
	No te gusta el fútbol.	*You don't like soccer.*

Actividades

1 ¿Qué te gusta? With a partner, ask each other what you like to do. If you answer in the affirmative, add a second activity that you also like to do. If you answer in the negative, add an activity that you like. Follow the model.

► MODELO: —¿Te gusta leer libros? —*Do you like to read books?*
—Sí, me gusta leer libros. También me gusta escribir cartas. —*Yes, I like to read books. I also like to write letters.*

or

—No, no me gusta leer libros, pero me gusta escribir cartas. —*No, I don't like to read books, but I do like to write letters.*

1. ¿Te gusta el arte?
2. ¿Te gustan las clases de ciencias?
3. ¿Te gusta navegar por Internet?
4. ¿Te gusta el fútbol?
5. ¿Te gustan los deportes?
6. ¿Te gusta caminar?
7. ¿Te gusta la música jazz?
8. ¿Te gusta hablar con amigos?

▶ MODELO:
—¿Qué te gusta hacer los lunes? —*What do you like to do on Mondays?*

—Me gusta estudiar y escuchar música. —*I like to study and to listen to music.*

—¿Qué no te gusta hacer? —*What don't you like to do?*

—No me gusta hacer ejercicio. —*I don't like to exercise.*

	Te gusta	No te gusta
lunes	estudiar, escuchar música	hacer ejercicio
martes	_____	_____
miércoles	_____	_____
jueves	_____	_____
viernes	_____	_____
sábado	_____	_____
domingo	_____	_____

EXPRESSING LOCATION AND EMOTION WITH *ESTAR*

La señora **está** en el sofá. **Está** aburrida.

La niña **está** en la sala. **Está** triste.

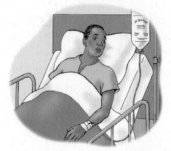

El señor **está** en el hospital. **Está** enfermo.

El chico **está** en la escuela. **Está** contento.

El chico y la chica **están** en el restaurante.
Están enamorados.

The verb **estar** is used to indicate the location of people or objects. **Estar** is also used to express emotional states at a specific moment in time or in a particular situation.

estar *(to be)*			
Singular		**Plural**	
yo	est**oy**	nosotros / nosotras	est**amos**
tú	est**ás**	vosotros / vosotras	est**áis**
Ud. / él / ella	est**á**	Uds. / ellos/ ellas	est**án**

Note that the first person singular is irregular, and that all the other forms, except for the first person plural, carry written accents.

Useful adjectives of emotion

aburrido/a	*bored*	enamorado/a	*in love*
alegre	*happy*	enfermo/a	*sick*
alterado/a	*upset*	enojado/a	*angry*
borracho/a	*drunk*	entusiasmado/a	*enthusiastic*
calmado/a	*calm*	fascinado/a	*fascinated*
cansado/a	*tired*	harto/a	*fed up, disgusted*
celoso/a	*jealous*	listo/a	*ready*
confundido/a	*confused*	nervioso/a	*nervous*
contento/a	*happy*	preocupado/a	*worried*
deprimido/a	*depressed*	seguro/a	*sure*
desilusionado/a	*disappointed*	triste	*sad*
emocionado/a	*excited*		

Actividades

1 Memoria perfecta. You are constantly misplacing things, but luckily you have a roommate who remembers where you put them. You call him/her to ask for help. With your partner, take turns asking each other questions.

► **MODELO:** llaves / estante
—¿*Dónde están las llaves?*
—*Están en el estante.*

1. cuadernos / cama
2. radio / cuarto de baño
3. mi libro de español / mochila
4. reloj / escritorio
5. papeles / silla
6. teléfono / mesa

2 ¿Dónde están?
Make a list of all the people and things in the house pictured below. Then, ask your partner where each one can be found. Take turns.

▶ MODELO: televisión
—¿Dónde está la televisión?
—La televisión está en la cocina.

3 Reacciones.
How would you feel in the following situations? Write your reactions and then share them with a classmate.

▶ MODELO: Your paycheck is late.
—Estoy preocupado/a.

1. You have an exam tomorrow.
2. You just found your true love.
3. You have the flu.
4. Your favorite aunt or uncle died.
5. You passed your most difficult class.
6. Your roommate stole some money.

4 Entrevista.
Interview six of your classmates to find out how they're doing today. Report your findings to the class.

▶ MODELO: —¿Cómo estás?   —How are you?
—Estoy muy contento/a.   —I am very happy.
—¿Por qué?   —Why?
—Porque mañana hay fiesta. —Because there is a party
                             tomorrow.

5 Emociones.
Complete these ideas.

1. Estoy contento/a cuando...
2. Estoy triste cuando...
3. Estoy enojado/a porque...
4. Estoy cansado/a porque...
5. Estoy desilusionado/a porque...
6. Estoy entusiasmado/a porque...

TALKING ABOUT PLACES IN A CITY

¿Qué hay en la ciudad? (*What's in the city?*)

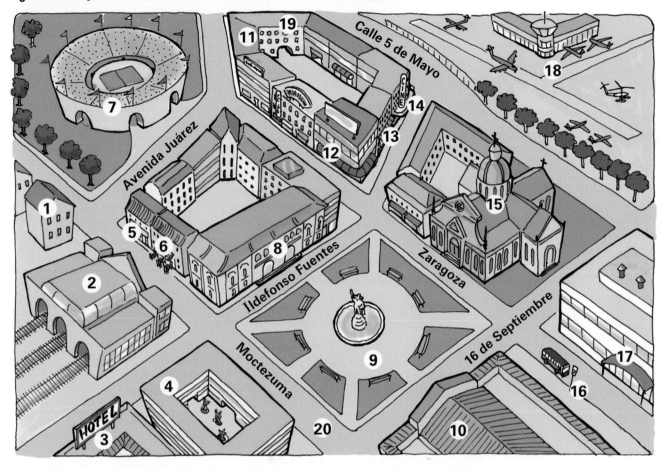

1. el edificio (*building*)
2. la estación de tren (*train station*)
3. el hotel
4. el museo
5. la librería (*bookstore*)
6. el café
7. el estadio
8. el correo (*post office*)
9. la plaza
10. la biblioteca (*library*)

11. el centro comercial (*shopping center*)
12. la tienda (*store*)
13. el restaurante
14. el cine (*movie theater*)
15. la iglesia (*church*)
16. la parada de autobús (*bus stop*)
17. el hospital
18. el aeropuerto
19. el almacén (*department store*)
20. la calle (*street*)

Actividades

1 **¿Dónde está?** Work with a partner to identify and locate the buildings in the city map above. Follow the model.

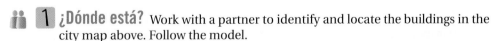

▶ **MODELO:** —¿Dónde está la tienda?   —*Where is the store?*
                —Está en la calle Zaragoza. —*It's on Zaragoza Street.*

2 ¿Dónde están? Teresa has received a phone message from her friend Lisa who is traveling in Mexico City. While looking at the map on page 71, listen to what Lisa says. On a sheet of paper, write down all the things she does and the places she mentions.

3 Una ciudad ideal. Create your own city by drawing and labeling an original city plan. Include at least seven buildings and places from the city map on page 71.

4 Los planes. Now work with a partner and compare your city plans. Follow the model.

▶ MODELO:
—¿Hay un restaurante en la ciudad? —*Is there a restaurant in the city?*
—Sí, hay un restaurante. (No, no hay un restaurante.) —*Yes, there is a restaurant. (No, there isn't a restaurant.)*
—¿Dónde está el restaurante? —*Where is the restaurant?*
—Está en la calle Carolina. —*It's on Carolina Street.*

5 ¿Qué haces? *(What do you do?)* Now work in pairs, and state where you do the following activities. Follow the model.

▶ MODELO:
—¿Dónde lees libros? —*Where do you read books?*
—Leo libros en la biblioteca. —*I read books in the library.*

beber café	esperar el autobús	mirar una película
caminar	estudiar	pagar mucho dinero
comer	hablar con amigos	tomar el tren
comprar	mirar arte	tomar un avión

DESCRIBING PRESENT ACTIONS IN PROGRESS

Present Progressive Tense

Gente en acción (*People in action*)

Natalia y José
están hablando.

Iván
está comiendo.

La señora Cortés
está escribiendo.

To describe an action in progress, use the *present progressive* tense. It is formed with the verb **estar** and the *present participle*. The present participle of regular verbs is formed by dropping the **-ar, -er,** or **-ir** ending of the verb and adding **-ando** for **-ar** verbs and **-iendo** for **-er** and **-ir** verbs.

Present participle of regular verbs		
-ar	**-er**	**-ir**
hablar: habl**ando** *speak — speaking*	comer: com**iendo** *eat — eating*	escribir: escrib**iendo** *write — writing*

Present Participles with a Spelling Change

In Spanish, whenever the unaccented letter **i** appears between two vowels, it changes to **y**. Present participles of verbs such as **leer, creer,** and **construir** *(to build)* include this change (le**ye**ndo, cre**ye**ndo, constru**ye**ndo). Most verbs ending in **–uir** [for example, **incluir** *(to include)* and **destruir** *(to destroy)*] also have this spelling change.

Liliana **está leyendo** el menú.
Los señores López **están construyendo** una casa nueva.

Liliana is reading the menu.
Mr. and Mrs. López are building a new house.

Expressions

Since the simple present tense can often be translated as "am / is / are reading / eating, etc.," the following expressions are frequently used with the present progressive tense to show that this tense focuses on the action in progress.

ahora
en este momento

now
at this moment, now

Actividades

1 Situaciones. Create complete sentences combining the phrases below in a meaningful way. Use the present progressive tense. Follow the model.

▶ MODELO: Gabriel / beber café / restaurante
Gabriel está bebiendo café en el restaurante.

A	B	C
1. Anabel	subir al autobús	la tienda
2. Julia y Nicolás	practicar el fútbol	la biblioteca
3. Mi profesora	alquilar un cuarto	la computadora
4. El Sr. Rodríguez	comprar una computadora	el correo
5. Mis amigos	leer un libro	el hotel
6. Tu amiga Nubia	pagar el cartel	el centro comercial
7. Nuestro profesor	mandar una carta	el estadio
8. Su compañero de clase	comer pizza	la parada de autobús
9. Yo	navegar por Internet	el aeropuerto
10. Nosotros	tomar el avión	el restaurante

2 ¿Qué están haciendo?

Use the present progressive tense to ask your partner what Leonor and Mario are doing. Add a place in the city or in the house where you think the action is occurring. Follow the model.

▶ **MODELO:** —¿Qué está haciendo Mario en la librería?
—Mario está comprando un libro.

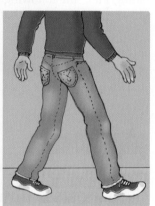

3 **En este momento...** With a partner, discuss what people are doing right now in the places listed.

▶ MODELO: tus amigos en la plaza
—¿Qué están haciendo tus amigos en la plaza?
—Mis amigos están caminando.

—*What are your friends doing in the plaza?*
—*My friends are walking.*

1. tus compañeros/as en la escuela
2. tu profesor/a en la clase
3. la gente en las calles
4. los / las estudiantes en la escuela
5. las personas en un restaurante
6. la gente en el cine
7. tus amigos/as en el centro comercial
8. la gente en el museo

4 **En el parque.** Refer to the picture on page 66 and, with a partner, discuss what the people are doing in the park.

_____

_____

_____

_____

_____

_____

_____

_____

Jaguares gemelos

Oficina de Nayeli en su casa, en Puebla.

Este jeroglífico, ¿qué significa? ¿Pájaro...? ¡Avión! El número de un vuelo. ¡Vuelo número novecientos cuarenta y nueve! ¿Adónde? ¡Claro, Madrid! ¡Nayeli está en Madrid!

En la sala de la casa de Nayeli.

¿Qué dice la nota?

Creo que Nayeli está en Madrid.

¿Madrid? ¿Pero por qué en Madrid?

Vamos a Madrid, pero es muy caro.

Pero Adriana, ¿y la excavación?

Nuestra profesora está en peligro.

Soy amigo de Nayeli y yo pago el viaje. No es difícil: los boletos aéreos, una tarjeta de crédito, dinero y una computadora para la comunicación.

¿Qué crees, Adriana?

No sé. Estoy preocupada.

Adriana, es necesario confiar en él.

Sí, claro.... No hay muchas opciones...

Su oferta es generosa.

... y sincera.

Muchas gracias. Usted es un amigo muy bueno.

Aquí está la nota para el Sr. Guzmán.

Sí, señorita, muchas gracias.

¡Gracias!

En la oficina de Armando

Armando, ¿cómo está todo?

Señora, todo está bien. Y ¿usted, en Costa Rica?

Bien, pero ¿todo está bien?

Claro, Adriana y Felipe viajan a Madrid.

¡Perfecto!

Muy bien. ¿Hablamos todos los días?

¡Todo está bajo control!

Si los jaguares no están juntos, México va a sufrir problemas económicos.

La profesora Nayeli Paz Ocotlán es la figura principal de la investigación de la policía.

Actividades

Online Study Center

For additional practice with this episode, visit the *Caminos* website at http://college.hmco.com/ languages/spanish/ renjilian/caminos/3e/ student_home.html.

1 Comprensión. Based on this episode of *Caminos del jaguar*, choose the logical response.

1. Adriana y Felipe están en...
   a. la universidad.
   b. la casa de Nayeli.

2. El jeroglífico describe...
   a. el número de un vuelo *(flight)*.
   b. el título de un libro.

3. Nayeli está en...
   a. México.
   b. Madrid.

4. Felipe está preocupado por...
   a. Adriana.
   b. la excavación.

5. ¿Quién paga el viaje de Adriana y Felipe a Madrid?
   a. Felipe
   b. Armando

6. Armando habla por teléfono con...
   a. doña Carmen.
   b. Esperanza.

2 Situaciones. Dramatize one of the following situations.

1. Adriana and Felipe discuss Armando's offer to pay for their trip to Madrid.
2. Armando's phone conversation with someone in Costa Rica.

3 Escritura. Write a brief summary of this episode of *Caminos del jaguar* in Spanish. (4–6 sentences).

NOTA CULTURAL

Los códices mayas

The Mayans employed a writing system of hieroglyphs (similar to the Aztecs of Central Mexico), and left engraved symbols and pictures on animal skin, papyrus (paper made from tree bark), or stone. The greatest examples of Mayan writing can be found in four documents (**códices**), located today in Dresden (Germany), Paris, Madrid, and the Distrito Federal (Mexico City). The códices describe ceremonies for the new year, and contain prophecies, astronomical data, and agricultural records. The Madrid codex describes daily activities such as bee keeping and hunting. It is thought to be a kind of manual used by Mayan priests to counsel the public.

Lectura

Online Study Center

For further reading practice online, visit the *Caminos* website at http://college.hmco.com/languages/spanish/renjilian/caminos/3e/student_home.html.

PRELECTURA

Reading Strategy

Asking questions

To achieve effective skills as a reader, training yourself to read in another language is one important step. Asking yourself questions *before* you read, *while* you are reading, and *after* you read facilitates your comprehension and memory.

1 Antes de leer. Before you read this article, ask yourself these questions.

1. What theme(s) or topic(s) does the title indicate?
2. Do I already know something about the topic?
3. What clues do the photos and captions reveal about the reading?
4. Before I begin reading, what else seems relevant?

2 Al leer. While you are reading, ask yourself these questions.

1. What topic(s) and theme(s) can I identify? After reading the title of the article, have I guessed correctly?
2. Which vocabulary words do I already know? Do they relate to the topic and themes? In order to understand the passage, which words are essential for me to know?
3. Can I understand the gist of the reading without looking up many words in a dictionary?
4. Which words can I skim over and still understand the reading?
5. Can I summarize each each paragraph?
6. As I read, what else can I identify as important to know?

Bienvenidos[1] a Puebla: Ciudad de ángeles

La casa de las muñecas, Puebla, México

Una leyenda mexicana indica que los ángeles llegaron[2] a Puebla y trazaron[3] las calles rectas[4] para[5] usarlas más fácilmente. Por eso, se llama Puebla de los Ángeles. Es la capital del estado de Puebla y está en el altiplano[6] central de México. Está a noventa minutos de la ciudad de México en automóvil, a tres horas de la ciudad de Oaxaca, a tres horas y media del Puerto de Veracruz y a seis horas de Acapulco. La temperatura media[7] varía entre 20 °C y 30 °C.

---

[1]Welcome; [2]arrived; [3]designed; [4]straight; [5]in order to; [6]high plain; [7]average

La Capilla de la Virgen del Rosario

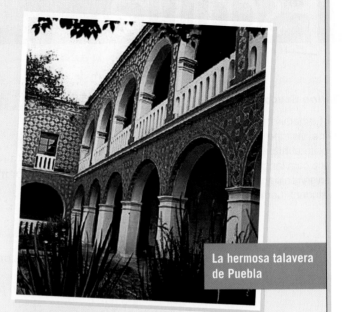

La hermosa talavera de Puebla

Puebla es famosa por sus estructuras barrocas[8] de ladrillo[9] rojo, piedra[10] gris, estuco[11] blanco y por los espectaculares azulejos de Talavera. La Catedral de Puebla tiene altas torres[12] y un hermoso altar con adornos de ónice[13], mármol[14] y oro[15], diseñado[16] por Manuel Tolsá, el famoso arquitecto de origen español.

La Biblioteca Palafoxiana es un espectacular edificio de la época colonial. Tiene más de 40.000 libros, todos muy valiosos[17]. Algunos[18] especialistas consideran la Capilla[19] de la Virgen del Rosario como la octava maravilla[20] del mundo por los impresionantes adornos interiores. El Convento Colonial de Santa Rosa es hoy un museo de cerámica. El Museo Amparo, con muchos adelantos[21] tecnológicos, es uno de los más modernos de América Latina. La Universidad Benemérito de Puebla, construida en 1578, es muy importante también.

[8]baroque; [9]brick; [10]stone; [11]stucco; [12]towers; [13]onyx; [14]marble; [15]gold; [16]designed [17]valuable; [18]Some; [19]Chapel; [20]eighth wonder; [21]advances

POSTLECTURA

3 Después de leer. After you read the article, ask yourself these questions.

1. What are the main ideas of the reading?
2. What themes or topics does the reading reveal?
3. To help me better understand the reading, which words do I need to look up?
4. What other information is relevant?

4 Ciudad de ángeles. With a partner, ask each other these questions based on the reading.

1. ¿Dónde está Puebla de los Ángeles? ¿Por qué se llama así?
2. ¿En automóvil, a cuántas horas está Puebla de Oaxaca? ¿de la capital? ¿del Puerto de Veracruz? ¿de Acapulco?
3. ¿Cuál es la temperatura media de la ciudad?
4. Menciona tres edificios importantes de Puebla.
5. ¿De dónde es el arquitecto de la Catedral de Puebla? ¿Cómo se llama?
6. ¿De qué color son los edificios del centro de la ciudad?
7. ¿Cómo se llama el museo moderno con avances tecnológicos?
8. El artículo menciona una biblioteca y una universidad. ¿Cuáles son?

Escritura

Writing Strategy

Brainstorming ideas

Before writing an essay or a report, it is often useful to brainstorm your ideas, especially with a partner or in a group. In order to do this effectively, write only in Spanish.

Workshop

1. Write down your ideas on paper as they occur to you. They can be single words, phrases, or questions.
2. Write quickly and in no particular order. Do not stop to evaluate which ideas are good.
3. Once the ideas are written, read the list and circle the ideas that you will use in your writing.

The following is a possible brainstorm for an essay that describes your apartment.

grande	*me gusta*
cocina fea	*azul*
comedor	*un compañero arrogante*
no hay sofá	*jardín bonito*
dos dormitorios	*hace frío*
una buena compañera	*un dormitorio pequeño*

Strategy in Action

For additional practice with the strategy of brainstorming ideas, turn to the *Escritura* section for *Unidad 2* in your Student Activities Manual.

1 Tu casa. Create a diagram of your home. Include the rooms and the furniture in each room. Then write a description to match the diagram.

2 Un fin de semana espectacular. Write a description of the activities you do during an ideal weekend. Use the expressions you've learned to indicate likes and dislikes, and verbs in the present tense.

Resumen de vocabulario

PRIMER PASO

DESCRIBING AN APARTMENT
Sustantivos

el alquiler, la renta	rent
el balcón	balcony
la bañera, la tina	bathtub
el (cuarto de) baño	bathroom
la casa	house
el clóset	closet
la cocina	kitchen
el comedor	dining room
el dormitorio	bedroom
la ducha	shower
el/la dueño/a	owner
el garaje	garage
el/la inquilino/a	tenant
el jardín	garden, yard
la oficina	office
la piscina, la alberca	swimming pool
el piso	floor, apartment (Spain)
la sala	living room
la terraza	terrace

Otras expresiones

amplio/a	spacious
barato/a	inexpensive
caro/a	expensive
completo/a	complete
con	with
moderno/a	modern
pequeño/a	small
pero	but
privado/a	private

POSSESSIVE ADJECTIVES

mi/mis	my
tu/tus	your (fam., sing.)
su/sus	your (formal), his, her, their
nuestro/a/nuestros/as	our
vuestro/a/vuestros/as	your (fam. plural, Spain)

IDENTIFYING FURNISHINGS AND HOUSEHOLD CHORES
Los muebles

la alfombra	rug
la aspiradora	vacuum cleaner
la cómoda	dresser
las escaleras	stairs
la escoba	broom
el espejo	mirror
la estufa	stove
el inodoro	toilet
el lavabo/el lavamanos	bathroom sink
la mesita	coffee table
la mesita de noche	night stand
el/la refrigerador/a	refrigerator
el ropero/el armario	wardrobe
el/la secadora/a de pelo	blow dryer
el sillón	armchair
el sofá	sofa

Los quehaceres (Household chores)

arreglar (la cama)	to make / fix up (the bed)
aspirar, pasar la aspiradora (por la alfombra)	to vacuum (the rug)
barrer (el piso)	to sweep (the floor)
cocinar	to cook
lavar (los platos)	to wash (the dishes)
limpiar/ordenar (el cuarto)	to clean / tidy (the room)
planchar (la ropa)	to iron (clothes)
sacar (la basura)	to take out (the garbage)
sacudir (los muebles)/ sacar el polvo de (los muebles) (Spain)	to dust (the furniture)
secar (los platos, la ropa)	to dry (the dishes, clothes)

REGULAR -AR, -ER, AND -IR VERBS

-ar verbs

acabar / acabar de + (infinitive)	to finish / to have just (done something)
alquilar	to rent
andar	to walk, move
bailar	to dance
buscar	to look for
caminar	to walk
cantar	to sing
comprar	to buy
desear	to wish for
escuchar	to listen
estudiar	to study
hablar	to speak
investigar	to research
lavar	to wash
llamar	to call
llegar	to arrive
llevar	to bring
mandar	to send
mirar	to look at
necesitar	to need
pasar	to happen, pass
practicar	to practice
preguntar	to ask
terminar	to finish
tomar	to take
trabajar	to work
usar	to use
viajar	to travel
visitar	to visit

-er verbs

aprender	to learn
beber	to drink
comer	to eat
comprender	to understand
correr	to run
creer	to believe
leer	to read
responder	to answer

-ir verbs

abrir	to open
compartir	to share
decidir	to decide
describir	to describe
escribir	to write
recibir	to receive
subir	to climb
vivir	to live

SEGUNDO PASO

INDICATING LIKES AND DISLIKES

Verbos

alquilar videos	to rent videos
dar un paseo	to take a walk
escribir cartas	to write letters
gustar	to like (be pleasing)
hablar con amigos	to talk with friends
hacer ejercicio	to exercise
jugar al volibol	to play volleyball
leer libros	to read books
mirar una película	to watch a movie
navegar por Internet (la Red/la web)	to surf the Internet (Web)
pintar	to paint
practicar deportes	to play sports
tocar (un instrumento)	to play (an instrument)
ver televisión	to watch television

Otras expresiones

mucho	a lot, very much
(un) poco	(a) little
también	also, too

EXPRESSING LOCATION AND EMOTION WITH ESTAR

Verbos

estar	to be

Adjetivos

aburrido/a	bored
alegre	happy
alterado/a	upset
borracho/a	drunk
calmado/a	calm
cansado/a	tired

celoso/a	*jealous*
confundido/a	*confused*
contento/a	*happy*
deprimido/a	*depressed*
desilusionado/a	*disappointed*
emocionado/a	*excited*
enamorado/a	*in love*
enfermo/a	*sick*
enojado/a	*angry*
entusiasmado/a	*enthusiastic*
fascinado/a	*fascinated*
harto/a	*fed up, disgusted*
listo/a	*ready*
nervioso/a	*nervous*
preocupado/a	*worried*
seguro/a	*sure*
triste	*sad*

TALKING ABOUT PLACES IN A CITY

el aeropuerto	*airport*
el almacén	*department store / warehouse*
la biblioteca	*library*
el café	*café*
la calle	*street*
el centro comercial	*shopping center*
el cine	*movie theater*
la ciudad	*city*

el correo	*post office*
el edificio	*building*
la estación de tren	*train station*
el estadio	*stadium*
el hospital	*hospital*
el hotel	*hotel*
la iglesia	*church*
la librería	*bookstore*
el museo	*museum*
la parada de autobús	*bus stop*
la plaza	*plaza*
el restaurante	*restaurant*
la tienda	*store*

DESCRIBING PRESENT ACTIONS IN PROGRESS

Sustantivos

| la gente | *people (singular)* |

Verbos

construir	*to build*
destruir	*to destroy*
incluir	*to include*

Otras expresiones

| ahora | *now* |
| en este momento | *at this moment, now* |

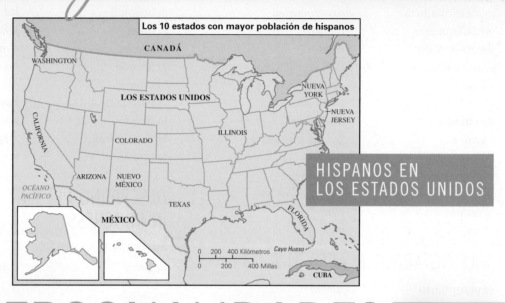

Los 10 estados con mayor población de hispanos

Online Study Center

To learn more about the people featured in this section, visit the *Caminos* website at http://college.hmco.com/languages/spanish/renjilian/caminos/3e/student_home.html.

HISPANOS EN
LOS ESTADOS UNIDOS

PERSONALIDADES

Hay aproximadamente cuarenta y dos millones de hispanos en los Estados Unidos. Son de familias de las veintiuna naciones hispanas. En su libro *La ola¹ latina,* el periodista² Jorge Ramos, nacido³ en México, analiza las contribuciones de los hispanos a la sociedad estadounidense. Ramos ofrece la siguiente descripción de los hispanos estadounidenses cuando observa, "El latino, por definición es mezcla⁴: de culturas, de idiomas, de identidades, de posibilidades, de tiempos⁵, de pasado y de futuro".

En las artes y las letras, las personalidades hispanas se destacan⁶ en la literatura, el arte, la música y el cine. La revista⁷ *Time* describe a los 25 hispanos más influyentes de los Estados Unidos de 2005. Incluyen también las categorías de la política y los negocios⁸. Muchas personas de habla española se identifican como "hispanos" y muchas como "latinos".

En la lista de los hispanos mencionados en *Time* están las puertorriqueñas Jennifer López (actriz y cantante) y Mari Carmen Ramírez (conservadora de arte moderno). También están los chicanos Robert Rodríguez (director de cine), Arturo Moreno (dueño⁹ del equipo¹⁰ de béisbol, los Anaheim Angels), Carmen Lomas Garza (artista) y Bill Richardson (gobernador de Nuevo México). Están adicionalmente el argentinoamericano Gustavo Santaolalla (músico y ganador¹¹ de un Óscar en 2006); los cubanoamericanos Narciso Rodríguez (modisto¹²), Cristina Saralegui (personalidad de televisión) y Andy García (actor).

Esta es una lista parcial de los hispanos influyentes estadounidenses. Visita el sitio web de *Caminos* para leer más en español sobre las personalidades mencionadas aquí¹³ y otras¹⁴ como Edward James Olmos, Eva Méndez, Amaury Nolasco, Jimmy Smits, Zoe Saldaña, (actores), Bárbara Bermudo (presentadora), George López (comediante), Eduardo Xol (decorador de exteriores) y Denise Quiñones (modelo y actriz).

¹wave; ²journalist; ³born; ⁴mix; ⁵times; ⁶stand out; ⁷magazine; ⁸business; ⁹owner; ¹⁰team; ¹¹winner; ¹²fashion designer; ¹³here; ¹⁴others

Jorge Ramos

Jennifer López

America Ferrera

Robert Rodríguez

Arturo Moreno

Zoe Saldaña

Bill Richardson

Gustavo Santaolalla

Narciso Rodríguez

Cristina Saralegui

"Un poema nos hace ver todo
por primera vez°". *makes us see everything*
for the first time
—Francisco X. Alarcón (Estados Unidos) del libro
Laughing Tomatoes / Jitomates Risueños

Comprensión

Working in pairs, ask each other the following questions.

1. ¿Qué definición ofrece Jorge Ramos del latino? En tu familia, ¿qué idioma/s hablan? ¿Con qué cultura conectan su identidad?
2. Nombra a hispanos influyentes en cinco categorías diferentes. ¿Cuál es más impresionante, en tu opinión? ¿Por qué?

ARTE

CARMEN LOMAS GARZA

Carmen Lomas Garza es una artista chicana. Ella es de una familia mexicana que reside en los Estados Unidos en Texas. Pero ahora°, la artista vive en San Francisco, donde pinta y escribe libros sobre las tradiciones mexicanas. En la introducción de uno de sus libros de cuadros° y relatos°, *Cuadros de familia*, la autora chicana Sandra Cisneros analiza las obras artísticas de Lomas Garza, "Éstos° son cuadros de familia y no importa si tu familia es de Kingsville o el Cairo, Sarajevo o Katmandú, también son imágenes° de tu familia". Lomas Garza pinta escenas típicas como ferias, fiestas, cumpleaños° y celebraciones.

  La Tamalada° es un cuadro en que° los miembros de la familia de la artista preparan tamales.

But now

portraits / stories
These

images

birthdays

Making tamales
in which

Tamalada (Making Tamales)

Comprensión

Working in pairs, ask each other the following questions.

1. ¿Qué preparan los miembros de la familia de la artista?
2. ¿Cuántos adultos hay en el cuadro? ¿Y cuántos adolescentes y niños°? ¿Cómo son? ¿Hay animales?   *children*
3. En tu opinión, ¿es de día o de noche? ¿Qué hora es?
4. ¿Qué temas observas en las dos obras de arte en el cuadro?
5. Nombra los colores que la artista usa en el cuadro.
6. ¿Cómo es el cuadro—interesante, aburrido°, excelente, positivo, tradicional, feliz?   *boring*
7. ¿Quién es un artista famoso/a de tu país?
8. ¿Qué te gusta comer más—los tacos, los tamales o los burritos?

Conéctate a Internet para ver el arte de Carmen Lomas Garza y para aprender sobre otros artistas hispanos estadounidenses como Daniel Desiga, Paul Botello, Abelardo Morell, Joe Bravo, Judy Baca, Celina Hinojosa, José Esquivel, Patssi Valdez y Carlos Almaraz.

MÚSICA

LUIS FONSI

El cantante° Luis Fonsi (=Luis Alfonso Rodríguez) nació° en Puerto Rico en 1978. A los cuatro años, participó° en el famoso Coro de Niños° de San Juan. A los diez años, su familia se estableció en la Florida. Sus dos primeros álbumes se llaman "Comenzaré°" y "Eterno". Es famoso por sus baladas y su voz espectacular. Su tremendo talento está en cantar y también en crear coreografía. Cantó° también duetos con las populares cantantes latinas Cristina Aguilera, Olga Tañón y Jaci Velázquez. En su álbum de 2005, "Paso a paso°", hay canciones en honor de su esposa, la talentosa actriz latina, Adamari López. Fonsi revela que "la vida está llena° de pruebas° y las pruebas son las que nos definen como seres° humanos".

singer / was born
participated /
   Children's Chorus
I will begin

He sang

Step by Step
full / challenges
beings

👥 Comprensión

Working in pairs, ask each other the following questions.

1. ¿Cuál es el nombre original de Luis Fonsi?
2. ¿De dónde es?
3. ¿Cuántos álbumes mencionan en el texto? ¿Cómo se llaman?
4. Fonsi es famoso por una categoría de música que canta. ¿Cuál es?
5. ¿Qué cantantes latinas cantan duetos con Fonsi?
6. ¿Cómo se llama la esposa de Fonsi? ¿Cuál es su profesión?
7. ¿Te gusta la balada como forma musical?
8. ¿Quién es otro/a cantante contemporáneo/a excelente?

Conéctate a Internet para escuchar la música de Fonsi, aprender más sobre él y otros cantantes hispanos estadounidenses como Cristina Aguilera, Vicki Carr, Gloria Estefan, Diego García, Jennifer López, Los Lonely Boys, Tito Puente, Carlos Santana, Selena y Jaci Velázquez.

LITERATURA

FRANCISCO X. ALARCÓN

Francisco X. Alarcón es un poeta chicano. Tiene más de siete libros de poesía y es ganador° de honores por sus creaciones literarias. También es profesor universitario.

winner

"En estos momentos de conflicto, el mundo necesita paz . . . Y nosotros podemos empezar desde el interior de nuestro ser."

—Ricky Martin (Puerto Rico / Estados Unidos)

"Espiral universal"

no hay
finales
sólo° nuevos principios°   *only / beginnings*

👥 Comprensión

Working in pairs, ask each other the following questions.

1. ¿Cómo es la forma de un espiral: rectangular, circular o triangular?
2. Según° el poeta, ¿está el espiral limitado a un punto o lugar en el espacio?   *According to*
3. El poeta comenta que no hay finales, sólo nuevos principios. ¿Estás de acuerdo°?   *in agreement*
4. En tu opinión, ¿es elocuente, optimista, pesimista, provocativo, sentimental o universal el poema?

MARJORIE AGOSIN

Marjorie Agosin es de una familia chilena. La poeta estadounidense es autora de más de treinta libros de poesía. Profesora de literatura latinoamericana en Wellesley College, es también activista por los derechos° humanos. La selección aquí es del poema "La noche del jaguar".   *rights*

"La noche del jaguar"

Yo toda la noche pinto
y me busco entre° el claroscuro°.   *between / light and dark*
Devorando° los colores,   *devouring*
me llamo entre la sombra carcomida°   *disappearing shadow*
en la noche del jaguar.
Soy veloz° como una honda° canción°.   *swift / deep / song*

👥 Comprensión

Working in groups, ask each other the following questions.

1. ¿Cuándo ocurre la acción en el poema?
2. ¿Qué devora el / la artista?
3. ¿Con qué animal se asocian la noche y la velocidad?
4. En tu opinión, ¿cómo es el poema —creativo, elegante, emocional, fascinante, hondo, interesante, original, realista... ?

Conéctate a Internet para aprender más sobre los poetas aquí u otros escritores hispanos estadounidenses como Isabel Allende, Sandra Cisneros, Chiqui Vicioso, Pedro Juan Soto, Francisco Jiménez, Tomás Rivera, Sandra Benítez, Rodolfo Gonzales y Norma Cantú.

3
De viaje

VOCABULARIO Y LENGUA

- ► Talking about weather and seasons
- ► Describing actions in the present: Present indicative of stem-changing verbs: **tener, ir, venir**
- ► Discussing transportation
- ► Talking about daily routines: Reflexive actions
- ► Ordering food in a restaurant
- ► Expressing actions in the present: Verbs with irregular **yo** forms: **saber** and **conocer**
- ► Using large numbers: 200 to 2,000,000
- ► Showing location of people, places, and things: Demonstratives, adverbs of location

CAMINOS DEL JAGUAR

- ► Información confidencial
- ► Las reglas son las reglas

LECTURA

- ► Sevilla, ciudad sensacional

NOTAS CULTURALES

- ► Los terremotos en México
- ► España y el uso de **vosotros**

ESTRATEGIAS

- ► **Reading:** Skimming; Scanning
- ► **Writing:** Providing supporting details

Salvador Dalí, *Muchacha en la ventana*

Preguntas del tema

- ► ¿Dónde vives?
- ► ¿Te gusta el clima de tu ciudad?
- ► ¿Hay transporte público en tu ciudad?
- ► ¿Te gusta viajar en auto o en tren?

PRIMER PASO

Vocabulario y lengua

TALKING ABOUT WEATHER AND SEASONS

¿Qué tiempo hace? *(What's the weather like?)*

Buenos días, con ustedes, Gloria López. Es un buen día para viajar por España. Hace mucho sol en la región central de España. Si viajan a Madrid hoy, hace sol con una temperatura máxima de 34 grados. Si viajan a Pamplona en el norte de España, hay chubascos fuertes. En Barcelona, en el este, está parcialmente nublado con una temperatura promedio de 31 grados centígrados. Si no les gusta el calor, es posible viajar a La Coruña en el noroeste porque hay una temperatura de sólo 23 grados centígrados. Por lo general, hace muy buen tiempo hoy.

Temperatures in most Hispanic countries are expressed in degrees Celsius (°C) using the centigrade scale.

La temperatura está a 32 grados centígrados.　　　*The temperature is 32 °C.*

The freezing point is 0 °C, while the boiling point is 100 °C. Use the following formulas to convert from Fahrenheit to Celsius and vice versa:

$$°C = (°F - 32) \div 1.8 \qquad °F = (°C \times 1.8) + 32$$

°C	0	10	20	30	40	50	60	70	80	90	100
°F	32	50	68	86	104	122	140	158	176	194	212

¿En qué estación estamos? *(What season is it?)*

la primavera

el verano

el otoño

el invierno

Más palabras y expresiones

Cognados

la brisa

húmedo/a

el huracán

los kilómetros (por hora)

el/la meteorólogo/a

las millas (por hora)

la probabilidad

la temperatura (mínima /máxima)

el tornado

Sustantivos

el aguacero / el chubasco	*downpour*
el cielo	*sky*
el clima	*climate*
el este	*east*
los grados centígrados / Celsius / Fahrenheit	*degrees centigrade / Celsius / Fahrenheit*
la lluvia	*rain*
la nieve	*snow*
el noreste / el noroeste	*northeast / northwest*
el norte	*north*
la nube	*cloud*
el oeste	*west*
el porcentaje	*percentage*
el promedio	*average*
el pronóstico del tiempo	*weather forecast*
el sur	*south*
el sureste / el suroeste	*southeast / southwest*
la tormenta / la tronada	*storm*

Otras expresiones

¿A cuánto está la temperatura?	*What is the temperature?*
está (parcialmente) nublado	*it's (partly) cloudy*
fuerte	*strong*
hace buen / mal tiempo	*it's good / bad weather*
hace calor / frío / fresco	*it's hot / cold / cool*
hace viento	*it's windy*
llovizna	*it's drizzling*
llueve	*it's raining*
nieva	*it's snowing*
por ciento	*percent*
seco/a	*dry*

Actividades

1 **¿Qué hay?** Match the art in the left column with the vocabulary word in the right column.

1. _____

2. _____

3. _____

4. _____

5. _____

6. _____

7. _____

   a. la nieve
   b. la lluvia
   c. el aguacero / el chubasco
   d. la tormenta / la tronada
   e. el cielo
   f. la nube
   g. la brisa

2 El tiempo. You are planning your next trip and need to pack accordingly. Listen to the weather reports for the various cities you are considering and indicate the order in which each city is mentioned on the lines below.

El tiempo de hoy 27 de septiembre

BUENOS AIRES	SAN JUAN	CIUDAD DE MÉXICO	MADRID	BOGOTÁ	CARACAS
9°C/48°F	24°C/75°F	17°C/63°F	20°C/68°F	14°C/57°F	29°C/84°F

____   ____   ____   ____   ____   ____

3 ¿Cuál es la estación? With a partner, imagine that you are traveling together to the following cities and countries around the world. Determine the season for each month listed and describe the weather at that time of year. (Remember, the seasons are reversed in the northern and southern hemispheres. Refer to the maps included in your textbook if you need to.) Follow the model.

► MODELO: Nueva York, NY / julio
—Viajamos a Nueva York en julio. ¿En qué estación estamos?
—Estamos en verano.
—¿Qué tiempo hace?
—Hace mucho calor.

—We are traveling to New York in July. What season is it?
—It's summer.
—What's the weather like?
—It's very hot.

1. Santiago, Chile / enero
2. Boston, MA / agosto
3. Buenos Aires, Argentina / junio
4. Los Ángeles, CA / abril
5. México, D.F. / noviembre
6. San Antonio, TX / mayo
7. La Habana, Cuba / septiembre
8. Burlington, VT / febrero
9. Asunción, Paraguay / diciembre
10. Miami, FL / octubre

4 ¿Qué tiempo hace? Work with a partner to compare the weather conditions for Santander, Valencia, Zaragoza, and Sevilla in the map at the beginning of this section. Prepare a brief report for each city with general weather conditions, season, and temperature. Present your findings to the class.

5 El noticiero. You were just hired by a Spanish-speaking cable network to present weather forecasts for people making travel plans. Use the Internet to find the current weather report for a city in a Spanish-speaking country, and prepare a weather forecast to present to the class. **Useful keywords:** pronóstico del tiempo, meteorología.

Present indicative of stem-changing verbs: *tener, ir, venir*

Esta tarde

At last / we found	Mauro	Aquí está el Hotel Prisma. ¡Por fin° **encontramos**° nuestro hotel!
I intend	Rosalía	Sí, ¡por fin! Yo **pienso**° dormir toda la tarde.
I prefer	Mauro	Pues yo no voy a dormir. Esta tarde **prefiero**° ir a un buen restaurante.
I'm dying of hunger	Rosalía	¡Ah! Buena idea. Me **muero** de hambre°. Vamos al restaurante Plácido Domingo.
then / you won't sleep	Mauro	¿Entonces° no **duermes**° esta tarde?
I'll request / you'll get	Rosalía	No, yo **pido**° el cuarto y tú **consigues**° el taxi. ¿De acuerdo?
	Mauro	¡Sí, de acuerdo!

Stem-changing verbs use the same present tense endings as regular **–ar, –er,** and **–ir** verbs, but a vowel change also occurs in the stem of certain forms.

Notice that the **nosotros** and **vosotros** forms do not contain a stem change.

Stem-changing verbs			
	e → ie: **empezar** *to start, begin*	e → i: **servir** *to serve*	o → ue: **volver** *to return, come back*
yo	emp**ie**zo	s**i**rvo	v**ue**lvo
tú	emp**ie**zas	s**i**rves	v**ue**lves
Ud. / él / ella	emp**ie**za	s**i**rve	v**ue**lve
nosotros/as	empezamos	servimos	volvemos
vosotros/as	empezáis	servís	volvéis
Uds. / ellos / ellas	emp**ie**zan	s**i**rven	v**ue**lven

Common stem-changing verbs					
e → ie		**e → i**		**o → ue**	
cerrar	*to close*	conseguir	*to get, obtain*	almorzar	*to have lunch*
comenzar	*to start, begin*	decir*	*to say, tell*	contar	*to count*
concernir	*to concern*	pedir	*to ask for*	costar	*to cost*
entender	*to understand*	perseguir	*to follow, pursue*	dormir	*to sleep*
mentir	*to lie*	repetir	*to repeat*	encontrar	*to find*
pensar	*to think*	seguir	*to follow, continue*	morir	*to die*
perder	*to lose*	servir	*to serve*	mostrar	*to show*
preferir	*to prefer*			poder	*to be able*
querer	*to want*			probar	*to taste, try*
recomendar	*to recommend*			recordar	*to remember*
				soñar	*to dream*
				(con)	*(about)*

*__Decir__ also has an irregular form in the first person singular: **yo digo.**

¡Yo siempre **digo** "*no*"!   *I always say "no"!*

Jugar (al) *(to play games, sports)* is the only verb whose stem changes from **u** to **ue**. (j**ue**go, j**ue**gas, j**ue**ga, jugamos, jugáis, j**ue**gan)

Remember that the weather terms **nieva** *(nevar)* and **llueve** *(llover)* that you learned on page 92 are stem-changing verbs and are used only in the third person singular.

The verb **costar** *(to cost)* is usually used, as in English, in the third person singular or plural.

Las computadoras c**ue**stan mucho dinero.   *Computers cost a lot of money.*
Viajar en autobús no c**ue**sta mucho.   *Traveling by bus doesn't cost a lot.*

The verbs **empezar a** and **pensar** are often followed by an infinitive.

emp**e**zar a + *infinitive*   *to begin doing something*
Los atletas **empiezan a correr.**   *The athletes begin running.*

p**e**nsar + *infinitive*   *to plan, intend*
Los estudiantes **piensan viajar** a Sevilla.   *The students plan to travel to Sevilla.*

Present participles

Stem-changing verbs ending in **–ar** and **–er** have regular present participle forms. Stem-changing verbs ending in **–ir** have irregular forms.

Present participle of stem-changing *-ir* verbs	
e → i	**o → u**
p**e**dir: p**i**diendo	d**o**rmir: d**u**rmiendo
Las chicas están p**i**diendo la comida.	El bebé está d**u**rmiendo.

More verbs that follow this pattern include:

e → i	o → u
decir: diciendo	morir: muriendo
preferir: prefiriendo	
repetir: repitiendo	
seguir: siguiendo	
servir: sirviendo	

Tener (to have)

Tener is an irregular verb because the first person singular form **(yo)** ends in **-go** but the remaining forms follow the pattern of stem-changing verbs.

tener (to have)			
Singular		**Plural**	
yo	ten**go**	nosotros / nosotras	tenemos
tú	ti**e**nes	vosotros / vosotras	tenéis
Ud. / él / ella	ti**e**ne	Uds. / ellos / ellas	ti**e**nen

Many verbs that are built from **tener** are conjugated the same way: **contener** *(to contain)*, **entretener** *(to entertain)*, **mantener** *(to maintain)*, etc.

The verb **tener** is used to express possession in the same way the verb *to have* is used in English.

—¿**Tienes** buenas amigas?　　　—*Do you have good friends?*
—Sí, **tengo** muchas buenas amigas.　　—*Yes, I have many good friends.*

Expressions with *tener*

¿Qué tienen?

Tiene frío.　　　Tiene calor.　　　Tiene hambre.　　　Tiene sed.

Tiene sueño.　　　Tiene miedo.　　　Tiene prisa.　　　Tiene cinco años.

Additional expressions with *tener*	
tener cuidado	*to be careful*
tener la culpa	*to be at fault*
tener éxito	*to be successful*
tener ganas de + *infinitive*	*to want to (do something)/*
	to feel like (doing something)
tener que + *infinitive*	*to have to (do something)*
tener razón	*to be right*
tener sentido	*to make sense*

Using *ir* and *venir*

Ir *(to go)* and **venir** *(to come)* are common irregular verbs that have many uses.

	ir *(to go)*	venir *(to come)*
yo	**voy**	**vengo**
tú	**vas**	**vienes**
Ud. / él / ella	**va**	**viene**
nosotros / nosotras	**vamos**	**venimos**
vosotros / vosotras	**vais**	**venís**
Uds. / ellos / ellas	**van**	**vienen**

Common uses of *ir* and *venir*		
To talk about future actions:		
ir + a + *infinitive*	¿Cómo **voy a pagar** el viaje?	*How am I going to pay for the trip?*
To express destination or origin:		
ir + a + *location*	Uds. **van a** la universidad.	*You go to the university.*
venir + de + *location*	Uds. **vienen de** la universidad.	*You are coming from the university.*
To say "Let's go!":		
¡Vamos!	Yo sé dónde está la clase.	*I know where the class is.*
	¡Vamos!	*Let's go!*
To say "*Let's . . .*" + action:		
vamos a + *infinitive*	**Vamos a buscar** un buen restaurante.	*Let's look for a good restaurant.*
To go (somewhere else) to get / for something:		
ir + por	Ella **va por** el café.	*She goes (somewhere else) to get the coffee.*
To come (here) to get / to come for something:		
venir + por	Ella **viene por** el café.	*She comes (here) to get the coffee.*

Contraction: a + el = al

Just like **de + el** = **del,** when the preposition **a** precedes the article **el,** they contract
to form **al.** There is no contraction with the pronoun **él** *(he).*

Voy **al** museo.   *I'm going to the museum.*
Vamos **al** hotel.   *Let's go to the hotel.*

Actividades

1 Recomendaciones del portero (doorman). Manuel is a doorman in a large downtown hotel in Madrid. Work with a partner to complete the dialog. Use the present tense.

Manuel Me llamo Manuel Gascón y soy portero en el hotel Prisma.

Tú ¿Qué restaurante _____ (**1.** recomendar) Ud. en Madrid?

Manuel _____ (**2.** poder, yo) recomendar muchos, ¿ _____ (**3.** preferir) Ud. comida española?

Tú ¡Por supuesto! Estamos en Madrid.

Manuel Entonces, _____ (**4.** recomendar, yo) el restaurante Casa de la Paella.

Tú ¿ _____ (**5.** costar) mucho dinero la comida allí?

Manuel No, no. Allí _____ (**6.** servir, ellos) platos de varios precios.

Tú _____ (**7.** querer, yo) probar la paella.

Manuel ¡Buena idea! La gente _____ (**8.** decir) que es magnífica.

Tú Pues entonces, necesito un taxi de inmediato para ir allí.

Manuel Yo _____ (**9.** pedir) el taxi para Ud. ¡Buen provecho!

2 Los planes de Vicente. Fill in the correct forms of the verbs in the following passage. Then answer the questions that follow.

Yo _____ (**1.** pensar) viajar por España. Voy a empezar mi viaje en Madrid y después *(after)* yo _____ (**2.** querer) visitar Granada, Málaga y Jerez en la provincia de Andalucía. Yo _____ (**3.** preferir) ir en verano porque no _____ (**4.** llover) mucho. Luis Fernando, mi amigo andaluz, _____ (**5.** decir) que yo _____ (**6.** poder) dormir y comer en su casa. Es fantástico porque yo sé que su familia _____ (**7.** servir) comidas deliciosas todos los días.

Now answer the following questions about Vicente's plans.

1. ¿Dónde piensa Vicente empezar su viaje?
2. ¿Dónde puede dormir Vicente?
3. ¿Qué lugares piensa visitar?
4. ¿Llueve mucho en Andalucía en verano?
5. ¿Cuándo prefiere ir Vicente a Andalucía?

3 ¿Qué tengo? Use the word **si** *(if)* to create complete sentences by matching a situation (Column A) with an expression with **tener** (Column B). Follow the model.

▶ **MODELO:** Hay poco tiempo. / tener prisa
Si hay poco tiempo, tengo prisa.

A	B
1. Veo un tigre *(tiger)*.	a. tener hambre
2. Hay un examen mañana.	b. tener miedo
3. No hay agua.	c. tener que estudiar
4. Hace mucho sol.	d. tener ganas de leer
5. Es invierno.	e. tener sueño
6. Saco una A en el examen.	f. tener frío
7. Es medianoche.	g. tener calor
8. No hay comida.	h. tener éxito
9. Estoy seguro/a.	i. tener razón
10. Compro un buen libro.	j. tener sed

4 **¿Adónde van? ¿De dónde vienen?** The following people are going to (**ir** + **a**) or coming from (**venir** + **de**) different places. Follow the model to indicate their destinations or origins.

> ► **MODELO:** las mamás y sus hijos / ir / parque
> *Las mamás y sus hijos van al parque.*

1. Gonzalo / venir / el centro comercial
2. nosotros / ir / las clases de español
3. ellas / ir / el estadio
4. Liliana / venir / la tienda
5. Uds. / ir / el mercado
6. tú / venir / la discoteca
7. el doctor / venir / el hospital
8. los chicos / ir / el museo
9. yo / venir / la universidad
10. Mi profesora / ir / Madrid

 5 **¿Qué vas a hacer?** With a partner, ask each other what you will be doing (Column B) based on the circumstances in Column A. Follow the model.

> ► **MODELO:** hay programas interesantes / mirar televisión
> —*¿Qué vas a hacer si hay programas interesantes?*
> —*Voy a mirar televisión.*

A	B
1. hace buen tiempo	a. bailar en la discoteca
2. hay un tornado	b. comprar una computadora
3. los tacos son buenos	c. salir al parque
4. el examen es mañana	d. estudiar hoy
5. tu amigo está enfermo	e. llamar al teléfono de emergencias
6. es sábado	f. comer mucho
7. hoy llueve todo el día	g. no salir de casa
8. tienes dinero	h. ir a la farmacia

 6 **¿Qué piensan hacer tú y tu compañero/a?** With a partner, ask each other questions to find out what each of you are planning to do next weekend. Discuss whether you can do some activities together. Try your best to persuade your friend to join you in your planned activities.

> ► **MODELO:** —¿Qué piensas hacer (quieres hacer / vas a hacer) el viernes por la noche?
> —Quiero cenar en un buen restaurante.
>
> — *What are you planning to (going to) do on Friday night?*
> — *I want to have dinner at a good restaurant.*

día	Estudiante A	Estudiante B
viernes (por la noche)	cenar en el restaurante Taco Loco	cenar en un buen restaurante
sábado (por la tarde)	jugar al básquetbol en el estadio	jugar al golf
domingo (por la tarde)	ir al centro comercial	comprar unos libros
domingo (por la noche)	ir al cine	mirar televisión

¿Cómo te gusta viajar?

Me gusta viajar en **bicicleta**.

Me gusta viajar en **avión**.

Más palabras y expresiones

Cognados

el chofer *(L. Am.)* / chófer *(Sp.)*	el taxi
la motocicleta	el tren
la ruta	el/la turista

Sustantivos

el autobús	*bus*
el barco	*boat*
el billete / boleto / pasaje	*ticket, passage*
el camión	*truck; bus (Mex.)*
la camioneta	*pick-up truck; van*
el coche / el auto(móvil) / el carro	*car, automobile*
el crucero	*cruise ship*
la dirección	*address*
el metro	*subway*
el viaje	*trip*

Verbos

alcanzar	*to reach, catch up with*
estar cerca / lejos (de)	*to be close / far away (from)*
llegar	*to arrive*
manejar / conducir	*to drive*
quedar	*to be (located)*
viajar	*to travel*

Otras expresiones

a pie	*on foot*
en	*by (with transportation), in, on*

Actividades

1 El viaje de una tarjeta postal. Trace the route of the postcard from Claudia to Octavio. Follow the model.

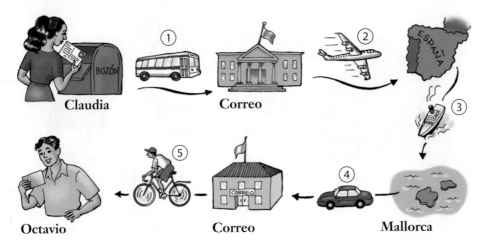

Claudia   Correo   ESPAÑA

Octavio   Correo   Mallorca

▶ MODELO: La tarjeta va al correo en autobús.   *The postcard goes to the post office by bus.*

1. La tarjeta va a España...
2. La tarjeta va a Mallorca...
3. La tarjeta va al correo...
4. La tarjeta va a la casa de Octavio...

2 Asociaciones. What means of transportation do you associate with these names?

1. Harley
2. Greyhound
3. Trek
4. Toyota
5. Delta
6. Amtrak
7. Checker
8. Royal Caribbean

3 ¿Cómo viajan? Working in pairs, ask each other these questions about transportation habits.

1. ¿Usas el transporte público?
2. Si vives en la universidad, ¿cómo viajas a casa en tus vacaciones?
3. Si vives en casa o en un apartamento, ¿cómo vas a la escuela?
4. ¿Te gusta viajar en motocicleta? ¿Por qué?
5. ¿Cómo vas al centro de tu ciudad?
6. Si vas a Europa, ¿vas en barco o en avión?
7. ¿Adónde vas en taxi? ¿Cuándo?
8. ¿Cómo va tu compañero/a de cuarto a la biblioteca?
9. Cuando vas al centro comercial, ¿cómo llegas a las tiendas?

4 Un viaje especial. You decide to take a trip to a Spanish-speaking country with a classmate. In pairs, discuss where you are going to go and how you are going to get there. Plan an itinerary that includes at least four different means of transportation.

▶ MODELO: Vamos a Puerto Rico en crucero.

Reflexive actions

Identify who performs and who receives the action of the verbs in these illustrations.

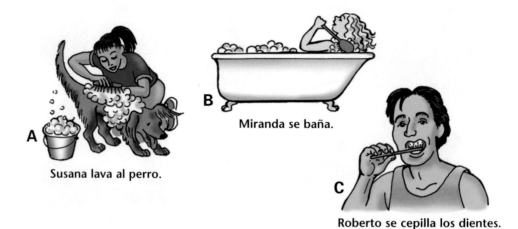

A Susana lava al perro.

B Miranda se baña.

C Roberto se cepilla los dientes.

When the subject both performs and receives the action of the verb, as in **B** and **C** above, the action is called *reflexive*. Reflexive verbs are used to discuss many daily routines in Spanish. Reflexive verbs are conjugated as shown below.

lavarse *(to wash oneself)*			
Subject Pronouns	**Reflexive Pronouns**	**Conjugated Verb**	
yo	**me**	lavo	*I wash (myself)*
tú	**te**	lavas	*you wash (yourself)*
Ud.	**se**	lava	*you wash (yourself)*
él / ella	**se**	lava	*he / she washes (himself / herself)*
nosotros/as	**nos**	lavamos	*we wash (ourselves)*
vosotros/as	**os**	laváis	*you wash (yourselves)*
Uds.	**se**	lavan	*you wash (yourselves)*
ellos / ellas	**se**	lavan	*they wash (themselves)*

To indicate that a verb is reflexive, the infinitive is usually listed with **se** attached at the end of the word. Otherwise the verb is not reflexive.

> **levantarse** = *to get (oneself) up*
>
> **levantar** = *to lift (something) up*

A verb is reflexive when the subject performs an action on itself. When the recipient of an action is different from the subject, the verb is not reflexive. Compare these examples.

Acuesto al niño.	*I put the child to bed.*
Me acuesto a las once.	*I go to bed at eleven o'clock.*
Despiertas a tu amigo.	*You wake up your friend.*
Tu amigo **se despierta** a las ocho.	*Your friend wakes up at eight o'clock.*

When a reflexive verb is conjugated, reflexive pronouns are always placed before the verb.

Los chicos **se** visten.	*The boys get dressed.*

When reflexive verbs are used together with an infinitive or present participle, the reflexive pronouns may either be attached to the end of these words, or precede the conjugated verb.

Los chicos van a vestir**se.**	*The boys are going to get dressed.*
Los chicos **se** van a vestir.	
Los chicos **se** están vistiendo.	*The boys are getting dressed.*
Los chicos están vistiéndo**se.**	

Reflexive verbs can sometimes be translated into English as *to get* or *to become* (+ action).

Yo **me** visto.	*I get dressed.*
Ella **se** levanta.	*She gets up.*

When using reflexive verbs to talk about parts of the body in Spanish, use the definite article, not the possessive adjective.

Nos lavamos **las** manos.	*We wash **our** hands.*
Tienes que cepillarte **los** dientes.	*You have to brush **your** teeth.*

Parts of the body frequently used with reflexive verbs include:

la cara	*face*	las manos	*hands*
los dientes	*teeth*	el pelo	*hair*

Common reflexive verbs

acostarse (ue)	*to go to bed; to lie down*
afeitarse	*to shave*
bañarse	*to take a bath*
cepillarse	*to brush*
despertarse (ie)	*to wake up*
divertirse (ie)	*to have a good time, enjoy oneself*
dormirse (ue)	*to fall asleep*
ducharse	*to take a shower*
irse	*to go away, leave*
levantarse	*to get up*
maquillarse	*to put on makeup*
peinarse	*to comb one's hair*
preocuparse	*to worry*
quedarse	*to stay*
quitarse (la ropa)	*to take off* (one's clothes)
secarse	*to dry off*
sentarse (ie)	*to sit down*
sentirse (ie)	*to feel*
vestirse (i)	*to get dressed*

To express the sequence in which you do things, use words such as:

primero *first*	luego *later, then, next*	por fin *finally*
entonces *then, at that time*	después *after, afterwards*	

Primero me despierto a las seis de la mañana, **luego** me baño y **por fin** me visto.	*First, I wake up at six in the morning, then I take a bath, and finally, I get dressed.*

Actividades

1 Nuestras rutinas. You are describing the routines of several people. Follow the model to complete your descriptions. Remember to change the reflexive pronouns to agree with the subjects.

> **MODELO:** tú / despertarse temprano todos los días
> Tú te despiertas temprano   *You wake up early every day.*
> todos los días.

1. yo / ducharse con agua caliente
2. Ud. / levantarse tarde
3. los chicos / quitarse el sombrero
4. el señor / afeitarse por la mañana
5. tú / vestirse con ropa moderna
6. las niñas / dormirse a las ocho y media
7. Marina / secarse el pelo

2 ¿Qué vas a hacer? Working with a partner, ask each other questions, following the model.

> **MODELO:** —¿Te vas a afeitar mañana?   —*Are you going to shave tomorrow?*
> *or*
> —¿Vas a afeitarte mañana?
> —Sí, me voy a afeitar mañana. —*Yes, I am going to shave tomorrow.*
> *or*
> —Sí, voy a afeitarme mañana.

1. despertarse / a las 6:00 A.M.
2. bañarse / temprano
3. secarse el pelo / por la mañana
4. acostarse / tarde
5. quitarse los zapatos *(shoes)* / antes de dormir
6. divertirse en la discoteca / los sábados
7. cepillarse los dientes / por la mañana
8. divertirse / los fines de semana

3 En este momento. State what the people in the pictures are doing right now. Use the present progressive tense of the appropriate reflexive verb.

1. _____   2. _____   3. _____

4. _____   5. _____   6. _____

4 Un día típico. What does Jaime do on a typical day? Look at the pictures below and decide in which order Jaime does the following activities. Number the activities in a logical order, then write a sentence to describe each action shown in the pictures. Use reflexive verbs.

_____

_____

_____

_____

_____

_____

_____

_____

_____

Información confidencial

En el hotel de Nayeli.

Hija mía, vas a Dresden por el jaguar y llevas el jaguar a México...

¡Y después, hay un terremoto!

Sí, hija, porque llegas con el jaguar en los días mayas de la mala suerte.

¡Y Hernán muere en el terremoto!

No es tu culpa, hija mía. Tu esposo, Hernán, te ama.

¡Hernán!

En la casa de la familia Covarrubias.

Mira, mi amor, con el jaguar, vamos a ser ricos.

Tú siempre estás en problemas.

No hay problemas, ¡de verdad!

Ay Gerardo. ¡Tú y tus fantasías!

En el cuarto de hotel de Nayeli.

Señora arqueóloga: ¡con este microfonito, no te voy a perder!

En el hotel de Nayeli.

Buenas tardes.

Por favor, buscamos a Nayeli Paz Ocotlán.

Ah, sí, claro. La Sra. Paz es una huésped muy buena en nuestro hotel.

La Sra. Paz se despierta, se ducha y se viste.

Hoy, la Sra. Paz solamente va al teléfono, busca un número, escribe en un papelito...

... y hace una llamada.

Después, ella me pide la dirección de una compañía de transporte.

¿Tiene usted la dirección?

Sí, tengo la dirección. Está cerca!

¡Gracias! ¡Vamos, Adriana!

En la compañía de transportes.

¿Me puede decir cuál chofer tiene la ruta de Madrid a Sevilla.

Esa información es confidencial, señora.

¿Confidencial? ¡Soy cliente y quiero buen servicio!

¡Estos turistas! ¿Quién les entiende?

Bueno, escribo la dirección aquí: Gerardo H. Covarrubias. Callejón del Agua número 7.

Actividades

Online Study Center

For additional practice with this episode, visit the *Caminos* website at http://college.hmco.com/ languages/spanish/ renjilian/caminos/3e/ student_home.html.

1 Comprensión. Based on this episode of *Caminos del jaguar*, choose the logical response.

1. Nayeli lleva el jaguar a...
   a. México.
   b. Dresden.

2. El jaguar llega en los días mayas...
   a. de los terremotos.
   b. de la mala suerte.

3. ¿Quién muere en el terremoto?
   a. un estudiante de Nayeli
   b. el esposo de Nayeli

4. La Sra. Covarrubias cree que el jaguar...
   a. es un buen negocio.
   b. es un problema.

5. Con el microfonito, Gafasnegras puede...
   a. escuchar a Nayeli.
   b. ver a Nayeli.

6. El portero del hotel...
   a. no tiene la dirección.
   b. tiene la dirección.

7. Nayeli busca...
   a. un número.
   b. una dirección.

8. En la compañía de transportes, Nayeli está...
   a. alterada.
   b. enamorada.

2 Situaciones. With a partner, dramatize one of the following situations.

1. The conversation between Sr. and Sra. Covarrubias.
2. Nayeli is trying to get information from the clerk at the truck company.

3 Escritura. Write a brief summary of what Nayeli does at the hotel before she leaves for the trucking company (4–6 sentences).

NOTA CULTURAL

Los terremotos *(earthquakes)* en México

At 7:17 A.M., on September 19, 1985, Mexico suffered two consecutive earthquakes that devastated the nation's capital, Mexico City. Ten thousand Mexicans died, 50,000 were injured, and 250,000 lost their homes as a result of this natural disaster. The psychological effects of these quakes still haunt many "capitalinos" to this day.

SEGUNDO PASO

Vocabulario y lengua

ORDERING FOOD IN A RESTAURANT

¿Qué van a tomar?

Online Study Center

For additional practice with this unit's vocabulary and grammar, visit the *Caminos* website at http://college.hmco.com/languages/spanish/renjilian/caminos/3e/student_home.html. You can also review audio flashcards, quiz yourself, and explore related Spanish-language sites.

Restaurante Dalí

Precio en euros

Entremeses	Tortilla española	2,1	**Appetizers**	Spanish omelette with potatoes and onions	
	Chorizo y pan	2,7		Sausage and bread	
	Queso manchego	3,0		Manchego (goat) cheese	
Sopas	Gazpacho	2,4	**Soups**	Gazpacho (cold vegetable soup)	
	Sopa de pescado	3,6		Fish soup	
	Sopa del día	2,7		Soup of the day	
Ensaladas	Ensalada mixta	3,6	**Salads**	Mixed salad	
	Ensalada rusa	2,4		Potato salad	
Entradas	Especialidad de la casa:		**Entrées**	Specialty of the house:	
	Paella valenciana	8,4		Paella valenciana (rice dish usually with meat, fish and vegetables)	
	Gambas al ajillo	5,4		Shrimp in garlic Sauce	
	Bistec asado con patatas fritas	6,6		Steak with French fries	
Postres	Helado de chocolate, vainilla o fresa	1,8	**Desserts**	Chocolate, vanilla, or strawberry ice cream	
	Fruta del día	1,2		Fruit of the day	
	Flan	1,8		Baked egg custard	
Bebidas	Sangría- 1 litro	5,4	**Drinks**	Beverage of wine, soda, or juice, and fruit pieces	
	Agua mineral con/sin gas	1,5		Mineral water (carbonated/uncarbonated)	
	Té o café	1,2		Tea or coffee	
	Refrescos variados	1,5		Assorted soft drinks	
	Zumo/Jugo de naranja	3,0		Orange juice	
	Cerveza	1,5		Beer	
	Vino tinto/blanco	1,2		Red/white wine	

108   ciento ocho ▶ Unidad 3

Más palabras y expresiones

Sustantivos

el almuerzo	*lunch*
el aperitivo/el entremés	*appetizer*
el/la camarero/a, el/la mesero/a	*waiter, waitress*
la carne	*meat*
la carta, el menú	*menu*
la cena	*dinner*
la comida	*food / dinner (in some places) / lunch (in others)*
la copa	*stemmed glass, goblet*
la cuchara	*tablespoon*
la cucharita	*teaspoon*
el cuchillo	*knife*
la cuenta	*bill*
el desayuno	*breakfast*
el hambre *(f.)*	*hunger*
la legumbre	*vegetable*
el marisco	*shellfish*
el pedido	*order*
la pimienta	*(black) pepper*
el plato	*plate, dish*
la propina	*tip*
la sal	*salt*
las tapas	*small servings of food (Sp.)*
la taza	*cup*
el tenedor	*fork*
el vaso	*glass (for drinks)*

Verbos

almorzar (ue)	*to have lunch*
cenar	*to have dinner*
dejar	*to leave (something behind)*
desayunar	*to have breakfast*
disfrutar	*to enjoy*
tomar	*to drink*

Adjetivos

caliente	*hot (temperature)*
dulce	*sweet*
fuerte (una comida)	*heavy (food)*
ligero/a	*light*
picante	*hot (spicy)*
preparado/a	*prepared*
rico/a	*rich, delicious*
sabroso/a	*delicious, tasty*

Otras expresiones

¡A sus órdenes!	*At your service!*
Tengo mucha hambre.	*I am very hungry.*
¿Qué desean comer / beber / tomar?	*What would you like to eat / drink?*
¿Qué nos recomienda?	*What do you recommend?*
Estoy muerto/a de hambre.	*I'm starving / famished.*
La cuenta, por favor.	*The check, please.*
Me gustaría / Quisiera (pedir)...	*I would like (to order) . . .*

Actividades

1 Una cena importante. You are dining with a friend in a nice restaurant. With a partner, talk about the foods each of you like and dislike.

▶ **MODELO:** el bistec

—¿Te gusta el bistec?   —*Do you like steak?*
—No, no me gusta.   —*No, I don't like it.*

or

—Sí, me gusta.   —*Yes, I like it.*

1. el helado de chocolate
2. el flan
3. la ensalada rusa
4. la sopa de pescado
5. la tortilla española
6. el jugo de naranja
7. las gambas al ajillo
8. el café

2 En el café. Help your partner decide what to order. Complete the chart by asking, then recording, your partner's choice for each category on the menu from Restaurante Dalí. After deciding on what to order, calculate the total cost of each meal. Remember to add a good tip depending on the service. Follow the model.

▶ **MODELO:** —¿Qué vas a pedir de entremés?   —*What are you going to order for an appetizer?*

—Voy a pedir queso manchego.   —*I am going to order Manchego cheese.*

	El pedido	El precio
Entremés	_____	_____
Sopa	_____	_____
Ensalada	_____	_____
Entrada	_____	_____
Postre	_____	_____
Bebida	_____	_____
Propina	_____	_____
Precio total:		_____

3 Entre nosotros. Role-play the following situation with a partner.

Turista	Camarero/a
You have just spent the whole day in Sevilla sightseeing. You have been enjoying yourself so much that you haven't had time to eat. The concierge has recommended a restaurant called "Los Arcos." You are very hungry and you want to eat everything on the menu. You especially want to try **sangría, tapas, paella,** and dessert.	You work at the restaurant called "Los Arcos." Today has been a difficult day. The cook is sick and the only person who knows anything about cooking is the dishwasher. In addition, there are no desserts, shrimp, or wine. Try to make the best of the situation.

EXPRESSING ACTIONS IN THE PRESENT

Verbs with irregular *yo* forms: *saber* and *conocer*

El verano es mi estación favorita. **Hago°** muchas cosas los fines de semana. **Salgo°** de mi casa a las seis de la mañana y **conduzco°** mi coche al parque. **Traigo°** mi guitarra y una novela interesante. Después de leer y tocar la guitarra, **doy un paseo°** por el parque y como en un buen restaurante que **conozco.**

I do / I leave
I drive / I bring
I take a walk

Some verbs are irregular only in the first person singular (**yo**), while the endings of the other forms remain the same as for regular verbs. For some of these verbs, the **yo** form ends in **-go** or **-zco.** The **yo** form of verbs that end in **-cer** and **-cir** tend to have **–zco** endings.

Verbs with irregular *yo* forms		
	-go verbs **hacer** *(to make; to do)*	**-zco verbs** **conducir** *(to drive)*
yo	ha**go**	condu**zco**
tú	haces	conduces
Ud. / él / ella	hace	conduce
nosotros / nosotras	hacemos	conducimos
vosotros / vosotras	hacéis	conducís
Uds. / ellos / ellas	hacen	conducen

Common verbs that follow these patterns:

-go verbs		**-zco verbs**	
oír (oi**go**)	*to hear*	conocer (cono**zco**)	*to know, be familiar with*
poner (pon**go**)	*to put, place*	parecer (pare**zco**)	*to seem*
salir (sal**go**)	*to go out; to leave*	producir (produ**zco**)	*to produce*
traer (tra**igo**)	*to bring*	traducir (tradu**zco**)	*to translate*

In addition to being a **–go** verb, the verb **oír** has these spelling changes: **oyes, oye, oímos, oís, oyen.**

The verb **salir** *(to go out; to leave)* is useful for expressing many actions. Here are just a few.

Common expressions with *salir*:

salir a + ***infinitive***	*to go out to + verb* Yo salgo a bailar los sábados.	**salir de**	*to leave from a place* Salimos de la biblioteca a las diez.
salir con	*to leave or go out with* Ramiro quiere salir con Yolanda.	**salir para**	*to leave for a place* ¿Cuándo sales para Europa?

Dar *(to give)*, **saber** *(to know)*, and **ver** *(to see)* are irregular in the **yo** form, but don't follow any particular pattern. The endings of the other forms remain the same as those for regular verbs.

	dar	**saber**	**ver**
yo	**doy**	**sé**	**veo**
tú	das	sabes	ves
Ud. / él / ella	da	sabe	ve
nosotros / nosotras	damos	sabemos	vemos
vosotros / vosotras	dais	sabéis	veis
Uds. / ellos / ellas	dan	saben	ven

Common expressions with **dar:**

dar un paseo	*to take a walk*	dar una conferencia	*to give a talk*
dar una clase	*to teach a class*	dar una fiesta	*to give a party*

Saber and conocer

Although the general meaning for both verbs is *to know,* each is used in Spanish to express that concept in distinct ways.

Uses of saber / conocer			
saber + *infinitive: to know how to do something*		conocer + *noun (place): to know / be familiar with (a place)*	
¿Sabes conducir?	*Do you know how to drive?*	**¿Conoces** Puerto Rico?	*Do you know Puerto Rico?*
Sabemos hablar español.	*We know how to speak Spanish.*	**Conozco** un buen restaurante.	*I know a good restaurant.*
saber + *noun (information): to know facts, such as time, dates, places, names, and pieces of information*		conocer a + noun *(person / people): to know someone*	
Sabemos el día y el lugar de la fiesta.	*We know the day and location of the party.*	**¿Conoces a** mi amigo Luis?	*Do you know / Have you met my friend Luis?*
No **sé** dónde están mis libros.	*I don't know where my books are.*	**Conozco a** mis compañeros de clase muy bien.	*I know my classmates very well.*

Personal *a*

A direct object is a word that receives the action of the verb. If the direct object is a person or implies a person, it must be preceded by the personal **a.** For **a** + **el,** remember to use the contraction **al.** If the direct object is a thing, then **a** is not used.

Veo la casa.	*I see **the house.** (thing)*
Veo **a** Marcos.	*I see **Marcos.** (person)*
Conozco la ciudad.	*I know **the city.** (thing)*
Conozco **a** la profesora.	*I know **the teacher.** (person)*
Conozco **al** profesor	

Actividades

1 **Una invitación.** Linda runs into her friend Pablo, and they talk about going to the movies. Complete their conversation with the correct form of the present tense of each verb in parentheses.

Linda ¡Hola, Pablo! ¿ _____ (saber) tú si hay películas (*movies*) buenas hoy?

Pablo Sí, hay muchas. Yo _____ (conocer) un cine muy bueno. Allí presentan películas francesas.

Linda ¿Francesas? ¡Yo no _____ (saber) francés! ¿Hay subtítulos?

Pablo No, no hay subtítulos, pero yo _____ (traducir) muy bien el francés.

Linda ¡Pablo, qué tonto eres! Es una broma (*joke*), ¿verdad?

Pablo ¡Claro que es una broma! Hay subtítulos. ¡Vamos al cine; yo _____ (conducir)!

Linda ¡Y yo pago, vamos!

2 ¡Yo también! Read what the following people do; then say whether you do these activities, too. With a classmate, take turns answering the questions.

▶ MODELO: —Nosotros salimos de casa a las siete, ¿y tú?
—*Yo también salgo de casa a las siete.*
or
—*No, no salgo de casa a las siete. Salgo a las siete y media.*

1. Ricardo sale para México, ¿y tú?
2. Nosotros conducimos autobuses grandes, ¿y tú?
3. Los estudiantes dan fiestas fantásticas, ¿y tú?
4. El profesor sale temprano, ¿y tú?
5. Ella pone la mesa antes de comer, ¿y tú?
6. El Sr. Rulfo conoce a mucha gente, ¿y tú?
7. Tu compañera traduce la tarea al inglés, ¿y tú?
8. Liliana ve televisión los domingos, ¿y tú?

3 ¿Quién sabe qué? Say what these people know or know how to do. Use **saber** or **conocer.** Follow the model and use the personal **a** if needed.

▶ MODELO: Elena / inglés
Elena sabe inglés.

1. Berta / muchos secretos
2. nosotros / Madrid
3. Verónica / no / bailar
4. ellos / el profesor Sánchez
5. Ud. / la hora
6. el chico / un buen restaurante mexicano
7. yo / planchar la ropa
8. el profesor / los nombres de los estudiantes
9. yo / no / la nueva estudiante
10. Gil y yo / cantar bien

4 Actividades. Using at least four of the verbs in the list, write a short e-mail to your best friend about things you do in a typical week. (Use the present indicative.) Then describe four things that you are going to do this weekend. (Use **ir a** + infinitive.)

hacer	conducir	ver	dar	ir
salir	poner	escribir	estudiar	traer

USING LARGE NUMBERS

¿Cómo contamos los números en español?

Los números de 200 a 2.000.000					
200	doscientos	600	seiscientos	1.999	mil novecientos noventa y nueve
201	doscientos uno	700	setecientos	2.000	dos mil
300	trescientos	800	ochocientos	2.001	dos mil uno
400	cuatrocientos	900	novecientos	1.000.000	un millón
500	quinientos	1.000	mil	2.000.000	dos millones

Note: In most Spanish-speaking countries, numbers are punctuated with periods instead of commas.

doscientos – novecientos	The numbers from 200 to 900 agree in gender with the nouns they modify. These words are always plural. *200 stores* = **doscientas** tiendas *300 rooms* = **trescientos** cuartos
mil	**Mil** remains unchanged and does not agree in gender or number with the noun it modifies. *one thousand pesos* = **mil** pesos *two thousand trains* = **dos mil** trenes. Note that **mil** means *one thousand* or *a thousand*.
millón	**Millón** (singular) is used with **un**; in all other instances use **millones** (plural). *1.005.093 pesos* = **un millón, cinco mil, noventa y tres** pesos *2.400.671 dollars* = **dos millones, cuatrocientos mil, seiscientos setenta y**[1] **un** dólares
un millón de / millones de	**Un millón de / millones de** is used only when the number is rounded out in millions. Otherwise **millones** follows the other rules above. *1.000.000 pesos* = **un millón de** pesos *5.000.000 dollars* = **cinco millones de** dólares *but* *5.100.401 girls* = **cinco millones, cien mil, cuatrocientas una** niñas

[1]Remember that **y** is used between the "tens" and "ones" place in numbers.

Actividades

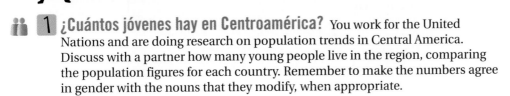

1 **¿Cuántos jóvenes hay en Centroamérica?** You work for the United Nations and are doing research on population trends in Central America. Discuss with a partner how many young people live in the region, comparing the population figures for each country. Remember to make the numbers agree in gender with the nouns that they modify, when appropriate.

▶ **MODELO:** —¿Cuántas niñas hay en El Salvador?
—Hay un millón, doscientas doce mil, doscientas dieciséis niñas en El Salvador.

—*How many girls are there in El Salvador?*
—*There are one million, two hundred twelve thousand, two hundred sixteen girls in El Salvador.*

Los jóvenes de Centroamérica		
País	**Niños 0–14 años de edad**	**Niñas 0–14 años de edad**
El Salvador	1.265.080	1.212.216
Costa Rica	590.261	563.196
Guatemala	2.573.359	2.479.098
Honduras	1.491.170	1.429.816
Nicaragua	1.031.897	994.633
Panamá	492.403	472.996

2 Eventos históricos.

Eventos históricos. Write out the following dates in Spanish on your own. Then work with a partner to see if you can match the events in Column A with the dates in Column B.

A	B
1. Cristóbal Colón llega a las Américas.	a. 1865
2. Los moros *(Moors)* llegan a España.	b. 1964
3. La segunda guerra mundial *(WWII)* termina (ends).	c. 1977
4. Un grupo de terroristas ataca Nueva York y el Pentágono.	d. 711
5. La disolución de la Unión Soviética ocurre.	e. 1492
6. Declaran la independencia de los Estados Unidos.	f. 2005
7. El huracán Katrina causa gran destrucción.	g. 1992
8. Los Beatles cantan en el *Ed Sullivan Show*.	h. 1776
9. La película *Saturday Night Fever* es muy popular.	i. 1945
10. John Wilkes Booth asesina al Presidente Abraham Lincoln.	j. 2001

Answers: 1. e; 2. d; 3. i; 4. j; 5. g; 6. h; 7. f; 8. b; 9. c; 10. a

3 ¿Cuántos hay?

¿Cuántos hay? Use the World Fact Book on the Internet (https://www.cia.gov/cia/publications/factbook/index.html) to determine the population for the following countries. Report your findings to the class in Spanish.

País	Población
España	_____
Bolivia	_____
México	_____
El Salvador	_____
Puerto Rico	_____
Argentina	_____
Perú	_____
Costa Rica	_____

SHOWING LOCATION OF PEOPLE, PLACES, AND THINGS

Demonstrative adjectives and pronouns: adverbs of location

¿Qué flores te gustan?

Cecilia, **esas** flores rojas me gustan mucho.

Sí, son muy bonitas, pero prefiero **aquellas** flores amarillas.

No, **aquellas** flores no me gustan. Prefiero **éstas**.

In the drawing above, which objects are the people talking about? Which words are used to indicate where these objects are?

Demonstrative adjectives and pronouns			
Demonstrative adjectives	Demonstrative pronouns	Neuter demonstrative pronouns	
este, esta	éste, ésta	esto	*this (one)*
estos, estas	éstos, éstas		*these (ones)*
ese, esa	ése, ésa	eso	*that (one)*
esos, esas	ésos, ésas		*those (ones)*
aquel, aquella	aquél, aquélla	aquello	*that (one) (over there)*
aquellos/as	aquéllos/as		*those (ones) (over there)*

Demonstrative adjectives are used to point out people or objects. They modify a noun and are placed directly before it. They agree in gender and number with the nouns they modify.

Esta tortilla me gusta.	*I like this tortilla.*
Esa ensalada parece deliciosa.	*That salad looks delicious.*

Demonstrative pronouns are used to replace nouns. These pronouns have the same forms as the adjectives, but carry a written accent over the stressed vowel. Like demonstrative adjectives, demonstrative pronouns also agree in gender and number with the nouns they replace.

Me gusta mucho este vino, **aquél** no.	*I like this wine very much, not **that one.***
Prefiero esta sopa. **Ésa** está muy salada.	*I prefer this soup. **That one** is very salty.*

Neuter demonstrative pronouns are used to refer to something indefinite or abstract: an object, an event, or an idea. Note that neuter pronouns don't have written accents.

Esto representa un problema enorme.	*This represents an enormous problem.*
Eso no me parece bien.	*That doesn't seem OK to me.*

Adverbs of location

When using demonstrative adjectives and pronouns, the following adverbs of place are useful to describe the relative location of things: **aquí** *(here)*; **allí / ahí** *(there)*; and **allá** *(over there)*.

—Por favor, necesito **esos** libros.　　　　—*Please, I need those books.*
—¿Cuáles libros? **¿Éstos** que están **aquí?**　—*Which books? These here?*
—Sí, **ésos** que están **allí.**　　　　　　—*Yes, those that are there.*

Actividades

1 **¿Qué galletitas?** Two friends are planning to buy a dessert to have after dinner. Complete their conversation with demonstrative adjectives or demonstrative pronouns, using the cues in parentheses.

Romeo　　¡Mira, Julieta, _____ (**1.** *these*) galletas María parecen muy ricas!
Julieta　　No, Romeo, no me gustan, quiero _____ (**2.** *those* [*over there*]) galletitas con piña.
Romeo　　De acuerdo, pero ¿ves alguna galletita de chocolate?
Julieta　　Claro, mira, _____ (**3.** *these*) son de chocolate.
Romeo　　¡Qué bien! Vamos a comprar _____ (**4.** *those*) galletas de chocolate y _____ (**5.** *these*) mazapanes.
Julieta　　Y yo quiero comprar también _____ (**6.** *those*) pastelitos de coco y _____ (**7.** *these*) galletas de almendra. ¿Quieres probar _____ (8. *those* [*over there*]) bollos de crema?
Romeo　　Por supuesto, quiero probar de todo. ¡Nuestra cena va a ser estupenda!

2 **En el restaurante.** You and a friend are enjoying some wonderful restaurant meals as you travel through Spain. Compare options on the menu as you decide what to order by completing the sentences with demonstrative adjectives and pronouns.

1. _____ *(This)* ensalada es grande. _____ *(That one)* es pequeña.
2. Mira _____ *(that* [*over there*]) paella valenciana tiene mariscos. Prefiero _____ *(that)* bistec.
3. _____ *(That)* mesero es simpático. _____ *(That one* [*over there*]) es antipático.
4. _____ *(This)* gazpacho está muy frío. _____ *(That)* sopa de pollo está caliente.
5. _____ *(This)* mesa está limpia. _____ *(Those ones* [*over there*]) están sucias.
6. _____ *(Those)* postres son de chocolate. _____ *(These ones)* son de piña.

3 Restaurante Delicias. Describe the items in the chart using demonstrative adjectives and the vocabulary you have learned in this chapter. The adverbs above each group of foods will help you decide which demonstrative adjective you'll need. Work with a partner.

▶ MODELO: (Aquí) Esta ensalada es grande y sabrosa.

CAMINOS DEL JAGUAR

Las reglas son las reglas

Actividades

1 Comprensión. Based on this episode of *Caminos del jaguar*, choose the logical response.

1. Adriana...
   a. no tiene hambre.
   b. tiene mucha hambre.

2. ¿Quién quiere comer algo rápido?
   a. Adriana.
   b. Felipe.

3. El mozo del restaurante recomienda...
   a. la especialidad de la casa.
   b. la especialidad española.

4. ¿Quién pide gazpacho y batido de frutas?
   a. Adriana
   b. Felipe

5. ¿Quién pide gazpacho y agua mineral con gas?
   a. Adriana
   b. Felipe.

6. El señor de la compañía de transportes no da la información...
   a. porque él está alterado.
   b. porque la información es confidencial.

7. ¿Adónde van Adriana y Felipe?
   a. a Sevilla
   b. a Madrid

8. Felipe tiene...
   a. el nombre del chofer.
   b. la dirección del hotel.

2 Situaciones. Dramatize one of the following situations.

1. Adriana and Felipe order a meal from the waiter at the coffee shop.
2. Adriana argues with the clerk at the trucking company.

3 Escritura. Write a brief summary (4–6 sentences) of this episode of *Caminos del jaguar.*

NOTA CULTURAL

España y el uso de *vosotros*

In Spain, the **vosotros** form is the plural of **tú** and is used to talk with friends and family. Adults often use **vosotros** to address younger people and children, who in turn will address them with **usted(es)** as a sign of respect. In Latin America, **ustedes** is the only plural form of address in all formal and informal situations. **Vosotros** is rarely used in Latin America but may occasionally be heard in very formal situations, such as religious ceremonies and political speeches.

Lectura

Online Study Center

For further writing practice online, visit the *Caminos* website at http://college .hmco.com/languages/ spanish/renjilian/caminos/ 3e/student_home.html.

PRELECTURA

1 Nuestras ciudades favoritas. In groups of three, take turns describing a city that each of you has visited with family or friends, or talk about the city in which you currently live. Answer the questions below.

1. ¿En qué país está la ciudad? ¿Cómo se llama? ¿Cuántos habitantes hay?
2. ¿Es una ciudad grande o pequeña? ¿Es vieja o nueva? ¿Cuántos años tiene?
3. ¿Qué edificios importantes hay? ¿Cómo son?
4. ¿Hay buenos restaurantes allí? ¿Qué tipo de comidas preparan? ¿Hay cibercafés?
5. ¿Cuáles son los principales sitios turísticos de interés?
6. ¿Qué actividades hacen ustedes de día y de noche con la familia o los amigos?
7. ¿Es famosa la ciudad por un evento, día o persona especial? Explica.

Reading Strategy

Skimming

Skimming is a reading strategy that you can apply when you want to learn information quickly from written articles. Skimming is the technique of quickly eliciting the general idea or main focus of a text or article. When reading in Spanish, skimming is very useful. First, glance quickly at any headings, titles, and obvious cognates (presented in *Unidad 1*). Second, rapidly glance at any visuals that the article or your instructor may provide. Skim the selection below and complete the activities that follow.

Sevilla, ciudad sensacional

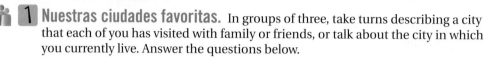
El exquisito Parque María Luisa

La capital de la provincia de Andalucía, Sevilla, tiene cerca de[1] 700.000 habitantes. Es la cuarta[2] ciudad más grande de España. Es posible llegar a Sevilla en el AVE, el tren rápido de alta velocidad. Sevilla es conocida por sus parques muy bonitos y sus museos, iglesias, conventos, torres y palacios, que presentan una rica variedad de estilos de arquitectura.

El Parque de María Luisa

El Parque de María Luisa es extraordinario. Con sus jardines preciosos, árboles latinoamericanos y zonas sombrías[3], es un buen sitio para dar un paseo a pie o en auto.

La Catedral

La Catedral de Sevilla, de estilo gótico, es una de las catedrales más famosas del mundo. Es la tercera en tamaño[4], después de la Catedral de San Pedro en Roma y la de San Pablo en Londres[5]. Los Reyes[6] de España seleccionaron[7] la Catedral de Sevilla para la gran boda[8] de su hija Elena.

La Catedral de Sevilla, España

[1]close to; [2]fourth; [3]shady; [4]third in size; [5]London; [6]King and Queen; [7]selected; [8]wedding.

Unos jóvenes hablan y comen tapas

La Giralda

Una pareja baila flamenco

La Giralda

La Giralda es un ejemplo maravilloso del arte islámico. Una alta torre[9] rectangular de casi 117.5 metros de altura, está junto a[10] la Catedral de Sevilla. En 1184 se empezó[11] su construcción de arquitectura musulmana[12] y en 1555 el arquitecto Hernán Ruiz agregó[13] el campanario[14], como el de una iglesia cristiana, con una gran figura de bronce como veleta[15]. Desde la torre hay una magnífica vista[16] panorámica de la ciudad de Sevilla.

La música y danza flamencas

La música y danza flamencas son típicas de Sevilla, donde los bailes se llaman "sevillanas", en honor de su origen en esta ciudad. Las sevillanas están llenas de ritmos hipnóticos, pasión y drama. Es fascinante mirar esta danza y escuchar la música de Sevilla.

Las tapas al aire libre[17]

En Sevilla hay bares al aire libre donde muchas personas comen tapas. La hora más animada para disfrutar de las tapas es de la una a las cuatro de la tarde, cerca de la orilla[18] del río Guadalquivir.

---

[9]tower; [10]next to; [11]was begun; [12]Muslim; [13]added; [14]bell tower; [15]weather vane; [16]view; [17]outside; [18]shore

POSTLECTURA

2 Información general. In the selection above, skim the headings of the text for the different characteristics that make Sevilla an exciting Spanish city. In pairs, ask each other, **Menciona cinco aspectos atractivos de Sevilla.** Then, study the photos, taking turns reading the captions under each one to gather further information rapidly about the content of the selection. Ask each other, **¿Qué cognados hay y qué significan?**

Reading Strategy

Scanning

Scanning is a commonly used reading strategy, especially for reading selections that contain many new vocabulary terms. In scanning, look for specific details that support the general information you've already learned.

3 Aspectos básicos. After scanning this selection, jot down one basic characteristic of each of these attractions in Sevilla.

1. El Parque de María Luisa
2. La Catedral y La Giralda
3. La música y la danza flamencas
4. Las tapas al aire libre

Escritura

Online Study Center

For further writing practice online, visit the *Caminos* website at http://college .hmco.com/languages/ spanish/renjilian/caminos/ 3e/student_home.html.

Writing Strategy

Providing supporting details

One way of making your writing interesting for the reader is to provide details about your topic that support or explain your main idea. The result is more vivid and convincing prose. Read the Workshop below to see how providing supporting details about a character from *Caminos del jaguar* makes the sample passage much more interesting.

Workshop

Main idea	Gafasnegras es mala.
Supporting details	Ella siempre lleva gafas de sol.
	Piensa robar el jaguar.
	Ella persigue a Nayeli.
	Pone un microfonito en la agenda de Nayeli.
Sample passage	No sabemos quién es, pero sabemos que lleva sus famosas gafas de sol. Desde el primer episodio de la historia, ella persigue a Nayeli porque piensa robar el jaguar. Desordena la habitación de Nayeli y pone un microfonito en su agenda para saber dónde está Nayeli.

Strategy in action

For additional practice in providing supporting details, turn to the *Escritura* section of *Unidad 3* in your Student Activities Manual.

1 Nuestro viaje. You and your friend are planning on spending the summer in Spain. You each have limited resources ($750). Create an itinerary of cities and sites to visit, where to stay, and what to eat. Plan to travel to a minimum of four places and to use at least three different means of transportation. Use the map in the front of the book for reference. Write a postcard to your friend describing the itinerary you plan. Include a main idea and supporting details.

2 Mi universidad. Get a copy of your campus map or sketch one out. Plan a tour for a prospective student to show her/him where everything is. Use demonstrative adjectives and pronouns.

Resumen de vocabulario

TALKING ABOUT WEATHER AND SEASONS

Sustantivos

el aguacero/el chubasco	*downpour*
la brisa	*breeze*
el cielo	*sky*
el clima	*climate*
el este	*east*
los grados centígrados/ Celsius/Fahrenheit	*degrees centigrade/ Celsius / Fahrenheit*
el huracán	*hurricane*
el invierno	*winter*
los kilómetros (por hora)	*kilometers (per hour)*
la lluvia	*rain*
el/la meteorólogo/a	*meteorologist*
las millas (por hora)	*miles (per hour)*
la nieve	*snow*
el noreste/el noroeste	*northeast/northwest*
el norte	*north*
la nube	*cloud*
el oeste	*west*
el otoño	*autumn, fall*
el porcentaje	*percentage*
la primavera	*spring*
la probabilidad	*probability*
el promedio	*average*
el pronóstico del tiempo	*weather forecast*
el sur	*south*
el sureste/el suroeste	*southeast/southwest*
la temperatura (mínima/máxima)	*(minimum/maximum) temperature*
la tormenta/la tronada	*storm*
el tornado	*tornado*
el verano	*summer*

Otras expresiones

¿A cuánto está la temperatura?	*What is the temperature?*
está (parcialmente) nublado	*it's (partly) cloudy*
fuerte	*strong*
hace buen/mal tiempo	*it's good/bad weather*
hace calor/frío/fresco	*it's hot/cold/cool*
hace viento	*it's windy*
húmedo/a	*humid*
llovizna	*it's drizzling*
llueve	*it's raining*
nieva	*it's snowing*
por ciento	*percent*
seco/a	*dry*

VERBS

almorzar (ue)	*to have lunch*
cerrar (ie)	*to close*
comenzar (ie)	*to start, begin*
concernir (ie)	*to concern*
conseguir (i)	*to get, obtain*
contar (ue)	*to count*
contener	*to contain*
costar (ue)	*to cost*
decir (i)	*to say, tell*
dormir (ue)	*to sleep*
empezar (ie)	*to begin*
encontrar (ue)	*to find*
entender (ie)	*to understand*
entretener	*to entertain*
ir	*to go*
jugar (ue) (al)	*to play (a sport)*
mantener	*to maintain*
mentir	*to lie*
morir (ue)	*to die*
mostrar (ue)	*to show*
pedir (i)	*to ask for*
pensar (ie)	*to think*
perder (ie)	*to lose*
perseguir (i)	*to follow, pursue*
poder (ue)	*to be able*
preferir (ie)	*to prefer*
probar (ue)	*to taste, try*
querer (ie)	*to want*
recomendar (ie)	*to recommend*
recordar (ue)	*to remember*
repetir (i)	*to repeat*
seguir (i)	*to follow, continue*
servir (i)	*to serve*
soñar (ue) (con)	*to dream (about)*
tener	*to have*
venir	*to come*
volver (ue)	*to return*

EXPRESSIONS WITH *TENER*

tener calor	*to be hot; to feel hot*
tener cuidado	*to be careful*
tener la culpa	*to be at fault*

tener éxito	to be successful
tener frío	to be cold
tener ganas de + *infinitive*	to feel like (doing something)
tener hambre	to be hungry
tener miedo	to be afraid
tener prisa	to be in a hurry
tener que + *infinitive*	to have to (do something)
tener razón	to be right
tener sed	to be thirsty
tener sentido	to make sense
tener sueño	to be sleepy, tired
tener *X* años	to be X years old

DISCUSSING TRANSPORTATION

Sustantivos

el autobús	bus
el avión	plane
el barco	boat
la bicicleta	bicycle
el billete/boleto/pasaje	ticket, passage
el camión	truck; bus (Mex.)
la camioneta/el camión	pick-up truck; van
el chofer (L. Am.)/ el chófer (Sp.)	driver; chauffeur
el coche/el auto (móvil)/el carro	car, automobile
el crucero	cruise ship
la dirección	address
el metro	subway
la motocicleta	motorcycle
la ruta	route
el taxi	taxi
el tren	train
el/la turista	tourist
el viaje	trip

Verbos

alcanzar	to reach, catch up with
estar cerca / lejos (de)	to be close/far away (from)
llegar	to arrive
manejar/conducir	to drive

quedar	to be (located)
viajar	to travel

Otras expresiones

a pie	on foot
después	after
en	by (with transportation), in, on

TALKING ABOUT DAILY ROUTINES

Sustantivos

la cara	face
los dientes	teeth
las manos	hands
el pelo	hair

Verbos

acostarse (ue)	to go to bed; to lie down
afeitarse	to shave
bañarse	to take a bath
cepillarse	to brush
despertarse (ie)	to wake up
divertirse (ie)	to have a good time, enjoy oneself
dormirse (ue)	to fall asleep
ducharse	to take a shower
irse	to go away, leave
levantarse	to get up
maquillarse	to put on makeup
peinarse	to comb one's hair
preocuparse	to worry
quedarse	to stay
quitarse (la ropa)	to take off (one's clothes)
secarse	to dry off
sentarse (ie)	to sit down
sentirse (ie)	to feel
vestirse (i)	to get dressed

Otras expresiones

después	afterwards
entonces	then, at that time
luego	later, then, next
por fin	finally
primero	first

SEGUNDO PASO

ORDERING FOOD IN A RESTAURANT

Sustantivos

el agua (f.) (mineral)	(mineral) water
el almuerzo	lunch
el aperitivo/el entremés	appetizer

el bistec	steak
el café	coffee
el/la camarero/a, el/ la mesero/a	waiter, waitress
la carne	meat
la carta, el menú	menu

la cena	*dinner*
la cerveza	*beer*
el chorizo	*sausage*
la comida	*food/dinner/lunch*
la copa	*stemmed glass, goblet*
la cuchara	*tablespoon*
la cucharita	*teaspoon*
el cuchillo	*knife*
la cuenta	*bill*
el desayuno	*breakfast*
la ensalada (mixta/rusa)	*(mixed/potato) salad*
el flan	*baked egg custard*
la fruta	*fruit*
la gamba	*shrimp*
el gazpacho	*cold vegetable soup*
el hambre (f.)	*hunger*
el helado (de chocolate, vainilla, fresa)	*(chocolate, vanilla, strawberry) ice cream*
la legumbre	*vegetable*
el marisco	*shellfish*
la paella (valenciana)	*rice, meat, and seafood dish (from Valencia)*
el pan	*bread*
la patata/papa	*potato*
el pedido	*order*
el pescado	*fish*
la pimienta	*(black) pepper*
el plato	*plate, dish*
la propina	*tip*
el queso	*cheese*
el refresco	*soft drink*
la sal	*salt*
la sangría	*wine, fruit, soda drink*
la sopa	*soup*
las tapas	*small servings of food (Sp.)*
la taza	*cup*
el té	*tea*
el tenedor	*fork*
la tortilla española	*Spanish omelette*
el vaso	*glass (for drinks)*
el vino (tinto/blanco)	*(red/white) wine*
el zumo/jugo	*juice*

Verbos

almorzar (ue)	*to have lunch*
cenar	*to have dinner*
dejar	*to leave (something behind)*
desayunar	*to have breakfast*
disfrutar	*to enjoy*
tomar	*to drink*

Adjetivos

caliente	*hot (temperature)*
dulce	*sweet*
frito/a	*fried*
fuerte (una comida)	*heavy (food)*
ligero/a	*light*
picante	*hot (spicy)*
preparado/a	*prepared*
rico/a	*rich, delicious*
sabroso/a	*delicious, tasty*
variado/a	*assorted*

Otras expresiones

¡A sus órdenes!	*At your service!*
Tengo mucha hambre.	*I am very hungry.*
¿Qué desean comer/ beber/tomar?	*What would you like to eat/drink?*
¿Qué nos recomienda?	*What do you recommend?*
Estoy muerto/a de hambre.	*I'm starving/famished.*
La cuenta, por favor.	*The check, please.*
Me gustaría/ Quisiera (pedir)...	*I would like (to order) . . .*

VERBS WITH IRREGULAR *YO* FORMS

conducir	*to drive*
conocer	*to know, be familiar with*
dar	*to give*
hacer	*to do, make*
oír	*to hear*
parecer	*to seem*
poner	*to put, place*
producir	*to produce*
saber	*to know*
salir	*to go out; to leave*
traducir	*to translate*
traer	*to bring*
ver	*to see*

DEMONSTRATIVES

aquel, aquella (aquél, aquélla); aquello	*that (one) (over there)*
aquellos/as (aquéllos/as)	*those (over there)*
ese, esa (ése/ésa); eso	*that (one)*
esos, esas (ésos/as)	*those*
este, esta(éste, ésta); esto	*this (one)*
estos, estas (éstos/as)	*these*

Adverbs

allá	*over there*
allí (ahí)	*there*
aquí	*here*

4
La vida diaria

VOCABULARIO Y LENGUA

- ► Discussing professions
- ► Using indirect object pronouns
- ► Indicating likes and dislikes: **Gustar** and similar verbs
- ► Using affirmative, negative, and transitional expressions

- ► Talking about family members
- ► Distinguishing between **ser** and **estar**
- ► Expressing location: Prepositions
- ► Narrating events in the past: Preterite of regular verbs

CAMINOS DEL JAGUAR

- ► Un negocio sucio
- ► ¡Susto espantoso!

LECTURA

- ► A España le encantan los turistas

NOTAS CULTURALES

- ► Atocha
- ► El Archivo General de Indias

ESTRATEGIAS

- ► **Reading:** Making notes in the margin
- ► **Writing:** Creating a timeline

Joaquín Sorolla y Bastida, *El Jardín*

Preguntas del tema

▸ ¿Qué profesión piensas tener en el futuro?

▸ ¿Qué profesión es interesante? ¿Cuál es aburrida?

▸ ¿Cómo es tu familia?

▸ ¿Qué te gusta hacer con la familia?

PRIMER PASO

Vocabulario y lengua

DISCUSSING PROFESSIONS

Somos vecinos *(neighbors)*

[4A] Laura Guzmán piensa ser *abogada* y su compañera Lourdes Vardi es *música*.

[3A] Los hijos de los señores Terranova piensan ser *médicos*.

[2A] El *cocinero* le sirve la comida a la familia Lara.

[1A] Los *jardineros* trabajan en el jardín del Dr. Martín.

[4B] Los *artistas* trabajan intensamente. La *escultora* trabaja con madera (*wood*), mientras que el *fotógrafo* saca fotos (*takes pictures*).

[3B] El *plomero* arregla el baño de la *farmacéutica* Aída Sosa.

[2B] Una *pintora* pinta la sala de Eduardo Calasa, un *hombre de negocios*.

[1B] Pablo es *peluquero* y trabaja en la Peluquería Pablo.

Profesiones y oficios

For many professions and occupations, the masculine nouns end in –**o** and the feminine nouns end in –**a**:

el/la arqueólogo/a *archaeologist*
el/la arquitecto/a *architect*
el/la criado/a *servant, maid*

el/la psicólogo/a *psychologist*
el/la secretario/a *secretary*
el/la veterinario/a *veterinarian*

For other professions, the masculine nouns end in –**ero** and the feminine nouns end in –**era:**

el/la bombero/a *firefighter*
el/la carpintero/a *carpenter*
el/la cartero/a *mail carrier*

el/la consejero/a *counselor*
el/la enfermero/a *nurse*
el/la ingeniero/a *engineer*

Masculine nouns ending in –**or** are made feminine by adding an –**a:**

el/la contador/a *accountant*
el/la profesor/a *professor*
el/la vendedor/a *salesperson*

el/la programador/a
programmer
el/la trabajador/a *worker*

Nouns for professions ending in –**ista** or in –**e** have the same form for both masculine and feminine professions.

el/la agente de viajes *travel agent*
el/ la dentista *dentist*
el/la electricista *electrician*

el/la gerente *manager*
el/la periodista *journalist*
el/la recepcionista *receptionist*

Other occupations that have only one form include: **el / la atleta** *(athlete)* and **el / la policía** *(police officer)*. Exceptions such as **el jefe** *(male boss)* and **la jefa** *(female boss)*, **el presidente** and **la presidenta**, are examples of how Spanish has adapted to reflect changes in the workforce.

Online Study Center

For additional practice with this unit's vocabulary and grammar, visit the *Caminos* website at http://college.hmco.com/ languages/spanish/renjilian/ caminos/3e/student_home .html. You can also review audio flashcards, quiz yourself, and explore related Spanish-language sites.

Actividades

1 Querido amiguito. Laura, the law student in Apartment 4A, is writing a letter to her friend Mauro. Refer to the drawing on page 130 and complete her letter using vocabulary from the list below.

| artistas | jardineros | cocinero | música | criada | peluquero |
| farmacéutica | pintora | guitarra | plomero | hijos | médico |

Querido Mauro:

Saludos desde Puerto Rico. Aquí me estoy divirtiendo muchísimo, aunque *(although)* estudio demasiado. Mi compañera de cuarto se llama Lourdes y es (**1**) _____. Toca la (**2**) _____ y escucha el jazz y la música clásica. Es muy buena compañera. Mis vecinos, los señores Lara, son muy simpáticos. Son muy ricos y tienen un (**3**) _____ que prepara la comida y una (**4**) _____ que limpia la casa.
Mis vecinos están siempre muy ocupados. El Dr. Martín emplea a dos (**5**) _____ para arreglar su jardín. Pablo, el (**6**) _____, tiene clientes todo el día. Esta semana, desde el lunes, una (**7**) _____ está pintando el apartamento del vecino del 2B. Ya casi termina. A los dos (**8**) _____ de los vecinos de abajo les gusta mucho jugar al "(**9**) _____ y paciente" ¡con sus animales! La vecina del 3B es (**10**) _____ y, antes de salir para el trabajo, descubre que la llave *(faucet)* del agua no funciona y ahora el (**11**) _____ está en su apartamento para arreglar la llave. En el apartamento de al lado *(next door)*, los (**12**) _____ están trabajando toda la tarde. ¡Qué ruido! *(What noise!)* y qué tarde tan terrible. Bueno, tengo mucho sueño y necesito descansar un poco. ¡Me voy a acostar! Escríbeme pronto.

Abrazos de,
Laura

2 Asociaciones. Which professions do you associate with the following words? Provide both masculine and feminine forms for each.

1. las aspirinas
2. la pintura
3. las rosas
4. la bañera
5. el cepillo
6. el piano
7. el bistec
8. la justicia
9. el teléfono
11. los animales
12. el edificio

 3 Profesionales. Combining an element from each column, discuss with a partner what each person does in his/her profession. Follow the model.

▶ MODELO: El profesor   enseñar   español
—¿Qué hace el profesor?
—El profesor enseña español.

1. El arqueólogo	limpiar	edificios
2. La pintora	apagar	los muebles
3. Los criados	diseñar	los pacientes
4. La médica	hacer	la casa
5. El bombero	pintar	el dinero
6. La carpintera	construir	el fuego
7. El arquitecto	calcular	excavaciones arqueológicas
8. La contadora	examinar	las casas

4 Una nueva civilización. NASA has discovered a new uninhabited planet (**un planeta deshabitado**) that is very similar to Earth. They have enough money to send one spaceship (**nave espacial**) to the planet to start a new civilization. The spaceship can hold only six people. Work in groups to decide who from the list below gets to go and why. Report your decisions to the class.

María Hernández (56), ingeniera	Esteban Rosas (24), enfermero
Efraín Jaramillo (48), médico	Clara Cabañas (30), programadora de computadoras
Raúl Ramírez (18), estudiante	Pablo Pérez (36), periodista y esposo de Penélope
Jaime Méndez (23), policía	Penélope Pérez (23), consejera y esposa de Pablo
Luisa Ortiz (31), carpintera	Alicia Vázquez (26), psicóloga

5 En mi barrio *(neighborhood)*. Write a description of five people with different professions in your neighborhood. Describe who they are, what they do, and what they are like.

USING INDIRECT OBJECT PRONOUNS

*My parents buy a stereo **for me.***   *The girls sell cookies **to us.***

Indirect objects indicate *to, for,* or *from* whom an action is done. The highlighted pronouns in each example above correspond to the indirect objects of the sentences: "they buy the stereo *for me*" and "they sell cookies *to us.*"

Indirect object pronouns			
me	*(to, for, from) me*	**nos**	*(to, for, from) us*
te	*(to, for, from) you*	**os**	*(to, for, from) you*
le	*(to, for, from) you, him, her*	**les**	*(to, for, from) you, them*

Indirect object pronouns can either precede the conjugated verb or be attached to the end of the infinitive or present participle.

Te voy a comprar el pasaje.	*I am going to buy you the ticket.*
Voy a decir**te** una cosa.	*I am going to tell you something.*
La alumna **le** está haciendo preguntas.	*The student is asking him / her / you questions.*
La alumna está haciéndo**le** preguntas.	
Paco **me** quiere comprar el coche.	*Paco wants to buy the car for / from me.*
Paco quiere comprar**me** el coche.	

Common verbs used with indirect object pronouns					
agradecer	*to thank, be grateful for*	entregar	*to hand in, deliver*	pedir (i)	*to ask for, request*
comprar	*to buy*	enviar	*to send*	preguntar	*to ask a question*
contar (ue)	*to tell*	escribir	*to write*	prestar	*to lend*
contestar	*to answer*	explicar	*to explain*	regalar	*to give (gifts)*
dar	*to give*	hablar	*to speak*	servir (i)	*to serve*
deber*	*to owe*	mandar	*to send*	traer	*to bring*
decir (i)	*to tell*	ofrecer	*to offer*	vender	*to sell*
enseñar	*to teach*	pagar	*to pay*		

*__Deber__ + *infinitive* also means *should* as in: Debes contarme todo. *(You should tell me everything.)*

Prepositional pronouns

Pronouns that appear after a preposition are called *prepositional pronouns*. In Spanish, they have the same forms as the subject pronouns except for the first person (**mí**) and second person (**ti**) singular.

Prepositional pronouns							
mí	*me*	**usted**	*you*	**nosotros/as**	*us*	**ustedes**	*you (plural)*
ti	*you*	**él / ella**	*him / her*	**vosotros/as**	*you*	**ellos / ellas**	*them*

Spanish frequently uses *both* the indirect object pronoun *and* the preposition **a** + noun / prepositional pronoun to emphasize and/or clarify to whom the indirect object pronoun refers.

La profesora **le** explica la lección **a usted.**	*The teacher explains the lesson to you.*
La profesora **le** explica la lección **a Julia.**	*The teacher explains the lesson to Julia.*
Les mandan el paquete **a ellas.**	*They send the package to them.*
Les mandan el paquete **a los chicos.**	*They send the package to the boys.*
Nos escriben **a nosotros.**	*They write to us.*
Nos escriben **a Yolanda y a mí.**	*They write to Yolanda and me.*

While the prepositional phrase is optional, the indirect object pronoun must always be used.

Sus padres **le** dan un regalo.		*His / Her parents give **him / her** a gift.*
Sus padres **le** dan un regalo **a ella.**	*or*	*Her parents give a gift **to her.***

Making requests and asking questions: *Pedir* and *preguntar*

In Spanish there are two verbs that mean *to ask:* **pedir** and **preguntar.** Both verbs are often used with indirect object pronouns. **Pedir** is used *to ask for* or *to request* something from someone. **Pedir** is also used to order food or drinks, or to place an order when you want to buy something.

El profesor les **pide** la tarea a los estudiantes.	*The teacher asks the students for their homework.*
Mi amiga me **pide** dinero.	*My friend asks me for money.*

Preguntar is used to obtain information about someone or something. **Preguntar por** means *to inquire* about someone or something.

El turista le **pregunta** la hora al guía.	*The tourist asks the guide for the time.*
Javier me **pregunta** si tengo hambre.	*Javier asks me if I'm hungry.*
Mi tía Amalia siempre **pregunta por** ti.	*My aunt Amalia always asks about you.*

Actividades

1 **¿A quién?** Provide the correct form of the indirect object pronoun that corresponds to the **boldface** noun or pronoun in each sentence.

1. La arqueóloga _____ da una conferencia **a los estudiantes.**
2. Nosotros _____ pagamos los honorarios **a la ingeniera.**
3. La médica _____ escribe una receta **a ti.**
4. La vendedora _____ va a vender un estéreo **a mí.**
5. El abogado _____ va a decir la verdad **a usted.**
6. El cocinero _____ sirve la cena **a nosotros.**
7. Hoy _____ vamos a pagar **al plomero.**
8. Los pintores _____ están pintando la casa **a ustedes.**

2 **Conversación privada.** Ana and Laura are gossiping. You overhear their conversation and have to match the boldface pronouns they use with the people from the list below. Who are they talking about? Follow the model.

▶ **MODELO:** Ana: Oye, Laura, yo **les** dije **a ellas** que la fiesta es en tu casa...
Ana está hablando de las amigas de Laura.

el novio de Ana   las amigas de Laura   los padres de Laura
Laura   Ana   Ana y Laura

1. Laura: ¡Ay, Ana! Tengo que pedir**les** permiso a **ellos.** ¡Es su casa!
2. Ana: Laura, estoy segura de que ellos **nos** van a decir que sí.
3. Laura: Creo que sí, Ana. Puedes enviar**le** a **él** una invitación.
4. Ana: Gracias, **te** agradezco mucho.
5. Laura: ¡**Te** digo que tú eres mi mejor amiga!

3 **¿De quién hablas?** Combine the words to form complete sentences. Follow the model.

▶ **MODELO:** la profesora / preguntar / a los estudiantes
La profesora les pregunta   *The professor asks the students.*
a los estudiantes.

1. ellos / contestar las preguntas / a la profesora
2. los médicos / ofrecer ayuda / a nosotros
3. ustedes / pedir el horario del tren / al empleado
4. yo / escribir correo electrónico / a mis amigos
5. el empleado siempre / desear feliz viaje / a los pasajeros
6. mi mamá / pedir un favor / a mí
7. el chico / hablar cordialmente / a la policía

4 **¿Qué haces?** Based on the following situations, complete the sentences with the appropriate form of **pedir** or **preguntar (por)**. Follow the model.

▶ **MODELO:** Estás en un restaurante y   *You are in a restaurant and want*
quieres el menú.   *the menu. What do you do?*
¿Qué haces?
Yo le **pido** el menú al mesero. *I ask the waiter for the menu.*

1. Tu amigo le debe dinero al banco. ¿Qué hace el banco?
El banco le _____ el dinero a mi amigo.
2. Estoy en la playa y necesito hacer una llamada importante. ¿Qué hago?
Tú le _____ a alguien un teléfono celular.
3. Conoces a alguien muy interesante en una fiesta. ¿Qué haces?
Yo le _____ cómo se llama.
4. Estás enfermo/a y necesitas medicinas. ¿Qué haces?
Yo le _____ las medicinas al médico.

5. Quieres invitar a alguien al cine. ¿Qué haces?

Yo le _____ si quiere ir al cine conmigo.

6. No sabes cómo está tu amiga María Rosa. ¿Qué haces?

Yo _____ ella.

5 **Preguntas personales.** With a classmate, take turns asking and answering the following questions.

▶ MODELO: ¿Quién te da regalos? (mi amigo Juan)

—¿Quién te da regalos? —*Who gives you gifts?*

—Mi amigo Juan me da regalos. —*My friend Juan gives me gifts.*

1. ¿Quiénes te hablan por teléfono? (mis amigos)
2. ¿Quién te escribe cartas? (la familia)
3. ¿Quién nos prepara la comida? (el cocinero)
4. ¿Quién les enseña español a ellos? (la profesora)
5. ¿Quién te debe dinero? (Ramiro y Rafael)
6. ¿Quién les pide su opinión a ustedes? (el presidente)
7. ¿Quiénes te dicen la verdad? (los abogados)
8. ¿Quién te paga el alquiler de tu casa? (mis padres)

6 **¿Qué hacen?** Your young nephew is asking you about what different people do for work. Make a list of six professions and write a sentence about each to tell him what they do and for whom. Include indirect object pronouns in your statements.

▶ MODELO: **el cartero** El cartero les entrega cartas a los vecinos.

INDICATING LIKES AND DISLIKES: *GUSTAR* AND SIMILAR VERBS

As you have learned, the verb **gustar** is used to express likes and dislikes. In Spanish, **gustar** literally means "*is pleasing to.*" Spanish uses indirect object pronouns to show "to whom" something is pleasing. Notice how the structure works.

Indirect Object Pronoun	Verb	Subject	
Me	gustan	los deportes.	*I like sports.* *(literally: Sports are pleasing to me.)*
Te	gusta	pintar.	*You like to paint.* *(literally: Painting is pleasing to you.)*

Use **gusta** when the subject is a singular noun, an infinitive, or a series of infinitives. Use **gustan** when the subject is a plural noun or a series of nouns.

¿Te **gusta** tener una mascota?   *Do you like to have a pet?*
Sí, me **gustan** los animales.   *Yes, I like animals.*

Gustar and similar verbs are used with all of the indirect object pronouns in the same way.

Gustar

me gusta(n)	*I like it / them*	**nos** gusta(n)	*we like it / them*
te gusta(n)	*you like it / them*	**os** gusta(n)	*you (plural) like it / them*
le gusta(n)	*you like it / them; he / she likes it / them*	**les** gusta(n)	*you (plural) they like it / them*

Verbs like gustar

caer bien / mal	*to like / dislike (a person)*	**interesar**	*to interest, be of interest*
encantar	*to delight, like very much (love)*	**molestar**	*to bother, annoy*
faltar	*to lack, need; to be left (to do)*	**parecer**	*to seem, appear to be*
fascinar	*to fascinate*	**preocupar**	*to worry*
importar	*to matter, be important, be of concern*		

Note that many of these verbs are used in a similar way in English. We don't say "I interest reading," but rather "Reading interests me."

Me interesa leer.   *Reading interests me.*
Te molestan las personas   *Unfriendly people bother you.*
   antipáticas.

As with all indirect object pronouns, the preposition **a** + noun or prepositional pronoun can be used to emphasize or clarify the recipient of the action.

A mí me importa la comunidad.   *My community matters to me.*
Al arquitecto le interesan las casas.   *The arquitect is interested in houses.*

When verbs like **gustar** are used with reflexive verbs, the reflexive pronoun is attached to the infinitive of the reflexive verb. Remember that the reflexive pronoun must match the subject.

A Juan le fascina **vestirse** con   *Juan likes to dress in expensive clothes.*
   ropa cara.
Me molesta **levantarme** temprano.   *It annoys me to get up early.*
      (Getting up early annoys me.)

Actividades

1 **Gustos.** Combine the words and phrases to form complete sentences. Follow the model.

▶ **MODELO:** a tí / preocupar / ir al dentista
A ti te preocupa ir al dentista.

1. a mí / caer bien / el profesor
2. al pintor / encantar / pintar
3. a nosotros / preocupar / los problemas en el mundo
4. a la arquitecta / interesar / construir casas
5. a la médica / parecer / importante atender a sus pacientes
6. a los cocineros / faltar / los ingredientes para la sopa
7. a las arqueólogas / fascinar / excavar
8. a los abogados / importar / la opinión del juez *(judge)*
9. al músico / gustar / las canciones de Enrique Iglesias
10. a la vendedora / caer bien / los clientes

2 **¿Te gusta?** With a partner, take turns asking each other for the following information.

▶ **MODELO:** gustar / las ensaladas
—¿Te gustan las ensaladas?   —*Do you like salads?*
—Sí, me gustan las ensaladas.   —*Yes, I do like salads.*
—No, no me gustan las ensaladas.   —*No, I don't like salads.*

1. encantar / las canciones románticas
2. interesar / las novelas de misterio
3. gustar / los libros para jóvenes
4. molestar / el problema del tráfico
5. preocupar / los problemas ecológicos
6. fascinar / las nuevas tecnologías
7. gustar / el cine mexicano
8. caer mal / las personas que fuman

3 **¿Te caen bien o mal?** Work in pairs. Make a list of people you know or of fictional characters from TV, film, or literature. Then ask each other whether you like or dislike the people you've listed. Follow the model.

▶ **MODELO:** Jennifer López
—¿Te cae bien Jennifer López?   —*Do you like Jennifer López?*
—Sí, me cae bien porque...   —*Yes, I like her because . . .*

or

—No, me cae mal porque...   —*No, I don't like her because . . .*

4 **¿Te importa?** You have to prepare a report for your sociology class. Following the model, ask four to six students questions about the survey topics below. Write their answers in the chart. Write **M** for **mucho, P** for **poco,** and **N** for **nada.** Report your findings to the class and discuss why certain things are important and others are not.

▶ **MODELO:** la ecología   *ecology*
—Marcela, ¿te importa la   —*Marcela, is ecology important to*
  ecología?   *you?*
—Sí, me importa mucho.   —*Yes, it is important to me.*

or

—No, me importa poco.   —*No, it's not very important to me.*
—No, no me importa nada.   —*No, it's not important to me at all.*

Nombre del estudiante	La ecología	El dinero	Los amigos	Las clases
Marcela	M			

USING AFFIRMATIVE, NEGATIVE, AND TRANSITIONAL EXPRESSIONS

Affirmative expressions		Negative expressions	
algo	*something, anything*	**nada**	*nothing*
todo	*everything*		
todo el mundo	*everybody, everyone*	**nadie**	*no one, nobody*
alguien	*someone, somebody*		
algún, alguno/a/os/as	*some, any*	**ningún, ninguno/a**	*none, not any*
siempre	*always*	**nunca, jamás**	*never*
todos los días	*every day*		
también	*also, too*	**tampoco**	*neither, either*
(o) ... o	*(either) . . . or*	**(ni)...ni**	*neither . . . nor*

Transitional expressions	
a veces	*at times*
algunas veces	*sometimes*
casi siempre / nunca / nada	*almost always / never / nothing*
de vez en cuando	*from time to time*
muchas veces	*many times*

Affirmative expressions and affirmative transitional expressions can be placed before or after the verb.

Yo **siempre** hago la tarea.   *I always do my homework.*
Yo hago **siempre** la tarea.

Casi siempre hacemos   *We almost always do our homework.*
la tarea.

Nadie and **nunca** are often used before the verb, while **nada** is normally placed after it.

Nunca practico deportes.	*I never play sports.*
Nadie dice la verdad.	*No one tells the truth.*
No tengo **nada.**	*I don't have anything.*

When the negative expressions **nada**, **nadie**, or **nunca** follow the verb, Spanish uses an additional **no** before the verb as in the previous example: **no** + *verb* + ***negative expression.***

Los domingos **no** voy **nunca** al cine.	*I never go to the movies on Sundays.*
No viene **nadie.**	*No one is coming.*

Nadie and **alguien** refer to people and require the personal **a** when used as direct objects.

—¿Visitas **a alguien** los fines de semana?	*—Do you visit anyone on weekends?*
—No, **no** visito **a nadie.**	*—No, I don't visit anyone.*

All forms of **alguno** and **ninguno** agree in number and gender with the noun they modify, but drop the **-o** before a masculine singular form. **Ninguno** is mostly used in the singular form.

—¿Hay aquí **algunos** estudiantes de Miami?	*—Are there any students from Miami?*
—No, no hay **ningún** estudiante de Miami.	*—No, there are no students from Miami.*
—¿Tienes **algunos** problemas?	*—Do you have any problems?*
—No, no tengo **ninguno.**	*—No, I don't have any.*

Actividades

1 Los contrarios. Change the following affirmative statements to make them negative. Some statements require two changes.

▶ MODELO:　Necesito comer algo antes de la reunión.　　*I need to eat something before the meeting.*
　　　　　　No necesito comer nada antes de la reunión.　　*I don't need to eat anything before the meeting.*

1. Quiero conocer a alguien interesante.
2. Ellos siempre viajan en tren.
3. Algunas postales tienen la dirección correcta.
4. Tengo todo listo para el viaje en tren.
5. Elena siempre toma taxi para ir a la universidad.
6. Tengo que decirte algo.
7. Voy al cine mañana. También voy a la biblioteca.
8. Todo el mundo quiere vivir en Sevilla.

2 Sucede todos los días. You have just returned from a vacation. It was not a very good trip and you have some bad things to say about it. Follow the model and create a dialog with a partner.

▶ MODELO: —¿Hay muchos hoteles buenos?

—*Are there many good hotels?*

—No, no hay ningún hotel bueno.

—*No, there aren't any good hotels.*

1. ¿Siempre sirven buena comida en los restaurantes?
2. ¿Siempre hay actividades divertidas?
3. ¿Hay algunos viajes interesantes?
4. ¿Hay alguna discoteca buena?
5. ¿Hay algunos centros comerciales?
6. ¿Siempre encuentras transporte en la ciudad?

3 ¡Nunca hago nada! Use the timeline below to indicate the activities you do or don't do and how often. Write a sentence for each item on the timeline, then discuss them with a partner.

▶ MODELO: —Casi siempre asisto a clase, ¿y tú?
—Siempre asisto a clase.

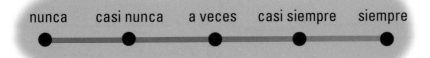

nunca   casi nunca   a veces   casi siempre   siempre

¿Hablas por teléfono?

¿Comes en restaurantes?

¿Vas al cine con tus amigos?

Un negocio sucio

Actividades

Online Study Center

For additional practice with this episode, visit the *Caminos* website at http://college.hmco.com/languages/spanish/renjilian/caminos/3e/student_home.html.

1 Comprensión. Based on this episode of *Caminos del jaguar,* choose the logical response.

1. Pacal es...
   a. un objeto de arte maya.   b. un rey maya.

2. El Sr. Covarrubias tiene el jaguar porque...
   a. es un negocio bien pagado.   b. es un objeto de arte.

3. La Sra.Covarrubias está...
   a. muy contenta con el jaguar.   b. preocupada.

4. A la Sra. Covarrubias...
   a. no le interesa el dinero.   b. le interesa el dinero.

5. El Sr. Covarrubias tiene que...
   a. guardar el jaguar en casa.   b. enviar el jaguar a otro país.

6. Adriana y Felipe viajan en el AVE porque...
   a. deben llegar rápido.   b. tienen poco dinero.

7. A Adriana...
   a. le cae bien Felipe.   b. no le cae bien Felipe.

8. ¿Qué le pide Nayeli al Sr. Covarrubias?
   a. la dirección en Quito   b. información sobre el negocio

2 Situaciones. Dramatize one of the following situations.

1. Mrs. and Mr. Covarrubias try to hide because they are afraid of the Jaguar Twin.
2. Mrs. Covarrubias tells her husband what she thinks about his business plan.

3 Escritura. Write a brief summary of what happens in this episode (4–6 sentences).

NOTA CULTURAL

La estación de Atocha

Atocha Station is the largest train station in Madrid. The station features beautiful, lush gardens with tropical palms and waterfalls. It was recently remodeled by Rafael Moneo, an internationally known Spanish architect. Local and long-distance trains arrive and depart from Atocha daily. The AVE (Alta Velocidad España), the high-speed train that connects Sevilla and Lérida to the capital, also uses Atocha as its terminal. On March 11, 2004, Spain suffered two deadly bomb attacks on passenger trains. One of the attacks occurred at Atocha.

SEGUNDO PASO

Vocabulario y lengua

TALKING ABOUT FAMILY MEMBERS

Online Study Center

For additional practice with this unit's vocabulary and grammar, visit the *Caminos* website at http://college.hmco .com/languages/spanish/ renjilian/caminos/3e/student _home.html. You can also review audio flashcards, quiz yourself, and explore related Spanish-language sites.

Pablo Rosas González
padre / papá

Marinela Suárez de Rosas
madre / mamá

Micifús
gata

Sultán
perro

Julio Ramón Iglesias
novio

Rosaura
hermana

Maricarmen
hermana

Me llamo Velia Rosas Suárez

Roberto
hermano

Aniela Gómez de Rosas
cuñada

Conchita
tortuga

Orejón
conejo

Leticia
sobrina

Pedro
sobrino

Beto
pájaro

Spanish speakers often use **somos** and not **son** to indicate how many people are in their own family. This form includes themselves in the number of family members.

The endings **–ito/-ita** are often added to nouns and adjectives to express affection or a smaller size. There must be gender and number agreement.

Mi hij**ita** está en la primaria.	*My dear / little daughter is in elementary school.*
Mi hij**ito** tiene 3 años.	*My dear / little son is 3 years old.*
Somos cinco en mi familia.	*There are five in our family.*

Más palabras y expresiones

Sustantivos

el/la abuelo/a	*grandfather / grandmother*
el/la bebé	*baby*
el/la bisabuelo/a	*great-grandfather / great-grandmother*
el/la chico/a	*boy / girl*
el/la esposo/a	*husband / wife*
el/la hermanastro/a	*stepbrother / stepsister*
el/la hijastro/a	*stepson / stepdaughter*
el/la hijo/a	*son / daughter*
la madrastra	*stepmother*
el marido	*husband*
la mascota	*pet*
el/la nieto/a	*grandson / granddaughter*
el/la niño/a	*boy / girl / child*
la nuera	*daughter-in-law*
el padrastro	*stepfather*
el/la pariente	*family member, relative*
el/la primo/a	*cousin*
el/la suegro/a	*father-in-law / mother-in-law*
el/la tío/a	*uncle / aunt*
el yerno	*son-in-law*

Verbos

abrazar	*to hug*
casarse (con)	*to get married (to)*
enamorarse (de)	*to fall in love (with)*
estar casado/a	*to be married*
estar divorciado/a	*to be divorced*
estar enamorado/a	*to be in love*
estar separado/a	*to be separated*
nacer	*to be born*
ser mayor	*to be older*
ser menor	*to be younger*
ser soltero/a	*to be single*

Actividades

1 La familia de Marinela. If Marinela were telling the story about her family, the family relationships would change. Look at the family tree on page 144 and describe the relationships between the following people from Marinela's point of view.

1. Me llamo Marinela y mi _____ se llama Pablo.
2. Tengo cuatro _____ .
3. Mi _____ se llama Roberto.
4. Su _____ se llama Aniela.
5. Mis _____ son Pedro y Leticia.
6. Mi _____ mayor se llama Rosaura.
7. Rosaura tiene un _____ muy guapo.

2 La familia de Velia. Listen to the story of Velia's family, and fill in the missing words.

La familia de Velia

Me llamo Velia Rosas Suárez y tengo una (**1**) _____ muy grande. Mi
(**2**) _____ se llama Pablo y mi (**3**) _____ se llama Marinela.
Mis (**4**) _____ son muy simpáticos. Somos cuatro (**5**) _____. Mi
(**6**) _____ Roberto tiene treinta y cinco años y es alto y guapo.
Su (**7**) _____ se llama Aniela. Aniela es mi (**8**) _____. Ellos tienen dos
(**9**) _____: el (**10**) _____ se llama Pedro y la (**11**) _____ se llama
Leticia. Leticia tiene tres mascotas, un (**12**) _____ que se llama Orejón, un
(**13**) _____ que se llama Beto y una (**14**) _____, Conchita. ¡Ella quiere
ser veterinaria! Quiero mucho a mis (**15**) _____. ¡Soy su (**16**) _____
favorita!

Mi (**17**) _____ mayor Rosaura tiene un (**18**) _____ que se llama
Julio. Ellos están muy enamorados y van a casarse este verano. Mi hermana
Maricarmen es (**19**) _____ y es estudiante. Ella tiene una
(**20**) _____ que se llama Micifús.

¿Y yo? Yo estoy (**21**) _____, no tengo (**22**) _____ y vivo con mi
(**23**) _____ Sultán.

3 ¿Quién es? Work with a partner to determine which family member is being described.

▶ MODELO: la esposa de mi hermano
—¿Quién es la esposa de mi hermano?
—*Es tu cuñada.*

1. el esposo de mi madre
2. el padre de mi madre
3. los hijos de mis hijos
4. la hija de mi tía
5. el hermano de mi prima
6. el esposo de mi hija
7. la hermana de mi padre
8. la madre de mi abuelo
9. las hijas de mi hermana
10. la única *(only)* hija de mi abuela

4 Entre nosotros. Interview a partner about his or her family. Use questions as provided in the model. Then draw a family tree that represents the family members, including their names and ages.

▶ MODELO: —¿Cuántos hermanos tienes?
—¿Cómo se llaman?
—¿Cuántos años tienen?

5 Mi familia. Write a paragraph about your family. Include a description of each family member, his or her name, age, relationship to you, profession, and other interesting facts.

DISTINGUISHING BETWEEN *SER* AND *ESTAR*

Mini historia de amor

Son novios y están enamorados

You have already learned some basic uses of **ser** and **estar** *(to be)*. The following short story summarizes the different ways these two verbs are used.

Uses of *ser:* El noviazgo *(The courtship)*

1. **States identity.**

   La novia **es** Juliana Castro; el novio **es** Luis Orozco.

   The fiancée is Juliana Castro; the fiancé is Luis Orozco.

2. **Describes origin of things and people.**

   Luis **es** de Buenos Aires y Juliana **es** de Quito.

   Luis is from Buenos Aires and Juliana is from Quito.

3. **Indicates someone's occupation or profession.**

   Juliana **es** médica y Luis **es** arquitecto.

   Juliana is a doctor and Luis is an architect.

4. **Describes nationality.**

   Él **es** argentino y ella **es** ecuatoriana.

   He is Argentinean and she is Ecuadorian.

5. **Describes inherent characteristics of things and people.**

   Juliana **es** muy bonita y Luis **es** encantador.

   Juliana is very pretty and Luis is charming.

6. **Describes the material of which something is made.**

   El anillo de Juliana **es** de oro y tiene un diamante enorme.

   Juliana's ring is made of gold and has an enormous diamond.

7. **States where an event takes place.**

   La boda **es** en la iglesia de San Felipe.

   The wedding is in the church of San Felipe.

Uses of *estar:* La boda *(The wedding)*

8. **Describes location of places, buildings, and things.**

   La iglesia de San Felipe **está** en el centro de la ciudad, cerca del parque.

   The San Felipe Church is downtown, close to the park.

9. **Describes location of people.**

   Cuando la novia llega, algunos invitados **están** en el parque, pero Luis ya **está** en la iglesia.

   When the bride arrives, some guests are in the park, but Luis is already at the church.

10. **Describes how things look or appear at a certain moment.**

    La novia **está** muy hermosa hoy, con su vestido blanco y largo. Luis también **está** guapísimo, con su traje negro.

    The bride is (looks) very beautiful today, in her long, white dress. Luis is (looks) also very handsome, in his black suit.

11. **Describes mental or emotional states.**

Todos **están** contentos: la novia,
el novio y los invitados; pero
una amiga de Juliana, Berta,
está muy emocionada.

*Everyone is happy: the bride,
the groom, and the guests; but
a friend of Juliana's, Berta,
is very moved.*

12. **Describes ongoing actions with a progressive tense.**

Cerca, un hombre guapo **está**
mirando a Berta intensamente...
¡Cupido **está** preparando
un nuevo romance!

*Close by, a handsome man is gazing
intensely at Berta . . .
Cupid is preparing
a new romance!*

FIN

THE END

Actividades

1 Comprensión Answer the following questions about the story.

1. ¿Quién es la novia?
2. ¿De dónde es la novia?
3. ¿De dónde es el novio?
4. ¿Cuál es la profesión de Juliana? ¿y la profesión de Luis?
5. ¿Dónde están los invitados cuando llega la novia?
6. ¿Cómo está la novia ese día? ¿y el novio?
7. ¿Cómo están todos los invitados?
8. ¿Dónde es la boda?
9. ¿Dónde está la iglesia?
10. ¿Qué está preparando Cupido?

2 ¡Adivina! Guess the subject of each riddle.

1. Es presidente de un país grande e importante. Su casa es blanca y está en la capital del país. ¿Quién es?
2. Son prácticos. Pueden ser grandes, pequeños, viejos, nuevos, bonitos y feos, buenos y malos, caros y baratos. Están generalmente en las calles contaminando el aire. Otras veces están en el garaje de la casa. ¿Qué son?
3. Son hermosas. Son de muchos colores y formas. Tienen perfume. Generalmente están en los jardines, pero a veces están adornando las casas. ¿Qué son?
4. Es clara y transparente. Está en el océano y en los ríos *(rivers)*, en el aire y en las nubes. En invierno es nieve y en verano puede ser vapor *(mist)*. ¿Qué es?

3 Ahora, ¡adivina tú! Now, create a riddle and ask a partner to guess what it is.

4 Mi historia. Now create your own story about two people who meet on your campus, demonstrating at least three uses of **ser** and three uses of **estar.** Some possible ideas:

1. amor en la cafetería
2. de compras en la tienda
3. los novios en la fiesta
4. el romance en el laboratorio de ciencia

EXPRESSING LOCATION: PREPOSITIONS

¿Dónde está la profesora Jaramillo?

1C: Sra. Coronado	
1B: Carlitos Coronado	**2C:** Profesora Jaramillo
1A: Sr. Coronado	

3C: Paula Peña	**4B:** Federica Fuentes
3B: Ricardo Ríos	**4A:** Manuel Mendoza

La Sra. Coronado está **junto a** la ventana.

Carlitos está **entre** la Sra. y el Sr. Coronado.

La profesora Jaramillo está **delante de** la Sra. Coronado.

Ricardo está **detrás de** Federica.

Paula está **al lado de** Ricardo.

Las bolsas están **debajo de** los asientos.

Las maletas están **encima del** portaequipajes.

El Sr. Coronado está **lejos de** Federica.

La profesora Jaramillo está **cerca de** la Sra. Coronado.

Mrs. Coronado is sitting next to the window.

Carlitos is between Mr. and Mrs. Coronado.

Professor Jaramillo is in front of Mrs. Coronado.

Ricardo is behind Federica.

Paula is next to Ricardo.

The bags are beneath the seats.

The suitcases are on top of the luggage rack.

Mr. Coronado is far from Federica.

Professor Jaramillo is close to Mrs. Coronado.

Prepositions can be used to state location, position in space, direction, sequence in time, or abstract relationships between objects, events, and people.

Additional prepositions of place			
bajo	*under*	**enfrente de**	*in front of, facing*
dentro de	*inside of*	**fuera de**	*outside of*
en	*in, on, at*	**sobre**	*on, on top of*

Prepositions of time					
a	*to, for*	**después de**	*after*	**para***	*for, to, in order to*
antes de	*before*	**durante**	*during*	**por***	*for, by means of*
con	*with*	**hacia**	*toward*	**según**	*according to*
de	*from, of*	**hasta**	*until*	**sin**	*without*
desde	*from, since*				

* You will learn more about the uses of **por** and **para** in *Unidad 6.*

Remember that the first and second person singular forms of prepositional pronouns are **mí** and **ti.** All the others retain the form of the subject pronoun (See pages **56–57**). The preposition **con** has its own forms for the first and second persons singular: **conmigo** *(with me),* **contigo** *(with you).*

Manuel va **conmigo** a la estación.	*Manuel goes to the station with me.*
Me gusta viajar **contigo**.	*I like traveling with you.*

Entre *(between, among)* is different from the other prepositions because it must always be followed by one or more subjects or subject pronouns.

¡Entre tú y yo no hay secretos!	*There are no secrets between you and me!*
Esta información es un secreto **entre nosotros**.	*This information is a secret between us.*

The preposition pairs **de/a** and **desde/hasta** are often used to express a time period or a distance covered from one place to another.

Trabajo **desde** las 3 P.M. **hasta** las 4 P.M.	*I work from 3 to 4 P.M.*
Estudio **desde** la mañana **hasta** la tarde.	*I work from morning to evening.*
El AVE viaja **de** Madrid **a** Sevilla.	*The AVE train travels from Madrid to Sevilla.*

Actividades

1 **¿Dónde están?** Refer back to the illustration of the passengers in the train on page 150. Say where the following people can be found. Follow the model.

▶ MODELO: Carlitos / el Sr. Coronado
Carlitos está al lado del   *Carlitos is next to Mr. Coronado.*
Sr. Coronado.

1. la Sra. Coronado / Carlitos
2. Manuel / Federica
3. la profesora Jaramillo /Paula / la Sra. Coronado
4. Ricardo / Federica
5. Manuel / Ricardo
6. Carlitos / Ricardo

2 Conversaciones.
You are in a disco and overhear the following exchanges and questions. Complete each dialog with a preposition from the list below. You can use some prepositions more than once.

con   conmigo   contigo   de   en   para   sin

1. —¡Estas flores son _____ ti, mi amor!
   —¿Son _____ mí las flores? ¡Qué cariñoso eres!
2. —¿Quién está _____ Mariana?
   —Francisco, su primo, está _____ ella.
3. —¿Quieres ir _____ al cine mañana?
   —No gracias, no puedo ir _____ .
4. —¿Eres la hermana _____ Jorge Vázquez?
   —Sí, soy la hermana mayor _____ él.
5. —Tú sabes que no puedes vivir _____ mí, ¿verdad?
   —Sí, yo sé muy bien que no puedo vivir _____ ti.
6. —¿Dónde está mi billete de tren?
   —Está _____ tu mochila.

3 Secuencia.
Choose the sentence ending that best describes the sequence in which you do the following things.

1. Por la noche...
   a. me duermo antes de acostarme.   **b.** me acuesto antes de dormirme.

2. Por la mañana...
   a. me ducho después de levantarme.   **b.** me ducho antes de levantarme.

3. En la universidad...
   a. pienso antes de hablar.   **b.** hablo antes de pensar.

4. En casa...
   a. estudio después de ver televisión.   **b.** veo televisión después de estudiar.

5. En mi auto...
   a. conduzco después de dormir poco.   **b.** no conduzco después de dormir poco.

6. Cuando viajo...
   a. llego antes de la salida del tren.   **b.** llego después de la salida del tren.

4 ¡Colas para todo!
Working with a partner, describe where each person is standing in the line to purchase bus tickets.

▶ **MODELO:** —El abuelo está detrás   —The grandfather is behind
                 de la señora alta, ¿verdad?   the tall lady, isn't he?
               —No, el abuelo está   —No, the grandfather is in
                 delante de ella.   front of her.

5 ¿Dónde están?
Have your partner use the questions below to ask where objects are in your room. As you give their locations, your partner will make a rough sketch placing the objects according to your instructions. Switch roles, then check each other's drawings to see if they are correct.

1. ¿Dónde están tu cama, tu lámpara y tu silla?
2. ¿En qué lugar está tu computadora?
3. ¿Qué cosas hay al lado de tu computadora?
4. ¿Tienes un teléfono en tu cuarto? ¿Dónde está?
5. ¿Qué tienes en la pared?
6. ¿Dónde están la puerta y la ventana? ¿Hay balcón? ¿Dónde está el balcón?
7. ¿Qué otros objetos hay en tu cuarto? ¿Dónde están?

NARRATING EVENTS IN THE PAST: PRETERITE OF REGULAR VERBS

Spanish uses two main verb tenses, the **preterite** and the **imperfect,** to describe past events. You will study the preterite in this unit and the imperfect in *Unidad 6.* The story below, *El sábado pasado,* illustrates the main uses of the preterite. The words in **boldface** are the preterite forms of regular verbs. The endings of these forms are added to the stem to form the preterite indicative tense. Identify these endings and then find them in the verb chart that appears after the story.

El sábado pasado

► To indicate a completed action or the start or the end of an action or event.

El sábado pasado, mi madre **invitó** a mis abuelos a cenar.

Last Saturday my mother invited my grandparents to dinner.

► To state or sum up opinions, attitudes, and beliefs.

Me **pareció** una gran idea.

It seemed like a great idea.

► To narrate a sequence of completed past actions.

Hablé con mi hermano y **decidimos** preparar algo especial. Él **compró** las bebidas, yo **compré** los ingredientes y **preparamos** la cena.

I spoke with my brother and we decided to prepare something special. He bought the drinks, I bought the ingredients, and we prepared the dinner.

► To narrate actions that happened within a fixed period of time.

Cenamos entre las 7 y las 9 de la noche. Nadie **se levantó** de la mesa hasta que **terminamos**. A mis abuelos les **encantó** la cena.

We ate dinner between 7 and 9 P.M. No one left the table until we finished. My grandparents loved the dinner.

Preterite of regular verbs			
	-ar hablar	**-er** comer	**-ir** decidir
yo	habl**é**	com**í**	decid**í**
tú	habl**aste**	com**iste**	decid**iste**
Ud. / él / ella	habl**ó**	com**ió**	decid**ió**
nosotros/as	habl**amos**	com**imos**	decid**imos**
vosotros/as	habl**asteis**	com**isteis**	decid**isteis**
Uds./ ellos / ellas	habl**aron**	com**ieron**	decid**ieron**

Note that the first and the third person singular forms have a written accent. Also, verbs that end in –**er** and –**ir** use the same set of endings in the preterite.

Most stem-changing verbs that end in –**ar** and –**er** in the present tense are regular in the preterite.

Encontr**é** las llaves de mi coche.	*I found my car keys.*
El carpintero volv**ió** tarde a su casa.	*The carpenter arrived home late.*

Actividades

1 ¿Comprendiste? Match the *El sábado pasado* story characters listed in the left-hand column with their actions in the right-hand column.

1. Los hermanos
2. El abuelo
3. A los abuelos
4. El chico
5. La madre
6. A la chica
7. La cena
8. Nadie

a. escuchó la conversación de la abuela.
b. invitó a los abuelos a cenar.
c. terminó a las nueve de la noche.
d. les encantó la cena.
e. prepararon la cena.
f. compró las bebidas.
g. le gustó mucho la idea.
h. se levantó de la mesa durante la cena.

2 Quehaceres. With a partner, ask each other questions following the model.

▶ MODELO: — ¿Lavaste los platos?   —*Did you wash the dishes?*
—Sí, lavé los platos.   —*Yes, I washed the dishes.*
or
—No, no lavé los platos.   —*No, I didn't wash the dishes.*

1. aspirar la alfombra de la sala
2. limpiar la cocina
3. barrer el piso
4. arreglar los estantes
5. guardar *(put away)* los platos
6. preparar la cena

3 Estudio y trabajo. Rewrite each sentence using the preterite forms of the verbs in **boldface**. Follow the model.

▶ MODELO: (Yo) **me quito** los zapatos antes de acostarme.
Me quité los zapatos antes de acostarme.

1. No **entiendo** nada en la clase.
2. Los estudiantes **celebran** toda la noche.
3. **Nos preocupamos** por el examen.
4. ¿**Usas** tu computadora nueva en la presentación?
5. Ustedes **conocen** la capital de España, ¿verdad?
6. Mi familia y yo **pasamos** un día feliz con mis abuelos.
7. Les **mando** los documentos por Internet.
8. ¿**Recibes** mis mensajes electrónicos?

4 Rutinas. Write a paragraph describing your day yesterday. Use at least five verbs from the list.

levantarse	despertarse	cepillarse	lavarse
ducharse	bañarse	volver	trabajar
acostarse	estudiar	caminar	comer

¡Susto espantoso!

En la casa del Sr. Covarrubias.

¿Podemos hablar con el Sr. Covarrubias?

Gerardo no está.

¿No sabe cuándo regresa?

Entonces, ¿no sabe usted nada?

No, no sé cuándo regresa.

No, lo siento, pero no sé nada.

Vámonos, Adriana, aquí no vamos a solucionar nada.

Quién sabe dónde está Gerardo en su camión.

Gracias, Sra. Covarrubias.

En la ciudad.

¿Y ahora qué hacemos?

Voy al Archivo de Indias para investigar. Nayeli pasa mucho tiempo allí.

Voy a leer el correo electrónico en el hotel. A ver si el Sr. de Landa tiene noticias de Nayeli.

Buena idea.

Nos vemos en el hotel más tarde.

En el hotel, habitación de Felipe.

Ah, ¡qué bien! Un mensaje del Sr. de Landa.

Queridos Adriana y Felipe: Todo está arreglado. Sus boletos están en Barajas, en la aerolínea Iberia. Tienen que volver a Madrid en dos días para tomar el avión desde allí. ¡Buena suerte!

¡Gol! ¡Ahhh, Nayeli está bien! ¡Nos vamos a encontrar con ella en la hermosa isla de Puerto Rico!

En el hotel, habitación de Felipe.

Adriana, ¡qué te pasa!

¡Qué miedo!

¿Cómo?

Al regresar del Archivo de Indias al hotel, vi a un hombre con un anillo raro.

¿Quién puede ser ese hombre del anillo?

¿A Puerto Rico?

No sé... pero no importa porque nos vamos para Puerto Rico.

¿Y los pasajes?

Sí, el Sr. de Landa dice que Nayeli está allí y está bien.

Están en Barajas. ¡Imagínate! ¡Nos vamos a la playa!

¡Nayeli está bien y nos vamos a encontrar con ella en San Juan!

En la agencia de viajes.

Un boleto a Quito, por favor, lo antes posible.

¿Mañana por la mañana?

Está bien, gracias, muy amable.

¿Quito? ¡Nos vamos a Quito!

Actividades

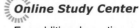
Online Study Center

For additional practice
with this episode, visit
the *Caminos* website at
http://college.hmco.com/
languages/spanish/
renjilian/caminos/3e/
student_home.html.

1 Comprensión. Based on this episode of *Caminos del jaguar*, choose the
logical response.

1. El Sr. Covarrubias...
   a. va a regresar pronto a casa.
   b. no está en casa.

2. En el Archivo de Indias, Adriana...
   a. busca a Nayeli.
   b. lee el correo electrónico.

3. El Sr. de Landa les da a Adriana y Felipe...
   a. dos pasajes para Barajas.
   b. dos pasajes de ida y vuelta para Puerto Rico.

4. Nayeli va a viajar a...
   a. Quito.
   b. San Juan.

5. Adriana vio a un hombre con...
   a. un anillo raro.
   b. una cara rara.

6. En San Juan, Adriana y Felipe...
   a. van a ver a Nayeli.
   b. van a ver al Sr. de Landa.

7. Gafasnegras sabe que Nayeli...
   a. va a viajar a Quito.
   b. va a viajar a Puerto Rico.

 2 Situaciones. Dramatize one of the following situations.

1. Armando tells Adriana and Felipe that the tickets are ready.
2. Adriana and Felipe talk to Sra. Covarrubias about her husband's whereabouts.

3 Escritura. Write a brief summary of this episode (4–6 sentences).

NOTA CULTURAL

El Archivo General de Indias

El Archivo General de Indias is the library in which
documents and records from three centuries of Spanish
colonial rule in the Americas (or Indies) are stored.
Among the documents contained in the archives is a
letter written in 1590 by Miguel de Cervantes, author of
the *Quijote,* requesting employment in the New World.
The Archivo is located in a beautiful colonial building
in the heart of Sevilla.

Lectura

Online Study Center

For further reading practice online, visit the *Caminos* website at http://college.hmco.com/languages/spanish/renjilian/caminos/3e/student_home.html.

PRELECTURA

1 Quiero ser turista. Describe a country that you would like to visit as a tourist. Then use the Internet or another source to learn particular characteristics that make this country popular for visitors. Read about some of the country's most attractive sites that not only beckon tourists from around the globe, but also provide many activities for local citizens. Answer the following questions as you research your chosen destination.

1. ¿Qué país quieres visitar? ¿En qué continente está el país? ¿Cuál es la población? ¿Qué idioma/s hablan allí?
2. ¿Cómo son la geografía y el clima del país?
3. ¿Cuántos turistas visitan el país en el verano? ¿Qué sitios son los más populares?
4. ¿De dónde son los nuevos inmigrantes que viven allí? ¿Qué culturas representan? ¿Qué idioma/s hablan?
5. Menciona una persona importante de allí. ¿Quién es?
6. ¿Por qué quieres visitar ese país?

Reading Strategy

Making notes in the margin

A useful reading strategy is to make notes in the margin of the text while you are reading. This technique allows you to respond actively to information and ideas presented by an author. As you read the following facts and features about Spain, jot these items in the margins:

a. The main topic of each paragraph.
b. Any questions you may have that stem logically from the information presented.
c. Your own answers or hunches about the questions you have formulated.
d. Information you can provide to supplement the reading based on written or other sources with which you are familiar.

A España le encantan los turistas

¿Sabes que cada año el número de turistas que visitan España es mayor que[1] el número de habitantes del país? ¡Pues así es! La población[2] del país suma 40.397.000, mientras que recibe a unos 65 millones de visitantes. Es un país muy popular porque ofrece no solamente mar y montañas, museos, castillos[3] y comidas ricas, sino[4] también un agradable espíritu de bienvenida[5].

---

[1]greater than; [2]population; [3]castles; [4]but; [5]welcome

El Parque Güell de Antonio Gaudí

Estadio olímpico de Barcelona

Barcelona

Barcelona es una ciudad de mucho prestigio, sofisticada y contemporánea. Se encuentra en Cataluña y allí hablan catalán y español. Más de 21 millones de turistas extranjeros escogen Cataluña para pasar sus vacaciones. Tiene importantes museos de arte, restaurantes y la famosa catedral, del arquitecto Antonio Gaudí, llamada La Sagrada Familia. La ciudad da al[6] mar y hay una playa muy popular con muchas diversiones para turistas y residentes.

Las Ramblas

Las Ramblas es el lugar favorito de la ciudad donde se pasean[7] muchos jóvenes y familias. Hay cafés y terrazas al aire libre[8], tiendas, kioskos, pintores y artistas. ¡Hay tanto que ver, comer y escuchar!

Estadio para las Olimpiadas

El inmenso estadio fue construido[9] para los Juegos Olímpicos de 1992. También construyeron una villa para atletas. Para esa ocasión, se hicieron muchos nuevos espacios deportivos que permanecen hoy en día[10].

"Puppy"

De Barcelona, vale la pena[11] hacer una excursión a Bilbao, en el País Vasco, ciudad famosa por la construcción del nuevo Museo Guggenheim, concebido por el arquitecto Frank O. Gehry. El notable edificio de titanio, caliza[12] y vidrio[13] es enorme. También es impresionante la escultura del perrito, "Puppy", símbolo del museo, que se compone de 60.000 plantas y flores y es casi tan alto como[14] el museo.

Artistas en las Ramblas, Barcelona

"Puppy", el enorme perrito enfrente del Museo Guggenheim

[6]faces; [7]stroll; [8]outdoor; [9]was built; [10]today; [11]it's worth; [12]limestone; [13]glass; [14]as tall as.

POSTLECTURA

2 **¡Me importan los números!** With a classmate, practice reading aloud the numbers and dates from the reading.

3 **Nuestras reacciones.** In groups of four, make a chart of your group's reactions to the reading by comparing the notes you each made in the margin. Follow these steps:

1. Jot down the main topics that you identified in the reading.
2. Write your own questions in the chart.
3. Write down your ideas regarding each question.
4. Add any references to other information that you may already know from other sources.

	Preguntas	Mi idea	Otra referencia
Tema 1: Aspectos atractivos	¿Por qué es tan popular España?	_____	_____
Tema 2:	_____	_____	_____
Tema 3:	_____	_____	_____
Tema 4:	_____	_____	_____

4 **Comprensión.** Working in pairs, answer these questions based on the reading.

1. ¿Cuántos habitantes tiene España?
2. ¿Cuántos turistas visitan el país anualmente? ¿Por qué?
3. ¿En qué parte del país está Barcelona? ¿Cómo es?
4. ¿Qué actividades hay en las Ramblas?
5. ¿Desde cuándo tiene Barcelona un estadio olímpico?
6. ¿Dónde está el Museo Guggenheim? ¿Quién es "Puppy" y cómo es?

5 **Comparaciones y contrastes.** In pairs, compare and contrast tourism in your country and in Spain. Ask each other these questions.

1. ¿En qué parte del mundo está tu país? ¿Cuál es la población? ¿Qué lengua/s hablan?
2. ¿Qué te gusta hacer con familia o amigos?
3. Describe el clima y la geografía en diferentes partes del país.
4. ¿Cuántos turistas visitan tu país en el verano? ¿Qué sitios son los más populares?
5. ¿De qué países vienen los visitantes?
6. ¿Cuál es la composición cultural de tu país? ¿De dónde son los nuevos inmigrantes que viven allí? ¿Qué lengua/s hablan? ¿Qué religiones practican?
7. Describe a una persona importante de tu región. ¿Cuál es su profesión?
8. Describe un lugar o monumento representativo de la cultura de tu país o región.

6 **De viaje a dos ciudades españolas.** You and a classmate have been invited to give a brief talk to a Spanish class about traveling to two destinations in Spain. Use the Internet to research and design a brochure with appealing visuals. Title your two-paragraph presentation "*Dos ciudades fascinantes de España.*"

Escritura

Online Study Center

For further writing practice online, visit the *Caminos* website at http://college.hmco.com/languages/spanish/renjilian/caminos/3e/student_home.html.

Writing Strategy

Creating a timeline

A good way to organize information visually is by use of a timeline. This strategy is useful when writing about a sequence of events, whether over a brief or lengthy period of time. A timeline helps you to see connections between earlier and subsequent events.

Workshop

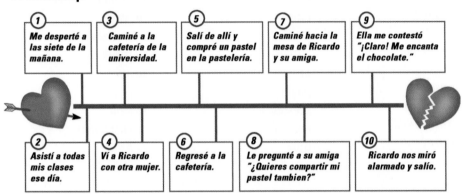

① Me desperté a las siete de la mañana.

② Asistí a todas mis clases ese día.

③ Caminé a la cafetería de la universidad.

④ Ví a Ricardo con otra mujer.

⑤ Salí de allí y compré un pastel en la pastelería.

⑥ Regresé a la cafetería.

⑦ Caminé hacia la mesa de Ricardo y su amiga.

⑧ Le pregunté a su amiga "¿Quieres compartir mi pastel tambien?"

⑨ Ella me contestó "¡Claro! Me encanta el chocolate."

⑩ Ricardo nos miró alarmado y salió.

Primero me desperté a las 7.00 de la mañana. Asistí a todas mis clases ese día y luego caminé a la cafetería para almorzar con mi novio, Ricardo. Entré en la cafetería media hora antes de nuestra cita y vi a Ricardo —¡besándose con otra chica! Ellos no me vieron. Compré un pastel de chocolate en la pastelería. Regresé a la cafetería y caminé a la mesa de Ricardo y su amiga. Le pregunté a su amiga: "¿Quieres compartir mi pastel también?" Ella me contestó: "¡Claro! Me encanta el chocolate". Ricardo nos miró alarmado y salió. Ahora, su amiga Laura es mi mejor amiga.

Strategy in action

For additional practice writing a timeline, turn to the *Escritura* section of *Unidad 4* in your Student Activities Manual.

1 Mi primer día de clase. Use a timeline to record at least five things that happened on your first day of class. Then, write a brief paragraph to describe the events of that day. Use the preterite tense.

2 Una fiesta familiar. Think of a special day that you spent with some members of your family (birthday, Thanksgiving, etc.) and write a story narrating the events of that day. Use the preterite tense.

PRIMER PASO

DISCUSSING PROFESSIONS

Sustantivos

el/la abogado/a	*attorney, lawyer*
el/la agente de viajes	*travel agent*
el/la arqueólogo/a	*archaeologist*
el/la arquitecto/a	*architect*
el/la artista	*artist*
el/la atleta	*athlete*
el/la bombero/a	*firefighter*
el/la carpintero/a	*carpenter*
el/la cartero/a	*mail carrier*
el/la cocinero/a	*cook*
el/la consejero/a	*counselor*
el/la contador/a	*accountant*
el/la criado/a	*servant, maid*
el/la dentista	*dentist*
el/la electricista	*electrician*
el/la enfermero/a	*nurse*
el/la escultor/a	*sculptor*
el/la fotógrafo/a	*photographer*
el/la gerente	*manager*
el hombre de negocios	*businessman*
el/la ingeniero/a	*engineer*
el/la jardinero/a	*gardener*
el/la jefe/a	*boss*
el/la médico/a	*doctor*
la mujer de negocios	*businesswoman*
el/la músico/a	*musician*
el/la peluquero/a	*hair stylist*
el/la periodista	*journalist*
el/la pintor/a	*painter*
el/la plomero/a	*plumber*
el/la policia	*police officer*
el/la presidente/a	*president*
el/la profesor/a	*professor*
el/la programador/a de computadoras	*computer programmer*
el/la psicólogo/a	*psychologist*
el/la recepcionista	*receptionist*
el/la secretario/a	*secretary*
el/la trabajador/a	*worker*
el/la vendedor/a	*salesperson*
el/la veterinario/a	*veterinarian*

COMMON VERBS USED WITH INDIRECT OBJECT PRONOUNS

agradecer	*to thank, be grateful for*
contestar	*to answer*
dar	*to give*
deber	*to owe, should*
enseñar	*to teach*
entregar	*to hand in, deliver*
enviar	*to send*
explicar	*to explain*
hablar	*to speak*
ofrecer	*to offer*
pagar	*to pay*
prestar	*to lend*
regalar	*to give (gifts)*
traer	*to bring*
vender	*to sell*

VERBS LIKE *GUSTAR*

caer bien/mal	*to like / dislike (a person)*
encantar	*to delight, like very much (love)*
faltar	*to lack, need; to be left (to do)*
fascinar	*to fascinate*
importar	*to matter, be important, be of concern*
interesar	*to interest, be of interest*
molestar	*to bother, annoy*
parecer	*to seem, appear to be*
preocupar	*to worry*

AFFIRMATIVE, NEGATIVE, AND TRANSITIONAL EXPRESSIONS

a veces	*at times*
algo	*something, anything*
alguien	*someone, somebody*
algún	*some, any*
algunas veces	*sometimes*
alguno/a/os/as	*some, any*
casi siempre/ nunca/nada	*almost always / never / nothing*

de vez en cuando	*from time to time*	(o) ... o	*(either) ... or*
muchas veces	*many times*	siempre	*always*
nada	*nothing*	también	*also, too*
nadie	*no one, nobody*	tampoco	*neither, either*
(ni) ... ni	*(neither) ... nor*	todo	*everything*
ningún	*none, not any*	todo el mundo	*everybody, everyone*
ninguno/a nunca, jamás	*never*	todos los días	*every day*

SEGUNDO PASO

TALKING ABOUT FAMILY MEMBERS

Sustantivos

el/la abuelo/a	*grandfather / grandmother*	enamorarse (de)	*to fall in love (with)*
el/la bebé	*baby*	estar casado/a	*to be married*
el/la bisabuelo/a	*great-grandfather / great-grandmother*	estar divorciado/a	*to be divorced*
		estar enamorado/a	*to be in love*
el/la chico/a	*boy / girl*	estar separado/a	*to be separated*
el conejo	*rabbit*	nacer	*to be born*
el/la cuñado/a	*brother-in-law / sister-in-law*	ser mayor	*to be older*
el/la esposo/a	*husband / wife*	ser menor	*to be younger*
el/la gato/a	*cat*	ser soltero/a	*to be single*
el/la hermanastro/a	*stepbrother / stepsister*		

Preposiciones

el/la hermano/a	*brother, sister*	a	*to, for*
el/la hijastro/a	*stepson / stepdaughter*	al lado de	*next to, side by side*
el/la hijo/a	*son / daughter*	antes de	*before*
la madrastra	*stepmother*	bajo	*under*
la madre / mamá	*mother, mom*	cerca de	*close to*
el marido	*husband*	con	*with*
la mascota	*pet*	de	*from, of*
el/la nieto/a	*grandson / granddaughter*	debajo de	*beneath, under*
el/la niño/a	*boy / girl / child*	delante de	*in front of*
el/la novio/a	*boyfriend / girlfriend*	dentro de	*inside of*
la nuera	*daughter-in-law*	desde	*from, since*
el padrastro	*stepfather*	después de	*after*
el padre / papá	*father, dad*	detrás de	*behind*
el pájaro	*bird*	durante	*during*
el/la pariente	*family member, relative*	en	*in, on, at*
el/la perro/a	*dog*	encima de	*on top of, above*
el/la primo/a	*cousin*	enfrente de	*in front of, facing*
el/la sobrino/a	*nephew / niece*	entre	*between, among*
el/la suegro/a	*father-in-law / mother-in-law*	fuera de	*outside of*
el/la tío/a	*uncle / aunt*	hacia	*toward*
la tortuga	*turtle*	hasta	*until*
el yerno	*son-in-law*	junto a	*next to*
		lejos de	*far from*
		para	*for, to, in order to*

Verbos

		por	*for, by means of*
		según	*according to*
abrazar	*to hug*	sin	*without*
casarse (con)	*to get married (to)*	sobre	*on, on top of*

ESPAÑA

PERSONALIDADES

Tomatito

Bebe

Julio Iglesias

España es un país multicultural. Además de español, muchos habitantes hablan otras lenguas españolas: vasco[1], catalán[2] y gallego[3]. La historia española refleja la influencia de tres culturas importantes: la cristiana, la judía[4] y la islámica (también llamada musulmana[5]). Estas influencias se ven en el arte, la arquitectura, el cine, la comida, la moda, la música y la literatura de España.

Hay muchas personalidades de España distinguidas en sus profesiones: la diseñadora de joyas[6] Paloma Picasso; el modista[7] Cristobal Balenciaga, el arquitecto Antonio Gaudí; los artistas Salvador Dalí y Joan Miró; los actores Penélope Cruz y Antonio Banderas; el director de cine Pedro Almodóvar; el Príncipe de Asturias[8] y su esposa doña Letizia; los escritores Miguel de Cervantes, Federico García Lorca y Ana María Matute son también personalidades famosas de España.

Enrique Iglesias

Alejandro Sanz

Manu Chao

[1]Basque; [2]Catalan; [3]Galician; [4]Jewish; [5]Muslim; [6]jewelry designer; [7]fashion designer; [8]Prince of Asturias

Comprensión

Working in pairs, ask each other the following questions.

1. ¿Es España unicultural?
2. ¿Cuántos idiomas hablan los españoles? ¿Cuáles son?
3. Nombra las diferentes culturas que han contribuido° a la civilización española.
4. ¿En qué areas se reflejan las influencias religiones en España?

have contributed

"Cuando quiero algo, lo busco con cabeza de hielo, corazón de fuego y mano de hierro".

Antonio Banderas, *Cristina La Revista* (España)

ARTE

JOSÉ MANUEL MERELLO

José Manuel Merello es un pintor expresionista. Nació° en el año 1960. Estudió° álgebra, geometría y filosofía en las universidades de España. Este artista contemporáneo ha tenido muchas exposiciones° y es ganador de varios premios / galardones por su arte. Esta obra de arte acrílica se titula *Niño soñando con°* su *bicicleta*.

He was born / He studied

exhibitions

dreaming about

Niño soñando con su bicicleta

👥 Comprensión

Working in pairs, ask each other the following questions.

1. ¿Cuántos años crees que tiene este niño?
2. ¿Con qué sueña el niño, según° el título de la pintura?   *according to*
3. ¿Adónde crees que quiere ir el niño?
4. ¿Qué colores usa el artista? ¿Qué temas interpretas en la obra?
5. Describe la pintura: ¿Es realista, surrealista, sentimental, original?

MÚSICA

En algunas familias españolas, las tradiciones musicales son notables. Por ejemplo, "Tomatito" (José Fernández Torres) toca la guitarra flamenca, como su padre y su abuelo. En 2005, ganó un Grammy Latino por el mejor álbum flamenco, "Aguadulce°".   *Sweet water*

Otro guitarrista con un nombre similar es el legendario "El Tomate" (Juan Muñoz), que tiene fama como el "gurú de la guitarra". Él tuvo influencia en tres de sus cinco hijas (Lucía, Lola y Pilar) para formar su grupo musical, "Las Ketchup". Su primer disco, "Las hijas del tomate" les ganó un premio europeo.

Bebe (Verónica Sánchez) ganó un Grammy Latino como el mejor Nuevo Artista del año 2005. De padres músicos, Bebe pasó la vida rodeada de° guitarras, baterías° y pianos. Su estilo es original.   *spent her life surrounded by / drums*

Julio Iglesias y su hijo Enrique Iglesias son de Madrid. Julio ha vendido° más de 250.000.000 millones de discos, mientras° Enrique Iglesias ha vendido más de 40.000.000 millones de álbumes. Estos dos artistas internacionales son ganadores de los premios más prestigiosos de la música. También, Julio está en el libro de   *has sold / while*

Las Ketchup

any records mundiales de Guinness por vender más discos en más idiomas que cualquier° otro cantante en la historia de la música. Él vive en Miami.

Otro madrileño influenciado musicalmente por su padre es Alejandro Sanz (Alejandro Sánchez Pizarro). Cuando recibió su primer *dedicated it to* Grammy Latino, Alejandro se lo dedicó° a su padre, ya muerto. Este cantante *sounds* español de fama internacional es popular por su música de sonidos° pop, flamenco y mediterráneo.

Los padres del cantante español "Manu Chao" (José-Manuel Thomas Arthur Chao) llevaron a la familia a vivir en Francia durante la dictadura de Francisco Franco. Con sus hermanos, tocaron conciertos en Latinoamérica. Su banda de hoy, "Manu Chao", es un grupo de cantantes y músicos de diferentes países. Canta en español, francés, árabe, gallego, inglés y portugués.

Otros distinguidos cantantes y grupos españoles son Miguel Bosé, Ana Belén, "Monja enana", "La oreja de Van Gogh", "El mago de Oz", Plácido Domingo, Rocío Durcal y José Carreras. Conéctate a Internet para aprender más sobre ellos.

Comprensión

Working in pairs, ask each other the following questions.

1. ¿Cuál de los cantantes dedicó su Grammy Latino a su padre?
has sold 2. ¿Quién ha vendido° más discos en muchas lenguas?
3. ¿Cuál de los músicos canta en español, francés, árabe y portugués?
4. ¿Cuáles de los artistas musicales tienen nombres similares?
5. ¿Quién tiene su residencia en los Estados Unidos?
gave 6. ¿A quién le dieron° el Grammy Latino por el Nuevo artista del año 2005?

LITERATURA

GUSTAVO ADOLFO BÉCQUER

Gustavo Adolfo Bécquer es uno de los poetas más importantes del movimiento romántico de la literatura española. Él vivió entre 1836–1870. Su poesía se nota por su tono íntimo, sus temas sobre los placeres° y las penas del amor, lo ideal y los sueños°.

pleasures / dreams
while / you gaze

"Rima XXI"

¿Qué es poesía?, dices mientras°
    clavas°en mi pupila tu pupila azul;
¿Qué es poesía? ¿Y tú me lo
    preguntas? Poesía... eres tú.

Comprensión

Working in pairs, ask each other the following questions.

1. ¿Qué pregunta el poeta? ¿De qué color es la pupila?
2. ¿Cuántas personas hay en el poema? ¿Con qué compara a la segunda persona?
3. El poeta dice, "Poesía eres tú". ¿Qué otra comparación es posible?

"Vengo a buscar lo que busco.
Mi alegría° y mi persona...." *joy*

Federico García Lorca, "Romance de la pena negra"

4. ¿Qué descripciones evoca el poema, en tu opinión? ¿Es elocuente, realista, apasionado°, bonito, tonto, sensual, positivo, romántico, idealista, exagerado? *de pasión*

5. Dramatiza el poema con un/a compañero/a de clase.

PALOMA PEDRERO

La española Paloma Pedrero es dramaturga°, directora / productora de cine, actriz y profesora de arte dramático. Nació en 1957. En sus obras, escribe sobre las diferentes tradiciones culturales de su país. En esta escena de su drama, *Resguardo° personal*, Pedrero nos presenta la relación conflictiva entre una pareja, Gonzalo y Marta.

playwright

Claim check

Resguardo personal

G: Marta, yo te quiero°. Te juro que te quiero.
M: Ya lo sé°. Me enseñaste algo que no conocía°...
G: Vuelve a casa. Podemos arreglar° las cosas...
M: Me enseñaste lo insólito° del amor: la destrucción.
G: Quiero seguir viviendo contigo. Creo que no está todo perdido°...
M: Puede ser que la destrucción sea° parte del amor...
G: ¡No me quieres escuchar!
M: No.
G: No tienes interés en hablar conmigo.
M: Sí.
G: ¿Sí?
M: Sí, que no, que no tengo interés.
G: ¿Vas a volver a casa?
M: No.
G: Te advierto° que no te lo voy a pedir más.
M: Te lo agradezco°. Tengo prisa.
G: Es tu última oportunidad.

I love you
I already know / I didn't know
fix
flip, weird side
lost
is

warn
thank

Comprensión

With a partner, dramatize the dialog. Then, answer these questions.

1. ¿Qué temas presenta la autora en esta escena dramática?
2. ¿Cuántos años tienen Gonzalo y Marta, en tu opinión?
3. ¿Cómo está Gonzalo? ¿Calmado, convincente, tolerante, decidido, flexible, desilusionado, determinado, romántico, estable, frustrado...?
4. ¿Con qué actitud reacciona Marta? ¿Calmada, convincente, tolerante, desilusionada, decidida, determinada, romántica, estable, flexible, frustrada?
5. ¿Quién tiene prisa? ¿Va a volver a casa? ¿Por qué?
6. Gonzalo le dice a Marta, "Es tu última oportunidad". En tu opinión, ¿qué le va a contestar Marta?
7. Describe el tono de este diálogo: alegre, melancólico, tenso, triste.
8. En el poema de Bécquer y el drama de Pedrero, ¿qué temas y tonos tienen en común y cuáles son diferentes?

5
Vacaciones en la playa

VOCABULARIO Y LENGUA

- ► Checking into a hotel
- ► Using direct object pronouns
- ► Talking about the beach and leisure activities
- ► Narrating events in the past: Preterite of verbs with spelling changes: *ir, ser, dar*

- ► Discussing vacations
- ► Using double object pronouns
- ► Narrating events in the past: Preterite of stem-changing *-ir* verbs
- ► Narrating events in the past: Preterite of irregular verbs

CAMINOS DEL JAGUAR

- ► Volibol y amor en la playa
- ► Dos espías

LECTURA

- ► Vamos al Caribe hispano: Cuba, Puerto Rico y la República Dominicana

NOTAS CULTURALES

- ► El turismo en el Caribe hispano
- ► Los parques nacionales

ESTRATEGIAS

- ► **Reading:** How to use the dictionary
- ► **Writing:** Using a dictionary

Luis Germán Cajiga, *Flamboyán entre palmeras*

Preguntas del tema

- ► ¿Adónde te gusta ir de vacaciones?
- ► ¿Qué actividades te gusta hacer?
- ► ¿Con quién/es vas de vacaciones?
- ► ¿Cuál es tu hotel favorito?

PRIMER PASO

Vocabulario y lengua

CHECKING INTO A HOTEL

luxury
first class
hotel industry / surrounded

views
guests
rooms

alarm clock

Online Study Center
For additional practice with this unit's vocabulary and grammar, visit the *Caminos* website at http://college.hmco.com/ languages/spanish/ renjilian/caminos/3e/ student_home.html. You can also review audio flashcards, quiz yourself, and explore related Spanish-language sites.

HOTEL NACIONAL, HABANA, CUBA

Inaugurado el 30 de diciembre de 1930, El Nacional es uno de los hoteles más clásicos de la Habana. Su **lujo°**, **elegancia**, distinción y servicios de **primera clase°**, se mantienen intactos después de seis décadas en la **industria hotelera°** cubana. **Rodeado°** por hermosos jardines, el hotel ocupa un lugar privilegiado cerca del Malecón habanero, ofreciendo una de las **vistas°** más bellas de la ciudad. Sus **huéspedes°** pueden disfrutar de **habitaciones°** espléndidas y cómodas.

FACILIDADES DE LAS HABITACIONES

TV satélite
Minibar
Radio despertador°
Teléfono

Aire acondicionado
Baño privado
Radio
Refrigerador

FACILIDADES DEL HOTEL

Bar
Centro de negocios
Elevador / Ascensor
Estacionamiento
Restaurante
Sala de ejercicios
Servicios médicos

Buró de turismo
Caja de seguridad
Jardín
Piscina
Sala de conferencias
Servicio de habitación
Tenis

Más palabras y expresiones

Cognados

el (mini) bar	el/la recepcionista
confirmar	la reservación
la recepción	reservar

Sustantivos

el alojamiento	*lodging, accommodations*
el botones	*bellhop*
el buzón	*mailbox*
el cajero automático	*automated teller machine (ATM)*
el cambio de dinero / moneda	*money exchange*
el cheque de viajero	*traveler's check*
el/la conserje	*concierge*
el (dinero en) efectivo	*cash*
el estacionamiento / aparcamiento	*parking lot*
el equipaje	*luggage*
la habitación	*room*
la maleta	*suitcase*
el salón (la sala) de conferencias	*conference room*
la tarifa	*rate, fare, tariff*
la tarjeta de crédito / débito	*credit / debit card*

Verbos

alojar(se)	*to stay (in a hotel)*
atender (ie)	*to attend to, wait on*
hacer una llamada (de larga distancia/ por cobrar)	*to make a (long distance / collect) phone call*

Adjetivos

cómodo/a	*comfortable*
doble	*double*
lujoso/a (de lujo)	*luxurious*
sencillo/a	*single (room or bed)*

Otras expresiones

¿A nombre de quién?	*In whose name?*
¿En qué le(s) puedo servir?	*How can I help you?*
con desayuno	*with breakfast*
con media pensión	*with two meals*
con vista al mar	*with an ocean view*
¿Cuánto cuesta... ?	*How much does . . . cost?*
¿Dónde puedo cambiar el dinero?	*Where can I exchange money?*
Lo siento.	*I'm sorry.*
por supuesto	*of course*
¡Que disfrute/n de su estadía / estancia!	*Enjoy your stay!*

Actividades

1 **Hotel Real de Minas.** Listen to the description of a hotel in Guanajuato, México, then determine whether the statements are **verdadero (V)** or **falso (F)**. Correct the false statements.

1. _____ Guanajuato es una ciudad bonita.
2. _____ El Hotel Real de Minas es un hotel económico.
3. _____ Hay 12 restaurantes en el hotel.
4. _____ Hay 175 habitaciones en el hotel.
5. _____ Veinte suites tienen aire acondicionado.
6. _____ No hay estacionamiento.
7. _____ Hay un bar cerca de la alberca.
8. _____ Su número de teléfono es el 63-215-80.

2 **¿Qué es?** Write the correct word that matches each definition.

1. Cuando viajas, pones mucha ropa (*clothing*) allí.
2. Es una forma de pagar el hotel si no tienes dinero en efectivo.
3. Se usa para abrir una puerta.
4. Allí descansas en el hotel.
5. Allí los turistas reciben la llave de la habitación.
6. Es un aparato para ir al piso doce.
7. Es la persona que ayuda a los huéspedes a encontrar sitios turísticos.
8. Es un lugar donde guardar el coche.

3 **Símbolos internacionales.** Match the international hotel symbols on the right with their meanings on the left.

_____ piscina (alberca)
_____ dos camas sencillas
_____ tarjetas de crédito
_____ cama sencilla
_____ cambio de moneda
_____ restaurante
_____ salón de conferencias
_____ teléfono
_____ ascensor
_____ bar
_____ estacionamiento
_____ cama doble
_____ televisión
_____ perros no
_____ minibar

4 **¿Qué necesitas?** State what hotel amenities you will need in the following situations. Follow the model.

▶ **MODELO:** Tienes hambre.
   Necesito un restaurante.

1. No tienes dinero.
2. Debes llamar a tu madre.
3. Tus maletas son muy grandes.
4. Tu habitación está en el piso veinticuatro.
5. Tienes sed.
6. Quieres hacer ejercicio.
7. Tienes hambre a medianoche y el restaurante está cerrado (*closed*).
8. Llegas al hotel en coche.

5 En el hotel. Complete the following conversation between a guest and the receptionist at a hotel using the vocabulary from the word bank below.

con vista al mar	¿En qué le puedo servir?	tarjeta de crédito
reservar	¡Que disfruten de su estadía!	habitación
sencilla	¿A nombre de quién?	

—Buenas tardes. _____

—Buenas tardes. Quisiéramos _____ una habitación para esta noche.

—_____

—De los Señores Guzmán.

—¿Por cuántas noches?

—Por dos, por favor.

—¿Qué tipo de _____ prefiere Ud.?

—Nos gustaría una habitación _____ .

—¿Con cama _____ o doble?

—Con una cama doble. ¿Cuánto cuesta?

—La habitación cuesta $132 por noche.

—Muy bien. ¿Se puede pagar con _____?

—Claro que sí. _____

6 Entre nosotros. Role-play the following situation with a partner.

Turista:	Recepcionista:
You are traveling through Spain by bicycle. After a difficult day, you arrive at your hotel very tired. When you arrive, the receptionist tells you that he or she doesn't have your reservation. You have a copy of your confirmation. Do whatever you can to get a room for the night.	A young bicyclist arrives at your hotel, but you can't find his or her reservation in the computer. There's a medical conference (**congreso**) in the hotel and there are no rooms left. Do your best to solve this dilemma.

USING DIRECT OBJECT PRONOUNS

Preparando el viaje

Amanda   No encuentro mi bolsa azul. **La** necesito para empacar mis cosas.

Arturo   Yo **la** tengo. Aquí está la bolsa. También tengo los boletos de avión.

Amanda   **Los** tienes también. ¡Qué bien! Mil gracias.

Amanda	¿Y el dinero?
Arturo	También **lo** tengo aquí. Supongo que llamaste a la embajada norteamericana y sacaste las visas, ¿verdad?
Amanda	¿Las visas? Claro, ayer hablé con la embajada para pedir**las**.
Arturo	Es importante tener**las**.
Amanda	Tienes razón. Sin visas no podemos viajar.

A direct object is the person or thing that directly receives the action of the verb. In the first sentence on page 173, **mi bolsa azul** is a direct object. Once the object is stated, it is often replaced by a direct object pronoun to avoid redundancy: *La necesito para empacar mis cosas.*

In the dialog above, can you identify the direct object nouns that correspond to the direct object pronouns in boldface? Note that third person direct object pronouns agree in number and gender with the nouns that they replace.

Direct object pronouns			
me	*me*	**nos**	*us*
te	*you*	**os**	*you*
lo, la	*him, her, you, it*	**los, las**	*them, you*

The direct object **lo** is often used to express a previously mentioned idea as in, *Sí **lo** sé.* (Yes, I know it.)

Direct object pronouns precede the conjugated verb.

—¿Y **los boletos?**	—*And the tickets?*
—**Los** recogemos en Madrid.	—*We'll pick them up in Madrid.*

When the direct object pronoun is used with a conjugated verb and an infinitive (**tengo que comprar, voy a hacer, acabo de escribir,** etc.) the pronoun can go either before the conjugated verb or attached to the end of the infinitive.

Quiero pedir **una habitación** más grande.	*I want to ask for a larger room.*
La quiero pedir.	*I want to ask for it.*
Quiero pedir**la**.	

Direct object pronouns are attached to the end of the infinitive when the infinitive is used with expressions such as **es importante / bueno / necesario,** etc., or in prepositional expressions such as **para recibir*las*, de visitar*la*.**

—Me gusta tener **un buen mapa.**	—*I like to have a good map.*
—Sí, es bueno tener**lo**.	—*Yes, it's good to have it.*

When the direct object pronoun is used with progressive forms (**estar** + present participle), the pronoun can go either before the conjugated form of **estar** or attached to the end of the participle. When attached to the participle, you must add a written accent.

—¿Estás escribiendo **la tarjeta postal?**	—*Are you writing the postcard?*
—Sí, **la** estoy escribiendo.	—*Yes, I'm writing it.*
—Sí, estoy escribiéndo**la**.	

Actividades

1 Sin repeticiones. Write sentences replacing the direct object nouns with direct object pronouns. Follow the model.

▶ MODELO: Miranda compra los pasajes. *Miranda buys the tickets.*
Miranda los compra. *Miranda buys them.*

1. Quiero mucho a Manuela.
2. Compré unas gafas.
3. Miro los balcones de Sevilla.
4. Los turistas escuchan música.
5. Acuesto al niño en su cama.
6. Desperté a mi hermano temprano.
7. Usted llamó al médico.
8. Podemos tomar el autobús.
9. Llamamos a nuestra profesora.

 2 Preguntas personales. You are making final preparations for a trip with a friend. Use direct object pronouns to answer your friend's questions. Be careful with the verb tenses in your answers. Follow the model.

► MODELO: ¿Llamaste al agente de viajes?
Sí, lo llamé. / No, no lo llamé.

1. ¿Depositaste dinero en el banco?
2. ¿Compraste un nuevo traje de baño?
3. ¿Tienes una maleta grande?
4. ¿Vas a empacar tus maletas?
5. ¿Terminaste todo tu trabajo?
6. ¿Tienes la reservación de hotel?
7. ¿Escogiste un hotel bonito?
8. ¿Tu familia te va a ayudar con el perro?
9. ¿Alquilaste un coche?
10. ¿Tienes todo listo?

 3 Un viaje a Uruguay. You and your friend are getting ready for a trip to Uruguay. You check with each other to see if everything is done. Follow the model and use direct object pronouns.

► MODELO: reservar el hotel   *reserve the hotel*
—¿Reservaste el hotel?   —*Did you reserve the hotel?*
—Sí, lo reservé.   —*Yes, I reserved it.*

1. recibir la visa
2. escribir las cartas
3. comprar los pasajes
4. recibir la confirmación del hotel
5. comprar las nuevas maletas
6. mandar las cuentas
7. encontrar las maletas
8. confirmar los planes para el viaje

 4 Un viaje. You and two of your friends are planning to go on vacation this weekend. Make a list of things to do using both an infinitive and a direct object noun. Then divide the tasks evenly by taking turns asking each other questions about who is going to do each item. Be sure to use direct object pronouns in your answers. Follow the model.

► MODELO: llevar / la radio   *take / the radio*
—¿Quién va a llevar la radio?   —*Who's going to take the radio?*
—Yo puedo llevarla.   —*I can take it.*
   Yo la puedo llevar.

TALKING ABOUT THE BEACH AND LEISURE ACTIVITIES

Vamos a la playa.

1.	jugar (al) volibol	*to play volleyball*
2.	las gafas de sol	*sunglasses*
3.	la novela	*novel*
4.	tomar el sol	*to sunbathe*
5.	el traje de baño	*bathing suit*
6.	el/la radio	*radio*
7.	la toalla	*towel*
8.	el protector / bronceador solar	*sunscreen*
9.	el balón	*beach ball*
10.	buscar conchas	*to look for shells*
11.	pasearse / dar un paseo	*to take a walk / stroll*
12.	el sombrero	*hat*
13.	las sandalias	*sandals*
14.	el picnic	*picnic*
15.	la sombrilla	*beach umbrella*
16.	hacer castillos de arena	*to make sand castles*
17.	hacer esquí acuático	*to water ski*
18.	nadar	*to swim*

Más palabras y expresiones

Verbos

broncearse	*to get a tan*
bucear	*to go skindiving, snorkeling*
hacer surfing	*to go surfing*
ir de pesca (pescar)	*to go fishing (to fish)*
montar a caballo	*to go horseback riding*
montar en bicicleta	*to go bicycling*
navegar en velero	*to go sailing*
protegerse	*to protect oneself*
quemarse	*to get a sunburn*

Actividades

1 ¿Qué es? Choose the best word or expression for each definition. There may be more than one correct answer.

1. una actividad que haces en el agua
2. algo que usas para protegerte del sol
3. algo que puedes leer
4. es un buen ejercicio
5. algo que buscas en la playa para una colección
6. algo que te pones en los pies (*feet*)
7. la comida que llevas a la playa
8. algo que usas cuando quieres escuchar música

2 Me toca a mí. Now write three of your own definitions similar to those in *Actividad 1*. Read them to a classmate and have him or her guess the vocabulary words being defined.

3 Memoria. As a class, create a chain sentence that describes what you all like to do at the beach. One person starts by stating what he or she likes to do. The next person repeats the statement, then adds his or her own activity. Take turns and try to remember what each of your classmates has said before you. Follow the model.

▶ **MODELO:** Student A: *Cuando voy a la playa, juego al volibol.*
Student B: *Cuando voy a la playa, juego al volibol y monto en bicicleta.*
Student C: *Cuando voy a la playa, juego al volibol, monto en bicicleta y...*

4 Playas caribeñas. You are planning a vacation to the Caribbean next summer. Find a beach where you would like to go on vacation and prepare a three-day travel itinerary for your trip. State 3–5 activities you plan to do each day. Use your favorite online search engine to find information on beaches in the Caribbean. The following phrases will help you find information in Spanish: "playas Puerto Rico," "playas Venezuela," "playas República Dominicana," "playas Colombia," and "playas Cuba".

Actividades en la playa

Ayer **fui** a la playa con mi hermano Miguel. Yo **busqué** conchas, **jugué** al volibol y **almorcé** un sandwich y fruta. Mi hermano Miguel **leyó** las tiras cómicas, **construyó** bonitos castillos de arena, pero se **cayó** y **destruyó** todo. ¡**Fue** un día muy divertido!

There are two irregular verbs and seven verbs with spelling changes in the preterite in the selection above. Identify the infinitives for each boldfaced verb. Which infinitives have irregular forms in the preterite? What spelling changes do you notice?

Preterite of verbs with spelling changes

Verbs ending in –**car**, –**gar**, and –**zar** have regular preterite endings except for spelling changes in the first person singular **yo** form. There are no spelling changes in the other forms.

Verbs with spelling changes in the first person		
c → qu	g → gu	z → c
buscar *(to look for)*	**jugar** *(to play)*	**abrazar** *(to hug)*
yo	bus**qué**	ju**gué**	abra**cé**
tú	buscaste	jugaste	abrazaste
Ud., él/ella	buscó	jugó	abrazó
nosotros/as	buscamos	jugamos	abrazamos
vosotros/as	buscasteis	jugasteis	abrazasteis
Uds., ellos/as	buscaron	jugaron	abrazaron

Other verbs with spelling changes in the yo form include:

c → qu		g → gu		z → c	
explicar	**expliqué**	llegar	**llegué**	almorzar	**almorcé**
practicar	**practiqué**	pagar	**pagué**	comenzar	**comencé**
tocar	**toqué**	entregar	**entregué**	empezar	**empecé**

Te **expliqué** el itinerario del viaje.			*I explained the trip itinerary to you.*		
Llegué a Costa Rica en barco.			*I arrived in Costa Rica by boat.*		
Empecé la excursión en San Juan.			*I started the tour in San Juan.*		

In the following verbs, the **i** changes to **y** in the third person singular and plural forms in the preterite.

El criminal **huyó** de la policía.		*The criminal fled from the police.*
Los turistas **leyeron** las revistas.		*The tourists read the magazines.*

creer *(to believe)*		Other verbs with *y* in the third person ending			
yo	creí	caer	*to fall*	cayó	cayeron
tú	creíste	leer	*to read*	leyó	leyeron
Ud., él, ella	creyó	construir	*to build*	construyó	construyeron
nosotros/as	creímos	huir	*to flee*	huyó	huyeron
vosotros/as	creísteis	oír	*to hear*	oyó	oyeron
Uds., ellos/as	creyeron				

Preterite indicative of *ir, ser,* and *dar*

The verbs **ir, ser,** and **dar** are irregular in the preterite. Notice that **ir** and **ser** have the same forms.

Preterite indicative of *ir, ser* and *dar*			
	ir *(to go)*	**ser** *(to be)*	**dar** *(to give)*
yo	**fui**	**fui**	**di**
tú	**fuiste**	**fuiste**	**diste**
Ud., él, ella	**fue**	**fue**	**dio**
nosotros/as	**fuimos**	**fuimos**	**dimos**
vosotros/as	**fuisteis**	**fuisteis**	**disteis**
Uds., ellos/as	**fueron**	**fueron**	**dieron**

Stating how long ago something happened

To ask and answer questions about how long *ago* you did something, use the structure below with **hace** plus the preterite.

¿Cuánto tiempo **hace que** + *verb in preterite tense?*
Hace + *period of time* + **que** + *verb in preterite tense*

¿Cuánto tiempo **hace que** Carlos visitó a sus amigos en Perú?		*How long ago did Carlos visit his friends in Peru?*
Hace dos años **que** los visitó.		*He visited them two years ago.*

Actividades

1 Mi primer día de práctica.
Mario's internship at the travel agency started yesterday, and he describes his day to his friend Lupe. Change all the verbs to the preterite to tell Mario's story in the past. Follow the model.

> **MODELO:** **Me levanto** a las siete...
> **Me levanté** a las siete...

Me levanto (1) a las siete. **Me ducho (2), desayuno (3)** y **tomo (4)** el autobús número setenta y tres para la oficina. **Llego (5)** a la agencia a las ocho y media. **Bebo (6)** un café con leche con mi jefa y **converso (7)** con ella sobre mis responsabilidades en el trabajo. Después **llegan (8)** muchos clientes y me **preguntan (9)** por ofertas de viajes a diferentes lugares. A mediodía, **almuerzo (10)** con mi jefa y con otro de los empleados en un pequeño café cerca de la agencia. Por la tarde, **empieza (11)** a llegar la gente después de las cuatro. Algunas personas **buscan (12)** información sobre viajes, otras **confirman (13)** y **pagan (14)** sus pasajes. A las seis de la tarde, **salgo (15)** para casa, pero antes **ceno (16)** en el restaurante La Buena Mesa con Ricardo, otro de los chicos de la agencia. ¡Qué día tan interesante y productivo!

2 Un fin de semana maravilloso.
Nela describes her weekend in Boston. Use the preterite of each of the verbs in parentheses to complete her paragraph.

El fin de semana pasado _____ (**1.** ser) muy divertido. Mis amigas Rosa, Marta y yo _____ (**2.** ir) de vacaciones a Boston porque _____ (**3.** comprar) un viaje muy barato en la agencia de viajes "Viajes Boston". _____ (**4.** Salir, nosotras) de Nueva York muy tarde el viernes por la noche y_____ (**5.** llegar) a medianoche a la ciudad. El sábado, Rosa y Marta _____ (**6.** visitar) primero a su abuela que vive allí. Después, _____ (**7.** entrar, nosotras) a la famosa tienda Filene's Basement y _____ (**8.** probarse) unos zapatos y unas chaquetas. El domingo, _____ (**9.** ir, nosotras) a comer a un restaurante elegante en la calle Newbury. Marta y Rosa _____ (**10.** comer) arroz con pollo pero yo solamente _____ (**11.** beber) un jugo de frutas. Por la tarde, _____ (**12.** visitar, nosotras) el Museo de Ciencias y por la noche _____ (**13.** ir, nosotras) a una discoteca. Allí _____ (**14.** conocer, nosotras) a unos chicos muy simpáticos y con ellos, _____ (**15.** escuchar, nosotras) música y _____ (**16.** bailar) toda la noche. _____ (**17.** Salir, nosotras) de Boston el lunes a las 6.00 de la mañana. ¡Queremos regresar muy pronto a Boston!

3 Ayer.
In pairs, discuss what you did yesterday using the preterite for the following settings. Choose two verbs from each of the lists in parentheses.

> **MODELO:** En casa (despertarse tarde / limpiar la cocina / descansar)
> —Ayer, me desperté tarde y limpié la cocina.
>
> *At home (wake up late / clean the kitchen / rest)*
> *—Yesterday, I woke up late and cleaned the kitchen.*

1. En casa (almorzar / despertarse / tocar música).
2. En la escuela (estudiar / leer mi libro de español / ir a la biblioteca).
3. En el gimnasio (jugar al volibol / practicar deportes / caminar rápido).
4. En el cine (mirar una película/ beber un refresco / reunirse con amigos).
5. En la tienda (comprar / buscar / pagar) muchas cosas.
6. En el parque (practicar deportes/ jugar al béisbol / correr).

4 Eventos de la vida.

Complete the chart below by filling in the year in which you experienced each of the events listed in the second column. Then, in pairs, ask your partner how long ago these events occurred. Follow the model.

▶ **MODELO:** 1997 / llevar ropa formal
—*¿Cuánto tiempo hace que llevaste ropa formal?*
—*Hace (diez) años que llevé ropa formal.*

año	eventos
_____	nacer
_____	comenzar la escuela primaria
_____	abrazar a mi primer amor
_____	graduarse de la escuela secundaria
_____	asistir a una fiesta
_____	tocar un instrumento
_____	aprender a montar en bicicleta
_____	ir de vacaciones a una playa
_____	comprar un disco compacto
_____	manejar un coche

5 Actividades en la playa.

Look at the illustration on page 76, and, in pairs, describe which of these activities you did or didn't do during your last trip to the beach or during a vacation. Be sure to indicate how long ago you did the activities and whether or not you liked them.

6 De vacaciones en la playa.

Imagine that you are one of the people in the photograph and describe what you did on vacation last summer. Write a postcard to your best friend using the preterite tense.

Volibol y amor en la playa

Adriana y Felipe llegan a San Juan, Puerto Rico buscando a Nayeli. Van al hotel y se registran.

Buenas tardes, señor y señora Reyes. ¿Desean una habitación doble?

No. Mi reservación es para "Adriana Reyes".

Y mi reservación está bajo "Felipe Luna".

¡Aquí hay tanto que hacer! Se puede navegar en velero.

¡Y la isla es bellísima! Ay, Adriana, hay momentos perfectos, como éste.

Sí. También se puede montar a caballo o hacer surfing.

¡Vamos a jugar al volibol con esos chicos!

Mientras tanto, en México y Sevilla.

Hay malas noticias: Tus estudiantes, Adriana Reyes y Felipe Luna, están en Puerto Rico.

¡No puede ser! ¿Por qué no están todavía en Puebla? Les dejé instrucciones clarísimas.

Parece que no las recibieron.

Esto es muy peligroso. Adriana y Felipe no tienen ninguna experiencia.

Aquí hay algo extraño. Tengo que hacer algo para protegerlos. ¡Ay! ¡Adriana y Felipe!

Abuelita, la suerte me volvió la espalda. ¿Qué debo hacer?

Descubriste el jaguar y volviste a México con él. Ahora debes de estar con tu familia y con tus amigos. Los seres humanos son más importantes que las cosas.

Agencia de viajes. Buenas tardes.

Beatriz, ya no voy a viajar a Quito. Por favor, necesito un billete para San Juan, Puerto Rico.

Ah... ya sé para dónde va Nayeli.

En Sevilla, Gafasnegras habla por teléfono con otro criminal:

Nayeli va a San Juan. No la voy a perder de vista. En Puerto Rico, se acaba el juego.

Actividades

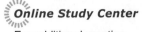
Online Study Center

For additional practice with this episode, visit the *Caminos* website at http://college.hmco.com/languages/spanish/renjilian/caminos/3e/student_home.html.

1 Comprensión. Based on this episode of ***Caminos del jaguar***, choose the logical response.

1. El recepcionista del hotel cree que la reservación es para los señores Reyes.
   a. Cree que están casados.
   b. Cree que son amigos.

2. Adriana y Felipe no quieren quedarse en el hotel.
   a. Quieren conocer las playas.
   b. Quieren descansar un poco.

3. En la playa, Adriana y Felipe se divierten.
   a. Montan a caballo.
   b. Juegan al volibol.

4. Nayeli recibió la noticia que Adriana y Felipe fueron a Puerto Rico.
   a. Nayeli está muy contenta.
   b. Nayeli está muy preocupada.

5. Nayeli cambia sus planes de viaje.
   a. Quiere proteger a Adriana y Felipe.
   b. Quiere conocer otra ciudad.

6. Gafasnegras vigila a Nayeli...
   a. para saber dónde están Adriana y Felipe.
   b. para saber adónde va Nayeli.

 2 Situaciones. Dramatize one of the following situations.

1. Adriana y Felipe hablan con el recepcionista del hotel sobre los deportes que juega la gente en la playa.

2. El recepcionista del hotel conversa con Adriana y Felipe sobre su reservación.

3 Escritura. Write a brief summary of this episode of *Caminos del jaguar*. (4–6 sentences)

NOTA CULTURAL

El turismo en el Caribe hispano

Cada año, millones de turistas de todas partes del mundo visitan las playas del Caribe. Muchos llegan en avión o en barco a Puerto Rico, a Cuba y a la República Dominicana. En estas islas, el turismo es muy importante para su economía. Los turistas disfrutan de las hermosas playas y temperaturas agradables, que varían entre los 27 °C y 29 °C. En Puerto Rico, mucha gente visita el Yunque, un famoso parque nacional con plantas y animales exóticos.

SEGUNDO PASO

Vocabulario y lengua

DISCUSSING VACATIONS

Unas vacaciones maravillosas

Borinquen

CRUCERO CARIBEÑO

Disfrute de una fantástica aventura en Puerto Rico, a bordo°
de los espectaculares barcos de la compañía Cruceros S.A.
Duración: 9 días y 8 noches
Precio: 925 dólares americanos
Incluye desayuno continental. Otras comidas son adicionales.

ATRACCIONES

Comida Buffet • Bar a bordo
Discoteca nocturna° • Tiendas
Clases de baile con excelentes instructores

GIMNASIO COMPLETO

Ejercicios aeróbicos en grupo
Médico especialista en medicina deportiva
Equipos de ejercicios con pesas°
Masaje terapéutico°

on board

nightly

weights
therapeutic massage

Más palabras y expresiones

Cognados

la aerolínea	la limosina
el club	el transporte
la confirmación	las vacaciones
la excursión / el tour	

Sustantivos

el (des)embarque	*(un)loading*
la despedida	*farewell*
el folleto	*brochure*
el/la guía	*tour guide*
la guía	*guidebook*
la isla	*island*
el paquete	*package (tour)*
el recreo	*recreation*
el traslado	*transfer*

Verbos

averiguar	*to find out*
avisar	*to advise, to warn*
descansar	*to rest*
encontrarse (ue) (con)	*to meet (with) someone*
estar a punto de	*to be on the verge of*
estar de acuerdo	*to agree*
estar/irse de vacaciones	*to be / go on vacation*
gozar (de)	*to enjoy*
recoger	*to pick up, to get*
reunirse (con)	*to meet (with) someone*

Otras expresiones

bello/a	*beautiful*
¡Buen viaje!/¡Feliz viaje!	*Have a nice trip!*
libre	*free (independent)*
Ni idea.	*I haven't got a clue.*
¡Oye!	*Hey! ; Listen!*
¡Qué gusto!	*What a pleasure!*

Actividades

1 Vacaciones en Puerto Rico. You and your friends just came back from the cruise to Puerto Rico shown on page 184. When you return to school, a classmate asks you questions about your trip. Work with a partner to ask and answer questions about what you did on your cruise. Follow the model. **¡OJO!** Be sure to use the preterite.

> **MODELO:** ¿Adónde / ir / tú?
> —¿Adónde fuiste?
> —Fui a Puerto Rico.

1. ¿Cómo / viajar / tú?
2. ¿Por / cuántos / días y noches / durar / el crucero?
3. ¿Cuánto / costar / el crucero?
4. ¿Qué / tipo de desayuno / comer / tú?
5. ¿Dónde / bailar / tú y tus amigos?
6. ¿Enfermarse / los viajeros?
7. ¿Disfrutar / Uds. / del viaje?

2 Un viaje a Chiapas. Listen to the advertisement about a vacation in Chiapas, México, and fill in the missing words.

¿Sueña Ud. con tener una (**1**) _____, repleta de (**2**) _____, (**3**) _____ y (**4**) _____? Nosotros tenemos el (**5**) _____ que Ud. busca.

Venga a Chiapas, uno de los estados más bellos de la República (**6**) _____. Es un mosaico que combina la (**7**) _____ histórica de la región con una inmensa riqueza natural, marcando así en su gente un estilo de vida lleno de tradiciones y de admiración por su medio.

En Chiapas se mezcla el (**8**) _____ clima de la (**9**) _____ montaña con el calor de la selva (**10**) _____; es un lugar siempre (**11**) _____ con una gran diversidad de fauna.

Paseando por el río Grijalva se puede ver el impresionante Cañón del Sumidero. Se pueden admirar las (**12**) _____ de Agua Azul, unas de las más bellas de México, o (**13**) _____ las Lagunas de Montebello.

La región de Chiapas es escenario de una de las más (**14**) _____ culturas prehispánicas, los mayas, con sus misteriosas ciudades, como Palenque, Yaxchilán y Bonampak, entre otras.

Nuestras (**15**) _____ duran entre cinco y ocho días con (**16**) _____, (**17**) _____, visitas y alimentación. Todo esto cuesta solamente $5.700 hasta $6.900 pesos, dependiendo del (**18**) _____ y del tipo de alojamiento.

Hacemos (**19**) _____ todo el año con excursiones diarias.

No pierda esta (**20**) _____. Llámenos hoy para pedir más información.

3 Disfruten de un viaje. Working in groups of three, create a brochure for a vacation to a place where everyone in your group wants to go. Be sure to include the destination, price, what the package includes, and special offers.

4 En la agencia de viajes. Using the sample brochures you created in *Actividad* 3, work in pairs or groups of three to role-play a conversation between travel agent and traveler(s). Be sure your conversation includes the following:

- Greetings
- Where to go and why (likes / dislikes, etc.)
- Examination of different brochures and what each destination offers
- Discussion of prices and what they include
- Decision on a trip and purchase / sale of a package
- Thank-you's / Good-bye's

USING DOUBLE OBJECT PRONOUNS

Fiesta sorpresa

Pedro	¡La fiesta sorpresa de Maricarmen va a ser fenomenal!
Marisa	¿Y ya sabes cuál es el precio de todo esto?
Pedro	No, Rosaura **nos lo** está calculando.
Marisa	¿Ya les mandaste las invitaciones a todos?
Pedro	**Se las** mandé a casi todos. Falta Rosaura. Voy a enviár**sela** mañana.
Marisa	¿Ya pediste las flores?
Pedro	Sí, la tienda **me las** va a enviar aquí. Y la torta, ¿quién **nos la** trae?
Marisa	**Nos la** trae Sofía.
Pedro	Muy bien. Creo que a Maricarmen le va a gustar la fiesta.

The indirect object pronoun always precedes the direct object pronoun when both are in the same sentence.

¿Quién **te** manda <u>flores?</u>	*Who sends you flowers?*
Mi novio **me las** manda.	*My boyfriend sends them to me.*

The indirect object pronouns **le** or **les** change to **se** when they precede the direct object pronouns **lo/s** or **la/s.**

—¿**Les** mandaste <u>las</u> <u>invitaciones</u> a los niños?	—*Did you send the invitations to the children?*
—Sí, hoy **se las** mandé.	—*Yes, I sent them to them today.*
—¿**Le** mandaste <u>la invitación</u> a Susana?	—*Did you send the invitation to Susana?*
—Sí, **se la** mandé.	—*Yes, I sent it to her.*

In verbal expressions with an infinitive or a progressive form, the two pronouns can precede the conjugated verb or be attached to the end of the infinitive or the present participle. A written accent needs to be added when two pronouns are attached to the infinitive.

—¿**Le** vas a mandar <u>los documentos</u> a Esther?	—*Are you going to send the documents to Esther?*
—Sí, voy a mandár**selos**.	—*Yes, I'm going to send them to her.*
—Sí, **se los** voy a mandar.	
—¿**Les** estás calculando <u>el precio</u>?	—*Are you calculating the price quote for them?*
—Sí, estoy calculándo**selo**.	—*Yes, I'm calculating it for them.*
—Sí, **se lo** estoy calculando.	

The pronoun **se** can refer to many people. Use a prepositional pronoun, a noun, or a proper name to clarify its meaning.

—¿Cuándo **le** mandaste las invitaciones a Rosana?	—*When did you send the invitations to Rosana?*
—**Se las** mandé **a ella** anteayer.	—*I sent them to her the day before yesterday.*

Reflexive verbs follow the same rules for the position of the pronouns. Note that the reflexive pronoun always precedes the direct object pronoun.

—¿No **te** vas a lavar <u>las manos</u>?	—*Aren't you going to wash your hands?*
—Sí, voy a lavár**melas** / **me las** voy a lavar.	—*Yes, I am going to wash them.*
—¿**Te** lavaste <u>el pelo</u>?	—*Did you wash your hair?*
—Sí, **me lo** lavé.	—*Yes, I washed it.*

Actividades

1 Una fiesta para los padres. Nora is planning a surprise anniversary party for her parents, and her Aunt Teresa offers to help her. Fill in the correct form of the direct and/or indirect object pronouns in the passage. Some phrases require two object pronouns.

Tía Nora, ¿es cierto que tú estás preparando la fiesta de aniversario de tus papás?

Nora Sí, tía, yo _____ (**1**) estoy preparando. Va a ser el seis de mayo.

Tía ¿Con quién _____ (**2**) estás preparando? ¿Con Emilita?

Nora Sí, Emilita _____ (**3**) está ayudando a preparar todo.

Tía ¿Quién _____ (**4**) está comprando los refrescos (a ti)?

Nora Mi hermano Jorge _____ (**5**) está comprando. Vamos a servir vino, también.

Tía Necesitan música, ¿no? Nosotros podemos ayudar _____ a Uds. (**6**) también.

Nora Sí, tía, ¿puedes comprar _____ (**7**) (a nosotros) el último CD de Shakira?

Tía Claro, _____ (**8**) voy a comprar mañana mismo.

Nora Gracias. ¡Eres la tía más maravillosa del mundo!

2 ¿Para quién es? You bought some gifts for your family. Review your shopping list with your aunt. She's going to help you wrap and mark all the gifts. Following the model, work with a partner to create a dialog.

▶ MODELO: estas medias / a mi abuelita

—*¿A quién le compraste estas medias?*

—*Se las compré a mi abuelita Adela.*

1. este traje de baño / a mi sobrina Mercedes
2. este sombrero de playa / a mi madrastra René
3. esta toalla de colores / a mi hermana mayor
4. este protector solar / a mi mamá
5. estos pantalones deportivos / a mi novio/a
6. estas fotos del verano / a todos

3 **¿Qué haces si... ?** You would like to find out what your friends would do if you or another person needed help. Work with a partner and ask each other the following questions, answering with direct and indirect object pronouns.

▶ **MODELO:** —*Si tus amigos se casan, ¿les regalas muchas flores?*
—*Sí, se las regalo.*

1. Si tengo frío y necesito un suéter, ¿me lo prestas?
2. Si vamos a un restaurante, ¿me pides un plato delicioso?
3. Si un/a amigo/a está enfermo/a, ¿le compras las medicinas?
4. Si necesitamos una sombrilla de playa, ¿nos la traes?
5. Si tus amigos/as están de vacaciones, ¿te escriben muchas tarjetas postales?
6. Si necesitamos un protector solar, ¿nos lo traes?
7. Si la policía te pide decir la verdad, ¿se la dices?
8. Si necesito tu juego de dominó, ¿me lo prestas?

4 **¿Y tú qué haces?** Work in pairs. Discuss the following activities with your partner, asking each other which things you do and for whom. Follow the model.

▶ **MODELO:** escribir tarjetas de cumpleaños
—*¿Escribes tarjetas de cumpleaños? ¿A quiénes se las escribes?*
—*Se las escribo a mis amigos y a mis hermanos.*

1. preparar la cena
2. reservar las habitaciones en el hotel
3. servir buena comida
4. dar dinero para ir de compras
5. escribir muchas cartas
6. comprar regalos
7. hablar español
8. mandar una postal

NARRATING EVENTS IN THE PAST: PRETERITE OF STEM-CHANGING –*IR* VERBS

En la playa

El domingo pasado, Roberto y su esposa Ana fueron a la playa con su perro. Llevaron sombreros, gafas de sol, un radio y libros para leer. Ellos caminaron **sonriendo°** a la playa y su perrito los **siguió°** con mucha alegría.
En el kiosko, Roberto **pidió°** refrescos y su esposa **se sirvió°** una porción grande de fruta.

smiling / followed
asked for / served herself

preferred / fell asleep
had fun

Ana se acostó debajo de una gran sombrilla para escuchar la radio. Roberto **prefirió°** estar en la arena leyendo su novela, pero **se durmió°** y no leyó nada. Todos **se divirtieron°** mucho.

Stem-changing **–ir** verbs in the present are also stem-changing in the preterite. In the present, these verbs have three kinds of stem changes: **e→ie, e→i,** and **o→ue.** In the preterite, there are two kinds of stem changes: **e→i** and **o→u.** These changes occur in the third person singular and plural of the preterite forms.

Note that the first and third person singular preterite forms carry the stress on the last syllable and have written accents.

–ir verbs: e → i		
preferir		**Other verbs with the same pattern**
yo	preferí	divertirse, sugerir *(to suggest)*
tú	preferiste	pedir, despedirse *(to say good-bye)*
Ud., él, ella	**prefirió**	repetir, vestirse
nosotros/as	preferimos	seguir, conseguir, perseguir
vosotros/as	preferisteis	sentirse
Uds., ellos/as	**prefirieron**	servir; reír *(to laugh)*, sonreír *(to smile)*, freír *(to fry)*

–ir verbs: o → u		
dormir		**Another verb with the same pattern**
yo	dormí	morir
tú	dormiste	
Ud., él, ella	**durmió**	
nosotros/as	dormimos	
vosotros/as	dormisteis	
Uds., ellos/as	**durmieron**	

Stem-changing **–ir** verbs have the same vowel change in the preterite as in their progressive forms.

El mesero **está sirviendo** la cena.   *The waiter is serving dinner.*
Él nos la **sirvió** ayer.   *He served it to us yesterday.*
Los huéspedes del hotel   *The hotel guests are sleeping.*
   están durmiendo.
Ellos no **durmieron** bien anoche.   *They did not sleep well last night.*

The third person preterite forms of the verbs **(son)reír** and **freír** have simplified spellings: **sonrió, rio, (son)rieron, frio, frieron.** Note that the verbs **rio** and **frio** do not need a written accent in the preterite.

Actividades

1 ¿Qué pasó? You are telling everyone at a family reunion about your recent cruise to Cancún. Join the words to create sentences in the preterite that describe what everyone did during the vacation. Follow the model.

▶ **MODELO:** Ana y Tomás /preferir ir a la playa
Ana y Tomás prefirieron ir a la playa.

1. Nosotros/ despedirse / de la familia
2. Mis padres / conseguir / los vuelos a un buen precio
3. Mi hermana menor / vestirse / de blanco en la playa
4. Nadie /dormir / mucho en el crucero
5. Los niños / pedir / tacos cada noche
6. Yo /preferir / comer chiles rellenos
7. Los meseros / servirnos / mucha comida
8. Toda la familia / divertirse / en Cancún

2 Punto de vista. Retell the story **En la playa** on page 190 from a different point of view. Make all necessary changes. Begin the story like this:

El domingo pasado mi amigo Mario y yo...

3 Pasatiempos de verano. Interview a friend about his / her last vacation trip, asking questions using the phrases below. After the interview, report your findings to the class.

▶ **MODELO:** sentirse contento/a / en la playa
—Sandra, ¿te sentiste contenta en la playa?
—Sí, me sentí contenta en la playa.
(To the class:) *Sandra se sintió contenta en la playa.*

1. preferir / bailar en la discoteca o bucear en el mar
2. dormir bien / todas las noches
3. divertirse / en la playa
4. vestirse / elegantemente para salir por la noche
5. pedir / un pasaje de primera clase o de clase económica
6. conseguir / un buen hotel
7. reír / mucho
8. despedirse / de todos antes de salir

4 Querido diario. Write a journal entry of ten sentences in the preterite to describe what you did yesterday. Choose from the following verbs.

acostarse	dormir	practicar
bailar	ducharse	levantarse
buscar	empezar	llegar
caminar	estudiar	pedir
despertarse	ir	sentirse
divertirse	jugar	vestirse

NARRATING EVENTS IN THE PAST: PRETERITE OF IRREGULAR VERBS

Profesionales en el trabajo

La cartera **puso** la carta en el buzón.

El electricista **vino** a mi casa para instalar mi nueva estufa.

Los bomberos **condujeron** el camión al incendio.

There are three main groups of irregular verbs in the preterite. They can be categorized by the changes they share in their stems.

Group 1: Verbs with **u** in the stem.

Group 2: Verbs with **i** in the stem.

Group 3: Verbs with **j** in the stem.

Notice that these verbs have a different set of endings than those used for regular verbs. Unlike regular verbs, there are no written accents on the **yo** or **él / ella / Ud.** forms.

Group 1: Verbs with *u* in the stem			
	tener → u	Other verbs with the same pattern	
yo	tuv**e**	andar	and**uv**-
tú	tuv**iste**	estar	est**uv**-
Ud., él, ella	tuv**o**	haber	**hubo**
nosotros/as	tuv**imos**	poder	**pud**-
vosotros/as	tuv**isteis**	poner	**pus**-
Uds., ellos/as	tuv**ieron**	saber	**sup**-

Hubo (*there was, there were*) is the preterite of **haber.** Like **hay** (*there is, there are*), there is only one form for singular and plural meanings.

No **hubo** problemas con la
  reservación.
Ayer **hubo** un accidente.

*There were no problems with
  the reservation.*
There was an accident yesterday.

Saber in the preterite means *to find out; to learn.*

Group 2: Verbs with *i* in the stem			
	venir → i	Other verbs with the same pattern	
yo	vin**e**	hacer	**hic**-
tú	vin**iste**	querer	**quis**-
Ud., él, ella	vin**o**		
nosotros/as	vin**imos**		
vosotros/as	vin**isteis**		
Uds., ellos/as	vin**ieron**		

In the third person singular form of **hacer,** the **c** becomes **z** before the vowel **o: usted / él / ella hizo.** This spelling change keeps the pronunciation of all forms consistent.

Group 3: Verbs with *j* in the stem			
	decir → j	Other verbs with the same pattern	
yo	dij**e**	conducir	**conduj**-
tú	dij**iste**	producir	**produj**-
Ud., él, ella	dij**o**	reducir	**reduj**-
nosotros/as	dij**imos**	traducir	**traduj**-
vosotros/as	dij**isteis**	traer	**traj**-
Uds., ellos/as	dij**eron**		

The endings of these verbs are the same as the endings in Groups 1 and 2, except in the third person plural where the ending is –**eron: producir** → **produjeron.**

Note the vowel change in **decir** from **e** to **i** in the verb stem.

Actividades

1 Cosas. Working in pairs, create logical sentences with elements from each of the columns below. Follow the model.

> ▸ MODELO: Tú hiciste paella para la cena.
> *You made paella for dinner.*

A	B	C
Yo	decir	viajar a Cancún
Los profesores	hacer	paella para la cena
El chofer	conducir	cosas muy buenas sobre
El cocinero del restaurante	poner	sus alumnos
Los programadores	querer	las invitaciones en el buzón
de computadoras	traer	las nuevas impresoras a la
Tú		oficina
		el auto hasta el hotel

2 En la playa. Your cousin has a summer job at a beach resort. Working with a partner, take turns asking and answering questions (using the preterite) about what happened yesterday. Follow the model.

> ▸ MODELO: ustedes (traducir el menú al español)
> —¿Qué hicieron ustedes?　—*What did you do?*
> —Nosotros tradujimos　—*We translated the menu to Spanish.*
> 　el menú al español.

1. los empleados (poner revistas en las habitaciones)
2. el conserje (hacer llamadas por teléfono)
3. ustedes (tener que subir las maletas de los huéspedes)
4. los huéspedes (estar en la playa)
5. tú (no poder descansar)
6. los turistas (ponerse protector solar)
7. el recepcionista (decirnos "Buenos días".)
8. el gerente del hotel (reducir el precio de algunas habitaciones)

3 Encuesta. Interview your classmates to find out who in your class has completed the following activities. Your goal is to find someone who did and someone who did not do each of the activities. Report your findings to the class. Follow the model.

> ▸ MODELO:　　　　traer el libro a la clase
> Student A:　—¿Trajiste el libro a clase?　—*Did you bring your book to class?*
> Student B:　—Sí, lo traje a clase.　—*Yes, I brought it to class.*
> Student C:　—No, no lo traje a clase.　—*No, I did not bring it to class.*
> 　　　　　　Lo dejé en mi coche.　　*I left it in my car.*
> (To the class)　—Pablo trajo su libro a　—*Pablo brought his book to class*
> 　　　　　　clase pero Alicia no lo　*but Alicia didn't bring it.*
> 　　　　　　trajo.

1. venir a clase a tiempo
2. llegar tarde
3. conducir a la universidad
4. andar a la universidad a pie
5. decirle "Hola" al / a la profesor/a
6. hacer la tarea
7. traducir el vocabulario al inglés
8. poner la mochila en el piso

4 Una vacación familiar. Write a short paragraph (8–10 sentences) describing a memorable family vacation from the past. Use these questions to guide your writing.

¿Qué ocasión celebraron?
¿Adónde fueron de vacaciones?
¿Quiénes fueron?
¿Qué hicieron?
¿Quién hizo una comida especial?
¿Qué comieron?
¿Hubo un incidente interesante? ¿Qué pasó?
¿Quién dijo un cuento chistoso *(funny)*?
¿Se divirtieron?

5 Un día en Acapulco. Work with a partner. Imagine that you and your friends are in Acapulco and just had a busy day enjoying the attractions. Look at the drawings and number them according to the sequence in which you both prefer to have done the activities. Then, write a caption for each one using the suggested verbs and linking words in the two lists below.

bailar	comer	comprar	descansar	llegar
nadar	pasear	pedir	tomar el sol	tomar un taxi

luego	primero	finalmente / por último	cuando
todo el día	después	toda la noche	toda la tarde

Dos espías

En el Yunque...

Qué belleza, ¿no?

¡Ah, sí! La belleza del Yunque es impresionante.

¿Estás pensando en Cuba?

En Cuba, no; estoy pensando en una linda leyenda cubana sobre el primer hombre y la primera mujer. Es también sobre el principio de la humanidad.

¡Qué interesante!

Mientras los primos siguen vigilando a Adriana y Felipe...

Luis, tenemos que vigilar a Adriana y a Felipe. La Sra. Gafasnegras nos va a matar si los perdemos de vista.

Sí, pero anoche no dormí. Pensé en mis exámenes toda la noche. Los presenté esta mañana.

Ay, Luis, no estamos aquí para hablar de tus exámenes. Tienes que estar alerta.

Tú debes tranquilizarte. No pasa nada.

¿Sabes que, yo —tu primo— estoy a punto de recibir mi título de programador?

Luis, ¡no estamos aquí para hablar de tus estudios de programador!

¿Por qué no puedes compartir mi alegría?

Luis, ¿no ves que estamos en medio de algo muy serio? Tienes que concentrarte, por favor.

¡Ay! Ya se van Adriana y Felipe. ¡No sé quién te va a matar, la Sra. Gafasnegras o yo!

Perro que ladra no muerde.

Luis, ¿cómo piensas sacar fotos si tienes la lente tapada[1]?

Perdón, señor Primo "Perfecto"...

Nayeli llega a San Juan de Puerto Rico y alguien la está esperando...

Nayeli, busco el jaguar Yax-Balam, el héroe gemelo. ¿Dónde está? Tú lo sabes.

No lo sé, no lo sé. No tengo idea de dónde está. ¿Quién es usted?

Actividades

Online Study Center

For additional practice with this episode, visit the *Caminos* website at http://college.hmco.com/languages/spanish/renjilian/caminos/3e/student_home.html.

1 Comprensión. Based on this episode of *Caminos del jaguar*, choose the logical response.

1. Luis y su primo están vigilando a Adriana y Felipe.
   a. Están en Sevilla
   b. Están en el Yunque.

2. Felipe le cuenta una historia a Adriana.
   a. Es un cuento puertorriqueño.
   b. Es una leyenda cubana.

3. Luis no se puede concentrar en su trabajo.
   a. Piensa en la Sra. Gafasnegras.
   b. Quiere un futuro mejor.

4. El primo de Luis está furioso con él.
   a. El primo quiere estudiar para ingeniero.
   b. El primo no quiere perder a Adriana y Felipe.

5. Luis tiene problemas en sacar una foto de Adriana y Felipe.
   a. No funciona la cámara.
   b. Tiene la lente tapada.

6. Nayeli tiene mucho miedo en Puerto Rico.
   a. Gafasnegras la ataca en el coche.
   b. No puede encontrar a Adriana y Felipe.

2 Situaciones. Dramatize one of the following situations.

1. Nayeli y Gafasnegras hablan sobre dónde están Adriana y Felipe.
2. Luis y su primo hablan sobre los estudios de Luis.

3 Escritura. Write a brief summary of this episode of *Caminos del jaguar.* (4–6 sentences)

NOTA CULTURAL

Los parques nacionales

Los Estados Unidos estableció el primer parque nacional del mundo en 1872 para proteger el ecosistema del parque Yellowstone. Desde entonces, y con el crecimiento de las ciudades, estos parques son más y más importantes para proteger la naturaleza, la fauna (animales) y la flora (plantas, flores y árboles) y mantener el equilibrio ecológico del planeta. En los países hispanos, hay numerosos parques nacionales, muchos de ellos declarados por las Naciones Unidas como Patrimonio Cultural de la Humanidad *(World Heritage Site),* por ejemplo el Parque de Doñana en España, el Parque de Ischigualasto en la Argentina y el Parque Nacional de Tikal en Guatemala.

Parque Nacional de Tikal

Lectura

Online Study Center

For further reading practice online, visit the *Caminos* website at http://college.hmco.com/languages/spanish/renjilian/caminos/3e/student_home.html.

Reading Strategy

How to use the dictionary

When reading a text in Spanish, go through it several times, checking for words you already know as well as for cognates, which you have studied in earlier chapters. You should also try to guess the meaning of words you do not know through the context of the sentence and the text. Once you have applied this strategy, use the dictionary to confirm your guesses. The dictionary may give you several different meanings for a word. It is important to determine the grammatical form of the word because that can affect its meaning. Note the following facts about Spanish dictionaries.

► Verbs (**verbos**) appear in the infinitive form. If you are looking up a conjugated form of a verb, you will have to determine its infinitive before you start your search.

► Masculine and feminine forms of nouns (**sustantivos**) are listed and marked *m.* or *f.* The meaning of a noun may change depending on its form.

► Only the masculine singular form of an adjective (**adjetivo**) is usually listed and marked *adj.*

► Idiomatic expressions (**expresiones idiomáticas**) are listed by their most important word. Sometimes you need several attempts to determine the main word.

► The letter **ñ** is listed as a separate letter after **n.** In older dictionaries, the letter combinations **ll** (as in **llover**) and and **ch** are listed as separate letters, after **l** and **c** respectively.

Vamos al Caribe hispano: Cuba, Puerto Rico y la República Dominicana

Las tres islas caribeñas de habla española, Cuba, Puerto Rico y la República Dominicana, tienen una herencia[1] tricultural común: la indígena[2] de cada región, la española y la africana. Esta mezcla[3] étnica les da gran riqueza a sus tradiciones, a su música, a su literatura y a su vida diaria, pero cada isla tiene también su identidad propia. Las islas tienen bellas playas y hermosa arquitectura colonial. Estas islas del Caribe comparten aspectos de su cultura, herencia y tradiciones con otras regiones hispanas como las costas caribeñas de Costa Rica, Panamá, Colombia y Venezuela.

[1]heritage; [2]indigenous; [3]mix

La Playa de Varadero,
La Habana, Cuba

Pareja dominicana
en la playa

Cuba

Cuba es la más grande de las tres islas caribeñas.
Fue el segundo lugar[4] al que llegó Cristóbal Colón[5].
Los españoles llevaron esclavos africanos para
trabajar en las plantaciones de azúcar[6]. Al azúcar lo
llamaban "el oro blanco" por su valor económico en
esa época. Con el tiempo, se mezclaron los africanos
con los españoles para producir la rica mezcla racial
que hoy existe en la isla. En 1959 Fidel Castro lideró
una revolución en Cuba y por más de treinta años,
hasta 1990, Cuba estuvo bajo el socialismo de la
Unión Soviética. Actualmente[7] la isla está en
transición económica. Tiene más de once millones de
habitantes.

Puerto Rico

Puerto Rico es la más pequeña de las tres islas
hispanas y es un Estado Libre Asociado[8] de los
Estados Unidos. Los puertorriqueños pueden viajar
libremente entre la isla y los EE. UU.[9] La población
indígena de la isla de Puerto Rico, los taínos o
arauacos, tenía[10] una sociedad bastante avanzada en
esta isla de 175 kilómetros de largo[11] y 56 kilómetros
de ancho[12]. La población hoy en día[13] es de casi
cuatro millones de habitantes.

La República Dominicana

La República Dominicana comparte[14] la misma isla
que la República de Haití. Este país fue el primer
centro administrativo español en América y sus

habitantes indígenas, los taínos, la llamaban
"Quisqueya". La población de la isla tiene también
herencia europea y africana debido a[15] los esclavos
que llevaron a trabajar allí. Actualmente es un gran
centro turístico en la región caribeña, aunque
también sufre de mucha pobreza económica y
desigualdad social. Tiene casi[16] ocho millones de
habitantes.

Un arrecife de coral
en el Mar Caribe

[4]place; [5]Christopher Columbus; [6]sugar; [7]Today; [8]free associated state; [9]U.S.; [10]had; [11]in length; [12]in width; [13]today; [14]shares; [15]because of; [16]almost.

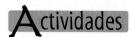

Actividades

1 **¿Verdadero o falso?** Write **V** if the following ideas are **verdaderas** or **F** if they are **falsas.** Correct the false sentences.

1. _____ El azúcar fue importante para la economía de Cuba.
2. _____ Cuba es la más pequeña de las islas de habla española.
3. _____ Los taínos llamaban *(called)* "Quisqueya" a Puerto Rico.
4. _____ En las islas caribeñas de habla española hay una mezcla étnica de influencia indígena, española y africana.
5. _____ Puerto Rico es un Estado Libre Asociado de los Estados Unidos.
6. _____ Haití y Cuba comparten la misma isla.
7. _____ Puerto Rico tiene ocho millones de habitantes.

2 **Cómo buscar palabras en el diccionario.** Keep a list of the words that you needed to look up in the dictionary for this reading and compare them with that of a friend. Are there any that you could have guessed without looking them up? Which ones?

3 **Compara y contrasta.** Compare and contrast the different characteristics of Cuba, the Dominican Republic, and Puerto Rico. Which island do you find the most interesting? Why? Work with a partner.

	Cuba	Puerto Rico	La República Dominicana
Población	_____	_____	_____
Etnicidad	_____	_____	_____
Sistema político	_____	_____	_____
Productos económicos	_____	_____	_____
Otros aspectos	_____	_____	_____

4 **Conversaciones cortas.** Work with a partner to answer the following questions.

1. ¿Qué islas hay en tu región? ¿Cómo son? ¿Tienen playas?
2. ¿A qué isla del mundo quieres viajar? ¿Dónde está? ¿Cómo es?
3. ¿Qué influencia étnica hay en tu región o estado?
4. ¿A qué grupo étnico pertenecen los padres y los abuelos de tu compañero/a de cuarto?
5. ¿Qué idiomas hablan en tu país actualmente? ¿Y en tu familia?

Escritura

Writing Strategy

Using a dictionary

Review the reading strategy prior to reading this strategy. To use a dictionary effectively, be sure to keep the following in mind.

There are many translations for some words. Look for the definition that best suits your needs. Once you have selected a word in the English–Spanish section, cross check its meaning in the Spanish–English section of the dictionary to assure accuracy, and be sure to read any grammar notes that will tell you about irregular forms, different translations, and so on. Always review the guide to using a particular dictionary to understand important symbols and abbreviations. Below are some common abbreviations and sample dictionary entries.

Workshop

f.	femenino	*adv.*	adverbio	*adj.*	adjetivo
m.	masculino	*s.*	sustantivo (*noun*)		

fan¹ (fan) **I.** s. (*paper*) abanico; (*electric*) ventilador *m;* AGR. aventadora **II.** tr. **fanned, fan-ning** (*to cool*) abanicar; FIG. (*to stir up*) avivar, excitar; AGR. aventar —intr. • **to f. out** abrirse en abanico

fan² (fan) s. FAM. (*enthusiast*) aficionado, hincha *m.*

support (se-port`) **I.** tr. (*weight*) aguantar, sostener, corroborar; (*a spouse, child*) mantener; (*a cause, theory*) sostener, respaldar; (*with money*) ayudar ∗ **to s. oneself** (*to earn one's living*) ganarse la vida; (*to learn*) apoyarse **II.** s. (*act*) apoyo; (*maintenance*) mantenimiento; ARQ., TEC. soporte *m.*

Strategy in Action

For additional practice using a dictionary, complete the exercises below and in the *Escritura I* section of your Student Activities Manual for *Unidad 5.*

 1 Usando el diccionario. Refer to the dictionary entries above to translate the italicized words. Be sure to use the appropriate form of the word or phrase. Work in groups.

1. Can I count on your *support*?.
2. I can't *support* myself on this salary.
3. My psychology instructor *supports* the Freudian school of thought.
4. The house has good *support* beams.
5. I'm a sports *fan.*
6. It's hot outside and you need to *fan* yourself to keep cool.
7. Turn on the *fan*! It's hot in here.

2 Querido/a amigo/a. You are on vacation. Write a postcard to your best friend, telling about your trip. Describe the hotel, its amenities, what there is to do, and what you like and don't like about the hotel. Then narrate a sequence of events to tell your friend what you did on your first day there. Be sure to use the preterite tense to talk about the things you did.

3 Mi primer día del trabajo. Congratulations! You just landed your dream job. Your first day on the job, however, was not what you expected. By the end of the day you are very frustrated and decide to write an email to your best friend to tell him / her all about your bad day. Describe your day to your friend, and don't forget to include all the details. Remember to use the preterite.

Online Study Center

For further writing practice, visit the *Caminos* website at http://college.hmco.com/ languages/spanish/ renjilian/caminos/3e/ student_home.html.

Resumen de vocabulario

PRIMER PASO

CHECKING INTO A HOTEL

Sustantivos

el alojamiento	*lodging, accommodations*
el ascensor/elevador	*elevator*
el botones	*porter*
el buzón	*mailbox*
el cajero automático	*automated teller machine (ATM)*
el cambio de dinero/ moneda	*money exchange*
el cheque de viajero	*traveler's check*
el/la conserje	*concierge*
el despertador	*alarm clock*
el (dinero en) efectivo	*cash*
la elegancia	*elegance*
el equipaje	*luggage*
el estacionamiento	*parking lot*
la habitación	*room*
el/la huésped	*guest*
el lujo	*luxury*
la maleta	*suitcase*
el (mini) bar	*(mini)bar*
la primera/ segunda clase	*first / second class*
la recepción	*reception*
el/la recepcionista	*receptionist*
la reservación	*reservation*
el salón (la sala) de conferencias	*conference room*
la tarifa	*rate, fare, tariff*
la tarjeta de crédito	*credit card*
la vista	*view*

Verbos

alojar(se)	*to stay (in a hotel)*
atender (ie)	*to attend to, wait on*
confirmar	*to confirm*
hacer una llamada (de larga distancia/ por cobrar)	*to make a (long distance / collect) phone call*
registrar	*to register*
reservar	*to reserve*

Adjetivos

cómodo/a	*comfortable*
doble	*double*
lujoso/a (de lujo)	*luxurious*
sencillo/a	*single (room or bed)*

Otras expresiones

¿A nombre de quién?	*In whose name?*
¿En qué le(s) puedo servir?	*How can I help you?*
con desayuno	*with breakfast*
con media pensión	*with two meals*
con vista al mar	*with an ocean view*
¿Cuánto cuesta... ?	*How much does . . . cost?*
¿Dónde puedo cambiar el dinero?	*Where can I exchange money?*
Lo siento.	*I'm sorry.*
por supuesto	*of course*
¡Que disfrute/n de su estadía/estancia!	*Enjoy your stay!*

TALKING ABOUT THE BEACH

Sustantivos

el balón *(beach) ball*	
las gafas de sol	*sunglasses*
la novela	*novel*
el picnic	*picnic*
la playa	*beach*
el protector/ bronceador solar	*sunscreen*
el/la radio	*radio*
la sandalia	*sandal*
el sombrero	*hat*
la sombrilla	*parasol / beach umbrella*
la toalla *towel*	
el traje de baño	*bathing suit*

Verbos

broncearse	*to get a tan*
bucear	*to go skindiving, snorkeling*
buscar conchas	*to look for shells*

hacer castillos de arena	*to make sandcastles*	nadar	*to swim*
hacer esquí acuático	*to water ski*	navegar en velero	*to go sailing*
hacer surfing	*to go surfing*	pasearse/dar un paseo	*to go for a walk*
ir de pesca (pescar)	*to go fishing (to fish)*	protegerse	*to protect oneself*
jugar (al) volibol	*to play volleyball*	quemarse	*to get a sunburn*
montar a caballo	*to go horseback riding*	tomar el sol	*to sunbathe*
montar en bicicleta	*to go bicycling*		

SEGUNDO PASO

DISCUSSING VACATIONS

Sustantivos

la aerolínea	*airline*
el club	*club (nightclub)*
la confirmación	*confirmation*
el (des)embarque	*(un)loading*
la despedida	*farewell*
la discoteca	*discotheque*
la excursión / tour	*excursion / tour*
el folleto	*brochure*
el/la guía	*tour guide*
la guía	*guidebook*
la isla	*island*
la limosina	*limousine*
el paquete	*package (tour)*
el recreo	*recreation*
el transporte	*transportation*
el traslado	*transfer*
la vacación	*vacation*

Verbos

averiguar	*to find out*
avisar	*to advise, warn*
descansar	*to rest*
encontrarse (ue) (con)	*to meet (with) someone*
estar a punto de	*to be on the verge of*
estar de acuerdo	*to agree*
estar/irse de vacaciones	*to be / go on vacation*
gozar (de)	*to enjoy*
recoger	*to pick up, get*
reunirse (con)	*to meet (with) someone*

Otras expresiones

a bordo	*on board*
bello/a	*beautiful*
¡Buen viaje! / ¡Feliz viaje!	*Have a nice trip!*
libre	*free (independent)*
Ni idea.	*I haven't got a clue.*
¡Oye!	*Hey! / Listen!*
¡Qué gusto!	*What a pleasure!*

IRREGULAR AND STEM-CHANGING VERBS IN THE PRETERITE

despedirse	*to say good-bye*
freír	*to fry*
reducir	*to reduce*
reír	*to laugh*
sonreír	*to smile*
sugerir	*to suggest*

6
El tiempo libre

Dania Sierra, *Guajiro verde*

Preguntas del tema

- ► ¿Qué haces en tu tiempo libre?
- ► ¿Qué música prefieres escuchar?
- ► ¿Cuáles son tus deportes favoritos?
- ► ¿Qué programas de televisión te gusta ver? ¿Por qué?

PRIMER PASO

Vocabulario y lengua

ENJOYING MUSIC AND DANCE

Mosaico musical hispano

play a role — En todo el mundo hispano, la música y el baile **juegan un papel**° central en la vida diaria. A la gente le gusta escuchar o bailar algunos de estos **ritmos** tradicionales.

El flamenco

La **guitarra** y las **castañuelas** son los instrumentos principales del *flamenco.* El *cantaor* o la *cantaora* transmite con

voice — su **voz**° los sentimientos más profundos

soul — del **alma**° de Andalucía. Otros ritmos españoles son el *pasodoble*, del centro de España y la *jota*, del norte.

El mariachi

musicians — Los **músicos**° del **mariachi** llevan el hermoso traje de *charro* mexicano. Sus instrumentos principales son los **violines** y las **trompetas.** El Mariachi Vargas de Tecalitlán es el más famoso de México. La *ranchera* es el ritmo típico que **interpreta** el mariachi. Dos conocidos cantantes de música mexicana son Vicente Fernández y su hijo, Alejandro Fernández, que también canta *baladas*.

Online Study Center

For additional practice with this unit's vocabulary and grammar, visit the *Caminos* website at http://college.hmco.com/languages/spanish/renjilian/caminos/3e/student_home.html. You can also review audio flashcards, quiz yourself, and explore related Spanish-language sites.

El rock latino y la música pop

El rock latino y la música pop tienen influencias de la música internacional, especialmente de los grandes conjuntos de Norteamérica. Uno de los

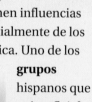

grupos hispanos que

reflects — más **refleja**° estas influencias es Maná de México, que combina la música rock con temas sociales. Otros populares **cantantes**° y

singers — compositores latinos son Shakira, Carlos Vives y Juanes de Colombia, Alejandro Sanz de España y Carlos Santana de México.

Los ritmos caribeños

Los **tambores**° marcan el ritmo bailable° del Caribe. El *merengue* es de la República Dominicana, el *son* es de Cuba y la *cumbia* es de Colombia. La *salsa* combina los ritmos caribeños con el jazz. Mark Anthony, Celia Cruz, Juan Luis Guerra, el Buena Vista Social Club y Joe Arroyo son intérpretes muy conocidos de los ritmos caribeños.

drums / danceable

El tango

El **tango** tiene su origen en los barrios populares de Buenos Aires. El instrumento tradicional que acompaña el tango es el **acordeón.** Poco a poco, esta hermosa música **se volvió**° popular en toda la Argentina y finalmente, en todo el mundo.

became

La música de los Estados Unidos

Las comunicaciones modernas facilitan la transmisión de la música de los Estados Unidos a través de **los discos compactos,** de la televisión y del Internet. Por eso, los jóvenes de los países hispanos conocen los ritmos estadounidenses por su nombre original, como: **el rock, el jazz, el hip-hop, los blues.**

Más palabras y expresiones

Cognados

la banda	la percusión
el concierto	el piano
la flauta	el saxofón

Sustantivos

los audífonos	*headphones*
el bailarín / la bailarina	*dancer*

la batería	*drum set*
la canción	*song*
el conjunto	*group, band*
la guitarra bajo	*bass guitar*
la letra	*lyrics*
el parlante	*speaker*
el reproductor MP3	*MP3 player*

Verbos

bailar	*to dance*
cantar	*to sing*
grabar	*to record, tape*
tocar (un instrumento)	*to play (an instrument)*

The ending **–ista** is often used to refer to the person who plays a particular instrument: el/la **guitarrista** *(guitarist)*, el/la **pianista** *(pianist)*.

Actividades

1 Juanes. Listen to a brief description of the life of Juanes, and complete the following statements with the correct answer.

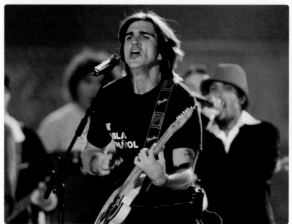

1. Juanes nació en _____.
   a. 1969　　　　　b. 1972　　　　　c. 1960

2. El verdadero nombre de Juanes es _____.
   a. Juan Ernesto　　b. Juan Esteban　　c. Juan Sebas

3. Juanes empezó su carrera con Ekhimosis, un grupo de _____.
   a. música hip-hop　　b. música rock　　c. música jazz

4. "A Dios le pido" es el título de _____.
   a. un disco compacto　　b. una canción　　c. un concierto

5. Juanes ganó tres premios Grammy Latinos en _____.
   a. 2000　　　　　b. 2002　　　　　c. 2001

6. "Mi sangre" es _____.
   a. un disco compacto　　b. una canción　　c. un concierto

7. Luna y Paloma son _____ de Juanes.
   a. hermanas　　　b. hijas　　　c. amigas

2 **Asociaciones.** Look at the CD covers below and match each with its corresponding musical style.

a. Mariachi   b. Rock   c. Tango   d. Flamenco   e. Merengue

1. _____

2. _____

3. _____

4. _____

5. _____

3 **Instrumentos.** What instruments do or did the following people play? Compare your answers with a partner.

1. Elton John
2. Itzhak Perlman
3. Louis Armstrong
4. Carlos Santana
5. Kenny G.
6. Paul McCartney
7. Alicia Keyes
8. Tito Puente

4 **Preguntas personales.** With a partner, answer these questions.

1. ¿Qué tipo de música te gusta?
2. ¿Te gusta bailar? ¿cantar? ¿dónde? ¿cuándo?
3. ¿Cuál es tu grupo musical favorito? ¿Por qué?
4. ¿Quién es tu cantante favorito/a? ¿Por qué?
5. ¿Toca algún miembro de tu familia un instrumento? ¿Cuál?
6. ¿Tocas tú algún instrumento musical? ¿Cuál?
7. ¿Asistes a conciertos de música? ¿A cuáles?
8. ¿Tienes un reproductor MP3? ¿Cuál? ¿Dónde lo escuchas?
9. ¿Prefieres usar audífonos o usas parlantes para escuchar música? ¿Por qué?
10. ¿Compras música en disco compacto o en Internet? ¿Por qué?

5 **La música del mundo hispano.** Choose one of the music genres presented on page 206–207 and find information about one of its artists. You can listen to samples of music on the Internet at websites like Amazon.com or by using iTunes. Then search for additional information to present to your classmates. Include the following information in your presentation: name of the artist, country of origin, type of music, instruments played, lyrics of a song you like, most popular songs or albums, and your personal opinion of the musician.

DESCRIBING IN THE PAST: IMPERFECT

You have learned to use the preterite to talk about completed actions in the past. In addition to this form, Spanish uses a second past form called the **imperfect.** The imperfect may have several meanings in English, for example: **el perro saltaba** = *the dog was jumping, the dog used to jump, the dog would jump, the dog jumped.*

Read the following description of the drawings and note the highlighted verbs in the imperfect. Time expressions like **a veces** *(sometimes),* **unas (otras) veces** *(sometimes / other times),* **todos los días (semanas)** *(every day / week)* are generally used with the imperfect to emphasize the habitual or repetitive nature of this tense.

Las mascotas de Fernando y sus hermanos

Use the imperfect...

▶ To talk about one's age and weather in the past.

Aquí estoy yo cuando **tenía** diez años. Ese día **hacía** buen tiempo.

▶ To describe past states of mind, feelings, likes, and dislikes.

Este es mi hermano Tomás. Él **prefería** los canarios y los gatos. A mí me **gustaban** las mariposas.

▶ To describe how people, things or places seemed or looked.

Ayer, el perro de Felicia, mi hermana, **estaba** muy inquieto.

▶ To describe how things used to be.

Unas veces, las mascotas **vivían** en paz. Otras veces, **había** caos total.

▶ To describe what people normally used to do, their habits, and routines, and how often they used to do them.

Todos los veranos **pasábamos** unas semanas en el campo y **jugábamos** juntos.

Todos los días **nos acostábamos** cansados y satisfechos.

Almost all Spanish verbs are regular in the imperfect.

The imperfect			
	–ar	**–er**	**–ir**
	estar	**tener**	**sentir** *(to be sorry, regret)*
yo	est**aba**	ten**ía**	sent**ía**
tú	est**abas**	ten**ías**	sent**ías**
Ud. / él /ella	est**aba**	ten**ía**	sent**ía**
nosotros/as	est**ábamos**	ten**íamos**	sent**íamos**
vosotros/as	est**abais**	ten**íais**	sent**íais**
Uds. / ellos / ellas	est**aban**	ten**ían**	sent**ían**

Note that **–er** and **–ir** verbs have the same endings. Note also that **–er** and **–ir** verbs have written accents in all forms, whereas **–ar** verbs have an accent only on the **nosotros** form.

All verbs that have stem changes in the present or the preterite are regular in the imperfect.

Había *(there was, there were)* is the imperfect of **haber.** Like **hay** *(there is, there are),* there is only one form for singular and plural meanings.

Había un gato en el parque.	*There was a cat in the park.*
Había muchos insectos allí.	*There were many insects there.*

There are only three irregular verbs in the imperfect.

	ser	**ir**	**ver**
yo	era	iba	veía
tú	eras	ibas	veías
Ud./ él /ella	era	iba	veía
nosotros/as	éramos	íbamos	veíamos
vosotros/as	erais	ibais	veíais
Uds./ ellos / ellas	eran	iban	veían

Actividades

1 Eventos. Match the events listed in Column A with the information in Column B.

A

1. _____ íbamos todos los años a Madrid.
2. _____ me sentía feliz.
3. Nunca hacía _____
4. _____ eran enemigos.
5. No había _____
6. ¿Tenías mascotas _____?
7. _____ siempre se levantaba temprano.
8. _____ le gustaba saltar.

B

a. Al perro
b. tú
c. Yo
d. El perro y el gato
e. buen tiempo.
f. Nosotros
g. Usted
h. muchos insectos.

2 Mi pasado. Fill in the blanks with the imperfect form of the verbs in parentheses.

Cuando yo _____ (**1.** ser) joven, siempre _____ (**2.** comer) mucho. Yo _____ (**3.** ir) a restaurantes y _____ (**4.** pedir) hamburguesas, leche y muchos postres. En verano mis hermanos y yo _____ (**5.** ir) de vacaciones a la playa y _____ (**6.** divertirse) muchísimo. Yo siempre _____ (**7.** jugar) con mis amigos y no _____ (**8.** tener) que trabajar. También mis amigos y yo _____ (**9.** navegar) mucho por Internet cuando _____ (10. tener) tiempo por las tardes.

3 Un trabajo de verano. You are describing a previous summer job, talking about what you used to do and how often you did it. Complete the description using the following adverbial expressions of time. Then, compare your answers with those of a partner.

con frecuencia   generalmente
todos los días   siempre
a veces   otras veces

El verano pasado trabajé como recepcionista en un canal de televisión. Cuando sucedía algo muy interesante, (**1**) _____ salían varios periodistas para ver los eventos. (**2**) _____ viajaban en auto, (**3**) _____ iban en dos autos, con los técnicos. (**4**) _____, yo atendía a muchas personas y (**5**) _____ llegaba gente muy importante para hablar por televisión. Y (**6**) _____ yo les pedía su autógrafo.

4 El vecindario (neighborhood). A friend of yours visited relatives in another city. Ask your friend questions about their neighborhood. Then, present the description of the neighborhood to your class.

1. ¿Estaba el vecindario cerca del centro de la ciudad?
2. ¿Cómo era? ¿grande? ¿pequeño?
3. ¿Había discoteca?
4. ¿Tenía muchas tiendas?
5. ¿Cómo eran las tiendas?
6. ¿Estaba cerca de la playa?
7. ¿Tenía buenos supermercados?
8. ¿Era deliciosa la comida en los restaurantes?
9. ¿La gente podía jugar al tenis? ¿al golf? ¿al básquetbol?
10. ¿...?

5 Así era yo. Tell your classmates about yourself and your life when you were a child. Answer questions such as: What did you look like? What was your family like? Who were your friends? What did you like to do? What did you usually do together? What was your favorite TV show? Who were your favorite singers or groups?

¿Qué deporte quieres practicar?

Más palabras y expresiones

Cognados

entrenar	el gimnasio
el/la espectador/a	practicar
esquiar	el uniforme

Sustantivos

el/la aficionado/a, fanático/a	*fan*
la cancha	*court, field*
el/la deportista	*athlete; sports enthusiast*
el/la entrenador/a	*trainer*
el equipo	*team; equipment*
el/la jugador/a	*player*
el partido	*game*
la pista	*ice rink; running track*

Verbos

ganar	*to win*
jugar (ue) (al)	*to play (a sport or game)*
patear	*to kick*
perder (ie)	*to lose*

Actividades

1 **Soy atleta.** Match the descriptions of the sports in Column A with the name of the sport in Column B.

A	B
_____ 1. En la escuela tenemos dos equipos. Ponemos la pelota en una cesta alta.	**a.** ciclismo
_____ 2. Este deporte es violento. Lo juegan dos personas con guantes grandes.	**b.** baloncesto
_____ 3. Solamente necesitamos una pelota y buenos zapatos. Somos dos equipos.	**c.** béisbol
_____ 4. Practico este deporte en la piscina de mi escuela.	**d.** fútbol
_____ 5. ¡Este deporte es también un medio de transporte! El vehículo tiene dos ruedas.	**e.** boxeo
_____ 6. Somos dos equipos. Golpeamos la pelota con un bate y ¡corremos mucho!	**f.** natación

2 ¿Qué necesitamos? Work with a partner and talk about the equipment that you need to play or to practice the following sports. Follow the model.

▶ MODELO: —*¿Qué necesitas para jugar al béisbol?*
—*Para jugar al béisbol, necesitamos una pelota, unos guantes y....*

1.

2.

3.

4.

5.

6.

7.

8.

3 ¿Cómo son los deportes? Work with a partner to decide which sport(s) you associate with each of these words. Explain the reasons for your choices.

violento/a	caro/a	rápido/a	barato/a
entretenido/a	aburrido/a	interesante	peligroso/a

4 Encuesta. Ask three classmates the following questions about sports. Write down their answers and present your findings to the class.

1. ¿Cuál es tu deporte favorito? ¿Por qué?
2. ¿Cuál es tu equipo favorito? ¿Por qué?
3. ¿Quién es tu jugador/a favorito/a? ¿Por qué? ¿Qué deporte juega?

Persona	Deporte favorito	Equipo favorito	Jugador/a favorito/a

DISTINGUISHING BETWEEN *POR* AND *PARA*

Por and **para** correspond in general to the English preposition *for,* but they are not interchangeable in Spanish. These are their main uses.

Uses of *por*	Uses of *para*
1A. To state the cause or motive of an action. (*because, on account of, for the sake of*)	**1B.** To state the purpose of actions, things, and tools. (*in order to, for*)

Trabajo **por** mi equipo... y el equipo es famoso **por** mí.
I work for my team's sake . . . and my team is famous because of me.

¡Jugamos **para** ganar la copa!
We play to win the cup!

2A. To describe spatial motion. (*by, around, through, along, via*)

2B. To specify destination. (*to, headed to*)

Tomás jugó fútbol **por** todos los Estados Unidos.
Tomás played soccer all around the United States.

Salí temprano **para** el estadio.
I left early for the stadium.

3A. To indicate acting in someone's place, on his/her behalf.

3B. To indicate the recipient of an action or an object.

Ayer jugué **por** Luis.
Yesterday, I played in Luis's place.

Esta copa es **para** mi novia.
This cup is for my girlfriend.

Uses of *por*	Uses of *para*
4A. To describe the period of time of an action, period of time in a day, percentages, and units of measure.	**4B.** To indicate a future deadline to meet.

Entrené **por** tres horas sin pausa. *I trained for three hours without a break.*	Tengo que entrenar **para** el cinco de mayo. *I have to train for May fifth.*

5A. To indicate the physical media used to send messages or things: radio, TV, Internet, fax, mail, and telephone. *(on, by, through)*	**5B.** To explain that something or someone falls short or exceeds your expectations.

Para ser tan joven, Tomás es un excelente jugador de fútbol.
For one so young, Tomás is an excellent soccer player.

Tomás habla **por** televisión y las cartas de sus aficionados le llegan **por** aire, **por** tierra y **por** mar.
Tomás talks on TV. He receives his fan mail by air, land, and sea.

Common expressions with *por*

ir **por** + *person / thing to go for;* *to pick up*	**por** favor *please*
pagar **por** *to pay for*	**por** fin *finally*
pasar **por** *to stop by*	**por** lo menos *at least*
por ejemplo *for example*	**por** lo tanto *therefore*
	por supuesto *of course*

Common expressions with *para*

para mí / ti / etc. *in my / your opinion ; for me / you*	**para** nada *no way, not at all*
para siempre *forever*	estar **para** + *verb to be about to + verb*

Actividades

1 Usos. Without translating the following sentences, discuss which preposition (**por / para**) would be the best to use in each situation. Work with a partner. Then, exchange your selections with another pair and evaluate their answers.

1. I am always doing things *on your behalf*.
2. Laura, here is a letter *for* you.
3. You have to be done with the project *by* tomorrow morning.
4. Will you miss me, honey? I am going to be away *for* a whole month!
5. Students are working hard *in order to* pass the exam.
6. Would you please teach this class *for* me? I can't make it tomorrow.
7. Where are you *headed for* at this hour?
8. *For* whom are all those gifts that you bought?

2 ¿Por o para? Work with a partner and fill in the correct preposition in the following sentences.

1. Compramos el casco _____ su bajo precio.
2. Mis papás compraron unos patines _____ mí.
3. Vamos a estar en el estadio _____ una hora.
4. La discoteca me gustó mucho _____ su música moderna.
5. Voy a imprimir el programa _____ ellos.
6. Si no quieres jugar tenis, yo juego _____ ti.
7. Debes tener tu equipo listo _____ mañana.
8. Estuvimos en Madrid y ¡viajamos _____ todas partes!

3 Música. Create sentences for the situations depicted based on the following drawings. Use **por** and/or **para.** Use the text that applies to each drawing as a hint.

4 **El palacio deportivo.** Read the following ad for a sporting goods store. Then, using the same format, create your own ad for a boutique, an event, or a product. Use **por** to describe why your specific event, boutique, or product is so attractive. Use **para** to describe your target audience: who is this event, product, or boutique for?

El Palacio Deportivo
¡Para todas sus necesidades deportivas!

¡Para niños y adultos!

¡Para deportes de invierno y de verano!

¡Para todas las edades!

Somos su tienda deportiva preferida…

…por los bajos precios
…por la alta calidad
…por la gran variedad de productos

Visítenos
en el Centro Comercial
Villa Nueva

¡Prisioneros en peligro!

Actividades

Online Study Center

For additional practice with this episode, visit the *Caminos* website at http://college.hmco.com/languages/spanish/renjilian/caminos/3e/student_home.html.

1 Comprensión. Based on this episode of *Caminos del jaguar,* choose the logical response.

1. ¿Vio Felipe al hombre que persiguió a Adriana?
   a. Sí, lo vio.
   b. No, no lo vio.

2. ¿Estaba segura Adriana que era el hombre del anillo raro?
   a. Estaba muy segura.
   b. No estaba muy segura.

3. ¿Adriana llama a Nayeli?
   a. No, Nayeli llama a Adriana.
   b Sí, Adriana llama a Nayeli.

4. Antes de hablar con Nayeli, Adriana y Felipe estaban muy...
   a. alterados.
   b. preocupados.

5. Después de la llamada, Adriana piensa que...
   a. hay algo extraño.
   b. hay algo interesante.

6. Nayeli dice que Felipe y Adriana...
   a. no son sus estudiantes.
   b. son inocentes.

7. El plan de Gafasnegras...
   a. no va muy bien.
   b. va muy bien.

 2 Situaciones. Dramatize one of the following situations.

1. Gafasnegras tells Nayeli that she already has the information.
2. Adriana and Felipe discuss what they have to do.

3 Escritura. Write a summary of what Nayeli tells Adriana on the phone. (4–6 sentences)

NOTA CULTURAL

El Yunque

El Yunque es el parque nacional más importante de Puerto Rico. Es un bosque lluvioso extraordinario. Tiene más de 240 especies de árboles y cientos de especies de animales diferentes. Allí encontramos la boa puertorriqueña, el papagayo *(parrot)* y el coquí. El coquí es una ranita *(small frog)* nativa de la isla de Puerto Rico.

SEGUNDO PASO

Vocabulario y lengua

DISCUSSING TELEVISION AND MOVIES

Online Study Center

For additional practice with this episode, visit the *Caminos* website at http://college.hmco.com/languages/spanish/renjilian/caminos/3e/student_home.html.

direct

wider

foreign / honor

genres

box-office draw

worker / unemployed

fire

causing

fearless

El cine de Pedro Almodóvar

Pedro Almodóvar Caballero es un famoso **director** del cine español. Comenzó a **dirigir**° películas en 1980 con su primera película *Pepi, Luci, Bom y otras chicas del montón*. En 1985 con la película *Matador* se dio a conocer a un público más amplio° y al año siguiente con *La ley del deseo* inicia una nueva etapa más moderada. En 1987 con *Mujeres al borde de un ataque de nervios* consigue que su **fama** se extienda a Europa e incluso llegue a América. Consiguió ser **nominado** a los Óscar con la película *Mujeres al borde de un ataque de nervios* en la **categoría** de mejor película **extranjera**°, pero no obtuvo el **galardón**°.

Su trabajo *Todo sobre mi madre* se ha confirmado como una de sus mejores películas por su solidez y la emoción que provoca; de hecho ganó su primer Óscar en el año 2000.

Sus películas son una miscelánea de **géneros**° que van desde la **comedia** como su película *Volver*, hasta el **drama,** como *Matador*. Almodóvar es uno de los directores más **taquilleros**° del cine español e internacional.

Sinopsis de *Volver* (2006)

Volver cuenta la historia de tres mujeres que sobreviven muchos obstáculos, que incluyen el fuego, la superstición, la locura e incluso la muerte. Las protagonistas son Raimunda, casada con un obrero° desempleado° y una hija adolescente; Sole, su hermana, se gana la vida como peluquera; y la madre de ambas, muerta en un incendio°, junto a su marido.

Volver es una comedia donde los vivos y los muertos conviven provocando° situaciones cómicas o de una emoción intensa y genuina. El modo en que los muertos continúan presentes en sus vidas hace que los muertos no mueran nunca. *Volver* muestra una España espontánea, divertida e intrépida°.

Más palabras y expresiones

Cognados

el actor	de acción	la escena	la nominación
la actriz	de ciencia ficción	filmar	romántico/a
cómico/a	de horror, de terror	el filme	la secuencia
criticar	de misterio	la narración	la sinopsis

Sustantivos

el acontecimiento	*event*
la actuación	*acting*
el argumento	*plot*
el billete, la entrada	*ticket*
la cartelera	*listing*
la crítica	*criticism*
el guión	*script*
el largometraje	*feature film*
la pantalla	*screen*
el papel	*role*
el personaje (principal, secundario)	*(main, secondary) character*
el/la protagonista	*main character*
la reseña	*review*
la taquilla	*box office*
la trama	*plot*

Verbos

actuar	*to act*
estrenar	*to premiere*
hacer el papel	*to play a role*
juzgar	*to judge*
presentar (pasar) una película	*to show a movie*
reseñar	*to review*
suceder	*to occur*
tratar de	*to deal with, treat*

Adjetivos

de amor	*love (adj.)*
de suspenso	*thriller (adj.)*
de vaqueros	*western (adj.)*

Actividades

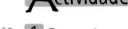 **1 Preguntas personales.** Work with a partner and answer the following questions.

1. ¿Te gusta ir al cine? ¿Por qué?
2. ¿Qué tipo de películas te gustan? ¿de amor? ¿cómicas? ¿de horror? ¿... ?
3. ¿Quién es tu actor/actriz favorito/a? ¿Por qué? ¿Cómo es?
4. ¿Cuál es tu película favorita? Explica la trama y menciona quiénes actúan en ella.
5. ¿Vas a ver una película porque lees las reseñas, ves los anuncios o por tus amigos?

2 **¿Qué película vieron?** Work with a partner and match what people describe in Column A with the type of movie listed in Column B.

A	B
_____ **1.** Al principio, era aburrida, pero finalmente, nos reímos muchísimo.	**a.** película de terror
_____ **2.** Había muchos caballos *(horses)*, revólveres, sombreros y mucho ruido.	**b.** película de suspenso
_____ **3.** Era una película muy lenta, pero por fin, la policía encontró al culpable.	**c.** película de amor
_____ **4.** ¡Al final de la película se casaron y fueron muy felices!	**d.** película de ciencia ficción
_____ **5.** Todos los personajes eran robots o personas de otros planetas.	**e.** comedia
_____ **6.** Durante toda la película tuve mucho miedo.	**f.** película de vaqueros

3 **Las películas de hoy.** Choose a movie that's showing this week in your area and write a sinopsis or review. Present it to the class.

GIVING INSTRUCTIONS AND MAKING REQUESTS: FORMAL COMMANDS

Deme dos entradas

The highlighted words in the drawings are commands, or imperative forms, which are used to request something from people whom you address formally with **usted or ustedes.**

Regular verbs

To create the formal imperative (**Ud.** and **Uds.** commands), drop the **–o** of the first person singular **yo** form in the present tense and add the opposite ending. Add **–e** or **–en** to **–ar** verbs and **–a** or **–an** to **–er** and **–ir** verbs to create the **Ud.** or **Uds.** commands respectively. To make a command negative, add **no** before the verb.

–ar verbs	–er and –ir verbs		Subject
tomar	**comer**	**escribir**	
tom**e**	com**a**	escrib**a**	usted
no tom**e**	no com**a**	no escrib**a**	
tom**en**	com**an**	escrib**an**	ustedes
no tom**en**	no com**an**	no escrib**an**	

If a verb has a stem change in the **yo** form of the present (**pienso, sirvo, duermo**), it maintains that change in the formal command forms: **piense(n), sirva(n), duerma(n).**

If a verb is irregular in the **yo** form of the present (**salgo, conduzco, veo**), it maintains that change in the formal command forms: **salga(n), conduzca(n), vea(n).**

Verbs with spelling changes

If an infinitive ends in **–car, –gar,** or **–zar,** it undergoes a spelling change in order to maintain the same sound as in the infinitive.

	infinitive	yo present indicative	usted / ustedes command
-car	buscar	busco	bus**que** / bus**quen**
-gar	pagar	pago	pa**gue** / pa**guen**
-zar	empezar	empiezo	empie**ce** / empie**cen**

Irregular verbs

	dar	estar	ir	saber	ser
usted	dé	esté	vaya	sepa	sea
ustedes	den	estén	vayan	sepan	sean

Position of pronouns with commands

Direct and indirect object pronouns and reflexive pronouns are attached to an affirmative command and precede a negative command. When a pronoun is added to an affirmative command of two or more syllables, a written accent is generally needed to maintain the original stress.

¿Quiere ver una buena película? **¡Alquíle*la*** en nuestra tienda!	*Do you want to see a good movie? Rent it in our store.*
En el teatro, **no *se* siente** en la silla equivocada.	*Don't sit in the wrong seat at the theater.*
Enví*enos* su pedido, pero **no *nos* pague** la película todavía.	*Send us your order today, but don't pay us for the movie yet.*

The subject pronoun is used infrequently with commands and is only used to emphasize the request. Subject pronouns always follow the verb in both negative and affirmative commands.

Vaya usted a la taquilla para comprar el billete.	*Go to the box office to buy the ticket.*
No hablen ustedes durante la película, por favor.	*Don't talk during the movie, please.*

Remember: When speaking about someone with a title (**señor/a, señorita, profesor/a, doctor/a,** etc.), Spanish uses the definite article: **La doctora Beatriz Pinzón trabaja en la compañía EcoModa.** The article is omitted when the person is addressed directly: **Doctora Pinzón, pase a mi oficina, por favor.**

Actividades

1 Está prohibido. You have been asked to write rules and instructions for students in your film class. Use the list below to tell them what they are allowed and not allowed to do. Use **Uds.** commands. Work with a partner.

1. No / llegar tarde.
2. No / comer o beber en la clase.
3. Ver todas las películas asignadas.
4. Elegir las películas de la lista aprobada *(approved)*.
5. No / hacer ruido en la clase.
6. No / tocar el DVD sin permiso.
7. Tomar apuntes durante la película
8. Leer reseñas en Internet como modelos.
9. Escribir una reseña de cada película.

2 Para nuestros visitantes. You are preparing a brochure for a hotel describing the attractions that you offer. Use the formal **Uds.** command form of the verbs below to write the brochure. Use each verb only once.

visitar	comenzar	leer	enviar	nadar
sentarse	cenar	pagar	ver	divertirse

1. _____ en nuestro restaurante Ricascosas, en la terraza.
2. _____ todas sus cuentas con cualquier tarjeta de crédito.
3. _____ en la piscina desde las ocho de la mañana hasta las nueve de la noche.
4. _____ los periódicos del día gratis *(free)* en nuestra recepción.
5. _____ en nuestras cómodas sillas y sofás a leer tranquilamente.
6. _____ las cartas en la oficina de correos del hotel.
7. _____ el día con un desayuno continental en su habitación.
8. _____ la ciudad en nuestros buses turísticos.
9. _____ en nuestra discoteca, la mejor de la ciudad.
10. _____ una selección exclusiva de películas desde su habitación.

3 El nuevo ayudante. A movie-theater owner has a new assistant who constantly asks what to do. Role-play the situation in pairs, asking the following questions. Follow the model, using formal commands and object pronouns.

> ▶ MODELO: —¿Les envío el horario a los periódicos?
> —*Sí, envíeselo.*
> *or*
> —*No, no se lo envíe.*

1. ¿Le pido dos cafés al bar?
2. ¿Les doy el horario de trabajo a los empleados?
3. ¿Pago las cuentas hoy?
4. ¿Les pido las películas nuevas a los distribuidores?
5. ¿Les entrego la lista a ellos mañana?
6. ¿Quito los carteles viejos de la sala de entrada?
7. ¿Pongo el dinero en la taquilla?
8. ¿Les mando los cheques a los empleados hoy?

4 Consejero. Choose one of the situations described below and give instructions regarding what to do or what not to do in each case. Use as many verbs as you can.

1. You have rented a movie and are showing your friends how to play it on the DVD and watch on the television screen.
2. You are organizing a sports tournament. Tell various people which sports are allowed and what they have to do regarding invitations, food for the visitors, selling the tickets, transportation, and so on.
3. You are taking care of your neighbor's big, mischievous dog. You usually address the dog with the **usted** form because he looks so impressive. Tell him what to do and what not to do while you are taking care of him.
4. Explain to prospective students how to succeed at your college or university.

USING ADVERBS ENDING IN -*MENTE*

Adverbs of manner describe how an action is done. These adverbs are usually formed in Spanish by adding **–mente** to the singular form of the adjective. If the adjective has **–a** and **–o** endings, **–mente** is added to the feminine form. When the adjective ends in another vowel or in a consonant, no change is necessary and **–mente** is added directly to the end of the adjective. The **–mente** ending in Spanish corresponds to the *–ly* ending of many English adverbs *(easy→ easily)*. Note that written accents on the adjectives are retained when the **–mente** ending is added.

generoso/a	genero**samente**	*generously*
impaciente	impaciente**mente**	*impatiently*
difícil	difícil**mente**	*with difficulty*

Nosotros trabajamos **continuamente**.	*We work continuously.*
Soy **inmensamente** feliz.	*I am enormously happy.*

These very commonly used adverbs may be used with or without **–mente:**
fácil / fácilmente; difícil / difícilmente; rápido / rápidamente.

Actividades

1 Cine. Complete the following sentences with the adverb form of the adjective given in parenthesis.

1. Voy al cine _____ (frecuente) con mis amigos o hermanos.
2. _____ (General) vemos películas cómicas.
3. El protagonista actuaba muy _____ (lento).
4. Los otros actores trabajaron _____ (perfecto).
5. El director contó la historia muy _____ (claro).
6. A mí me gustó _____ (especial) la actriz principal.

2 ¿De qué manera? Use adverbs to tell how the following people do these activities.

▶ MODELO: *El examen es fácil. Yo hago el examen fácilmente.*

1. La explicación de Julia es muy clara. Julia explica las cosas muy _____.
2. Nuestras conversaciones son agradables. Luis y yo conversamos _____.
3. Mi trabajo es muy duro. Yo trabajo _____.
4. Ese tren es muy rápido. Ese tren anda muy _____.
5. La ropa de Verónica es elegante. Verónica se viste _____.
6. Carlos es un escritor profesional. Carlos escribe _____.

3 Estilo personal. In pairs, ask each other the following questions about how you, your family, or friends usually do things. Then, create five new questions with different adverbs about life at the university. Ask another pair your questions.

1. ¿Caminas rápidamente? ¿lentamente?
2. ¿Llegas a clase puntualmente todos los días?
3. ¿Chateas con tus amigos frecuentemente? ¿infrecuentemente?
4. ¿Esperas a tus amigos pacientemente? ¿impacientemente?
5. ¿Tus amigos se visten elegantemente para las fiestas?
6. ¿Te duchas inmediatamente después de levantarte todos los días?

4 Invitación. Discuss with your friend which type of movies you frequently like to see, those you generally don't like to see and where you normally see them. Use adverbs ending in **–mente** in your conversation.

CAMINOS DEL JAGUAR

¡Bomba!

Actividades

1 Comprensión. Based on this episode of *Caminos del jaguar,* choose the logical response.

1. Gafasnegras piensa que Nayeli...
   a. piensa demasiado.   b. pregunta demasiado.

2. Nayeli no sabe...
   a. adónde van.   b. dónde está Adriana.

3. Luis está muy interesado en...
   a. los prisioneros.   b. la computadora.

4. El primo de Luis está...
   a. muy importante.   b. muy impaciente.

5. Al final, Gafasnegras...
   a. le da la computadora a Luis. b. no le da la computadora a Luis.

6. Gafasnegras no necesita...
   a. el jaguar   b. a Nayeli.

2 Situaciones. Dramatize one of the following situations.

1. Gafasnegras tells Nayeli, Adriana, and Felipe that she is going to detonate the bomb.
2. Nayeli tells Gafasnegras and the cousins that Adriana and Felipe are innocent and should be let free.

3 Escritura. Write a brief summary of what happens in this episode with Adriana, Felipe and Nayeli. (4–6 sentences)

NOTA CULTURAL

El Centro Ceremonial Indígena de Tibes

Éste es el sitio arqueológico más importante del Caribe. Está cerca de la ciudad de Ponce, Puerto Rico y representa más de mil años de la historia de los indios taínos en la época precolombina. La excavación empezó en 1975 y el lugar es ahora un gran parque arqueológico con un importante museo. Todos los años llegan allí más de 80.000 visitantes para ver las casas de los taínos, llamadas *bohíos* y para ver los sitios dónde practicaban su religión y jugaban deportes como el fútbol.

Lectura

Online Study Center

For further reading practice online, visit the *Caminos* website at http://college .hmco.com/languages/ spanish/renjilian/caminos/ 3e/student_home.html.

PRELECTURA

Reading Strategy

Identifying main ideas

In *Unidad 3* you learned about skimming to determine the content and main ideas of a reading. In this unit you will focus on skimming to identify the main ideas of paragraphs. A reading or passage generally contains three important elements:

1. **Topic:** The topic or theme can often be found in titles and subtitles.
2. **Topic sentence:** The topic sentence, usually the first sentence in a paragraph, states the main idea of a paragraph.
3. **Supporting details:** These can be facts about the topic or anecdotes to make the subject more interesting.

Locating the topic sentence of each paragraph gives you critical clues about the main ideas of a passage. To identify the details that support the main ideas, you must read the selection more closely.

1 Sin diccionario. Without using a dictionary, quickly read the following selection about Caribbean sports. For each paragraph, identify and write the topic and topic sentence. Do not worry about the details.

▶ MODELO: Topic: *el béisbol*
Topic sentence: *En los países de Cuba, Puerto Rico y la República Dominicana, el deporte nacional es el béisbol.*

Diversos deportes del Caribe

El béisbol

En los países de Cuba, Puerto Rico y la República Dominicana, el deporte nacional es el béisbol. Muchos caribeños lo practican desde la llegada de los estadounidenses a las islas. Los chicos jóvenes juegan en las calles y en los parques y los partidos despiertan[1] gran interés en la población. Muchos jugadores dominicanos, cubanoamericanos y puertorriqueños juegan en las ligas profesionales de los Estados Unidos y varios de ellos han tenido grandes éxitos[2]. Cuba es el único país que por ahora prohíbe la participación de cubanos en las ligas norteamericanas. Este deporte es popular también en las regiones caribeñas de Panamá y Colombia, donde también hay exitosos equipos femeninos.

David Ortiz, jugador dominicano de béisbol en Estados Unidos

[1]awaken; [2]have been very successful.

El futbolista cubano Mikal Galindo, ahora juega en los Estados Unidos

Niños hispanos jugando al fútbol americano

El fútbol

Los indígenas mayas de Centroamérica y México y los arauacos[3] de la zona caribeña practicaban el fútbol en los juegos ceremoniales. Jugaban con una pesada[4] pelota de caucho[5] y usaban la cintura[6] para mantener la pelota en el aire sin tocar el suelo[7]. Este juego fue un precursor del juego moderno que conocemos hoy, con millones de aficionados en todo el mundo[8].

El fútbol americano

Los caribeños no juegan mucho este deporte, pero los partidos norteamericanos tienen espectadores en todo el mundo hispano porque se transmiten por los canales hispanos de televisión desde Miami. La gente de muchos países sabe los nombres de los equipos más populares de los Estados Unidos y es común encontrar a jóvenes que usan camisetas[9] y gorras con los emblemas de equipos populares de fútbol americano.

El básquetbol

El básquetbol es otro de los deportes populares en el Caribe y en gran parte de las regiones hispanas. La televisión de los Estados Unidos tuvo mucha influencia en su introducción en las islas del Caribe.

Jugadores puertorriqueños de básquetbol

---

[3]Arawak Indians [4]heavy; [5]rubber; [6]waist; [7]ground; [8]in the whole world; [9]T-shirts.

POSTLECTURA

👥 **2** **Información adicional.** In order to obtain additional information, read the selection again. Then, working in pairs, discuss these questions.

1. Describe la importancia en el Caribe de cada deporte mencionado en la lectura.
2. ¿Cuál es el deporte más popular en tu región? ¿Quiénes lo practican? ¿Cuál es tu equipo preferido?
3. ¿Cuál es el jugador más talentoso de este año en béisbol, fútbol o básquetbol? ¿Para qué equipo juega?
4. Compara tus preferencias deportivas con las de tus compañeros.

3 **Deportes en mi vida.** Write a paragraph about favorite sports in your school and your life. If you do not play sports, write about a friend or relative. Include answers to these questions.

1. ¿Qué deportes practican en tu universidad en las diferentes estaciones (en invierno, primavera, verano y otoño)? ¿Juegas tú en algún equipo de la escuela?
2. ¿Qué deportes prefieres como jugador/a o espectador/a? ¿Por qué?

4 **Un partido de béisbol.** You went to a baseball game during spring training and took this foto. Write a letter to a friend to describe your experience. Include the following information in your letter. Where did you go? What was the weather like? Who did you see play? What did you eat? Who won the game? What did you do after the game?

Escritura

Writing Strategy

Freewriting

One way to jump-start the writing process is to practice freewriting. This is a good way to see what ideas you may have about a subject before organizing your writing. The workshop provides some guidelines for generating ideas.

Online Study Center

For further writing practice online, visit the *Caminos* website at http://college .hmco.com/languages/ spanish/renjilian/caminos/ 3e/student_home.html.

Workshop

1. Choose a topic that you are going to write about in Spanish—one of your own or one that has been assigned. Write it at the top of the page.
2. You may either sit in front of the computer or write in longhand. Avoid the temptation you may have to correct errors while writing.
3. Write about the idea in Spanish for five to ten minutes without stopping. For now, don't correct grammar, spelling, accents, or punctuation.
4. If you do not know the conjugation of a verb, write the infinitive.
5. If you do not know the Spanish word, write the word in English so you don't lose your train of thought.
6. If you can't think of the next word, write the last word over and over again until you have an idea.
7. After you are finished, read over your writing. Underline or highlight the important ideas and organize them as part of your outline.
8. Now you can begin to write your composition using these ideas.

Strategy in Action

For additional practice with freewriting, complete the exercises below and in the *Escritura* section of your Student Activities Manual for *Unidad 6*.

1 El concierto ideal. You have been chosen to represent your school to organize a concert with two different artists or groups that represent your school population. Write a letter to the Dean of Students explaining who you want to invite and why.

2 Mi película favorita. Write a synopsis of your favorite movie of all time. Include the main characters, plot, and why you like the movie.

PRIMER PASO

ENJOYING MUSIC AND DANCE

Sustantivos

el acordeón	accordion
los audífonos	headphones
el bailarín/la bailarina	dancer
la balada	ballad
la banda	band
la batería	drum set
los blues	blues
la canción	song
el/la cantante	singer
las castañuelas	castanets
el concierto	concert
el conjunto	group, band
el disco compacto, CD	compact disc, CD
el flamenco	Spanish-style music
la flauta	flute
el grupo	group
la guitarra	guitar
la guitarra bajo	bass guitar
el/la guitarrista	guitarrist
el hip-hop	hip-hop
el jazz	jazz
la letra	lyrics
el mariachi	mariachi musician
el merengue	Dominican-style music
el/la músico/a	musician
el parlante	speaker
la percusión	percussion
el/la pianista	pianist
el piano	piano
la ranchera	Mexican-style music
el ritmo	rhythm
el rock	rock
la salsa	salsa (music)
el saxofón	saxophone
el tambor	drum
el tango	tango
el reproductor MP3	MP3 player
la trompeta	trumpet
el violín	violin
la voz	voice

Verbos

bailar	to dance
cantar	to sing
grabar	to record, tape
interpretar	to interpret
jugar un papel	to play a role
tocar (un instrumento)	to play (an instrument)
volverse	to become

TALKING ABOUT SPORTS AND EXERCISE

Sustantivos

el/la aficionado/a, fanático/a	fan
los anteojos	swim goggles
el básquetbol/baloncesto	basketball
el bate	baseball bat
el béisbol	baseball
la bicicleta	bicycle
el boxeo	boxing
la caminata	walking
la cancha	court, field
el casco	helmet
la cesta	wicker basket
el ciclismo	biking
el deporte	sport
el/la deportista	athlete; sports enthusiast
el/la entrenador/a	trainer
el equipo	team; equipment
el/la espectador/a	spectator
el esquí	ski; skiing
el fútbol	soccer
el fútbol americano	football
la gimnasia	gymnastics
el gimnasio	gym
el golf	golf
el gorro de baño	swim cap
el guante	baseball glove
el hockey	hockey
el jai alai	jai alai
el/la jugador/a	player
la natación	swimming

el palo de golf	*golf club*	el uniforme	*uniform*
el palo de hockey	*hockey stick*	el vestido de baño	*swimwear*
el partido	*game*	los zapatos de tenis	*tennis shoes, sneakers*
el patinaje	*skating*		
los patines de ruedas	*inline skates*	**Verbos**	
los patines para hielo	*ice skates*	entrenar	*to train*
la pelota, el balón	*ball*	esquiar	*to ski*
la pista	*ice rink; running track*	ganar	*to win*
la raqueta	*tennis racket*	jugar (ue) (al)	*to play (a sport or game)*
la ropa de gimnasia	*gymwear*	patear	*to kick*
el tenis	*tennis*	perder (ie)	*to lose*
		practicar	*to practice*

SEGUNDO PASO

DISCUSSING TELEVISION AND MOVIES

		la taquilla	*box office*
Sustantivos		la trama	*plot*
el acontecimiento	*event*	**Verbos**	
el actor	*actor*	actuar	*to act*
la actriz	*actress*	criticar	*to criticize*
la actuación	*acting*	dirigir	*to direct*
el argumento	*plot*	estrenar	*to premiere*
el billete, la entrada	*ticket*	filmar	*to film*
la cartelera	*listing*	hacer el papel	*to play a role*
la categoría	*category*	juzgar	*to judge*
el cine	*movies; movie theater*	nominar	*to nominate*
la comedia	*comedy*	presentar (pasar) una película	*to show a movie*
la crítica	*criticism*		
el director	*director*	reseñar	*to review*
el drama	*drama*	sentir (ie)	*to be sorry, regret*
la escena	*scene*	suceder	*to occur*
la fama	*fame*	tratar de	*to deal with, treat*
el filme	*film*		
el género	*genre*	**Adjetivos**	
el guión	*script*	ciencia ficción	*science fiction*
el largometraje	*feature film*	cómico/a	*funny (adj.)*
la narración	*narration*	de acción	*action (adj.)*
la nominación	*nomination*	de amor	*love (adj.)*
la pantalla	*screen*	de ciencia ficción	*science fiction (adj.)*
el papel	*role*	de horror, de terror	*horror (adj.)*
la película	*movie*	de misterio	*mystery (adj.)*
el personaje (principal, secundario)	*(main, secondary) character*	de suspenso	*thriller (adj.)*
		de vaqueros	*western (adj.)*
el/la protagonista	*main character*	extranjero/a	*foreign*
la reseña	*review*	romántico/a	*romantic*
la secuencia	*sequence*	taquillero/a	*box office draw / hit*
la sinopsis	*synopsis*		

EL CARIBE

Online Study Center

To learn more about the people featured in this section, visit the *Caminos* website at http://college .hmco.com/languages/ spanish/renjilian/caminos/ 3e/student_home.html.

PERSONALIDADES

Wilfredo Lam

Marc Anthony

José Alicea

Bebo Valdés

Juan Luis Guerra

Obie Bermúdez

Lila Downs

Israel "Cachao" López

Esmeralda Santiago

Elvis Crespo

Hay muchas personalidades importantes en las artes de las islas del Mar Caribe. Las influencias en muchas de sus creaciones de arte, música y literatura son de origen africano, indígena y europeo. Entre los artistas cubanos están Wilfredo Lam, pintor surrealista y Yamilys Brito, que incluye imágenes con palabras en algunas de sus obras artísticas. Entre los artistas importantes de Puerto Rico hay dos que crean carteles de acontecimientos en la isla: José Alicea y Lyzette Rosado. En la República Dominicana dos artistas famosos son Enriquillo Rodríguez y Clara Ledesma.

Muchos caribeños recibieron un Grammy Latino en 2005. De Puerto Rico ganaron Marc Anthony por el Mejor Álbum de Salsa; Elvis Crespo por el Mejor Álbum de Merengue y Mejor Álbum de Rock Vocal; y Obie Bermúdez, por el Mejor Vocal Pop Masculino. También el dominicano Juan Luis Guerra ganó en dos categorías: el Mejor Álbum Cristiano en español y la Mejor Canción Tropical del año. Entre los cubanos, Bebo Valdés ganó por el Mejor Álbum de Jazz Latino; Israel "Cachao" López por el Mejor Álbum Tropical Tradicional y la cantante Lila Downs, que nació en Cuba, recibió el Grammy Latino por el Mejor Álbum Folklórico de 2005.

Hay muchos escritores caribeños de importancia en las épocas recientes. La puertorriqueña Esmeralda Santiago, la dominicana Julia Álvarez y la cubana Cristina García son tres novelistas que viven en Estados Unidos y escriben sobre la condición humana de los caribeños. Visita el sitio web de *Caminos* para leer más en español sobre estas personalidades y otros caribeños influyentes.

> "Crecer no tiene que ver con ser famoso, crecer está dentro de ti. Y llevar la música de mi pueblo es lo que me ha hecho crecer". —Carlos Vives (Colombia)

Comprensión

Trabajando en parejas, háganse las preguntas.

1. ¿Qué influencias hay sobre el arte, la música y la literatura del Caribe? ¿Conoces alguna obra de los artistas mencionados?
2. ¿En qué categorías ganaron los cantantes los Grammy Latinos? ¿Cuál prefieres escuchar tú? ¿Por qué?

ARTE

AIMÉE GARCÍA

Aimée García es una artista cubana que nació en 1972 en la ciudad de Matanzas. Su arte apareció en muchas exhibiciones en Cuba, México, Corea del Sur y Estados Unidos. En el año 1999 pintó *La guía*°, pintura que es una combinación de óleo en lienzo°, con hilo° y madera°.

guide

La guía

oil on canvas
string / wood

Comprensión

Trabajando en parejas, estudien esta pintura y contesten las preguntas.

1. La artista está pintando una escena con árboles°. ¿Qué colores usa para pintar la escena? En tu opinión, ¿qué hora del día es?   *trees*
2. Describe a la artista en la pintura. ¿De qué color es su vestido? ¿Cuántos años crees que tiene ella? ¿Cuántos años tiene la artista Aimée García?
3. ¿Qué función tiene la jirafa°? ¿Hay otro animal posible?   *giraffe*
4. ¿De qué colores es la jirafa? En tu opinión, ¿qué efecto produce en la pintura? ¿cómico? ¿absurdo? ¿interesante? ¿...? ¿Por qué?
5. ¿Qué relación hay entre la fotografía de la artista y la artista en la pintura? ¿Son dos mujeres diferentes o es la misma persona?
6. ¿Te gusta o no te gusta esta pintura? ¿Por qué?

MÚSICA

OLGA TAÑÓN

La artista musical, Olga Tañón, es puertorriqueña. Ganó
un Grammy Latino de la Mejor Interpretación Vocal
Femenina de 2003 por su álbum, "Sobrevivir°". Ella canta
diversos estilos musicales como merengue y balada pop.
Tañón incluye en su nuevo álbum, "A puro fuego°", sus
discos más celebrados de los diez años pasados de su
carrera.

Survive

Pure Fire

Comprensión

Trabajen en parejas para contestar las preguntas.

1. ¿De dónde es Olga Tañón?
2. Según la lectura, ¿qué tipo de música canta? ¿Qué premio ganó?
3. ¿Cómo se llaman dos de sus álbumes musicales? ¿Qué emociones despiertan
   los títulos?
4. ¿A qué otro/a cantante hispánico/a conoces? ¿De dónde es? ¿Qué canta?

LITERATURA

NORBERTO JAMES RAWLINGS

El autor Norberto James Rawlings nació en la República Dominicana
en 1945. Este poeta dominicano es también profesor de español.
Se graduó de la Universidad de La Habana y, en 1992, recibió su
doctorado en lengua y literatura hispánica de Boston University.
Los poemas aquí son de su nuevo libro, *La urdimbre del silencio*
(*The Weaving of Silence*), que se publicó en 2000 en La República
Dominicana.

> "...tengo el gusto de andar por mi país,
> dueño de cuanto hay en él".
> —Nicolás Guillén (Cuba), "Tengo"

"Estatuas"

Las estatuas
mueren también,
si nadie las mira.

Comprensión

En parejas, contesten las preguntas.

1. ¿Es el poema sobre las personas, los lugares o las cosas?
2. En la opinión del poeta, ¿cuándo mueren las estatuas?
3. El poeta indica que las estatuas son como personas. ¿Qué opinas tú?
4. Describe una estatua famosa de tu región: ¿De qué color es? ¿Dónde está? ¿Es grande o pequeña? ¿De qué o de quién es? ¿Por qué es importante? ¿Por qué (no) te gusta?

"Apuntes° para el poema"

Hice apuntes
para escribir un poema a la primavera,
y de tanto (re)escribirlo,
sólo quedó de las flores,
el recuerdo° de su aroma,
y mi asombro° ante tanto verdor°.

Notes

memory
amazement / greenness

Comprensión

Trabajando en parejas, contesten las preguntas.

1. Antes de crear el poema, ¿qué escribió el poeta?
2. ¿A qué estación del año le escribió el poema?
3. ¿Qué quedó de las flores que el poeta puso en el poema?
4. Al final del poema, ¿qué color asocia el poeta con la primavera?
5. ¿De qué color es tu flor favorita? ¿Tiene un aroma delicado o fuerte?
6. ¿Te gustan más las flores de la primavera o del verano? En tu región, ¿hay flores también en el otoño o en el invierno?

7

De compras

VOCABULARIO Y LENGUA

► Talking about stores and shopping
► Shopping for clothes
► Contrasting the preterite and the imperfect: Verbs with different meanings in the preterite: **Conocer, poder, querer, saber**

► Bargaining in a marketplace
► Asking for and giving directions
► Making comparisons; Superlatives; Possessive pronouns

CAMINOS DEL JAGUAR

► Ganas de vivir
► Magia en Mitad del Mundo

LECTURA

► Soy Rumiaya, el alma de la roca

NOTAS CULTURALES

► Quito, Ecuador
► El nombre del Ecuador

ESTRATEGIAS

► **Reading:** Tapping background knowledge
► **Writing:** Paraphrasing

Rafael González y González, *Mercadito*

Preguntas del tema

- ► ¿Te gusta ir de compras? ¿Por qué?

- ► ¿Cuál es tu tienda favorita? ¿Qué venden?

- ► ¿Qué ropa prefieres llevar a las fiestas? ¿y a las clases?

- ► ¿Qué regalos compras para tus amigos?

PRIMER PASO

Vocabulario y lengua

TALKING ABOUT STORES AND SHOPPING

En el almacén Márquez

Store clerk	**Dependiente**°	Buenos días señor, ¿en qué le puedo servir?
customer	Sebastián (**Cliente**°)	Es el cumpleaños de mi novia Raquel, y necesito un regalo especial para ella. ¿Tiene Ud. alguna sugerencia?
Of course!	Dependiente	**¡Claro que sí!**° Tenemos muchas cosas bonitas... joyas, perfumes, ropa.
shop window / size	Sebastián	Vi unos suéteres en el **escaparate**°, pero no sé su **talla**°.
	Dependiente	¿Quizás un reloj o un perfume?
	Sebastián	¿Cuánto cuestan los relojes?
[1]**nuevo sol** = currency in Perú	Dependiente	Tenemos una selección amplia desde 475 nuevos soles[1].
to spend	Sebastián	Uf, realmente no puedo **gastar**° tanto. ¿Tiene algo **a un precio más bajo**°?
at a lower price		
display case	Dependiente	Pues, aquí en el **mostrador**° tenemos perfumes finos desde 167 nuevos soles.
on sale	Sebastián	¿Hay alguna fragancia **en oferta**°?
	Dependiente	Bueno, en oferta tenemos la fragancia "Pasión". Si la compra, Ud. recibe una bufanda **gratis**°.
free		
deal / I'll take it!	Sebastián	¡Qué **ganga**°! **¡Me la llevo!**°
register / receipt	Dependiente	Bueno, puede pagar en la **caja**°. Aquí tiene el **recibo**° si la quiere **devolver**°.
to return		
	Sebastián	Gracias.

Many store names are formed by adding **-ería** to the type of products they sell or services they provide. Others, such as music or department stores, tend to have individual brand names. Note that the word farmacia does not have an accent on the **"i"**. The stress falls on the syllable **"ma"**.

Online Study Center

For additional practice with this unit's vocabulary and grammar, visit the *Caminos* website at http://college.hmco.com/ languages/spanish/ renjilian/caminos/3e/ student_home.html. You can also review audio flashcards, quiz yourself, and explore related Spanish-language sites.

Actividades

1 ¿Dónde se compra? ¿En qué tipo de tienda puedes comprar estos artículos?

1. aspirina
2. unos guantes
3. una fragancia Armani
4. maquillaje *(makeup)*
5. una novela de amor
6. un cuaderno
7. unas rosas
8. un reloj
9. una raqueta de tenis

2 Quiero devolver el perfume. Raquel decide devolver el perfume que le compró su novio, Sebastián, porque no le gustó la fragancia. Escucha su conversación con el dependiente del almacén y completa las frases.

1. Raquel habló con...

   a. Sebastián.
   b. el dependiente.
   c. Patricia.

2. Raquel no tenía el recibo porque...

   a. lo perdió.
   b. el perfume fue un regalo.
   c. compró el perfume en otra tienda.

3. El dependiente le podía ofrecer...

   a. el dinero.
   b. otra fragancia.
   c. crédito.

4. El dependiente le dijo a Raquel que...

   a. el perfume estaba en oferta.
   b. el perfume era caro.
   c. el perfume era verde y azul.

5. El perfume incluía...

   a. un pastel de cumpleaños.
   b. una bufanda verde y azul.
   c. una bufanda azul y roja.

6. La mujer en la joyería...

   a. compraba un reloj.
   b. compraba perfume.
   c. llevaba una bufanda.

7. Raquel estaba sorprendida porque...

   a. la mujer con la bufanda era su amiga.
   b. no le gustaba la bufanda.
   c. la bufanda era bonita.

3 En la tienda. Estás en una tienda comprando algo para tus vacaciones. Completa la conversación entre el/la cliente y el/la dependiente. Trabajen en parejas. parejas.

Dependiente Buenas tardes. ¿ _____ servir?

Cliente Buenas tardes. Voy de vacaciones este fin de semana y necesito _____.

Dependiente ¿Adónde va?

Cliente _____.

Dependiente ¡Ah, qué bien, es un lugar maravilloso y además lo que *(what)* Ud. busca está en _____!

Cliente ¡Qué suerte! También necesito _____ porque allí hace mucho sol.

Dependiente	Pues tenemos una gran variedad. Hay en todos los colores.
Cliente	¿Dónde están?
Dependiente	Aquí en el _____.
Cliente	¿ _____ ?
Dependiente	Sí, lo tenemos en rojo.
Cliente	¿ _____ ?
Dependiente	Todo le cuesta $25. Puede Ud. pagar en la _____.
Cliente	Gracias.

4 El triángulo amoroso. Raquel decide hablar con Sebastián y Patricia para decirles lo que pasó cuando ella fue a la tienda para devolver el perfume. Inventa su conversación. Trabajen en grupos de tres.

SHOPPING FOR CLOTHES

Comprando ropa *(Buying clothes)*

1. la chaqueta
2. el traje
3. la camisa
4. la ropa interior
5. los pantalones
6. el abrigo
7. el impermeable
8. el saco
9. el vestido
10. la blusa
11. la falda
12. las botas
13. los zapatos
14. los calcetines
15. las medias
16. el cinturón
17. la bolsa
18. los guantes
19. el sombrero
20. la gorra
21. la bufanda
22. la corbata

de puntos

de rayas

de cuadros

La ropa del golfista
le queda floja/grande.
(fits him loosely)

de manga larga   de manga corta

de tacón alto   de tenis

La ropa de la muchacha
le queda estrecha/pequeña.
(fits her tightly)

La ropa del golfista **le queda floja / grande.**
(is loose / big)

La ropa de la muchacha **le queda estrecha /
pequeña.** *(is tight / small)*

Más palabras y expresiones

Sustantivos

el algodón	*cotton*
la camiseta	*T-shirt*
la lana	*wool*
la mancha	*stain*
el par	*pair*
el paraguas	*umbrella*
la ropa interior	*underwear*
la seda	*silk*
la sudadera	*sweatsuit, sweatshirt*
el suéter	*sweater*

Verbos

(des)atar	*to (un)tie*
estar / de moda	*in style*
estar	*to be in style*
estar roto/a, sucio/a, manchado/a	*to be ripped, dirty, stained*
ir de compras	*to go shopping*
llevar	*to wear*
probarse (ue)	*to try on*
quedarle (a alguien)	*to fit (someone)*

Actividades

 1 ¿Qué piensas comprar? ¿Qué ropa piensas comprar para estas ocasiones?
Haz una lista para cada ocasión y compárala con la lista de un/a compañero/a.

1. asistir a un partido de fútbol americano
2. ir a una discoteca nueva
3. ir a la fiesta de cumpleaños de tu novio/a
4. presentarte a tu primera entrevista *(interview)* de trabajo
5. ir a la playa
6. ir a esquiar
7. asistir a una boda muy elegante
8. ir a la clase de español

2 ¿Qué está de moda? Describe lo que llevan estas personas.

3 ¿Qué lleva? Trae una foto de un/a amigo/a o de una persona famosa a la clase y describe lo que lleva.

4 Entre nosotros. Trabaja con un/a compañero/a para crear un diálogo entre un/a dependiente de una tienda de ropa y un/a cliente que llega a última hora.

Cliente	Dependiente
Hoy estuviste de compras en una tienda de ropa. Cuando llegas a casa, te das cuenta de que la ropa que compraste tiene una mancha y no la puedes usar en la fiesta de esta noche. Decides regresar a la tienda para devolverla y comprar algo diferente. Estás de muy mal humor y tienes mucha prisa porque ya es bastante tarde. ¿Qué haces?	Trabajas en una tienda de ropa pequeña. Estás muy cansado/a porque hoy fue un día muy largo. Faltan quince minutos para cerrar y de repente llega un/a cliente para cambiar ropa que está manchada. Tu jefe/a se llevó las llaves de la caja y no puedes abrirla para atender al /a la cliente. Soluciona el dilema.

CONTRASTING THE PRETERITE AND THE IMPERFECT

Preterite or imperfect?

In narration, the imperfect establishes the context of the story by describing the background of what happened, the physical and mental states of the speakers or characters, what things looked like, and how they used to be. In contrast, the preterite moves the story forward in time by providing an account of what happened at a specific moment in time: what people said or did, and what events took place. Review what you have learned about these forms in *Unidades 4, 5,* and *6* before you read the following summary of their uses.

The preterite is used . . .	The imperfect is used . . .
▶ To indicate a completed action in the past.	▶ To set up a continuous background or a scenario in which events or actions occur in the past. This includes telling time, indicating age, and describing weather in the past.

Ayer **fui** a la tienda.

Yesterday I went to the store.

Eran las siete de la mañana. **Hacía** sol y no **llovía.**

It was seven o'clock A.M. It was sunny and it wasn't raining.

▶ To indicate a series of completed actions in the past.	▶ To describe mental, emotional, or physical states or conditions in the past.

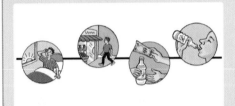

Esta mañana **me desperté, fui** a la tienda, **compré** un refresco y lo **bebí.**

This morning I woke up, went to the store, bought a soft drink and drank it.

Yo **pensaba** que mis llaves **estaban** en la mesita de noche.

I thought that my keys were on the nightstand.

▶ To indicate the beginning of an action or a condition.	▶ To describe actions and events that were in progress in the past without emphasis on when they started or ended.

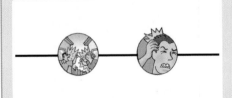

A las seis de la mañana, mis vecinos **empezaron** a gritar y me **dio** dolor de cabeza.

At 6 A.M. my neighbors started to yell and it gave me a headache.

Corría rápidamente en el parque.

I was running very fast in the park.

(continued)

▶ To indicate the ending of an action or condition.

La fiesta **terminó** a las *2 A.M.*

The party ended at 2 A.M.

▶ To describe repetitive or habitual past actions—what one used to do.

Almorzábamos juntas todos los sábados.

We used to eat lunch together every Saturday.

▶ To sum up a past action, condition, or opinion.

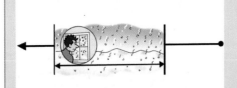

Nevó todo el día ayer. **Fue** un día horrible. No me **gustó** estar en casa.

It snowed all day yesterday. It was a horrible day. I didn't like staying at home.

▶ With **ir a** + *infinitive* to anticipate "what was going to (would) happen."

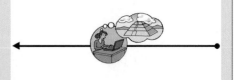

Iba a viajar a Teotihuacán pero tuve que trabajar.

I was going to travel to Teotihuacán but I had to work.

Using the preterite and the imperfect together

When you are talking about the past in Spanish, the imperfect and the preterite often appear together. The combination of these two tenses adds interest and suspense to the narration.

1. Background / scenario
The imperfect describes the scene or provides background information while the preterite narrates the events that happened at that moment.

Estaba lloviendo cuando **salimos** del cine.

It was raining when we left the movie theater.

2. Interrupted actions

In this case, the ongoing action doesn't continue because it is interrupted by what happens.

Lorenzo **miraba** sus telenovelas cuando el teléfono **sonó**.

Lorenzo was watching his soap operas when the phone rang.

3. Retelling: Indirect speech

Use the preterite to introduce indirect speech. The imperfect is used when retelling what someone said, thought, believed, wanted to do, or knew.

Lo siento, pero no te quiero.

Adelaida le **dijo** a Lorenzo que no lo **quería**.

Adelaida told Lorenzo that she didn't love him.

Verbs with different meanings in the preterite:
Conocer, poder, querer, saber

Some Spanish verbs have different English translations when used in the preterite. The meaning of these verbs in the imperfect remains consistent with their meaning in the present and infinitive forms. Below is a list of these verbs:

Infinitive	Preterite	Imperfect
conocer	*met a person or visited a place for the first time*	*knew, was familiar with, used to know*
poder	*managed (to do something)*	*was able to, was allowed to, could*
no poder	*was not able to do it (and didn't do it), didn't manage (to do something)*	*was not able to do it, could not do it (unknown outcome)*
querer	*intended to; wanted to but didn't do it*	*wanted to (unknown outcome)*
no querer	*refused (to do something)*	*didn't want to, wasn't feeling up to it (unknown outcome)*
saber	*found out; realized*	*used to know, knew (information)*

Conocí a Pablo en la fiesta.	*I met Pablo at the party.*
Conocimos París en la primavera.	*We visited Paris in the spring. (for the first time)*
Pude terminar la novela.	*I managed to finish the novel.*
No **pudieron** venir a la fiesta.	*They weren't able to come to the party. (and didn't)*
Quise llamarte, pero mi teléfono no funcionó.	*I intended to call you, but my phone didn't work.*
Supe la verdad ayer.	*I found out the truth yesterday.*

Actividades

1 ¡De perezoso a heroico! El dramático día de Diego. Lee este cuento en voz alta *(aloud)* y haz las actividades.

1. Identifica las formas del pretérito y del imperfecto.
2. En parejas, identifiquen el uso de los verbos según la lista de arriba.
3. Inventen y contesten preguntas en el pasado sobre la historia de Diego. Pongan atención al uso del pretérito y del imperfecto.

Era muy tarde.

Perdí el tren.

El jefe no tenía ningún interés.

Vimos a dos personas que salían del almacén.

Me llamo Diego y trabajo en el Almacén Rodríguez de las cuatro de la tarde hasta las once de la noche. El jueves pasado fue un día horrible. Era muy tarde cuando me desperté, entonces salí corriendo de casa y se me olvidó el horario del tren. Por supuesto, perdí el tren de las tres y diez de la tarde y tuve que tomar el siguiente tren, una hora después. Cuando hablé con el jefe, se puso furioso porque llegué tarde. Traté de explicarle mi problema, pero él no tenía ningún interés en escuchar mis excusas. Me dijo que yo era un irresponsable; me criticó por ser perezoso y me hizo sentir muy mal.

Mi amiga Julia trabaja en el departamento de computadoras de la misma tienda, y yo soy dependiente en el departamento de música. Ese jueves por la tarde estuve muy ocupado con muchos clientes, y vendí bastantes artículos caros. Luego, a las nueve, Julia y yo salimos a cenar. Fuimos a nuestro restaurante ecuatoriano favorito. Comimos en una hora porque teníamos que regresar al trabajo.

Cuando regresamos al almacén, no había ni una estrella en el cielo. Eran las diez de la noche y todo estaba oscuro. Al acercarnos, vimos a dos personas que salían del almacén cargando máquinas pequeñas: eran una mujer alta, rubia, bien vestida y un hombre grande, de pelo oscuro y también muy elegante. A pesar de *(Despite)* las apariencias, yo estaba seguro de que eran dos ladrones *(thieves)*. De inmediato corrí hacia ellos y Julia llamó a los detectives de la tienda. Los guardias llegaron junto con la policía y se llevaron a los ladrones. ¡Fue un día muy dramático!

2 ¿Pretérito o imperfecto? Completa las oraciones con el pretérito o imperfecto según el contexto.

1. Cuando Delmira _____ (tener) diez años, todas las noches _____ (escuchar) los cuentos *(stories)* de su abuela.

2. Los jóvenes del conjunto Maná _____ (tocar) continuamente. Ellos _____ (ir) a ser ricos y famosos algún día. Y en efecto, en los años 80 y 90 el grupo _____ (vender) millones de discos.

3. Hoy yo _____ (levantarse), _____ (hacer) la cama, _____ (lavar) la ropa y _____ (pasar) la aspiradora por la alfombra. _____ (Ser) una mañana muy productiva.

4. La noche _____ (estar) muy oscura cuando un hombre misterioso _____ (salir) a la calle.

3 **Un viaje por El Caribe.** Olga y Rubén hicieron un viaje por el Caribe. Completa la historia de su viaje con los verbos **conocer, querer, poder,** y **saber** en el pretérito o el imperfecto, según el contexto.

En junio Olga y Rubén hicieron un viaje por el Caribe. Fueron a la República Dominicana porque ellos _____ (**1.** querer) conocerla. En este viaje Olga y Rubén _____ (**2.** conocer) Santo Domingo y otras ciudades dominicanas. Ellos no _____ (**3.** poder) ir a Puerto Rico porque Rubén no _____ (**4.** querer = *refused*); él prefirió ir a Cuba, el país de sus antepasados (*ancestors*). Cuando llegaron a Cuba, Olga _____ (**5.** saber) que los bisabuelos de Rubén eran de Aragón, España. Esto le pareció interesantísimo y ella _____ (**6.** querer) saber más sobre la familia de Rubén. Una señora cubana que _____ (**7.** saber) mucho sobre genealogía la ayudó. De esta manera, ellos _____ (**8.** saber) que un bisabuelo de Rubén ¡era puertorriqueño! Por esta razón van a buscar sus raíces (*roots*) en la isla de Puerto Rico el año que viene.

4 **Fractura.** Completa el cuento del accidente de Yolanda con la forma correcta del pretérito o imperfecto.

Siempre _____ (**1.** hacer) deportes cuando _____ (**2.** ser) joven. A veces me _____ (**3.** gustar) mucho patinar en línea (*to rollerblade*). Una vez, cuando yo _____ (**4.** tener) quince años, patinaba con unos amigos, y de pronto, yo _____ (**5.** caerse). Ellos me _____ (**6.** llevar) al hospital. Mientras yo _____ (**7.** estar) en mi cama con mucho dolor, _____ (**8.** llegar) el médico y me _____ (**9.** decir): "Tú no _____ (**10.** llevar) casco cuando tú _____ (**11.** caerse), ¿verdad?" Yo le _____ (**12.** preguntar) al doctor: "¿Cómo sabe usted que yo no _____ (**13.** llevar) el casco?" Y el doctor _____ (**14.** contestar), "No es difícil saberlo. ¡Me lo _____ (**15.** decir) la fractura que tienes en la cabeza (*head*)!"

5 **Yolanda.** Iris y Lilia hablan de lo que le ocurrió a Yolanda. Crea su conversación usando el pretérito e imperfecto. Palabras y frases útiles: patinar (*to skate, rollerblade*), (no) aceptar, (no) ponerse el casco, chocarse contra un poste (*to crash into a post*), tener un accidente, terminar en el hospital (*to end up in the hospital*).

Ganas de vivir

Actividades

Online Study Center

For additional practice with this episode, visit the *Caminos* website at http://college.hmco.com/languages/spanish/renjilian/caminos/3e/student_home.html.

1 Comprensión. Basándote en este episodio de *Caminos del jaguar,* elige la alternativa lógica.

1. Don Gustavo...
   a. no sabe lo que pasó en Puerto Rico.
   b. sabe lo que pasó en Puerto Rico.

2. Felipe dice que...
   a. estaban disfrutando de Puerto Rico.
   b. estaban estudiando en Puerto Rico.

3. Felipe quedó libre porque...
   a. se desató los pies.
   b. Adriana le desató los pies.

4. Felipe movió la cubeta...
   a. con las manos.
   b. con los pies.

5. ¿Quién tenía mucho miedo?
   a. Adriana y Felipe
   b. Gafasnegras

6. Para poder escapar, Adriana y Felipe...
   a. quebraron la computadora.
   b. quebraron la ventana.

7. Gafasnegras se sorprende porque...
   a. Miguel vio a Adriana y Felipe.
   b. Adriana y Felipe están vivos.

8. El jaguar Hun-Ahau está en...
   a. la casa de Nayeli.
   b. la casa de doña Carmen.

9. El paquete con el jaguar llegó a...
   a. Puerto Rico.
   b. Ecuador

2 Situaciones. Dramaticen una de las siguientes situaciones.

1. La conversación de don Gustavo y Adriana sobre lo que pasó en Puerto Rico.
2. La conversación entre Gafasnegras y Miguel.

3 Escritura. Escribe un resumen de lo que hacen Adriana y Felipe en Mitad del Mundo. (4–6 frases)

NOTA CULTURAL

Quito, Ecuador

Entre las capitales latinoamericanas, Quito —a 2.640 metros de altura— es la segunda en altura después de La Paz, Bolivia. Su población, de más de un millón de habitantes, comparte las herencias inca y española. La capital está al pie del volcán Pichincha. El centro antiguo de la ciudad conserva su arquitectura colonial: calles estrechas y empinadas (*steep*), casas blancas y hermosas iglesias con altares de oro. Al norte se encuentra el Quito moderno: anchas avenidas, parques y contemporáneos edificios y casas.

SEGUNDO PASO

Vocabulario y lengua

BARGAINING IN A MARKETPLACE

Los mercados y el arte del regateo

bargaining	El **regateo°** es el arte de negociar un precio más bajo. En los mercados de
handicrafts	**artesanías°** y en las tiendas pequeñas de España y América Latina, todavía es usual
to bargain	**regatear°** por el precio. En los mercados de las ciudades pequeñas, como Otavalo,
	al norte de Quito, los
street vendors	**vendedores ambulantes°**
jewelry / weavings	ofrecen **joyas°**, ropa, **tejidos°**
	y artesanías, y los
buyers	**compradores°** tienen la
discount	costumbre de pedir **rebaja°**
	en el precio.

Cómo regatear

Para regatear en español como un experto, sigue los pasos y usa las expresiones que se detallan abajo.

1. Pide el precio: **¿Cuánto cuesta/n?, ¿En cuánto me lo(s) / la(s) deja?, ¿Qué precio tiene/n...?**
2. Reacciona: **¿20 pesos? ¿Tanto?** *(That much?)* **(¿Tan caro?)** *(That expensive?)*
3. Ofrece un precio más bajo u otra estrategia para conseguir una rebaja en el precio:

Es muy caro/a.	**¿Qué tal _____ pesos?**
Son muy caros/as.	**¿Me puede dar un descuento**
No voy a pagar tanto.	*(discount)***?**
No me alcanza el dinero.	**¿Son más baratos/as si compro dos?**
Le puedo dar _____ pesos.	

4. Si el vendedor no te ofrece un precio más bajo, repite los pasos anteriores para negociar un precio promedio *(average)*.
5. Si el vendedor no quiere ofrecer una rebaja, indica que vas a buscar en otro lugar: **Bueno, voy a ver si no lo/la compro por menos en otro lado** *(somewhere else)*.
6. Si se ponen de acuerdo en *(you both agree on)* un precio, haz la compra y no te olvides de darle las gracias al vendedor: **Muchas gracias. Lo agradezco.**

Estas son algunas de las cosas que venden en los mercados.

Joyas

un anillo de esmeralda

un collar de plata con un pendiente de turquesa

una pulsera de cobre

unos aretes de piedra

un prendedor de oro

Artesanías

un tapete de lana

un plato de Talavera

un recipiente de barro

un tapiz de algodón

un juguete de madera

una máscara de jaguar

Actividades

1 **Un regateo.** Escucha la conversación de un regateo entre una turista y un vendedor en un mercado hispano y contesta las preguntas.

1. ¿Qué busca la turista? ¿Para quién?
2. ¿Cuánto cuestan las joyas originalmente?
3. ¿Cuánto dinero ofrece la turista después?
4. ¿Cómo contesta el vendedor?
5. ¿Qué decide hacer la turista?
6. ¿Cómo responde el vendedor?
7. ¿Cuál es el último precio que paga la turista?
8. ¿Cuánto dinero ahorra en el regateo? ¿Fue una ganga?

2 Comprando regalos. Estás de vacaciones y tienes que comprar regalos para las personas de la lista. Describe los regalos que les vas a comprar y por qué.

1. tu hermano/a
2. tu mejor amigo
3. tu mejor amiga
4. tu novio/a
5. tu madre
6. tu padre
7. una prima de quince años
8. un niño de diez años

3 El regateo. Estás en el mercado comprando regalos, pero todos los vendedores te dan precios diferentes. Crea una conversación con un/a vendedor/a. Tú regateas para obtener el mejor precio. Trabajen en parejas.

ASKING FOR AND GIVING DIRECTIONS

¿Dónde está?

Perdone la molestia, pero ¿nos puede decir dónde está el museo?

Sí, señores, sigan derecho por tres cuadras, pasen por la catedral y doblen a la izquierda. El museo está a tres cuadras a la derecha.

Más palabras y expresiones

Sustantivos

la cuadra	*street block*
la esquina	*corner*
la intersección	*intersection*
el semáforo	*traffic light*

Verbos

acelerar	*to accelerate*	parar	*to stop*
bajar (por)	*to go (down) (a street)*	pasar (por)	*to pass (by)*
cruzar	*to cross*	seguir derecho, recto	*to go straight*
dar la vuelta	*to turn around*	subir (por)	*to go up (a street)*
doblar (a)	*to turn*	tener cuidado	*to be careful*
estacionar	*to park*		

continued

Otras expresiones

a la (mano) derecha / izquierda	*on the right / left(hand) side*
¿Cómo se llega a...?	*How does one get to . . . ?*
despacio	*slowly*
hasta	*until*
¿Me puede decir dónde está/n...?	*Can you tell me where . . . is / are?*
medio/a *(adj.)*	*half*

Note: Be sure to review formal commands in *Unidad 6,* pages 224–225, so that you can use the appropriate forms for giving directions.

Actividades

1 ¿Dónde están ustedes? Tú y tu amigo están de vacaciones y piden instrucciones de cómo se llega de un lugar al otro. Mientras escuchas las instrucciones, sigue el mapa para determinar hasta dónde llegan Uds.

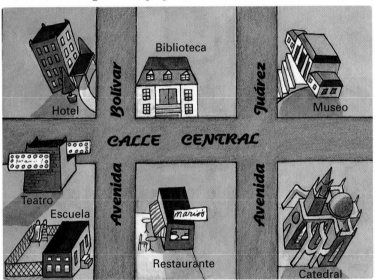

¿Dónde están Uds.?

1. _____   3. _____
2. _____   4. _____

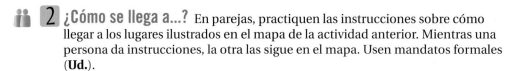

2 ¿Cómo se llega a...? En parejas, practiquen las instrucciones sobre cómo llegar a los lugares ilustrados en el mapa de la actividad anterior. Mientras una persona da instrucciones, la otra las sigue en el mapa. Usen mandatos formales (**Ud.**).

¿Cómo se llega...

1. del museo al teatro?
2. del hotel al restaurante?
3. de la catedral al hotel?
4. de la escuela a la catedral?
5. de la biblioteca al museo?

3 ¿Dónde está? Una persona importante visita tu universidad y necesita saber cómo llegar a estos lugares desde la clase de español. Trabajen en parejas y usen mandatos formales (**Ud.**).

1. la cafetería
2. el edificio de la administración
3. el gimnasio
4. la biblioteca
5. la librería
6. la Facultad de Ciencias Naturales
7. la Facultad de Artes
8. la cancha de fútbol americano
9. el centro estudiantil

MAKING COMPARISONS

Making unequal comparisons

Spanish uses the following structures to compare adjectives *(age, size, appearance, and other characteristics of people and things)*, adverbs *(how people do things)*, and nouns *(people and things themselves)* that are different, and verbs *(things that people do)*.

Comparing adjectives

más (*more*) / **menos** (*less*) + (adjective) + **que** (*than*)

El edificio es **más** alto **que** la casa.
The building is taller than the house.
La casa es **menos** alta **que** el edificio.
The house is less tall than the building.

Comparing adverbs

más (*more*) / **menos** (*less*) +
(adverb) + **que** (*than*)

El auto rojo va **más** rápido **que** el auto azul.
The red car goes faster than the blue car.
El auto azul va **menos** rápido **que** el auto rojo.
The blue car goes slower than the red car.

Comparing nouns

más (*more*) / **menos** (*less*) +
(noun) + **que** (*than*)

El muchacho tiene **más** dinero **que** la muchacha.
The boy has more money than the girl.
La muchacha tiene **menos** dinero **que** el muchacho.
The girl has less money than the boy.

Comparing verbs

verb + **más** / **menos** + **que**

Yo trabajo **más que** mi compañera.
I work more than my roommate.
Mi compañera trabaja **menos que** yo.
My roommate works less than I do.

When comparing people using pronouns, use the subject pronouns.

Tú sabes muchas **más**
cosas **que yo.**
Ellos tienen **menos** dinero
que nosotros.

*You know a lot more
things than I do.*
*They have less money than
we do.*

When a number is mentioned in the comparison, the equivalent of *than* is **de:**
más / menos + **de** + *number*.

Hay **más de tres** kilómetros
hasta el centro.
La cena me costó **menos de
diez** dólares.

*It's more than three
kilometers to downtown.*
*Dinner cost me less than ten
dollars.*

Some comparisons have an irregular form:

Adjective		Irregular comparative form	
bueno/a buenos/as	*good*	mejor/es	*better*
malo/a malos/as	*bad*	peor/es	*worse*
joven / jóvenes	*young*	menor/es	*younger*
viejo/a viejos/as	*old*	mayor/es	*older*

Adverb		Irregular comparative form	
bien	*well*	mejor	*better*
mal	*bad, ill*	peor	*worse*
mucho	*a lot*	más	*more*
poco	*a little*	menos	*less*

Superlatives

To form the superlative, English adds *-est* to the adjective *(the cleanest, the newest)* or uses expressions such as *the most* or *the least* with the adjective *(the most convenient, the least expensive)*. In Spanish, superlatives are formed as follows:

Superlatives

el / la / los / las (+ noun) + **más /menos** + adjective (+ **de**...)

el / la / los / las + mejor(es) / peor(es) (+ noun) (+ **de**...)

el / la / los / las (+ noun) + **mayor(es) / menor(es)** (+ **de**...)

Antonio Banderas es **el actor más famoso de** España.	*Antonio Banderas is the most famous actor of Spain.*
Ellas son **las más elegantes del** grupo.	*They are the most elegant of the group.*
¿Cuál es **la mejor película de** este año?	*Which is the best movie of the year?*
Ésta es **la peor hora del** día.	*This is the worst time of the day.*
Yo soy **la hermana mayor de** todos.	*I am the oldest sister of all the siblings.*

The superlative uses the preposition **de** to express *in* or *of.* Note that the irregular forms **mejor/es** and **peor/es** usually appear before the noun while **mayor/es** and **menor/es** usually appear after the noun.

Comparisons of equality

Spanish uses the following structures to compare adjectives *(age, size, appearance, and other characteristics of people and things)*, adverbs *(how people do things)*, nouns *(people and things themselves)*, and verbs *(actions)* that are the same.

Comparing adjectives and adverbs

tan + adjective / adverb + **como** = *as* + adjective / adverb + *as*

El muchacho es **tan alto como** la muchacha.
The boy is as tall as the girl.
La muchacha es **tan alta como** el muchacho.
The girl is as tall as the boy.

Comparing nouns

tanto/a/os/as + noun + **como** = *as much / many* + noun + *as*

La niña tiene **tantos juguetes como** el niño.
The girl has as many toys as the boy.
El niño tiene **tantos juguetes como** la niña.
The boy has as many toys as the girl.

Comparing verbs

verb + **tanto como** = *as much as*

La alumna canta **tanto como** el alumno.
The (female) student sings as much as the (male) student.
El alumno canta **tanto como** la alumna.
The (male) student sings as much as the (female) student.

Possessive pronouns

When making comparisons, it is common to avoid redundancy by using possessive pronouns.

el/la	mío/a	*mine*
los/las	míos/as	
el/la	tuyo/a	*yours*
los/las	tuyos/as	
el/la	suyo/a	*yours, his, hers*
los/las	suyos/as	
el/la	nuestro/a	*ours*
los/las	nuestros/as	
el/la	vuestro/a	*yours*
los/las	vuestros/as	
el/la	suyo/a	*yours, theirs*
los/las	suyos/as	

These possessive pronouns agree in gender and number with the noun they refer to.

Mi carro es más económico que **tu carro.**	*My car is more economical than* **your car.**
Mi carro es más económico que **el tuyo.**	*My car is more economical than* **yours.**
Nuestra universidad es mejor que **su universidad.**	*Our university is better than* **their university.**
Nuestra universidad es mejor que **la suya.**	*Our university is better than* **theirs.**

Actividades

1 **¡Vamos a comparar!** Compara las siguientes cosas, personas y lugares. Sigue el modelo. Utiliza los verbos **ser, estar** y **tener.** Trabaja con un/a compañero/a.

▶ **MODELO:** Nueva York / Boston (grande)
Nueva York es más grande que Boston.

1. Guatemala / Argentina (pequeña)
2. metro / autobús (rápido)
3. la computadora / el teléfono celular (eficiente)
4. mi casa / tu casa (lejos de la universidad)
5. una pequeña tienda de ropa / un almacén (atención personal)
6. una rosa roja / una rosa amarilla (bonita)
7. yo / tú (alto/a)
8. los estadounidenses / los europeos (vacaciones)

2 **¿Más comparaciones?** Reescribe las oraciones haciendo comparaciones **de igualdad o desigualdad.** Sigue el modelo.

▶ **MODELO:** El perfume *Amor* cuesta sesenta dólares. El perfume *Flor* cuesta ochenta dólares.
El perfume Flor *cuesta más que el perfume* Amor.
Nancy es muy inteligente. Su hermano Federico también es muy inteligente.
Federico es tan inteligente como Nancy.

1. En la universidad, Sonia tiene seis cursos. Abraham tiene ocho.
2. El coche *Divino* cuesta sesenta mil dólares. El coche *Elegante* cuesta setenta mil.
3. La casa de Antonio tiene siete cuartos. La casa de Guadalupe también tiene siete cuartos.
4. La casa de Eduardo tiene tres dormitorios. La casa de Pilar tiene cinco.
5. El museo de la ciudad es nuevo. El parque central también es nuevo.
6. Jorge maneja rápidamente. Alicia también maneja rápidamente.
7. En la familia de Anita hay nueve personas. En la familia de Carlos hay siete.
8. La tortuga avanza lentamente. La liebre *(hare)* avanza rápidamente.
9. La Librería Cervantes tiene muchos libros. La Librería Cortázar también tiene muchos libros.
10. A Mercedes y a Luis les gusta dar paseos por la ciudad. A nosotros también.

3 **¿Cuál es mejor?** Completa el texto con el superlativo. Usa **mayor, más** o **menos + de.** Usa artículo si es necesario. Sigue el modelo.

> ▶ MODELO: Mi clase era la _____ grande _____ colegio.
> Mi clase era la *más* grande *del* colegio.

1. Hace poco, estuvimos en una de las ciudades _____ grandes _____ mundo: La Ciudad de México.
2. Mis dos hermanos son menores que yo. Yo soy la _____ _____ familia.
3. La selva del Amazonas es la _____ importante _____ tierra.
4. La Librería Paz es magnífica, es la librería _____ completa _____ ciudad.
5. ¿Es el inglés el idioma _____ popular _____ países occidentales?
6. Las cataratas del Niágara son las _____ grandes _____ mundo, pero no son las _____ altas. El Salto Ángel, en Venezuela, es el _____ alto.

 4 **Más comparaciones.** Describe a las personas en la tabla. Luego haz comparaciones de estas personas con las de un/a compañero/a. Sigue el modelo.

> ▶ MODELO: Estudiante A: Mi primo, Carlos, tiene 23 años.
> *My cousin Carlos is 23 years old.*
> Estudiante B: Mi primo, Renato, tiene 16 años.
> *My cousin Renato is 16 years old.*
> Estudiante A: Entonces mi primo es mayor que el tuyo.
> *Therefore my cousin is older than yours.*
> Estudiante B: Mi primo es menor que el tuyo.
> *My cousin is younger than yours.*

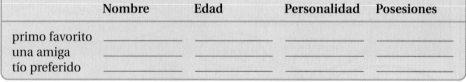

	Nombre	Edad	Personalidad	Posesiones
primo favorito	_____	_____	_____	_____
una amiga	_____	_____	_____	_____
tío preferido	_____	_____	_____	_____

5 **¿Qué piensan Uds.?** Lean las oraciones siguientes y digan si están de acuerdo o no. Si no están de acuerdo, modifiquen la oración. Comparen sus opiniones con las de sus compañeros/as.

1. El dinero es menos importante que el amor.
2. Hoy en día los hombres tienen tanta ropa elegante como las mujeres.
3. Los estudiantes universitarios trabajan más que los profesores de la universidad.
4. En los Estados Unidos, el béisbol es tan importante como el fútbol americano.
5. La comida tailandesa es mejor que la comida italiana.
6. El mejor coche de los Estados Unidos es el Ford.
7. Es más fácil hablar con los amigos que con los padres.
8. Jugar al baloncesto es menos difícil que jugar al volibol.
9. El béisbol es el deporte más popular de los Estados Unidos.
10. En California hay universidades tan buenas como en Massachusetts.

CAMINOS DEL JAGUAR

Magia en Mitad del Mundo

Actividades

1 Comprensión. Basándote en este episodio de **_Caminos del jaguar_,** elige la alternativa lógica.

Online Study Center

For additional practice with this episode, visit the _Caminos_ website at http://college.hmco.com/ languages/spanish/ renjilian/caminos/3e/ student_home.html.

1. En el restaurante, Adriana pide...
   a. locro.   b. llapingachos con fritada.

2. Don Gustavo piensa que Adriana y Felipe parecen...
   a. unos turistas sospechosos.   b. unos turistas inocentes.

3. Originalmente, ¿dónde estaban los jaguares?
   a. En un museo   b. En la tumba de un rey maya

4. La historia del continente de las Américas empieza...
   a. antes de 1492.   b. después de 1492.

5. ¿Cuál es el plan de Gafasnegras?
   a. Eliminar a Nayeli   b. Eliminar a Yax-Balam

6. Los desastres sucedieron porque el jaguar Yax-Balam llegó...
   a. solo.   b. durante _Uayeb_.

7. La fecha para reunir los jaguares es el día que...
   a. murió Pacal.   b. nació Pacal.

8. En la Mitad del Mundo, Adriana y Felipe...
   a. están en un hemisferio.   b. están en dos hemisferios.

2 Situaciones. Dramaticen una de estas situaciones.

1. La conversación de Gafasnegras y Miguel.
2. La conversación de Adriana y Felipe en la Mitad del Mundo.

3 Escritura. Escribe un corto resumen sobre este episodio.
(3–4 oraciones)

NOTA CULTURAL

El nombre del Ecuador

En el siglo dieciocho, un grupo de científicos franceses midieron la circunferencia de la tierra cerca de Quito, en el meridiano cero. Las medidas demostraron que la tierra no es una esfera perfecta porque es más ancha en el Ecuador que entre el Polo Sur y el Polo Norte. Los especialistas usaron en su informe "las tierras del Ecuador" para referirse al sitio de la medida. Desde entonces, el nombre del **Ecuador** se volvió popular y posteriormente se adoptó como nombre oficial del país.

Lectura

PRELECTURA

A legend is a story that people pass down from generation to generation. Legends are often based on historical events, although these may not be verifiable. In addition, legends may combine magical or fantastic elements with factual components. Through this Ecuadorean legend, you will learn the story of a shepherd boy who tends llamas and whose soul becomes entrapped in a rock. Known as Rumiaya, the rock watches over a small lake in the Limpiopungo plains at the foot of Cotopaxi, a majestic snow-covered volcano in Ecuador. The God of the Cotopaxi allows Rumiaya to change back into a human and tell his story whenever travelers show interest in the isolated stone.

In **quechua,** the Inca language spoken in Bolivia, Ecuador, and Perú, **rumi** means *stone* or *rock*. **Aya** means *spirit* or *soul*. **Limpiopungo** is the combination of the Spanish adjective **limpio** *(clean)* and the quechua noun **pungo** *(plains).*

Reading Strategy

Tapping background knowledge

Previous knowledge of the reading topic, plus your own experience, influence your interpretation and understanding of a text. The activities here will help activate background knowledge you have about legends.

 1 Asociaciones. Antes de leer, trabajen en grupos para repasar sus conocimientos sobre los siguientes temas.

1. Cuenta una leyenda popular de tu región. ¿Es misteriosa o melancólica, heroica, triste? ¿Se combinan elementos verdaderos con elementos fantásticos o mágicos en esa leyenda? Explica.
2. ¿Qué famosos elementos naturales hay en tu país: océanos, ríos, bosques, montañas, cañones, lagos, valles? ¿Cuál te impresiona más?
3. ¿Qué elemento natural figura en una leyenda nacional o regional de tu país?
4. Los pastores cuidan ovejas *(watch over sheep)* que pastan *(graze)* en los campos. ¿Dónde hay pastores en el mundo de hoy? ¿Cómo es su vida?

Soy Rumiaya, el alma de la roca

El gran volcán Cotopaxi, cubierto de nieve

Limpiopungo es una planicie[1] junto al Cotopaxi, el gran volcán nevado[2] del Ecuador. En este valle hay un hermoso lago de aguas limpias y cristalinas. Junto a este hermoso lago hay una piedra[3] que parece un vigía[4]. Las personas que van a este lugar dicen que, a veces, el alma[5] de esta piedra, Rumiaya, sale de ella para contar su historia.

Esto solamente sucede[6] cuando los viajeros[7] expresan mucho interés en la gran piedra y miran la piedra intensamente. De pronto, el alma de Rumiaya sale de la piedra. Lleva un grueso[8] poncho de lana de llama, zamarros[9] y un gorro muy abrigado[10] para protegerse del frío. Los ojos negros le brillan como cristales. Deslumbra[11] con su mirada[12] a los viajeros y empieza a hablar:

—Me llamo Rumiaya, el alma de la piedra. Vivo en la roca. Esta noche es especial y puedo contar mi historia. Hace mucho tiempo, solamente las llamas y los nativos del Cotopaxi vivíamos aquí. Yo era un pastorcito[13] de llamas y cuando amanecía[14], sacaba[15] las llamas a pastar[16] por la mañana. Me sentaba en la orilla[17] de la laguna y me ponía a mirar sus tranquilas y hermosas aguas durante muchas horas sin cansarme. Un día, cuando miraba embelesado[18] la laguna, una de las pequeñas llamas se acercó mucho y cayó al agua.

Sin dudarlo ni un momento, entré a la laguna para salvarla, pero empecé a hundirme[19]. No pude salir y me hundí hasta que todo se volvió[20] oscuro[21]. Un terrible frío me llenó el cuerpo[22]. Yo ya no era de esta vida.

De pronto, el gran dios de la montaña vino hacia mí y yo le dije:

—¡Gran dios de la montaña, creo que voy a morir! ¿Qué va a hacer mi alma sin mi amada[23] laguna? Si muero, ¡déjame junto a ella!

Con voz[24] de viento, el gran dios de la montaña me dijo:

—Voy a concederte[25] tu deseo. Vas a permanecer[26] eternamente junto al agua en forma de roca. Como quieres tanto a la laguna, tú mereces[27] que tu historia se conozca. Desde ahora[28] vas a ser Rumiaya, el alma de la piedra. Cuando alguien demuestre[29] interés por ti, puedes tomar la forma humana y contar tu historia.

Tan misteriosamente como viene, Rumiaya desaparece en la noche, dejando un aire de melancolía.

---

[1]plain; [2]snow-capped; [3]stone; [4]watchman; [5]soul; [6]occurs; [7]travelers; [8]heavy; [9]chaps covering pants; [10]warm; [11]Dazzles; [12]glance; [13]humble shepherd; [14]at dawn; [15]I took out; [16]graze; [17]edge; [18]spellbound; [19]to sink; [20]became; [21]dark; [22]body; [23]beloved; [24]voice; [25]grant you; [26]remain; [27]deserve; [28]From now on; [29]shows

POSTLECTURA

2 **La historia de Rumiaya: Eventos y personajes.** Trabajen en grupos para contestar las preguntas.

1. ¿Quiénes son los personajes de la leyenda? Describan sus personalidades.
2. ¿Quién narra la historia?
3. ¿Qué llevaba el pastorcito al salir de la piedra?
4. ¿Quién vive en la planicie? Según la ropa que lleva, ¿cómo es el clima allí?
5. ¿Por qué se cayó a la laguna una de las pequeñas llamas?
6. ¿Encontró el pastorcito la llama? ¿Qué pasó después?
7. Describe la voz del gran dios de la montaña.
8. ¿En qué convirtió el dios de la montaña al pastorcito?
9. ¿Cuándo puede contar Rumiaya su historia?
10. En tu opinión, ¿qué visión tenían de la naturaleza los nativos del Cotopaxi?

3 Suciopungo. Escribe la forma del imperfecto o del pretérito del verbo en esta breve historia.

La planicie _____ (**1.** estar) sucia y llena de basura. Los viajeros que _____ (**2.** pasar) por allí no _____ (**3.** preocuparse) ni de la ecología ni de las plantas y animales que _____ (**4.** vivir) en ella. Un día, el rey de aquel país _____ (**5.** prohibir) tirar papeles y restos de comida en la planicie porque él _____ (**6.** querer) conservarla limpia. Desde ese día, el rey _____ (**7.** empezar) a castigar personalmente a todos los infractores (*offenders*) hasta que Suciopungo _____ (**8.** convertirse) en Limpiopungo.

4 Nuestro planeta. El rey tiene muchas órdenes para los habitantes de su reino. Elige el infinitivo apropiado de la lista de abajo para completar las ideas. Se puede usar más de uno para completarlas.

aceptar   tirar   obedecer   cuidar   limpiar   tener   castigar   proteger

1. El rey quiere _____ el reino más limpio del mundo.
2. Para los habitantes es necesario _____ las órdenes del rey siempre.
3. Es importante _____ la planicie sucia y no _____ basura en ella.
4. El rey va a _____ a los infractores.
5. Todos los habitantes tienen que _____ la responsabilidad de cuidar los lagos y las lagunas.
6. Es esencial _____ la naturaleza para disfrutar de un planeta limpio.

5 Clasificaciones. Trabajen en parejas. Una persona de cada pareja hace una lista de los eventos que le parecen verdaderos en la historia de Rumiaya; la otra persona hace una lista de los eventos que le parecen de fantasía. Discutan las razones de cada uno/a para clasificar los eventos como fantasía o realidad.

6 Una leyenda original. Escribe en español una corta leyenda de dos párrafos sobre un tema de tu región, del campo o de la ciudad. Incluye elementos de la realidad y de la fantasía.

Una representación del dios Quetzalcoatl

Escritura

Writing Strategy

Paraphrasing

One good way to check your understanding of something you have heard, seen, or read is to paraphrase, or to put information and ideas in your own words. This is a common technique for practicing new language structures and reinforcing new vocabulary without copying or quoting the source verbatim.

Online Study Center

For further writing practice online, visit the *Caminos* website at http://college .hmco.com/languages/ spanish/renjilian/caminos/ 3e/student_home.html.

Workshop

The following examples show possible ways to paraphrase descriptions from the story of Rumiaya.

Original: Limpiopungo es una planicie junto al Cotopaxi, el gran volcán nevado del Ecuador.

Paraphrase: Limpiopungo es un lugar en Ecuador. Está al lado de un volcán que se llama Cotopaxi.

Original: Junto a este hermoso lago hay una piedra que parece un vigía.

Paraphrase: Una piedra grande está junto al lago. La piedra está cuidándolo.

Strategy in Action

For additional practice with paraphrasing, complete the exercises below and in the *Escritura* section of your Student Activities Manual for *Unidad 7*.

1 Limpiopungo. En tus propias palabras, escribe un resumen de dos párrafos de la leyenda de Limpiopungo.

2 Un cuento de niños. ¿Recuerdas los cuentos de tu niñez? Escribe un resumen de tu cuento favorito de cuando eras niño/a con tus propias palabras. Unos cuentos populares son: La cenicienta *(Cinderella)*, El patito feo *(The Ugly Duckling)*, Los tres cerditos *(The Three Little Pigs)*, La Bella Durmiente *(Sleeping Beauty)* y Blancanieves *(Snow White)*.

La lista de abajo contiene vocabulario útil para los cuentos de niños. Si las palabras que necesitas no se encuentran en la lista, búscalas en un buen diccionario inglés-español.

Once upon a time	*Érase una vez*	king	*el rey*	princess	*la princesa*
broom	*la escoba*	knight /	*caballero*	prison	*la cárcel*
castle	*el castillo*	gentleman		queen	*la reina*
crown	*la corona*	magic *(adj.)*	*mágico/a*	thief	*el ladrón /*
devil	*el diablo*	magic *(n.)*	*la magia*		*la ladrona*
dragon	*dragón*	magic wand	*la varita*	to have bad /	*tener mala /*
fairy tale	*cuento de hadas*		*mágica*	good luck	*buena suerte*
forest, woods	*el bosque*	magician	*el / la mago/a*	treasure	*el tesoro*
ghost	*el fantasma*	monster	*el / la monstruo/a*	witch	*el / la brujo/a*
giant	*el / la gigante*	palace	*el palacio*	wizard	*el / la mago/a*
godfather	*padrino*	pirate	*el / la pirata*	wolf	*el lobo*
godmother	*madrina*	prince	*el príncipe*		

Resumen de vocabulario

PRIMER PASO

TALKING ABOUT STORES AND SHOPPING

el almacén	*department store*
la boutique	*boutique*
la caja	*cash register*
el la cliente	*customer*
el/la dependiente	*store clerk*
el disco	*album, record*
el escaparate	*store window*
la farmacia	*pharmacy*
la florería	*florist*
la ganga	*deal, bargain*
la joyería	*jewelry store*
la lavandería	*laundromat*
la librería	*bookstore*
el maquillaje	*makeup*
el mostrador	*display case; counter*
la papelería	*stationery store; office supply store*
la perfumería	*perfume store*
el recibo	*receipt*
la talla	*size*
la tintorería	*dry cleaner*
la zapatería	*shoe store*

Verbos

devolver	*to return (something)*
gastar	*to spend (money)*

Otras expresiones

a un precio más bajo	*at a lower price*
¡Claro que sí!	*Of course!*
en oferta	*on sale*
gratis	*free*

SHOPPING FOR CLOTHES

Sustantivos

el abrigo	*coat*
el algodón	*cotton*
la blusa	*blouse*
la bolsa	*purse, bag*
la bota	*boot*
la bufanda	*scarf*
el calcetín	*sock*
la camisa	*shirt*
la camiseta	*T-shirt*
la chaqueta	*jacket*
el cinturón	*belt*
la corbata	*tie*
la falda	*skirt*
el guante	*glove*
el impermeable	*raincoat*
la lana	*wool*
la mancha	*stain*
las medias	*stockings, hose*
los pantalones	*pants*
el par	*pair*
el paraguas	*umbrella*
la ropa interior	*underwear*
el saco	*jacket, blazer*
la seda	*silk*
el sombrero	*hat*
la sudadera	*sweat suit, sweatshirt*
el suéter	*sweater*
el traje	*suit*
el vestido	*dress*
el zapato	*shoe*

Verbos

(des)atar	*to (un)tie*
estar de moda	*to be in style*
ir de compras	*to go shopping*
llevar	*to wear; to take*
probarse (ue)	*to try on*
quedarle (a alguien)	*to fit (someone)*

Adjetivos

estrecho/a	*tight / small*
flojo/a	*loose / big (clothes)*
grande	*large / big (clothes)*
manchado/a	*stained*
pequeño/a	*tight, small (clothes)*
roto/a	*ripped*
sucio/a	*dirty*

SEGUNDO PASO

BARGAINING IN A MARKETPLACE

Sustantivos

el anillo	*ring*
los aretes	*earrings*
la artesanía	*craft*
el barro	*clay*
el cobre	*copper*
el collar	*necklace*
el/la comprador/a	*buyer*
el descuento	*discount*
la esmeralda	*emerald*
el jaguar	*jaguar*
la joya	*jewelry*
el juguete	*toy*
el (otro) lado	*somewhere else*
la madera	*wood*
la máscara	*mask*
el mercado	*marketplace*
el oro	*gold*
el pendiente	*pendant*
la piedra	*stone*
la plata	*silver*
el plato	*dish*
el precio	*price*
el prendedor	*pin, brooch*
la pulsera	*bracelet*
la rebaja	*discount*
el recipiente	*container*
el regateo	*bargaining*
el tapete	*rug*
el tapiz	*tapestry*
el tejido	*weaving*
la turquesa	*turquoise*
el/la vendedor/a	*seller*

Verbos

rebajar	*to lower (a price)*
regatear	*to bargain*

Otras expresiones

ambulante	*mobile*
¿En cuánto me lo(s)/ la(s) deja?	*How much will you charge me for it / them?*

ASKING FOR AND GIVING DIRECTIONS

Sustantivos

la cuadra	*street block*
la esquina	*corner*
la intersección	*intersection*
el semáforo	*traffic light*

Verbos

acelerar	*to accelerate*
bajar (por)	*to go (down) (a street)*
cruzar	*to cross*
dar la vuelta	*to turn around*
doblar (a)	*to turn*
estacionar	*to park*
parar	*to stop*
pasar (por)	*to pass (by)*
seguir derecho, recto	*to go straight*
subir (por)	*to go up (a street)*
tener cuidado	*to be careful*

Otras expresiones

a la (mano) derecha/ izquierda	*on the right/ left(hand) side*
¿Cómo se llega a...?	*How does one get to . . . ?*
despacio	*slowly*
hasta	*until*
¿Me puede decir dónde está/n...?	*Can you tell me where . . . is / are?*
medio/a *(adj.)*	*half*

POSSESSIVE PRONOUNS

el/la	mío/a	*mine*
el/la	tuyo/a	*yours*
el/la	suyo/a	*yours, his, hers, theirs*
el/la	nuestro/a	*ours*
el/la	vuestro/a	*yours*

8
Salud y bienestar

VOCABULARIO Y LENGUA

- ► Identifying parts of the body
- ► Making a doctor's appointment
- ► Expressing requests and emotions: Present subjunctive

- ► Learning about foods and nutrition
- ► Discussing progressive actions in the past: Past progressive
- ► Expressing doubt or certainty: Present subjunctive / indicative

CAMINOS DEL JAGUAR

- ► La curandera carismática
- ► Un plan secreto

LECTURA

- ► Salud y bienestar: Toma control de tu vida

NOTAS CULTURALES

- ► Curanderos
- ► Los tejidos

ESTRATEGIAS

- ► **Reading:** Comparing and contrasting
- ► **Writing:** Using visual organizers (Venn diagrams)

Mola de Panamá con el símbolo médico

Preguntas del tema

▶ Cuando estás enfermo/a ¿vas al médico?

▶ ¿Haces ejercicio todos los días?

▶ ¿Qué más haces para mantener buena salud?

▶ ¿Comes una dieta balanceada?

PRIMER PASO

Vocabulario y lengua

IDENTIFYING PARTS OF THE BODY (LAS PARTES DEL CUERPO)

En la clase de anatomía

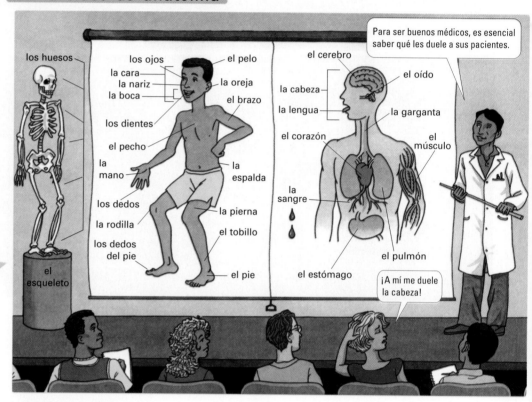

Para ser buenos médicos, es esencial saber qué les duele a sus pacientes.

los huesos
los ojos
la cara
la nariz
la boca
el pelo
la oreja
el brazo
los dientes
el pecho
la mano
los dedos
la rodilla
los dedos del pie
el esqueleto
la espalda
la pierna
el tobillo
el pie

el cerebro
la cabeza
la lengua
el corazón
la sangre
el oído
la garganta
el músculo
el pulmón
el estómago

¡A mí me duele la cabeza!

Actividades

1 **Asociaciones.** ¿Qué partes del cuerpo asocias con estas actividades?

1. jugar al volibol
2. escuchar música
3. comer
4. tocar la guitarra
5. pensar
6. nadar en la piscina
7. leer una novela
8. maquillarse
9. saludar a un/a amigo/a
10. patear

2 **En el sitio correcto.** Completa cada oración con la parte del cuerpo más adecuada para la acción.

1. Me pongo el sombrero en la _____.
2. Me pongo guantes porque tengo frío en las _____.
3. Uso gafas de sol para protegerme los _____.
4. Me pongo los calcetines en los _____.
5. Por la mañana me peino el _____.
6. Pruebo la comida con la _____.
7. Marco los números de teléfono con los _____.
8. Si fumo cigarrillos me duelen los _____.

3 **¿Qué les duele?** Identifica las partes del cuerpo que les duelen a estas personas. Sigue el modelo.

▶ **MODELO:** A ella le duele el brazo.
Her arm hurts.

4 **La rutina diaria.** Escribe oraciones completas con las palabras de cada columna. Utiliza cada uno de los sujetos y verbos por lo menos una vez. Después, en parejas, intercambien las frases y comparen las oraciones.

A	B	C
Yo	lavarse	las manos
Tú	cepillarse	el pelo
Los niños	peinarse	los dientes
Nosotras	maquillarse	el cuerpo
Tu mejor amiga	afeitarse	la cara
Mi hermano y yo	secarse	las piernas

appointment ## Una cita° con la médica

Recepcionista	Buenos días. Oficina de la Dra. Medina.
Sr. Jaramillo	Buenos días. Habla el Sr. Jaramillo.
Recepcionista	¿En qué le puedo ayudar, Sr. Jaramillo?

twisted   *Sr. Jaramillo*   Mi hija Claudia **se torció**° el tobillo y es necesario llevarla a la Dra. Medina hoy.

Recepcionista	¿Su hija puede caminar?

broken   *Sr. Jaramillo*   No, no puede. Parece que tiene el tobillo **fracturado**°.

Recepcionista   Entonces es mejor llevarla a **la sala de emergencia** inmediatamente para tomarle una **radiografía.**

Sr. Jaramillo   ¿Y la Dra. Medina no puede atenderla?

Recepcionista   No, lo siento. La Dra. Medina está ahora en el hospital atendiendo a otros **pacientes.** Al llegar al hospital, llame Ud. a la Dra. Medina. Ella puede atender a Claudia allí.

Sr. Jaramillo   Muchas gracias, señorita.

Recepcionista   No hay de qué, con mucho gusto.

Más palabras y expresiones

Cognados

el antibiótico	la inflamación
la aspirina	la inyección
curar	la medicina
el examen físico	la operación
la fractura	reducir
grave	el remedio
la infección	el síntoma

Sustantivos

el bienestar	*well-being*
el consultorio médico	*doctor's office*
el/la curandero/a	*healer*
la enfermedad	*illness*

el hielo	*ice*
el jarabe	*syrup*
la píldora, pastilla	*pill*
la presión (sanguínea)	*blood pressure*
la prueba, el análisis	*test, exam (medical)*
la receta	*prescription*
el soroche	*altitude sickness*
la vacuna	*vaccine*
la venda	*bandage*
el yeso	*cast*

Verbos

aliviarse	*to get better*
cuidarse	*to take care of oneself*
dañar	*to harm*
doler (ue)	*to hurt*
enfermarse	*to get sick*
estornudar	*to sneeze*
evitar	*to avoid*
hacer una cita	*to make an appointment*
mejorar	*to get better*
respirar	*to breathe*
romper(se) (el brazo)	*to break (one's arm)*
sangrar	*to bleed*
ser alérgico/a a..., tener alergia a...	*to be allergic to . . .*
toser	*to cough*
vendar	*to bandage*
vomitar	*to vomit*

Expresiones con *estar*

estar embarazada	*to be pregnant*
estar inflamado/a	*to be inflamed, swollen*
estar mareado/a	*to be dizzy*
estar resfriado/a	*to have a cold*

Expresiones con *tener*

tener apetito	*to have an appetite*
tener buena / mala salud	*to be in good / bad health*
tener catarro, resfrío	*to have a cold*
tener dolor	*to have pain*
tener escalofríos	*to shiver, have a chill*
tener fiebre	*to have a fever*
tener gripe	*to have the flu*
tener náuseas	*to be nauseous*
tener tos	*to have a cough*

Actividades

🎧 **1 En la sala de emergencia.** Escucha la conversación entre Claudia y la Dra.Medina, luego contesta las preguntas.

1. ¿Cómo sigue Claudia?
2. ¿Cuál es la buena noticia que tiene la doctora? ¿Y la mala?
3. ¿Cuándo es el próximo partido de fútbol?
4. ¿Por cuánto tiempo tiene Claudia que llevar una venda en el tobillo?
5. ¿Qué más tiene que hacer Claudia para mejorarse?
6. ¿Cuándo es el campeonato?
7. ¿Puede jugar Claudia en el campeonato?
8. ¿Qué necesita hacer Claudia para no tener problemas con el tobillo?

👥 **2 Recomendaciones médicas.** ¿Qué recomienda un/a médico/a en estas circunstancias? Trabajen en parejas para inventar recomendaciones para estos síntomas. Sigan el modelo.

> ▶ **MODELO:** PACIENTE: Me duele la garganta.
> MÉDICO/A: *Debes (Necesitas) tomar té caliente.*

1. No tengo mucho apetito.
2. Me torcí el brazo.
3. Tengo fiebre y náuseas.
4. Me duele el estómago.
5. Estoy mareado/a y tengo dolor de cabeza.
6. Tengo catarro y no puedo respirar.
7. Me duele la cabeza.
8. Fui a bailar anoche y me torcí el pie.
9. ¿...?

👥 **3 Remedios tradicionales.** Haz una lista de cinco remedios caseros que conoces para curar dolores o enfermedades, por ejemplo: **sopa de pollo para un catarro.** Con una pareja comparen sus listas y hablen de los beneficios de estos remedios tradicionales en comparación con las medicinas modernas.

EXPRESSING REQUESTS AND EMOTIONS: PRESENT SUBJUNCTIVE

Look at the verbs in boldface. What infinitives do they come from? Notice that these verbs are identical to the formal (**Ud.**) commands that you learned in *Unidad 6,* pages 224–225. Compare the sentence structure here with the sentence structures you have learned so far. How is it different? How many subjects do you find in each sentence? These sentences are examples of the present subjunctive.

What is the present subjunctive?

The term subjunctive refers to a *mood,* not to a tense. Up to now you have primarily been using verbs in the indicative *mood.* The indicative mood expresses actions that are definite, clear, and which state factual events and outcomes. The subjunctive is a mood that expresses:

► **R**equests, wishes, needs, and desires
► **E**motions and subjective feelings
► **D**oubt and uncertainty

Think of the letters **RED** to help you remember what triggers the use of the subjunctive. Not only does the subjunctive express these moods, it appears within a particular sentence structure. As you have seen in the exchange on page 278: a main clause in the indicative is linked by **que** to a dependent or subordinate clause in the subjunctive. Note also that the subject in the main clause is different from the subject in the dependent clause.

Le recomiendo	**que**	coma alimentos nutritivos.
I recommend (to you)	*that*	*you eat nutritious foods.*
No es bueno	**que**	usted fume.
It isn't good	*that*	*you smoke.*

In this unit, we will study how to form the present subjunctive and how to use it to express requests and emotions. In these cases, it is the meaning of the verb or verb phrase in the main clause that triggers the use of the subjunctive in the dependent clause.

Formation of the present subjunctive

To form the present subjunctive, follow the same rule as for formal commands.

Verb	1. Start with the present indicative yo form.	2. Drop the –o.	3. Add the opposite endings.
comprar	compro	compr-	compre
beber	bebo	beb-	beba
escribir	escribo	escrib-	escriba

Once you have the stem of the verb, add the following endings:

Present subjunctive of *–ar, –er, –ir* verbs			
Subject pronouns	comprar	beber	escribir
yo	compre	beba	escriba
tú	compres	bebas	escribas
Ud., él, ella	compre	beba	escriba
nosotros/as	compremos	bebamos	escribamos
vosotros/as	compréis	bebáis	escribáis
Uds., ellos, ellas	compren	beban	escriban

To form the subjunctive of the following groups of verbs, start with the present indicative **yo** form as shown in the preceding charts.

► Irregular **yo** verbs
- salir: **salga, salgas, salga, salgamos, salgáis, salgan**
- conducir: **conduzca, conduzcas, conduzca, conduzcamos, conduzcáis, conduzcan**
- ver: **vea, veas, vea, veamos, veáis, vean**

► Verbs with spelling changes
- llegar: **llegue, llegues, llegue, lleguemos, lleguéis, lleguen**
- buscar: **busque, busques, busque, busquemos, busquéis, busquen**
- cruzar: **cruce, cruces, cruce, crucemos, crucéis, crucen**
- escoger: **escoja, escojas, escoja, escojamos, escojáis, escojan**

► Stem-changing -**ar** and -**er** verbs
- pensar (e → ie): **pie**nse, **pie**nses, **pie**nse, pensemos, penséis, **pie**nsen
- probar (o → ue): pr**ue**be, pr**ue**bes, pr**ue**be, probemos, probéis, pr**ue**ben
- perder (e → ie): p**ie**rda, p**ie**rdas, p**ie**rda, perdamos, perdáis, p**ie**rdan
- volver (o → ue): v**ue**lva, v**ue**lvas, v**ue**lva, volvamos, volváis, v**ue**lvan

Irregular verbs

Any verb that has an irregular stem in the formal command forms (*Unidad 6*, p. 225) has the same irregular stem in the present subjunctive.

► estar: **esté, estés, esté, estemos, estén**
► dar: **dé, des, dé, demos, den**
► ir: **vaya, vayas, vaya, vayamos, vayan**
► saber: **sepa, sepas, sepa, sepamos, sepan**
► ser: **sea, seas, sea, seamos, sean**

Like **hay** *(there is, there are)*, **haber** only has one form meaning *there is, there are* in the present subjunctive: **haya.**

Stem-changing -*ir* verbs

Verbs that end in –**ir** and have a stem change from **e → ie** or **o → ue** in the present indicative, have the same change in the present subjunctive. They have an additional change from **e → i** and **o → u** in the **nosotros** and **vosotros** forms of the present subjunctive.

mentir (e → ie)		servir (e → i)		dormir (o → ue)	
m**ie**nta	m**i**ntamos	s**i**rva	s**i**rvamos	d**ue**rma	d**u**rmamos
m**ie**ntas	m**i**ntáis	s**i**rvas	s**i**rváis	d**ue**rmas	d**u**rmáis
m**ie**nta	m**ie**ntan	s**i**rva	s**i**rvan	d**ue**rma	d**ue**rman

Use of the present subjunctive with verbs of request or emotion

As shown in the examples above when the meaning of the main verb or expression conveys a request or an emotion, it triggers the subjunctive in the dependent or subordinate clause. Remember that the subject in the main clause must be different from the subject in the dependent clause.

Quiero **que tú me ayudes** un poco.   *I want you to help me a little.*

When there is only one subject in both clauses, use the **infinitive** after a conjugated verb or after an impersonal expression. Impersonal expressions do not have an explicit subject (**Es necesario que…, Es importante que…**) and are often used to soften a request.

Quiero **ayudarte** un poco.   *I want to help you a little.*
Es importante no **fumar.**   *It is important not to smoke.*

When the verb in the main clause is accompanied by an indirect object pronoun, the verb in the dependent clause agrees with the person that the pronoun refers to.

Les sugerimos a Uds. que
    regresen mañana.

We suggest that you return tomorrow.

Los médicos nos piden que
    hagamos ejercicio todos los días.

Doctors ask us to exercise every day.

Le aconsejo a mi padre que se
    mantenga en forma.

I advise my father to stay in shape.

Verbs and impersonal expressions of request and emotion

The following verbs and impersonal expressions convey wishes, requests, needs, desires and emotions, or subjective feelings. When they appear in the main clause, they trigger the use of the subjunctive in the dependent or subordinate clause.

Verbs		Impersonal expressions	
aconsejar	*to advise*	es bueno	*it's good*
alegrarse (de)	*to be happy*	es esencial	*it's essential*
desear	*to want*	es extraño	*it's strange*
enojarse	*to be angry*	es importante	*it's important*
esperar	*to hope*	es malo	*it's bad*
estar contento/a de	*to be happy*	es mejor	*it's better*
gustarle	*to like; to be pleasing*	es necesario	*it's necessary*
(a alguien)	*(to someone)*		
lamentar	*to lament, regret*	es peor	*it's worse*
mandar	*to order*	es preciso	*it's necessary*
molestarle (a alguien)	*to bother (someone)*	es preferible	*it's preferable*
necesitar	*to need*	es ridículo	*it's ridiculous*
pedir (i)	*to request, ask for*	es terrible	*it's terrible*
preferir (ie)	*to prefer*	es una lástima	*it's a shame*
preocupar(se)	*to worry*	es urgente	*it's urgent*
querer (ie)	*to want*		
recomendar (ie)	*to recommend*		
rogar (ue)	*to beg, plead*		
sentir (ie)	*to be sorry, regret*		
sorprender	*to surprise*		
sugerir (ie)	*to suggest*		
temer	*to fear, be afraid of*		
tener miedo (de)	*to be afraid of*		

When the verb **decir** is used to give an order, it requires the subjunctive in the dependent clause. When used to inform it requires the indicative.

La médica me dice que **haga** ejercicio.

The doctor tells me to exercise.

La médica me dice que **tengo**
    un infección del oído.

*The doctor tells me that I have an
    ear infection.*

Ojalá

The word **ojalá** is used to express hope and is followed by the subjunctive. The origin of this word is the Arabic expression *God (Allah) willing*. Unlike the verbs and expressions in the preceding list, **ojalá** does not change form and the use of **que** is optional. **Ojalá** may also stand alone as an interjection that means "I / We / Let's hope so."

—**¡Ojalá** (que) te **mejores** pronto!

—*I hope that you get well soon!*

—¿Van a descubrir una cura para
    el cáncer?

—*Are they going to discover a cure for
    cancer?*

—**¡Ojalá!**

—*Let's hope so!*

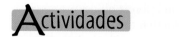

Actividades

1 Consejos del médico. Completa los consejos del médico con la forma correcta del verbo. Decide si necesita el presente del subjuntivo o el infinitivo.

1. Es necesario que tú _____ tu medicina regularmente.
   - a. tomes
   - b. tomar
   - c. tomas

2. El médico espera que tú _____ sus consejos.
   - a. sigas
   - b. sigues
   - c. seguir

3. Si no le gusta su médico, es urgente _____ otro.
   - a. buscar
   - b. busca
   - c. busque

4. Es necesario _____ muchas frutas cada día.
   - a. comes
   - b. comas
   - c. comer

5. Es urgente que los jóvenes _____ de fumar.
   - a. dejen
   - b. dejar
   - c. dejan

6. Quiero que tú _____ la lengua y que _____ "Aaaaaaa".
   - a. sacar / decir
   - b. sacas / dices
   - c. saques / digas

7. Es mejor _____ una cita en dos semanas.
   - a. pedir
   - b. pida
   - c. pide

2 ¿Qué necesitas hacer? Completa los deseos de estas personas con la forma correcta del subjuntivo. Sigue el modelo.

> ▸ **MODELO:** Mi profesora de español quiere que yo haga la tarea.   *My Spanish professor wants me to do the homework.*

1. Mi profesor/a de español quiere que yo...
   - a. _____ (poner) atención.
   - b. _____ (asistir) a clase.
   - c. _____ (no llegar) tarde.
   - d. _____ (estudiar) mucho.
   - e. _____ (no traducir) todo al inglés.
   - f. _____ (hablar) más en clase.

2. Mis padres quieren que yo...
   - a. _____ (sacar) buenas notas.
   - b. _____ (escoger) una buena profesión.
   - c. _____ (llamarlos) cada semana.
   - d. _____ (no gastar) mucho dinero en las fiestas.
   - e. _____ (no conducir) mi auto muy rápido.
   - f. _____ (no enfermarme).

3 Salud y bienestar. Completa estas oraciones sobre preferencias y consejos sobre la salud con el subjuntivo de los verbos entre paréntesis.

1. Doctor, quiero que usted me _____ (examinar) de inmediato.
2. Es inaceptable que tú no nos _____ (decir) la verdad.
3. Ricardo, es esencial que tú _____ (cuidarse).
4. A nadie le gusta que el doctor le _____ (poner) inyecciones.
5. Es necesario que usted nos _____ (dar) su información médica.
6. A nosotros nos preocupa que tú _____ (tener) alergias.
7. Si usted se siente mal, le sugiero que _____ (consultar) a un médico.
8. Es muy bueno que Uds. _____ (mantenerse) en forma.

4 Episodios de la vida. Varias personas expresan sus reacciones sobre estas situaciones. Pon la forma adecuada del presente del indicativo o del presente del subjuntivo del verbo entre paréntesis según el contexto. Sigue el modelo.

▶ **MODELO:** Yo _____ (esperar) que Paco _____ (comer) menos grasa.
Yo espero que Paco coma menos grasa.

1. Es bueno que la gente _____ (ser) saludable.
2. Mauro _____ (lamentar) que tú no _____ (hacer) ejercicio.
3. Ojalá que la doctora me _____ (enseñar) buena nutrición.
4. A mí me _____ (molestar) que la gente _____ (fumar).
5. Nosotros _____ (sentir) mucho que el bebé _____ (tener) fiebre.
6. Los profesores _____ (alegrarse) de que sus estudiantes _____ (saber) mucho español al final del curso.
7. Mis amigos me _____ (pedir) que no _____ (beber) y que los _____ (llevar) a casa.
8. Yo no _____ (querer) que mis amigos _____ (preocuparse) por mí.

5 Amistad. Tus buenos amigos te ayudan cuando lo necesitas. Trabajando con un/a compañero/a, conversen sobre estas situaciones posibles. Sigue el modelo.

▶ **MODELO:** Te sientes solo/a. ¿Quieres que alguien te acompañe?
Sí, quiero que alguien me acompañe. or
No, no quiero que nadie me acompañe.

1. Tienes dificultades económicas. ¿Les pides a tus amigos que te presten dinero?
2. Estás enfermo/a. ¿Quieres que yo te compre alguna medicina?
3. Te tuerces el tobillo. ¿Prefieres que el médico te ponga una venda?
4. No tienes con quién salir a pasear. ¿Quieres que yo salga contigo?
5. Te rompes el brazo y no puedes cocinar. ¿Le pides a alguien que haga tu cena?
6. Tienes un virus y no vas a la escuela. ¿Quieres que un/a amigo/a te explique la lección?
7. Tienes que estudiar para un examen difícil. ¿Quieres que tus amigos estudien contigo?
8. Es tu cumpleaños. ¿Deseas que tus padres te manden dinero o un regalo?

6 Consejos. Trabajen en parejas para darles consejos a estas personas. Usen los verbos **aconsejar, recomendar** y **sugerir.** Recuerden el uso del subjuntivo.

▶ **MODELO:** —Quiero salir a cenar en un restaurante elegante, pero no tengo mucho dinero y tengo que pagar unas cuentas. ¿Qué me aconsejas?
—*Te aconsejo que pagues las cuentas primero y que comas en McDonald's.*

1. Tengo dos invitaciones: una para asistir a un concierto con mis amigos y otra para salir a cenar con mi familia. ¿Qué me aconsejas que haga?
2. Pablo quiere romper *(to break up)* con su novia. Ella lo quiere mucho, pero Pablo está enamorado de otra muchacha. ¿Qué le sugieres a Pablo que haga?
3. Mi compañera de cuarto escucha música toda la noche y yo no puedo estudiar. ¿Qué le digo a mi compañera?
4. Había tres amigos en mi cuarto y desapareció mi reloj de oro. ¿Debo preguntarles si alguno de ellos tiene mi reloj o no debo hacerlo? ¿Qué me aconsejas que haga?
5. Toda mi ropa está sucia y mañana tengo una entrevista para un trabajo. ¿Qué me recomiendas que haga?
6. La semana que viene es el cumpleaños de mi tía, una señora mayor. ¿Qué me sugieres que le regale a ella?
7. Mi abuelo está en el hospital y quiero ir a verlo, pero tengo un examen muy importante. ¿Qué me recomiendas que haga?
8. Mi hermana debe hacer ejercicio, pero no lo hace. ¿Qué le sugiero?

La curandera carismática

Actividades

Online Study Center

For additional practice with this episode, visit the *Caminos* website at http://college.hmco.com/languages/spanish/renjilian/caminos/3e/student_home.html.

1 Comprensión. Basándote en este episodio de *Caminos del jaguar,* elige la alternativa lógica.

1. Zulaya dice que su obligación es...
   a. devolver el jaguar.
   b. guardar el jaguar.

2. La gente que quiere el jaguar...
   a. conoce a Zulaya.
   b. no conoce a Zulaya.

3. La organización de Mario confía...
   a. en el jaguar.
   b. en Zulaya.

4. Adriana se siente mal por...
   a. el viaje a Quito.
   b. el soroche.

5. El curandero quiere que vayan a la casa...
   a. del curandero.
   b. de una curandera.

6. Doña Remedios le dice a Adriana que...
   a. busque el jaguar.
   b. no busque el jaguar.

7. Gafasnegras...
   a. no busca a Zulaya.
   b. busca a Zulaya.

2 Situaciones. Dramaticen una de las siguientes situaciones.

1. La conversación de Zulaya con Mario.
2. La conversación de Adriana con doña Remedios.

3 Escritura. Describe qué sucede en el mercado cuando Adriana se siente mal. (4–6 oraciones)

NOTA CULTURAL

Curanderos

En muchas regiones de América Latina, la coexistencia de los remedios tradicionales y modernos es una práctica común. Los curanderos son tradicionalmente personas con profundos conocimientos sobre las plantas medicinales y sus usos. Muchos curanderos cultivan estas plantas o las recogen en las selvas para curar a las personas enfermas. Algunos curanderos celebran rituales para la curación, mientras que otros ya no lo hacen.

SEGUNDO PASO

Vocabulario y lengua

LEARNING ABOUT FOODS AND NUTRITION

La pirámide de la alimentación *(The food pyramid)*

to keep ourselves / healthy

foods

to eat / quantity / upper

weight

Mantener una **dieta** balanceada es importante para **conservarnos**° **sanos**°. La pirámide de la alimentación nos muestra los productos recomendados en cada grupo de **alimentos**°. En los niveles más bajos de la pirámide están los alimentos que debemos **consumir**° en mayor **cantidad**° y en la parte superior°, están los alimentos que solamente debemos consumir en cantidades mínimas. En la base de la pirámide, vemos que controlar el **peso**° y hacer ejercicio son muy importantes para la salud.

Online Study Center

For additional practice with this units vocabulary and grammar, visit the *Caminos* website at http://college.hmco.com/languages/spanish/renjilian/caminos/3e/student_home.html. You can also review audio flashcards, quiz yourself, and explore related Spanish-language sites.

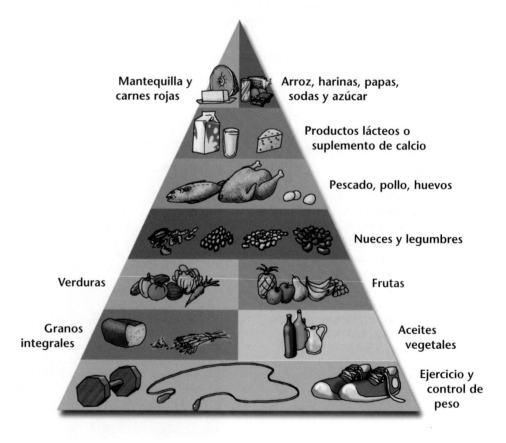

Mantequilla y carnes rojas

Arroz, harinas, papas, sodas y azúcar

Productos lácteos o suplemento de calcio

Pescado, pollo, huevos

Nueces y legumbres

Verduras

Frutas

Granos integrales

Aceites vegetales

Ejercicio y control de peso

Las porciones

El número recomendado de **porciones** depende de cuántas **calorías** necesite la persona **diariamente**. Las calorías **dependen,** a su vez, del **nivel°** de actividad que **mantenga°** la persona, de su edad, de su sexo y de sus circunstancias. Por ejemplo, una persona muy **sedentaria** necesita menos calorías que una persona **activa,** las personas jóvenes consumen, por lo general, más calorías que las personas ancianas y las mujeres embarazadas deben mantener una dieta **nutritiva°** con mucho calcio. Las personas que sufren de alergias o de alguna insuficiencia **física** pueden necesitar dietas especiales.

level
maintains

nutritious

Actividades

1 Ponlas en su grupo. Pon las comidas de la lista en el grupo de alimentos que les corresponde en la pirámide. Algunas comidas pueden pertenecer a más de un grupo. Trabajen en parejas.

verduras
jugo de naranja
yogur
taco
plátano
cereal
huevo
crema de cacahuate
manzana
mantequilla
pechuga de pollo (chicken breast)
papa (patata) al horno
queso
refrescos
frijoles (beans)
pan

2 **¿Comes una dieta balanceada?** Haz una lista de lo que comiste ayer. Después, en parejas, comparen sus listas. Hablen de lo que necesitan hacer para mantener una dieta balanceada. Presenten sus ideas a la clase.

3 **Encuesta.** Hazles una encuesta a dos compañeros sobre sus hábitos alimenticios *(eating habits)*. Después, clasifica cada uno de los alimentos nombrados en el sitio que le corresponda en la pirámide. Entonces, haz un resumen de la información que conseguiste. Dale un informe a la clase.

1. ¿Qué bebes cuando tienes sed? ¿Cuál es tu bebida favorita?
2. ¿Bebes alcohol? ¿Cuántas veces por semana? ¿Cuándo?
3. ¿Cuál es la fruta que más te gusta? ¿Cuál es la fruta que menos te gusta? ¿Por qué?
4. ¿Cuál es la verdura que más te gusta? ¿Cuál es la verdura que menos te gusta? ¿Por qué?
5. ¿Cuál es tu comida favorita? ¿Por qué?
6. ¿Cuál es la comida que menos te gusta? ¿Por qué?
7. ¿Cuántos vasos de agua tomas al día?
8. ¿Qué comes cuando tienes hambre entre las comidas?

4 **Planeando el menú.** Tienes que planear la comida de una semana para la cafetería de tu universidad. Planea un menú balanceado para todos los días.

Menú diario				
lunes	martes	miércoles	jueves	viernes

5 **Para todas las edades.** ¿Cómo cambiarías *(would you change)* el menú de la Actividad 4 para niños de siete a nueve años? ¿Para personas mayores? ¿Para personas con problemas cardíacos?

Menú		
Para niños	Para personas mayores	Para personas con problemas cardíacos

DISCUSSING PROGRESSIVE ACTIONS IN THE PAST: PAST PROGRESSIVE

¿Qué estaban haciendo esta mañana?

Mi padre **estaba bebiendo** café.

Mis gatos **estaban jugando** en el jardín.

Mi hermano menor **estaba durmiendo**.

A las siete de la mañana mi mamá **estaba preparando** el desayuno.

Y en ese momento, mi primo Luis y yo **estábamos divirtiéndonos**.

The past progressive corresponds to the English *we were running, they were watching television, I was talking.* It describes what people were doing during a given period or at a specific moment in the past. Its use in Spanish is often accompanied by a time expression such as **en aquella época, en esos días, en ese momento.** The past progressive is formed with **estar** and a present participle. (Review the formation of the present participle in *Unidad 2,* page 63.)

Past progressive
imperfect of **estar** + present participle

Cuando me encontré con Luis, yo **estaba comprando** unas manzanas.	*When I ran into Luis, I was buying some apples.*
Estaba pensando en ti, ¡y en ese momento, tú apareciste!	*I was thinking of you, and at that moment, you appeared!*

As with the present progressive tense, direct, indirect, and reflexive object pronouns may precede **estar** or attach to the end of the present participle. In the latter case, a written accent needs to be added to show the stressed syllable.

Nos estaban llamando. Estaban llamándo**nos**.	*They were calling us.*
Le estábamos escribiendo una carta. Estábamos escribiéndo**le** una carta.	*We were writing a letter to him.*

Actividades

1 Comprensión. Selecciona la expresión más lógica para describir lo que estaban haciendo las personas en estas situaciones.

1. En la cocina, Margarita...
   a. estaba limpiando la alfombra.
   b. estaba sirviendo los refrescos.

2. En la tienda de alimentos, nosotros...
   a. estábamos escogiendo las verduras.
   b. estábamos pagando las cuentas.

3. En el hospital, tú...
   a. estabas mirando el menú.
   b. estabas buscando a un médico.

4. En la farmacia, la dependiente...
   a. estaba comprando papel.
   b. estaba vendiendo antibióticos.

5. En la cafetería, Carolina y tú...
   a. estaban cocinando.
   b. estaban tomando un café.

6. En el dormitorio, Feliciano y su hermano Toño...
   a. estaban lavando los platos.
   b. estaban recogiendo la ropa.

2 Ayer por la tarde. ¿Qué estaban haciendo ayer por la tarde las personas de los dibujos? Trabajen en parejas.

1. Mónica 2. Mamá 3. Papá

4. Abuela 5. El gatito 6. Guillermo

3 ¿Qué estabas haciendo...? En parejas, conversen sobre las actividades de cada uno/a de ustedes en los días y horas descritas.

▶ MODELO: *ayer, a las tres de la tarde*
   —¿Qué estabas haciendo ayer a las tres de la tarde?
   —Estaba comiendo con amigos en la cafetería de la universidad.

1. ayer, a las once de la mañana
2. esta mañana, a las seis
3. el pasado 4 de julio por la noche
4. el sábado, a las once de la noche
5. anoche, a las siete de la noche
6. ayer, antes de la clase de español
7. el 31 de diciembre del año pasado
8. el jueves al mediodía

Notice in the preceding examples that when the main verb expresses doubt, uncertainty, or denial, the dependent verb is in the **subjunctive.**

Indicative			Subjunctive
Main clause expressing doubt, uncertainty, denial, disbelief	+	**que** +	dependent clause (what is doubted, denied, uncertain, not believed)

No creemos	**que**	el mercado **tenga** mangos.
We don't believe	*that*	*the market will have mangos.*
Es imposible	**que**	hoy **estén** cerradas las tiendas.
It's impossible	*that*	*the stores are closed today.*
Dudo	**que**	**podamos** llegar temprano.
I doubt	*that*	*we will arrive early.*

When the main verb expresses certainty, the **indicative** is used.

Creemos	**que**	el mercado **tiene** mangos.
We believe	*that*	*the market has mangos.*
Estoy seguro de	**que**	hoy **están** cerradas las tiendas.
I am sure	*that*	*the stores are closed today.*
No hay duda de	**que**	**podemos** llegar temprano.
There is no doubt	*that*	*we can arrive early.*

Verbs and expressions of doubt, uncertainty, denial, and disbelief			
Use the subjunctive			
dudar	*to doubt*	no es evidente	*it's not evident*
es imposible	*it's impossible*	no es seguro	*it's not sure*
es posible	*it's possible*	no es verdad	*it's not true*
es probable	*it's probable*	no está claro	*it isn't clear*
negar (ie)	*to deny*	no estar seguro/a de	*to be unsure*
no creer	*to not believe*	no pensar (ie)	*to not think*
no es cierto	*it's not certain*	puede ser	*it can be*

Common verbs and expressions of certainty			
Use the indicative			
creer	*to think; to believe*	estar seguro/a de	*to be sure*
es cierto	*it's certain, true*	no dudar	*to not doubt*
es evidente	*it's evident*	no hay duda (de)	*there's no doubt*
es obvio	*it's obvious*	no negar (ie)	*to not deny*
es seguro	*it's sure*	opinar	*to think (have an opinion)*
es verdad	*it's true*	pensar (ie)	*to think (opinion)*
está claro	*it's clear*		

In a question with **creer, opinar,** and **pensar** the indicative or the subjunctive may be used in the dependent clause. The subjunctive stresses uncertainty about the issue.

> ¿Crees que la comida **esté** mala?   *Do you think that the food is spoiled?*

Quizás and **tal vez** both mean *perhaps* and are generally used with the subjunctive. Note that the word **que** is not used.

> ¿Ves mucha televisión? ¡Quizás   *Do you watch a lot of TV? Perhaps you*
>   **seas** teleadicto!   *are a TV-addict!*

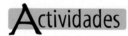

Actividades

1 Dudas y certezas. Completa las oraciones de una manera lógica.

1. Es probable que...
   a. vaya al gimnasio.   b. va al gimnasio.

2. Dudo que...
   a. sea bueno comer mucha azúcar.   b. es bueno comer mucha azúcar.

3. Es seguro que la ensalada...
   a. sea buena para la salud.   b. es buena para la salud.

4. No hay duda de que...
   a. seas mi mejor amigo.   b. eres mi mejor amigo.

5. No creo que...
   a. tienes tiempo para todo.   b. tengas tiempo para todo.

6. Es obvio que...
   a. estés en buena forma.   b. estás en buena forma.

2 Momentos de la vida. Completa los diálogos con el subjuntivo o el indicativo según el contexto.

Ernesto y Amanda están en un restaurante de comida rápida.

Ernesto	No creo que nosotros _____ (**1.** deber) comer un almuerzo con mucha grasa, pero dudo que tú _____ (**2.** seguir) mis consejos. Recuerda, nunca es demasiado pronto para pensar en la nutrición.
Amanda	No niego que las papas fritas _____ (**3.** ser) malas para la salud y es cierto que la ensalada _____ (**4.** contribuir) a la buena nutrición; pero, es imposible que la gente _____ (**5.** comer) solamente ensaladas y verduras. Es muy aburrido.
Ernesto	Es verdad que nosotros _____ (**6.** deber) tener una dieta balanceada. Vamos a pedir ensalada y hamburguesas, ¿de acuerdo?

Gregorio y Adelita, dos novios, se declaran su amor y amistad.

Gregorio	Adelita, es verdad que tú me _____ (**7.** querer), ¿no?
Adelita	Corazón, es cierto que te _____ (**8.** adorar) y es verdad que _____ (**9.** querer) vivir el resto de mi vida contigo.
Gregorio	Estoy seguro de que nosotros _____ (**10.** ir) a ser muy felices.
Adelita	Creo que tú y yo nos _____ (**11.** respetar) mucho.

Sami está en la oficina de la doctora Colón, una psicóloga excelente.

Sami	Es verdad que yo no _____ (**12.** sentirse) muy bien. Estoy triste.
Dra. Colón	Todos tenemos momentos bajos en la vida. Sami, no niego que _____ (**13.** estar, tú) deprimido. Es importante que _____ (**14.** hablar, tú) de tus problemas.

3 ¿Es verdad? Tú no estás de acuerdo con las opiniones de tu amigo/a. En parejas, expresen su desacuerdo usando estas expresiones: **no es verdad, niego que, dudo que, no creo que.** Sigan el modelo.

▶ MODELO: Comes muy poca fruta.
No es verdad que coma muy poca fruta.

1. La pizza es más rica que la lasaña.
2. Yo soy un/a cocinero/a excelente.
3. Mi dieta no tiene carne roja.
4. Los estudiantes prefieren comer tacos y sodas.
5. Todos los domingos hago huevos fritos.
6. En mi casa siempre hay crema de cacahuate.
7. Las manzanas y los plátanos contienen sal.
8. Los perritos comen ensalada.

4 Verdades y dudas. Escríbele un correo electrónico a tu prima, contándole las cosas que sabes y las dudas que tengas. Incluye diez ideas sobre la vida académica, social, familiar y profesional, utilizando las expresiones de duda, negación y certeza *(certainty).*

Un plan secreto

En el mercado de Otavalo.

¡Mira, Felipe, es el amanecer!

¿Quieres entrar?

Claro.

En la tienda de Zulaya.

¡Hola!

Buenas tardes, señorita. ¿Busca algo en especial?

Me llamó la atención el tejido del amanecer. Queremos verlo.

¡Dios mío! ¡Qué coincidencia! ¿Está usted leyendo este libro?

Sí, me fascinan los objetos de arte precolombinos...

...y el misterio de las piezas perdidas, como esas dos.

¡Los héroes gemelos!

¿Qué sabe usted de ellos?

La autora es nuestra profesora de arqueología.

¿Lo dice en serio?

Sí, en este momento, Yax-Balam y Hun-Ahau son muy importantes en nuestras vidas.

¿Qué quiere decir con eso?

Pues... los gemelos están separados. Y nosotros debemos reunirlos el 31 de agosto, ni antes ni después.

Pero, ¿por qué el treinta y uno de agosto?

Ése es el día que murió Pacal, el gran rey de los mayas. Los jaguares tienen que estar con él en Xibalbá.

Pero, no entiendo. ¿Qué hacen ustedes aquí en el Ecuador?

Creemos que Yax-Balam está aquí, en Otavalo. Pero esta información es confidencial.

Adriana, tenemos que irnos.

¿Por qué? ¿Qué pasa?

¡Vámonos! ¡Vámonos!

Señorita, gracias por su compra. Deben salir por aquí.

¿Perdón?

Aquí tiene, gracias, gracias.

Señorita, la estaba esperando. Usted es la mensajera de Armando de Landa, ¿no es así?

No es el momento oportuno. Su paquete ya está listo. Aquí está.

Sí, pero ¿cómo lo sabía?

En las montañas.

¡Era Gafasnegras, la que trató de matarnos en Puerto Rico! ¿Ése es el jaguar auténtico?

Estoy segura de que es Yax-Balam. La suerte sigue con nosotros.

¡Qué mala suerte! Pero aquí no termina la historia. ¡Van a ver!

Actividades

Online Study Center

For additional practice with this episode, visit the *Caminos* website at http://college.hmco.com/languages/spanish/renjilian/caminos/3e/student_home.html.

1 Comprensión. Basándote en este episodio de *Caminos del jaguar,* elige la alternativa lógica.

1. Adriana y Felipe quieren...
   a. ver el tejido del amanecer.   b. comprar el tejido del amanecer.

2. A Zulaya le interesa...
   a. el misterio del amanecer.   b. el libro de Nayeli.

3. A Zulaya le fascinan...
   a. los jaguares.   b. las piedras.

4. Los gemelos tienen que estar juntos en México...
   a. el 31 de agosto.   b. el 31 de julio.

5. Adriana y Felipe creen que ellos...
   a. pueden confiar en Zulaya.   b. no pueden confiar en Zulaya.

6. ¿Dónde está Yax-Balam?
   a. En la bolsa de Adriana.   b. En la bolsa de Gafasnegras.

2 Situaciones. Dramaticen una de las siguientes situaciones.

1. Zulaya y Adriana hablan sobre el libro de Nayeli.
2. Zulaya le entrega una bolsa a Gafasnegras.

3 Escritura. Describe qué sucede cuando Gafasnegras se acerca a la tienda de Zulaya. (4–6 oraciones)

NOTA CULTURAL

Los tejidos

En muchas regiones andinas de América Latina, los tejidos son parte de la herencia cultural y el arte de hacerlos pasa de generación en generación. En Ecuador, Bolivia y Perú se usa la lana de las llamas y alpacas para tejer ropa y alfombras que después se venden en los mercados. Para teñir la lana de diferentes colores se usan tintes naturales extraídos de varios tipos de plantas. Actualmente, se usan también fibras artificiales. En el mercado de Otavalo, en Ecuador, se pueden ver las hermosas formas y colores de tejidos tradicionales.

Lectura

PRELECTURA

The readings that follow describe various health and wellness issues for people of different ages. They were published in several contemporary magazines in Spanish, including *GeoMundo*, *Cristina*, *Vanidades*, and *Newsweek en Español*.

Reading Strategy

Comparing and contrasting

In this reading section, there are six short articles that are different in many respects, but that also have similarities. Before reading them, do these pre-reading activities in which you will be comparing and contrasting medical conditions. This will prepare you for the reading content and will enable you to compare the ideas, solutions, or advice presented in the six articles.

1 **Cuerpos y condiciones.** En parejas, pronuncien e indiquen lo que significa cada uno de los siguientes cognados.

alcoholismo	alergia	detectar	cortisona	demencia
diabetes	infecciones	congénito	estafilococos	artritis
antibióticos	resultados	anatomía	eliminar	prevenir

2 **Opinión.** Di si cada enfermedad de la tabla te preocupa poco, algo o mucho.

Condición	Me preocupa poco	Me preocupa algo	Me preocupa mucho
la artritis	_____	_____	_____
infecciones	_____	_____	_____
la hipertensión	_____	_____	_____
el Alzheimer	_____	_____	_____
alergias	_____	_____	_____
el alcoholismo	_____	_____	_____
el cáncer	_____	_____	_____

3 **¿Más o menos?** Con un/a compañero/a, discutan cuál de las siete enfermedades es más o menos seria. Sigue el modelo.

▶ MODELO: *Yo creo que el Alzheimer es menos / más (tan) serio que (como) el cáncer. ¿Qué crees tú?*

4 **Comparaciones y contrastes.** Trabajen en parejas para comparar y contrastar los síntomas y las características de tres de las condiciones médicas de la tabla de la *Actividad 2*.

Salud y bienestar: Toma control de tu vida

Curar la artritis con piquetes de abejas[1]

La artritis a veces ataca a personas de mediana[2] edad, y los dolores que sufren son aliviados[3] mediante[4] un método tradicional. La curación consiste en obligar a una abeja a picar[5] al enfermo en el área afectada. Los pacientes que han recibido[6] el tratamiento aseguran[7] que, aunque al principio[8] el dolor del piquete es muy fuerte, con el tiempo este dolor se reduce.

Los niños y las alergias

La rinitis alérgica[9] puede afectar hasta un 42 por ciento de los niños que se encuentran en la edad escolar[10]. En un día típico, más de 10.000 niños faltan a[11] la escuela debido a problemas por las alergias estacionales[12].

Alergias en la familia es un factor muy importante para predecir[13] alergias en los niños. Por lo general, el riesgo[14] de que un niño desarrolle alergias estacionales aumenta cuando uno de los padres tiene una alergia, y es todavía más grande cuando ambos padres sufren de alergias.

¿Qué bebes — café, té o agua?

¿Te sientes cansado/a en la mañana? Es quizás porque tienes sed. Es buena idea beber un vaso de agua inmediatamente después de levantarte. De esta manera, no vas a necesitar café o té. El café y el té son populares, pero es importante que consumas ocho vasos de agua cada día.

Venciendo[15] el mal de Alzheimer

El mal de Alzheimer es una enfermedad muy seria que borra la personalidad de la persona afectada e impacta a toda la familia. No hay todavía[16] cura para esta enfermedad devastadora. Pero, la gente puede ofrecerse al Brain Endowment Bank como donante[17] para el estudio de enfermedades neurológicas.

Los científicos[18] anunciaron la semana pasada los resultados preliminares de estudios de una vacuna que podría ayudar a tratar o prevenir el mal[19] de Alzheimer. Una de las principales características del Alzheimer son los depósitos de una proteína llamada betaamiloide en el cerebro. No se sabe si estos depósitos son la causa de la pérdida[20] de memoria y demencia, pero algunos investigadores creen que eliminarlas podría reducir los síntomas.

Pequeños corazoncitos[21]

La medicina y la tecnología hacen posible milagros[22] para alargar[23] la vida, y para hacer posible la de bebés por nacer[24]. Hoy se pueden detectar enfermedades congénitas del corazón en bebés que todavía están en el vientre[25], gracias al ultrasonido[26] de frecuencia más elevada, que permite ver claramente la anatomía del pequeño corazón. Este nuevo recurso es crucial, ya que el uno por ciento de los bebés nace con problemas del corazón.

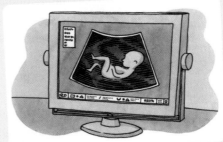

---

[1]bee stings; [2]middle; [3]relieved; [4]by means of; [5]to sting; [6]have received; [7]assure; [8]at first; [9]nasal allergy; [10]school; [11]miss; [12]seasonal; [13]predict; [14]risk; [15]Conquering; [16]yet; [17]organ donor; [18]scientists; [19]disease; [20]loss; [21]Little hearts; [22]miracles; [23]lengthen; [24]unborn; [25]womb; [26]ultrasound exam

Prevenir las infecciones

Los estafilococos[27] han causado[28] muertes[29] infantiles. Hay muchas maneras de prevenir las infecciones en general:

Lavarse es la mejor manera de combatir infecciones. Los niños deben de lavarse las manos antes de las comidas, y si es posible antes de comer cualquier cosa, y después de usar el baño.

Desinfectarse todas las heridas y cortaduras[30], pues es por donde pueden entrar los microbios al organismo.

No tocar ningún tipo de insecto, conocido o desconocido, y mucho menos escarbar[31] en la tierra buscándolos. Mantenerse alejados[32] de animales pequeños cuyos dueños[33] no sean perfectamente conocidos.

Vigilar[34] cualquier infección. Si observas que el lugar infectado empeora[35], o si no está visible, si notas que tu niño tiene una fiebre alta, llévalo inmediatamente a su médico. Si el estado del niño no mejora en 2 o 3 días, es el momento de comenzar a administrarle antibióticos.

[27]bacteria; [28]have caused; [29]deaths; [30]cuts; [31]dig; [32]far away; [33]owners; [34]Watch; [35]worsens

POSTLECTURA

1 ¿Verdadero o falso? Trabajando en parejas, discutan si las oraciones siguientes son falsas o verdaderas según las lecturas. Corrijan las oraciones falsas.

1. El mal de Alzheimer afecta a todos en la familia.
2. El uno por ciento de los bebés nace con problemas del corazón.
3. El agua es mala para la salud.
4. Más de veinte mil estudiantes faltan a la escuela cada día a causa de las alergias.
5. Si estás cansado/a, la sed puede ser la causa.
6. Los pacientes que tienen mal de Alzheimer pierden la memoria.
7. Las alergias pueden pasar de padres a hijos.
8. La tecnología no es buena para detectar enfermedades infantiles.
9. Lavarse las manos es una buena manera de evitar infecciones.
10. Hay una nueva vacuna que reduce los síntomas del mal de Alzheimer.
11. Es mejor jugar con animales desconocidos.
12. El piquete de una abeja puede reducir los dolores de la artritis.

2 Recomendaciones. Imagínate que tú eres especialista en salud y bienestar. Trabaja con un/a compañero/a y dale algunas recomendaciones para mantener a toda la familia sana. Combina un elemento de la columna A con otro de la columna B. Cuidado con los verbos reflexivos. Sigue el modelo.

▶ MODELO: es mejor / tener un examen médico cada año
Es mejor que tengas un examen médico cada año.

A	B
(no) es importante	llevar a tu niño al médico si tiene una fiebre alta
(no) es malo	lavarse las manos antes de comer
(no) es necesario	consultar a un/a médico/a si tienes un problema serio
(no) es mejor	desinfectarse las heridas
(no) es preferible	no caminar todos los días
(no) es bueno	hacer ejercicio todos los días
(no) es urgente	no tocar los insectos para no infectarse
(no) es esencial	beber mucha agua

3 Comparaciones y contrastes. Trabaja con un/a compañero/a para comparar y contrastar los diferentes tratamientos de dos de las condiciones médicas de la lectura: las infecciones, la artritis, las alergias, el Alzheimer. ¿Qué tratamiento es mejor? ¿Por qué?

Escritura

Writing Strategy

Using visual organizers (Venn diagrams)

One way to organize your ideas visually when comparing or contrasting two or more items is by creating a Venn diagram. Below is a sample of a Venn diagram that has been done to compare two different popular diets **La dieta South Beach** and **La dieta Atkins.**

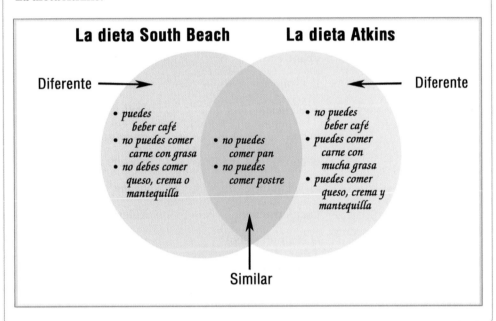

La dieta South Beach   **La dieta Atkins**

Diferente →   ← Diferente

- *puedes beber café*
- *no puedes comer carne con grasa*
- *no debes comer queso, crema o mantequilla*

- *no puedes comer pan*
- *no puedes comer postre*

- *no puedes beber café*
- *puedes comer carne con mucha grasa*
- *puedes comer queso, crema y mantequilla*

↑ Similar

Workshop

1. Draw a Venn diagram on a piece of paper.
2. Choose a topic to compare or contrast.
3. Begin by listing the things that are unique to the items in the outer rings of each circle.
4. Then list the things that the items have in common in the center, where the circles overlap.
5. Refer to this diagram to help organize your writing.

Strategy in Action

For additional practice using visual organizers, complete the exercises below and in the *Escritura* section of your Student Activities Manual for *Unidad 8.*

1. **Dos dietas.** Compara dos diferentes dietas que son populares hoy día. Después, escribe tus recomendaciones de qué dieta sugieres y por qué.

2. **Combatir el estrés.** Compara dos diferentes métodos para combatir el estrés. Después escribe un cartel para el centro de salud de tu universidad.

Resumen de vocabulario

PRIMER PASO

IDENTIFYING PARTS OF THE BODY
Sustantivos

la boca	*mouth*
el brazo	*arm*
la cabeza	*head*
la cara	*face*
el cerebro	*brain*
el corazón	*heart*
el cuerpo	*body*
los dedos	*fingers*
los dedos del pie	*toes*
los dientes	*teeth*
la espalda	*back*
el estómago	*stomach*
la garganta	*throat*
los huesos	*bones*
la lengua	*tongue*
la mano	*hand*
el músculo	*muscle*
la nariz	*nose*
el oído	*ear (inner)*
los ojos	*eyes*
la oreja	*ear (outer)*
el pecho	*chest*
el pelo	*hair*
el pie	*foot*
la pierna	*leg*
el pulmón	*lung*
la rodilla	*knee*

la sangre	*blood*
el tobillo	*ankle*

MAKING A DOCTOR'S APPOINTMENT
Sustantivos

el antibiótico	*antibiotic*
la aspirina	*aspirin*
el bienestar	*well-being*
la cita	*appointment*
el consultorio médico	*doctor's office*
el/la curandero/a	*healer*
la enfermedad	*illness*
el examen físico	*physical exam*
la fractura	*fracture*
el hielo	*ice*
la infección	*infection*
la inflamación	*inflamation*
la inyección	*injection*
el jarabe	*syrup*
la medicina	*medicine*
la operación	*operation*
el/la paciente	*patient*
la píldora, pastilla	*pill*
la presión (sanguínea)	*blood pressure*
la prueba, el análisis	*test, exam (medical)*
la radiografía	*x-ray*
la receta	*prescription*
el remedio	*remedy*

la sala de emergencia	emergency room
el síntoma	symptom
el soroche	altitude sickness
la vacuna	vaccine
la venda	bandage
el yeso	cast

Verbos

aliviarse	to get better
cuidarse	to take care of oneself
curar	to cure
dañar	to harm
doler (ue)	to hurt
enfermarse	to get sick
estornudar	to sneeze
evitar	to avoid
hacer una cita	to make an appointment
mejorar	to get better
reducir	to reduce
respirar	to breathe
romper(se) (el brazo)	to break (one's arm)
sangrar	to bleed
ser alérgico/a a..., tener alergia a...	to be allergic to . . .
torcer(se) (el tobillo)	to twist, sprain (one's ankle)
toser	to cough
vendar	to bandage
vomitar	to vomit

Adjetivos

fracturado/a	broken, fractured
grave	grave, serious

Expresiones con *estar*

estar embarazada	to be pregnant
estar inflamado/a	to be inflamed
estar mareado/a	to be dizzy
estar resfriado/a	to have a cold

Expresiones con *tener*

tener apetito	to have an appetite
tener buena / mala salud	to be in good / bad health
tener catarro, resfrío	to have a cold
tener dolor	to have pain
tener escalofríos	to shiver, have a chill
tener fiebre	to have a fever
tener gripe	to have the flu
tener náuseas	to be nauseous
tener tos	to have a cough

VERBS AND EXPRESSIONS OF REQUEST AND EMOTION

Verbs

aconsejar	to advise
alegrarse (de)	to be happy
desear	to want
enojarse	to be angry

VERBS AND EXPRESSIONS OF REQUEST AND EMOTION cont.

Verbs

esperar	*to hope*
estar contento/a de	*to be happy*
gustarle (a alguien)	*to like; to be pleasing*
lamentar	*to lament, regret*
mandar	*to order*
molestarle (a alguien)	*to bother (someone)*
necesitar	*to need*
ojalá	*I / We / Let's hope so*
pedir (i)	*to request, ask for*
preferir (ie)	*to prefer*
preocupar(se)	*to worry*
querer (ie)	*to want*
recomendar (ie)	*to recommend*
rogar (ue)	*to beg, plead*
sentir (ie)	*to be sorry, regret*
sorprender	*to surprise*

sugerir (ie)	*to suggest*
temer	*to fear, be afraid of*
tener miedo (de)	*to be afraid (of)*

Impersonal expressions

es bueno	*it's good*
es esencial	*it's essential*
es extraño	*it's strange*
es importante	*it's important*
es malo	*it's bad*
es mejor	*it's better*
es necesario	*it's necessary (to someone)*
es peor	*it's worse*
es preciso	*it's necessary*
es preferible	*it's preferable*
es ridículo	*it's ridiculous*
es terrible	*it's terrible*
es urgente	*it's urgent*
es una lástima	*it's a shame*

SEGUNDO PASO

LEARNING ABOUT FOODS AND NUTRITION

Sustantivos

el alimento	*food*
la caloría	*calorie*
la cantidad	*quantity*
la dieta	*diet*
los frijoles	*beans*
el peso	*weight*
la pirámide de la alimentación	*food pyramid*
la porción	*portion*

Verbos

conservarse	*to keep*
consumir	*to consume*
depender	*to depend*

Adjetivos

activo/a	*active*
físico/a	*physical*
nutritivo/a	*nutritious*
sano/a	*healthy*
sedentario/a	*sedentary*

Adverbio

diariamente	*daily*

VERBS AND EXPRESSIONS OF DOUBT, UNCERTAINTY, DENIAL, AND DISBELIEF

dudar	*to doubt*
es imposible	*it's impossible*
es posible	*it's possible*
es probable	*it's probable*
negar (ie)	*to deny*
no creer	*to not believe*
no es cierto	*it's not certain*
no es evidente	*it's not evident*
no es seguro	*it's not sure*
no es verdad	*it's not true*
no está claro	*it isn't clear*
no estar seguro/a de	*to be unsure*
no pensar (ie)	*to not think*
puede ser	*it can be*
quizás	*maybe, perhaps*
tal vez	*maybe, perhaps*

Common verbs and expressions of certainty

creer	*to think; to believe*
es cierto	*it's certain, true*
es evidente	*it's evident*
es obvio	*it's obvious*
es seguro	*it's sure*
es verdad	*it's true*
está claro	*it's clear*
estar seguro/a de	*to be sure*
no dudar	*to not doubt*
no hay duda (de)	*there's no doubt*
no negar (ie)	*to not deny*
opinar	*to think (have an opinion)*
pensar (ie)	*to think (opinion)*

SUDAMÉRICA

Online Study Center

To learn more about the people featured in this section, visit the *Caminos* website at http://college .hmco.com/languages/ spanish/renjilian/caminos/ 3e/student_home.html.

Michelle Bachelet

Carolina Herrera

Víctor Jara

Inca Son

Evo Morales

PERSONALIDADES

Pablo Neruda

Mercedes Sosa

Gabriel García Márquez

Los sudamericanos

Los artistas sudamericanos tratan muchos temas: el amor, la familia, el medio ambiente[1], la guerra, la política, la cultura. El tema de los derechos humanos[2] también se refleja en el arte, la música, la literatura y el cine sudamericano. En las últimas décadas del siglo[3] XX, muchos países latinoamericanos sufrieron bajo dictaduras[4] represivas. El resultado fue la desaparición[5] o muerte de miles de personas que protestaron contra los actos discriminatorios y tiránicos de sus gobiernos.

Entre[6] los chilenos, el poeta Pablo Neruda y la novelista Isabel Allende critican en sus obras la opresión sociopolítica contra los ciudadanos de su país y de otras naciones hispanoamericanas.

Los argentinos Quino, en sus tiras cómicas[7], y Mercedes Sosa, en sus canciones, cubren temas de las violaciones de derechos humanos. En el cine argentino, las películas "La historia oficial",

---

[1]environment; [2]human rights; [3]century; [4]dictatorships; [5]disappearance; [6]among; [7]comic strips

"En el arte, la única competencia que tengo
es con lo que hice ayer."
—Shakira (Colombia)

"Tango", "Kamchatka" y otras tratan[8] de los ciudadanos desaparecidos en la Argentina durante las décadas de los setenta y ochenta.

Cien años de soledad[9] es una novela extraordinaria escrita por el colombiano Gabriel García Márquez. Varias de sus obras literarias, junto con las de Mario Vargas Llosa (Perú) y Mario Benedetti (Uruguay), que tratan de temas políticos y sociales, han sido[10] interpretadas en películas.

Visita el sitio web de ***Caminos*** para leer más en español sobre estas personalidades y otros sudamericanos influyentes como Michelle Bachelet, la primera mujer presidente de Chile; Evo Morales, el primer presidente indígena de Bolivia; Carolina Herrera, diseñadora venezolana; la escritora chilena Gabriela Mistral, ganadora del Premio Nobel de Literatura; los cantantes Victor Jara (Chile) y Shakira (Colombia); y los grupos Inca Son (Perú), Los Jaira (Bolivia) y Kandela y Son (Ecuador).

Mario Vargas Llosa

Shakira

Comprensión

Trabajando en parejas, háganse las preguntas.

1. ¿Cuáles son algunos de los temas de las artes y letras en Sudamérica?
2. Indiquen las profesiones de tres diferentes personalidades sudamericanas.

ARTE

FERNANDO BOTERO

El escultor° y pintor Fernando Botero nació en Colombia en 1932. Las obras de este artista prolífico aparecen en museos, plazas y avenidas famosas en las Américas, Europa y África. El volumen y la grandeza son características de su estilo artístico para pintar a personas, lugares y cosas. Es importante notar la preocupación de Botero por los derechos humanos y su crítica a la violencia que se vive en su país natal. Actualmente° tiene residencias en París, Nueva York y la Toscana.

sculptor

currently

Naturaleza muerta con helado

---

[8]deal with; [9]*One Hundred Years of Solitude* [10]have been.

Comprensión

Trabajando en parejas, háganse las preguntas sobre la obra de Botero.

1. ¿Cuáles son posibles temas de esta naturaleza muerta°? Describe el estilo del artista.   *still life*
2. ¿Qué frutas hay en la pintura? ¿De qué colores son? ¿Cuál es la más jugosa°?   *juicy*
3. Describe los postres. ¿Cuál te apetece° más?   *appeals to*
4. ¿De qué sabor° es el helado? ¿A cuántas personas puede servir?   *flavor*
5. ¿En qué cuarto puede estar la mesa? Nombra una probable ocasión para servir estos postres y frutas.
6. ¿Cómo te parece esta naturaleza muerta —deliciosa, exagerada, llamativa°, divertida, aburrida?   *bright, sho*
7. ¿Prefieres pastel de chocolate, de vainilla o de limón? ¿Por qué? ¿Cuál tiene más calorías, en tu opinión?
8. De las frutas que se ven en la pintura, ¿cuáles son buenas para la salud? ¿Cuál es tu favorita?

MÚSICA

JUANES

El cantante, guitarrista, productor y compositor, Juanes nació en Medellín, Colombia, bajo el nombre de Juan Esteban Aristizábal. A los siete años, su padre y sus tres hermanos mayores le enseñaron a tocar la guitarra. Ganador de casi dos docenas de premios prestigiosos de la música internacional (Premios Grammy Latinos, Premios MTV, Premios Lo Nuestro), incorpora muchos ritmos autóctonos° en sus canciones. Sus influencias musicales incluyen   *indigenous*
tango, ranchera, bolero, salsa, guasca y trova cubana. Sus temas son variados°: el amor, la búsqueda de la identidad, la guerra civil en Colombia.   *varied*

Comprensión

Trabajando en parejas, háganse las siguientes preguntas sobre Juanes.

1. Además de cantar, ¿qué hace Juanes en su carrera profesional?
2. ¿Dónde nació el cantante?
3. ¿Quiénes fueron los profesores de música de Juanes?
4. ¿A qué edad empezó a tocar la guitarra?
5. ¿Cómo se llaman los premios ganados por° Juanes?   *won by*
6. ¿Qué ritmos incorpora Juanes en sus canciones? ¿Qué estilos de música influyen a este cantante colombiano?
7. Nombra algunos de los temas musicales de Juanes.
8. Describe a un/a cantante de tu país que canta sobre el amor, la identidad o la guerra. ¿Quién es y qué expresa en su música?

Conéctate a Internet para escuchar la música de Juanes y aprender más sobre él.

> "Creo que la vida es como jugar un juego de cartas donde para ganar tienes que jugar lo mejor posible. Pero a menudo nuestra vida, como las cartas, suelen estar marcadas."
>
> —Isabel Allende (Chile)

LITERATURA

ISABEL ALLENDE

short story writer
war

Novelista y cuentista°, Isabel Allende nació en 1942 en Perú, de padres chilenos. En su cuento "Dos palabras", el carácter de los políticos y los efectos de la guerra° están entre los varios temas que la autora incorpora en esta narración corta. En el fragmento que sigue, una mujer llamada Belisa Crepusculario escribe discursos° para la gente. El Coronel°, soldado° y candidato para la presidencia de Chile, le pide que le escriba un discurso.

speeches
colonel / soldier

Dos palabras

...

—¿Eres la que vende palabras?—...

—Para servirte—...

El Coronel se puso de pie°. La mujer vio su piel oscura y sus fieros° ojos de puma.

stood up / fierce, wild

—Quiero ser Presidente—dijo él.

Estaba cansado de recorrer esa tierra maldita° en guerras inútiles y derrotas° que ningún subterfugio podía transformar en victorias.

wretched / defeats

...al Coronel no le interesaba convertirse en otro tirano...Su idea consistía en ser elegido° por votación popular.

elected

—Para eso necesito hablar como un candidato. ¿Puedes venderme las palabras para un discurso?— preguntó el coronel a Belisa Crepusculario.

—¿Cuánto te debo por tu trabajo, mujer?—...

—Un peso, Coronel.

—No es caro—dijo él abriendo la bolsa° que llevaba colgadaº del cinturón...

bag/he wore hanging right/ bonus

—Además tienes derecho° a una ñapa°. Te corresponden dos palabras secretas dijo Belisa Crepusculario.

👥 Comprensión

Con un/a compañero/a, háganse las preguntas sobre la lectura.

1. Nombra las partes del cuerpo que la autora menciona en el cuento.
2. ¿Qué animal menciona?
3. ¿Qué vende Belisa Crepusculario? ¿A quién?
4. ¿De qué estaba cansado el Coronel como soldado? ¿Qué adjetivo usa el Coronel para describir las guerras? ¿Estás de acuerdo?
5. ¿Qué quiere ser el Coronel? ¿Por qué necesita él las palabras de Belisa? ¿Cómo prefiere ser elegido él?
6. ¿Cuánto tiene que pagar el Coronel a Belisa por el discurso? ¿Es caro o barato? ¿Qué más le regala Belisa al Coronel?
7. ¿Qué tipo de Presidente quiere ser el Coronel?
8. La época de política represiva de los años pasados en Chile es un tema importante de esta selección. ¿Qué es lo contrario de una dictadura? ¿Cómo son los políticos de tu región?

9
La tecnología

VOCABULARIO Y LENGUA

- ► Talking about technology
- ► Contrasting the indicative and subjunctive in adjective clauses
- ► Giving instructions: Familiar *tú* commands

- ► Discussing cars
- ► Contrasting the indicative and subjunctive in adverbial clauses
- ► Describing actions in the recent and remote past: Present and past perfect indicative

CAMINOS DEL JAGUAR

- ► ¿Misión cumplida?
- ► Intuiciones y acusaciones

LECTURA

- ► Coches de hoy y mañana

NOTAS CULTURALES

- ► El padrino / La madrina
- ► Los parques nacionales de Costa Rica

ESTRATEGIAS

- ► **Reading:** Defining audience and purpose
- ► **Writing:** Developing a point of view

Gilbert "Magú" Luján, *Cruising Turtle Island*

Preguntas del tema

- ► ¿Pasas mucho tiempo navegando por Internet? ¿Por qué?
- ► ¿Cuál es el aparato de tecnología que más usas?
- ► ¿Cuál es el mejor coche? ¿el peor coche?
- ► ¿Cómo es el coche ideal?

PRIMER PASO

Vocabulario y lengua

TALKING ABOUT TECHNOLOGY

Hotel moderno con alta tecnología

Los días en los que un teléfono y un televisor eran los aparatos tecnológicos más avanzados dentro de una habitación ya son cosa del pasado. Hoy en día, la tecnología tiene un papel° muy importante en los servicios del hotel. Aquí hay algunos de los cambios.

role

La alta tecnología

Casi todas las habitaciones están equipadas con computadoras para **acceder a Internet**° con conexiones de **alta velocidad**° o de **conexión sin cables**° (WiFi).

access the Internet
high speed / wireless

Los televisores están colgados o **instalados**° en la pared. Tienen **pantallas planas**° de plasma o de LCD interactivos. A través de estos televisores se puede acceder a Internet con un **teclado**° **inalámbrico**°, mantener videoconferencias y ver quién llama a la puerta. Además, hay videoconsolas con cientos de **videojuegos**° para mantener entretenidos a los niños y aparatos de **realidad virtual.** *cont. on next page*

installed

flat screen

keyboard / wireless

videogames

Para la comodidad

Las habitaciones tienen climatización inteligente, programas informáticos que controlan las luces, **robots** de limpieza, sensores de luz, **control remoto** universal para hacer todo desde la cama, hasta subir la persiana°.

Venetian blinds

Páginas electrónicas

En las estanterías de la habitación hay libros electrónicos con pantallas **táctiles**° y numerosos textos **almacenados**°.

touch
saved

Cara a cara

El teléfono tiene una pantalla en la que el huésped ve a la persona que le atiende en recepción.

Un buen despertar

Las mesitas tienen un sistema emisor de ondas° que favorece el sueño. En algunos casos integran teléfono, **fax,** televisor y computadora. Y, si uno quiere desayunar en la cama, puede hacerlo en una bandeja° equipada con una pantalla en la que se puede ver las noticias o leer el **correo electrónico**°.

soundwave machine

tray

e-mail

Más palabras y expresiones

Cognados

el aparato
la aplicación
automático/a
la batería
el botón

la cámara
copiar
digital
el directorio
el documento
en línea
entrar

la función
el icono
el módem
multimedia
el programa
el teléfono celular
la videocámara

Sustantivos

el archivo	*computer file*
la ayuda	*help*
el buscador	*search engine*
la computadora portátil	*laptop*
la contraseña	*password*
el disco duro	*hard drive*
la (alta) definición	*(high) definition*
el entretenimiento	*entertainment*
la (video) grabadora	*(video) recorder*
el mensaje	*message*
el paso	*step*
el ratón	*mouse*
la red	*network*

Verbos

apagar	*to turn off, to shut off*
apuntar	*to point, to jot down*
archivar, guardar	*to save, to file*
bajar	*to download*
cargar	*to charge*
colgar (ue)	*to hang (up)*

desempeñar	*to carry out*
imprimir	*to print*
iniciar	*to begin*
mover (ue)	*to move; to shift*
prender, encender (ie)	*to turn on*
presionar, hacer clic, pulsar, oprimir	*to click (with the mouse); to push (a button)*

Adjetivos

disponible	*available*

Actividades

1 Habitación 2020. Lee la descripción del hotel del futuro (pp. 310–311) y determina qué servicios ofrece. Pon una X al lado de cada servicio que se ofrece.

_____ computadora
_____ desayuno virtual
_____ juegos electrónicos
_____ libros electrónicos
_____ máquina fax
_____ procesador automático de comidas
_____ robot-camarero
_____ teléfono con pantalla
_____ teclado inalámbrico
_____ teléfonos táctiles
_____ minibar automático
_____ televisor interactivo

2 ¿Qué describe? Escucha las descripciones de unos nuevos aparatos tecnológicos y escribe el número de la descripción al lado del aparato que le corresponda.

a. _____

b. _____

c. _____

d. _____

e. _____

3 **¡Qué buena es la tecnología!** A veces la tecnología no funciona como debe. Acabas de recibir un correo electrónico de una amiga, pero no puedes leer todo el mensaje. Completa el mensaje con las siguientes palabras.

mensaje   computadora   ayuda   impresora
programa   teléfono   tecnología

Tema:
Fecha:
Para:

¡Hola!

Hoy compré una nueva _*_. Traté de instalar el *$_ < para
mandarte un mensaje electrónico, pero dice que hay errores.
La *$* tampoco funciona y no puedo imprimir este *$<*.
Yo sé que soy nueva con la *&$v**_, pero esto es ridículo.
Por favor, necesito tu $*&_*. ¡Llámame, porque sé que por
lo menos funciona mi *&_!_!

Tu amiga,
Leticia

---

4 **Combinaciones.** Trabaja con un/a compañero/a para crear siete oraciones. Combinen palabras de cada columna y agreguen más palabras para hablar de la tecnología. Sigan el modelo.

▶ MODELO: *Yo prendo mi computadora por la mañana para leer mi correo electrónico.*

A	B	C
Yo	prender	archivo
Tú	mandar	párrafo
Mis amigos	abrir	computadora
Los profesores	cerrar	palabras
Ud.	buscar	mensaje
Tú y yo	imprimir	programa
Mi mamá	escribir	documento

5 **Nuevos productos.** Usa el Internet para buscar un nuevo producto tecnológico. Primero, busca en una página web en español como las siguientes y trae una copia del producto a la clase. Luego, en grupos de tres, hablen de sus productos y escojan el que más les guste para presentar a la clase.

http://www.apple.com/es

http://www.microsoft.com/argentina

http://www.palm.com/mx

http://www.sony.com.co

Dilema

Trabajo en una oficina que **tiene** tecnología vieja e ineficiente, pero sueño con una oficina que **tenga** tecnología moderna y eficiente.

Adjective clauses: An adjective clause is a subordinate clause introduced by **que** that modifies a noun, in the same way that a simple adjective does.

Simple adjective	Adjective clause
Tengo una computadora **vieja**. *I have an old computer.* Quiero una computadora **nueva**. *I want a new computer.*	Tengo una computadora **que es vieja**. *I have a computer that is old.* Quiero una computadora **que sea nueva**. *I want a computer that is new.*

The indicative is used when the verb in the subordinate clause refers to a specific or existent person or thing.

Trabajo en una compañía que **está** lejos de mi casa.	*I work at a company that is far from my home.*
Tengo un secretario que **sabe** muchísimo de computadoras.	*I have a secretary who knows a lot about computers.*

The subjunctive is used when the verb in the subordinate clause refers to an indefinite, non-existent, or unknown person or thing.

Quiero una computadora que **tenga** los últimos avances tecnológicos.	*I want a computer that has the latest technological advances.*
Busco una cámara digital que **saque** buenas fotos de acción.	*I'm looking for a digital camera that takes good action pictures.*

Many double negative expressions introduce adjective clauses that require the subjunctive: **No conozco a nadie que..., No hay nada que..., No hay ningún lugar que...,** etc.

Necesitamos a alguien que **sepa** hacer páginas web.	*We need someone who knows how to do web pages.*
No hay nadie que **tenga** la computadora perfecta.	*There isn't anyone who has the perfect computer.*

Actividades

1 Gustos y preferencias. Completa las preguntas con el presente del subjuntivo de los verbos entre paréntesis. Luego, contesta las preguntas con un/a compañero/a.

1. ¿Quieres una computadora de mano que _____ (venir) con correo electrónico?
2. ¿Prefieres un televisor que _____ (tener) una pantalla de plasma o de LCD?
3. ¿Buscas videojuegos que no _____ (contener) mucha violencia?
4. ¿Necesitas una computadora portátil que _____ (ser) más pequeña?
5. ¿Buscas restaurantes que _____ (ofrecer) una conexión sin cables?
6. ¿Sólo bajas música que te _____ (gustar) del Internet?

2 Cambios necesarios. A veces hay cosas que queremos cambiar en nuestras vidas. Usa el verbo **tener** o **conocer** para explicar lo que tienes y verbos como **querer, necesitar** y **buscar** para explicar lo que necesitas. Sigue el modelo.

► MODELO: un/a profesora
Tengo una profesora que enseña español pero necesito una profesora que enseñe portugués.

1. una clase
2. un coche
3. una grabadora de música
4. un teléfono
5. una conexión al Internet
6. una película
7. una cámara
8. un/a presidente
9. un apartamento
10. una televisión

3 Un/a compañero/a ideal.

Necesitas buscar un/a compañero/a de cuarto. ¿Cuáles son las cualidades más importantes? ¿Cuáles son las cualidades menos importantes? Pon estas cualidades en orden de importancia. Luego, trabajen en parejas y decidan cuáles son las tres cosas más importantes y las tres cosas menos importantes. Sigue el modelo.

▶ **MODELO:**   —*Busco un/a compañero/a que me trate bien.*
              —*No quiero un/a compañero/a que fume.*

_____ (no) limpiar su cuarto
_____ (no) fumar
_____ (no) tocar música a todas horas
_____ ser amable
_____ pagar las cuentas a tiempo

_____ tener computadora
_____ tratarme bien
_____ (no) estudiar mucho
_____ (no) hacer mucho ruido
_____ (no) tener mascotas

4 Un trabajo ideal.

Necesitas buscar un trabajo nuevo. Decides escribir un anuncio clasificado en el periódico. Escribe un anuncio que describa tu trabajo ideal, incluyendo la tecnología que conoces. Comienza tu anuncio con esta frase: "Se busca un trabajo que..."

GIVING INSTRUCTIONS: FAMILIAR *TÚ* COMMANDS

Cómo bajar música
con iTunes

Conéctate al Internet.
Abre el programa de iTunes.
Haz clic en la tienda de música.
Busca tu música favorita.
Escucha la canción para asegurar que
es la que quieres.
Haz clic en "Comprar canción" o
"Comprar álbum".
Escribe tu contraseña. (¡No olvides tu
tarjeta de crédito!)
Oprime el botón "Comprar" y baja la
música a iTunes.
Escucha la música en tu computadora
y ponla en tu iPod.
¡Disfrútala!

In *Unidad 6*, you learned the formation and uses of the formal **Ud. / Uds.** commands. Look at the **tú** commands in the preceding instructions. Do you recognize some of the forms? Which forms are new? Where are the pronouns placed in the affirmative and the negative commands?

Affirmative *tú* commands

To form the *affirmative tú* command, use the third person singular of the present tense. All verbs with irregular third person singular forms have an irregular **tú** command form. Review the formation of the present tense on pages 94, 95, and 96.

Infinitive	affirmative *tú* command	Infinitive	affirmative *tú* command
cantar	canta	entender (ie)	entiende
beber	bebe	pedir (i)	pide
escribir	escribe	oír	oye
recordar (ue)	recuerda	leer	lee

The subject pronoun **tú** is sometimes used for emphasis. If used in a command, the pronoun follows the command form.

Busca tú un nuevo juego electrónico para tu primo.   *Look for a new videogame for your cousin.*

Irregular affirmative *tú* commands

The following verbs have irregular forms for the affirmative **tú** commands:

Infinitive	affirmative *tú* command	Infinitive	affirmative *tú* command
decir	di	salir	sal
hacer	haz	ser	sé
ir	ve	tener	ten
poner	pon	venir	ven

Negative *tú* commands

The *negative familiar* commands are the same as the present subjunctive forms for **tú,** which you learned in *Unidad 8*. Review these forms on pages 278–281.

Infinitive	negative *tú* command	Infinitive	negative *tú* command
cantar	no cantes	oír	no oigas
beber	no bebas	ir	no vayas
escribir	no escribas	ser	no seas
recordar (ue)	no recuerdes	poner	no pongas
entender (ie)	no entiendas	conducir	no conduzcas
pedir (i)	no pidas	ver	no veas

Object pronouns

Direct and indirect object pronouns and reflexive pronouns are attached to the end of affirmative commands. When pronouns are attached, a written accent is needed if the stress falls on the third or fourth syllable from the end of the word.

¡**Dinos** la contraseña, por favor!	*Tell us the password, please!*
¡**Dínosla,** por favor!	*Tell it to us, please!*
Escríbeme pronto.	*Write to me soon.*

Direct and indirect object pronouns and reflexive pronouns precede the verb in all negative commands.

No **le** saques la foto a Juan todavía.	*Don't take the photo of Juan yet.*
No **se la** saques todavía.	*Don't take it (the photo) of him yet.*
No **te** duermas.	*Don't fall asleep.*

Actividades

1 Consejos. Dale consejos a un/a compañero/a de clase de cómo tener éxito en la universidad. Sigue el modelo.

> ► **MODELO:** _____ (Despertarse) temprano.
> *Despiértate temprano.*

1. _____ (Salir) de casa a tiempo.
2. No _____ (llegar) tarde a las clases.
3. _____ (Mantenerse) alerta en clase.
4. _____ (Escuchar) a los profesores.
5. _____ (Estudiar) todos los días.
6. _____ (Ir) a la biblioteca y _____ (leer) la tarea.
7. _____ (Hacer) ejercicios en el gimnasio con un/a amigo/a.
8. Si estás enfermo/a y no puedes ir a clase, _____ (mandarle) un correo electrónico a un/a compañero/a de clase y _____ (pedirle) la tarea.
9. No _____ (acostarse) tarde.
10. _____ (Dormir) bien cada noche para reducir el estrés.

2 Instrucciones. Tu profesor/a te pide que escribas un informe (*report*) para tu clase de español y necesitas buscar la información en Internet. Le pides sugerencias al /a la profesor/a. En parejas, pongan en orden sus sugerencias. Usen mandatos informales afirmativos (**tú**).

abrir la primera página web	escribirlo en tus propias palabras
abrir tu buscador favorito	escribir palabras clave en español
apuntar la información importante	repetir los pasos hasta encontrar la información que necesitas
entregárselo al/a la profesor/a	organizar la información para el informe
hacer clic en "Búsqueda"	leerla

3 Ayuda. Tu primo viene de visita y, como tu dormitorio está muy desorganizado, un amigo te ayuda a arreglarlo antes de la visita. Contesta sus preguntas con mandatos informales. No te olvides de usar los pronombres necesarios. Sigue el modelo.

> MODELO: ¿Dónde pongo los libros?
> Ponlos en el estante.

1. ¿Dejo los CDs en la mesa?
2. ¿Te presto mi cama de aire?
3. ¿Qué hago con la ropa que está en el piso?
4. ¿Cierro la puerta del armario?
5. ¿Apago la computadora?
6. ¿Hago la cama?
7. ¿Barro el piso?
8. ¿Dónde guardo tu iPod?
9. ¿Qué hago con el dinero que encontré en el escritorio?
10. ¿Pongo los zapatos debajo de la cama?

4 De visita. Tu primo está de visita, pero no sabe usar las cosas en tu apartamento. Mientras estás en clase, él te llama varias veces para preguntarte cómo usar las siguientes cosas. Trabajen en parejas y escriban de 2 a 4 mandatos informales para cada situación.

1. ¿Cómo funciona el televisor?
2. Tengo hambre y no sé usar tu microondas.
3. Quiero mandar un correo electrónico, pero no tengo tu contraseña.
4. Quiero escuchar música pero no sé como usar tu iPod.
5. Veo que tienes TiVO. ¿Cómo puedo grabar una película?
6. Me gustaría jugar con los videojuegos. ¿Cómo lo hago?

5 Apoyo técnico. En parejas, escriban diez consejos para una amiga que va a empezar a trabajar para un servicio de apoyo técnico. Va a recibir muchas llamadas al día y a veces las personas que llaman van a ser poco amables. ¿Qué debe hacer ella cuando hable con los clientes? ¿Qué no debe hacer?

¿Mision cumplida?

Actividades

Online Study Center

For additional practice with this episode, visit the *Caminos* website at http://college.hmco.com/languages/spanish/renjilian/caminos/3e/student_home.html.

1 Comprensión. Basándote en este episodio de *Caminos del jaguar,* elige la alternativa lógica.

1. Nayeli se siente segura con su madrina porque...
   a. la madrina se preocupa.
   b. se siente protegida.

2. La madrina quiere escuchar la historia...
   a. inmediatamente.
   b. después.

3. Nayeli dice que...
   a. tiene mucho tiempo.
   b. tiene poco tiempo.

4. Doña Carmen dice que...
   a. no recuerda a Armando.
   b. recuerda a Armando.

5. Nayeli dice que Armando...
   a. es brillante y serio.
   b. se robó el jaguar.

6. Armando está furioso con Zulaya porque...
   a. Zulaya no quiere su dinero.
   b. Zulaya no esperó sus instrucciones.

7. Adriana y Felipe le llevan a Nayeli el jaguar...
   a. Yax-Balam.
   b. Hun-Ahau.

8. Adriana dice que la misión está...
   a. casi cumplida.
   b. cumplida.

2 Situaciones. Dramaticen una de las siguientes situaciones.

1. Doña Carmen recibe a Nayeli en su casa.
2. Armando habla con Zulaya por teléfono.

3 Escritura. Escribe un resumen de lo que dice Adriana cuando le entrega el jaguar a Nayeli. (4–6 oraciones)

NOTA CULTURAL

El padrino / La madrina

En las culturas hispanas es un honor ser elegido/a como padrino o madrina. Se elige generalmente a algún miembro de la familia o a un amigo íntimo. Su función es tomar el lugar del padre o de la madre cuando sea necesario para asegurar el bienestar del ahijado o la ahijada. Generalmente hay una relación importante entre padrinos y ahijados. Muchas veces, la madrina o el padrino contribuye a pagar los gastos de celebraciones especiales como el bautizo y algunos cumpleaños especiales como la fiesta de quinceañera de la ahijada.

SEGUNDO PASO

Vocabulario y lengua

DISCUSSING CARS

Online Study Center

For additional practice with this unit's vocabulary and grammar, visit the *Caminos* website at http://college.hmco.com/languages/spanish/renjilian/caminos/3e/student_home.html. You can also review audio flashcards, quiz yourself, and explore related Spanish-language sites.

Necesitamos comprar un coche

—**Mire mamá, el limpiaparabrisas funciona muy bien.**

1. el baúl, maletero
2. el espejo retrovisor
3. el limpiaparabrisas
4. la llanta, rueda
5. las luces
6. el parabrisas
7. el pito, claxon
8. la placa
9. la puerta
10. el tanque de gasolina

Más palabras y expresiones

Cognados

el acelerador
el auto, automóvil
el carro
compacto/a

económico/a
la gasolina
híbrido/a
el motor

Sustantivos

el aire acondicionado	*air conditioning*
el asiento	*seat*
el coche	*car*
la batería, pila	*battery*
la bolsa de aire, el airbag	*airbag*

la carretera	highway
el choque	crash
el cinturón de seguridad	seatbelt
el/la conductor/a	driver
el deportivo	sports car
los frenos	brakes
la licencia de manejar/conducir	driver's license
la llanta pinchada	flat tire
la multa	fine
el volante	steering wheel

Verbos

abrocharse (el cinturón)	to buckle up (seatbelt)
arrancar	to start (a car, a race)
chocar	to collide
conducir, manejar	to drive
dañar	to injure; to damage
frenar	to brake
parar	to stop
pitar	to beep the horn

Actividades

1 ¿Qué es? Identifica la parte del coche que se describe.

1. El chofer se sienta en este lugar.
2. Son absolutamente necesarios cuando llueve.
3. Se necesita para llamar la atención, ¡no para hacer ruido!
4. El coche no puede parar sin ellos.
5. Protege a los pasajeros en los accidentes.
6. Si tu coche no lo tiene, te va a dar mucho calor en el verano.
7. Allí pones tu pie y ¡el coche anda!
8. Se vende por litros en España y en los Estados Unidos por galones.
9. Si dejas las luces encendidas muchas horas, se acaba.

2 ¡Quiero comprar un Jaguar! Contesta las siguientes preguntas sobre el tipo de coche que quieres comprar.

1. ¿Qué clase de auto te gusta? ¿deportivo? ¿compacto? ¿híbrido? ¿económico? ¿de lujo? ¿camioneta? ¿Por qué?
2. ¿Qué color prefieres? ¿Por qué?
3. ¿Cuál es tu presupuesto (budget)?
4. ¿Qué características son esenciales en tu coche?
5. ¿Qué características son deseables pero no esenciales?

3 ¿Qué auto compramos? Tú y tu mejor amigo/a deciden comprar un coche juntos. En parejas, comparen sus respuestas a la *Actividad 2* y decidan cuál de los coches van a comprar y por qué.

4 El coche ideal. Trae a clase una foto del coche que te piensas comprar (o dibújalo) y descríbelo a la clase.

Siempre estacionaba mi coche enfrente de la oficina **cuando llegaba** al trabajo por la mañana.

Pero ayer **cuando llegué,** tuve un pequeño accidente porque no vi la motocicleta que estaba allí.

La policia llegó y ¡me dio una multa de $100! Debo tener más cuidado **cuando manejo.**

Mañana, **cuando vaya** al trabajo, voy en metro.

As shown in the preceding examples, an adverbial conjunction (like **cuando**) can introduce a dependent clause. What forms are used after **cuando** in each of the examples? Why do you think the present indicative is used in the third sentence while the present subjunctive is used in the last one?

Adverbial clauses, introduced by conjunctions such as **cuando,** give information such as when, how, or under what circumstances an action may occur. When using adverbial conjunctions, choose the...

▶ **Imperfect** in the dependent clause to narrate *past habitual* actions.

▶ **Preterite** in the dependent clause to describe *specific past* actions.

► **Present indicative** in the dependent clause to report *present habitual* actions.

► **Present subjunctive** in the dependent clause to indicate a *future* action.

Adverbial conjunctions that are followed by the indicative or the subjunctive according to the preceding patterns are the following:

a pesar de que	*even though, even if*
aunque	*even when, even though, even if, although*
cuando	*when*
después (de) que	*after*
en cuanto	*as soon as*
hasta que	*until*
tan pronto como	*as soon as*

Notice that with **aunque** and **a pesar de que,** the English translation changes to indicate the difference between a concrete condition or fact (present indicative) and a condition or situation that may or may not happen (present subjunctive).

Rafael siempre va al trabajo **a pesar de que se siente** enfermo.	*Rafael always goes to work even though he feels ill.*
Rafael va al trabajo **aunque se sienta** enfermo.	*Rafael goes to work even if he feels ill.*

Notice that the sentence order is flexible with adverbial conjunctions.

Leo el correo electrónico **tan pronto como** llego al trabajo.	*I read my e-mail as soon as I get to work.*
Tan pronto como llego al trabajo, leo el correo electrónico.	*As soon as I get to work, I read my e-mail.*

Actividades

1 En camino. Determina si lo que sucede son situaciones habituales (indicativo) o futuras (subjuntivo). Selecciona la posibilidad correcta.

1. Cada jueves, Roberto sale de la casa cuando...
   a. llega su colega Jaime.
   b. llegue su colega Jaime.

2. Katie piensa comprar una motocicleta tan pronto como...
   a. ahorra el dinero.
   b. ahorre el dinero.

3. Isabel va a salir de viaje después de que el mecánico...
   a. arregla su coche.
   b. arregle su coche.

4. Con el precio tan alto de la gasolina, Pepito siempre maneja su coche hasta que...
   a. se le acabe la gasolina.
   b. se le acaba la gasolina.

5. El jefe siempre maneja su carro deportivo a pesar de que la gasolina...
   a. cuesta mucho.
   b. cueste mucho.

6. Roberto piensa comprar un coche híbrido en cuanto...
   a. le pagan.
   b. le paguen.

2 La conferencia. Lorena y Sami preparan una conferencia para sus clientes. Completa la descripción de algunas de sus actividades con el indicativo o subjuntivo de los verbos en paréntesis, según el contexto.

Lorena   Tenemos que preparar el café tan pronto como _____ (**1.** llegar) los clientes de hoy.

Sami   Sí, especialmente hay que tener todo listo cuando el jefe _____ (**2.** venir).

Lorena	Sami, ¿hiciste el registro en cuanto _____ (**3.** recibir) la lista de clientes?
Sami	Por supuesto, lo hice tan pronto como el secretario me _____ (**4.** traer) la lista.
Lorena	¿Piensas salir temprano hoy, después de que _____ (**5.** hacer, nosotros) la última presentación del día?
Sami	No, Lorena, es importante quedarme en la oficina hasta que _____ (**6.** terminar, yo) de escribir todos los informes para el archivo. ¿Y tú?
Lorena	Voy a buscar mi coche que está con el mecánico. Por eso, aunque _____ (**7.** dejar, yo) algunas cosas sin hacer, tengo que salir a las cinco.

3 **Ayer y mañana.** Escríbele un correo electrónico a tu amigo/a, describiéndole lo que tú ya hiciste y lo que van a hacer tú y tus compañeros de apartamento. Sigue el modelo.

▶ **MODELO:** El verano pasado, tan pronto como tuve el dinero, alquilé una cabaña en la playa con mis amigos.
El mes que viene, tan pronto como... *tenga dinero, voy a alquilar otra cabaña en la playa con mis amigos.*

1. Anoche cuando llegué a casa, me preparé una bebida de frutas en mi batidora.
   Mañana, cuando...
2. En cuanto recibimos nuestros salarios el mes pasado, pagamos la cuenta de teléfono, pero no pagamos la cuenta de la electricidad. Este mes, en cuanto...
3. Ayer no cenamos hasta que todos llegaron de la universidad.
   Hoy, tampoco vamos a cenar hasta que...
4. Yayo se duchó esta mañana tan pronto como se levantó.
   Mañana, Yayo también va a ducharse tan pronto como...
5. El año pasado, cuando recibí dinero de mi abuela, me compré ropa nueva.
   Esta semana, cuando...

DESCRIBING ACTIONS IN THE RECENT AND REMOTE PAST: PRESENT PERFECT AND PLUPERFECT (PAST PERFECT) INDICATIVE

Un día muy ocupado

Tomás	¿Qué **has hecho**° hoy, Mario?	*have you done*
Mario	**He estudiado**° mucho, **he limpiado** la casa, **he ido**° al supermercado y ahora estoy preparando la cena. Voy a preparar un plato que nunca **había preparado**° antes.	*I have studied / I have cleaned / have gone* *had prepared*
Tomás	Oye, pues yo **no he cenado**° todavía...	*I haven't had dinner*
Mario	Entonces ven a cenar conmigo.	
Tomás	Mil gracias. ¿Eres buen cocinero?	
Mario	Por supuesto. Nos vemos más tarde. Hasta luego.	

Present perfect and pluperfect (past perfect) indicative

A perfect tense has two parts: a conjugated form of the helping verb **haber** and the past participle of the main verb.

The present perfect uses the present tense of **haber.** The pluperfect (past perfect) uses the imperfect of **haber.**

The past participle of regular verbs is formed by adding –**ado** to the stem of –**ar** verbs and –**ido** to the stems of –**er** and –**ir** verbs.

hablar: habl + -ado = **hablado**
querer: quer + -ido = **querido**
venir: ven + -ido = **venido**

The present perfect and pluperfect indicative *(El presente perfecto y el pluscuamperfecto del indicativo)*				
	Present perfect		**Pluperfect**	
yo	he		había	
tú	has	hablado	habías	hablado
Ud. / él / ella	ha	querido	había	querido
nosotros/as	hemos	venido	habíamos	venido
vosotros/as	habéis		habíais	
Uds. / ellos / ellas	han		habían	

The present perfect indicative

The present perfect tense is used to talk about a recently completed action with reference to the present. It is also used to indicate an indefinite point in the past with reference to the present.

¿Ya **has hecho** la tarea?	*Have you already done the homework?*
Nunca **he estado** en España.	*I have never been to Spain.*

The pluperfect (past perfect) indicative

Like the present perfect tense, the past perfect is used to talk about an action or event that happened before another past action or event.

Cuando yo tenía dieciséis años, ya **había comprado** mi propio coche.	*When I was sixteen years old, I had already bought my own car.*
Antonio todavía no **había comido** cuando pasé a recogerlo.	*Antonio hadn't eaten yet when I went by to pick him up.*

The perfect tenses often use the word **ya** to express *already* and the word **todavía** when answering a question negatively. It expresses *yet.*

Sentence structure

Direct and indirect object pronouns and reflexive pronouns come directly before the conjugated form of **haber.**

—¿**Has manejado** el nuevo coche híbrido?

—No, todavía no <u>lo</u> **he manejado**.

—*Have you driven the new hybrid car?*

—*No, I have driven it yet.*

—¿<u>Te</u> **habías alojado** en ese hotel antes?

—Sí, <u>me</u> **había alojado** allí.

—*Had you stayed in that hotel before?*

—*Yes, I had stayed there.*

Irregular past participles

Infinitive	Past participle	
abrir	**abierto**	*opened*
cubrir	**cubierto**	*covered*
decir	**dicho**	*said, told*
descubrir	**descubierto**	*discovered*
escribir	**escrito**	*written*
hacer	**hecho**	*made, done*
morir	**muerto**	*died*
poner	**puesto**	*put, placed*
resolver	**resuelto**	*resolved*
romper	**roto**	*broken, torn*
ver	**visto**	*seen*
volver	**vuelto**	*returned*

You must write an accent over the **i** of the **–ido** ending for those **–er** and **–ir** verbs whose stems end in -**a**, -**e**, or -**o**.

Infinitive	Stem	Past participle	
creer	cre-	creído	*believed*
leer	le-	leído	*read*
oír	o-	oído	*heard*
traer	tra-	traído	*brought*

Actividades

1 Hecho. Combina las palabras para crear oraciones en los tiempos perfectos. Primero, usa el **presente perfecto** y después, el **pluscuamperfecto** de los verbos. Sigue el modelo.

▶ MODELO: los científicos / descubrir / nuevas tecnologías

Los científicos han descubierto nuevas tecnologías.

Los científicos habían descubierto nuevas tecnologías.

The scientists have discovered new technologies.

The scientists had discovered new technologies.

1. las compañías de coches / producir / menos coches
2. el gobierno / limpiar / las carreteras
3. nosotros / leer / el folleto
4. yo / romper / el teclado inalámbrico
5. mi madre / no / manejar / su nuevo coche
6. ¿tú / ver / mi nuevo blog?
7. nadie / decirme / nada
8. la profesora / apagar / la computadora

2 ¿Quién lo ha hecho?

Utiliza un verbo de la columna A y una expresión de la columna B para relatar qué han hecho diferentes personas. Usa el presente perfecto y un sujeto diferente para cada oración. Intenta usar las palabras **ya** y **todavía.** Sigue el modelo.

► MODELO:

A	B
ver	la película

Mi novio y yo todavía no hemos visto la nueva película de Johnny Depp.

A	B
escribir	el coche
abrocharse	la mesa
abrir	la música
oprimir	la verdad
manejar	la composición
escuchar	el botón
poner	el cinturón
decir	la puerta

3 ¿Lo has hecho?

En parejas, averigüen cuáles de las siguientes cosas ha hecho tu compañero/a durante la semana pasada.

► MODELO: manejar sin abrocharte el cinturón de seguridad
—*¿Has manejado sin abrocharte el cinturón de seguridad?*
—*Sí, (No, no) he manejado sin abrocharme el cinturón de seguridad.*

1. abrir la puerta para una persona del sexo opuesto
2. bajar canciones del Internet
3. ver una página web interesante
4. hacer un viaje en coche
5. leer un libro
6. ir a todas tus clases
7. hablar por teléfono mientras manejabas

4 ¿Qué había pasado antes?

Francisco llegó muy tarde a la fiesta de cumpleaños de una amiga. Utiliza el pluscuamperfecto de indicativo para relatar qué había pasado antes de que llegara Francisco. Sigue el modelo.

► MODELO: La celebración (empezar) a las nueve.
La celebración había empezado a las nueve.

1. La banda (tocar) por dos horas.
2. Algunas parejas (bailar) mucho.
3. Muchos invitados (comer) aperitivos y (beber) cerveza y vino.
4. Todos sus amigos (divertirse) muchísimo.
5. En camino a la fiesta Francisco (tener) una llanta pinchada.
6. Él no (poder) arreglarlo solo y (llamar) a un mecánico.
7. Sus amigos no (preocuparse) porque él les (decir) que iba a llegar tarde.
8. Afortunadamente no le (pasar) nada malo.

5 Las distintas épocas de mi vida.

Indica cinco actividades que ya habías hecho durante diferentes épocas de tu vida: cuando tenías tres, seis, nueve, doce, quince o dieciséis años, por ejemplo. Utiliza el pluscuamperfecto del indicativo. Después, indica cinco actividades que todavía no has hecho. Sigue el modelo.

► MODELO: *Cuando yo tenía un año, ya había aprendido a caminar.*
Todavía no he aprendido a nadar.

Intuiciones y acusaciones

Adriana y Felipe dan un paseo.

Costa Rica tiene una gran diversidad biológica.

Sí, es como un paraíso de novela.

Sí, Adriana, pero es real y lo estamos disfrutando.

Sí, ... ¡Mira la cantidad de mariposas!

Felipe, quiero comentar algo contigo.

Te estoy escuchando, Adriana, ¿de qué se trata?

Se trata de doña Carmen.

Fue muy amable con nosotros, ¿no crees?

Sí, nos trató como familia, pero me sentí muy incómoda con ella

¿Por qué te sentiste incómoda?

No lo sé. Quizás debo escuchar mi intuición y mi corazón.

Adriana, doña Carmen es la madrina de Nayeli. No puedes dudar de ella.

Lo sé, pero la personalidad que ella muestra no es la verdadera.

Adriana, hemos pasado por momentos muy difíciles. ¡Tu imaginación está trabajando horas extras!

No, Felipe, escúchame. Doña Carmen no es buena persona, estoy segura, pero no tengo pruebas.

Claro que no tienes pruebas. Dale a doña Carmen una oportunidad.

Felipe, a mí nunca me ha fallado la intuición.

Entonces, ¿qué quieres hacer?

Tengo que hablar con Nayeli, pero va a ser muy difícil. No va a comprender.

Tú sabes lo que haces. Confío en ti.

Gracias, Felipe. Eres fiel como un perro ... ¡y perdona la comparación!

¡Y tú eres astuta como un zorro!

¿Qué planean los pintores?

Esto es fácil. Mira aquí.

Sí, se apaga la electricidad y está listo.

Nayeli y Adriana dan un paseo.

Nayeli, tengo la sospecha de que doña Carmen está involucrada en el robo de Yax-Balam.

Adriana, ¡cómo puedes decir eso! Yo le debo toda mi vida a mi madrina.

Lo siento, Nayeli. Tú misma has dicho que debemos escuchar nuestras intuiciones.

Entonces no tienes pruebas, Adriana. Esta vez, tu intuición te ha engañado.

Todos cenan en la casa de doña Carmen.

¡Qué cena más sabrosa, madrina!

Es un honor tener aquí a los tres arqueólogos que salvaron a México.

¿Qué paso? Felipe, ¿dónde estás?

Aquí estoy, Adriana.

Actividades

Online Study Center

For additional practice with this episode, visit the *Caminos* website at http://college.hmco.com/languages/spanish/renjilian/caminos/3e/student_home.html.

1 Comprensión. Basándote en este episodio de *Caminos del jaguar,* elige la alternativa lógica.

1. Costa Rica tiene...
   a. un paraíso real.   b. mucha diversidad biológica.

2. Felipe y Adriana...
   a. disfrutan de la naturaleza.   b. cuidan la naturaleza.

3. Felipe opina que doña Carmen es una señora...
   a. muy nerviosa.   b. muy amable.

4. Adriana opina que la personalidad de doña Carmen...
   a. es verdadera.   b. no es verdadera.

5. La opinión de Adriana sobre doña Carmen se basa en...
   a. pruebas.   b. intuición.

6. Las acusaciones de Adriana...
   a. irritan a Nayeli.   b. preocupan a Nayeli.

7. Cuando la luz se fue en la casa de doña Carmen, todos...
   a. estaban descansando.   b. estaban cenando.

2 Situaciones. Dramaticen una de las siguientes situaciones.

1. Adriana le dice a Nayeli que no confía en su madrina.
2. Felipe y Adriana hablan sobre la madrina de Nayeli.

3 Escritura. Escribe una descripción de quiénes son los pintores que aparecen en este episodio. (4–6 oraciones)

NOTA CULTURAL

Los parques nacionales de Costa Rica

Costa Rica se conoce por la inmensa variedad biológica de su flora y de su fauna. Hay numerosas especies de pájaros, de mariposas y de otros animales, y también de flores y plantas. Este país se distingue también por los recursos económicos que dedica para preservar los grandes parques nacionales que se han establecido en el país. Entre ellos están el parque de **Braulio Carrillo**, **Monteverde, Pax Natura** y **Valle Escondido.**

Lectura

Online Study Center

For further reading practice online, visit the *Caminos* website at http://college .hmco.com/languages/ spanish/renjilian/caminos/ 3e/student_home.html.

PRELECTURA

In this selection, we will learn some characteristics of cars advertised on the Internet. The short articles in this reading, based on different Internet sites and *Quo* magazine, include information regarding cars and technological innovations.

Reading Strategy

Defining audience and purpose

Defining the target audience and determining the intended purpose of a reading helps you read with greater focus. Ask yourself if the reading is targeted for you and your university peers, for your parents, for adolescent readers, or for readers in particular professional fields. Decide the intended purpose of the reading, as well. For example, is the purpose of the article to inform, to convince, to entertain, to react, to refute? Defining your audience and purpose also helps you think more critically and express your thoughts and feelings about what you read with clarity.

1 Coches del pasado. Antes de leer la lectura, trabajen en parejas para repasar sus conocimientos sobre los coches del pasado y del presente.

1. ¿Qué marca de coche manejaban tus abuelos? ¿y tus padres u otros parientes mayores? ¿Eran coches importados o nacionales *(domestic)*?
2. ¿Qué colores preferían? ¿Qué tipo de coche les gustaba manejar: deportivo, familiar *(station wagon)*, camioneta?
3. ¿De qué tamaño era: pequeño, grande, mediano?
4. Era automático o de cambios *(stick shift)*? ¿de dos o cuatro puertas? ¿con aire acondicionado? ¿con radio, casetes, CDs?
5. ¿Cuál es la edad legal para manejar un coche en tu estado? Algunos dicen que los jóvenes no deben sacar la licencia de manejar antes de los dieciocho años. ¿Estás de acuerdo? ¿Por qué?
6. ¿Cuál es el mejor coche si vives en la ciudad? ¿y en el campo? ¿en la playa? Explica.

2 Transporte del presente. En parejas, describan a la persona que prefiere usar cada uno de los siguientes medios de transporte.

1. una bicicleta
2. una moto
3. una camioneta
4. un "segway"
5. un coche compacto
6. un descapotable *(convertible)*
7. un coche "Zip"
8. una limosina

3 Preferencias. Escribe cinco cosas que buscas en un coche contemporáneo. Después, compara tu lista con la de un/a compañero/a. Explícale por qué.

Coches de hoy y mañana

¿Está muerto el coche eléctrico?

Hay mucha controversia sobre el coche eléctrico. Según Piers Ward, de la revista *Top Gear,* "el auto eléctrico tiene un problema de imagen[1]". Parece que la gente necesita incentivos para comprar los coches eléctricos, como, por ejemplo, no tener que pagar impuestos[2] de coche. El futuro está incierto[3].

Combatiendo la contaminación

Para reducir la contaminación del aire causada por los coches, General Motors y otras firmas de coches invirtieron[4] cientos de millones de dólares en desarrollar[5] un coche eléctrico.

Los consumidores y las leyes

Los consumidores mostraron poco interés en el coche eléctrico. Por eso, el gobierno cambió las leyes para promover[6] autos con células[7] de combustible, autos híbridos[8] y otros que combaten la contaminación.

La compañía Ford

La compañía Ford cree que hay, quizás, un futuro para el coche eléctrico, pero ha dicho, "Estamos decepcionados[9] por el bajo nivel[10] de aceptación[11] por parte de los consumidores".

Un auto con dos motores

Según el artículo, "el presente pertenece a los autos híbridos, como el Toyota Prius y el Honda Civic Hybrid, que vienen con dos motores, uno eléctrico y otro a gasolina".

El lavacoche[12] económico del futuro

En Inglaterra un equipo de expertos diseñadores[13] de coches ha diseñado un lavacoche más económico. También es mejor para el medio ambiente durante el verano cuando no llueve tanto en muchas partes del mundo. El lavacoche funciona como un lavaplatos, usando vapores de agua. Lavar un coche con una manguera[14] usa ciento treinta y cinco litros de agua comparado con el lavacoche que usa solamente cuatro litros. Además, se puede filtrar el agua y usarla otra vez. El lavacoche es inflable[15].

Relaja y maneja

La compañía Bosch en España anuncia una innovación técnica para el automóvil: El "asiento Drive Dynamic Seat". Es un asiento que ofrece al/a la conductor/a más diversión y confort mientras[16] maneja. Además, con el sistema Bosch instalado en el coche, el / la conductor/a tiene un apoyo[17] dinámico para la columna vertebral[18] que le da masaje a la espalda durante el viaje. Es una saludable[19] innovación tecnológica, especialmente durante viajes muy largos.

El asiento Drive Dynamic

---

[1]image; [2]taxes; [3]uncertain; [4]invested; [5]to develop; [6]promote; [7]cells; [8]hybrids; [9]disillusioned; [10]level; [11]acceptance; [12]carwash; [13]designers; [14]hose; [15]inflatable; [16]while; [17]support; [18]spine; [19]healthy

El coche BMW compacto 1

BMW Serie 1, compacto

La marca alemana BMW ofrece un coche compacto con su Serie 1. La firma lo describe como "un automóvil con carácter propio[20], con el diseño[21], la tecnología y el espíritu de un auténtico BMW". Con este modelo, BMW quiere atraer[22] a los consumidores más jóvenes.

Atascos en España

Adiós, atascos[23]

Millones de españoles están desesperados[24] a causa de los atascos de circulación[25], especialmente durante las vacaciones.

Una solución puede ser la instalación de sensores fuera[26] y dentro del coche y en diferentes partes de la carretera[27], como tienen en Italia.

La idea para los conductores es detectar peligros como congestión de tráfico, adversidades climáticas y condiciones de las calles. Los sensores avisan[28] a los conductores con mensajes sobre los peligros para evitarlos[29]. Por ejemplo, el hielo negro[30], que no se ve, es un peligro serio.

---

[20]own; [21]design; [22]to attract; [23](traffic) jams; [24]desperate; [25]traffic jams; [26]outside of; [27]highway; [28]warn; [29]avoid them; [30]black ice

POSTLECTURA

1 Conéctate. Trabajando en parejas, emparejen la información con el artículo apropiado.

La información

¿Qué artículo lees...

_____ **1.** si quieres un coche con un motor eléctrico y otro a gasolina.

_____ **2.** si tienes miedo del hielo negro.

_____ **3.** si deseas limpiar tu coche y usar poca agua.

_____ **4.** si prefieres un coche compacto con carácter propio.

_____ **5.** si tienes interés en tu confort mientras manejas.

_____ **6.** si deseas evitar peligros en la carretera en el futuro.

_____ **7.** si buscas datos sobre los coches eléctricos.

Artículo

a. ¿Está muerto el coche eléctrico?

b. El lavacoche económico del futuro

c. Relaja y maneja

d. BMW Serie 1

e. Adiós, atascos

f. Un auto con dos motores

2 Propósitos. ¿Cuál es el propósito de cada lectura sobre los coches? Usa las letras de la actividad anterior para identificar cada artículo. (Hay tres descripciones extras.)

1. _____ Hablar del confort que provee un asiento que apoya la columna vertebral.
2. _____ Inspirarnos a comprar un coche particular.
3. _____ Convencernos de los beneficios de un lavacoche que usa poca agua.
4. _____ Entretenernos con imágenes y datos atractivos sobre los coches.
5. _____ Informarnos sobre unas innovaciones tecnológicas que ayudan a los conductores cuando manejan.
6. _____ Animarnos a construir un coche híbrido.
7. _____ Darnos opiniones sobre los coches del futuro que ayudan a proteger el medio ambiente.

3 Opiniones. En parejas, lean dos de los artículos en voz alta y discútanlos. ¿Qué datos revelan sobre los coches y para qué consumidores existen?

4 ¿Quiénes son los lectores? Determina quiénes van a ser los lectores de esta lectura y por qué. Puedes indicar más de una categoría para cada artículo:

► los jóvenes entre los 20 y 30 años
► los estudiantes universitarios
► los adultos mayores de 50 años
► modelos, hombres/mujeres de negocios
► los padres de familia
► atletas
► médicos
► actores/actrices.

5 Coche clásico contemporáneo. Trabajen en parejas para escribir un folleto sobre el coche clásico contemporáneo o para diseñar una página web. Primero, diseñen un coche que tenga características que sean atractivas para una de las siguientes personas: un/a estudiante universitario/a, un padre o una madre de familia, un/a entrenador/a (*coach*), una persona famosa. Invéntenlo (categoría, marca, símbolo o logo particular, tamaño, color, componentes, precio, consumo de gasolina, consideraciones ecológicas, placa especial). Después de diseñarlo y dibujarlo, escriban el folleto y preséntenlo a la clase.

Escritura

Online Study Center

For further writing practice online, visit the *Caminos* website at http://college .hmco.com/languages/ spanish/renjilian/caminos/ 3e/student_home.html.

Writing Strategy

Developing a point of view

An important consideration when writing is to think about who is telling the story. You can create different ways to view your topic depending on the voice you use or the perspective taken. For example, if you are addressing children, writing from the perspective of a child may serve to reach your audience more effectively. Or, you may want to reach children by addressing their parents.

Workshop

The following technological gadgets have been created specifically for children, seniors, or both. With a partner, decide who would use each item.

Strategy in Action

For additional practice with creating a point of view, complete the following exercises and those in the *Escritura* section of your Student Activities Manual for *Unidad 9*.

1 Para niños. Escoge uno de los productos anteriores y escribe un párrafo o anuncio específicamente para niños que les anime a pedirles el aparato a sus padres. Habla del uso del aparato y de sus ventajas (*advantages*). Incluye mandatos informales **(tú).**

2 Para adultos de tercera edad. Escoge uno de los productos anteriores y escribe una descripción dirigida específicamente a personas mayores de los 60 años. Habla de los atractivos del aparato y de lo fácil que es usarlo. Incluye mandatos formales **(Ud.).**

Resumen de vocabulario

TALKING ABOUT TECHNOLOGY

Sustantivos

la alta velocidad	high speed
el aparato	apparatus
la aplicación	application
el archivo	computer file
la ayuda	help
la batería	battery
el botón	button
el buscador	search engine
la cámara	camera
la computadora portátil	laptop
la conexión (sin cables)	(wireless) connection (WiFi)
la contraseña	password
el control remoto	remote control
el correo electrónico	e-mail
la (alta) definición	(high) definition
el directorio	directory
el disco duro	hard drive
el documento	document
el entretenimiento	entertainment
el fax	fax
la función	function
el icono	icon
el mensaje	message
el módem	modem
la pantalla (plana)	(flat) screen
el paso	step
el plasma	plasma
el programa	program
el ratón	mouse
la realidad virtual	virtual reality
la red	network

el robot	robot
el teclado	keyboard
el teléfono celular	cell phone
la videocámara	videocamera
la (video) grabadora	(video)recorder
el videojuego	videogame

Verbos

acceder	to access
almacenar	to store
apagar	to turn off, to shut off
apuntar	to point
archivar, guardar	to save; to file
bajar	to download
cargar	to charge
colgar (ue)	to hang (up)
copiar	to copy
desempeñar	to carry out
entrar	to enter
imprimir	to print
iniciar	to begin
instalar	to install
mover (ue)	to move; to shift
prender, encender (ie)	to turn on
presionar, hacer clic, pulsar, oprimir	to click (with the mouse); to push (a button)

Adjetivos

automático/a	automatic
digital	digital
disponible	available
en línea	online
inalámbrico/a	wireless
multimedia	multimedia
táctil	touch, tactile

SEGUNDO PASO

Adverbial conjunctions

a pesar de que	*even though, even if*
aunque	*even when, even though, even if, although*
cuando	*when*
después (de) que	*after*
en cuanto	*as soon as*
hasta que	*until*
tan pronto como	*as soon as*

DISCUSSING CARS

Sustantivos

el acelerador	*accelerator*
el aire acondicionado	*air conditioning*
el asiento	*seat*
el auto, automóvil, carro, coche	
la batería, pila	*battery*
el baúl, maletero	*trunk*
la bolsa de aire, el airbag	*airbag*
la carretera	*highway*
el choque	*crash*
el cinturón de seguridad	*seatbelt*
el/la conductor/a	*driver*
el deportivo	*sports car*
el espejo (retrovisor)	*(rear-view) mirror*
los frenos	*brakes*
la gasolina	*gasoline*
la licencia de manejar/conducir	*driver's license*
el limpiaparabrisas	*windshield wiper*
la llanta pinchada	*flat tire*
la llanta, rueda	*wheel, tire*
la luz	*light*
el motor	*motor*
la multa	*fine*
el parabrisas	*windshield*
el pito, claxon	*horn*
la placa	*license plate*
la puerta	*door*
el tanque de gasolina	*gas tank*
el volante	*steering wheel*

Verbos

abrocharse (el cinturón)	*to buckle up (seatbelt)*
arrancar	*to start (a car, a race)*
chocar	*to collide*
conducir, manejar	*to drive*
dañar	*to injure; to damage*
frenar	*to brake*
parar	*to stop*
pitar	*to beep the horn*

Adjetivos

compacto/a	*compact*
económico/a	*economical*
híbrido/a	*hybrid*

PRESENT AND PAST PERFECT INDICATIVE

todavía	*yet*
ya	*already*

UNIDAD 10

Tradiciones y artes

VOCABULARIO Y LENGUA

- Learning about holidays and traditions
- Indicating subjective feelings, emotions, and attitudes in the past: Imperfect subjunctive
- Linking actions: Subjunctive with adverbial clauses
- Talking about art and artists
- Discussing crafts and folk art
- Using relative pronouns

CAMINOS DEL JAGUAR

- En la oscuridad
- ¿Traición o verdad?

LECTURA

- Fiestas centroamericanas: Nicaragua, Honduras, El Salvador

NOTAS CULTURALES

- El maíz
- Cuauhtémoc

ESTRATEGIAS

- **Reading:** Taking notes in a chart
- **Writing:** Summarizing

Rafael González y González, *Mercado de Palín*

Preguntas del tema

▸ ¿Cuál es tu día festivo favorito? ¿Por qué?

▸ ¿Cómo celebras tu cumpleaños? ¿con amigos? ¿con familia? ¿sólo/a?

▸ ¿Qué tipo de arte te gusta? ¿Por qué?

▸ ¿Quién es el/la artista que más admiras? Explica.

PRIMER PASO

Vocabulario y lengua

LEARNING ABOUT HOLIDAYS AND TRADITIONS

Días festivos y celebraciones

events
are celebrated / parades
fireworks

resolutions

custom
costumes

plaque

commemorate

Palm Sunday
Easter Sunday

Los **hechos° históricos o religiosos** y otras fechas significativas del mundo hispano **se festejan°** de muchas maneras como por ejemplo, con **desfiles°, festivales,** bailes, conciertos, **exhibiciones públicas, fuegos artificiales°** y **ceremonias** o **ritos** especiales. En muchos de estos eventos, la gente lleva los trajes **folclóricos** del país.

Las celebraciones familiares típicamente incluyen la preparación de comidas especiales y algunas veces, música y bailes. El fin del año se celebra con fiestas y fuegos artificiales y la gente también hace **propósitos°** para el nuevo año.

En las fiestas populares como los carnavales, a veces es **costumbre°** llevar máscaras y **disfraces°.** Cuando se celebran fechas históricas o eventos oficiales importantes, se exhiben con frecuencia placas° o alguna **obra de arte** como **estatuas** y **murales** para conmemorar° el hecho.

Dos fiestas importantes del mundo hispano son la Semana Santa y el Día de los Muertos.

Procesión de Semana Santa, Sevilla, España.

SEMANA SANTA

Semana Santa es una celebración católica que comienza el Domingo de Ramos° y termina el Domingo de Resurrección°. Las **tradiciones** de la Semana Santa comenzaron en el siglo XVI cuando la Iglesia Católica intentó presentar la vida de Jesucristo de una manera popular. En los países hispanos hay ceremonias y ritos religiosos durante esa semana. Las celebraciones más famosas tienen lugar en Sevilla, España. Las cofradías° llevan pasos°, que representan la muerte y la resurrección de Jesucristo o la Virgen María, por las calles estrechas de la ciudad. Miles de turistas visitan Sevilla durante Semana Santa para ver las impresionantes procesiones.

brotherhoods, guilds / floats

El Día de los Muertos en México

Para los mexicanos, el Día de los Muertos o Día de los Fieles Difuntos° representa algo más que la veneración a sus muertos. En México, a diferencia de otros países, la gente se pasa el día **burlándose°**, jugando y **conviviendo°** con la **muerte.** Se **celebra** con expresiones muy originales como las **calaveras°** de azúcar, el pan de muertos, calaveras de papel maché que se burlan de la muerte, y las tradicionales **ofrendas°,** las cuales se preparan con respeto por los familiares para recordar a los que se han ido. Los alimentos, flores y objetos personales del difunto son parte esencial del altar y según la creencia, los fieles difuntos regresan este día para gozar lo que más disfrutaban cuando estaban vivos. Esta fiesta se celebra entre el 31 de octubre y el 2 de noviembre.

Dearly Departed

making fun of
living

skulls

offerings

Un grabado de "La Catrina" por el famoso artista, José Guadalupe Posada.

Una ofrenda para el Día de los Muertos, que incluye pan de muertos, calaveras de azúcar, papel picado y las flores típicas, los cempasúchiles.

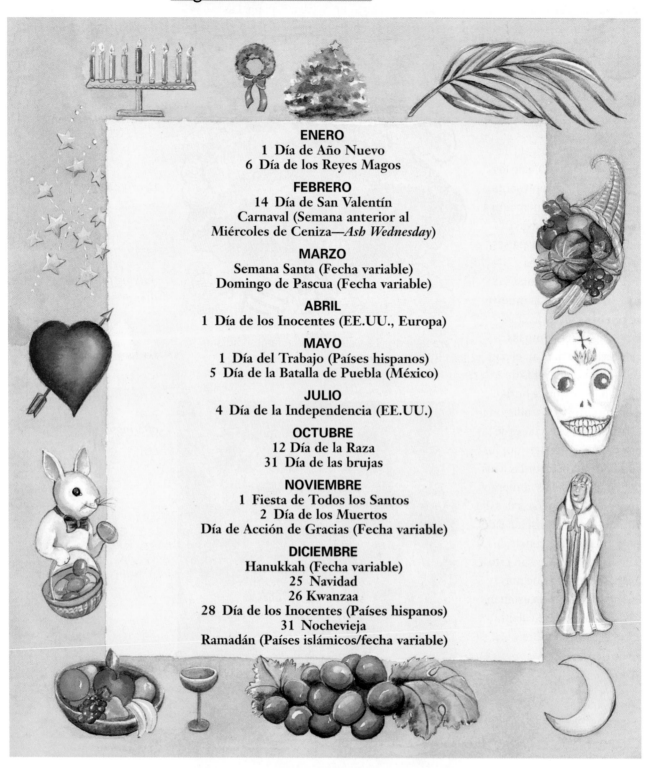

ENERO
1 Día de Año Nuevo
6 Día de los Reyes Magos

FEBRERO
14 Día de San Valentín
Carnaval (Semana anterior al
Miércoles de Ceniza—*Ash Wednesday*)

MARZO
Semana Santa (Fecha variable)
Domingo de Pascua (Fecha variable)

ABRIL
1 Día de los Inocentes (EE.UU., Europa)

MAYO
1 Día del Trabajo (Países hispanos)
5 Día de la Batalla de Puebla (México)

JULIO
4 Día de la Independencia (EE.UU.)

OCTUBRE
12 Día de la Raza
31 Día de las brujas

NOVIEMBRE
1 Fiesta de Todos los Santos
2 Día de los Muertos
Día de Acción de Gracias (Fecha variable)

DICIEMBRE
Hanukkah (Fecha variable)
25 Navidad
26 Kwanzaa
28 Día de los Inocentes (Países hispanos)
31 Nochevieja
Ramadán (Países islámicos/fecha variable)

Actividades

1 La Nochevieja. Escucha la presentación de cómo se celebra la Nochevieja en algunos países hispanos y contesta las preguntas.

1. ¿Cuándo celebramos la Nochevieja?
2. ¿Por qué hacemos propósitos para el año nuevo?
3. ¿Cuáles son algunos propósitos que solemos hacer?
4. ¿Qué ritual especial hay en España?
5. ¿Qué hacen para celebrar la Nochevieja en Colombia?

2 Mis celebraciones. Habla con un/a compañero/a sobre cómo celebras tú la llegada del año nuevo.

1. ¿Celebras el año nuevo? ¿Cómo lo celebras? ¿Con quién?
2. ¿Existen en tu ciudad o estado ceremonias o rituales para recibir el año nuevo?
3. ¿Es útil hacer propósitos de año nuevo? ¿Por qué?
4. ¿Cuáles son algunos propósitos que has hecho? ¿Pudiste cumplirlos?

3 Asociaciones. ¿Qué fiestas asocias con estas cosas?

1. el verano
2. un árbol verde con decoraciones y luces
3. un picnic
4. un corazón rojo
5. el otoño
6. la primavera
7. el invierno
8. un desfile
9. un regalo
10. un disfraz

4 El Día de los Inocentes. ¿Le has hecho bromas a alguien el Día de los Inocentes? ¿A quién? ¿Qué broma le hiciste y cómo reaccionó la persona? ¿Alguien te ha hecho bromas a ti? ¿Quién? Describe las bromas y cómo reaccionaste.

5 Fiestas importantes. Haz una lista de las fiestas que celebras durante el año. Incluye fiestas familiares (cumpleaños y aniversarios), fiestas universitarias (la graduación) o fiestas nacionales y regionales. Compara tu lista con la lista de un/a compañero/a y conversen sobre cómo se celebran las fiestas que han seleccionado.

6 El Día de la Independencia. Describe qué hacías para celebrar el Día de la Independencia cuando eras niño/a. Compáralo con lo que haces ahora.

Día de la Independencia

Yo quería que **celebráramos** juntos el 4 de julio.

Sí, pero mi jefe me pidió que **viniera** a Madrid.

Lo sé, era necesario que **fueras** a España.

¡Feliz 4 de julio para todos! Ojalá yo **pudiera** celebrarlo con ustedes.

MADRID

The highlighted words in the illustration are in the imperfect subjunctive. To form the imperfect subjunctive of both regular and irregular verbs, eliminate the **–ron** of the *third person plural* of the *preterite* tense and add the endings shown in the table below to the stem.

Imperfect subjunctive forms

All verbs that are irregular in the preterite are also irregular in the imperfect subjunctive. (To review the forms of the preterite, see pages 153, 178, and 189.)

Imperfect Subjunctive			
	celebrar	poner	venir
Preterite 3rd person plural	celebra~~ron~~	pusie~~ron~~	vinie~~ron~~
Stem	celebra-	pusie-	vinie-
yo	celebra**ra**	pusie**ra**	vinie**ra**
tú	celebra**ras**	pusie**ras**	vinie**ras**
Ud. / él /ella	celebra**ra**	pusie**ra**	vinie**ra**
nosotros/as	celebrá**ramos**	pusié**ramos**	vinié**ramos**
vosotros/as	celebra**rais**	pusie**rais**	vinie**rais**
Uds. / ellos / ellas	celebra**ran**	pusie**ran**	vinie**ran**

Notice that the nosotros form needs a written accent.

Hubiera (*there was, there were*) is the imperfect subjunctive of **haber**. Like **hay** (*there is, there are*), there is only one form for singular and plural meanings.

Fue excelente que **hubiera** tanta gente en la celebración del 4 de julio.	*It was excellent that there were so many people at the 4th of July celebration.*
Me encantó que **hubiera** tantos platos diferentes en la cena del Día de Acción de Gracias.	*It made me happy that there were so many different dishes for the Thanksgiving dinner.*

You may occasionally see the alternative imperfect subjunctive endings **–se, -ses, -se, -semos, -seis, -sen.**

Uses of the imperfect subjunctive

Noun clauses

When the verb in the main clause expresses a request, emotion, doubt or uncertainty in the past, the verb in the dependent clause is in the imperfect subjunctive. (Review the present subjunctive with noun clauses on pages 278–281 and 291–292.)

Request:	Yo **quería** que nosotros **celebráramos** el Carnaval.	*I wanted us to celebrate Carnival.*
Emotion:	**Fue** fantástico que **nos visitaras** el Día de Acción de Gracias.	*It was wonderful that you could visit us on Thanksgiving.*
Doubt:	La familia **dudaba** que **pudieras** venir en Semana Santa.	*The family doubted that you could come during Holy Week.*

Adjective clauses

The imperfect subjunctive is used in adjective clauses that describe people, things, or events that are uncertain, unknown or non-existent in the past. (Review the present subjunctive with adjective clauses on page 314.)

En la tienda no **había** ningún disfraz que me **gustara**.	*There wasn't a single costume that I liked in the store.*
Pedro **buscaba** un disfraz que no le **costara** mucho.	*Pedro was looking for a costume that didn't cost him a lot.*

Actividades

1 Amor, amor. Completa este párrafo sobre el Día de San Valentín usando el imperfecto de subjuntivo.

El día del amor y la amistad, el Día de San Valentín, me encantaba que mis amigos me _____ (**1.** enviar) tarjetas y regalos. Una vez, recibí una tarjeta de Héctor, en la que me pedía que _____ (**2.** salir, yo) con él. En mi respuesta, le dije que yo quería que _____ (**3.** venir, él) a mi casa y que _____ (**4.** conocer) a mis padres.

Antes de salir a cenar, mis padres nos pidieron que _____ (**5.** regresar, nosotros) temprano y así lo hicimos. Queríamos cenar en un restaurante que _____ (**6.** servir) comida italiana. Encontramos un restaurante pequeño y romántico. Desde entonces, estamos juntos y hace poco Héctor me pidió que _____ (**7.** casarse, yo) con él. Yo le sugerí que _____ (**8.** esperar, nosotros) un poco, pero creo que nos vamos a casar pronto.

2 Celebraciones. Escribe cada oración en el pasado. Sigue el modelo.

► MODELO: *Danilo insiste en que celebremos su cumpleaños*
en un restaurante.

Danilo insistió en que celebráramos su cumpleaños
en un restaurante.

1. Rita se alegra de que yo pueda visitarla en Navidad.
2. Luis pide un disfraz que no sea muy caro.
3. Es una sorpresa que mis amigos celebren mi cumpleaños.
4. Dudo que tú sepas mi nombre.
5. Me gusta mucho que me describas las tradiciones de tu país.
6. Anita les pide a sus padres que le compren un iPod para la Navidad.
7. Rafael quiere que vayamos al desfile.
8. Mi primo me sugiere que haga un pastel para la fiesta.

3 Mis opiniones. Elige una frase de la columna A y complétala de una manera lógica con una frase de la columna B. Tienes que cambiar el verbo entre paréntesis en la columna B al imperfecto del subjuntivo. Después, compara tus oraciones con las de un/a compañero/a.

A	B
1. No nos gustó que	a. algunas personas no (celebrar) los días de fiesta.
2. Fue una lástima que	b. la gente no (participar) en el desfile.
3. Me pareció mal que	c. tú no (querer) regalarme nada el Día de los Reyes Magos.
4. Dudé que	d. no (haber) más gente en el Carnaval.
5. Me alegré de que	e. Pedro me (enviar) una tarjeta para el Día de San Valentín.
6. Esperábamos que	f. no (haber) disfraces el Día de las brujas.

4 ¿Padres estrictos? Haz una lista de las cosas que tus padres te pedían que hicieras con más frecuencia cuando eras pequeño/a. Utiliza algunos de estos verbos en el pasado para comenzar tus frases. Después, pregúntale a un/a compañero/a qué le pedían sus padres.

► MODELO: *Mis padres me pedían que me acostara temprano.*

querer	preferir	ser importante	sugerir
pedir	insistir	decir	rogar

LINKING ACTIONS: SUBJUNCTIVE WITH ADVERBIAL CLAUSES

El altar de mi abuelito

You have already learned that some adverbial conjunctions can take the indicative or the subjunctive. (Review adverbial clauses, page 324.) Other adverbial conjunctions are *always* followed by the subjunctive regardless of the tense.

Conjunctions always followed by the subjunctive	
a fin de que	*in order that*
a menos que	*unless*
antes (de) que	*before*
con tal (de) que	*provided that*
en caso de que	*in case*
para que	*so that*
sin que	*without*

If the verb in the main clause is in the present, then the present subjunctive is used in the dependent clause. If the verb in the main clause is in the preterite or imperfect, then the imperfect subjunctive is used in the dependent clause.

No voy a la fiesta **a menos que termine** mi tarea de química.

I'm not going to the party unless I finish my chemistry homework.

Los incas adoraban al sol **para que** los **protegiera.**

The Incas worshiped the sun, so that it would protect them.

Hice un bonito altar para mi abuelo **sin que** nadie me **ayudara.**

I made a beautiful altar for my grandfather without anyone helping me.

The imperfect subjunctive is always used after the adverbial expression **como si** *(as if, as though).*

Mis amigos me hicieron bromas **como si** hoy **fuera** el Día de los Inocentes.

My friends played tricks on me as if today were April Fool's Day.

When there is no change of subject, the adverbial conjunctions above (except for **a menos que**) may be followed by an infinitive after the preposition: **antes** *de* **salir,** *para* **escuchar,** *sin* **terminar,** and so on. The sentence may begin with either clause. Note that the **que** is omitted in these cases.

Antes de ir al Carnaval, tenemos que buscar la dirección.
Tenemos que buscar la dirección **antes de ir** al Carnaval.

Before going to the Carnival, we have to look for the address.
We have to look for the address before going to the Carnival.

Actividades

1 El Carnaval. Completa las oraciones con la alternativa correcta.

1. Los vecinos organizaron una fiesta para que todos...
   a. se conozcan.
   b. se conocieran.

2. Nadie debe faltar a menos que...
   a. estuviera enfermo.
   b. esté enfermo.

3. El año pasado los chicos llevaron música sin que nadie la...
   a. pida.
   b. pidiera.

4. Mis vecinos se fueron antes de que todos...
   a. llegaran.
   b. lleguen.

5. Siempre hay bebidas sin alcohol en caso de que alguien...
   a. conduzca.
   b. condujera.

6. Generalmente el desfile termina sin que nada malo...
   a. sucediera.
   b. suceda.

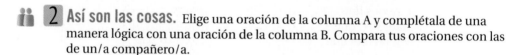

2 Así son las cosas. Elige una oración de la columna A y complétala de una manera lógica con una oración de la columna B. Compara tus oraciones con las de un/a compañero/a.

A	B
1. Te compré el estéreo	a. antes de que te envíen los libros.
2. Llegamos a tiempo	b. en caso de que el avión llegara antes de la hora.
3. Les voy a decir la verdad	c. a menos que nos ganemos la lotería.
4. Debes preguntar el precio	d. sin que tuviéramos que preguntar la dirección.
5. No podemos comprar ese auto	e. a fin de que me explicaras el problema.
6. Te llamé	f. para que tú escucharas tu música favorita.
7. Fuimos más temprano al aeropuerto	g. con tal de que Uds. no se la cuenten a nadie.

3 Nochevieja. Juan Carlos y Beatriz están haciendo una paella para la cena de Nochevieja. Completa el diálogo con la forma correcta del presente o del imperfecto del subjuntivo.

1. Mira, Juan, estos ingredientes son para que tú _____ (hacer) la paella.
2. Está bien, Beatriz, la voy a hacer con tal de que tú me _____ (ayudar).
3. Mira, te escribí la receta con letras grandes en caso de que tú no _____ (poder) leerla en el libro de cocina.
4. Todo tiene que estar listo antes de que _____ (llegar) los invitados.
5. Van a llegar temprano, a menos que _____ (ocurrir) algo inesperado.

4 Condiciones. Trabaja con un/a compañero/a para completar estas oraciones con tus propias ideas.

1. Yo siempre les ayudo a mis amigos con tal de que ellos...
2. Es bueno ahorrar dinero en caso de que...
3. Es terrible tener problemas sin que nadie te...
4. No puedo salir de vacaciones a menos que...
5. Llamé a mis padres para que ellos...
6. Ayer gasté mucho dinero, como si yo...

5 El día internacional. Tú y tus amigos/as organizaron un desfile para el día internacional del pueblo. Creen una conversación para hablar de los preparativos. Usen cuatro cláusulas adverbiales en su conversación. (antes de que, en caso de que, con tal de que, a menos que, sin que, a fin de que, para que)

▶ **MODELO:** Tuvimos que limpiar la calle antes de que llegara la gente.

En la oscuridad

Actividades

Online Study Center

For additional practice with this episode, visit the *Caminos* website at http://college.hmco.com/languages/spanish/renjilian/caminos/3e/student_home.html.

1 Comprensión. Basándote en este episodio de *Caminos del jaguar,* elige la alternativa lógica.

1. No hay luz y Adriana pregunta si...
   a. Nayeli está tranquila.
   b. Felipe está allí.

2. Nayeli piensa que doña Carmen quizás esté...
   a. en la cocina.
   b. investigando el problema.

3. A Adriana, la situación le parece...
   a. extraordinaria.
   b. extraña.

4. Según Felipe, las fallas eléctricas son...
   a. normales.
   b. irregulares.

5. A Adriana no le gusta que doña Carmen...
   a. no esté con ellos.
   b. diga que no pasa nada.

6. Según doña Carmen, la falla ocurrió porque...
   a. la casa es muy vieja.
   b. alguien dañó el generador.

7. Doña Carmen dice que...
   a. hay videocámaras.
   b. el generador funcionó.

 2 Situaciones. Dramaticen una de las siguientes situaciones.

1. La luz se va mientras Nayeli, Adriana, Felipe y doña Carmen cenan.
2. Adriana, Felipe, Nayeli y doña Carmen se dan cuenta de que los jaguares han desaparecido.

3 Escritura. Describe quién crees que robó el jaguar y por qué. (6–8 oraciones)

NOTA CULTURAL

El maíz

En América Latina se producen muchas variedades de maíz: blanco, amarillo, rojo y azul oscuro, casi negro. El maíz es muy importante en la alimentación de casi todos los países latinoamericanos. Es también un ingrediente esencial en muchas comidas regionales como sopas, salsas, pasteles, tamales y tortillas. En Colombia y Venezuela las arepas son tortillas similares a las mexicanas e igualmente populares.

SEGUNDO PASO

Vocabulario y lengua

TALKING ABOUT ART AND ARTISTS

Online Study Center

For additional practice with this unit's vocabulary and grammar, visit the *Caminos* website at http://college.hmco.com/languages/spanish/renjilian/caminos/3e/student_home.html. You can also review audio flashcards, quiz yourself, and explore related Spanish-language sites.

El estudio de arte *(The Art Studio)*

el pintor
el pincel
la paleta
el cuadro
el retrato
el marco

la pintura
(painting)

la madera
la escultora
el bronce
el mármol

la escultura
(sculpture)

la ceramista
la vasija
la arcilla (el barro)

la cerámica
(ceramics)

el bosquejo
el dibujante

el dibujo
(drawing)

Most artistic periods are described in English with the suffix *–ism*. The corresponding Spanish term ends in **–ismo.** For example:

modernism = **modernismo**   *impressionism* = **impresionismo**

An artist who belongs to a particular school of painting is referred to in English with the suffix *–ist*. The corresponding Spanish term ends in **–ista.** Note that the ending is the same whether the artist is male or female.

modernist = **el / la modernista**   *impressionist* = **el /la impresionista**

What do you think the Spanish terms for the following words might be: *cubism, cubist, realism, realist, surrealism, surrealist, expressionism, expressionist, romanticism, romanticist, muralism, muralist?*

Más palabras y expresiones

Cognados

el arte clásico, contemporáneo, moderno, abstracto	la forma
el/la artista	la ilustración
el contraste	la imagen
el detalle	el/la modelo
la figura	

Sustantivos

la acuarela	*watercolor*
el aurorretrato	*self-portrait*
la exposición, exhibición	*art exhibit*
el lienzo	*canvas*
la luz y sombra	*light and shadow*
la naturaleza muerta	*still life*
el paisaje	*landscape, countryside*
la pintura al óleo	*oil-painting*
la vida cotidiana	*daily life*

Verbos

colgar (ue)	*to hang*
crear	*to create*
dibujar	*to draw*
ilustrar	*to illustrate*
pintar	*to paint*
significar	*to mean*

Otras expresiones

claro/a	*light*
en blanco y negro	*(in) black and white*
en color(es)	*(in) color*
oscuro/a	*dark*

Actividades

1 Museo de arte. El museo de arte de tu ciudad escribe una invitación a una exposición. Completa el texto con las palabras más adecuadas.

Lo invitamos a nuestro Museo Comunal. En el primer piso, están las vasijas de una _____ muy conocida, Rosa Flores. Al lado de esta sala están los dibujos de Arturo Mesa, un _____ de fama internacional. En el segundo piso, tenemos las _____ de cobre y madera de la escultora Marina Valle. Finalmente, queremos que usted vea los cuadros del _____ Ricardo Urrutia, nuestro artista invitado este mes.

2 Arte moderno. ¿Qué piensas de estas obras de arte? En grupos, contesten las preguntas y describan cada cuadro.

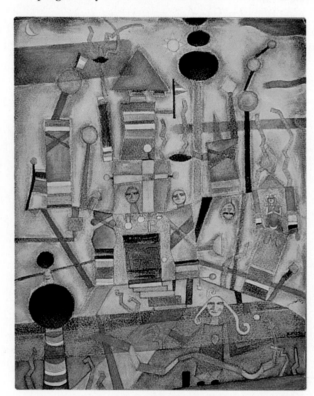

Xul Solar, *Patria B*

1. ¿Qué colores usa el artista?
2. ¿Cuáles son las formas dominantes del cuadro?
3. ¿Qué símbolos reconocen? ¿Qué relación tienen con el tema del cuadro?
4. Según su opinión, ¿tiene el artista una visión positiva del mundo? ¿Por qué?

Frida Kahlo, *Las dos Fridas* (1939)

1. ¿Es serio o divertido el cuadro? ¿Qué elementos expresan esa emoción?
2. ¿Qué diferencia hay entre las dos Fridas del cuadro?
3. ¿Qué elementos en común tienen las dos Fridas?
4. ¿Por qué creen que los corazones son visibles?
5. ¿Qué les dice este autorretrato de Frida Kahlo sobre ella?

Marisol (Marisol Escobar), *The Family* (1962)

1. ¿Cómo es la familia? ¿Parece rica, pobre, feliz o infeliz? ¿Cómo lo saben?
2. Describan a cada miembro de esta familia. ¿Dónde está el padre?
3. ¿Por qué creen que la artista usa la escultura para expresar sus ideas?
4. Describan los colores.

3 Preguntas personales. Contesta las preguntas.

1. ¿Qué tipo de arte te gusta más? ¿Por qué?
2. ¿Quién es tu artista favorito/a? ¿De dónde es? ¿Qué tipo de obras crea?
3. ¿Te gusta ir a museos? ¿Por qué sí o por qué no?
4. ¿Conoces a algunos artistas hispanos? ¿Cuáles? ¿De dónde son? Describe sus obras.

4 Preséntala. En Internet, una revista o libro de arte, escoge una foto de una obra de arte de un/a artista hispano/a que te guste. Tráela a la clase y descríbesela.

Objetos artesanales

ALEBRIJES

En Oaxaca se hacen artesanías como estas figuritas de madera pintadas **a mano.** Son muy populares entre los **coleccionistas,** y además se consideran como talismanes de la buena suerte. Hay alebrijes en forma de unicornios, jaguares, jirafas, iguanas, jaguares, armadillos, etcétera.

Alebrijes en forma de jaguar,
Oaxaca, México

OJO DE DIOS

Muchos símbolos indígenas fueron destruidos durante la colonización española de América, pero el Ojo de Dios **ha permanecido**° desde entonces porque tiene forma de **cruz**°. Se hacen de palitos° de madera con hilos° de lana de colores brillantes. En muchas partes se usa como talismán porque se cree que trae buena suerte.

has remained
cross
sticks / yarn

are made

Chica mexicana con un
"Ojo de Dios" en la mano

RÉPLICAS PRECOLOMBINAS

En Colombia **se fabrican**° actualmente **réplicas** de objetos precolombinos de oro. Estas **piezas** se usan como joyas, como decoración en las casas o como **adornos** de bolsos o cinturones.

Una máscara precolombina,
Museo del Oro, Bogotá

Artesano toledano

skillful

golden

EL DAMASQUINADO

En la ciudad española de Toledo, **hábiles**° **artesanos** trabajan con la técnica del damasquinado, es decir, la decoración de metales preciosos. Allí se fabrican hermosos objetos como el que vemos en la foto, con adornos **dorados**° de diseños de influencia árabe.

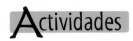

Actividades

1 Clasificación. Con un/a compañero/a, construyan una tabla para clasificar los cuatro objetos artesanales descritos *(described)* en la lectura.

	Alebrijes	Ojo de Dios	Réplicas precolombinas	Damasquinado
origen	_____	_____	_____	_____
material	_____	_____	_____	_____
uso	_____	_____	_____	_____
colores	_____	_____	_____	_____

2 Las arpilleras. En algunos países de Suramérica, las mujeres forman grupos económicos y a veces políticos para hacer unos tapices que se llaman arpilleras. Escucha el texto y escribe (**P**) si la descripción pertenece a las arpilleras del Perú y (**C**) si pertenece a las de Chile.

Una arpillera peruana

Una arpillera chilena

1. _____ expresión social
2. _____ la vida diaria
3. _____ bodas y celebraciones
4. _____ la historia del país
5. _____ dictadura militar
6. _____ historia de la artista

3 Interpretación. Compara las escenas de las dos arpilleras en la *Actividad 2.* ¿Qué o quiénes están en la escena? ¿Qué hacen?

4 Artesanías personales. Diseña un objeto artesanal que represente la historia de tus antepasados. Puede ser real o imaginario. Dibújalo y describe su historia incluyendo qué es, para qué se usa y con qué material se hace.

Exposición

Irene	Hola Elena. Te presento a Roberto.	*Elena*	Gracias, Roberto.
Roberto	Mucho gusto, Elena.	*Roberto*	¿Cuál es la técnica que usas actualmente?
Elena	Encantada. ¿Eres el periodista **con quien** hablé ayer?	*Elena*	Ahora pinto principalmente al óleo, pero **lo que** más quiero es experimentar con otras técnicas.
Roberto	Sí, soy yo. Gracias por darme esta entrevista.		
Elena	Con mucho gusto. Me dice Irene que eres el único periodista **que** sabe de arte.	*Roberto*	¿Como cuáles?
		Elena	La acuarela y la fotografía son **las que** más me interesan.
Roberto	¡Irene es **la que** más sabe! Ella dice que los cuadros **que** exhibes hoy son excelentes.	*Roberto*	Entonces me tienes que invitar a tu próxima exposición.
		Elena	¡Por supuesto!

Relative pronouns combine two sentences that have a noun or pronoun in common. The main relative pronouns in English are *that, which,* and *who/whom,* all of which are sometimes omitted. In Spanish, they must be used.

Que refers to things as well as people *(that, which, who).*

Compré un pequeño cuadro **que** quiero regalarte.	*I bought a small painting that (which) I want to give you.*
Tengo un primo **que** es escultor.	*I have a cousin who is a sculptor.*

Quien/quienes refers to people *(who / whom)* and usually follows a preposition.

Maricarmen Hernández es la médica **a quien** siempre consulto.	*Maricarmen Hernandez is the doctor whom I always consult.*
Éste es el artista **con quien** hablé de arte latinoamericano.	*This is the artist with whom I talked about Latin American art*

El/la/los/las que may refer to people or things *(the one(s) who/that, those who/that).*

Esta pintura es **la que** quiero comprar.	*This painting is the one that I want to buy.*
No quiero esa pintura, **la que** voy a comprar es aquélla.	*I don't want that painting, the one that 1 am going to buy is that one over there.*

Lo que refers to an idea or a previous situation (*what, that which*).

A mi papá no le gustó **lo que** le pintó el artista.	*My dad did not like what the artist painted for him.*

Actividades

1 Referencias. Completa de una manera lógica las oraciones de la columna A con las oraciones de la columna B.

A	B
1. La casa en	a. lo que dices.
2. Queremos unas vacaciones	b. la que vivimos es nuestra.
3. El museo	c. que no sean muy caras.
4. Betty es la persona con	d. al que fui ayer me gustó mucho.
5. La exposición	e. quien debes hablar.
6. No comprendo	f. que tenemos hoy es excelente.

2 José y Josefina. José y Josefina están planeando sus actividades para el fin de semana. Completa su conversación con el pronombre relativo que corresponda. Usa **que, quien, lo que** o **el / la / los / las que.**

Josefina	¿Qué quieres hacer hoy?
José	Me gustaría ver la exhibición de Fernando Botero (**1**) _____ se presenta en el museo de arte.
Josefina	Pues no sé. (**2**) _____ realmente quiero hacer es ir al cine. ¿Qué tal si vamos al cine hoy y al museo mañana?
José	Pero, es que ya compré las entradas para el museo.
Josefina	A ver... ¿son éstas (**3**) _____ compraste?
José	Sí, ésas son.
Josefina	Pues, la persona (**4**) _____ te las vendió se equivocó. Las entradas son para el domingo.
José	Entonces la chica con (**5**) _____ hablé se equivocó. Vamos al museo el domingo y hoy podemos ir al cine. ¿Cuál es la película (**6**) _____ quieres ver?
Josefina	(**7**) _____ quiero ver es la nueva película de Pedro Almodóvar.
José	Estupendo. Es el director español a (**8**) _____ más admiro.

3 Comprensión. Conecta lógicamente las ideas en las dos oraciones con el pronombre relativo **que.**

► MODELO: Laura es una buena artista. Sabe mucho sobre pintura al óleo.
Laura es una buena artista que sabe mucho sobre pintura al óleo.

1. Diana tiene un dibujo. El dibujo es nuevo.
2. Me regalaron una escultura. La escultura es de bronce.
3. Voy al museo mañana. El museo está cerca de mi casa.
4. ¿Dónde está la arcilla? Compré la arcilla ayer.
5. Le regalé un cuadro a Yolanda. Pinté el cuadro en junio.
6. Tengo un bosquejo. El bosquejo representa una naturaleza muerta.
7. Alicia es una artista guatemalteca. Ella enseña arte a los niños.
8. Hay autorretratos de Frida Kahlo. Sus autorretratos son interesantes.

4 Lo mejor. En parejas, conversen sobre lo que más les gusta de estas situaciones.

► MODELO: visitar un museo
¿Qué es lo que más te gusta de visitar un museo?
Lo que más me gusta de visitar un museo es ver cuadros famosos.

1. estudiar idiomas	4. ir al cine
2. viajar a otros países	5. pintar cuadros
3. trabajar	6. ¿...?

¡Traición o verdad?

Actividades

1 Comprensión. Basándote en este episodio de *Caminos del jaguar,* elige la alternativa lógica.

Online Study Center

For additional practice with this episode, visit the *Caminos* website at http://college.hmco.com/languages/spanish/renjilian/caminos/3e/student_home.html.

1. Adriana piensa que doña Carmen...
   a. dice la verdad.
   b. miente.

2. Doña Carmen quiere hablar primero con...
   a. la policía.
   b. los vecinos.

3. Armando dice que Mariluz Gorrostiaga se fue para...
   a. Puerto Rico.
   b. San Antonio.

4. Según Armando, Mariluz...
   a. sigue trabajando para él.
   b. ya no trabaja para él.

5. Es obvio que Armando ...
   a. tiene el jaguar.
   b. está trabajando para doña Carmen.

6. Nayeli ahora sabe que Adriana...
   a. tenía razón.
   b. no tenía razón.

7. Según doña Carmen, Armando es...
   a. incompetente.
   b. competente.

2 Situaciones. Dramaticen una de las siguientes situaciones.

1. La conversación de Armando y doña Carmen.
2. La conversación de Nayeli y Adriana después de escuchar a Armando.

3 Escritura. Describe cómo se siente Nayeli con la noticia de la traición de su madrina. (4–6 oraciones)

NOTA CULTURAL

Cuauhtémoc

Toda civilización tiene sus héroes, los cuales pueden ser míticos como los héroes gemelos o históricos como Cuauhtémoc. Cuauhtémoc fue el último emperador que gobernó el pueblo azteca, entre 1495 y 1525. Era sobrino de Moctezuma II y defendió los territorios aztecas contra los ataques de los conquistadores españoles. Por su gran valentía y determinación, Cuauhtémoc se considera un héroe nacional en México. Su imagen aparece en los billetes mexicanos de 100 pesos.

Lectura

PRELECTURA

Reading Strategy

Taking notes in a chart

Often, reading passages are filled with many facts and dates. A useful strategy to apply when reading this kind of article is to keep track of the information by jotting down answers to the questions *who?*, *what?*, *when?*, *where?*, and *why?*

1 Datos básicos. Antes de leer sobre unas fiestas centroamericanas, prepara una tabla como la siguiente. Después, mientras lees, completa la tabla con la información indicada. La tabla ya contiene los nombres de los países.

País	Festival Celebración	Geografía Clima	Gobierno Economía	Población	Otros datos
Nicaragua	_____	_____	_____	_____	_____
Honduras	_____	_____	_____	_____	_____
El Salvador	_____	_____	_____	_____	_____

Fiestas centroamericanas: Nicaragua, Honduras, El Salvador

Nicaragua, Honduras y El Salvador son tres países de Centroamérica que tienen unas características en común y algunos aspectos diferentes.

Nicaragua

En área, Nicaragua es el país más grande de Centroamérica. Tiene costas tanto en el Atlántico como en el Pacífico y montañas en el centro del país. Su historia se caracteriza por muchas guerras[1] y poca paz[2]. Managua, la capital y la ciudad más grande, sufrió gran destrucción en el terremoto de 1972 y en la Revolución de 1978–1979. En agosto, hay festivales en honor al santo patrón de Nicaragua, Santo Domingo. Estos festivales se celebran con ceremonias religiosas, corridas de toros[3], carreras de caballos[4] y peleas de gallos[5].

Un desfile en el Festival de Santo Domingo, Nicaragua

---

[1]wars; [2]peace; [3]bullfights; [4]horse races; [5]cock fights

Honduras

La república de Honduras es muy montañosa; tiene una historia de inestabilidad con muchos cambios de gobierno y guerras. Económicamente, es el país más pobre de Centroamérica y también es el país de mayor población en Centroamérica. Durante dos semanas de enero, se celebra en Cedro, un pueblo al norte de Tegucigalpa, la capital hondureña, el festival del Señor del Buen Fin. Durante esta fiesta se sirven comidas tradicionales y se celebran ceremonias religiosas. Como en muchos países hispanos, el ocho de diciembre se celebra el día de la Virgen de la Concepción y las festividades se prolongan durante una semana.

El festival de la Virgen de la Concepción en Tegucigalpa, Honduras

Un festival en El Salvador

El Salvador

El Salvador es la república más pequeña y más densamente poblada de Centroamérica. Ha sufrido muchas guerras y catástrofes naturales. Es el único país de Centroamérica sin acceso al mar Caribe, pero su geografía es variada y sus numerosos volcanes producen una tierra excelente para el cultivo del café. Tiene también más de doscientas variedades de orquídeas. En El Salvador se celebran muchos festivales tanto religiosos como populares como la fiesta de El Salvador, en la que hay desfiles de carrozas[7] decorativas por las calles. El doce de diciembre es la celebración del Día del Indio, en el que hay desfiles muy coloridos en honor a la Virgen de Guadalupe.

[7]floats

POSTLECTURA

 2 Comprensión. Trabajen en grupos y contesten las preguntas sobre la lectura.

1. ¿Qué desastre natural sufrió Managua?
2. ¿Cuál es el país de más población en Centroamérica?
3. ¿Cuál es la capital de Honduras?
4. ¿Cómo es Honduras geográficamente?
5. ¿Cuál es la capital salvadoreña?
6. ¿Tiene El Salvador playas en el mar Caribe?
7. ¿Qué flores hay en El Salvador? ¿Por qué se puede cultivar mucho café?
8. Menciona un festival de cada país.

3 Datos de mi tabla. En parejas, comparen la información que han puesto en la tabla de la *Actividad 1*.

4 Otros festivales centroamericanos. Trabajen en grupos para buscar información sobre algunas de las características de las otras repúblicas centroamericanas: Panamá, Costa Rica y Guatemala. Usen una tabla para escribir y comparar los datos.

5 Celebraciones cerca de mí. Trabajen en grupos de dos o tres personas. Cada estudiante describe una celebración, un festival, día de fiesta, carnaval o ceremonia religiosa especial de su estado, región o país. Incluyan detalles sobre diferentes aspectos de la celebración.

Escritura

Writing Strategy

Summarizing

A summary is a concise version of something that you have read or seen. It contains the most important information and leaves out much of the detail. Once you have identified the main ideas and supporting details of a passage, you can connect the ideas in paragraph form. Unlike paraphrasing, the intent of a summary is to condense the material and present it in a straightforward way.

Online Study Center

For further writing practice online, visit the *Caminos* website at http://college .hmco.com/languages/ spanish/renjilian/caminos/ 3e/student_home.html.

Workshop

Review the following strategies to prepare for writing a summary:

► Providing supporting details *(Unidad 3)*

► Making notes in the margin *(Unidad 4)*

► Paraphrasing *(Unidad 7)*

Strategy in Action

For additional practice with summarizing, complete the exercises below and in the *Escritura* section of the Student Activities Manual for *Unidad 10.*

1 Resumen. Investiga información en Internet sobre una fiesta del mundo hispano y escribe un resumen de la celebración. Compara tu composición con la de un/a compañero/a.

2 ¿Qué pasó en Costa Rica? Escribe un resumen de los dos episodios de *Caminos del jaguar* de esta unidad. Compara tu composición con la de un/a compañero/a.

PRIMER PASO

LEARNING ABOUT HOLIDAYS AND TRADITIONS

Susantivos

la calavera	skull
la ceremonia	ceremony
la costumbre	custom
el desfile	parade
el disfraz	costume
la estatua	statue
la exhibición	exhibition
el festival	festival
los fuegos artificiales	fireworks
el hecho	event
la muerte	death
el mural	mural
la obra de arte	work of art
la ofrenda	offering
el propósito	resolution, purpose, intention
el rito	rite; ritual
la tradición	tradition

Verbos

burlarse (de)	to make fun of
celebrar	to celebrate
convivir	to live with
festejarse	to celebrate

Adjetivos

folclórico/a, folklórico/a	folkloric
histórico/a	historical
público/a	public
religioso/a	religious

CONJUNCTIONS ALWAYS FOLLOWED BY THE SUBJUNCTIVE

a fin de que	in order that
a menos que	unless
antes (de) que	before
con tal (de) que	provided that
en caso de que	in case
para que	so that
sin que	without

SEGUNDO PASO

TALKING ABOUT ART AND ARTISTS

Sustantivos

la acuarela	watercolor
la arcilla / el barro	clay
el arte clásico, contemporáneo, moderno, abstracto	classic, contemporary, modern, abstract art
el/la artista	artist
el aurorretrato	self-portrait
el bosquejo	sketch
el bronce	bronze
la cerámica	ceramics
el/la ceramista	ceramist, potter
el contraste	contrast
el cuadro	painting, picture
el detalle	detail
el/la dibujante	illustrator
el dibujo	drawing
el/la escultor/a	sculptor
la escultura	sculpture
la exposición, exhibición	art exhibit
la figura	figure
la forma	form
la ilustración	illustration
la imagen	image
el lienzo	canvas
la luz y sombra	light and shadow
la madera	wood

el marco	*frame*
el mármol	*marble*
el/la modelo	*model*
la naturaleza muerta	*still life*
el paisaje	*landscape*
la paleta	*palette*
el pincel	*paintbrush*
el/la pintor/a	*painter*
la pintura	*painting*
la pintura al óleo	*oil-painting*
el retrato	*portrait*
la vasija	*vase*
la vida cotidiana	*daily life*

Verbos

colgar (ue)	*to hang*
crear	*to create*
dibujar	*to draw*
ilustrar	*to illustrate*
pintar	*to paint*
significar	*to mean*

Otras expresiones

claro/a	*light*
en blanco y negro	*(in) black and white*
en color(es)	*(in) color*
oscuro/a	*dark*

DISCUSSING CRAFTS AND FOLK ART

Sustantivos

el adorno	*decoration, adornment*
el/la artesano/a	*artisan*
el/la coleccionista	*collector*
la cruz	*cross*
la pieza	*piece*
la réplica	*replica*

Verbos

fabricar	*to make*
permanecer	*to remain*

Otras expresiones

a mano	*by hand*
dorado/a	*golden*
hábil	*skillful*

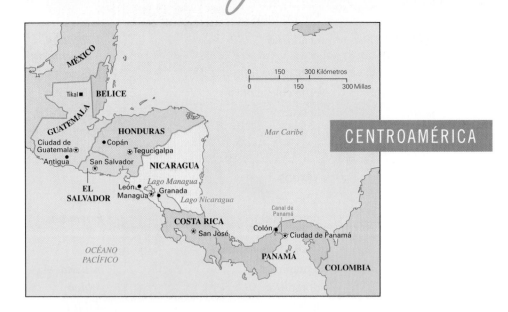

CENTROAMÉRICA

Online Study Center

To learn more about the people featured in this section, visit the *Caminos* website at http://college .hmco.com/languages/ spanish/renjilian/caminos/ 3e/student_home.html.

PERSONALIDADES

Óscar Arias

Arzobispo Óscar Romero

Katia Cardenal

Guillermo Anderson

Los centroamericanos

Las artes y letras de América Central incorporan una gran variedad de temas: las raíces culturales, las tradiciones indígenas del pasado y presente, las expresiones sentimentales, las distintas actitudes hacia la vida y la muerte, la juventud[1] y la vejez[2], la guerra[3] y la paz[4], lo familiar y lo desconocido[5], la religión, el amor y la identidad nacional.

Hay una larga historia de conflictos y violencia en Centroamérica. Las injusticias contra los pueblos indígenas han caracterizado[6] ciertas regiones. Miles de centroamericanos se exiliaron por razones[7] políticas para escaparse de peligros y mal tratamiento.

En sus obras, muchos escritores, músicos, artistas y otros intelectuales revelan la importancia de las culturas indígenas, afirmando las diversas raíces culturales. Dos centroamericanos ganaron el Premio Nobel de la Paz por su activismo a favor de los grupos indígenas: la escritora indígena Rigoberta Menchú de Guatemala (1992) y el ex presidente Óscar Arias de Costa Rica (1987).

El Arzobispo Óscar Romero, de El Salvador, perdió su vida por la causa de la igualdad[8] y los derechos socioeconómicos de su pueblo. El director de cine guatemalteco, Luis Argueta, examina la historia y las raíces culturales guatemaltecas en sus películas, como hace también la directora costarricense Guita Schyfter.

---

[1]youth; [2]old age; [3]war; [4]peace; [5]unknown; [6]have characterized; [7]reasons; [8]equality

Claribel Alegría

Moisés Gadea

Franklin Chang-Díaz

Ricardo Arjona

"Prefiero... tener la libertad de expresar
todo lo que quiero como cantante."
—Ricardo Arjona (Guatemala)

Otros centroamericanos han hecho contribuciones a las artes y letras con el enfoque[9] sobre las raíces culturales como fondo[10]. En la música, se destacan el hondureño Guillermo Anderson, que canta sobre la gente nativa de su región; el trío costarricense Editus, que combina jazz moderno y tradicional con auténticos sonidos latinoamericanos; el nicaragüense Moisés Gadea, que canta sobre condiciones sociales en su país.

Miguel Ángel Asturias

Es importante reconocer los logros de Franklin Chang-Díaz, astronauta costarricense; y de escritores distinguidos como Claribel Alegría de El Salvador, Carmen Naranjo de Costa Rica y Miguel Ángel Asturias de Guatemala.

Visita el sitio web de *Caminos* para leer más en español sobre estas personalidades centroamericanas.

[9]focus; [10]background

Comprensión

Trabajando en parejas, háganse estas preguntas.

1. ¿Qué centroamericanos ganaron el Premio Nobel de la Paz?
2. Nombra las profesiones de las personalidades de América Central mencionadas aquí. ¿Cuál te parece más interesante?

ARTE

Ritos: Hombres del maíz, 2000

PEDRO RAFAEL GONZÁLEZ CHAVAJAY

Para muchos pueblos indígenas hispanoamericanos del pasado y del presente, el maíz° ha tenido importancia agrícola y religiosa. El maíz sirve de comida para la familia. Como elemento de las ceremonias religiosas, refleja el respeto y el amor por la tierra. Esto se puede observar también en las artes. El tema de las raíces culturales se ve en una multitud de imágenes artísticas. La obra *Ritos°: Hombres de maíz,* es del artista guatemalteco, Pedro Rafael González Chavajay.

corn

ceremonias

Comprensión

Trabajando en parejas, háganse estas preguntas.

1. ¿Cómo se llama esta obra de arte? ¿De dónde es el artista?
2. ¿Cómo son las personas? ¿Qué ropa llevan?
3. ¿Cuándo ocurre este rito? ¿Qué instrumentos tocan durante la ceremonia?
4. En la cesta hay una jarra°. ¿Cómo es? ¿Para qué se usa?   *jug*
5. ¿Qué ambiente° crea el uso artístico de luz y sombra?   *atmosphere*
6. ¿De qué colores es el maíz en esta obra? ¿En qué comidas populares de hoy encontramos el maíz?
7. ¿Qué producto agrícola representa tu país en el pasado y en el presente? ¿En qué comidas lo encontramos?
8. En tus propias palabras, describe esta obra.

MÚSICA

RUBÉN BLADES

Rubén Blades es una personalidad que ha hecho grandes contribuciones en los campos de la música, del cine, del derecho° y de la política. Nació en Panamá en 1948, de padre colombiano y madre cubana. Blades dice que su abuela le enseño a cultivar el sentido° de la justicia. Al terminar sus estudios en la Universidad de Panamá, se hizo abogado.

    Su visión de solucionar problemas sociales y su dedicación a sus raíces caracterizan su música. Ganó su primer Grammy en 1985 y otro tres años más tarde. Canta en español y en inglés, y ha participado° con otros grupos hispanos en la fusión de música irlandesa, árabe y afro-cubana, además de° salsa. Ganó también premios como actor de cine y de televisión.

    En 1994, fue candidato para la presidencia panameña, pero perdió la elección. En el año 2000, sirvió de Embajador de Buena Voluntad° para las Naciones Unidas.

law

sense

has participated

in addition to

Good Will Ambassador

"¿De dónde viene mi canto? Y yo ¿adónde voy?"

—Rubén Darío (Nicaragua), "¡Eheu!".

Comprensión

Trabajando en parejas, háganse estas preguntas.

1. ¿De dónde son Rubén Blades y sus padres?
2. ¿Qué le enseñó su abuela? ¿En qué campo profesional se graduó Blades en la universidad?
3. ¿Cuáles son sus otras profesiones?
4. Describe su música y sus premios. ¿En qué idioma canta?
5. ¿Qué le pasó a Blades en las elecciones presidenciales de Panamá?
6. ¿Qué hace un/a Embajador/a de Buena Voluntad? En tus propias palabras, resume el trabajo que hacen en las Naciones Unidas.

Conéctate a Internet para escuchar la música de Rubén Blades, aprender más sobre él, los cantantes ya mencionados u otros: los nicaragüenses Salvador Cardenal, "Alux Nahual", Carlos Mejía Godoy y Katia Cardenal; el guatemalteco Ricardo Arjona; el costarricense Juan Carlos Ureña y el panameño Luis Russell.

LITERATURA

ROQUE DALTON

Roque Dalton vivió entre los años 1935 y 1975. Por su activismo político fue condenado° a muerte, pero el poeta salvadoreño logró exiliarse a otras partes de Latinoamérica y Europa. Tristemente, al regresar a El Salvador, fue asesinado. Amaba la poesía y a su país; murió por sus ideales de justicia e igualdad.

condemned

"Cómo tú"

Creo que el mundo es bello,
que la poesía es como el pan,
      de todos.
Y que mis venas no terminan en mí
sino° en la sangre unánime
de los que luchan por la vida,
el amor,
las cosas,
el paisaje y el pan,
la poesía de todos.

but rather

👥 Comprensión

Trabajando en parejas, háganse estas preguntas.

1. ¿Qué adjetivo usa el poeta para describir el mundo? ¿Es negativa o positiva su actitud?
2. ¿Con qué compara la poesía? Inventa otra comparación para la poesía.
3. ¿De quiénes es la poesía?
4. ¿Para qué luchan todos, según el poeta?
5. En tu opinión, ¿cuál es más importante: el amor o las cosas?
6. En tu opinión, ¿Cuál es el mensaje central de este poema? ¿Te gusta este mensaje o no? ¿Por qué?

message

RIGOBERTA MENCHÚ

Rigoberta Menchú es una indígena guatemalteca nacida en 1959. Lucha por tener un país libre de violencia contra la gente indígena. En su novela autobiográfica, *Yo, Rigoberta Menchú*, habla de la vida de su familia indígena y de las condiciones difíciles para el pueblo quiché, el grupo indígena en el norte de Guatemala del cual ella es miembro. Algunas de las memorias y actitudes que presenta en el libro siguen aquí.

ethnic groups	*Me llamo Rigoberta Menchú. Tengo veintitrés años.
includes / people	*...en Guatemala, existen veintidós etnias° indígenas...
	*Mi situación personal engloba° toda la realidad de un pueblo°....
	*...tengo mis costumbres, costumbres indígenas quichés.
paradise	*Precisamente mi tierra es un paraíso° de todo lo lindo que es la naturaleza....
in the middle	Yo casi vivo en medio° de muchas montañas.
número seis	*...yo soy la sexta° de la familia....
hardly	*Nosotros vivimos más en las montañas...que apenas° dan maíz, frijol...
	*...mis padres...han vivido una situación muy difícil y son muy pobres.

👥 Comprensión

Trabajando en parejas, háganse estas preguntas.

1. ¿Dónde tiene sus raíces Rigoberta Menchú? ¿Cuántos años tiene en el cuento y en el año 2007?
herself 2. ¿Quiere representarse solamente a sí misma°?
3. ¿Qué costumbres practica? ¿Cuántas etnias hay en Guatemala?
4. ¿Es de una familia pequeña?
5. ¿Qué cultivaba la familia en las montañas?
6. ¿Cómo era la vida de Menchú y su familia?
7. Cuenta brevemente una autobiografía que conozcas tú.
8. ¿Hay grupos indígenas en tu región? ¿Dónde viven? Describe algo de su vida.

ERNESTO CARDENAL

Ernesto Cardenal es un poeta nicaragüense. Dedicó una gran parte de su vida a luchar contra la dictadura del general Anastasio Somoza en Nicaragua. En este poema, compara el amor por su país con el amor por una mujer.

"Epigramas"°

Yo he repartido° papeletas clandestinas°,
gritando, ¡VIVA LA LIBERTAD! en plena° calle
desafiando° a los guardias armados.
Yo participé en la rebelión de abril°:
pero palidezco° cuando paso por tu casa
y tu sola mirada me hace temblar°.

Inscriptions

I have distributed/secret messages
in the middle of
challenging
nombre de una protesta grande
I turn pale
tremble

👥 Comprensión

Trabajando en parejas, háganse estas preguntas.

1. ¿En qué actividad política participó el narrador del poema? ¿Por qué estaba gritando?
2. ¿En qué mes ocurrió la rebelión?
3. ¿Cómo es el narrador en sus acciones políticas y amorosas: fuerte, débil, personal, popular, inestable, estable, emocional, miedoso?
4. En tu opinión, ¿por qué le hace temblar la "mirada" de la otra persona?
5. Nombra dos temas de este poema.
6. ¿Qué libertades tienes en tu país: votar, reunirse en grupos, expresar tus ideas, practicar la religión de tu preferencia, llevar armas? ¿En qué regiones no existen estas libertades?

11
Temas de la sociedad

VOCABULARIO Y LENGUA

► Talking about contemporary society
► Reacting to societal issues
► Using the future tense and future of probability

► Discussing environmental issues
► Expressing emotions and doubt in the past: Present and past perfect subjunctive
► Using the conditional tense and conditional of probability

CAMINOS DEL JAGUAR

► Trampa de trampas
► ¡Gol!

LECTURA

► ¡Milenios de miedos!

NOTAS CULTURALES

► El Instituto de Culturas Texanas
► El Paseo del Río en San Antonio

ESTRATEGIAS

► **Reading:** Distinguishing facts from opinions
► **Writing:** Narrowing a topic

Michael Rios, *Maya Garden*

Preguntas del tema

- ▶ ¿Qué haces para ayudar a tu comunidad?
- ▶ ¿Qué problema social te preocupa más?
- ▶ ¿Qué cosas contribuyen a la contaminación del aire? ¿del agua?
- ▶ ¿Cómo podemos reducir la cantidad de basura en el mundo?

PRIMER PASO

Vocabulario y lengua

TALKING ABOUT CONTEMPORARY SOCIETY

Jóvenes de hoy

uncertainty

worries / AIDS

increased

employment

turned into

to reach

has led to

delinquent acts

consumption

pregnancies

La juventud mexicana de hoy es una generación que está preocupada por su futuro. Para ellos, la **incertidumbre**° de la vida está siempre presente, pero la muerte no es una de sus **angustias**° principales. Sin embargo, el **SIDA**° y las drogas sí están entre sus preocupaciones. Además, estos jóvenes modernos tienen más consciencia social y por eso han **aumentado**° sus demandas de educación, **empleo**°, servicios de salud, espacios de expresión cultural y representación política.

Antes de casarse, los jóvenes del país piensan en estudiar y en **obtener** un empleo, pero en México, el trabajo se ha **convertido en**° un sueño más difícil de **alcanzar**° que el amor.

Diversos estudios indican que la crisis en la población joven ha propiciado° un aumento en el número de suicidios, **actos delictivos**°, **consumo**° de drogas y alcohol, **embarazos**° no deseados y enfermedades psicológicas.

Online Study Center

For additional practice with this unit's vocabulary and grammar, visit the *Caminos* website at http://college .hmco.com/languages/ spanish/renjilian/caminos/ 3e/student_home.html. You can also review audio flashcards, quiz yourself, and explore related Spanish-language sites.

Más palabras y expresiones

Cognados

la adicción	el/la delinquente	la solución
el/la adolescente	la depresión	el terrorismo
el beneficio	la drogadicción	el/la terrorista
la comunidad	la justicia	el tráfico de drogas
el crimen	la libertad	el/la voluntario/a
la cura	el/la policía	
la delincuencia	el programa social	

Sustantivos

las armas	*weapons*
el asesinato	*assassination, murder*
el/la asesino/a	*murderer*
la cárcel, prisión	*prison*
el consejo	*advice*
los desamparados	*homeless people*
el desempleo	*unemployment*
la guerra	*war*
el lío	*problem, trouble, mess*
el logro	*achievement*
el/la niñero/a	*nanny, babysitter*
la patria	*homeland*
el peligro	*danger*
la pobreza	*poverty*
el robo	*robbery*
la seguridad	*security*
el seguro médico	*health insurance*
la sociedad	*society*
la terapia	*therapy*
el/la trabajador/a social	*social worker*

Verbos

amenazar	*to threaten*
arrestar	*to arrest*
asesinar	*to assassinate, murder*
encarcelar	*to imprison*
enfrentar	*to confront, face up to*
estar desesperado/a	*to be desperate*
fracasar	*to fail*
lograr	*to achieve; to attain*
luchar	*to fight*
matar	*to kill*
tener remedio	*to have a solution*
triunfar	*to succeed, triumph*

Actividades

1 ¿Verdadero o falso? Di si estas frases son verdaderas (**V**) o falsas (**F**) según la lectura. Si son falsas, corrígelas.

1. Los jóvenes de México están preocupados por el futuro.
2. La muerte está entre sus angustias principales.
3. La educación es importante para los jóvenes mexicanos.
4. Los jóvenes piensan obtener un empleo después de casarse.
5. Es difícil encontrar empleo.
6. El consumo de drogas ha aumentado.

2 Querida Catalina. Una joven le escribe a Catalina, una psicóloga que da consejos en el Internet, para pedirle ayuda. Escucha lo que dice en el correo electrónico y completa la siguiente información. Después, trabajen en parejas para darle consejos a Laura.

1. Laura tiene _____ años.
   a. veinte   **b.** treinta   **c.** trece

2. Ella está _____.
   a. casada   **b.** separada   **c.** divorciada

3. Ella trabaja en una tienda de _____.
   a. zapatos   **b.** discos   **c.** ropa

4. Su trabajo _____.
   a. paga mal   **b.** tiene beneficios sociales   **c.** paga bien

5. Mientras trabaja, su _____ cuida a la hija.
   a. tía   **b.** madre   **c.** vecina

6. Laura quiere _____.
   a. quedarse en casa   **b.** cambiar de trabajo   **c.** estudiar

3 Titulares. Eres reportero/a para el periódico de tu pueblo. Escribe titulares para presentar los artículos sobre los siguientes temas.

▶ **MODELO:** tráfico de drogas
Los Estados Unidos anuncian un nuevo plan para eliminar el tráfico de drogas.

1. el consumo de alcohol
2. el terrorismo
3. la pobreza
4. el SIDA
5. los actos delictivos
6. las enfermedades psicológicas
7. el desempleo
8. el asesinato

4 Soluciones. Trabajando en grupos, creen soluciones posibles para tres de los problemas sociales mencionados en la *Actividad 3*. La lista siguiente tiene algunas soluciones posibles.

contratar más policías   aumentar los impuestos sobre el alcohol
crear más trabajos   aumentar el sueldo mínimo

5 A escribir.
Escribe una composición de dos párrafos sobre uno de los problemas sociales de la *Actividad 3* y ofrece algunas soluciones. Organiza tu composición de esta manera.

Problema
1. *Causas*
2. *Soluciones*

REACTING TO SOCIETAL ISSUES

Una encuesta nacional

En México, se les hizo una encuesta a quinientos jóvenes entre los trece y los veinticuatro años de edad sobre los problemas a los que ellos se enfrentan. Aquí hay algunas de sus respuestas.

Autoestima
¿Te sientes con capacidad para resolver todos tus problemas?

	Edad		
Frecuencia	13 a 17 años	18 a 24 años	Promedio
Siempre	22%	35%	29%
Casi siempre	47%	53%	50%
A veces	29%	12%	20%
Casi nunca	2%	–	1%

¿Te gusta tu aspecto físico?

	Sexo		Promedio
Frecuencia	Hombres	Mujeres	Hombres y mujeres
Mucho	25%	25%	25%
Algo	62%	53%	57,5%
Poco	8%	11%	9,5%
Nada	5%	11%	8%

Adicciones
¿Acostumbras tomar alcohol?

	Sexo		Promedio
Frecuencia	Hombres	Mujeres	Hombres y mujeres
Sí	55%	35%	45%
No	45%	65%	55%

¿Conoces directamente a alguien que tenga problemas con...?

	Sí	No
su forma de beber	68%	32%
el consumo de drogas	63%	37%

Actividades

1 Opiniones. Contesta las preguntas de la encuesta. Después, en grupos, recojan la información y calculen los porcentajes según las respuestas de la clase. Comparen sus opiniones con las de los jóvenes mexicanos.

2 Nuestra cápsula del tiempo. Aunque hay muchos problemas sociales en el mundo, también hay muchas cosas buenas. ¿Qué objetos representativos de nuestra época puedes poner en una cápsula del tiempo para abrir en el futuro? Con una pareja, hagan una lista de diez objetos.

Para considerar: Eventos importantes, música, comida, tecnología, ropa, cosas personales y comunicaciones.

3 En grupos. Trabajen en grupos de tres. Comparen sus listas personales de la *Actividad 2* y elijan diez objetos de sus listas. Preséntenle la nueva lista a la clase y expliquen por qué escogieron finalmente esos diez objetos.

USING THE FUTURE TENSE AND FUTURE OF PROBABILITY

Haré un buen trabajo

I will start	Sonia	Tío Efraín, el año entrante **empezaré**° mi especialización.
Will you study / will you do	Efraín	¿**Estudiarás**° para ser psicóloga o **harás**° algo diferente?
I will become / I will help	Sonia	Algo diferente, tío Efraín. **Seré**° trabajadora social y **ayudaré**° a los jóvenes que tengan problemas con las drogas y el alcohol.
you will be very successful	Efraín	Te felicito, Sonia. Estoy seguro de que **tendrás** mucho éxito°.

Most verbs in Spanish are regular in the future. The stem for most **-ar, -er,** and **-ir** verbs is the infinitive. All verbs share a common set of endings in the future tense.

Future tense of regular verbs				
Infinitive	Subject	Stem	Ending	Future tense
trabajar	yo	trabajar-	**é**	trabajar**é**
creer	tú	creer-	**ás**	creer**ás**
escribir	Ud., él, ella	escribir-	**á**	escribir**á**
sentir	nosotros/as	sentir-	**emos**	sentir**emos**
dar	vosotros/as	dar-	**éis**	dar**éis**
ir	Uds., ellos, ellas	ir-	**án**	ir**án**

Notice that all endings carry written accents except the **nosotros/as** form.

There are very few verbs that are irregular in the future. The following verbs have irregular stems, but the endings are the same as for regular verbs.

Future tense of irregular verbs		
Infinitive	Stem	Future tense example
decir	dir-	yo **diré**
hacer	har-	tú **har**ás
poder	podr-	Ud. **podr**á
poner	pondr-	él **pondr**á
querer	querr-	ella **querr**á
saber	sabr-	nosotros/as **sabr**emos
salir	saldr-	vosotros/as **saldr**éis
tener	tendr-	Uds. **tendr**án
venir	vendr-	ellos, ellas **vendr**án

Habrá *(there will be)* is the future of **haber.** Like **hay** *(there is, there are),* **habrá** is used only in the singular where it means *there will be.*

Habrá una conferencia sobre los jóvenes en América Latina.	*There will be a talk about youth in Latin America.*
Habrá muchos participantes.	*There will be many attendees.*

The English equivalent of the future tense is *will* or *shall* plus a *verb:*

Mañana **haré** la encuesta.	*I will / shall do the survey tomorrow.*

In addition to the future tense, you have already learned two other ways of expressing the future in Spanish: **ir a** + infinitive or present indicative.

Mañana **voy a hacer** la encuesta.	*I am going to do the survey tomorrow.*
Mañana **hago** la encuesta.	*I'll do the survey tomorrow.*

The future may be used to express *probability* or *to wonder* about a present situation or action. The equivalent in English can be *probably, I / we wonder, it must be,* and so on.

Luisa	Luzmila no ha llegado. ¿Qué hora **será**?	*Luzmila hasn't arrived. I wonder what time it is.*
Guillermo	No lo sé. **Serán** las tres de la tarde.	*I don't know. It's probably around three P.M.*
Luisa	¿Dónde **estará** Luzmila?	*Where can Luzmila be?*

Actividades

1 Nuestras preocupaciones. Completa estas preguntas con el futuro de los verbos entre paréntesis. Después, con un/a compañero/a, discutan si estas cosas ocurrirán cuando ustedes sean mayores.

1. ¿ _____ (Haber) buena atención médica para los mayores?
2. ¿ _____ (Pagar, nosotros) mucho por nuestro seguro médico?
3. ¿ _____ (Eliminar) el gobierno la pobreza en que viven muchos ancianos?
4. ¿ _____ (Ser) posible quedarnos en nuestra casa?
5. ¿ _____ (Sufrir, nosotros) de alguna enfermedad grave?
6. ¿Nuestros hijos _____ (querer) cuidarnos cuando lo necesitemos?

2 ¿Qué será será? Tú y tu compañero/a de estudio hablan sobre lo que harán en el futuro. Pon en futuro, en la forma de **tú,** los verbos que están entre paréntesis. Cuando termines, hazle la encuesta a tu compañero/a.

▶ MODELO: ¿En qué región _____ (vivir)?
¿En qué región vivirás?

1. ¿ _____ (Hacer) una maestría o un doctorado antes de empezar a trabajar?
2. ¿Qué profesión _____ (tener)? ¿ _____ (Ganar) más o menos de cien mil dólares al año?
3. ¿ _____ (Preocuparse) por los problemas sociales y económicos de los jóvenes?
4. ¿ _____ (Usar) transporte público para llegar al trabajo? ¿Qué marca de coche _____ (preferir)?
5. ¿ _____ (Alquilar) o _____ (comprar) tu apartamento o casa?
6. ¿ _____ (Fumar) o no? ¿ _____ (Consumir) alcohol o no?
7. ¿Cuántas semanas de vacaciones _____ (tomar) al año? ¿Adónde _____ (viajar) y con quién?
8. ¿ _____ (Casarse) antes de cumplir los treinta años? ¿ _____ (Querer) tener hijos? ¿Por qué sí o por qué no?

3 ¿Dónde estará? Margarita y Enrique están esperando a su amiga Reyes, que ya está atrasada *(late)* para el almuerzo. Con un/a compañero/a, creen una conversación entre ellos sobre las posibles razones.

4 **¿Qué opinas tú?** Muchas cosas pueden suceder en nuestra sociedad durante los próximos diez años. Trabajando en parejas, discutan estas afirmaciones y expliquen si están de acuerdo o no y por qué.

1. El número de suicidios entre los jóvenes aumentará.
2. Habrá menos casos de SIDA en el país.
3. Los jóvenes conseguirán trabajo muy fácilmente.
4. Todo el mundo tendrá seguro médico.
5. La pobreza y el hambre disminuirán en todo el mundo.
6. Descubrirán nuevas medicinas para curar las enfermedades mentales.
7. No habrá más ataques de terroristas en los EE.UU.
8. El gobierno permitirá la clonación de seres humanos.
9. Los jóvenes tendrán más educación.
10. El gobierno prohibirá la venta de cigarrillos en todo el país.

5 **Predicciones.** Escribe una composición sobre la situación de uno de estos problemas sociales en el año 2020: (a) el consumo de alcohol y drogas, (b) la cura definitiva del SIDA, del cáncer o de otra enfermedad, (c) el costo de la educación universitaria, (d) la delincuencia en el país o (e) soluciones al terrorismo.

Trampa de trampas

En el apartamento de Adriana, en San Antonio.

¿Dónde estará Gafasnegras?

No sé, pero ella tiene que vender los jaguares.

Los jaguares son difíciles de vender.

Pero, ¿cuántos anticuarios habrá en San Antonio?

Busquemos en la guía telefónica. Yo busco desde la *a* hasta la *m* y tú comienzas con la *n*.

Los anticuarios de San Antonio ya deben saber que son robados porque ven la televisión mexicana.

En el anticuario, en San Antonio.

Mmm...

Bueno, ¿cuál es su conclusión?

Tengo un cliente al que le interesaría mucho. Aquí tiene la dirección y el teléfono.

Raúl, valió la pena poner el anuncio. ¡El criminal cayó en la trampa! Le di tu número.

Bien, entonces espero la llamada. Gracias, compadre.

De nada. Por la patria, haré lo que sea necesario.

Mira este anuncio de "Arte precolombino".

Queda muy cerca, iré a ver qué puedo averiguar.

Suerte, Adriana.

Señor, vi su anuncio en el periódico. ¿No ha venido una señora delgada, de pelo negro a venderle unos objetos de arte maya?

¿Y usted por qué quiere saberlo?

Estamos buscando dos objetos que pertenecen a México.

¿Puede usted darme más detalles?

Son dos objetos de barro y representan a los héroes gemelos, Yax-Balam y Hun-Ahau. Los teníamos juntos en Costa Rica y se los robaron de nuevo.

¡Usted sabe mucho y creo que dice la verdad! Debe hablar con el Sr. Guzmán.

¿Quién es él?

Es un agente mexicano, pero se hace pasar por coleccionista de arte. Aquí tiene la dirección.

Esa mujer que usted describió estuvo aquí hace poco.

¿Cómo puede ser?

No se preocupe, el Sr. Guzmán tiene todo bajo control. Ya lo verá.

Actividades

Online Study Center

For additional practice with this episode, visit the *Caminos* website at http://college.hmco.com/languages/spanish/renjilian/caminos/3e/student_home.html.

1 Comprensión. Basándote en este episodio de *Caminos del jaguar,* elige la alternativa lógica.

1. Felipe cree que Gafasnegras tiene que...
   a. esconder los jaguares.
   b. vender los jaguares.

2. Felipe y Adriana encuentran a un anticuario que sabe algo sobre...
   a. el arte precolombino.
   b. Nayeli.

3. El anticuario está contento porque Gafasnegras...
   a. va a llamar a Raúl.
   b. va a llamar a Adriana.

4. Para el anticuario, la patria es...
   a. algo indiferente.
   b. algo importante.

5. Adriana sale para averiguar la información que encontró en...
   a. el periódico.
   b. la guía telefónica.

6. El anticuario dice que Gafasnegras...
   a. ya compró los jaguares.
   b. quiere vender los jaguares.

7. El anticuario le pide a Adriana que no se preocupe porque...
   a. todo va a salir mal.
   b. el Sr. Guzmán tiene todo bajo control.

2 Situaciones. Dramaticen una de las siguientes situaciones.

1. Adriana y Felipe hacen planes para buscar los jaguares.
2. El anticuario y Gafasnegras hablan sobre los jaguares.

3 Escritura. Escribe la conversación telefónica que Adriana va a tener con el Sr. Guzmán. (4–6 oraciones)

NOTA CULTURAL

El Instituto de Culturas Texanas

Este museo de San Antonio tiene exposiciones que muestran la variada cultura del estado de Texas y sus orígenes hispanos. Se exhiben también varios objetos arqueológicos representativos de las culturas que han formado el estado. Hay una tienda en el museo donde se venden libros y videos sobre las tradiciones culturales de Texas. También se venden reproducciones de algunas obras de arte de su colección.

SEGUNDO PASO

Vocabulario y lengua

DISCUSSING ENVIRONMENTAL ISSUES

Consejos ecológicos

unequal

A muchos nos preocupan **el deterioro del planeta** y las **consecuencias** de nuestras desiguales° relaciones con la **naturaleza**. Pero gran parte de la gente considera que no puede hacer nada o que los problemas son tan grandes que se escapan de sus manos. Nada más falso.

It isn't about / fight
remaining species / Being aware
environment / The only thing

behavior

Existen innumerables cosas que podemos hacer día a día para ayudar a **conservar el planeta** y llevar una **existencia** más **armoniosa** con la naturaleza. **No se trata de**° una lucha° a muerte entre tecnología y naturaleza, entre el hombre y las **demás especies**°. Tomando consciencia° de nuestra **responsabilidad ecológica,** podemos aprender a coexistir adecuadamente con el medio ambiente°. Lo único° que se requiere en muchas ocasiones es una pequeña modificación en nuestro **comportamiento**°. No debemos dejar de hacer o usar las cosas que nos gustan o nos son cómodas. Tan sólo debemos hacerlas de una manera más ecológica.

own

USA TU PROPIA° TAZA...

garbage

discarded
avoids

Lleva un vaso o taza a la oficina y úsalo para beber agua o café. Así no producirás **basura**° cada vez que tengas sed. Piensa en el montón de vasos **desechados**° que acumulas al año y la cantidad de basura que se evita° si tú y tus compañeros de trabajo usan su propia taza.

save (rescue)

save (collect)

sheet of paper / sides

¿QUIERES SALVAR° EL MUNDO?

Empieza por **ahorrar**° papel. El papel es producido de fibra vegetal procesada que se obtiene **explotando** los bosques del mundo. Toda hoja° tiene dos caras°. **Reusándolas** y escribiendo o imprimiendo en su reverso, reduces tu consumo de papel. Al reducir tu consumo, reduces la presión sobre los bosques y la cantidad de basura.

¡APÁGALO!

Apaga un **bombillo**° o la computadora, impresora, televisión o cualquier otro aparato eléctrico que no estés usando. La **energía** consumida por estos equipos se produce quemando° **combustible**° caro, que **contamina** el medio ambiente o explotando nuestros **recursos**° hidroeléctricos naturales limitados y cada vez más **escasos**°.

lightbulb

burning
fuel
resources / scarce

APOYA° LAS ORGANIZACIONES QUE AYUDAN A LOS ANIMALES

Support

Hay muchas organizaciones como el WWF (World Wildlife Fund) que ayudan a proteger los animales en peligro de **extinción,** como los **elefantes, ballenas**°, **delfines, pingüinos, osos panda**°, **tigres,** tortugas y **monos**°. También hay organizaciones como el ASPCA que se dedica a prevenir la crueldad a los animales como los perros, gatos, **gallos**°, **caballos**° y pájaros. Puedes apoyarlas con contribuciones o puedes escribirles cartas a los políticos, ser voluntario o ¡adoptar una mascota!

whales
panda bears / monkeys

roosters / horses

Más palabras y expresiones

Cognados

la contaminación   la deforestación

Sustantivos

el calentamiento global   *global warming*
la capa de ozono   *ozone layer*
los desperdicios nucleares   *nuclear waste*
el dióxido de carbono   *carbon dioxide*
el efecto invernadero   *the greenhouse effect*
la lluvia ácida   *acid rain*

Actividades

1 ¿Verdadero o falso? Di si las oraciones son verdaderas (**V**) o falsas (**F**). Si son falsas, corrígelas según la lectura. Trabaja con una pareja.

1. Una sola persona no puede hacer nada para resolver los problemas ecológicos.
2. Se puede vivir en armonía con la naturaleza.
3. Debemos modificar nuestras vidas modernas por completo.
4. La tecnología no puede coexistir con la naturaleza sin destruirla.
5. Debemos usar muchas tazas de plástico.
6. Debemos ahorrar papel.
7. No es necesario que apaguemos los aparatos eléctricos cuando no se usan.
8. No se puede hacer nada por los animales en peligro.
9. Los combustibles no contaminan ni el aire ni el agua.
10. Todo el mundo tiene responsabilidades ecológicas.

2 **Noticias ecológicas.** Escucha las noticias que hablan del problema de la extinción de especies y contesta las preguntas.

1. ¿Cuántas especies en peligro de extinción hay en el mundo?
2. ¿Cuáles son las causas de este problema?
3. Nombra tres especies de animales en peligro de extinción.
4. ¿Qué pasa cuando se extingue una especie?
5. ¿Por qué nos afecta a nosotros?

3 **¿Qué más podemos hacer?** Haz una lista de cinco cosas que se puede hacer para ayudar a conservar el planeta.

4 **A escribir.** ¿Cuál es el problema ecológico que más te preocupa? ¿Por qué? ¿Cómo se puede resolver?

EXPRESSING EMOTIONS AND DOUBT IN THE PAST: PRESENT AND PLUPERFECT (PAST PERFECT) SUBJUNCTIVE

Un planeta en peligro

have contaminated	Lilia	Es terrible que **hayamos contaminado**° el aire con tantos productos químicos. Ahora vivimos con el resultado.
have produced	Inés	Es verdad, pero los coches también han contribuido a esa contaminación. No me gusta para nada que las compañías de autos **hayan producido**° tantos coches grandes.
has (not) stopped	Lilia	A mí tampoco, pero también es triste que la gente no **haya dejado**° de comprarlos.
had (not) approved	Inés	Estoy de acuerdo. Los políticos no hacen mucho. A mí no me gustó que el gobierno no **hubiera aprobado**° leyes más estrictas para proteger el medio ambiente.
	Lilia	¿Y la solución?
	Inés	Tenemos que seguir luchando por la naturaleza.

You have learned that verbs expressing wishes, emotions, and similar feelings in the main clause require the use of the subjunctive in the subordinate or dependent clause.

Espero que ustedes **lean** las instrucciones.

I hope that you read the instructions.

Esperaba que ustedes **leyeran** las instrucciones.

I was hoping that you read the instructions.

When the verb in the main clause is in the present and the dependent clause refers to the recent past, the *present perfect subjunctive* is used.

Espero que **hayan leído** las instrucciones.

I hope that you have read the instructions.

When the verb in the main clause is in a past tense and the dependent clause refers to an action that occurred before the one described in the main clause, the pluperfect *(past perfect) subjunctive* appears in the subordinate clause.

Me alegró mucho que **hubieran leído** las instrucciones.

It made me happy that you had read the instructions.

The present perfect and pluperfect subjunctive
(El presente perfecto y pluscuamperfecto del subjuntivo)

	present subjunctive	+ past participle	imperfect subjunctive	+ past participle
yo	**haya**		**hubiera**	
tú	**hayas**	hablado	**hubieras**	hablado
Ud. / él / ella	**haya**	querido	**hubiera**	querido
nosotros/as	**hayamos**	venido	**hubiéramos**	venido
vosotros/as	**hayáis**		**hubierais**	
Uds. / ellos / ellas	**hayan**		**hubieran**	

Remember to review how to form past participles and sentence structure with object pronouns in *Unidad 9,* pages 327–328.

Actividades

1 La contaminación.

Un grupo de amigos expresan sus opiniones sobre la contaminación. Completa cada frase con la forma correcta del presente perfecto del subjuntivo. Sigue el modelo.

► MODELO: Es bueno que las autoridades *hayan limpiado* (limpiar) el agua contaminada en las ciudades.

1. No es verdad que todos los países _____ (solucionar) los problemas de la contaminación del medio ambiente.
2. Es una lástima que los coches _____ (ser) la causa de la contaminación del aire.
3. Temo que el número de águilas _____ (reducirse) este año.
4. Ojalá que no _____ (morirse) muchas ballenas este año en las aguas contaminadas.
5. Es bueno que el gobierno de los Estados Unidos _____ (darse cuenta) de la urgencia de proteger los animales.
6. Estoy contento de que los jóvenes _____ (utilizar) menos agua en la ducha.
7. Es bueno que los parques nacionales _____ (preservar) las flores y los bosques en peligro de extinción.
8. Me alegro de que recientemente los ecólogos _____ (preocuparse) por los animales marinos como el delfín y la ballena.

2 Las preferencias de la familia.

Tú hiciste las siguientes actividades durante una visita a casa. Cuéntale a un/a compañero/a la reacción de diferentes miembros de tu familia. Sigue el modelo y emplea el pluscuamperfecto del subjuntivo.

► MODELO: No apagué las luces cuando salí de casa.
A mi padre no le gustó que yo no hubiera apagado las luces cuando salí de casa.

1. Le di cincuenta dólares al WWF.
2. Pasé media hora en la ducha.
3. Tiré basura en el piso.
4. Compré un coche híbrido.
5. Reciclé mis botellas de plástico.
6. Participé en una protesta contra las fábricas nucleares.

3 Emociones.

Haz una lista de cinco cosas que has hecho recientemente. Luego, comparte tu lista con un/a compañero/a. Dale tu opinión a la otra persona de cada cosa en su lista. Sigue el modelo.

► MODELO: He comprado un nuevo coche.
Me alegro de que hayas comprado un nuevo coche.

4 Mis memorias.

Imagínate que tienes noventa y cinco años y estás escribiendo tus memorias. Allí dices que te arrepientes de haber hecho cinco cosas en tu vida. Usa **ojalá** y el pluscuamperfecto del subjuntivo para describirlas. Explica también por qué te arrepientes de ellas. Sigue el modelo.

► MODELO: *Ojalá que yo no hubiera roto el antiguo plato de cerámica de mi mamá cuando era niño/a.*

USING THE CONDITIONAL TENSE AND CONDITIONAL OF PROBABILITY

Planes

Irene	¿**Te gustaría**° mirar esta película de amor?	*Would you like*
Carlos	No, querida. En vez de mirar la televisión, **preferiría**° navegar por Internet.	*I would prefer*
	Podríamos ver° qué oportunidades hay para ser voluntario en nuestra comunidad.	*We could see*
Irene	Buena idea. **Me encantaría**° trabajar con los jóvenes de nuestro vecindario.	*I would love*

Most verbs in Spanish are regular in the conditional. As with the future, the infinitive is the conditional stem for most **-ar, -er,** and **-ir** verbs. All verbs share a common set of endings in the conditional. Notice that these endings carry a written accent.

Conditional tense of regular verbs				
Infinitive	**Subject**	**Stem**	**Ending**	**Conditional tense**
trabajar	yo	trabajar-	**ía**	trabajar**ía**
creer	tú	creer-	**ías**	creer**ías**
escribir	Ud., él, ella	escribir-	**ía**	escribir**ía**
preferir	nosotros/as	preferir-	**íamos**	preferir**íamos**
dar	vosotros/as	dar-	**íais**	dar**íais**
ir	Uds., ellos, ellas	ir-	**ían**	ir**ían**

Irregular verbs in the conditional tense are the same verbs that have an irregular stem in the future (page 382). Conditional tense endings for irregular verbs are the same as those for regular verbs.

Conditional tense of irregular verbs		
Infinitive	Stem	Conditional tense
decir	dir-	yo **diría**
hacer	har-	tú **harías**
poder	podr-	Ud. **podría**
poner	pondr-	él **pondría**
querer	querr-	ella **querría**
saber	sabr-	nosotros/as **sabríamos**
salir	saldr-	vosotros/as **saldríais**
tener	tendr-	Uds. **tendrían**
venir	vendr-	ellos, ellas **vendrían**

Habría *(there would be)* is the conditional form of **haber.** Like **hay** *(there is, there are),* **habría** is used only in the singular and means *there would be.*

Pensé que **habría** soluciones para este problema.	*I thought that there would be solutions for this problem.*

The English equivalent of the conditional tense is *would* or *could* plus a *verb.*

—Pensé que **vendrías** hoy.	*—I thought that you would come today.*
—No, te dije que no **tendría** tiempo.	*—No, I told you that I wouldn't have time.*

The conditional can be used to show politeness or to soften a command.

—¿**Podrías** ayudarme?	*—Could you help me?*
—Me **gustaría,** pero no puedo hoy.	*—I would like to, but I can't today.*

The conditional may be used to express *probability* when there is doubt or questioning about a past situation or action. The equivalent in English can be *probably, I / we wonder* plus the past tense.

—Catalina no vino a ayudar con los niños ayer. ¿Qué le **pasaría**?	*—Catalina didn't come to help with the children yesterday. I wonder what happened to her.*
—Me imagino que **estudiaría** para su examen de cálculo.	*—I imagine that she was probably studying for her calculus exam.*

Actividades

1 **Soy profesor/a.** Tú sueñas con ser el / la profesor/a de la clase de español. Explica qué harías tú y qué harían tus alumnos en la clase.

1. Yo _____ (hablar) español con los alumnos siempre.
2. Mis alumnos siempre _____ (hacer) la tarea.
3. Yo _____ (ayudar) a todos los alumnos.
4. Mis alumnos _____ (sacar) buenas notas en todos los exámenes.
5. Nosotros _____ (ir) a restaurantes mexicanos, españoles y cubanos todos los meses.
6. Toda la clase _____ (llegar) a tiempo.
7. Mis alumnos _____ (escribir) composiciones excelentes.
8. Nosotros _____ (aprender) algo sobre todos los países hispanos.

2 Posibles reacciones. ¿Qué harías o dirías tú en estas situaciones? Usa diferentes verbos en el condicional para cada situación.

▶ MODELO: al ganar la lotería
Yo compraría una nueva casa para mis padres y viajaría por el mundo.

1. al recibir una llamada telefónica pidiendo dinero para salvar los osos polares
2. al saber que se murió la mascota de tu mejor amigo/a
3. al aceptar un trabajo en un parque nacional de Costa Rica
4. al ver a una amiga dejar basura en una mesa de la cafetería
5. al conseguir un pasaje gratis a las Galápagos
6. al ver muchos papeles en el piso de la clase
7. al ser elegido director/a de un programa de reciclaje en la universidad
8. al ir a Antártida para estudiar los pingüinos

3 ¿Qué le pasaría? Roberta llega a la oficina tarde y parece muy cansada. Luz y Rafael conversan sobre qué le pasaría a Roberta anoche. Con un/a compañero/a, creen una conversación en la que ellos discuten las posibilidades.

4 Soy reportero/a. Haz una lista de cuatro preguntas para entrevistar a dos compañeros/as de tu clase sobre el medio ambiente. Usa el condicional de algunos de los verbos de la lista. Después haz la entrevista a tus compañeros/as.

▶ MODELO: *¿Dejarías de usar tazas de papel?*
¿Qué harías para ayudar al medio ambiente de nuestro vecindario?

apoyar	comprar	dejar	hacer	dirigir
preocuparse	usar	reusar	tener	ayudar
ser	ahorrar	apagar	evitar	participar

¡Gol!

Actividades

Online Study Center

For additional practice with this episode, visit the *Caminos* website at http://college.hmco.com/languages/spanish/renjilian/caminos/3e/student_home.html.

1 Comprensión. Basándote en este episodio de *Caminos del jaguar,* elige la alternativa lógica.

1. Adriana le agradece al Sr. Guzmán porque...
   - a. llegó muy temprano.
   - b. aceptó verla.

2. Raúl es el responsable de encontrar...
   - a. los jaguares robados.
   - b. a Adriana y a Felipe.

3. Raúl no le había explicado nada a Adriana porque nunca pudo...
   - a. verla.
   - b. alcanzarla.

4. Raúl dice que en su trabajo, el anonimato...
   - a. es esencial.
   - b. no es esencial.

5. ¿Dónde había visto Adriana la nota que tiene Raúl?
   - a. En México.
   - b. En San Antonio.

6. ¿Qué golpea a Gafasnegras en la cabeza?
   - a. La bolsa con los jaguares.
   - b. Una pelota de fútbol.

7. ¿Qué palabra es ILEYAN al revés?
   - a. Yelani.
   - b. Nayeli.

2 Situaciones. Dramaticen una de las siguientes situaciones.

1. Adriana y el Sr. Guzmán se presentan en el restaurante.
2. Gafasnegras cae en la trampa del Sr. Guzmán.

3 Escritura. Escribe un resumen de la reacción de Adriana cuando se da cuenta de que Raúl es el hombre del anillo raro. (4–6 oraciones)

NOTA CULTURAL

El Paseo del Río en San Antonio

El Paseo del Río de San Antonio es uno de los lugares más atractivos de la ciudad y lo visitan miles de turistas cada año. En este sitio ocurren unos eventos muy importantes de los últimos episodios de *Caminos del jaguar.* El Paseo del Río tiene una variedad inmensa de restaurantes, hoteles, tiendas de ropa y galerías de arte. Los habitantes de San Antonio y los turistas suelen pasear por el área en barcos especiales o pasear por las anchas aceras a las orillas del río.

Lectura

Online Study Center

For further reading practice online, visit the *Caminos* website at http://college.hmco.com/languages/spanish/renjilian/caminos/3e/student_home.html.

PRELECTURA

Throughout the ages, people have been frightened by many different events and things, as the author of this reading details. He believes that fright itself is probably the most human—and animal—of feelings. He compares the fears of people in the Middle Ages, a thousand years ago, to the different worries people have in the 21st century.

Reading Strategy

Distinguishing facts from opinions

Informational texts contain descriptions of facts, situations, or events. News and historical descriptions are informational texts. These texts are not necessarily impartial and the writer may seek to influence readers in a certain way by using strategies such as giving examples that support his or her ideas, using quotes, introducing doubt, or making strong assertions. In order to distinguish facts from opinions when reading this type of text, try to become familiar with the devices used by writers to influence their readers.

1 **Los miedos de mis abuelos.** Escoge de la lista de abajo, según tu opinión, cinco cosas que les daban miedo a tus abuelos. Cuando termines, con un/a compañero/a, discutan qué cosas les dan miedo a las personas de su generación. Pongan sus ideas en orden de importancia y compárenlas. Pueden usar las palabras de la lista o añadir otras ideas.

la violencia
la contaminación
los terremotos
la falta de trabajo
el robo de identidad
la falta de petróleo
la falta de vivienda
las drogas
la discriminación

la soledad
los problemas económicos
el terrorismo
la guerra
los desastres naturales
la desaparición de los bosques
el deterioro del planeta
las enfermedades
el hambre

2 **Mis preocupaciones y miedos.** Trabaja con un/a compañero/a para identificar los problemas sociales que aparecen en el dibujo. Luego, discutan las tres cosas que más debe temer su comunidad o su país en los próximos diez años.

¡Milenios de miedos!

Si no le temes a Dios, ¡témele a la peste[1]! Si no le tienes miedo a la bomba atómica, ¡témele al SIDA! Los miedos de ayer y de hoy son una muestra[2] de que esas sensaciones también tienen historia y están sometidas[3] a procesos culturales, religiosos y políticos.

Ahora, en este milenio, podemos preguntarnos cuáles son los miedos más característicos del hombre contemporáneo. Y ayudados, por ejemplo, por el historiador francés Georges Duby, comparemos algunas de las angustias[4] del año dos mil con las del año mil.

Tal vez lo más humano (y también lo más animal) es el miedo. El más antiguo de los miedos es, quizás, el miedo a lo desconocido[5] y de él nacen múltiples terrores. Sin embargo, ha habido otras cosas peores aguardando[6] al hombre.

El hombre de hoy está lleno de inquietudes[7] y preguntas y, la mayoría de las veces, sus miedos difieren de los de hace mil años, aunque se pueden encontrar similitudes[8] entre unos y otros, como el miedo a la miseria[9], a las catástrofes naturales y a las enfermedades. A pesar de los avances tecnológicos y los descubrimientos científicos, el hombre contemporáneo está sometido[10] a nuevos desamparos[11].

Tal vez los miedos de hoy son más agudos[12] que los del medioevo, como el miedo a la desaparición de la raza humana, a la destrucción de la naturaleza, a una catástrofe nuclear, a una nueva guerra mundial.

Con todo, el miedo puede ser una especie de estimulador de búsquedas espirituales y de vuelos imaginativos. Por lo demás, a la persona que tiene miedo, todavía no se le ha acabado el mundo.

[1]plague; [2]sample; [3]bound; [4]anxieties; [5]the unknown; [6]awaiting; [7]worries; [8]similarities; [9]poverty; [10]is subjected to; [11]troubles; [12]acute

POSTLECTURA

3 **Miedos de los milenios.** Trabajen en grupos para contestar las preguntas sobre la lectura.

1. ¿Qué épocas compara el autor del texto?
2. ¿Cuál es el miedo más humano de todos?
3. ¿Qué miedos tenía la gente a partir del año mil?
4. Según el autor, ¿de qué condiciones tiene miedo el hombre moderno?
5. Cuando el autor dice que los miedos de hoy son más agudos que los del pasado, ¿qué ejemplos da?
6. ¿Qué significa el título del artículo?

4 **Estrategias.** Trabaja con un/a compañero/a. Busquen frases del texto para ilustrar estas estrategias que usa el autor.

a. mencionar a expertos
b. dar ejemplos
c. comparar épocas

5 **¿Estás de acuerdo?** Trabaja con un/a compañero/a. Analicen esta frase del autor y discutan por qué contiene un pensamiento positivo sobre el miedo.

"A la persona que tiene miedo, todavía no se le ha acabado el mundo".

6 **Mi punto de vista.** Con tus propias palabras, resume los temas de la lectura. Expone brevemente cuáles son las ideas principales del autor del texto.

Escritura

Writing Strategy

Narrowing a topic

The secret of writing a compelling paragraph is to choose a topic that is focused. If the topic is very broad, there is too much information to cover adequately. It may be necessary to narrow your topic several times before it is focused enough for a clear, concise paragraph.

Online Study Center

For further writing practice online, visit the *Caminos* website at http://college .hmco.com/languages/ spanish/renjilian/caminos/ 3e/student_home.html.

Workshop

Here is an example of a topic that has been narrowed down several times.

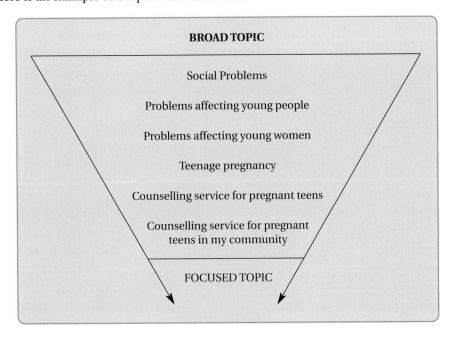

BROAD TOPIC

Social Problems

Problems affecting young people

Problems affecting young women

Teenage pregnancy

Counselling service for pregnant teens

Counselling service for pregnant teens in my community

FOCUSED TOPIC

Strategy in Action

For additional practice with narrowing a topic, complete the exercises below and in the *Escritura* section of your Student Activities Manual for *Unidad 11.*

1 Problemas del futuro. Si no resolvemos los problemas sociales de hoy, habrá muchos problemas en el futuro. Escoge un problema social y escribe tus predicciones de lo que pasará.

2 El mundo del futuro. Si no cuidamos el medio ambiente, habrá muchos problemas ecológicos en el futuro. Escoge un problema ecológico y escribe tus predicciones de lo que pasará.

PRIMER PASO

TALKING ABOUT CONTEMPORARY SOCIETY

Sustantivos

el acto delectivo	delinquent act
la adicción	addiction
el/la adolescente	adolescent
la angustia	worry
las armas	weapons
el asesinato	assassination, murder
el/la asesino/a	murderer
el beneficio	benefit
la cárcel, prisión	prison
la comunidad	community
el consejo	advice
el consumo	consumption
el crimen	crime
la cura	cure
la delincuencia	delinquency
el/la delincuente	delinquent
la depresión	depression
los desamparados	homeless people
el desempleo	unemployment
la drogadicción	drug addiction
el embarazo	pregnancy
el empleo	employment
la guerra	war
la incertidumbre	uncertainty
la justicia	justice
la libertad	freedom
el lío	problem, trouble, mess
el logro	achievement
el/la niñero/a	nanny, babysitter
la patria	homeland
el peligro	danger

la pobreza	poverty
el/la policía	police; police officer
el programa social	social program
el robo	robbery
la seguridad	security
el seguro médico	health insurance
el SIDA	AIDS
la sociedad	society
la solución	solution
la terapia	therapy
el terrorismo	terrorism
el/la terrorista	terrorist
el/la trabajador/a social	social worker
el tráfico de drogas	drug trafficking
el/la voluntario/a	volunteer

Verbos

alcanzar	to reach
amenazar	to threaten
arrestar	to arrest
asesinar	to assassinate, murder
aumentar	to increase
convertir	to change, convert
encarcelar	to imprison
enfrentar	to confront, face up to
estar desesperado/a	to be desperate
fracasar	to fail
lograr	to achieve; to attain
luchar	to fight
matar	to kill
obtener	to obtain
tener remedio	to have a solution
triunfar	to succeed, triumph

SEGUNDO PASO

DISCUSSING ENVIRONMENTAL ISSUES

Sustantivos

la ballena	*whale*
la basura	*garbage*
el bombillo	*lightbulb*
el caballo	*horse*
el calentamiento global	*global warming*
la capa de ozono	*ozone layer*
el combustible	*fuel*
el comportamiento	*behavior*
la consecuencia	*consequence*
la contaminación	*pollution, contamination*
la deforestación	*deforestation*
el delfín	*dolphin*
los desperdicios nucleares	*nuclear waste*
el deterioro	*deterioration*
el dióxido de carbono	*carbon dioxide*
el efecto invernadero	*the greenhouse effect*
el elefante	*elephant*
la energía	*energy*
la especie	*species*
la existencia	*existence*
la extinción	*extinction*
el gallo	*rooster*
la lluvia ácida	*acid rain*

la mascota	*pet*
el mono	*monkey*
la naturaleza	*nature*
el oso (panda)	*(panda) bear*
el pingüino	*penguin*
el planeta	*planet*
el recurso	*resource*
la responsabilidad	*responsibility*
el tigre	*tiger*

Verbos

ahorrar	*to save (collect)*
apoyar	*to support*
conservar	*to conserve, preserve*
contaminar	*to pollute, contaminate*
desechar	*to dispose, discard*
explotar	*to exploit*
reusar	*to reuse*
salvar	*to save (rescue)*
tratarse de	*to deal with; to be about*

Adjetivos

armonioso/a	*harmonious*
desechado/a	*discarded, disposed*
ecológico/a	*ecological*
escaso/a	*scarce*

12
Del pasado al presente

VOCABULARIO Y LENGUA

- ► Comparing the Aztecs, Mayans, and Incas
- ► Using **si** clauses in the present
- ► Expressing hypothetical actions: **Si** clauses

- ► Discussing Hispanic contributions in the United States
- ► Contrasting **pero, sino,** and **sino que**
- ► Using passive forms

CAMINOS DEL JAGUAR

- ► ¿Chocolate o cárcel?
- ► Amor y paz

LECTURA

- ► Ecos del pasado: Héroes mayas

NOTAS CULTURALES

- ► El Zócalo
- ► El Museo Nacional de Antropología

ESTRATEGIAS

- ► **Reading**: Using a genealogical chart with notes
- ► **Writing**: Editing one's own work

Benigno Gómez, *6 Birds*

Preguntas del tema

▶ ¿Has visitado algún sitio arqueológico de una cultura antigua? Explica.

▶ ¿Qué quieres estudiar sobre la historia de las civilizaciones antiguas?

▶ ¿A qué hispanos famosos conoces?

▶ ¿Cuáles son algunas contribuciones de los hispanos en los Estados Unidos?

PRIMER PASO

Vocabulario y lengua

COMPARING THE AZTECS, MAYANS, AND INCAS

Tres grandes civilizaciones: Los aztecas, los mayas y los incas

developed

Tres civilizaciones muy **desarrolladas**° antes de la **exploración** y la **conquista** españolas, fueron la azteca, la maya y la inca.

LOS AZTECAS

La cultura azteca se componía de varios grupos del valle central de México, los que llegaron a formar el gran **imperio** azteca desde el siglo XIV hasta la llegada de Hernán Cortés en 1519 y la muerte de su emperador, Moctezuma. Los aztecas pertenecían al grupo **étnico** y **lingüístico** de los *nahuas* y tenían una organización social y política compleja, necesaria para gobernar un gran imperio. Sus prácticas religiosas se basaban en un calendario de ceremonias y sacrificios celebrados por los sacerdotes. Los aztecas fundaron la capital de su imperio, Tenochtitlán en medio del lago Texcoco que llegó a tener entre ocho y más de trece kilómetros cuadrados de área. Aunque no se

Para los aztecas, el dios Quetzalcóatl era el creador de la humanidad y su protector.

sabe por seguro, dicen que había entre doscientos y trescientos cincuenta mil habitantes a principios del siglo XV. Cortés **venció**° a Moctezuma, el emperador azteca, y en las **ruinas** de Tenochtitlán, **fundó**° la Ciudad de México.

defeated
founded

Conocemos la historia azteca a través de las investigaciones arqueológicas y de las crónicas españolas, escritas por misioneros españoles y por cronistas aztecas en español o en náhuatl, usando el alfabeto latino. Los libros sagrados o códices se guardaban en los templos y la mayoría fue destruida durante la colonia española. Sin embargo, algunos de ellos sobrevivieron, como el Códice Borbónico que describe los días del calendario y sus ceremonias, lo mismo que el Códice Borgia.

in addition to
weavers

Los **descendientes** de los nahuas, **además de**° desempeñar oficios y profesiones modernas, cultivan la tierra y son hábiles **tejedores**° de lana y algodón.

Los mayas

La gran civilización maya es una de las más importantes culturas prehispánicas del continente americano. Tuvo su **apogeo**° entre los años 200 y 900 después de Cristo, cuando construyeron grandes ciudades como Chichén Itzá, Uxmal, Itzamal y Mayapán, además de **imponentes**° **templos** y **pirámides,** muchos de los cuales podemos apreciar hoy en día. A partir del siglo X y hasta que llegaron los españoles a la región, en el siglo XVI, la cultura maya fue **decayendo**° poco a poco.

El universo maya tiene tres niveles cósmicos: el cielo, *Caan*; la tierra, *Cab*; y el inframundo, *Xibalbá*.

height

imposing

declining

Durante su época de esplendor, los mayas extendieron su imperio por lo que hoy conocemos como Centroamérica y parte de Yucatán y Mérida, en México. La cultura de este pueblo **se destacó**° por la creación y el uso de la **escritura**° **jeroglífica,** la que nos ha llegado en los hermosos libros o **códices** que se conservan en las bibliotecas de Dresden, París, Madrid y la Ciudad de México. Además de tener profundos conocimientos de astronomía, los mayas fueron también matemáticos, usaban el cero y un sistema numérico basado en múltiplos de veinte.

stood out / writing

Los incas

En el sur, el imperio de los incas **se distinguió**° por su admirable organización, arquitectura, orfebrería° y textiles. Los incas construyeron imponentes ciudades de piedra y tenían una red de más de veinte mil kilómetros de caminos que comunicaban a los 12 millones de habitantes del imperio. Entre las ciudades de piedra están Cuzco, la antigua capital del imperio incaico, y Machu Picchu, las ruinas de una ciudad que permaneció **perdida**° por muchos **siglos**°. Cuzco fue fundada en el año 1100 y es la ciudad que lleva más tiempo **habitada**° en Suramérica.

La majestuosa ciudad de Machu Picchu

was distinguished
gold or silver work

lost / centuries

inhabited

El imperio inca duró hasta 1527, cuando el explorador y conquistador español Francisco Pizarro venció a Atahualpa, el emperador, en la batalla de Cajamarca. **Sin embargo**°, hubo muchas rebeliones y el último emperador, Túpac Amaru, fue ejecutado° en 1572.

Los descendientes de los incas siguen hablando su idioma nativo, el quechua, y participan activamente en las sociedades a las que **pertenecen**° en Bolivia, el Ecuador, el Perú, al sur de Colombia y al norte de Chile y de la Argentina.

Nevertheless
executed

belong

Actividades

1 Identificación. Trabajen en parejas y, según los textos anteriores, determinen si las cosas de esta lista están relacionadas con los aztecas, los mayas, los incas o con más de una de estas culturas.

1. caminos
2. ciudades de piedra
3. Chichén Itzá
4. la astronomía
5. códices
6. Tenochtitlán
7. el uso de la escritura
8. Xibalbá
9. pirámides
10. matemáticas

2 Comprensión. Contesta las preguntas según el texto sobre los aztecas, mayas e incas.

1. ¿Quiénes fueron Hernán Cortés? ¿Moctezuma? ¿Francisco Pizarro? ¿Atahualpa? ¿Túpac Amaru?
2. ¿Cuándo venció Cortés a los aztecas? ¿Qué hizo después?
3. ¿Cuáles son algunos lugares importantes del mundo maya?
4. ¿Cuándo comenzó a decaer el mundo maya?
5. ¿Cuándo venció Pizarro a los incas? ¿Dónde?
6. Menciona algunos de los logros de los aztecas, los mayas y los incas.
7. ¿Para qué construyeron caminos los incas?
8. ¿Cuántas personas vivían en el imperio inca?
9. ¿Por qué es importante la ciudad de Cuzco?
10. ¿Qué idioma hablan los descendientes de los incas?

3 Las artesanías del mundo maya. Escucha la descripción de las artesanías y escribe tres frases que describan cada uno de estos artículos.

1. _____
2. _____
3. _____
4. _____
5. _____
6. _____

USING *SI* CLAUSES IN THE PRESENT

Herencia cultural

Elena, **si miras** bien la foto de tu bisabuela, **vas a ver** que tú te pareces mucho a ella.

Es cierto, abuelita, y **si no te importa**, **¿puedo** sacar una copia?

Tengo varias copias y **si quieres** una, te la **doy** hoy mismo.

Si me das una foto de mi bisabuela, **será** fantástico, abuelita.

In Spanish **si** (if) introduces a condition that must be fulfilled for something to happen. When **si** is followed by a verb in the present, the condition is likely to be fulfilled. In this case, the verb in the main clause may be in the present indicative or future, or it can be a command. The verb that immediately follows **si** can never be in the present subjunctive.

> **Si quieres** una foto, te **doy / daré** una. *If you want a photo, I'll give you one.*
> **Si tienes** varias fotos, ¡**dame** una, por favor! *If you have several photos, give me one, please!*

Sentences can begin with either the main clause or the **si** clause.

> Te **sentirás** bien **si ayudas** a otras personas. *You will feel good if you help other people.*
> **Si ayudas** a otras personas, te **sentirás** bien. *If you help other people, you will feel good.*

Actividades

1 Condiciones. Combina las frases de una manera lógica.

A	B
1. Si queremos aprender sobre los incas	a. es posible encontrar objetos antiguos.
2. Si haces excavaciones arqueológicas	b. aprenderás sobre el calendario azteca.
3. Si lees el Códice Borbónico	c. entenderás a 400 millones de personas.
4. Si vamos a Chichén Itzá	d. debes visitar también Machu Picchu.
5. Si aprendes español	e. conoceremos imponentes monumentos.
6. Si se dañan los códices	f. verás un hermoso paisaje desde allí.
7. Si te subes a una pirámide	g. perderemos un tesoro histórico.
8. Si viajas a la ciudad de Cuzco	h. debemos estudiar su historia.

2 Excavación arqueológica. Lee el texto siguiente y completa las oraciones con el presente, el futuro o una orden o consejo (mandato), según sea necesario.

Si _____ (**1.** querer / tú) ser arqueólogo, _____ (**2.** deber) estudiar esta carrera en la universidad. Luego, si _____ (**3.** participar) en una excavación, _____ (**4.** poner) mucha atención a las instrucciones que te den. Si _____ (**5.** estar) excavando y _____ (**6.** encontrar) un objeto de valor arqueológico, _____ (**7.** deber) siempre avisarle al jefe de la excavación. Si tú no _____ (**8.** saber) extraer el objeto o si no _____ (**9.** poder) porque es difícil, _____ (**10.** ser) necesario buscar ayuda. Si _____ (**11.** hacer) un buen trabajo, tu jefe te _____ (**12.** aumentar) el sueldo. Si _____ (**13.** tener) un poco más de dinero, _____ (**14.** vivir) mejor también. Si no _____ (**15.** cumplir) con tus deberes, _____ (**16.** perder) tu trabajo.

3 Si esto sucede... Explícale a un/a compañero/a qué haces o qué vas a hacer en estas situaciones.

1. Si alguien necesita mi ayuda...
2. Si no he estudiado la lección....
3. Si no puedo pagar mi educación...
4. Si ocurre un accidente en la calle...
5. Si estoy deprimido/a...
6. Si mi mejor amigo/a se enoja...
7. Si mi novio/a no me quiere...
8. Si alguien me insulta...

EXPRESSING HYPOTHETICAL ACTIONS: *SI* CLAUSES

¿Qué pasaría si...?

As you have learned, a **si** clause expresses a condition and the main clause in a sentence describes the expected result if the condition is fulfilled. When talking about hypothetical or contrary-to-fact situations, as shown in the drawing, the **si** clause is in the *imperfect* subjunctive and the verb in the main clause is in the *conditional* tense. Note that sentences expressing hypothetical or contrary-to-fact situations can begin with either the main clause or the **si** clause.

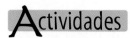

Actividades

1 Imaginación. Completa las oraciones siguientes de una manera lógica.

1. Leería sobre Hernán Cortés si _____ mi libro de historia.
   a. encontrara   b. encontraría

2. Sabríamos mucho más sobre la historia maya si _____ más investigación.
   a. hubiera   b. habría

3. Si yo _____ quechua, podría hablar con los descendientes de los incas.
   a. sabría   b. supiera

4. Seríamos buenos tejedores de lana si _____ descendientes de los nahuas.
   a. seríamos   b. fuéramos

5. Si _____ más códices, sabríamos mucho más sobre la cultura maya.
   a. tuviéramos   b. tendríamos

6. Aprenderías mucha historia si _____ leer la escritura jeroglífica maya.
   a. podrías   b. pudieras

2 Suposiciones. Basándote en las siguientes oraciones, crea suposiciones usando el imperfecto del subjuntivo y el condicional. Sigue el modelo.

▶ **MODELO:** Si mis padres *visitan* el Perú, *conocerán* Machu Picchu.
*Si mis padres **visitaran** el Perú, **conocerían** Machu Picchu.*

1. Si nosotros tenemos dinero, iremos a Chichén Iztá.
2. Si subimos a las pirámides, veremos un paisaje hermoso.
3. Si viajas al Perú, podrás conocer unas iglesias muy hermosas.
4. Si mi hermana va a Cuzco, conocerá la antigua capital inca.
5. Si quieres saber más sobre los aztecas, debes estudiar historia.
6. Si me convierto en un dios maya, viviré en Xibalbá.

3 ¿Qué harías? Con un/a compañero/a, contesten las preguntas creando oraciones hipotéticas. Después, preséntenle las respuestas a la clase.

1. ¿Qué harías si tuvieras un accidente en el coche de tus padres?
2. ¿Cómo reaccionarías si te ofrecieran un trabajo en una planta nuclear?
3. Si conocieras al presidente de los Estados Unidos, ¿qué le dirías?
4. ¿Qué harías si no estudiaras en la universidad?
5. ¿Adónde viajarías si tuvieras un año libre y el dinero no fuera un obstáculo?
6. ¿Qué harías si fueras profesor/a de historia?
7. ¿En qué país te gustaría trabajar si fueras arqueólogo/a?

4 Si esto sucediera... Trabaja con un/a compañero/a para explicar qué harías en estas situaciones.

1. Si fuera un perro...
2. Si tuviera 100 años...
3. Si tuviera 6 años...
4. Si fuera descendiente de los incas...
5. Si supiera pintar...
6. Si viviera en el Perú...
7. Si pudiera cambiar algo en mi vida...
8. Si mis padres me dieran 5 mil dólares...

CAMINOS DEL JAGUAR

¿Chocolate o cárcel?

Actividades

Online Study Center

For additional practice with this episode, visit the *Caminos* website at http://college.hmco.com/languages/spanish/renjilian/caminos/3e/student_home.html.

1 Comprensión. Basándote en este episodio de *Caminos del jaguar,* elige la alternativa lógica.

1. Gafasnegras cree que todavía puede...
   a. quedarse con los jaguares.   b. hacer muchas cosas.

2. El primo de Luis se preocupa por la opinión de...
   a. su esposa.   b. sus amigos.

3. Luis se preocupa porque ha perdido...
   a. su trabajo con Gafasnegras.   b. su futura carrera.

4. El primo de Luis reconoce que el culpable es...
   a. él mismo.   b. Luis.

5. Armando le ofrece al policía...
   a. una confesión.   b. dinero.

6. Doña Carmen está segura de que no...
   a. irá a la prisión.   b. tendrá otro abogado.

7. Felipe se siente muy orgulloso de Adriana porque...
   a. ella le regaló chocolates.   b. ella lo resolvió todo.

8. Según Felipe, el chocolate es...
   a. tan dulce como Adriana.   b. algo simbólico.

 2 Situaciones. Dramaticen una de las siguientes situaciones.

1. Adriana le regala una caja de chocolates a Felipe.
2. Doña Carmen habla con el policía.

3 Escritura. Describe a cuántas personas arrestó la policía y dónde. ¿Cómo reaccionaron estas personas? (5–6 oraciones)

NOTA CULTURAL

El Zócalo

El nombre oficial del Zócalo es "Plaza de la Constitución" y es la segunda plaza más grande del mundo, solamente sobrepasada por la Plaza Roja de Moscú. Para los mexicanos, el Zócalo representa no sólo el corazón del Distrito Federal sino también el corazón de todo México. En su centro hay una enorme bandera mexicana. El Zócalo es un lugar de reunión, y allí se celebran los actos públicos del día de la Independencia, el 16 de septiembre. La gente se pasea por el Zócalo y frecuenta los restaurantes que hay alrededor, las tiendas y los vendedores ambulantes. Cerca del Zócalo está el Templo Mayor, uno de los monumentos más importantes de la cultura mexicana.

SEGUNDO PASO

Vocabulario y lengua

DISCUSSING HISPANIC CONTRIBUTIONS IN THE UNITED STATES

⁘ Online Study Center

For additional practice with this unit's vocabulary and grammar, visit the *Caminos* website at http://college.hmco.com/languages/spanish/renjilian/caminos/3e/student_home.html. You can also review audio flashcards, quiz yourself, and explore related Spanish-language sites.

La población hispana actual

DATOS ESTADÍSTICOS

Según la Oficina del Censo de los Estados Unidos (*U.S. Census Bureau*), los hispanos constituyen la minoría más grande de los Estados Unidos. En el año 2005, la **población**° hispana era de 42,7 millones de habitantes, lo cual representa un **crecimiento**° del 90% desde 1990 cuando había solamente 22,4 millones de hispanos en el país. Esta **cifra**° constituye aproximadamente el 14% de la población del país y no incluye a los habitantes de Puerto Rico. Esta población hispana convierte a los Estados Unidos en el quinto país **de habla española**° del mundo, después de México, Colombia, Argentina y España.

population

growth

figure

Spanish-speaking

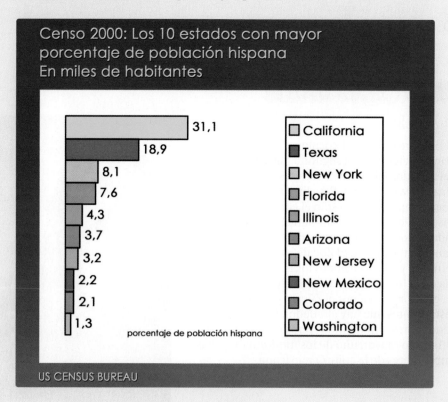

Censo 2000: Los 10 estados con mayor porcentaje de población hispana
En miles de habitantes

31,1	☐ California
18,9	■ Texas
8,1	☐ New York
7,6	■ Florida
4,3	■ Illinois
3,7	■ Arizona
3,2	■ New Jersey
2,2	■ New Mexico
2,1	■ Colorado
1,3	☐ Washington

porcentaje de población hispana

US CENSUS BUREAU

Más del 60% de los hispanos nacieron en los Estados Unidos y la mayoría son de origen mexicano. Se **pronostica**° que para el año 2050 los hispanos llegarán a ser más de 100 millones, es decir, casi la cuarta parte de la población de los Estados Unidos.

predict

Estas cifras resaltan° la importancia económica de la población hispana del país. Se calcula que el **poder adquisitivo**° de este grupo llegó a los 700 mil millones de dólares en 2006 y crecerá el 30% para llegar a 1.000.000 de millones en el año 2010.

highlight
purchasing power

Los estados con mayor población hispana son California con 12,4 millones y Texas con 7,8 millones, pero también hay una población hispana grande en los estados de Nueva York y la Florida.

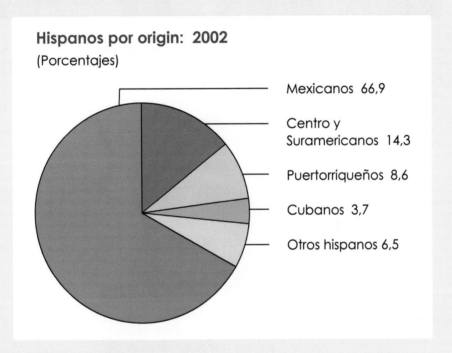

Hispanos por origin: 2002
(Porcentajes)

Mexicanos 66,9

Centro y Suramericanos 14,3

Puertorriqueños 8,6

Cubanos 3,7

Otros hispanos 6,5

GANADORES DE LOS PREMIOS° HISPANIC HERITAGE 2006

Awards

Premio de Arte: Antonio Banderas, actor de cine conocido internacionalmente.

Premio a la Educación: Dra. Juliet Villarreal García, primera latina presidente de una universidad, en la Universidad de Texas en Brownsville.

Premio al Liderazgo (*Leadership*): Teniente Coronel (retirada) Consuelo Castillo Kickbusch, la latina con el rango más alto en el 'Combat Support Field' del ejército estadounidense.

Premio al Deporte: Juan Marichal, uno de los jugadores más celebrados en la historia de la Liga Mayor de Béisbol.

Premio de Trayectoria Artística: José Feliciano, reconocido como uno de los primeros artistas latinos que entró exitosamente al mercado de música en inglés.

Actividades

 1 Comprensión. En grupos de tres, estudien la información estadística sobre los hispanos en los Estados Unidos y contesten las siguientes preguntas.

1. ¿Cuántos hispanos viven en el país?
2. ¿Cuánto aumentó la población hispana desde 1990?
3. ¿En qué estados vive la mayoría de los hispanos? ¿Por qué creen que es así?
4. ¿Cuáles son los cinco países con mayor número de personas de habla española?
5. ¿De dónde son los hispanos que viven en el país?
6. ¿Qué porcentaje de la población serán los hispanos en el año 2050?
7. ¿Cuánto es el poder adquisitivo de los hispanos? ¿Cuánto será en 2010?

 2 Los Premios Hispanic Heritage. Trabajando en parejas, lean la información sobre las personas que recibieron premios de honor en 2006 y discutan estas preguntas.

1. ¿Conoces a alguno de los ganadores de los premios?
2. ¿Qué premio te parece más importante? ¿Por qué?
3. ¿Te gustaría crear otro premio? ¿Cuál sería? ¿Por qué?

3 **Los premios Emmy latinos.** Escucha el pasaje sobre los premios Emmy latinos de 2006 y haz las siguientes actividades.

Seis estrellas latinas. En la tabla que sigue, empareja la persona con la descripción de su actividad artística.

Arista	Descripción
1. Fernando Arau	**a.** Reconocido presentador deportivo de Telemundo.
2. Saúl Lisazo	**b.** Presentadora de un popular *talk show* de Univisión.
3. Jessi Losada	**c.** Estrella de telenovelas en Televisa.
4. Lucero	**d.** Veterano actor de telenovelas.
5. María Elena Salinas	**e.** Popular presentador de un programa de la mañanas en Univisión.
6. Cristina Saralegui	**f.** Presentadora de noticias.

Comprensión. Di si las siguientes afirmaciones son verdaderas o falsas.

1. Las mayores compañías de medios de comunicación están en Los Ángeles.
2. Nueva York es el tercer mercado de televisión en español del país.
3. San Francisco es la ciudad con la población latina más diversa del mundo.
4. Nueva York es el centro de la industria del espectáculo y de los medios latinos.
5. La National Academy of Television piensa que la televisión en español no es importante.

4 **La influencia hispana.** Trabajen en grupos para completar el cuadro con los conocimientos que tienen sobre los hispanos de los Estados Unidos. Escriban qué influencia han tenido los grupos hispanos, según su país de origen, en la lengua, la comida y la música de este país. Añadan otras categorías a su gusto.

Grupo	Lengua	Comida	Música	Deportes

CONTRASTING *PERO, SINO,* AND *SINO QUE*

Planes

José	Sueño con un negocio propio, **pero** no sé si podré tenerlo.
Pedro	No solamente es una ilusión **sino** también una posibilidad.
José	¿Por qué lo dices?
Pedro	No sólo debes soñar, **sino que** ¡debes pedir un préstamo en el banco!

In Spanish, **pero** and **sino** mean *but;* however, they are used differently. Use **sino** or **sino que** when the first element in a sentence is negative and the second element contradicts it. **Sino** connects nouns or phrases whereas **sino que** connects verb clauses. In most other cases **pero** is used to express *but*.

En el país no hay una sola minoría, **sino** muchas.
There is not one single minority in the country, but many.

Los hispanos eran la segunda minoría antes, **pero** ahora son la primera.
Hispanics were the second minority, but now they are the first.

Actividades

1 Los hispanos. Completa estas oraciones sobre lo que hacen algunas personas con **pero, sino** o **sino que** según el caso.

1. El actor Eduardo Verástegui es mexicano _____ tiene una casa en Miami.
2. Los hispanos no solamente hablan español, _____ también hablan inglés.
3. El deporte hispano más popular es el fútbol, _____ hay muchos jugadores hispanos de béisbol en los Estados Unidos.
4. Los premios Emmy latinos de 2006 no fueron en Dallas, _____ en Nueva York.
5. La población hispana no está disminuyendo, _____ sigue creciendo.
6. Penélope Cruz empezó su carrera en España _____ hace películas en Hollywood.
7. La mayoría de los hispanos vive en California, _____ también hay muchos hispanos en otros estados.
8. La población hispanohablante en el país no es pequeña _____ grande.

2 No estoy de acuerdo. Con un/a compañero/a, conversen sobre estas preferencias personales contestando la pregunta con **pero** o **sino,** según el modelo.

▶ MODELO: ¿Quieres aprender sobre historia? / no tengo tiempo / literatura
Sí, quiero aprender sobre historia, pero no tengo tiempo.
No, no quiero aprender sobre historia sino sobre literatura.

1. ¿Quieres votar por un candidato hispano? / no conozco a ninguno / candidato asiático
2. ¿Quieres aprender a bailar salsa? / no puedo / merengue
3. ¿Quieres colaborar en el desfile? / solamente un poco / la venta de comida
4. ¿Quieres ver los Premios Oscar en la televisión? / es muy tarde / los premios Emmy latinos

USING PASSIVE FORMS

Speech bubbles:
- Este formulario del censo **se llena** muy fácilmente.
- Sí, es cierto.
- ¡Eso no **se juega** así!
- **¡Se me dañó** el juego!

Los formularios del censo **fueron enviados** a todos los hogares del país.

Passive structures point out actions and their consequences without focusing on who performs them. The focus is on the action itself. In Spanish, passive structures can be expressed with **se** and the passive voice.

Passive *se*

To express an action without regard to who or what performs it, Spanish uses **se** + verb preceded or followed by a subject in the third-person singular or plural.

Se presentará el *programa* mañana.	*The program will be presented tomorrow.*
Se darán los *premios* a seis personas.	*The awards will be given to six persons.*
Se prohíbe *fumar* en sitios públicos.	*Smoking is prohibited in public places.*

Passive **se** is often used in signs or advertisements.

Se vende	*For sale*
Se habla español	*Spanish is spoken*
Se prohíbe estacionar	*No parking*

Impersonal *se*

If no subject is expressed, **se** + the third-person singular of the verb is used. The impersonal **se** may be expressed in English by *one, you, they* + verb.

Se vive bien en San Diego.	*One lives well in San Diego.*
Se dice que Salma Hayek va a ganar un premio este año.	*They say that Salma Hayek will win an award this year.*

Note that **la gente dice que** or the third person plural form of the verb also introduce impersonal expressions with no particular subject, similar to impersonal **se**.

La gente dice que hay más ciudades como Machu Picchu.	*People say that there are more cities like Machu Picchu.*
Dicen que nunca vamos a encontrar esas ciudades.	*It is said that we will never find those cities.*

Passive voice

In Spanish, the passive voice is formed with **ser** + past participle. The verb agrees in number with the preceding noun (the subject) and the past participle agrees with the subject in number and in gender.

<u>Los premios Emmy latinos</u> **son celebrados** en Nueva York.	*The Latin Emmy Awards are celebrated in New York.*
<u>El censo</u> **fue realizado** en el año 2000.	*The census was done in 2000.*

Information about who performs the action may be added with the preposition **por** followed by a pronoun or a noun.

El artículo sobre los hispanos fue escrito **por ti.**	*The article about the Hispanics was written by you.*

When the person performing the action is known, a regular active sentence structure is often preferred.

Tú escribiste el artículo sobre los actores hispanos.	*You wrote the article about Hispanic actors.*

Se with unintentional actions

English expressions such as *it slipped my mind, it got late, it took on a life of its own,* and so on, refer to unintentional or unplanned occurrences. To express unintentional actions in Spanish, use **se** + indirect object pronoun + verb in the third person + subject. In addition to the verbs in the examples, other verbs that are typically used with this construction include **acabar, dañar, descomponer, quedar,** and **romper.**

Se me cayeron los platos y se quebraron.	*I dropped the plates and they broke.*
Se nos perdió tu informe.	*We lost your report (by mistake).*
¿**Se te olvidó** ir a clase?	*Did you forget to go to class?*
¿Cómo **se te ocurrió** eso?	*How did that occur to you?*

Actividades

1 ¿Dónde? Trabajando en parejas, conversen sobre dónde o cómo se hacen las siguientes actividades. Sigan el modelo.

> ▶ **MODELO:** hablar español / Colombia
> —¿Dónde se habla español?   —*Where do they speak Spanish?*
> —Se habla español en Colombia.   —*Spanish is spoken in Colombia.*

1. celebrar el 4 de julio / en los Estados Unidos.
2. presentar telenovelas / en la televisión
3. encontrar mucha información / en Internet
4. ver los partidos de fútbol / en el estadio
5. oír noticias en español / en los medios hispanos
6. hablar inglés / en muchas partes
7. conseguir información sobre la población / en las estadísticas del censo
8. pronosticar el crecimiento del país / en los informes del censo

2 Los Estados Unidos. Crea oraciones pasivas con el verbo **ser.** Sigue el modelo.

> ▶ **MODELO:** Las familias *celebran* el Día de Acción de Gracias.
> *El Día de Acción de Gracias es celebrado por las familias.*

1. Los estadounidenses *celebran* el 4 de julio.
2. Los californianos *cultivan* las mejores frutas.
3. Las fábricas de los Estados Unidos *exportan* muchos productos.

4. Muchos inmigrantes mexicanos *recogen* las cosechas.

5. Los especialistas *calculan* las estadísticas del censo.

6. Las leyes del país *protegen* a los grupos minoritarios.

3 Historia. Paquita está estudiando en el Perú y le escribe a su familia sobre algunas características de las culturas precolombinas. Reconstruye lo que ella escribió siguiendo el modelo.

> **MODELO:** Los nazcas *fabricaron* hermosos tejidos.
> *Hermosos tejidos fueron fabricados por los nazcas.*

1. Los aztecas *usaron* el chocolate como bebida sagrada.

2. Los aztecas *realizaron* sacrificios humanos.

3. Diferentes grupos indígenas *practicaron* el juego de pelota.

4. Los artesanos *usaron* el oro y otros metales en objetos decorativos y religiosos.

5. Los mayas *estudiaron* la astronomía.

6. Los aztecas *conquistaron* grandes territorios.

4 ¿Un buen plan? Completa las oraciones de la columna A con las de la columna B en forma lógica. Sigue el modelo.

> **MODELO:** **A:** *Josefa no pudo comprar nada en la tienda porque...*
> **B:** *se le olvidó el dinero en casa.*

A	B
1. Decidió ir a México porque...	**a.** se le olvidó el horario.
2. No tomó el tren a tiempo para el aeropuerto porque...	**b.** se le perdió el pasaporte.
3. Tenía los ojos muy rojos porque...	**c.** se le ocurrió la idea de conocer la tierra de los mayas.
4. No pudo subir al avión para ir a México porque...	**d.** se le perdieron las llaves de la casa.
5. No pudo entrar a su casa porque...	**e.** se le rompieron las gafas de sol.

5 ¿Qué le pasó a Mario? Trabajando con un/a compañero/a, miren los dibujos y describan lo que le sucedió a Mario un día de mala suerte. Sigan el modelo. Después, cuenten algunas experiencias similares que tuvieron ustedes.

> **MODELO:** A Mario **se le cayó** el papelito con la dirección.

1. olvidar / ponerle gasolina al auto

2. acabar / la gasolina al auto

3. quedar / las llaves en el auto

4. dañar / la visita a su amiga Irma

Amor y paz

Templo Mayor, Ciudad de México.

México tiene una gran deuda con la Sra. Nayeli Paz Ocotlán y con sus dos estudiantes, Adriana y Felipe. Sin ellos, los héroes gemelos estarían en manos de criminales.

Fue un honor devolver los héroes gemelos.

¡Nayeli, no seas modesta!

Armando culpó a Nayeli porque ella era la última persona que había visto el jaguar. Él planeó el robo de Yax-Balam cuando lo transportaban de México a Sevilla.

¿Cómo encontró usted sola a los gemelos, el primero en Dresden y el otro, en España, cinco años después?

En la vida no hay coincidencias. Según los mayas, todo tiene su ciclo.

¿Puede explicar eso, por favor?

La espiritualidad de Nayeli la guió a ella y nos guió a todos.

Los héroes gemelos fueron recuperados por personas que creen en la voz del corazón...

Esto es como un sueño, ¿no?

Sí, pero sigo pensando en qué sigue ahora.

¿Y cuál es la respuesta?

Pues... conseguir la armonía universal, con paz, sin enemigos...

Un mundo sin asesinos ni criminales...

¡Precisamente!

Algún día será.

Sí, algún día será.

Una rosa amarilla significa que todo está bien, una roja es peligro, pero ¿qué significa una rosa blanca?

Es un símbolo de tu sinceridad.

¿Y ahora qué sigue, Raúl?

¡Mira esto!

Ah... Éste es nuestro nuevo proyecto. ¿Qué haría yo sin ti?

El peso resurge a niveles inexplicables
La economía mexicana se fortalece

Actividades

1 Comprensión. Basándote en este episodio de *Caminos del jaguar,* elige la alternativa lógica.

1. Sin la ayuda de Nayeli, Adriana y Felipe, los héroes gemelos...
   - a. estarían en México.
   - b. no estarían en México.

2. Nayeli dice que para ella es un honor...
   - a. estar en México.
   - b. que los héroes estén en México.

3. Adriana dice que Nayeli es demasiado...
   - a. honesta.
   - b. modesta.

4. Armando robó los jaguares cuando iban...
   - a. de Sevilla a México.
   - b. de México a Sevilla.

5. Armando culpó a Nayeli del robo de Yax-Balam porque...
   - a. ella lo encontró.
   - b. ella fue la última que lo vio.

6. Nayeli encontró a los jaguares en...
   - a. España y México.
   - b. España y Alemania.

7. Según la periodista, Nayeli y Adriana creen en...
   - a. la voz del corazón.
   - b. la voz de la razón.

2 Situaciones. Dramaticen una de las siguientes situaciones.

1. Nayeli y Raúl hablan sobre el significado de las rosas y su trabajo futuro.
2. Adriana y Felipe hablan de un mundo ideal.

3 Escritura. Al final de esta historia, Adriana y Felipe han resuelto un caso difícil. ¿Qué crees que sucederá ahora en las vidas de Adriana y Felipe? (6–7 oraciones)

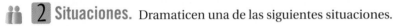

Online Study Center

For additional practice with this episode, visit the *Caminos* website at http://college.hmco.com/languages/spanish/renjilian/caminos/3e/student_home.html.

NOTA CULTURAL

El Museo Nacional de Antropología

En el Museo Nacional de Antropología de la Ciudad de México, hay muchos objetos arqueológicos de gran valor. En 1964, cuando el museo fue inaugurado, el presidente de México expresó lo siguiente sobre la importancia de la institución:

"La gente mexicana levanta este monumento para honrar las culturas admirables que florecieron durante la época precolombina en las regiones que ahora son territorios de la República. Ante los testigos de esas culturas, el México contemporáneo da un homenaje a nuestra cultura indígena en cuyo ejemplo reconocemos las características de nuestros orígenes nacionales".

Lectura

Online Study Center

For further reading practice online, visit the *Caminos* website at http://college.hmco.com/languages/spanish/renjilian/caminos/3e/student_home.html.

PRELECTURA

The *Popol Vuh was* the sacred book of the Mayans. The second part narrates how the Mayan Hero Twins overpowered the frightening Lords of the Mayan underworld, Xibalbá, a parallel world beneath ours, full of plants, animals, and people. The version of the *Popol Vuh* that we know today is a Spanish version of an old Quiché Maya book translated by the Jesuit Francisco Jiménez. The translator included, side-by-side with the Spanish text, a transcript of the original Maya Quiché language, which probably was an interpretation of a lost Mayan codex. The classical Mayan names of the Hero Twins, Hun-Ahau and Yax-Balam, are transcribed as Hunahpú and Ixbalamqué in the *Popol Vuh*.

Reading Strategy

Using a genealogical chart with notes

When you read a narration that describes many different family members, it is useful to develop a family genealogy to keep track of the people mentioned. You can also jot down a trait of each character while you create a family tree to help remember who's who. You will have an opportunity to practice this technique when you read the passage that follows.

 1 **Un árbol genealógico.** Antes de leer sobre los héroes gemelos, haz un árbol genealógico de tres generaciones de tu familia o de otra familia que conoces bien. Al lado de cada miembro familiar, escribe una característica o acción especial de esa persona entre paréntesis. Luego, usando el árbol genealógico y tus apuntes, descríbele esa familia a un/a compañero/a.

Ecos del pasado: Héroes mayas

El Popol Vuh, el libro sagrado de los mayas, cuenta la historia de Hunahpú[1] y de Ixbalamqué[2], los grandes Héroes Gemelos que vencieron[3] a los malvados Señores[4] de Xibalbá: Hun-Camé[5] y Vucub-Camé[6].

El padre de Hunahpú e Ixbalamqué era otro famoso gemelo maya: Hun-Hunahpú. Éste y su hermano Vucub-Hunahpú eran los mejores jugadores de pelota de la tierra y los Señores de Xibalbá los invitaron para jugar con ellos en Xibalbá. Cuando llegaron allí, los Señores de Xibalbá los mataron porque los gemelos no pudieron cumplir con las pruebas imposibles que les habían puesto. Los Señores de Xibalbá enterraron[7] a Vucub-Hunahpú en la plaza de juego de pelota y colgaron[8] la cabeza de Hun-Hunahpú en un árbol de calabazas[9].

---

[1]Lord One; [2]Little Jaguar; [3]defeated; [4]evil lords, gods; [5]Death One; [6]Death Seven; [7]buried; [8]hung; [9]pumpkin tree

Un día, Ixquic, una princesa de Xibalbá, se acercó al árbol para coger[10] una calabaza. En ese momento, la cabeza de Hun-Hunahpú le escupió[11] en la palma de la mano y ella quedó embarazada con los Héroes Gemelos. Al poco tiempo, Ixquic tuvo que escapar de Xibalbá porque los Señores iban a matarla y se refugió en casa de Ixmucané, la madre de Hun-Hunahpú y Vucub-Hunahpú. Allí nacieron los Héroes Gemelos. Cuando crecieron, llegaron a ser los mejores jugadores de pelota, tal como lo habían sido su padre y su tío.

Los Señores de Xibalbá, Hun-Camé y Vucub-Camé, se dieron cuenta de que los Héroes Gemelos jugaban tan bien como su padre y su tío y, enfurecidos, decidieron invitarlos a Xibalbá con la intención de matarlos a ellos también.

Al llegar a Xibalbá, Hunahpú e Ixbalamqué descubrieron los trucos[12] de los Señores de Xibalbá con la ayuda de varios animales. De esa manera tuvieron éxito en todas las pruebas en las que su padre y su tío habían fracasado[13]: se fumaron un cigarro sin fuego, quemaron una antorcha[14] sin gastarla[15]; sobrevivieron en la casa de la oscuridad[16], en la casa del frío, en la casa de las navajas[17], y en la casa de los murciélagos[18]. Por último, pudieron vencer[19] la misma muerte, destruyeron a los Señores de Xibalbá y se convirtieron en dioses auténticos. Desde entonces, brillan como astros en el firmamento[20].

---

[10]to pick; [11]spit; [12]tricks; [13]failed; [14]torch; [15]using it up [16]darkness; [17]knives; [18]bats; [19]defeat; [20]sky

POSTLECTURA

2 **Los Héroes Gemelos: Su genealogía.** Con un/a compañero/a, hagan un árbol geneológico de la familia de los Héroes Gemelos. Escriban entre paréntesis una o dos características o acciones de ellos y su familia.

3 **Personajes y personalidades.** Usa tus apuntes y la lectura para contestar las preguntas.

1. ¿Qué lugar era Xibalbá y quién vivía allí?
2. ¿Quiénes eran Hun-Hunahpú y Vucub-Hunahpú? ¿Y Hun-Camé y Vucub-Camé?
3. ¿Qué significan las palabras "Hun" y "Vucub", según la lectura?
4. ¿Por qué se enojaron los Señores de Xibalbá con los Héroes Gemelos?
5. ¿Cómo se llamaba la abuela de los Héroes Gemelos? ¿A quién recibió ella en su casa?
6. ¿Quién era Ixquic y por qué tuvo que huir de Xibalbá?
7. ¿Qué les gustaba hacer a los Héroes Gemelos?
8. ¿Qué cosas imposibles pudieron hacer con éxito los Héroes Gemelos?
9. ¿En qué se convirtieron los Héroes Gemelos después de vencer a los dioses de Xibalbá?

4 **¡Adelante con aventuras!** Ahora que las figuras de los gemelos están juntas en el museo en México, pueden tener más aventuras. Inventa otro mito de los Héroes Gemelos en el tiempo contemporáneo.

Escritura

Online Study Center

For further writing practice online, visit the *Caminos* website at http://college.hmco.com/languages/spanish/renjilian/caminos/3e/student_home.html.

Writing Strategy

Editing one's own work

An important, yet often overlooked, step in writing is to edit your own work. It is important to focus on content and organization as well as on form. Use this self-editing checklist as a guide to editing your own writing. You can also use it as a guideline for peer editing.

Workshop

A. Focus on content. Ask yourself these questions:

- ► Is the topic interesting?
- ► Is the main idea clearly expressed?
- ► Does the supporting detail enhance the main idea?
- ► Is the order of sentences and ideas logical and easy to follow?
- ► Does the conclusion summarize my ideas?

B. Focus on form. Check the following:

- ► gender of nouns
- ► subject / verb agreement
- ► noun /adjective agreement
- ► word order within the entire sentence
- ► word order within each phrase
- ► new vocabulary
- ► influences of English idioms on Spanish
- ► spelling and capitalization
- ► punctuation
- ► use of accents

After editing your work, remember to focus on appearance. If the composition is handwritten, be sure that it is legible and that you write on every other line. If it is computer-generated, be sure to print it out double-spaced and include all necessary accents and other punctuation.

Strategy in Action

For additional practice with editing your own work, complete the exercises below and in the *Escritura* section of your Student Activities Manual for *Unidad 12*.

1 ¿A quiénes invitarías? Si pudieras invitar a tres hispanos famosos a tu casa para una cena, ¿a quiénes invitarías y por qué?

2 La siguiente misión de I.L.E.Y.A.N. Al final de ***Caminos del jaguar,*** Raúl habla con Nayeli de otra misión para recuperar objetos arqueológicos perdidos. Inventa su siguiente aventura y escribe lo que pasará con Nayeli y Raúl.

Resumen de vocabulario

PRIMER PASO

COMPARING THE AZTECS, MAYANS, AND INCAS

Sustantivos

el apogeo	*height*
el códice	*codex*
la conquista	*conquest*
el/la descendiente	*descendent*
la escritura	*writing*
la exploración	*exploration*
el imperio	*empire*
la pirámide	*pyramid*
las ruinas	*ruins*
el siglo	*century*
el/la tejedor/a	*weaver*
el templo	*temple*

Verbos

decaer	*to decline*
destacar(se)	*to stand out*

distinguir(se)	*to distinguish*
fundar	*to found*
pertenecer	*to belong*
vencer	*to defeat*

Adjetivos

desarollado/a	*developed*
étnico/a	*ethnic*
habitado/a	*inhabited*
imponente	*imposing*
jeroglífico/a	*hieroglyphic*
lingüístico/a	*linguistic*
perdido/a	*lost*

Otras expresiones

además de	*in addition to*
sin embargo	*nevertheless*

SEGUNDO PASO

DISCUSSING HISPANIC CONTRIBUTIONS IN THE UNITED STATES

Sustantivos

la cifra	*figure, number*
el crecimiento	*growth*
la población	*population*
el poder adquisitivo	*purchasing power*
el premio	*award, prize*

Verbos

pronosticar	*to predict*

Otras expresiones

de habla española	*Spanish-speaking*
pero	*but*
sino, sino que	*but (rather)*

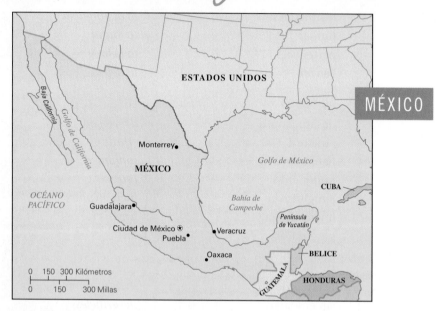

Online Study Center

To learn more about the people featured in this section, visit the *Caminos* website at http://college .hmco.com/languages/ spanish/renjilian/caminos/ 3e/student_home.html.

PERSONALIDADES

Los mexicanos

El tema de la identidad cultural se refleja en el arte, la música, la literatura y el cine de México. Los artistas de pintura mural —Diego Rivera (1886–1957), David Alfaro Siqueiros (1898–1974), José Clemente Orozco (1883–1949) y Rufino Tamayo (1899–1991)— interpretan las dificultades socioeconómicas y políticas del pueblo mexicano, mezcla[1] de raíces[2] indígenas, españolas y africanas. Los muralistas describen además[3], los sueños[4] y esperanzas de la gente de clase trabajadora[5]. Retratan la grandeza e importancia de las civilizaciones azteca y maya del pasado mientras expresan asimismo la realidad mexicana de una vida dura del siglo XX. La Revolución Mexicana de 1910 les había prometido a los campesinos tierras fértiles, pan y escuelas; pero la pobreza[6] continuaba marcando sus vidas.

Las obras de los escritores mexicanos reflejan diversas perspectivas sobre el pueblo mexicano. En su libro *El laberinto de la soledad*[7], Octavio Paz, quien ganó el Premio Nobel de Literatura, define para el mundo internacional la identidad mexicana. La cultura es también el tema de los escritores y periodistas[8] José Emilio Pacheco y Elena Poniatowska. El prolífico escritor Carlos Fuentes sirvió a su país como diplomático. Laura Esquivel es tanto novelista como guionista[9].

---

[1]mixture; [2]roots; [3]in addition; [4]dreams; [5]working class; [6]poverty; [7]*The Labyrinth of Solitude*; [8]journalists; [9]screenwriter

"Quiero utilizar la música como instrumento divino para plantar semillas° de esperanza".
—Carlos Santana (México)

seeds

Los artistas de la actualidad[10] siguen afirmando la identidad mexicana. En el cine mexicano, las películas *Ángeles negros*, *Como agua para chocolate*, *Novia que te vea*[11] y otras similares tratan diferentes cuestiones relacionadas con la identidad étnica, racial, política y cultural.

La legendaria actriz María Félix apareció en muchas películas con otros ídolos del cine mexicano del siglo veinte como Jorge Negrete y Pedro Infante. Los jóvenes actores mexicanos también son muy versátiles. Entre ellos están los actores Eduardo Verástegui y Jaime Camil, quienes empezaron su carrera como músicos.

Otro actor multitalentoso, Gael García Bernal ha recibido mucha buena crítica por su interpretación de Ernesto "Che" Guevara. La actriz y directora Salma Hayek también ha ganado mucha fama por sus películas y especialmente por su interpretación de la artista mexicana Frida Kahlo. Kate del Castillo manifiesta sus talentos dramáticos en dos dimensiones: las películas y la televisión.

Los mexicanos se destacan[12] en el mundo internacional de la música. Carlos Santana es un artista que ha tenido una larga carrera como compositor y cantante, representando a México y al mundo latino. Salvador López, el director del famoso Ballet Folklórico de México, es nieto de su fundadora, Amalia Hernández. Las danzas de la compañía, que baila en todas partes del mundo, combinan rituales indígenas y elementos modernos para representar la diversa identidad mexicana.

Visita el sitio web de ***Caminos*** para leer más en español sobre estas personalidades y otros mexicanos influyentes como Vicente Fox, el ex-presidente de México; María Elena Salinas, periodista y presentadora estrella de noticias[13]; Alejandro González Iñárritu, Arturo Ripstein, Marcela Fernández Violante, Alfonso Cuarón, directores de cine; Lorena Rojas, Valentino Lanús, Yolanda Andrade, José Ángel Llamas, Camila Sodi, actores; Carlos Monsiváis, Rosario Castellanos, escritores; Jacqueline Bracamontes, modelo; y Oswaldo Sánchez, jugador de fútbol.

[10]nowadays; [11]*May I see you a bride*; [12]stand out; [13]news anchor

Comprensión

Trabajando en parejas, háganse las siguientes preguntas.

1. ¿Cuáles son algunos de los temas de las artes y letras en México?
2. Describe a tres personalidades fascinantes de esta lectura.

ARTE

Frida y Diego, 1931

FRIDA KAHLO

Frida Kahlo nació en 1907 en México de padre judío europeo y madre mexicana con raíces indígenas. Tuvo una vida llena de prolífica producción artística, sufrimiento físico, activismo sociopolítico y dos matrimonios con el mismo hombre.

En sus pinturas Frida expresa la búsqueda de la identidad social y personal. De sus 143 pinturas, 55 son autorretratos. La pintora explora también la tempestuosa relación con su esposo, Diego Rivera, el gran artista mexicano. Cuando era joven, Frida sufrió un accidente que le causó dolores muy fuertes durante toda la vida. A ella la atormentaba la imposibilidad de tener hijos y su arte comunica también esta pena.

Sus obras se caracterizan por su estilo surrealista, sus colores vivos y los componentes culturales. Frida murió en 1954.

👥 Comprensión

Trabajando en parejas, háganse estas preguntas sobre el cuadro de Frida.

1. ¿Quiénes son estas dos personas?

stature, height 2. Compara a los dos en estatura°. ¿Cómo son?

3. ¿Qué ropa llevan ellos? ¿De qué colores? ¿Cuál es el más prominente?

4. El objeto que tiene Diego en la mano es una paleta con pinceles. ¿Qué profesión representa?

banner 5. Hay una cinta° con palabras sobre la cabeza de Frida. ¿Qué crees que dice el mensaje? ¿Quién lleva la cinta? Describe a la persona.

6. ¿Cómo te parece la pareja: contenta, descontenta, divertida, aburrida, serena, furiosa, resignada?

7. ¿Dónde estará la pareja: en su casa, en un baile, en una fiesta, en un museo, en un hotel?

8. ¿Qué piensas de este cuadro? ¿Te gusta? ¿Por qué? ¿Cuál es tu artista favorito/a?

MÚSICA

LUIS MIGUEL

Luis Miguel, un ídolo del pop, es hijo de un guitarrista español y de una cantante italiana. Grabó° su primer álbum a los doce años, con el título de "Enamorados°". Aunque nació en Puerto Rico en 1970, se crió° en México y el presidente de México le otorgó° la nacionalidad mexicana. Su música refleja su espíritu mexicano y su dedicación a celebrar las tradiciones musicales de su país de adopción.

He recorded
In love
was raised
bestowed on him

Este superestrella de la música latinomericana ha cantado en más de cien conciertos alrededor del° mundo, ha vendido más de cincuenta y dos millones de discos y ha ganado nueve Grammys, además de° docenas de otros premios y reconocimientos°. Tiene su propia estrella en el Paseo de la Fama de Hollywood. En 2006, celebró veinticinco años de carrera musical a la edad de treinta y seis años, algo extraordinario. Sus apodos° son "Sol de México", "Luismi" y "Micky".

around

besides
recognition

nicknames

Las canciones más populares de Luis Miguel son de tipo bolero° o canciones románticas. Algunos de sus discos famosos son los siguientes: "Decídete" (1983), "Fiebre de amor" (1985), "Soy como quiero ser" (1987), "América y en vivo" (1992), "Segundo romance" (1994), "Amarte es un placer" (1999), "Vivo" (2000), "México en la piel" (2004), "Grandes éxitos" (2005).

(a type of music that originated in Spain)

Comprensión

Con un/a compañero/a, háganse estas preguntas sobre Luis Miguel.

1. ¿Dónde nació Luis Miguel? ¿Y sus padres?
2. ¿A qué edad grabó su primer álbum?
3. ¿Cómo consiguió el cantante la nacionalidad mexicana?
4. ¿Cuántos discos ha vendido? ¿Cuántos Grammys ha ganado?
5. ¿Dónde ha cantado en conciertos? ¿Cuándo celebró los veinticinco años de carrera?
6. ¿Qué tipo de música caracteriza al cantante?
7. ¿Qué significan en inglés los títulos de sus discos?
8. Describe a un/a cantante de tu país que cante música romántica o que exprese tradiciones musicales importantes. Nombra en español algunos títulos. ¿Qué ideas revelan sus canciones?

Conéctate a Internet para escuchar la música de Luis Miguel y aprender más sobre él y otros cantantes y músicos como Alicia Villareal, Alejandro Fernández, Ana Gabriel, Julieta Venegas (también compositora) y Alicia Machado (también actriz).

LITERATURA

ÁNGELES MASTRETTA

Ángeles Mastretta es periodista y escritora mexicana de novelas y cuentos. Con muchos detalles culturales, ella describe la vida diaria y muchas tradiciones mexicanas. Ha ganado premios literarios y sus obras han sido traducidas° a muchos idiomas. Nació en Puebla, México.

En esta selección de su libro *Mujeres de ojos grandes*, la narradora nos cuenta la historia del noviazgo° inesperado° de su tía Cristina con el señor Arqueros, un español. Aquí vemos la reacción de la tía Cristina al recibir su anillo°.

have been translated

engagement / unexpected

engagement ring

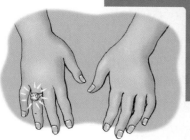

"Una sorpresa para Tía Cristina" (de *Mujeres de ojos grandes*)

anxiety
neighborhood
city square / Mexican dish / corn pancakes
stews / grated
aroma
pastures

news / sparkling
priest
=amigo de su esposo /
good-byes / As if her fiancé were

Cuando salió de la angustia° propia de las sorpresas, la tía Cristina miró su anillo y empezó a llorar por sus hermanas, por su madre, por sus amigas, por su barrio°, por la catedral, por el zócalo°, por los volcanes, por el cielo, por el mole°, por las chalupas°, por el himno nacional, por la carretera a México, por Cholula, por Coetzálan, ...por las cazuelas°, por los chocolates rasposos°, por la música, por el olor° de las tortillas, por el río San Francisco, por el rancho de su amiga Elena y los potreros° de su tío Abelardo, por la luna de octubre y la de marzo, por el sol de febrero....

Al día siguiente salió a la calle con la noticia° y su anillo brillándole°. Seis meses después se casó con el señor Arqueros frente a un cura°, un notario y los ojos de Suárez°. Hubo misa, banquete, baile y despedidas°. Todo con el mismo entusiasmo que si el novio estuviera° de este lado del mar. Dicen que no se vio novia más radiante en mucho tiempo.

👥 Comprensión

Trabajando en parejas, háganse las preguntas sobre el pasaje.

1. Cuando la tía Cristina recibió el anillo, lloró mucho. ¿Qué personas nombra ella?
2. ¿Qué comidas menciona ella?
3. ¿Cuáles son los meses del año a que se refiere?
4. ¿Qué referencias hay a la naturaleza?
5. Después de recibir el anillo, ¿a los cuántos meses se casaron la tía Cristina y el señor Arqueros? ¿De dónde es él?
6. Cuando se casó la tía Cristina, ¿quiénes estaban presentes? ¿Cómo celebraron después de la ceremonia en la iglesia?
7. ¿Quién, crees tú, está narrándonos la historia?
8. En tu opinión, ¿cómo estaba la novia el día en que se casó: deprimida, animada, radiante, pálida, alegre, triste, sentimental?

JUAN RULFO

El escritor mexicano Juan Rulfo vivió de 1918 hasta 1986. Era huérfano° y pasó una niñez difícil por la pobreza que sufría mucha gente en México en esa época. Además de su producción literaria, Rulfo ha dejado una extensa obra fotográfica. En sus obras literarias, se dedicó a describir el sufrimiento socioeconómico de su gente. Este texto es de su cuento "Es que somos muy pobres". Aquí sabemos lo que le pasa a la querida vaca° de Tacha, una joven muchacha.

orphan

beloved cow

"La vaca de Tacha" (de "Es que somos pobres")

Aquí todo va de mal en peor°. La semana pasada se murió mi tía Jacinta, y el sábado cuando ya la habíamos enterrado° y comenzaba a bajársenos la tristeza°, comenzó a llover como nunca. A mi papá eso le dio coraje°, porque toda la cosecha° de cebada° estaba asoleándose en el solar. Y el aguacero llegó de repente°, en grandes olas de agua, sin darnos tiempo ni siquiera a esconder aunque fuera un manojo°; lo único que pudimos hacer, todos los de mi casa, fue estarnos arrimados° debajo del tejabán°, viendo cómo el agua fría que caía del cielo quemaba aquella cebada amarilla tan recién cortada.

Y apenas ayer, cuando mi hermana Tacha acababa de cumplir doce años, supimos que la vaca que mi papá le regaló para el día de su santo° se la había llevado el río°.

from bad to worse
we had buried
sadness started to leave us
anger / harvest / barley
suddenly
handful
to take cover / roof

Saint's day / the river had
swept it away

Comprensión

Trabajando en parejas, contesten las preguntas sobre la lectura.

1. ¿Cuándo se murió la tía Jacinta?
2. ¿Llovió mucho o poco? ¿Por qué le dio coraje al papá?
3. ¿Cómo llegó el aguacero, rápido o despacio? ¿Dónde se quedaron arrimados los de la familia?
4. ¿Cómo estaba el agua, caliente o fría?
5. ¿Cuántos años tenía Tacha?
6. ¿Quién le regaló la vaca a Tacha? ¿Qué le pasó a la vaca?
7. ¿Qué relación tiene Tacha con la persona que narra la historia?
8. ¿Cómo te hace sentir esta selección: triste, alegre, furioso/a, optimista, pesimista, furioso/a, curioso/a?

Reference Materials

Regular verbs

Simple tenses

Infinitive	Past participle / Present participle	Indicative Present	Indicative Imperfect	Indicative Preterite	Indicative Future	Indicative Conditional	Subjunctive Present	Subjunctive Imperfect*
cantar *to sing*	cantado / cantando	canto	cantaba	canté	cantaré	cantaría	cante	cantara
		cantas	cantabas	cantaste	cantarás	cantarías	cantes	cantaras
		canta	cantaba	cantó	cantará	cantaría	cante	cantara
		cantamos	cantábamos	cantamos	cantaremos	cantaríamos	cantemos	cantáramos
		cantáis	cantabais	cantasteis	cantaréis	cantaríais	cantéis	cantarais
		cantan	cantaban	cantaron	cantarán	cantarían	canten	cantaran
correr *to run*	corrido / corriendo	corro	corría	corrí	correré	correría	corra	corriera
		corres	corrías	corriste	correrás	correrías	corras	corrieras
		corre	corría	corrió	correrá	correría	corra	corriera
		corremos	corríamos	corrimos	correremos	correríamos	corramos	corriéramos
		corréis	corríais	corristeis	correréis	correríais	corráis	corrierais
		corren	corrían	corrieron	correrán	correrían	corran	corrieran
subir *to go up, to climb up*	subido / subiendo	subo	subía	subí	subiré	subiría	suba	subiera
		subes	subías	subiste	subirás	subirías	subas	subieras
		sube	subía	subió	subirá	subiría	suba	subiera
		subimos	subíamos	subimos	subiremos	subiríamos	subamos	subiéramos
		subís	subíais	subisteis	subiréis	subiríais	subáis	subierais
		suben	subían	subieron	subirán	subirían	suban	subieran

*In addition to this form, another one is less frequently used for all regular and irregular verbs: **cantase, cantases, cantase, cantásemos, cantaseis, cantasen; corriese, corrieses, corriese, corriésemos, corrieseis, corriesen; viviese, vivieses, viviese, viviésemos, vivieseis, viviesen.**

Commands

Person	Affirmative	Negative	Affirmative	Negative	Affirmative	Negative
tú	canta	no cantes	corre	no corras	sube	no subas
usted	cante	no cante	corra	no corra	suba	no suba
ustedes	canten	no canten	corran	no corran	suban	no suban
nosotros	cantemos	no cantemos	corramos	no corramos	subamos	no subamos
vosotros	cantad	no cantéis	corred	no corráis	subid	no subáis

Stem-changing verbs: -ar and -er groups

Type of change in the verb stem	Subject	Indicative Present	Subjunctive Present	Commands Affirmative	Commands Negative	Other -ar and -er stem-changing verbs
-ar verbs e > ie pensar *to think*	yo	pienso	piense	—	—	atravesar *to go through, to cross;* cerrar *to close;* despertarse *to wake up;* empezar *to start;* negar *to deny;* sentarse *to sit down.*
	tú	piensas	pienses	piensa	no pienses	
	él/ella, Ud.	piensa	piense	piense	no piense	
	nosotros/as	pensamos	pensemos	pensemos	no pensemos	nevar *to snow* is only conjugated in the third person singular *nieva.*
	vosotros/as	pensáis	penséis	pensad	no penséis	
	ellos/as, Uds.	piensan	piensen	piensen	no piensen	
-ar verbs o > ue contar *to count, to tell*	yo	cuento	cuente	—	—	acordarse *to remember;* acostar(se) *to go to bed;* almorzar *to have lunch;* colgar *to hang;* costar *to cost;* demostrar *to demonstrate, to show;* encontrar *to find;* mostrar *to show;* probar *to prove, to taste;* recordar *to remember.*
	tú	cuentas	cuentes	cuenta	no cuentes	
	él/ella, Ud.	cuenta	cuente	cuente	no cuente	
	nosotros/as	contamos	contemos	contemos	no contemos	
	vosotros/as	contáis	contéis	contad	no contéis	
	ellos/as, Uds.	cuentan	cuenten	cuenten	no cuenten	
-er verbs e > ie entender *to understand*	yo	entiendo	entienda	—	—	encender *to light, to turn on;* extender *to stretch;* perder *to lose.*
	tú	entiendes	entiendas	entiende	no entiendas	
	él/ella, Ud.	entiende	entienda	entienda	no entienda	
	nosotros/as	entendemos	entendamos	entendamos	no entendamos	
	vosotros/as	entendéis	entendáis	entended	no entendáis	
	ellos/as, Uds.	entienden	entiendan	entiendan	no entiendan	
-er verbs o > ue volver *to return*	yo	vuelvo	vuelva	—	—	mover *to move;* torcer *to twist.*
	tú	vuelves	vuelvas	vuelve	no vuelvas	
	él/ella, Ud.	vuelve	vuelva	vuelva	no vuelva	
	nosotros/as	volvemos	volvamos	volvamos	no volvamos	llover *to rain* is only conjugated in the third person singular *llueve.*
	vosotros/as	volvéis	volváis	volved	no volváis	
	ellos/as, Uds.	vuelven	vuelvan	vuelvan	no vuelvan	

Stem-changing verbs: -ir verbs

Group I

Type of change in the verb stem	Subject	Indicative			Subjunctive		Commands	
		Present	Preterite		Present	Imperfect	Affirmative	Negative
-ir verbs **e > ie** or **i** Infinitive: sentir *to feel* Present participle: sintiendo	yo tú él/ella, Ud. nosotros/as vosotros/as ellos/as, Uds.	siento sientes siente sentimos sentís sienten	sentí sentiste **sintió** sentimos sentisteis **sintieron**		sienta sientas sienta sintamos sintáis sientan	**sintiera** **sintieras** **sintiera** **sintiéramos** **sintierais** **sintieran**	— siente sienta sintamos sentid sientan	— no sientas no sienta no sintamos no sintáis no sientan
-ir verbs **o > ue** or **u** Infinitive: dormir *to sleep* Present participle: durmiendo	yo tú él/ella, Ud. nosotros/as vosotros/as ellos/as, Uds.	**duermo** **duermes** **duerme** dormimos dormís **duermen**	dormí dormiste **durmió** dormimos dormisteis **durmieron**		**duerma** **duermas** **duerma** durmamos durmáis **duerman**	**durmiera** **durmieras** **durmiera** **durmiéramos** **durmierais** **durmieran**	— **duerme** **duerma** durmamos dormid **duerman**	— no **duermas** no **duerma** no durmamos no durmáis no **duerman**

Other similar verbs: advertir *to warn;* arrepentirse *to repent;* consentir *to consent, to pamper;* convertir(se) *to turn into;* divertir(se) *to amuse (oneself);* herir *to hurt, to wound;* mentir *to lie;* morir *to die;* preferir *to prefer;* referir *to refer;* sugerir *to suggest.*

Group II

Type of change in the verb stem	Subject	Indicative			Subjunctive		Commands	
		Present	Preterite		Present	Imperfect	Affirmative	Negative
-ir verbs **e > i** Infinitive: pedir *to ask for, to request* Present participle: pidiendo	yo tú él/ella, Ud. nosotros/as vosotros/as ellos/as, Uds.	pido pides pide pedimos pedís piden	pedí pediste pidió pedimos pedisteis pidieron		pida pidas pida pidamos pidáis pidan	pidiera pidieras pidiera pidiéramos pedierais pidieran	— pide pida pidamos pedid pidan	— no pidas no pida no pidamos no pidáis no pidan

Other similar verbs: competir *to compete;* despedir(se) *to say good-bye;* elegir *to choose;* impedir *to prevent;* perseguir *to chase;* repetir *to repeat;* seguir *to follow;* servir *to serve;* vestir(se) *to dress, to get dressed.*

Verbs with spelling changes

	Verb type	Ending	Change	Verbs with similar spelling changes
1	buscar *to look for*	-car	• Preterite: yo busqué • Present subjunctive: busque, busques, busque, busquemos, busquéis, busquen	comunicar, explicar, indicar, sacar, pescar
2	conocer *to know*	-cer or -cir	• Present indicative: conozco, conoces, conoce, and so on • Present subjunctive: conozca, conozcas, conozca, conozcamos, conozcáis, conozcan	nacer, obedecer, ofrecer, parecer, pertenecer, reconocer, conducir, traducir
3	vencer *to win*	-cer or -cir	• Present indicative: venzo, vences, vence, and so on • Present subjunctive: venza, venzas, venza, venzamos, venzáis, venzan	convencer, torcer *to twist*
4	leer *to read*	-eer	• Preterite: leyó, leyeron • Imperfect subjunctive: leyera, leyeras, leyera, leyéramos, leyerais, leyeran • Present participle: leyendo	creer, poseer *to own*
5	llegar *to arrive*	-gar	• Preterite: llegué • Present subjunctive: llegue, llegues, llegue, lleguemos, lleguéis, lleguen	colgar, navegar, negar, pagar, rogar, jugar
6	coger *to take*	-ger or -gir	• Present indicative: cojo • Present subjunctive: coja, cojas, coja, cojamos, cojáis, cojan	escoger, proteger, recoger, corregir, dirigir, elegir, exigir
7	seguir *to follow*	-guir	• Present indicative: sigo • Present subjunctive: siga, sigas, siga, sigamos, sigáis, sigan	conseguir, distinguir, perseguir
8	huir *to flee*	-uir	• Present indicative: huyo, huyes, huye, huimos, huís, huyen • Preterite: huí, huiste, huyó, huimos, huisteis, huyeron • Present subjunctive: huya, huyas, huya, huyamos, huyáis, huyan • Imperfect subjunctive: huyera, huyeras, huyera, huyéramos, huyerais, huyeran • Present participle: huyendo • Commands: huye tú, huya usted, huyan ustedes, huíd vosotros, huyamos nosotros; no huyas tú, no huya usted, no huyan ustedes, no huyamos nosotros, no huyáis vosotros	concluir, contribuir, construir, destruir, disminuir, distribuir, excluir, influir, instruir, restituir, substituir
9	abrazar *to embrace to hug*	-zar	• Preterite: abracé, abrazaste, abrazó, and so on • Present subjunctive: abrace, abraces, abrace, abracemos, abracéis, abracen	alcanzar, almorzar, comenzar, empezar, gozar, rezar

Verbs that need a written accent

Verb type	Ending	Change	Verbs with similar spelling changes
1 sonreír *to smile*	-eír	See p. 450 for a complete conjugation of these verbs.	freír, reír
2 enviar *to send*	-iar	• Present indicative: envío, envías, envía, enviamos, enviáis, envían • Present subjunctive: envíe, envíes, envíe, enviemos, enviéis, envíen	ampliar, criar, desviar, enfriar, guiar, variar
3 continuar *to continue*	-uar	• Present indicative: continúo, continúas, continúa, continuamos, continuáis, continúan • Present subjunctive: continúe, continúes, continúe, continuemos, continuéis, continúen	acentuar, efectuar, exceptuar, graduar, habituar, insinuar, situar

Compound tenses

	Indicative						Subjunctive	
Present perfect	Past perfect		Preterite perfect	Future perfect		Conditional perfect	Present perfect	Past perfect
he	había		hube	habré		habría	haya	hubiera
has	habías		hubiste	habrás		habrías	hayas	hubieras
ha cantado	había cantado		hubo cantado	habrá cantado		habría cantado	haya cantado	hubiera cantado
hemos corrido	habíamos corrido		hubimos corrido	habremos corrido		habríamos corrido	hayamos corrido	hubiéramos corrido
habéis vivido	habíais vivido		hubisteis vivido	habréis vivido		habríais vivido	hayáis vivido	hubierais vivido
han	habían		hubieron	habrán		habrían	hayan	hubieran

Irregular verbs: Compound tenses

All irregular verbs follow the same formation pattern as the regular verbs with **haber**, in all tenses. The only thing that changes is the form of the past participle of each verb. See the chart below and the individual charts of irregular verbs for these forms. In Spanish, no word can come between **haber** and the past participle.

Common irregular past participles

Infinitive	Past participle		Infinitive	Past participle	
abrir	**abierto**	*opened*	morir	**muerto**	*died*
caer	caído	*fallen*	oír	oído	*heard*
creer	creído	*belived*	poner	**puesto**	*put, placed*
cubrir	**cubierto**	*covered*	resolver	**resuelto**	*resolved*
decir	**dicho**	*said, told*	romper	**roto**	*broken, torn*
descubrir	**descubierto**	*discovered*	(son)reír	(son)reído	*(smiled) laughed*
escribir	**escrito**	*written*	traer	traído	*brought*
hacer	**hecho**	*made, done*	ver	**visto**	*seen*
leer	leído	*read*	volver	**vuelto**	*returned*

Regular and irregular reflexive verbs: Position of the reflexive pronouns in the simple tenses

Example 1: lavarse

Infinitive	Present participle	Reflexive pronouns	Indicative					Subjunctive	
			Present	Imperfect	Preterite	Future	Conditional	Present	Imperfect
lavarse *to wash oneself*	lavándome	**me**	lavo	lavaba	lavé	lavaré	lavaría	lave	lavara
	lavándote	**te**	lavas	lavabas	lavaste	lavarás	lavarías	laves	lavaras
	lavándose	**se**	lava	lavaba	lavó	lavará	lavaría	lave	lavara
	lavándonos	**nos**	lavamos	lavábamos	lavamos	lavaremos	lavaríamos	lavemos	laváramos
	lavándoos	**os**	laváis	lavabais	lavasteis	lavaréis	lavaríais	lavéis	lavarais
	lavándose	**se**	lavan	lavaban	lavaron	lavarán	lavarían	laven	lavaran

Example 2: ponerse

Infinitive	Present participle	Reflexive pronouns	Indicative					Subjunctive	
			Present	Imperfect	Preterite	Future	Conditional	Present	Imperfect
ponerse *to put on, to get (sad, happy, etc.)*	poniéndome	**me**	pongo	ponía	puse	pondré	pondría	ponga	pusiera
	poniéndote	**te**	pones	ponías	pusiste	pondrás	pondrías	pongas	pusieras
	poniéndose	**se**	pone	ponía	puso	pondrá	pondría	ponga	pusiera
	poniéndonos	**nos**	ponemos	poníamos	pusimos	pondremos	pondríamos	pongamos	pusiéramos
	poniéndoos	**os**	ponéis	poníais	pusisteis	pondréis	pondríais	pongáis	pusierais
	poniéndose	**se**	ponen	ponían	pusieron	pondrán	pondrían	pongan	pusieran

Example 3: vestirse

Infinitive	Present participle	Reflexive pronouns	Indicative					Subjunctive	
			Present	Imperfect	Preterite	Future	Conditional	Present	Imperfect
vestirse *to get dressed*	vistiéndome	**me**	visto	vestía	vestí	vestiré	vestiría	vista	vistiera
	vistiéndote	**te**	vistes	vestías	vestiste	vestirás	vestirías	vistas	vistieras
	vistiéndose	**se**	viste	vestía	vistió	vestirá	vestiría	vista	vistiera
	vistiéndonos	**nos**	vestimos	vestíamos	vestimos	vestiremos	vestiríamos	vistamos	vistiéramos
	vistiéndoos	**os**	vestís	vestíais	vestisteis	vestiréis	vestiríais	vistáis	vistierais
	vistiéndose	**se**	visten	vestían	vistieron	vestirán	vestirían	vistan	vistieran

Regular and irregular reflexive verbs: Position of the reflexive pronouns with commands

Person	Affirmative	Negative	Affirmative	Negative	Affirmative	Negative
tú	lávate	no te laves	ponte	no te pongas	vístete	no te vistas
usted	lávese	no se lave	póngase	no se ponga	vístase	no se vista
ustedes	lávense	no se laven	pónganse	no se pongan	vístanse	no se vistan
nosotros	lavémonos	no nos lavemos	pongámonos	no nos pongamos	vistámonos	no nos vistamos
vosotros	lavaos	no os lavéis	poneos	no os pongáis	vestíos	no os vistáis

Regular and irregular reflexive verbs: Position of the reflexive pronouns in compound tenses*

Reflexive Pronoun	Indicative						Subjunctive	
	Present Perfect	Past Perfect	Preterite Perfect	Future Perfect	Conditional Perfect		Present Perfect	Past Perfect
me	he	había	hube	habré	habría		haya	hubiera
te	has	habías	hubiste	habrás	habrías		hayas	hubieras
se	ha	había	hubo	habrá	habría		haya	hubiera
nos	hemos	habíamos	hubimos	habremos	habríamos		hayamos	hubiéramos
os	habéis	habíais	hubisteis	habréis	habríais		hayáis	hubiérais
se	han	habían	hubieron	habrán	habrían		hayan	hubieran

(participles for each group: lavado, puesto, vestido)

*The sequence of these three elements—the reflexive pronoun, the auxiliary verb **haber,** and the present perfect form—is invariable and no other words can come in between.

Regular and irregular reflexive verbs: Position of the reflexive pronouns with conjugated verb + infinitive**

Reflexive Pronoun	Indicative					Subjunctive	
	Present	Imperfect	Preterite	Future	Conditional	Present	Imperfect
me	voy a	iba a	fui a	iré a	iría a	vaya a	fuera a
te	vas a	ibas a	fuiste a	irás a	irías a	vayas a	fueras a
se	va a	iba a	fue a	irá a	iría a	vaya a	fuera a
nos	vamos a	íbamos a	fuimos a	iremos a	iríamos a	vayamos a	fuéramos a
os	vais a	ibais a	fuisteis a	iréis a	iríais a	vayáis a	fuerais a
se	van a	iban a	fueron a	irán a	irían a	vayan a	fueran a

(infinitives for each group: lavar, poner, vestir)

The reflexive pronoun can also be placed after the infinitive: voy a lavarme,** voy a poner**me,** voy a vestir**me,** and so on. Use the same structure for the present and the past progressive: **me** estoy lavando / estoy lavándo**me; me** estaba lavando / estaba lavándo**me.**

Andar, caber, caer

Infinitive	Past participle / Present participle	Indicative					Subjunctive	
		Present	Imperfect	Preterite	Future	Conditional	Present	Imperfect
andar *to walk; to go*	andado andando	ando andas anda andamos andáis andan	andaba andabas andaba andábamos andabais andaban	**anduve anduviste anduvo anduvimos anduvisteis anduvieron**	andaré andarás andará andaremos andaréis andarán	andaría andarías andaría andaríamos andaríais andarían	ande andes ande andemos andéis anden	**anduviera anduvieras anduviera anduviéramos anduvierais anduvieran**
caber *to fit; to have enough space*	cabido cabiendo	**quepo** cabes cabe cabemos cabéis caben	cabía cabías cabía cabíamos cabíais cabían	**cupe cupiste cupo cupimos cupisteis cupieron**	**cabré cabrás cabrá cabremos cabréis cabrán**	**cabría cabrías cabría cabríamos cabríais cabrían**	**quepa quepas quepa quepamos quepáis quepan**	**cupiera cupieras cupiera cupiéramos cupierais cupieran**
caer *to fall*	caído cayendo	**caigo** caes cae caemos caéis caen	caía caías caía caíamos caíais caían	caí caíste **cayó** caímos caísteis **cayeron**	caeré caerás caerá caeremos caeréis caerán	caería caerías caería caeríamos caeríais caerían	**caiga caigas caiga caigamos caigáis caigan**	**cayera cayeras cayera cayéramos cayerais cayeran**

Commands

Person	andar Affirmative	andar Negative	caber Affirmative	caber Negative	caer Affirmative	caer Negative
tú	anda	no andes	cabe	no **quepas**	cae	no **caigas**
usted	ande	no ande	**quepa**	no **quepa**	**caiga**	no **caiga**
ustedes	anden	no anden	**quepan**	no **quepan**	**caigan**	no **caigan**
nosotros	andemos	no andemos	**quepamos**	no **quepamos**	**caigamos**	no **caigamos**
vosotros	andad	no andéis	cabed	no **quepáis**	caed	no **caigáis**

Dar, decir, estar

Infinitive	Past participle / Present participle	Indicative					Subjunctive	
		Present	Preterite	Imperfect	Future	Conditional	Present	Imperfect
dar *to give*	dado / dando	doy / das / da / damos / dais / dan	di / diste / dio / dimos / disteis / dieron	daba / dabas / daba / dábamos / dabais / daban	daré / darás / dará / daremos / daréis / darán	daría / darías / daría / daríamos / daríais / darían	dé / des / dé / demos / deis / den	diera / dieras / diera / diéramos / dierais / dieran
decir *to say, tell*	dicho / diciendo	digo / dices / dice / decimos / decís / dicen	dije / dijiste / dijo / dijimos / dijisteis / dijeron	decía / decías / decía / decíamos / decíais / decían	diré / dirás / dirá / diremos / diréis / dirán	diría / dirías / diría / diríamos / diríais / dirían	diga / digas / diga / digamos / digáis / digan	dijera / dijeras / dijera / dijéramos / dijerais / dijeran
estar *to be*	estado / estando	estoy / estás / está / estamos / estáis / están	estuve / estuviste / estuvo / estuvimos / estuvisteis / estuvieron	estaba / estabas / estaba / estábamos / estabais / estaban	estaré / estarás / estará / estaremos / estaréis / estarán	estaría / estarías / estaría / estaríamos / estaríais / estarían	esté / estés / esté / estemos / estéis / estén	estuviera / estuvieras / estuviera / estuviéramos / estuvierais / estuvieran

Commands

Person	dar		decir		estar	
	Affirmative	Negative	Affirmative	Negative	Affirmative	Negative
tú	da	no **des**	**di**	no **digas**	**está**	no **estés**
usted	**dé**	no **dé**	**diga**	no **diga**	**esté**	no **esté**
ustedes	**den**	no **den**	**digan**	no **digan**	**estén**	no **estén**
nosotros	**demos**	no **demos**	**digamos**	no **digamos**	**estemos**	no **estemos**
vosotros	dad	no **deis**	decid	no **digáis**	**estad**	no **estéis**

Haber*, hacer, ír

Infinitive	Past participle / Present participle	Indicative					Subjunctive	
		Present	Imperfect	Preterite	Future	Conditional	Present	Imperfect
haber* *to have*	habido habiendo	**he** **has** **ha** **hemos** habéis **han**	había habías había habíamos habíais habían	**hube** **hubiste** **hubo** **hubimos** **hubisteis** **hubieron**	**habré** **habrás** **habrá** **habremos** **habréis** **habrán**	**habría** **habrías** **habría** **habríamos** **habríais** **habrían**	**haya** **hayas** **haya** **hayamos** **hayáis** **hayan**	**hubiera** **hubieras** **hubiera** **hubiéramos** **hubierais** **hubieran**
hacer *to do*	**hecho** haciendo	**hago** haces hace hacemos hacéis hacen	hacía hacías hacía hacíamos hacíais hacían	**hice** **hiciste** **hizo** **hicimos** **hicisteis** **hicieron**	**haré** **harás** **hará** **haremos** **haréis** **harán**	**haría** **harías** **haría** **haríamos** **haríais** **harían**	**haga** **hagas** **haga** **hagamos** **hagáis** **hagan**	**hiciera** **hicieras** **hiciera** **hiciéramos** **hicierais** **hicieran**
ír *to go*	**ido** **yendo**	**voy** **vas** **va** **vamos** **vais** **van**	**iba** **ibas** **iba** **íbamos** **ibais** **iban**	**fui** **fuiste** **fue** **fuimos** **fuisteis** **fueron**	iré irás irá iremos iréis irán	iría irías iría iríamos iríais irían	**vaya** **vayas** **vaya** **vayamos** **vayáis** **vayan**	**fuera** **fueras** **fuera** **fuéramos** **fuerais** **fueran**

Commands

Person	hacer		ir	
	Affirmative	Negative	Affirmative	Negative
tú	**haz**	no **hagas**	**ve**	no **vayas**
usted	**haga**	no **haga**	**vaya**	no **vaya**
ustedes	**hagan**	no **hagan**	**vayan**	no **vayan**
nosotros	**hagamos**	no **hagamos**	**vamos**	no **vayamos**
vosotros	haced	no **hagáis**	**id**	no **vayáis**

Note: The imperative of **haber** is not used.

*Haber also has an impersonal form **hay.** This form is used to express "There is, There are."

Jugar, oír, oler

Infinitive	Past participle / Present participle	Indicative Present	Indicative Imperfect	Indicative Preterite	Indicative Future	Indicative Conditional	Subjunctive Present	Subjunctive Imperfect
jugar *to play*	jugado jugando	**juego** **juegas** **juega** jugamos jugáis **juegan**	jugaba jugabas jugaba jugábamos jugabais jugaban	**jugué** jugaste jugó jugamos jugasteis jugaron	jugaré jugarás jugará jugaremos jugaréis jugarán	jugaría jugarías jugaría jugaríamos jugaríais jugarían	**juegue** **juegues** **juegue** **juguemos** **juguéis** **jueguen**	jugara jugaras jugara jugáramos jugarais jugaran
oír *to hear; to listen*	**oído** **oyendo**	**oigo** **oyes** **oye** oímos oís **oyen**	oía oías oía oíamos oíais oían	oí oíste **oyó** oímos oísteis **oyeron**	oiré oirás oirá oiremos oiréis oirán	oiría oirías oiría oiríamos oiríais oirían	**oiga** **oigas** **oiga** **oigamos** **oigáis** **oigan**	**oyera** **oyeras** **oyera** **oyéramos** **oyerais** **oyeran**
oler *to smell*	olido oliendo	**huelo** **hueles** **huele** olemos oléis **huelen**	olía olías olía olíamos olíais olían	olí oliste olió olimos olisteis olieron	oleré olerás olerá oleremos oleréis olerán	olería olerías olería oleríamos oleríais olerían	**huela** **huelas** **huela** olamos oláis **huelan**	oliera olieras oliera oliéramos olierais olieran

Commands

Person	jugar Affirmative	jugar Negative	oír Affirmative	oír Negative	oler Affirmative	oler Negative
tú	**juega**	no **juegues**	**oye**	no **oigas**	**huele**	no **huelas**
usted	**juegue**	no **juegue**	**oiga**	no **oiga**	**huela**	no **huela**
ustedes	**jueguen**	no **jueguen**	**oigan**	no **oigan**	**huelan**	no **huelan**
nosotros	**juguemos**	no **juguemos**	**oigamos**	no **oigamos**	olamos	no olamos
vosotros	jugad	no **juguéis**	**oíd**	no **oigáis**	oled	no oláis

Poder, poner, querer

Infinitive	Past participle / Present participle	Indicative					Subjunctive	
		Present	Imperfect	Preterite	Future	Conditional	Present	Imperfect
poder *to be able to, can*	podido pudiendo	**puedo** **puedes** **puede** podemos podéis **pueden**	podía podías podía podíamos podíais podían	**pude** **pudiste** **pudo** **pudimos** **pudisteis** **pudieron**	**podré** **podrás** **podrá** **podremos** **podréis** **podrán**	**podría** **podrías** **podría** **podríamos** **podríais** **podrían**	**pueda** **puedas** **pueda** podamos podáis **puedan**	**pudiera** **pudieras** **pudiera** **pudiéramos** **pudierais** **pudieran**
poner* *to put*	**puesto** poniendo	**pongo** pones pone ponemos ponéis ponen	ponía ponías ponía poníamos poníais ponían	**puse** **pusiste** **puso** **pusimos** **pusisteis** **pusieron**	**pondré** **pondrás** **pondrá** **pondremos** **pondréis** **pondrán**	**pondría** **pondrías** **pondría** **pondríamos** **pondríais** **pondrían**	**ponga** **pongas** **ponga** **pongamos** **pongáis** **pongan**	**pusiera** **pusieras** **pusiera** **pusiéramos** **pusierais** **pusieran**
querer *to want, wish; to love*	querido queriendo	**quiero** **quieres** **quiere** queremos queréis **quieren**	quería querías quería queríamos queríais querían	**quise** **quisiste** **quiso** **quisimos** **quisisteis** **quisieron**	**querré** **querrás** **querrá** **querremos** **querréis** **querrán**	**querría** **querrías** **querría** **querríamos** **querríais** **querrían**	**quiera** **quieras** **quiera** queramos queráis **quieran**	**quisiera** **quisieras** **quisiera** **quisiéramos** **quisierais** **quisieran**

Commands

Person	poner		querer	
	Affirmative	Negative	Affirmative	Negative
tú	**pon**	no **pongas**	**quiere**	no **quieras**
usted	**ponga**	no **ponga**	**quiera**	no **quiera**
ustedes	**pongan**	no **pongan**	**quieran**	no **quieran**
nosotros	**pongamos**	no **pongamos**	queramos	no queramos
vosotros	poned	no **pongáis**	quered	no queráis

*Similar verbs to **poner: imponer, suponer, componer, descomponer.**
Note: The imperative of **poder** is used very infrequently.

Saber, salir, ser

Infinitive	Past participle / Present participle	Indicative					Subjunctive	
		Present	Imperfect	Preterite	Future	Conditional	Present	Imperfect
saber *to know*	sabido sabiendo	sé sabes sabe sabemos sabéis saben	sabía sabías sabía sabíamos sabíais sabían	supe supiste supo supimos supisteis supieron	sabré sabrás sabrá sabremos sabréis sabrán	sabría sabrías sabría sabríamos sabríais sabrían	sepa sepas sepa sepamos sepáis sepan	supiera supieras supiera supiéramos supierais supieran
salir *to go out,* *to leave*	salido saliendo	salgo sales sale salimos salís salen	salía salías salía salíamos salíais salían	salí saliste salió salimos salisteis salieron	saldré saldrás saldrá saldremos saldréis saldrán	saldría saldrías saldría saldríamos saldríais saldrían	salga salgas salga salgamos salgáis salgan	saliera salieras saliera saliéramos salierais salieran
ser *to be*	sido siendo	soy eres es somos sois son	era eras era éramos erais eran	fui fuiste fue fuimos fuisteis fueron	seré serás será seremos seréis serán	sería serías sería seríamos seríais serían	sea seas sea seamos seáis sean	fuera fueras fuera fuéramos fuerais fueran

Commands

Person	saber		salir		ser	
	Affirmative	Negative	Affirmative	Negative	Affirmative	Negative
tú	sabe	no sepas	sal	no salgas	sé	no seas
usted	sepa	no sepa	salga	no salga	sea	no sea
ustedes	sepan	no sepan	salgan	no salgan	sean	no sean
nosotros	sepamos	no sepamos	salgamos	no salgamos	seamos	no seamos
vosotros	sabed	no sepáis	salid	no salgáis	sed	no seáis

Sonreír, tener*, traer

Infinitive	Past participle / Present participle	Indicative Present	Indicative Imperfect	Indicative Preterite	Indicative Future	Conditional	Subjunctive Present	Subjunctive Imperfect
sonreír *to smile*	sonreído sonriendo	sonrío sonríes sonríe sonreímos sonreís sonríen	sonreía sonreías sonreía sonreíamos sonreíais sonreían	sonreí sonreíste sonrió sonreímos sonreísteis sonrieron	sonreiré sonreirás sonreirá sonreiremos sonreiréis sonreirán	sonreiría sonreirías sonreiría sonreiríamos sonreiríais sonreirían	sonría sonrías sonría sonriamos sonriáis sonrían	sonriera sonrieras sonriera sonriéramos sonrierais sonrieran
tener* *to have*	tenido teniendo	tengo tienes tiene tenemos tenéis tienen	tenía tenías tenía teníamos teníais tenían	tuve tuviste tuvo tuvimos tuvisteis tuvieron	tendré tendrás tendrá tendremos tendréis tendrán	tendría tendrías tendría tendríamos tendríais tendrían	tenga tengas tenga tengamos tengáis tengan	tuviera tuvieras tuviera tuviéramos tuvierais tuvieran
traer *to bring*	traído trayendo	traigo traes trae traemos traéis traen	traía traías traía traíamos traíais traían	traje trajiste trajo trajimos trajisteis trajeron	traeré traerás traerá traeremos traeréis traerán	traería traerías traería traeríamos traeríais traerían	traiga traigas traiga traigamos traigáis traigan	trajera trajeras trajera trajéramos trajerais trajeran

Commands

Person	sonreír Affirmative	sonreír Negative	tener Affirmative	tener Negative	traer Affirmative	traer Negative
tú	sonríe	no sonrías	ten	no tengas	trae	no traigas
usted	sonría	no sonría	tenga	no tenga	traiga	no traiga
ustedes	sonrían	no sonrían	tengan	no tengan	traigan	no traigan
nosotros	sonriamos	no sonriamos	tengamos	no tengamos	traigamos	no traigamos
vosotros	sonreíd	no sonriáis	tened	no tengáis	traed	no traigáis

*Many verbs ending in -tener are conjugated like this verb: **contener, detener, entretener(se), mantener, obtener, retener.**

Valer, venir*, ver

Infinitive	Past participle / Present participle	Indicative Present	Imperfect	Preterite	Future	Conditional	Subjunctive Present	Imperfect
valer *to be worth*	valido / valiendo	**valgo** / vales / vale / valemos / valéis / valen	valía / valías / valía / valíamos / valíais / valían	valí / valiste / valió / valimos / valisteis / valieron	**valdré** / **valdrás** / **valdrá** / **valdremos** / **valdréis** / **valdrán**	**valdría** / **valdrías** / **valdría** / **valdríamos** / **valdríais** / **valdrían**	**valga** / **valgas** / **valga** / **valgamos** / **valgáis** / **valgan**	valiera / valieras / valiera / valiéramos / valierais / valieran
venir* *to come*	venido / viniendo	**vengo** / **vienes** / **viene** / venimos / venís / **vienen**	venía / venías / venía / veníamos / veníais / venían	**vine** / **viniste** / **vino** / **vinimos** / **vinisteis** / **vinieron**	**vendré** / **vendrás** / **vendrá** / **vendremos** / **vendréis** / **vendrán**	**vendría** / **vendrías** / **vendría** / **vendríamos** / **vendríais** / **vendrían**	**venga** / **vengas** / **venga** / **vengamos** / **vengáis** / **vengan**	**viniera** / **vinieras** / **viniera** / **viniéramos** / **vinierais** / **vinieran**
ver *to see*	visto / viendo	**veo** / **ves** / **ve** / **vemos** / **veis** / **ven**	**veía** / **veías** / **veía** / **veíamos** / **veíais** / **veían**	vi / viste / vio / vimos / visteis / vieron	veré / verás / verá / veremos / veréis / verán	vería / verías / vería / veríamos / veríais / verían	**vea** / **veas** / **vea** / **veamos** / **veáis** / **vean**	viera / vieras / viera / viéramos / vierais / vieran

Commands

	valer Affirmative	valer Negative	venir Affirmative	venir Negative	ver Affirmative	ver Negative
Person						
tú	vale	no **valgas**	**ven**	no **vengas**	**ve**	no **veas**
usted	**valga**	no **valga**	**venga**	no **venga**	**vea**	no **vea**
ustedes	**valgan**	no **valgan**	**vengan**	no **vengan**	**vean**	no **vean**
nosotros	**valgamos**	no **valgamos**	**vengamos**	no **vengamos**	**veamos**	no **veamos**
vosotros	valed	no **valgáis**	venid	no **vengáis**	ved	no **veáis**

*Similar verb to venir: prevenir

Appendix B: Prefixes and Suffixes

Prefixes

Prefix	Meaning and use	Example	English
ante-	*before*	antenoche, antepasado	*last night, ancestor*
des-	*lack of a quality*	desatento/a, desafortunado/a	*inattentive, unfortunate*
en-/em-	*used to form verbs*	envejecer, emparejar	*to get old, to pair/to match*
ex-	*previous; used with professions or roles*	el expresidente, el exmarido	*ex-president, ex-husband*
in-/im-	*lack of*	inconveniente, imperfecto/a	*inconvenient, imperfect*
infra-	*below a standard*	infrahumano/a	*subhuman*
mega-	*large, 1,000*	el megáfono, el megavatio	*megaphone, megawatt*
micro-	*small, 1/100*	el microondas, el microgramo	*microwave, microgram*
multi-	*many*	multicolor, multimedia	*multicolor, multimedia*
post-/pos-	*after*	posponer, postoperatorio, el postgrado	*postpone, postoperative, postgraduate*
pre-	*before*	predecir, el precontrato	*to predict, pre-contract*
super-	*high degree of a quality*	superbuen/a, el superhombre	*extra good, superman*
ultra-	*beyond, more than*	ultramoderno/a	*ultramodern*
vice-	*second*	el vicepresidente	*vice president*

Suffixes

Sufffix	Meaning and use	Example	English
-able	*able to; used in adjectives*	adorable, criticable, pasable	*adorable, criticizable, passable*
-ado, -ido	*past participle endings*	he hablado, he comido	*I have spoken, I have eaten*
-ado/a -ido/a	*ending of the past participle used as adjective*	está cansado/a, está vencido/a	*he/she is tired; he/she is defeated*
-ancia	*feminine noun ending*	la ambulancia, la importancia	*ambulance, importance*
-ano/a	*most common ending of adjectives of nationality*	cubano/a, colombiano/a, venezolano/a	*Cuban, Colombian, Venezuelan*
-ante	*ending of adjectives formed from verbs*	abundante, fascinante, interesante	*abundant, fascinating, interesting*
-ario	*collection*	el diario, el cuestionario, el diccionario, el horario, el vocabulario	*diary, questionnaire, dictionary, schedule, vocabulary*
-ción	*feminine noun ending*	la canción, la estación, la opción, la situación	*song, station, option, situation*
-dad	*feminine noun ending*	la ciudad, la vanidad	*city, vanity*

(continued)

Sufffix	Meaning and use	Example	English
-eño/a	*ending of some adjectives of nationality*	madrileño/a, panameño/a	*from Madrid, from Panama*
-ense	*ending of some adjectives of nationality*	costarricense, estadounidense	*from Costa Rica, from the United States*
-ería	*shop, store*	la cafetería, la lechería, la joyería, la panadería	*cafeteria, milk store, jewelry store, bakery*
-ísimo/a	*extremely; used with adjectives*	buenísimo/a, riquísimo/a	*extremely/very, very good/delicious*
-ista	*feminine or masculine ending; describes profession, skill or a specific quality*	el/la capitalista, el/la lingüista, el/la optimista, el/la dentista	*capitalist, linguist, optimist, dentist*
-ito/a	*diminutive ending*	Pedrito, Juanita, la casita, amarillito	*little Pedro, little Juana, little house, yellowish (a little yellow)*
-mente	*ending of some adverbs*	actualmente, claramente	*presently, clearly*
-or/a	*person or thing that does something; used with professions, machines and so on*	el/la autor/a, el/la editor/a, el/la computador/a, el detector	*author, publisher, computer, detector*
-s, -es	*plural ending of nouns and adjectives*	los secretarios, las secretarias, fáciles	*secretaries, easy*
-tad	*feminine noun ending*	la libertad, la voluntad	*freedom, will*

Appendix C: Classroom Expressions

Mandatos plurales (ustedes)	Mandatos singulares (usted)	Mandatos singulares (tú)	Commands
Abran el libro.	Abra el libro.	Abre el libro.	*Open your book(s).*
Aprendan el vocabulario.	Aprenda el vocabulario.	Aprende el vocabulario.	*Learn the vocabulary.*
Cierren el libro.	Cierre el libro.	Cierra el libro.	*Close your book(s).*
Escriban la tarea.	Escriba la tarea.	Escribe la tarea.	*Write the homework.*
Escuchen.	Escuche.	Escucha.	*Listen.*
Estudien la lección.	Estudie la lección.	Estudia la lección.	*Study the lesson.*
Hagan el ejercicio.	Haga el ejercicio.	Haz el ejercicio.	*Do the exercise.*
Lean la lectura.	Lea la lectura.	Lee la lectura.	*Read the passage.*
Levanten la mano.	Levante la mano.	Levanta la mano.	*Raise your hand(s).*
Repasen la gramática.	Repase la gramática.	Repasa la gramática.	*Review the grammar.*
Repitan.	Repita.	Repite.	*Repeat.*
Siéntense.	Siéntese.	Siéntate.	*Sit down.*
Sigan.	Siga.	Sigue.	*Continue.*
Tomen asiento.	Tome asiento.	Toma asiento.	*Have a seat.*
Vayan a la pizarra.	Vaya a la pizarra.	Ve a la pizarra.	*Go to the board.*

Appendix D: *Caminos del jaguar* Video Expressions

A veces se gana y a veces se pierde.   You win some and lose some., 6

A ver si...   Let's see if . . ., 5

¡Adelante!   Come in!, 4

Algo no me suena bien.   Something is not right., 6

¡Anda pronto!   Hurry up!, 4

¡Ánimo!   Cheer up! (Come on!), 11

Antes de que desapareciera...   Before it disappeared . . ., 12

¡Ay, caramba!   Good grief!, 2

¡Cálmese!   Calm down!, 3

Cayó en la trampa.   She fell into the trap., 11

Con permiso.   Excuse me., 2

Con tan corto plazo...   On such short notice . . ., 11

Creyeron que nos habían dejado en la tumba.   They thought they had left us for dead., 7

Cueste lo que cueste.   No matter what it costs., 2

¿De qué se trata?   What is it about?, 1

¡Deja en paz ese aparato!   Leave that machine alone!, 6

Di que sí.   Say yes., 1

El fin sí justifica los medios.   The end justifies the means., 11

¡El que ríe último, ríe mejor!   He who laughs last, laughs best!, 8

Ella tuvo que rendirse.   She had to give up., 7

Empecemos desde el principio.   Let's start from the beginning., 7

¿En qué puedo servirles? How may I help you?, 3

¡Eres astuta como un zorro!   You are as clever as a fox!, 9

Es bueno que escuches tu corazón.   It's good that you listen to your heart., 8

Es cuestión de vida o muerte.   It's a matter of life or death., 7

Es más bravo que un león.   He is more courageous than a lion., 7

Eso no importa.   That doesn't matter., 4

Espero que todo salga bien.   I hope all goes well., 8

Está por encima de toda sospecha. She's above suspicion., 9

Está un poco mareada.   She is a bit dizzy., 8

Esto es una despedida, mis amigos.   This is good-bye, my friends., 6

Estoy a punto de...   I'm about to . . ., 5

Estoy de acuerdo.   I agree., 2

Estoy muerto de hambre.   I'm starving., 3

Fuera de serie.   Out of this world., 12

¡Genial!   Great!, 3

Hace el papel de...   He/She plays the role of . . ., 3

Hágame el favor...   Do me the favor . . ., 6

¡Hay tanto que hacer!   There is so much to do!, 5

¡Imagínate!   Imagine!, 1

Las apariencias engañan.   Things are not always what they seem., 12

Le quita a uno el habla.   It takes your breath away., 5

¿Lo dice en serio?   Are you serious?, 8

Lo siento.   I'm sorry., 1

Me da igual.   It's all the same to me., 3

Me imagino que sí...   I imagine so . . ., 5

Me llamó la atención.   It caught my attention., 8

Me vendría bien...   I wouldn't mind . . ., 4

¡Ni locos!   No way!, 4

No corro el riesgo de ser descubierta.   I won't risk being discovered., 10

No empieces con tus indirectas.   Don't start with your little digs., 10
No es culpa tuya.   It is not your fault., 3
No es para tanto.   There's no need to make such a fuss., 10
No hay de qué preocuparse.   There's nothing to worry about., 9
No hay duda.   There's no doubt., 2
No hay por qué alarmarse.   There's no reason to be alarmed., 8
No le quiero alargar la historia...   To make a long story short . . ., 10
No les haga daño.   Don't harm them., 6
No me cae nada mal.   I don't dislike him at all., 4
No me queda otro recurso...   I have no other choice . . ., 12
No pasa nada.   Nothing is wrong., 5
No puedes perderte de vista.   You won't be out of sight., 3
No puedo quedarme con los brazos cruzados.   I can't just sit around and wait., 5
No queda más remedio.   We have no choice., 7
¿No sabe usted nada de...?   Don't you know anything about . . . ?, 12
No se me había ocurrido.   I hadn't thought of that., 10
No seas tan modesta.   Don't be so modest., 12
No te preocupes.   Don't worry., 4
No tenemos la contraseña.   We don't have the password., 6
No tengo ni la menor idea.   I don't have the slightest idea., 9
No tiene caso pensar en...   There is no point in thinking about . . ., 12
No vale la pena.   It's not worth it., 4
Nos falta lo más difícil.   The hardest part is yet to come., 11
Nunca me ha fallado.   It has never failed me., 9
Nunca se sabe.   One never knows., 10
Ojalá nunca te hubiera hecho caso.   I wish I had never listened to you., 12
Ojalá tengas razón.   I hope you are right., 8
Olvídalo.   Forget it., 1
¿Por qué le he de creer?   Why should I believe you?, 11
Pueden contar conmigo.   You can count on me., 7
Pues no sé.   I really don't know., 1
¡Qué alivio!   What a relief!, 4
¡Qué bueno!   Great!, 1
¡Qué bueno que ya te sientas mejor!   I'm glad you feel better!, 8
¡Qué envidia!   I'm so jealous!, 1
¡Qué exagerado eres!   You are so dramatic!, 1
¡Qué gusto oír tu voz!   It's so nice to hear from you!, 6
¿Qué haría sin ti?   What would I do without you?, 12
¡Qué horror!   How awful!, 3
¡Qué raro!   How strange!, 2
¡Qué sé yo!   What do I know!, 2
Quedé en verla...   We arranged to meet . . ., 11
Quizás ella pueda curarte.   She might be able to cure you., 8
Quizás hayan visto algo.   Perhaps they have seen something., 10
Quizás no lo sepas todo.   Maybe you don't know everything., 9
Se está haciendo pasar...   He is pretending to be . . ., 11
Se fueron sin dejar rastro.   They left without a trace., 10
Se le está acabando el tiempo.   She is running out of time., 11
Se nos fue la luz.   We had a power outage., 10
Se pinchó la llanta.   We have a flat tire., 7
Según sus cuentas...   According to her calculations . . ., 7
Será un placer.   It would be a pleasure., 12
Si no es molestia...   If you don't mind . . ., 2
Si no tiene ningún inconveniente...   If you don't mind . . ., 11
Siempre te metes en líos.   You're always getting in trouble., 3
Sin darse cuenta...   Without realizing it . . ., 7
Sin ti...   Without you . . ., 10
Sobre gustos, no hay nada escrito.   There is no accounting for taste., 9
¡Tenga piedad!   Have pity!, 6
Tengo fondos.   I have means (resources)., 2

Tengo un mal presentimiento.   I have a bad feeling., 2
¿Tienen reservación?   Do you have a reservation?, 5
Todo está arreglado.   Everything is taken care of., 4
Todo está saliendo muy bien.   Everything is turning out really well., 9
¡Vamos!   Let's go!, 1
Ve al grano.   Get to the point., 9
¿Y qué pasó después?   And, what happened afterward?, 5
Ya veremos...   We'll see . . . , 5
Yo cumplí con mi obligación.   I fulfilled my obligation., 9
Yo hago lo que me dé la gana.   I do as I please., 6

Spanish-English Vocabulary

This vocabulary includes most of the active vocabulary presented in the chapters. (Some exceptions are many numbers, some names of cities and countries, and some obvious cognates.) The list also includes many receptive words found throughout the chapters. The definitions are limited to the context in which the words are used in this book. Stem changes are shown for all stem-changing verbs; for example, **cerrar (ie); -ir** verbs that have both a present tense and preterite stem change are shown as **preferir (ie, i), dormir (ue, u).** Active words are followed by a number that indicates the chapter in which the word appears as an active item; the abbreviation **P** refers to the **Capítulo preliminar.**

The following abbreviations are used:

adj.	adjective	*m.*	masculine
adv.	adverb	*Mex.*	Mexican
f.	feminine	*pl.*	plural
inf.	infinitive	*pron.*	pronoun
Lat. Am.	Latin American	*s.*	singular

A

a to, for, 4; **a bordo** on board, 5; **a fin de que** in order that, 10; **a la (mano) derecha/izquierda** on the right/left(hand side), 7; **a mano** by hand, 10; **a menos que** unless, 10; **a pesar de que** even though, even if, 9; **a pie** on foot, 3; **¡A sus órdenes!** At your service!, 3; **a un precio más bajo** at a lower price, 7; **a veces** at times, 4

abeja (*f.*) bee

abogado/a (*m., f.*) attorney, lawyer, 4

abrazar to hug, embrace, 4

abrigo (*m.*) coat, 7

abril (*m.*) April, 1

abrir to open, 2

abrocharse (el cinturón) to buckle up (seatbelt), 9

abuelo/a (*m., f.*) grandfather/grandmother, 4

aburrido/a bored, 2

acabar to finish; **acabar de +** (*inf.*) to finish; to have just (done something), 2

acceder to access, 9

acción: de acción action (*adj.*), 6

acelerador (*m.*) accelerator, 9

acelerar to accelerate, 7

acercarse to approach

aconsejar to advise, 8

acontecimiento (*m.*) event, 6

acordión (*f.*) accordion, 6

acostarse (ue) to go to bed; to lie down, 3

actitud (*f.*) attitude

actividad (*f.*) activity, P

activo/a active, 8

acto delectivo (*m.*) delinquent act, 11

actor (*m.*) actor, 6

actriz (*f.*) actress, 6

actuación (*f.*) acting, 6

actualidad: de la actualidad at the present time

actuar to act, 6

acuarela (*f.*) watercolor, 10

acuerdo: estar de acuerdo to agree, 5

adelanto (*m.*) advance

además de in addition to, 12

adicción (*f.*) addiction, 11

adiós good-bye, P

adivinar to guess

adjetivo (*m.*) adjective

adolescente (*m., f.*) adolescent, 11

¿adónde? where (to)?

adorno (*m.*) decoration, adornment, 10

advertir (ie, i) to warn

aerolínea (*f.*) airline, 5

aeropuerto (*m.*) airport, 2

afeitarse to shave, 3

aficionado/a (*m., f.*) fan, 6

agente (*m., f.*) agent, 5; **agente de viajes** travel agent, 4

agosto (*m.*) August, 1

agradable pleasant, 1

agradecer (zc) to thank, 4

agregar to add

agua (el) (*f.*) water; **agua mineral** mineral water, 3

aguacero (*m.*) downpour, 3

agudo/a acute

ahí there, 3

ahijado/a (*m., f.*) godson/goddaughter

ahora now, 2

ahorrar to save, 11

airbag (*m.*) airbag, 9

aire (*m.*) air; **aire acondicionado** air conditioner, 9; **al aire libre** outdoors

al (a + el) to the, 3; **al lado de** next to, side by side, 4

alargar to lengthen

alberca (*f.*) swimming pool, 2

alcanzar to reach, catch up with, 3, 11

alcoba (*f.*) bedroom

alegrarse (de) to be happy, 8

alegre happy, 2

alemán (*m.*) German language, 1

alemán/alemana German

alergia (*f.*) allergy; **tener alergia a...** to be allergic to ..., 8

alérgico: ser alérgico/a a... to be allergic to ..., 8

alfombra (*f.*) rug, 2

algo something, anything, 4

algodón (*m.*) cotton, 7

alguien someone, somebody, 4

algún, alguno/a some, any, 4; **algunas veces** sometimes, 4

alimentación (*f.*) food; nutrition, 8

alimento (*m.*) food, 8

aliviarse to get better, 8

allá there, over there, 3

allí there, over there, 3

alma (el) (*f.*) soul

almacén (*m.*) department store; warehouse, 2, 7

almacenar to store, 9

almendra (*f.*) almond

almorzar (ue) to have lunch, 3

almuerzo (*m.*) lunch, 3

alojamiento (*m.*) lodging, accommodations, 5

alojar(se) to stay (in a hotel), 5

alquilar to rent, 2; **alquilar videos** to rent videos, 2

alquiler (*m.*) rent, 2

alrededor del around, about

alterado/a upset, 2

alto/a tall, 1; **alta velocidad** (*f.*) high speed, 9

alumno/a (*m., f.*) student, P

amable friendly, 1

amado/a loved

amanecer (zc) to dawn

amar to love

amarillo/a yellow, 1

ambiente (*m.*) atmosphere

ambulante mobile, 7

amenazar to threaten, 11

amigo/a (*m., f.*) friend, P

amistad (*f.*) friendship

amor (*m.*) love; **de amor** (*adj.*), 6

amplio/a spacious, 2

análisis (*m.*) test, exam, 8

anaranjado/a orange, 1

anatomía (*f.*) anatomy, 1

ancho (*m.*) width

andar to walk; to move, 2

ángel (*m.*) angel

angustia (*f.*) worry, 11

anillo (*m.*) ring, 7

anteojos (*m.*) swim goggles, 6

antes (de) before, 4; **antes (de) que** before, 10

antibiótico (*m.*) antibiotic, 8

antipático/a unfriendly, 1

antropología (*f.*) anthropology, 1

anuncio (*m.*) announcement

año (*m.*) year; **tener X años** to be X years old, 3

apagar to turn off, shut off, 9

aparato (*m.*) apparatus, 9

aparecer (zc) to appear

apenas hardly

aperitivo (*m.*) appetizer, 3

apetito (*m.*) appetite; **tener apetito** to have an appetite, 8

aplicación (*f.*) application (tech.), 9

apodo (*m.*) nickname

apogeo (*m.*) height, 12

apoyar to support, 11

apoyo (*m.*) support

aprender to learn, 2

apuntar to point; to make a note of, 9

apuntes (*m. pl.*) notes

aquel/aquella (*adj.*) that (over there), 3

aquél/aquélla (*pron.*) that one (over there), 3

aquellos/as (*adj.*) those (over there), 3

aquéllos/as (*pron.*) those ones (over there), 3

aquí here, 3

árbol (*m.*) tree

archivar to save; to file, 9

archivo (*m.*) computer file, 9

arcilla (*f.*) clay, 10

arena (*f.*) sand; **hacer castillos de arena** to make sandcastles, 5

arete (*m.*) earring, 7

argumento (*m.*) plot, 6

arma (*f.*) weapon, 11

armario (*m.*) wardrobe, 2

armonía (*f.*) harmony

armonioso/a harmonious, 11

arqueología (*f.*) archaeology, 1

arqueólogo/a (*m., f.*) archaeologist, 4

arquitecto/a (*m., f.*) architect, 4

arrancar to start (a car, a race), 9

arreglar (la cama) to make, fix up (the bed), 2

arrestar to arrest, 11

arte (*m.*) **(las artes)** (*f. pl.*) art (the arts), 1; **arte abstracto** abstract art, 10; **arte clásico** classic art, 10; **arte contemporáneo** contemporary art, 10; **arte moderno** modern art, 10

artesanía (*f.*) craft, 7

artesano/a (*m., f.*) artisan, 10

artículo (*m.*) article

artista (*m., f.*) artist, 1, 4, 10

ascensor (*m.*) elevator, 5

asesinar to assassinate, murder, 11

asesinato (*m.*) assassination, murder, 11

asesino/a (*m., f.*) murderer, 11

asiento (*m.*) seat, 9

aspiradora (*f.*) vacuum cleaner, 2

aspirar (la alfombra) to vacuum the rug, 2

aspirina (*f.*) aspirin, 8

atender (ie) to attend to, wait on, 5

atleta (*m., f.*) athlete, 4

atractivo/a attractive, 1

audífonos (*m. pl.*) headphones, 6

aumentar to increase, 11

aunque even when, though, even if, although, 9

aurorretrato (*m.*) self-portrait, 10

auto (*m.*) car, 9

autobús (*m.*) bus, 3

autóctono/a indigenous

automático/a automatic, 9

automóvil (*m.*) car, automobile, 3, 9

averiguar to find out, 5

avión (*m.*) plane, 3

avisar to advise; to warn, 5

ayer yesterday

ayuda (*f.*) help, 9

azúcar (*m., f.*) sugar

azul blue, 1

azulejo (*m.*) tile

B

bailar to dance, 2, 6

bailarín/bailarina (*m., f.*) dancer, 6

bajar to download, 9; **bajar (por) (la calle)** to go (down) (a street), 7

bajo under, 4

bajo/a short (in height), 1

balada (*f.*) ballad, 6

balcón (*m.*) balcony, 2

ballena (*f.*) whale, 11

balón (*m.*) (beach) ball, 5, 6

baloncesto (*m.*) basketball, 6

banda (*f.*) band, 6

bañarse to take a bath, 3

bañera (*f.*) bathtub, 2

baño (cuarto de) (*m.*) bathroom, 2

bar (mini) (*m.*) (mini)bar, 5

barato/a inexpensive, 2

barco (*m.*) boat, 3

barrer (el piso) to sweep (the floor), 2

barrio (*m.*) neighborhood

barro (*m.*) clay, 7, 10

básquetbol (*m.*) basketball, 6

bastante enough; **Bastante bien, gracias.** Pretty well, thanks., P

basura (*f.*) garbage

basurero (*m.*) garbage can, 1

bate (*m.*) baseball bat, 6

batería (*f.*) drum set, 6; battery, 9

baúl (*m.*) trunk, 9

bebé (*m., f.*) baby, 4

beber to drink, 2; **¿Qué desean beber?** What would you like to drink?, 3

béisbol (*m.*) baseball, 6

belleza (*f.*) beauty

bello/a beautiful, 5

beneficio (*m.*) benefit, 11

biblioteca (*f.*) library, 2

bicicleta (*f.*) bicycle, 3, 6

bien well; **Muy bien, gracias.** Very well, thank you., P

bienestar (*m.*) well-being, 8
¡Bienvenido! Welcome!, P
billete (*m.*) ticket, 6
biología (*f.*) biology, 1
bisabuelo/a (*m., f.*) great grandfather/great grandmother, 4
bistec (*m.*) steak, 3
blanco/a white, 1
blues (*m. pl.*) blues, 6
blusa (*f.*) blouse, 7
boca (*f.*) mouth, 8
boda (*f.*) wedding
bolígrafo (*m.*) pen, 1
bolsa (*f.*) purse, bag, 7; **bolsa de aire** airbag, 9
bombero/a (*m., f.*) firefighter, 4
bombillo (*m.*) lightbulb, 11
bonito/a pretty, 1
borracho/a drunk, 2
borrador (*m.*) chalkboard eraser, 1
bosque (*m.*) forest
bosquejo (*m.*) sketch, 10
bota (*f.*) boot, 7
botón (*m.*) button, 9
botones (*m.*) porter, 5
boutique (*m.*) boutique, 7
boxeo (*m.*) boxing, 6
brazo (*m.*) arm, 8
brillar to shine, sparkle
brisa (*f.*) breeze, 3
bronce (*m.*) bronze, 10
bronceador solar (*m.*) sunscreen, 5
broncearse to get a tan, 5
bucear to go skindiving, snorkeling, 5
bueno/a good, 1; **¡Buen viaje!** Have a nice trip!, 5; **Buenas noches.** Good evening./Good night., P; **Buenas tardes.** Good afternoon., P; **Buenos días.** Good morning., P; **es bueno** it's good , 8
bufanda (*f.*) scarf, 7
burlarse de to make fun of, 10
buscador (*m.*) search engine, 9
buscar to look for, 2; **buscar conchas** to look for shells, 5
búsqueda (*f.*) search
buzón (*m.*) mailbox, 5

C

caballo (*m.*) horse, 11
cabeza (*f.*) head, 8
caer to fall, 4; **caer bien/mal** to like/dislike (a person), 4
café (*m.*) (color) brown, 1; café, 2; coffee, 3
caja (*f.*) cash register, 7; box

cajero automático (*m.*) automated teller machine (ATM), 5
calavera (*f.*) skull, 10
calcetín (*m.*) sock, 7
calculadora (*f.*) calculator, 1
calendario (*m.*) calendar, 1
calentamiento global (*m.*) global warming
caliente hot (temperature), 3
calle (*f.*) street, 2
calmado/a calm, 2
calor: hace calor it's hot, 3; **tener calor** to be hot, feel hot, 3
caloría (*f.*) calorie, 8
cama (*f.*) bed, 1
cámara (*f.*) camera, 9
camarero/a, (*m., f.*) waiter/waitress, 3
cambiar to exchange; **¿Dónde puedo cambiar el dinero?** Where can I exchange money?, 5
cambio de dinero/moneda (*m.*) money exchange, 5
caminar to walk, 2
caminata (*f.*) walking, 6
camión (*m.*) truck, bus (*Mex.*), 3
camioneta (*f.*) minivan; pickup truck, 3
camisa (*f.*) shirt, 7
camiseta (*f.*) T-shirt, 7
cancha (*f.*) court, field, 6
canción (*f.*) song, 6
cansado/a tired, 2
cantante (*m., f.*) singer, 6
cantar to sing, 2, 6
cantidad (*f.*) quantity, 8
capa de ozono (*f.*) ozone layer, 11
cara (*f.*) face, 3, 8
cárcel (*f.*) prison, 11
cargar to charge, 9
caribeño/a Caribbean
carne (*f.*) meat, 3
caro/a expensive, 2
carpeta (*f.*) folder, 1
carpintero/a (*m., f.*) carpenter, 4
carretera (*f.*) highway, 9
carro (*m.*) car, automobile, 3, 9
carta (*f.*) menu, 3
cartel (*m.*) poster, 1
cartelera (*f.*) listing, billboard, 6
cartero/a (*m., f.*) mail carrier, 4
casa (*f.*) house, 2
casado: estar casado/a to be married, 4
casarse (con) to get married (to), 4
cascada (*f.*) waterfall
casco (*m.*) helmet, 6
casi almost; **casi siempre/nunca/nada** almost always/never/nothing, 4

caso: en caso de que in case, 10
castañuela (*f.*) castanet, 6
castillo (*m.*) castle; **hacer castillos de arena** to make sandcastles, 5
categoría (*f.*) category, 6
catarro (*m.*) cold; **tener catarro** to have a cold, 8
catorce fourteen, 1
CD (*m.*) compact disc, CD, 6
celebrar to celebrate, 10
celoso/a jealous, 2
cena (*f.*) dinner, 3
cenar to have dinner, 3
centro comercial (*m.*) shopping center, 2
cepillarse to brush, 3; **cepillarse los dientes** to brush one's teeth
cerámica (*f.*) ceramics, 10
ceramista (*m., f.*) ceramist, potter, 10
cerca de close to, 4; **estar cerca (de)** to be close (to), 3
cerebro (*m.*) brain, 8
ceremonia (*f.*) ceremony, 10
cereza (*f.*) cherry
cero zero, 1
cerrar (ie) to close, 3
certeza (*f.*) certainty
cerveza (*f.*) beer, 3
cesta (*f.*) wicker basket, 6
chaqueta (*f.*) jacket, 7
Chao. Bye., P
cheque de viajero (*m.*) traveler's check, 5
chico/a (*m., f.*) boy, girl, P, 4
chino (*m.*) Chinese language, 1
chino/a Chinese, 1
chistoso/a funny
chocar to collide, 9
chofer (*Lat. Am.*) **/ chófer** (*Spain*) (*m.*) chauffeur, 3
choque (*m.*) crash, 9
chorizo (*m.*) sausage, 3
chubasco (*m.*) downpour, 3
ciclismo (*m.*) biking, 6
cielo (*m.*) sky, 3
cien one hundred, 1
ciencia ficción science fiction, 6; **de ciencia ficción** (*adj.*), 6
ciencias (médicas, naturales, políticas, sociales) (*f. pl.*) (medical, natural, political, social) sciences, 1
científico/a scientific
ciento noventa y nueve one hundred ninety-nine, 1
ciento uno one hundred one, 1
cierto/a certain, true; **(no) es cierto** it's (not) certain, true, 8
cifra (*f.*) figure, 12

cinco   five, 1
cincuenta   fifty, 1
cine (*m.*)   movies; movie theater, 2, 6
cinturón (*m.*)   belt, 7; **abrocharse el cinturón**   to buckle up seatbelt, 9; **cinturón de seguridad** seatbelt, 9
cita (*f.*)   appointment, 8; **hacer una cita**   to make an appointment, 8
ciudad (*f.*)   city, 2
claro/a   light, 10; **¡Claro que sí!**   Of course!, 7; **(no) está claro**   it's (not) clear, 8
clase (*f.*)   class, P
claxon (*m.*)   horn, 9
cliente (*m., f.*)   customer, 7
clima (*m.*)   climate, 3
clóset (*m.*)   closet, 2
club (*m.*)   club (nightclub), 5
cobre (*m.*)   copper, 7
coche (*m.*)   car, automobile, 3, 9
cocina (*f.*)   kitchen, 2
cocinar   to cook, 2
cocinero/a (*m., f.*)   cook, 4
códice (*m.*)   codex, 12
cola (*f.*)   tail; **hacer cola**   to stand in line
coleccionista (*m., f.*)   collector, 10
colgar (ue)   to hang (up), 9, 10
collar (*m.*)   necklace, 7
colocar   to place, put
color: en color(es)   in color, 10
combustible (*m.*)   fuel, 11
comedia (*f.*)   comedy, 6
comedor (*m.*)   dining room, 2
comenzar (ie)   to start, begin, 3
comer   to eat, 2; **¿Qué desean comer?**   What would you like to eat?, 3
cómico/a   funny, 1, 6
comida (*f.*)   food; dinner/lunch, 3
¿cómo?   how?, P; **¿Cómo está usted?/¿Cómo estás tú?**   How are you?, P; **¿Cómo se dice...?**   How do you say . . . ?, P; **¿Cómo se llama usted?/¿Cómo te llamas?**   What's your name?, P; **¿Cómo se llega a...?**   How does one get to . . . ?, 7
cómoda (*f.*) dresser, 2
cómodo/a   comfortable, 5
compacto/a   compact, 9
compañero/a (de clase/de cuarto) (*m., f.*)   classmate, roommate, P
compartir   to share, 2
competencia (*f.*)   competition
completo/a   complete, 2
componer   to compose
comportamiento (*m.*)   behavior, 11

composición (*f.*)   composition, 1
comprador/a (*m., f.*)   buyer, 7
comprar   to buy, 2
compras: ir de compras   to go shopping, 7
comprender   to understand, 2
computador/a (*m., f.*)   computer, 1; **computadora portátil** (*f.*)   laptop, 9
comunidad (*f.*)   community, 11
con   with, 2, 4; **con desayuno** with breakfast, 5; **con media pensión**   with two meals, 5; **Con permiso.**   Excuse me., P; **con tal (de) que**   provided that, 10; **con vista al mar**   with an ocean view, 5
concernir (ie)   to concern, 3
concierto (*m.*)   concert, 6
condenar   to condemn
conducir (zc)   to drive, 3, 9
conductor/a (*m., f.*)   driver, 9
conejo (*m.*)   rabbit, 4
conexión (sin cables) (*f.*)   (wireless) connection (WiFi), 9
confirmación (*f.*)   confirmation, 5
confirmar   to confirm, 5
confundido/a   confused, 2
conjunto (*m.*)   group, band, 6
conocer (zc)   to know, be familiar with, 3
conquista (*f.*)   conquest, 12
consecuencia (*f.*)   consequence, 11
conseguir (i, i)   to get, obtain, 3
consejero/a (*m., f.*)   counselor, 4
consejo (*m.*)   advice, 11
conserje (*m., f.*)   concierge, 5
conservar   to conserve, preserve, 11
conservarse (sano/a)   to keep oneself (healthy), 8
construir   to construct, build, 2
consultorio médico (*m.*)   doctor's office, 8
consumir   to consume, 8
consumo (*m.*)   consumption, 11
contador/a (*m., f.*)   accountant, 4
contaminación (*f.*)   pollution, contamination, 11
contaminar   to pollute, contaminate, 11
contar (ue)   to count, 3; to tell
contener   to contain, 3
contento/a   happy, 2; **estar contento/a de**   to be happy, 8
contestar   to answer, 4
contraseña (*f.*)   password, 9
contraste (*m.*)   contrast, 10
contribuir   to contribute
control remoto (*m.*)   remote control, 9
convertir (ie, i)   to change, convert, 11

convivir   to live with, 10
copa (*f.*)   stemmed glass, goblet, 3
copiar   to copy, 9
coraje (*m.*)   anger
corazón (*m.*)   heart, 8
corbata (*f.*)   tie, 7
correo (*m.*)   post office, 2; **correo electrónico** e-mail, 9
correr   to run, 2
corrida de toros (*f.*)   bullfight
corto/a   short (length), 1
cosecha (*f.*)   harvest
costar (ue)   to cost, 3; **¿Cuánto cuesta... ?**   How much does . . . cost?, 5
costumbre (*f.*)   custom, 10
crear   to create, 10
creatividad (*f.*)   creativity
creativo/a   creative
crecimiento (*m.*)   growth, 12
creer   to think, believe, 2, 8; **no creer**   to not believe, 8
criado/a (*m., f.*)   servant, maid, 4
crimen (*m.*)   crime, 11
crítica (*f.*)   criticism, 6
criticar   to criticize, 6
crucero (*m.*)   cruise ship, 3
cruz (*f.*)   cross, 10
cruzar   to cross, 7
cuaderno (*m.*)   notebook, 1
cuadra (*f.*)   street block, 7
cuadro (*m.*)   painting, picture, 10
¿cuál?   which?, what?, P
cualquier (*adj.*)   any
cuando   when, 9
¿cuándo?   when?, P
cuanto: en cuanto   as soon as, 9
¿cuánto/a/s?   how much?, how many?, P; **¿A cuánto está la temperatura?**   What is the temperature?, 3; **¿Cuánto cuesta... ?** How much does . . . cost?, 5; **¿En cuánto me lo(s)/la(s) deja?**   How much will you charge me for it/them?, 7
cuarenta   forty, 1
cuarto/a   fourth
cuarto (*m.*)   quarter (of an hour), 1
cuarto de baño (*m.*)   bathroom, 2
cuatro   four, 1
cuchara (*f.*)   tablespoon, 3
cucharadita (*f.*)   teaspoon, 3
cuchillo (*m.*)   knife, 3
cuenta (*f.*)   bill, 3; **La cuenta, por favor.**   The check, please., 3
cuerpo (*m.*)   body, 8
cuidado: tener cuidado   to be careful, 3, 7
cuidarse   to take care of oneself, 8
culebra (*f.*)   snake

culpable (*m., f.*) guilty one
cumpleaños (*m.*) birthday
cuñado/a (*m., f.*) brother-in-law/
sister-in-law, 4
cura (*f.*) cure, 11; (*m.*) priest
curandero/a (*m., f.*) healer, 8
curar to cure, 8

D

dañar to harm, 8; to injure; to
damage, 9
dar to give, 3, 4; **dar la vuelta** to
turn around, 7; **dar un paseo** to
take a walk, 2
de of, from, 1, 4; **de acción**
action (*adj.*), 6; **de amor** love
(*adj.*), 6; **de ciencia ficción**
science fiction (*adj.*), 6; **de habla
española** Spanish-speaking, 12;
de horror, de terror horror
(*adj.*), 6; **de la mañana/tarde/
noche** in the morning/after-
noon/evening (for specific time
periods), 1; **de misterio** mystery
(*adj.*), 6; **De nada.** You're welcome., P; **de suspenso** thriller
(*adj.*), 6; **de vaqueros** western
(*adj.*), 6; **de vez en cuando** from
time to time, 4
debajo de beneath, under, 4
deber to owe, 4; should, 4
debido a because of
decaer to decline, 12
decidir to decide, 2
decir (i) to say, tell, 3; **¿Cómo se
dice...?** How do you say . . . ?,
P; **¿Qué quiere decir...?** What
does . . . mean?, P
dedo (*m.*) finger, 8; **dedo del pie**
toe, 8
definición (*f.*) definition; **alta
definición** high definition, 9
deforestación (*f.*) deforestation, 11
dejar to leave (something
behind), 3
del (de + el) of the, 2
delante de in front of, 4
delectivo: acto delectivo (*m.*)
delinquent act, 11
delfín (*m.*) dolphin, 11
delgado/a thin, 1
delincuencia (*f.*) delinquency, 11
delincuente (*m., f.*) delinquent, 11
dentista (*m., f.*) dentist, 4
dentro de inside of, 4
depender to depend, 8
dependiente (*m., f.*) store clerk, 7
deporte (*m.*) sport, 6

deportista (*m., f.*) athlete; sports
enthusiast, 6
deportivo (*m.*) sports car, 9
depresión (*f.*) depression, 11
deprimido/a depressed, 2
derecha: a la (mano) derecha on
the right(hand side), 7
derecho (*m.*) law, right; **seguir
derecho** to go straight, 7
desafiar to challenge
desagradable unpleasant, 1
desamparados (*m. pl.*) homeless
people, 11
desamparo (*m.*) trouble,
helplessness
desaparición (*f.*) disappearance
desarrollado/a developed, 12
desarrollar to develop
desastre (*m.*) disaster
desayunar to have breakfast, 3
desayuno (*m.*) breakfast, 3; **con
desayuno** with breakfast, 5
descansar to rest, 5
descendiente (*m., f.*) descendant, 12
desconocido/a unknown
describir to describe, 2
desde from, since, 4; **desde ahora**
from now on
desear to wish for, 2; to want, 8;
¿Qué desean comer/beber?
What would you like to eat/
drink?, 3
desechado/a discarded,
disposed, 11
desechar to dispose, discard, 11
desembarque (*m.*) unloading, 5
desempeñar to carry out, 9
desempleo (*m.*) unemployment, 11
desesperado: estar desesperado/a
to be desperate, 11
desfile (*m.*) parade, 10
desilusionado/a disappointed, 2
despacio slowly, 7; **más despacio**
more slowly, P
despedida (*f.*) farewell, 5
despedir (i, i) to fire (from a job)
despedirse (i, i) to say good-bye, 5
desperdicios nucleares (*m. pl.*)
nuclear waste, 11
despertador (*m.*) alarm clock, 5
despertarse (ie) to wake up, 3
después after, afterwards, 3;
después de after, 4; **después (de)
que** after, 9
destacar(se) to stand out, 12
destruir to destroy, 2
detalle (*m.*) detail, 10
deterioro (*m.*) deterioration, 11
detrás de behind, 4

devolver (ue) to return (something), 7
día (*m.*) day, 1
diariamente daily, 8
dibujante (*m., f.*) illustrator, 10
dibujar to draw, 10
dibujo (*m.*) drawing, 10
diciembre (*m.*) December, 1
dictador (*m.*) dictator
dictadura (*f.*) dictatorship
diente (*m.*) tooth, 3, 8
dieta (*f.*) diet, 8
diez ten, 1
difícil difficult, 1
digital digital, 9
dinero money; **cambio de dinero**
(*m.*) money exchange, 5; **(dinero
en) efectivo** (*m.*) cash, 5; **¿Dónde
puedo cambiar el dinero?** Where
can I exchange money?, 5
dióxido de carbono (*m.*) carbon
dioxide, 11
dirección (*f.*) address, 3, 7
director (*m.*) director, 6
directorio (*m.*) directory, 9
dirigir to direct, 6
disco (*m.*) record, album, 7; **disco
compacto, CD** compact disc,
CD, 6; **disco duro** hard drive, 9
discoteca (*f.*) discotheque, 5
discurso (*m.*) speech
diseñador/a (*m., f.*) designer
diseñar to design
diseño (*m.*) design
disfraz (*m.*) costume, 10
disfrutar to enjoy, 3; **¡Qué
disfrute/n de su estadía!** Enjoy
your stay!, 5
disponible available, 9
distinguir(se) to distinguish, 12
distinguido/a distinguished
divertirse (ie, i) to have a good
time, enjoy oneself, 3
divorciado: estar divorciado/a to
be divorced, 4
doblar (a) to fold, to bend,
to turn, 7
doble double, 5
doce twelve, 1
doctor/a (*m., f.*) doctor, P
documento (*m.*) document, 9
doler (ue) to hurt, 8
dolor (*m.*) pain; **tener dolor** to
have pain, 8
domingo (*m.*) Sunday, 1
don (D.) (*m.*) title of respect with
first name, P
¿dónde? where?, P; **¿Dónde puedo
cambiar el dinero?** Where can I
exchange money?, 5; **¿Me puede**

decir dónde está/n... ? Can you tell me where . . . is/are?, 7

doña (Dña.) (*f.*) title of respect with first name, P

dorado/a golden, 10

dormir (ue, u) to sleep, 3; **dormirse (ue, u)** to fall asleep, 3

dormitorio (*m.*) bedroom, 1, 2

dos two, 1

drama (*m.*) drama, 6

dramaturgo/a (*m., f.*) playwright

drogadicción (*f.*) drug addiction, 11

ducha (*f.*) shower, 2

ducharse to take a shower, 3

duda doubt; **no hay duda (de)** there's no doubt, 8

dudar to doubt, 8; **no dudar** to not doubt, 8

dueño/a (*m., f.*) owner, 2

dulce sweet, 3

durante during, 4

E

ecológico/a ecological, 11

economía (*f.*) economics, 1

económico/a economical, 9

edificio (*m.*) building, 2

efectivo: (dinero en) efectivo (*m.*) cash, 5

efecto invernadero (*m.*) greenhouse effect, 11

ejemplo (*m.*) example

ejercicio: hacer ejercicio to exercise, 2

el (*m.*) the, 1

él (*m.*) he, him, 1, 4

electricista (*m., f.*) electrician, 4

elefante (*m.*) elephant, 11

elegancia (*f.*) elegance, 5

elegir (i, i) to choose

elevador (*m.*) elevator, 5

ella (*f.*) she, her, 1, 4

ellos/as (*m., f.*) they, them, 1, 4

embarazada: estar embarazada to be pregnant, 8

embarazo (*m.*) pregnancy, 11

embarque (*m.*) loading, 5

emocionado/a excited, 2

empeorar to worsen

empezar (ie) to begin, 3

empleo (*m.*) employment, 11

en in, on, at, 1; by (with transportation), in, on, at, 3, 4; **en blanco y negro** (in) black and white, 10; **en caso de que** in case, 10; **en color(es)** in color, 10; **en cuanto** as soon as, 9; **en este momento** at this moment,

now, 2; **en grupos** in groups, P; **en línea** online, 9; **en oferta** on sale, 7; **en parejas** in pairs, P

enamorado/a in love, 2; **estar enamorado/a** to be in love, 4

enamorarse (de) to fall in love (with), 4

encantar to delight, like very much (love), 4

encarcelar to imprison, 11

encender (ie) to turn on, 9

encima de on top of, above, 4

encontrar (ue) to find, 3; **encontrarse (con)** to meet (with) someone, 5

encuesta (*f.*) survey

energía (*f.*) energy, 11

enero (*m.*) January, 1

enfermarse to get sick, 8

enfermedad (*f.*) illness, 8

enfermero/a (*m., f.*) nurse, 4

enfermo/a sick, 2

enfoque (*m.*) focus

enfrentar to confront, face up to, 11

enfrente de in front of, facing, 4

enojado/a angry, 2

enojarse to be angry, 8

enorme enormous, huge

ensalada (mixta/rusa) (*f.*) (mixed/potato) salad, 3

ensayo (*m.*) essay

enseñar to teach, 4

entender (ie) to understand, 3

enterrar (ie) to bury

entonces then, at that time, 3

entrada (*f.*) ticket, 6

entrar to enter, 9

entre between, among, 4

entregar to hand in, deliver, 4

entremés (*m.*) appetizer, 3

entrenador/a (*m., f.*) trainer, 6

entrenar to train, 6

entretener to entertain, 3

entretenimiento (*m.*) entertainment, 9

entusiasmado/a enthusiastic, 2

enviar to send, 4

envidioso/a envious, 1

equilibrio (*m.*) balance

equipaje (*m.*) luggage, 5

equipo (*m.*) team; equipment, 6

escaleras (*f. pl.*) stairs, 2

escalofríos: tener escalofríos to shiver, have a chill, 8

escapar to escape

escaparate (*m.*) store window, 7

escaso/a scarce, 11

escena (*f.*) scene, 6

escoba (*f.*) broom, 2

escolar scholastic

esconder to hide

escribir to write, 2; **escribir cartas** to write letters, 2

escritor/a (*m., f.*) writer

escritorio (*m.*) desk, 1

escritura (*f.*) writing, 12

escuchar to listen, 2

escuela (*f.*) school, 1

escultor/a (*m., f.*) sculptor, 4, 10

escultura (*f.*) sculpture, 10

ese/a (*adj.*) that, 3

ése/a, eso (*pron.*) that (one), 3

esencial: es esencial it's essential, 8

esmeralda (*f.*) emerald, 7

esos/as (*adj.*) those, 3

ésos/as (*pron.*) those (ones), 3

espalda (*f.*) back, 8

español (*m.*) Spanish language, 1

español/a Spanish, 1

especialización (*f.*) major, 1

especie (*f.*) species, 11

espectador/a (*m., f.*) spectator, 6

espejo (*m.*) mirror, 2; **espejo retrovisor** rear-view mirror, 9

esperanza (*f.*) hope

esperar to hope, 8

espíritu (*m.*) spirit

esposo/a (*m., f.*) husband/wife, 4

esquí (*m.*) ski; skiing, 6; **hacer esquí acuático** to water ski, 5

esquiar to ski, 6

esquina (*f.*) corner, 7

estable stable, firm

estación de tren (*f.*) train station, 2

estacionamiento (*m.*) parking lot, 5

estacionar to park, 7

estadía (*f.*) stay; **¡Qué disfrute/n de su estadía!** Enjoy your stay!, 5

estadio (*m.*) stadium, 2

estancia (*f.*) stay, 5

estante (*m.*) bookshelf, 1

estar to be, 2; **estar a punto de** to be on the verge of, 5; **estar cerca/lejos (de)** to be close/far away (from), 3; **estar de acuerdo** to agree, 5; **estar de moda** to be in style, 7; **estar muerto/a de hambre** to be starving, famished, 3; **estar resfriado/a** to have a cold, 8; **estar de vacaciones** to be on vacation, 5

estatua (*f.*) statue, 10

estatura (*f.*) stature

este (*m.*) east, 3

este/a (*adj.*) this, 3

éste/a, esto (*pron.*) this (one), 3

estilo (*m.*) style

estómago (*m.*) stomach, 8

estornudar to sneeze, 8

estos/as (*adj.*)   these, 3
éstos/as (*pron.*)   these (ones), 3
estrecho/a   tight, 7
estrenar   to premiere, 6
estuco (*m.*)   stucco
estudiante (*m., f.*)   student, P
estudiar   to study, 2
estufa (*f.*)   stove, 2
etnia (*f.*) ethnic group
étnico/a   ethnic, 12
europeo/a   European
evidente: (no) es evidente   it's (not) evident, 8
evitar   to avoid, 8
examen físico (*m.*)   physical exam, 8
excepcional   exceptional, 1
excursión (*f.*)   excursion, tour, 5
exhibición (*f.*)   exhibition, art exhibit, performance, 10
existencia (*f.*)   existence, 11
éxito: tener éxito   to be successful, 3
exitoso/a   successful
explicar   to explain, 4
exploración (*f.*)   exploration, 12
explotar   to exploit, 11
exposición (*f.*)   art exhibit, 10
extinción (*f.*)   extinction, 11
extranjero/a   foreign, 6
extraño/a   strange, 8

F

fabricar   to make, 10
fácil easy, 1
facultad (*f.*)   School (as in School of Humanities), 1
falda (*f.*)   skirt, 7
faltar   to lack, need; to be left (to do), 4
fama (*f.*)   fame, 6
fanático/a (*m., f.*)   fan, 6
farmacia (*f.*)   pharmacy, 7
fascinado/a   fascinated, 2
fascinante   fascinating, 1
fascinar   to fascinate, 4
fauna (*f.*)   animal life
fax (*m.*)   fax, 9
febrero (*m.*)   February, 1
fecha (*f.*)   date, 1
feliz happy; **¡Feliz viaje!**   Have a nice trip!, 5
feo/a   ugly, 1
festejarse   to celebrate, 10
festival (*m.*)   festival, 10
fiebre: tener fiebre   to have a fever, 8
figura (*f.*)   figure, 10
fijarse   to notice, pay attention

filmar   to film, 6
filme (*m.*)   film, 6
filosofía (*f.*)   philosophy, 1
finca (*f.*)   property; farm
física (*f.*)   physics, 1
físico/a   physical, 8
fisiología (*f.*)   physiology, 1
flamenco (*m.*)   Spanish-style music, 6
flan (*m.*)   baked egg custard, 3
flauta (*f.*)   flute, 6
flojo/a   lazy, 1; loose, 7
flor (*f.*)   flower
flora (*f.*)   flora
florería (*f.*)   florist, 7
folclórico/a, folklórico/a   folkloric, 10
folleto (*m.*)   brochure, 5
forma (*f.*)   form, 10
fotógrafo/a (*m., f.*)   photographer, 4
fracasar   to fail, 11
fractura (*f.*)   fracture, 8
fracturado/a   broken, fractured, 8
francés (*m.*)   French language, 1
francés/francesa   French, 1
freír (i, i)   to fry, 5
frenar   to brake, 9
frenos (*m.*)   brakes, 9
fresco: hace fresco   it's cool, 3
frijoles (*m.*)   beans
frío: hace frío   it's cold, 3; **tener frío** to be cold, 3
frito/a   fried, 3
fruta (*f.*)   fruit, 3
fuegos artificiales (*m. pl.*)   fireworks, 10
fuera de   outside of, 4
fuerte   strong, 3; **una comida fuerte**   heavy food, 3
función (*f.*)   function, 9
fundar   to found, 12
fútbol (*m.*)   soccer, 6; **fútbol americano**   football, 6

G

gabinete (*m.*)   closet
gafas de sol (*f. pl.*)   sunglasses, 5
galleta (*f.*)   cookie
gallo (*m.*)   rooster, 11
gamba (*f.*)   shrimp, 3
ganador/a (*m., f.*)   winner; earner
ganar   to win, 6
ganas: tener ganas de + *inf.*   to want to (do something); to feel like (doing something), 3
ganga (*f.*)   deal, bargain, 7
garaje (*m.*)   garage, 2
garganta (*f.*)   throat, 8
gasolina (*f.*)   gasoline, 9

gastar   to spend (money), 7
gato/a (*m., f.*)   cat, 4
gazpacho (*m.*)   cold vegetable soup, 3
gemelo/a (*m., f.*)   twin
género (*m.*)   genre, 6
gente (*f., s.*)   people, 2
gerente (*m., f.*)   manager, 4
gimnasia (*f.*)   gymnastics, 6
gimnasio (*m.*)   gym, 6
golf (*m.*)   golf, 6
gordo/a   fat, 1
gorra (*f.*)   cap, 7
gorro de baño (*m.*)   swim cap, 6
gozar (de)   to enjoy, 5
grabadora (*f.*)   recorder, 9
grabar   to tape, 6
grados centígrados/Fahrenheit (*m.*)   degrees centigrade/Fahrenheit, 3
grande   big, large, 1; loose (clothes), 7
gratis   free, 7
grave   grave, serious, 8
gripe: tener gripe   to have the flu, 8
gris   gray, 1
gritar   to shout
grupo (*m.*)   group, 6; **en grupos** in groups, P
guante (*m.*)   glove, baseball glove, 6, 7
guapo/a   handsome, good-looking, 1
guardar   to save; to file, 9
guerra (*f.*)   war, 11
guía (*m., f.*)   tour guide, 5; (*f.*) guidebook, 5
guión (*m.*)   script, 6
guionista (*m., f.*)   script writer
guitarra (*f.*)   guitar, 6; **guitarra bajo** bass guitar, 6
guitarrista (*m., f.*)   guitarrist, 6
gustar   to like (be pleasing), 2, 8; **Me gustaría (pedir)...**   I would like (to order) . . ., 3
gusto (*m.*)   pleasure; **El gusto es mío.**   The pleasure is mine., P; **¡Qué gusto!**   What a pleasure!, 5

H

haber (*auxiliary verb*)   to have, 9
hábil   skillful, 10
habitación (*f.*)   room, 5
habitado/a   inhabited, 12
habla: de habla española   Spanish-speaking, 12
hablar   to speak, 2, 4; **hablar con amigos**   to talk with friends, 2

hace: hace buen/mal tiempo it's good/bad weather, 3; **hace calor/frío/fresco** it's hot/cold/cool, 3; **hace viento** it's windy, 3

hacer to do; to make, 3; **hacer castillos de arena** to make sandcastles, 5; **hacer clic** to click (with the mouse); to push a button, 9; **hacer ejercicio** to exercise, 2; **hacer el papel** to play a role, 6; **hacer esquí acuático** to water ski, 5; **hacer surfing** to go surfing, 5; **hacer una cita** to make an appointment, 8; **hacer una llamada (de larga distancia/por cobrar)** to make a (long distance/collect) phone call, 5

hacia toward, 4

hallazgo (*m.*) finding, discovery

hambre (el) (*f.*) hunger, 3; **estar muerto/a de hambre** to be starving, famished, 3; **tener hambre** to be hungry, 3; **¡Tengo mucha hambre!** I am very hungry!, 3

harto/a fed up, disgusted, 2

hasta until, 4, 7; **Hasta la vista.** Until we meet again., P; **Hasta luego.** See you later., P; **Hasta mañana.** See you tomorrow., P; **hasta que** until, 9

hay there is, there are, 1; **no hay** there isn't; there aren't, 1; **no hay duda (de)** there's no doubt, 8

hecho (*m.*) event, 10

helado (de chocolate, vainilla, fresa) (*m.*) (chocolate, vanilla, strawberry) ice cream, 3

herencia (*f.*) heritage

hermanastro/a (*m., f.*) stepbrother/stepsister, 4

hermano/a (*m., f.*) brother/sister, 4

hermoso/a beautiful, 1

heroico/a heroic

híbrido/a hybrid, 9

hijastro/a (*m., f.*) stepson/stepdaughter, 4

hijo/a (*m., f.*) son/daughter, 4

hip-hop (*m.*) hip-hop, 6

historia (*f.*) history, 1

histórico/a historical, 10

hockey (*m.*) hockey, 6

hombre (*m.*) man, 1; **hombre de negocios** businessman, 4

hora (*f.*) hour; **¿Qué hora es?** What time is it?, 1

horario (*m.*) schedule, 1

horror: de horror horror (*adj.*), 6

hospital (*m.*) hospital, 2

hotel (*m.*) hotel, 2

hoy today, 1; **hoy en día** today; nowadays

huérfano/a (*m., f.*) orphan

hueso (*m.*) bone, 8

huésped (*m., f.*) guest, 5

huir to escape, 4

humanidades (*f. pl.*) humanities, 1

húmedo/a humid, 3

hundirse to drown

huracán (*m.*) hurricane, 3

I

icono (*m.*) icon, 9

idioma (*m.*) language, 1

igualdad (*f.*) equality

iglesia (*f.*) church, 2

Igualmente. Likewise., P

ilustración (*f.*) illustration, 10

ilustrar to illustrate, 10

imagen (*f.*) image, 10

imperio (*m.*) empire, 12

impermeable (*m.*) raincoat, 7

imponente imposing, 12

importante: es importante it's important, 8

importar to matter, be important, be of concern, 4

imposible: es imposible it's impossible, 8

impresora (*f.*) printer, 1

imprimir to print, 9

impuesto (*m.*) tax

inagotable inexhaustible

inalámbrico/a wireless, 9

incendio (*m.*) fire

incertidumbre (*f.*) uncertainty, 11

incierto/a uncertain

incluir to include, 2

indefinido/a indefinite

indígena indigenous

inesperado/a unexpected

infección (*f.*) infection, 8

inflamación (*f.*) inflammation, 8

inflamado/a: estar inflamado/a to be inflamed, 8

informe (*m.*) report

ingeniería (*f.*) engineering, 1

ingeniero/a (*m., f.*) engineer, 4

inglés (*m.*) English language, 1

inglés/inglesa English, 1

iniciar to begin, 9

inmenso/a immense, enormous

inodoro (*m.*) toilet, 2

inquietud (*f.*) worry

inquilino/a (*m., f.*) tenant, 2

instalar to install, 9

inteligente intelligent, 1

interesar to interest, be of interest, 4

---

interpretar to interpret, 6

intersección (*f.*) corner, 7

intrépido/a daring, fearless

invertir (ie, i) to invest

investigador/a (*m., f.*) researcher

investigar to research, 2

invierno (*m.*) winter, 3

inyección (*f.*) injection, 8

ir to go, 3; **ir de compras** to go shopping, 7; **ir de pesca** to go fishing, 5; **ir por** + person/thing to go for; to pick up, 6; **irse** to go away, leave, 3; **irse de vacaciones** to go on vacation, 5

isla (*f.*) island, 5

italiano (*m.*) Italian language, 1

italiano/a Italian, 1

izquierda: a la (mano) izquierda on the left(hand side), 7

J

jaguar (*m.*) jaguar, 7

jai alai (*m.*) jai alai, 6

jamás never, 4

japonés (*m.*) Japanese language, 1

japonés/japonesa Japanese, 1

jarabe (*m.*) syrup, 8

jardín (*m.*) garden, yard, 2

jardinero/a (*m., f.*) gardener, 4

jazz (*m.*) jazz, 6

jefe/a (*m., f.*) boss, 4

jeroglífico/a hieroglyphic, 12

joven young, 1

joya (*f.*) jewelry, 7

joyería (*f.*) jewelry store, 7

judío/a Jewish

jueves (*m.*) Thursday, 1

jugador/a (*m., f.*) player, 6

jugar (ue) (al) to play (a sport or game), 3, 6; **jugar (al) volibol** to play volleyball, 2, 5; **jugar un papel** to play a role, 6

jugo (*m.*) juice, 3

jugoso/a juicy

juguete (*m.*) toy, 7

julio (*m.*) July, 1

junio (*m.*) June, 1

junto a next to, 4

justicia (*f.*) justice, 11

juventud (*f.*) youth

juzgar to judge, 6

K

kilómetros (por hora) (*m.*) kilometers (per hour), 3

L

la (*f.*)   the

lado (*m.*)   side; **al lado de**   next to, side by side, 4; **(otro) lado**   somewhere else, 7

ladrillo (*m.*)   brick

ladrón/ladrona (*m., f.*)   thief

lago (*m.*)   lake

lamentar   to lament, regret, 8

lámpara (*f.*)   lamp, 1

lana (*f.*)   wool, 7

lápiz (*m.*)   pencil, 1

largo (*m.*)   length

largo/a   long, 1

largometraje (*m.*)   feature film, 6

lástima (*f.*)   shame; **es una lástima**   it's a shame, 8

lavabo (*m.*)   bathroom sink, 2

lavacoche (*m.*)   carwash

lavamanos (*m.*)   bathroom sink, 2

lavandería (*f.*)   laundromat, 7

lavar (los platos)   to wash (the dishes), 2

lección (*f.*)   lesson, 1

leer (libros)   to read (books), 2

legumbre (*f.*)   vegetable, 3

lejos (de)   far from, 4; **estar lejos (de)**   to be far away (from), 3

lengua (*f.*)   tongue, 8

lente (*m.*)   lens

lento/a   slow, 1

letra (*f.*)   lyrics, 6

levantarse   to get up, 3

libertad (*f.*)   liberty, 11

libre   free (independent), 5

librería (*f.*)   bookstore, 2, 7

libro (*m.*)   book, 1

licencia de manejar/conducir (*f.*)   driver's license, 9

lienzo (*m.*)   canvas, 10

ligero/a   light, 3

limón (*m.*)   lemon

limosina (*f.*)   limousine, 5

limpiaparabrisas (*m.*)   windshield wiper, 9

limpiar (el cuarto)   to clean, tidy (the room), 2

lindo/a   lovely, 1

línea: en línea   online, 9

lingüística (*f.*)   linguistics, 1

lingüístico/a   linguistic, 12

lío (*m.*)   problem, 11

listo/a   smart, clever, 1; **estar listo/a**   to be ready, 2

literatura (*f.*)   literature, 1

llamada: hacer una llamada (de larga distancia/por cobrar)   to make a (long distance/collect) phone call, 5

llamar   to call, 2; **¿Cómo se llama usted ?/¿Cómo te llamas?**   What's your name?, P; **Me llamo...**   My name is . . ., P

llamarse   to be named; to be called, P

llanta (*f.*)   tire, 9; **llanta pinchada**   flat tire, 9

llave (*f.*)   key, 1

llegar   to arrive, 2, 3; **¿Cómo se llega a... ?**   How does one get to . . . ?, 7

lleno/a   full

llevar   to bring, 2; to wear; to take, 7

llover (ue)   to rain

lloviznar   to drizzle (*weather*), 3

lluvia (*f.*)   rain, 3; **lluvia ácida**   acid rain, 11

lograr   to achieve; to obtain, 11

logro (*m.*)   achievement, 11

luchar   to fight, 11

luego   later, then, next, 3; **Hasta luego.**   See you later., P

lugar (*m.*)   place

lujo (*m.*)   luxury, 5

lujoso/a (de lujo)   luxurious, 5

lunes (*m.*)   Monday, 1

luz (*f.*)   light, 9; **luz y sombra**   light and shadow, 10

M

madera (*f.*)   wood, 7, 10

madrastra (*f.*)   stepmother, 4

madre (*f.*)   mother, 1, 4

madrina (*f.*)   godmother

maíz (*m.*)   corn

mal (*m.*)   disease; **estar mal**   to feel ill, P

maleta (*f.*)   suitcase, 5

maletero (*m.*)   trunk, 9

malo/a   bad, 1; **es malo**   it's bad, 8; **Muy mal, bastante mal.**   Very bad, quite bad., P

mamá (*f.*)   mom, 4

mancha (*f.*)   stain, 7

manchado/a   stained, 7

mandar   to send, 2; to order, 8

mandato (*m.*)   order

manejar   to drive, 3, 9

manguera (*f.*)   hose

mano (*f.*)   hand, 3, 8; **a mano**   by hand, 10

mantener   to maintain, 3

manzana (*f.*)   street block, 7

mañana   tomorrow, 1; **de/por la mañana**   in the morning, 1; **Hasta mañana.**   See you tomorrow., P

mapa (*m.*)   map, 1

maquillaje (*m.*)   makeup, 7

maquillarse   to put on makeup, 3

maravilla (*f.*)   wonder

marco (*m.*)   frame, 10

mareado: estar mareado/a   to be dizzy, 8

mariachi (*m.*)   mariachi musician, 6

marisco (*m.*)   shellfish, 3

mármol (*m.*)   marble, 10

martes (*m.*)   Tuesday, 1

marzo (*m.*)   March, 1

más   more; **más despacio**   more slowly, P

máscara (*f.*)   mask, 7

mascota (*f.*)   pet, 4

matar   to kill, 11

matemáticas (*f.*)   mathematics, 1

materia (*f.*)   subject matter, 1

mayo (*m.*)   May, 1

mayor   older, 1; **ser mayor**   to be older, 4

media (*f.*)   half (hour), 1; sock, stocking, 7

medianoche (*f.*)   midnight, 1

mediante   by means of

medicina (*f.*)   medicine, 8

médico/a (*m., f.*)   doctor, 4

medio/a (*adj.*)   half, 7; average; **en medio de**   in the middle of

mediodía (*m.*)   noon, 1

mejor: es mejor   it's better, 8

mejorar   to get better, 8

menor   younger; **ser menor**   to be younger, 4

menos   minus, 1

mensaje (*m.*)   message, 9

mentir (ie, i)   to lie, 3

menú (*m.*)   menu, 3

mercado (*m.*)   marketplace, 7

merecer (zc)   to deserve

merengue (*m.*)   Dominican-style music, 6

mesa (*f.*)   table, 1

mesero/a (*m., f.*)   waiter, waitress, 3

mesita (*f.*)   coffee table, 2; **mesita de noche**   night stand, 2

meteorólogo/a (*m., f.*)   meteorologist, 3

metro (*m.*)   subway, 3

mezcla (*f.*)   mix

mí   me (*direct object*), 4

mi(s)   my, 2

miedo   fear; **tener miedo (de)**   to be afraid (of), 3, 8

miedoso/a   fearful

miembro (*m.*)   member

mientras   while

miércoles (*m.*)   Wednesday, 1

milagro (*m.*)   miracle

millas (por hora) (*f.*)   miles (per hour), 3
minibar (*m.*)   mini bar, 5
mío/a(s) (*m., f.*)   mine, 7
mirada (*f.*)   glance
mirar   to look at, 2; **mirar una película**   to watch a movie, 2
miseria (*f.*)   poverty
misterio: de misterio   mystery (*adj.*), 6
mitad (*f.*)   half, 1
mochila (*f.*)   backpack, 1
moda: estar de moda   to be in style, 7
modelo (*m., f.*)   model, 10
módem (*m.*)   modem, 9
moderno/a   modern, 2
molestar   to bother, annoy, 4; **molestarle (a alguien)**   to bother (someone), 8
momento: en este momento   at this moment, now, 2
moneda: cambio de moneda (*m.*)   money exchange, 5
modista (*m., f.*)   designer
mono (*m.*)   monkey, 11
montaña (*f.*)   mountain
montar   to go, ride; **montar a caballo**   to go horseback riding, 5; **montar en bicicleta**   to go bicycling, 5
morado/a   purple, 1
moreno/a   dark-haired, 1
morir (ue, u)   to die, 3
mostrador (*m.*)   counter, 7
mostrar (ue)   to show, 3
motocicleta (*f.*)   motorcycle, 3
motor (*m.*)   motor, 9
mover (ue)   to move, shift, 9
movimiento (*m.*)   movement
mucho (*adv.*)   a lot, very much, 2; **mucho/a** (*adj.*)   a lot of, 2; **Mucho gusto.**   Pleased to meet you., P
muebles (*m. pl.*)   furniture; **sacudir los muebles**   to dust the furniture, 2
muerte (*f.*)   death, 10
muerto/a   dead; **estar muerto/a de hambre**   to be starving, famished, 3
mujer (*f.*)   woman, 1; **mujer de negocios**   businesswoman, 4
multa (*f.*)   fine, 9
multimedia   multimedia, 9
mural (*m.*)   mural, 10
murciélago (*m.*)   bat
músculo (*m.*)   muscle, 8
museo (*m.*)   museum, 2
música (*f.*)   music, 1

músico/a (*m., f.*)   musician, 4, 6
muy   very, 1; **Muy bien, gracias.** Very well, thank you., P; **Muy mal, bastante mal.**   Very bad, quite bad., P

N

nacer (zc)   to be born, 4
nada   nothing, 4; **casi nada**   nothing, 4; **Nada en particular.** Nothing special., P
nadar   to swim, 5
nadie   no one, nobody, 4
nariz (*f.*)   nose, 8
naranja (*f.*)   orange
narración (*f.*)   narration, 6
natación (*f.*)   swimming, 6
naturaleza muerta (*f.*)   still life, 10
náuseas: tener náuseas   to be nauseous, 8
navegar   to travel by boat; **navegar en velero**   to go sailing, 5; **navegar por Internet (la Red/la web)** to surf the Internet (Web), 2
necesario: es necesario   it's necessary, 8
necesitar   to need, 2, 8
negar (ie)   to deny, 8
negocio (*m.*)   business
negro/a   black, 1
nervioso/a   nervous, 2
nevado/a   snow-capped
nevar   to snow, 3
(ni)... ni   (neither) . . . nor, 4; **Ni idea.**   I haven't got a clue., 5; **ni siquiera**   not even
nieto/a (*m., f.*)   grandson/granddaughter, 4
nieve (*f.*)   snow, 3
ningún, ninguno/a   none, not any, 4
niñero/a (*m., f.*)   nanny, babysitter, 11
niñez (*f.*)   childhood
niño/a (*m., f.*)   little boy/girl (child), 4
nivel (*m.*)   level
noche (*f.*)   night, 1; **de/por la noche** in the evening, 1
nombre   name; **¿A nombre de quién?**   In whose name?, 5
nominación (*f.*)   nomination, 6
nominar   to nominate, 6
noreste (*m.*)   northeast, 3
noroeste (*m.*)   northwest, 3
norte (*m.*)   north, 3
nosotros/as   we, us, 1, 4
noticia (*f.*)   news item

noticiero (*m.*)   news program
novela (*f.*)   novel, 5
noventa   ninety, 1
noviazgo (*m.*)   courtship
noviembre (*m.*)   November, 1
novio/a (*m., f.*)   boyfriend/girlfriend, 4
nube (*f.*)   cloud, 3
nublado/a   cloudy; **está (parcialmente) nublado**   it's (partly) cloudy, 3
nuera (*f.*)   daughter-in-law, 4
nuestro/a(s) (*m., f.*)   our, 2, 7
nueve   nine, 1
nuevo/a   new, 1; **¿Qué hay de nuevo?**   What's new?, P
nunca   never, 4; **casi nunca**   almost never, 4
nutritivo/a   nutritious, 8

O

(o)... o   (either) . . . or, 4
obra de arte (*f.*)   work of art, 10
obrero/a (*m., f.*)   worker
obtener   to obtain, 11
obvio: es obvio   it's obvious, 8
ochenta   eighty, 1
ocho   eight, 1
octubre (*m.*)   October, 1
oeste (*m.*)   west, 3
oferta: en oferta   on sale, 7
oficina (*f.*)   office, 1, 2
ofrecer (zc)   to offer, 4
ofrenda (*f.*)   offering, 10
oído (*m.*)   ear (inner), 8
oír   to hear, 3
ojalá   I/we/let's hope so, 8
ojo (*m.*)   eye, 8; **¡Ojo!**   Be careful!, P
olor (*m.*)   odor
once   eleven, 1
operación (*f.*)   operation, 8
opinar   to think (have an opinion), 8
oprimir   to click (with the mouse); to push a button, 9
optimista   optimistic, 1
opuesto/a   opposite
oración (*f.*)   sentence
ordenar (el cuarto)   to clean, tidy (the room), 2
órdenes: ¡A sus órdenes!   At your service!, 3
oreja (*f.*)   ear (outer), 8
organizado/a   organized, 1
orilla (*f.*)   edge; shore
oro (*m.*)   gold, 7
oscuro/a   dark, 10
oso (panda) (*m.*)   (panda) bear, 11
otoño (*m.*)   autumn, fall, 3

otorgar to grant, give
otro lado (*m.*) somewhere else, 7
¡Oye! Hey!; Listen!, 5

P

paciente (*m., f.*) patient, 8
padrastro (*m.*) stepfather, 4
padre (*m.*) father, 1, 4
padrino (*m.*) godfather
paella (valenciana) (*f.*) rice, meat, and seafood dish (from Valencia), 3
pagar (por) to pay for, 4
paisaje (*m.*) landscape, countryside, 10
pájaro (*m.*) bird, 4
página (*f.*) page, P
país (*m.*) country
palabra (*f.*) word
paleta (*f.*) palette, 10
palidecer (zc) to turn pale
pálido/a pale
palo (*m.*) club; **palo de golf** golf club, 6; **palo de hockey** hockey stick, 6
pan (*m.*) bread, 3
pantalla (*f.*) screen, 6; **pantalla plana** flat screen, 9; **pantalla de plasma** plasma screen, 9
pantalones (*m. pl.*) pants, 7
papa (*f.*) potato, 3
papá (*m.*) dad, 4
papel (*m.*) paper, 1; role, 6; **hacer el papel** to play a role, 6
papelería (*f.*) stationery store; office supply store, 7
paquete (*m.*) package (*tour*), 5
par (*m.*) pair, 7
para for, to, in order to, 4; **estar para** + verb to be about to + verb, 6; **para nada** no way, not at all, 6; **para mí/ti** in my/your opinion; for me/you, 6; **para que** so that, 10; **para siempre** forever, 6
parabrisas (*m.*) windshield, 9
parada de autobús (*f.*) bus stop, 2
paraguas (*m.*) umbrella, 7
parar to stop, 7, 9
parecer (zc) to seem, appear to be, 3, 4
pared (*f.*) wall, 1
pareja (*f.*) pair, couple; **en parejas** in pairs, P
pariente (*m., f.*) family member, relative, 4
parlante (*m., f.*) speaker, 6
paro: en paro on strike
párrafo (*m.*) paragraph

partido (*m.*) game, 6
pasar to happen; to pass, 2; **pasar (por)** to pass (by), 6, 7; **pasar la aspiradora (por la alfombra)** to vacuum the rug, 2; **pasar una película** to show a movie, 6
pasearse to go for a walk, 5
pastilla (*f.*) pill, 8
patata (*f.*) potato, 3
patear to kick, 6
patinaje (*m.*) skating, 6
patín (*m.*) skate; **patines en línea** inline skates, 6; **patines para hielo** ice skates, 6
paz (*f.*) peace
pecho (*m.*) chest, 8
pedido (*m.*) order, 3
pedir (i, i) to ask for, request, 3, 8
peinarse to comb one's hair, 3
pelea de gallos (*f.*) cockfight
película (*f.*) movie, 6
peligro (*m.*) danger, 11
pelirrojo/a red-head, 1
pelo (*m.*) hair, 3, 8
pelota (*f.*) ball, 6
peluquero/a (*m., f.*) hair stylist, 4
pena (*f.*) sorrow; pain
pendiente (*m.*) pendant, 7; earring
pensar (ie) to think, 3; to think (opinion), 8
pensión: con media pensión with two meals, 5
peor: es peor it's worse, 8
pequeño/a small, 1; tight (clothes), 7
pera (*f.*) pear
percusión (*f.*) percussion, 6
perder (ie) to lose, 3, 6
pérdida (*f.*) loss
perdido/a lost, 12
Perdón. Pardon./Excuse me., P
perezoso/a lazy, 1
perfumería (*f.*) perfume store, 7
periodista (*m., f.*) journalist, 4
permanecer (zc) to remain, 10
permiso: Con permiso. Excuse me., P
pero but, 2
perro/a (*m., f.*) dog, 4
perseguir (i, i) to follow, pursue, 3
personaje (principal, secundario) (*m.*) (main, secondary) character, 6
pertenecer (zc) to belong, 12
pesar: a pesar de despite
pescado (*m.*) fish (*caught*), 3
pescar to fish; **ir de pesca** to go fishing, 5
pesimista pessimistic, 1
peso (*m.*) weight, 8

pianista (*m., f.*) pianist, 6
piano (*m.*) piano, 6
picante hot (spicy), 3
picnic (*m.*) picnic, 5
pie (*m.*) foot, 8; **a pie** on foot, 3
piedra (*f.*) stone, 7
piel (*f.*) skin
pierna (*f.*) leg, 8
pieza (*f.*) piece, 10
pila (*f.*) battery, 9
píldora (*f.*) pill, 8
pimienta (*f.*) (black) pepper, 3
pincel (*m.*) paintbrush, 10
pinchar la llanta to puncture the tire
pingüino (*m.*) penguin, 11
pintar to paint, 2, 10
pintor/a (*m., f.*) painter, 4, 10
pintura (*f.*) painting, 1, 10; **pintura al óleo** oil-painting, 10
piña (*f.*) pineapple
pirámide (*f.*) pyramid, 12
piscina (*f.*) swimming pool, 2
piso (*m.*) floor, apartment (*Spain*), 2; **barrer el piso** to sweep the floor, 2
pista (*f.*) ice rink; running track, 6
pitar to beep the horn, 9
pito (*m.*) horn, 9
pizarra (*f.*) chalkboard, 1
placa (*f.*) plate, 9
placer (*m.*) pleasure
planchar (la ropa) to iron (clothes), 2
planeta (*m.*) planet, 11
plata (*f.*) silver, 7
plato (*m.*) plate, dish, 3, 7
playa (*f.*) beach, 5
plaza (*f.*) plaza, 2
plena: en plena in the middle of
plomero/a (*m., f.*) plumber, 4
pluma (*f.*) pen, 1
población (*f.*) population, 12
pobreza (*f.*) poverty, 11
poco (*m.*) little, small amount; **un poco** a little, 2
poder (ue) to be able, 3
poder adquisitivo (*m.*) purchasing power, 12
poema (*m.*) poem
poesía (*f.*) poetry
poeta (*m., f.*) poet
policía (*m., f.*) police, 4, 11
poner to put, place, 3; **ponerse de pie** to stand up
popular popular, 1
popularidad (*f.*) popularity
por for, by means of, 4; **por ciento** percent, 3; **por ejemplo** for example, 6; **por favor** please, P, 6;

por fin   finally, 3, 6; **por la mañana/tarde/noche**   in the morning/afternoon/night (for general time periods), 1; **por lo menos**   at least, 6; **por lo tanto**   therefore, 6; **por supuesto**   of course, 5, 6
porcentaje (*m.*)   percentage, 3
porción (*f.*)   portion, 8
porque   because, P
¿por qué?   why, P
portero (*m.*)   doorman
portugués (*m.*)   Portuguese language, 1
portugués/portuguesa   Portuguese, 1
posible: es posible   it's possible, 8
postre (*m.*)   dessert
practicar   to practice, 2, 6; **practicar deportes**   to play sports, 2
precio (*m.*)   price, 7; **a un precio más bajo**   at a lower price, 7
preciso: es preciso   it's necessary, 8
predecir   to predict
preferible: es preferible   it's preferable, 8
preferir (ie, i)   to prefer, 3, 8
pregunta (*f.*)   question, P
preguntar   to ask, 2
premio (*m.*)   prize, 12
prendedor (*m.*)   pin, brooch, 7
prender   to turn on, 9
preocupado/a   worried, 2
preocupar(se)   to worry, 3, 4, 8
preparado/a   prepared, 3
presentar una película   to show a movie , 6
presidente/a (*m., f.*)   president, 4
presión (sanguínea) (*f.*)   blood pressure, 8
presionar   to click (with the mouse); to push a button, 9
prestar   to lend, 4
primavera (*f.*)   spring, 3
primer/o/a (*m.*)   first, 1, 3; **primera clase** (*f.*)   first class, 5
primo/a (*m., f.*)   cousin, 4
principio (*m.*)   beginning
prisa: tener prisa   to be in a hurry, 3
prisión (*f.*)   prison, 11
privado/a   private, 2
probabilidad (*f.*)   probability, 3
probable: es probable   it's probable, 8
probar (ue)   to try, taste, 3; **probarse (ue)**   to try on, 7
problema (*m.*)   problem, 1
producir (zc)   to produce, 3
profesor/a (*m., f.*)   professor, P, 4
profesorado (*m.*)   faculty, 1

programa (*m.*)   program, 9; **programa social** (*m.*)   social program, 11
programador/a de computadoras (*m., f.*)   computer programmer, 4
prohibir   to prohibit
promedio (*m.*)   average, 3
pronosticar   to predict, 12
pronóstico del tiempo (*m.*)   weather forecast, 3
propina (*f.*)   tip, 3
propio/a   own
propósito (*m.*)   resolution, purpose, intention, 10
protagonista (*m., f.*)   main character, 6
protector solar (*m.*)   sunscreen, 5
protegerse   to protect oneself, 5
provocar   to cause
prueba (*f.*)   test, exam, 8
psicología (*f.*)   psychology, 1
psicólogo/a (*m., f.*)   psychologist, 4
público/a   public, 10
pueblo (*m.*)   town, people
puede ser   it can be, 8
puerta (*f.*)   door, 1, 9
pulmón (*m.*)   lung, 8
pulsar   to click (with the mouse); to push a button, 9
pulsera (*f.*)   bracelet, 7
pupitre (*m.*)   writing desk, 1

Q

¿qué?   what?, P; **¿Qué quiere decir... ?**   What does . . . mean?, P; **¿Qué tal?**   How's it going?, P
quedar   to be (located), 3; **quedarle (a alguien)**   to fit (someone), 7; **quedarse**   to stay, 3
quehacer (*m.*)   chore
quemar   to burn; **quemarse**   to get a sunburn, 5
querer (ie)   to want, 3, 8; **¿Qué quiere decir... ?**   What does . . . mean?, P; **Quisiera (pedir)...**   I would like (to order) . . . , 3
queso (*m.*)   cheese, 3
¿quién?   who?, P; **¿A nombre de quién?**   In whose name?, 5
química (*f.*)   chemistry, 1
quince   fifteen, 1
quitarse (la ropa)   to take off (one's clothes), 3
quizás   maybe, perhaps, 8

R

radio (*m., f.*)   radio, 1, 5
radiografía (*f.*)   X-ray, 8

raíz (*f.*)   root
ranchera (*f.*)   Mexican-style music, 6
rápido/a   fast, 1
raqueta (*f.*)   tennis racket, 6
ratón (*m.*)   mouse, 9
razón (*f.*)   reason; **tener razón**   to be right, 3
realidad (virtual) (*f.*)   (virtual) reality, 9
realista   realistic
rebaja (*f.*)   discount, 7
rebajar   to lower (a price), 7
recámara (*f.*)   bedroom
recepción (*f.*)   reception, 5
recepcionista (*m., f.*)   receptionist, 4, 5
receta (*f.*)   prescription, 8
recibir   to receive, 2
recibo (*m.*)   receipt, 7
recipiente (*m.*)   container, 7
recoger   to pick up; to get, 5
recomendar (ie)   to recommend, 3, 8; **¿Qué nos recomienda?**   What do you recommend?, 3
recordar (ue)   to remember, 3
recreo (*m.*)   recreation, 5
recto/a   straight; **seguir recto**   to go straight, 7
recuerdo (*m.*)   memory
recurso (*m.*)   resource, 11
red (*f.*)   network, 9
reducir (zc)   to reduce, 5, 8
reflejar   to reflect
refresco (*m.*)   soft drink, 3
refrigerador/a (*m., f.*)   refrigerator, 2
regalar   to give (gifts), 4
regatear   to bargain, 7
regateo (*m.*)   bargaining, 7
registrar   to register, 5
regla (*f.*)   rule, P
regresar   to return
regular   OK, P
reír (i, i)   to laugh, 5
religioso/a   religious, 10
reloj (*m.*)   watch, clock, 1
remedio (*m.*)   remedy, 8; **remedio casero**   home remedy; **tener remedio**   to have a solution, 11
renta (*f.*)   rent, 2
repente: de repente   suddenly
repetir (i, i)   to repeat, P, 3
réplica (*f.*)   replica, 10
reproductor MP3 (*m.*)   MP3 player, 6
reseña (*f.*)   review, 6
reseñar   to review, 6
reservación (*f.*)   reservation, 5
reservar   to reserve, 5
resfriado: estar resfriado/a   to have a cold, 8

resfrío: tener resfrío to have a cold, 8
residencia (*f.*) dormitory, 1
respirar to breathe, 8
responder to answer, 2
responsabilidad (*f.*) responsibility, 11
restaurante (*m.*) restaurant, 2
resumen (*m.*) summary
retrato (*m.*) portrait, 10
reunirse (con) to meet (with) someone, 5
reusar to reuse, 11
revista (*f.*) magazine
rey (*m.*) king
rico/a rich, delicious, 3
ridículo: es ridículo it's ridiculous, 8
riesgo (*m.*) risk
río (*m.*) river
riqueza (*f.*) wealth
ritmo (*m.*) rhythm, 6
rito (*m.*) rite; ritual, 10
robo (*m.*) robbery, 11
robot (*m.*) robot, 9
rock (*m.*) rock, 6
rodeado/a de surrounded by
rodilla (*f.*) knee, 8
rogar (ue) to beg, plead, 8
rojo/a red, 1
romántico/a romantic, 1, 6
romper(se) (el brazo) to break (one's arm), 8
ropa (*f., s.*) clothes, clothing; **ropa de gimnasia** (*f.*) gymwear, 6; **ropa interior** (*f.*) underwear, 7
ropero (*m.*) wardrobe, 2
rosa (*f.*) rose, 1
rosado/a pink, 1
roto/a ripped, broken 7
rubio/a blond(e), 1
rueda (*f.*) wheel, 9
ruina (*f.*) ruin, 12
ruta (*f.*) route, 3

S

sábado (*m.*) Saturday, 1
saber to know, 3; **No sé.** I don't know., P; **saber a** to taste like
sabor (*m.*) taste; flavor
sabroso/a delicious, tasty, 3
sacar to take (away), to take out; **sacar la basura** to take out the garbage, 2; **sacar el polvo de (los muebles)** (*Spain*) to dust (the furniture), 2
saco (*m.*) jacket, blazer, 7
sacudir (los muebles) to dust (the furniture), 2

sal (*f.*) salt, 3
sala (*f.*) living room, 2; **sala de clase** classroom, 1; **sala de conferencias** conference room, 5; **sala de emergencia** emergency room, 8
salir to go out, leave, 3
salón (*m.*) living room; **salón de conferencias** conference room, 5
salsa (*f.*) salsa (music), 6
salud (*f.*) health; **tener buena/ mala salud** to be in good/bad health, 8
salvar to save (rescue), 11
sandalia (*f.*) sandal, 5
sandía (*f.*) watermelon
sangrar to bleed, 8
sangre (*f.*) blood, 8
sangría (*f.*) wine. fruit, and soda drink, 3
sano/a healthy, 8
saxofón (*m.*) saxphone, 6
secador/a de pelo (*m., f.*) hair dryer, 2
secar (los platos, la ropa) to dry (the dishes, clothes), 2; **secarse** to dry off, 3
seco/a dry, 3
secretario/a (*m., f.*) secretary, 4
secuencia (*f.*) sequence, 6
secuestrar to kidnap
secuestro (*m.*) kidnapping
sed (*f.*) thirst; **tener sed** to be thirsty, 3
seda (*f.*) silk, 7
sedentario/a sedentary, 8
seguir (i, i) to follow, continue, 3; **seguir derecho/recto** to go straight, 7
según according to, 4
segundo/a second; **segunda clase** (*f.*) second class, 5
seguro/a sure, 2; **no es seguro** it's not sure, 8; **(no) estar seguro/a de** to be (un)sure, 8
seguro médico (*m.*) health insurance, 11
seis six, 1
semáforo (*m.*) stoplight, 7
semilla (*f.*) seed
sencillo/a single (room or bed), 5
sentarse (ie) to sit down, 3
sentido (*m.*) sense; **tener sentido** to make sense, 3
sentir (ie, i) to be sorry, regret, 8; **sentirse (ie, i)** to feel, 3
señor (Sr.) (*m.*) Mr., P
señora (Sra.) (*f.*) Mrs., P
señorita (Srta.) (*f.*) Miss, P

separado/a: estar separado/a to be separated, 4
septiembre (*m.*) September, 1
ser to be, 1; **ser alérgico/a a...** to be allergic to . . ., 8; **ser mayor** to be older, 4; **ser menor** to be younger, 4; **ser soltero/a** to be single, 4
ser humano (*m.*) human being
serio/a serious, 1
servir (i, i) to serve, 3; **¿En qué le(s) puedo servir?** How can I help you?, 5
sesenta sixty, 1
setenta seventy, 1
sí yes; **Sí, cómo no.** Of course., P
SIDA (*m.*) AIDS, 11
siempre always, 4; **casi siempre** almost always, 4
siento: Lo siento. I'm sorry., P, 5
siete seven, 1
siglo (*m.*) century, 12
significar to mean, 10
silla (*f.*) chair, 1
sillón (*m.*) armchair, 2
simbolizar to simbolize
simpático/a nice, friendly, 1
sin without, 4; **sin embargo** nevertheless, 12; **sin que** without, 10
sino, sino que but (rather), 12
sinopsis (*f.*) synopsis, 6
síntoma (*m.*) symptom, 8
sistema (*m.*) system, 1
sobre on, on top of, 4; about, over, on top of
sobrepasar to exceed
sobrino/a (*m., f.*) nephew/niece, 4
sociología (*f.*) sociology, 1
sofá (*m.*) sofa, 2
sol (*m.*) sun
soldado/a (*m., f.*) soldier
solo/a alone
sólo only
soltero: ser soltero/a to be single, 4
solución (*f.*) solution, 11
solucionar to solve
sombra: luz y sombra (*f.*) light and shadow, 10
sombrero (*m.*) hat, 5, 7
sombrilla (*f.*) parasol, beach umbrella, 5
someter to subdue
sonido (*m.*) sound
sonreír (i, i) to smile, 5
soñar (ue) (con) to dream (about), 3
sopa (*f.*) soup, 3; **sopa de pollo** chicken soup
soroche (*m.*) altitude sickness, 8
sorprender to surprise, 8

su(s) your (*formal*), his, her, their, 2
subir to climb, 2; **subir (por)** to go up (a street), 7
suceder to occur, 6
sucio/a dirty, 7
sudadera (*f.*) sweatsuit, sweatshirt, 7
sudamericano/a South American
suegro/a (*m., f.*) father-in-law/mother-in-law, 4
suelo (*m.*) ground
sueño (*m.*) dream; **tener sueño** to be sleepy, tired, 3
suéter (*m.*) sweater, 7
sufrimiento (*m.*) suffering
sugerir (ie, i) to suggest, 5, 8
sujeto (*m.*) subject, 1
sur (*m.*) south, 3
sureste (*m.*) southeast, 3
suroeste (*m.*) southwest, 3
surfing: hacer surfing to go surfing, 5
suspenso: de suspenso thriller (*adj.*), 6
sustantivo (*m.*) noun
suyo/a (*m., f.*) yours, his, hers, theirs, 7

T

táctil pertaining to touch, tactile, 9
tal vez maybe, perhaps, 8
talla (*f.*) size, 7
tamaño (*m.*) size
también also, too, P, 4
tambor (*m.*) drum, 6
tampoco neither, either, 4
tan... como as . . . as, 7; **tan pronto como** as soon as, 9
tango (*m.*) tango, 6
tanque de gasolina (*m.*) gas tank, 9
tapa (*f.*) small serving of food (*Spain*), 3
tapado/a covered
tapete (*m.*) rug, 7
tapiz (*m.*) tapestry, 7
taquilla (*f.*) box office, 6
taquillero/a box office draw/hit, 6
tarde (*f.*) afternoon, 1; **de/por la tarde** in the afternoon/evening, 1
tarifa (*f.*) rate, fare, tariff, 5
tarjeta de crédito (*f.*) credit card, 5; **tarjeta postal** (*f.*) postcard
taxi (*m.*) taxi, 3
taza (*f.*) cup, 3
té (*m.*) tea, 3
teatro (*m.*) theater, 1
teclado (*m.*) keyboard, 9
tejedor/a (*m., f.*) weaver, 12
tejido (*m.*) weaving, 7

teléfono (*m.*) telephone, 1; **teléfono celular** cell phone, 9
telenovela (*f.*) soap opera
televisión (*f.*) television, 1
tema (*m.*) theme, 1
temblar (ie) to tremble
temer to fear, be afraid of, 8
temperatura (mínima/máxima) (*f.*) (minimum/maximum) temperature, 3; **¿A cuánto está la temperatura?** What is the temperature?, 3
templo (*m.*) temple, 12
tenedor (*m.*) fork, 3
tener to have, 3; **tener apetito** to have an appetite, 8; **tener buena/mala salud** to be in good/bad health, 8; **tener calor** to be hot, feel hot, 3; **tener catarro, resfrío** to have a cold, 8; **tener cuidado** to be careful, 3, 7; **tener dolor** to have pain, 8; **tener escalofríos** to shiver, have a chill, 8; **tener éxito** to be successful, 3; **tener fiebre** to have a fever, 8; **tener frío** to be cold, 3; **tener ganas de + *inf.*** to want to (do something), to feel like (doing something), 3; **tener gripe** to have the flu, 8; **tener hambre** to be hungry, 3; **tener miedo (de)** to be afraid (of), 3, 8; **tener náuseas** to be nauseous, 8; **tener prisa** to be in a hurry, 3; **tener que + *inf.*** to have to (do something), 3; **tener razón** to be right, 3; **tener remedio** to have a solution, 11; **tener sed** to be thirsty, 3; **tener sentido** to make sense, 3; **tener sueño** to be sleepy, tired, 3; **tener tos** to have a cough, 8; **tener X años** to be (X) years old, 3
tenis (*m.*) tennis, 6
teñir (i, i) to dye
terapia (*f.*) therapy, 11
terminar to finish, 2
terraza (*f.*) terrace, 2
terremoto (*m.*) earthquake
terrible: es terrible it's terrible, 8
terror: de terror horror (*adj.*), 6
terrorismo (*m.*) terrorism, 11
terrorista (*m., f.*) terrorist, 11
ti you (*direct object*), 4
tiempo (*m.*) time; **hace buen/mal tiempo** it's good/bad weather, 3; **tiempo libre** free time, 5
tienda (*f.*) store, 2
tierra (*f.*) Earth; land
tigre (*m.*) tiger, 11
tímido/a shy, timid, 1
tina (*f.*) bathtub, 2

tintorería (*f.*) dry cleaner, 7
tío/a (*m., f.*) uncle/aunt, 4
tira cómica (*f.*) comic strip
tiza (*f.*) chalk, 1
toalla (*f.*) towel, 5
tobillo (*m.*) ankle, 8
tocar to play (an instrument), 2, 6
todavía yet, 9
todo everything, 4; **todo el mundo** everybody, everyone, 4; **todos los días** every day, 4
tomar to take; to drink, 2, 3; **tomar el sol** to sunbathe, 5
torcer(se) (el tobillo) to twist, sprain (one's ankle), 8
tormenta (*f.*) storm, 3
tornado (*m.*) tornado, 3
toronja (*f.*) grapefruit
torre (*f.*) tower
tortilla española (*f.*) omelette with potatoes and onions (*Spain*), 3
tortuga (*f.*) turtle, 4
tos: tener tos to have a cough, 8
toser to cough, 8
tour (*m.*) excursion, tour, 5
trabajador/a hard-working, 1
trabajador/a (*m., f.*) worker, 4; **trabajador/a social** social worker, 11
trabajar to work, 2
trabajo social (*m.*) social work, 1
tradición (*f.*) tradition, 10
traducir (zc) to translate, 3
traer to bring, 3, 4
tráfico de drogas (*m.*) drug trafficking, 11
traje (*m.*) suit, 7; **traje de baño** bathing suit, 5
trama (*f.*) plot, 6
transporte (*m.*) transportation, 5
traslado (*m.*) transfer, 5
tratamiento (*m.*) treatment
tratar de to deal with, treat, 6; **tratarse de** to deal with; to be about, 11
trazar to design
trece thirteen, 1
treinta thirty, 1
tren (*m.*) train, 3
tres three, 1
triste sad, 2
tristeza (*f.*) sadness
triunfar to succeed, 11
trompeta (*f.*) trumpet, 6
tronada (*f.*) storm, 3
truco (*m.*) trick
tu(s) your, 2
tú you, 1; **¿y tú?** and you?, P
turista (*m., f.*) tourist, 3
turquesa (*f.*) turquoise, 7
tuyo/a (*m., f.*) yours, 7

U

unidad (*f.*) unit, P
uniforme (*m.*) uniform, 6
universidad (*f.*) university, 1
uno one, 1
urgente: es urgente it's urgent, 8
usar to use, 2
usted(es) you, 1, 4; **¿y usted?** and you?, P
uva (*f.*) grape

V

vaca (*f.*) cow
vacación (*f.*) vacation, 5; **estar/irse de vacaciones** to be/go on vacation, 5
vacuna (*f.*) vaccine, 8
valer la pena to be worth it
valioso/a valuable
¡Vamos! /¡Vámonos! Let's go!, P
vapor (*m.*) mist
vaquero: de vaqueros western (*adj.*), 6
variado/a assorted, 3
variedad (*f.*) variety
vasija (*f.*) vase, 10
vaso (*m.*) glass (for drinks), 3
vecindario (*m.*) neighborhood
veinte twenty, 1
vejez (*f.*) old age
velocidad: alta velocidad (*f.*) high speed, 9
vencer to defeat, 12

venda (*f.*) bandage, 8
vendar to bandage, 8
vendedor/a (*m., f.*) salesperson, 4; seller, 7; **vendedor/a ambulante** street vendor
vender to sell, 4
venir to come, 3
ventana (*f.*) window, 1
ver to see, 3; **ver televisión** to watch television, 2
verano (*m.*) summer, 3
verdad true; **(no) es verdad** it's (not) true, 8; **¿Verdad?** Really?, P
verdadero/a true
verde green, 1
vestido (*m.*) dress, 7; **vestido de baño** (*m.*) swimwear, 6
vestirse (i, i) to get dressed, 3
veterinario/a (*m., f.*) veterinarian, 4
vez: algunas veces sometimes, 4; **de vez en cuando** from time to time, 4; **muchas veces** many times, 4
viajar to travel, 2, 3
viaje (*m.*) trip, 3; **agente de viajes** (*m., f.*) travel agent, 4; **¡Buen viaje!/¡Feliz viaje!** Have a nice trip!, 5
viajero/a (*m., f.*) traveler
videocámara (*f.*) videocamera, 9
videograbadora (*f.*) video recorder, 9
videojuego (*m.*) video game, 9
viejo/a old, 1
viento: hace viento it's windy, 3
viernes (*m.*) Friday, 1

vigilar to watch
vino (tinto/blanco) (*m.*) (red/white) wine, 3
violín (*m.*) violin, 6
visitar to visit, 2
vista (*f.*) view, 5; **Hasta la vista.** Until we meet again., P
vivir to live, 2
volcán (*m.*) volcano
volante (*m.*) steering wheel, 9
voluntario/a (*m., f.*) volunteer, 11
volver (ue) to return, 3; **volverse** to become, 6; **volverse la espalda** to turn one's back
vomitar to vomit, 8
vosotros/as (*m., f. pl.*) you (*Spain*), 1, 4
voz (*f.*) voice, 6
vuestro/a (*m., f.*) your (*Spain*), 2, 7

Y

y and, 1
ya already, 9
yerno (*m.*) son-in-law, 4
yeso (*m.*) cast, 8
yo I, 1

Z

zapatería (*f.*) shoe store, 7
zapato (*m.*) shoe, 7; **zapatos de tenis** (*m.*) sneakers, tennis shoes, 6
zumo (*m.*) juice, 3

English-Spanish Vocabulary

A

above encima de, sobre, 4
accelerate acelerar, 7
accelerator acelerador (*m.*), 9
access acceder, 9
accommodations alojamiento (*m.*), 5
according to según, 4
accordion acordión (*f.*), 6
accountant contador/a (*m., f.*), 4
achieve lograr, 11
achievement logro (*m.*), 11
acid rain lluvia ácida (*f.*), 11
act actuar, 6
acting actuación (*f.*), 6
action de acción (*adj.*), 6
active activo/a, 8
activity actividad (*f.*), P
actor actor (*m.*), 6
actress actriz (*f.*), 6
add agregar, añadir
addiction adicción (*f.*), 11
address dirección (*f.*), 3, 7
adjective adjetivo (*m.*)
adolescent adolescente (*m., f.*), 11
adornment adorno (*m.*), 10
advance adelanto (*m.*)
advice consejo (*m.*), 11
advise avisar, 5; aconsejar, 8
after después (de), 4; después (de) que, 9
afternoon tarde (*f.*), 1; **Good afternoon** Buenas tardes., P
afterwards después, 3
agent agente (*m., f.*), 5; **travel agent** agente de viajes, 4
agree estar de acuerdo, 5
AIDS SIDA (*m.*), 11
air aire (m.); **air conditioner** aire acondicionado (*m.*), 9
airbag bolsa de aire (*f.*), airbag (*m.*), 9
airline aerolínea (*f.*), 5
airport aeropuerto (*m.*), 2
alarm clock despertador (*m.*), 5
album disco (*m.*), 7
almond almendra (*f.*)
almost always/never/nothing casi siempre/nunca/nada, 4
alone solo/a
already ya, 9
also también, P, 4
although aunque, 9
altitude sickness soroche (*m.*), 8
always siempre, 4
among entre, 4

anatomy anatomía (*f.*), 1
and y, 1
angel ángel (*m.*)
anger coraje (*m.*); enojo (*m.*)
angry enojado/a, 2
ankle tobillo (*m.*), 8
announcement anuncio (*m.*)
annoy molestar, 4
answer contestar, P, 4; responder, 2
anthropology antropología (*f.*), 1
antibiotic antibiótico (*m.*), 8
any algún, alguno/a/os/as, 4
anything algo, 4
apartment apartamento (*m.*), 2; piso (*m.*) (*Spain*), 2
apparatus aparato (*m.*), 9
appear to be parecer (zc), 4; aparecer (zc)
appetizer aperitivo (*m.*), entremés (*m.*), 3
application aplicación (*f.*), 9
appointment cita (*f.*), 8
approach acercarse
April abril (*m.*), 1
archaeologist arqueólogo/a (*m., f.*), 4
archaeology arqueología (*f.*), 1
architect arquitecto/a (*m., f.*), 4
arm brazo (*m.*), 8
armchair sillón (*m.*), 2
around alrededor
arrest arrestar, 11
arrive llegar, 2, 3
art (arts) arte (*m.*) (las artes) (*f. pl.*), 1; **classic, contemporary, modern, abstract art** arte clásico, contemporáneo, moderno, abstracto (*m.*), 10; **art exhibit** exposición (*f.*), exhibición (*f.*), 10
article artículo (*m.*)
artisan artesano/a (*m., f.*), 10
artist artista (*m., f.*), 1, 4, 10
as soon as en cuanto, tan pronto como, 9
ask preguntar, P, 2; **ask for** pedir (i, i), 3, 8
aspirin aspirina (*f.*), 8
assassinate asesinar, 11
assassination asesinato (*m.*), 11
assorted variado/a, 3
at en; **at a lower price** a un precio más bajo, 7; **at that time** entonces, 3; **at this moment** en este momento, 2; **at times** a veces, 4; **At your service!** ¡A sus órdenes!, 3
athlete atleta (*m., f.*), 4; deportista (*m., f.*), 6

atmosphere ambiente (*f.*)
attend to atender (ie), 5
attitude actitud (*f.*)
attorney abogado (*m., f.*), 4
attractive atractivo/a, 1
August agosto (*m.*), 1
aunt tía (*f.*), 4
automated teller machine (ATM) cajero automático (*m.*), 5
automatic automático/a, 9
automobile coche (*m.*), auto(móvil) (*m.*), carro (*m.*), 3, 9
autumn otoño (*m.*), 3
available disponible, 9
average promedio (*m.*), 3
avoid evitar, 8

B

baby bebé (*m., f.*), 4
baby-sitter niñero/a (*m., f.*), 11
back espalda (*f.*), 8
backpack mochila (*f.*), 1
bad malo/a, 1; **it's bad** es malo, 8; **Very bad, quite bad.** Muy mal, bastante mal., P
bag bolsa (*f.*), 7
balcony balcón (*m.*), 2
ball pelota (*f.*), balón (*m.*), 6; **beach ball** balón (*m.*), 5
ballad balada (*f.*), 6
band banda (*f.*), conjunto (*m.*), 6
bandage venda (*f.*), 8; vendar, 8
bar: (mini) bar minibar (*m.*), 5
bargain ganga (*f.*), 7; regatear, 7
bargaining regateo (*m.*), 7
baseball béisbol (*m.*), 6
baseball bat bate (*m.*), 6
basket, wicker basket cesta (*f.*), 6
basketball básquetbol (*m.*), baloncesto (*m.*), 6
bass guitar guitarra bajo (*f.*), 6
bathing suit traje de baño (*m.*), 5
bathroom (cuarto de) baño (*m.*), 2
bathtub bañera (*f.*), tina (*f.*), 2
battery batería (*f.*), pila (*f.*), 9
be ser, 1; estar, 2; **be able** poder (ue), 3; **be about** tratarse de, 11; **be afraid (of)** tener miedo (de), 3, 8; temer, 8; **be allergic to ...** ser alérgico/a a..., tener alergia a..., 8; **be angry** enojarse, 8; **be born** nacer (zc), 4; **be careful** tener cuidado, 7; **be close/far away (from)** estar cerca/lejos (de), 3; **be desperate** estar

desesperado/a, 11; **be divorced** estar divorciado/a, 4; **be dizzy** estar mareado/a, 8; **be familiar with** conocer (zc), 3; **be hungry** tener hambre, 3; **be important/ of concern** importar, 4; **be in a hurry** tener prisa, 3; **be in good/bad health** tener buena/mala salud, 8; **be in style** estar de moda, 7; **be inflamed** estar inflamado/a, 8; **be located** quedar, 3; **be nauseous** tener náuseas, 8; **be on the verge of** estar a punto de, 5; **be pregnant** estar embarazada, 8; **be right** tener razón, 3; **be separated** estar separado/a, 4; **be sorry** sentir (ie, i), 8; **be successful** tener éxito, 3; **be sure** estar seguro/a de, 8; **be unsure** no estar seguro/a de, 8; **be X years old** tener X años, 3
beach playa (f.), 5; **beach umbrella** sombrilla (f.), 5
beans frijoles (m.)
beautiful hermoso/a, 1; bello/a, 5
beauty belleza (f.)
become volverse (ue), 6
bed cama (f.), 1
bedroom dormitorio (m.), 1, 2; alcoba (f.)
bee abeja (f.)
beep the horn pitar, 9
beer cerveza (f.), 3
before antes (de) (que), 4, 10
beg rogar (ue), 8
begin comenzar (ie), empezar (ie), 3; iniciar, 9
behavior comportamiento (m.), 11
behind detrás de, 4
believe creer, 2, 8
belong pertenecer (zc), 12
belt cinturón (m.), 7
beneath debajo de, 4
benefit beneficio (m.), 11
better: it's better es mejor, 8
between entre, 4
bicycle bicicleta (f.), 3, 6
big grande, 1
biking ciclismo (m.), 6
bill cuenta (f.), 3
biology biología (f.), 1
bird pájaro (m.), 4
birthday cumpleaños (m.)
black negro/a, 1; **black and white** en blanco y negro, 10
blazer saco (m.), 7
bleed sangrar, 8
blond(e) rubio/a, 1

blood sangre (f.), 8; **blood pressure** presión sanguínea (f.), 8
blouse blusa (f.), 7
blue azul, 1
blues blues (music) (m. pl.), 6
boat barco (m.), 3
body cuerpo (m.), 8
bone hueso (m.), 8
book libro (m.), 1
bookshelf estante (m.), 1
bookstore librería (f.), 2, 7
boot bota (f.), 7
bored aburrido/a, 2
boss jefe/a (m., f.), 4
bother (someone) molestar (a alguien), 8
boutique boutique (m.), 7
box office taquilla (f.), 6; **box office draw/hit** taquillero/a, 6
boxing boxeo (m.), 6
boy chico (m.), P, 4; niño (m.), 4
boyfriend novio (m.), 4
bracelet pulsera (f.), 7
brain cerebro (m.), 8
brake frenar, 9; freno (m.), 9
bread pan (m.), 3
break (one's arm) romper(se) (el brazo), 8
breakfast desayuno (m.), 3
breathe respirar, 8
breeze brisa (f.), 3
bring llevar, 2; traer, 3, 4
brochure folleto (m.), 5
broken fracturado/a, 8
bronze bronce (m.), 10
brooch prendedor (m.), 7
broom escoba (f.), 2
brother hermano (m.), 4
brother-in-law cuñado (m.), 4
brown café, 1; marrón, castaño (hair)
brush cepillarse, 3
buckle up (seatbelt) abrocharse (el cinturón), 9
build construir, 2
building edificio (m.), 2
bullfight corrida de toros (f.)
bus autobús (m.), 3; camión (m.) (Mex.), 3
bus stop parada de autobús (f.), 2
businessman hombre de negocios (m.), 4
businesswoman mujer de negocios (f.), 4
but pero, 2; (*rather*) sino, sino que, 12
button botón (m.), 9
buy comprar, 2
buyer comprador/a (m., f.), 7

by (*with transportation*) en, 3; **by hand** a mano, 10; **by means of** por, 4
Bye. Chao., P

C

café café (m.), 2
calculator calculadora (f.), 1
calendar calendario (m.), 1
call llamar, 2; **to be called** llamarse, P
calm calmado/a, 2
calorie caloría (f.), 8
camera cámara (f.), 9
canvas lienzo (m.), 10
cap gorra (f.), 7
car auto (m.), automóvil (m.), carro (m.), coche (m.), 3, 9
carbon dioxide dióxido de carbono (m.), 11
careful: Be careful! ¡Ojo!, P
Caribbean caribeño/a; Caribe (m.)
carpenter carpintero/a (m., f.), 4
carry out desempeñar, 9
cash (dinero en) efectivo (m.), 5
cash register caja (f.), 7
castanet castañuela (f.), 6
cast yeso (m.), 8
cat gato/a (m., f.), 4
catch agarrar
catch up with alcanzar, 3
category categoría (f.), 6
celebrate celebrar, festejar, 10
cell phone teléfono celular (m.), 9
century siglo (m.), 12
ceramic cerámica (f.), 10
ceramist ceramista (m., f.), 10
ceremony ceremonia (f.), 10
certain: it's (not) certain (no) es cierto, 8
certainty certeza (f.)
chair silla (f.), 1
chalk tiza (f.), 1
chalkboard pizarra (f.), 1
challenge desafiar
change convertir, 11
character (main, secondary) personaje (principal, secundario) (m.), 6; **main character** protagonista (m., f.), 6
charge cargar, 9
chauffeur chofer (m.) (Lat. Am.), chófer (m.) (Spain), 3
check revisar: **The check, please.** La cuenta, por favor., 3
cheese queso (m.), 3
chemistry química (f.), 1
chest pecho (m.), 8

Chinese chino/a, 1; (*language*) chino (*m.*), 1

church iglesia (*f.*), 2

city ciudad (*f.*), 2

class clase (*f.*), P

classmate compañero/a de clase (*m., f.*), P

classroom sala de clase (*f.*), 1

clay arcilla (*f.*), barro (*m.*), 7, 10

clean (the room) limpiar/ordenar (el cuarto), 2

clear: it's (not) clear (no) está claro, 8

clerk (store) dependiente (*m., f.*), 7

clever listo/a, 1

click (with the mouse) presionar, hacer clic, pulsar, oprimir, 9

climate clima (*m.*), 3

climb subir, 2

clock reloj (*m.*), 1

close cerrar (ie), 3

close (to) cerca (de), 4

closet clóset (*m.*), 2; ropero (*m.*), 2

cloud nube (*f.*), 3

cloudy: it's (partly) cloudy está (parcialmente) nublado, 3

club (nightclub) club (*m.*), 5

coat abrigo (*m.*), 7

codex códice (*m.*), 12

coffee café (*m.*), 3

cold frío/a; **be cold** tener frío, 3; **it's cold** hace frío, 3

collector coleccionista (*m., f.*), 10

collide chocar, 9

color en color(es) (*adj.*), 10

comb (one's hair) peinar(se) (el pelo), 3

come venir, 3

comedy comedia (*f.*), 6

comfortable cómodo/a, 5

community comunidad (*f.*), 11

compact compacto/a, 9

compact disc, CD disco compacto, CD (*m.*), 6

competition competencia (*f.*)

complete completo/a, 2

composition composición (*f.*), 1

computer computador/a (*m., f.*), 1

computer file archivo (*m.*), 9

computer programmer programador/a de computadoras (*m., f.*), 4

concern concernir (ie), 3

concert concierto (*m.*), 6

concierge conserje (*m., f.*), 5

condemn condenar

conference room salón/sala de conferencias (*m., f.*), 5

confirm confirmar, 5

confirmation confirmación (*f.*), 5

confront enfrentar, 11

confused confundido/a, 2

conquest conquista (*f.*), 12

consequence consecuencia (*f.*), 11

conserve conservar, 11

construct construir, 2

consume consumir, 8

consumption consumo (*m.*), 11

contain contener, 3

container recipiente (*m.*), 7

contaminate contaminar, 11

contamination contaminación (*f.*), 11

continue seguir (i, i), 3

contrast contraste (*m.*), 10

contribute contribuir

convert convertir (ie, i), 11

cook cocinar, 2

cook cocinero/a (*m., f.*), 4

cool: it's cool hace fresco, 3

copper cobre (*m.*), 7

copy copiar, 9

corner esquina (*f.*), intersección (*f.*), 7

cost costar (ue), 3

costume disfraz (*m.*), 10

cotton algodón (*m.*), 7

cough toser, 8; tos (*f.*), 8

counselor consejero/a (*m., f.*), 4

count contar (ue), 3

counter mostrador (*m.*), 7

court cancha (*f.*), 6

cousin primo/a (*m., f.*), 4

craft artesanía (*f.*), 7,

crash choque (*m.*), 9

create crear, 10

creative creativo/a

creativity creatividad (*f.*)

credit card tarjeta de crédito (*f.*), 5

crime crimen (*m.*), 11

criticism crítica (*f.*), 6

criticize criticar, 6

cross cruz (*f.*), 10

cross cruzar, 7

cruise ship crucero (*m.*), 3

cup taza (*f.*), 3

cure cura (*f.*), 11; curar, 8

custard: baked egg custard flan (*m.*), 3

custom costumbre (*f.*), 10

customer cliente (*m., f.*), 7

D

dad papá (*m.*), 4

daily diariamente, 8

damage dañar, 9

dance bailar, 2, 6

dancer bailarín/ina (*m., f.*), 6; bailador/a (*m., f.*)

danger peligro (*m.*), 11

dark oscuro/a, 10

dark-haired moreno/a, 1

date fecha (*f.*), 1

daughter hija (*f.*), 4

daughter-in-law nuera (*f.*), 4

day día (*m.*), 1

deal ganga (*f.*), 7

deal with tratarse de, 11

death muerte (*f.*), 10

December diciembre (*m.*), 1

decide decidir, 2

decline decaer, 12

decoration adorno (*m.*), 10

defeat vencer, 12

definition definición (*f.*); **high definition** alta definición, 9

deforestation deforestación (*f.*), 11

degrees centigrade/Fahrenheit grados centígrados/Fahrenheit (*m.*), 3

delicious sabroso/a, rico/a, 3

delight encantar, 4

delinquency delincuencia (*f.*), 11

delinquent delincuente (*m., f.*), 11

delinquent act acto delectivo (*m.*), 11

deliver entregar, 4

dentist dentista (*m., f.*), 4

deny negar (ie), 8

department store almacén (*m.*), 2, 7

depend depender, 8

depressed deprimido/a, 2

depression depresión (*f.*), 11

descendent descendiente (*m., f.*), 12

describe describir, 2

design diseñar; diseño (*m.*);

designer diseñador/a (*m., f.*)

desk escritorio (*m.*), pupitre (*m.*), 1

destroy destruir, 2

detail detalle (*m.*), 10

deterioration deterioro (*m.*), 11

develop desarrollar

developed desarrollado/a, 12

dictator dictador (*m.*); **dictatorship** dictadura (*f.*)

die morir (ue, u), 3

diet dieta (*f.*), 8

difficult difícil, 1

digital digital, 9

dining room comedor (*m.*), 2

dinner cena (*f.*), 3; (*in some places*) comida (*f.*), 3

direct dirigir, 6

director/a director (*m., f.*), 6

directory directorio (*m.*), 9

dirty sucio/a, 7

disappointed desilusionado/a, 2

disaster desastre (*m.*)
discard desechar, 11
discarded desechado/a, 11
discotheque discoteca (*f.*), 5
discount rebaja (*f.*), 7
disgusted harto/a, 2
dish plato (*m.*), 3, 7
dislike (*a person*) caer mal, 4
dispose desechar, 11
disposed desechado/a, 11
distinguish distinguir(se), 12;
　distinguished distinguido/a
do hacer, 3
doctor médico/a, doctor/a
　(*m., f.*), 4
doctor's office consultorio médico
　(*m.*), 8
document documento (*m.*), 9
dog perro/a (*m., f.*), 4
dolphin delfín (*m.*), 11
Dominican-style music merengue
　(*m.*), 6
door puerta (*f.*), 1, 9
dormitory residencia (*f.*), 1
double doble, 5
doubt dudar, 8; **there's no doubt**
　no hay duda (de), 8
download bajar, 9
downpour aguacero (*m.*), chubasco
　(*m.*), 3
drama drama (*m.*), 6
draw dibujar, 10
drawing dibujo (*m.*), 10
dream (about) soñar (ue) (con), 3
dress vestido (*m.*), 7
dresser cómoda (*f.*), 2
drink beber, 2; **soft drink** refresco
　(*m.*), 3
drive conducir (zc), manejar, 3, 9
driver conductor/a (*m., f.*), 9
driver's license licencia de
　manejar/conducir (*f.*), 9
drizzle (*weather*) lloviznar, 3
drug addiction drogadicción
　(*f.*), 11
drug trafficking tráfico de drogas
　(*m.*), 11
drum tambor (*m.*), 6; **drum set**
　batería (*f.*), 6
drunk borracho/a, 2
dry seco/a, 3
dry (the dishes, clothes) secar (los
　platos, la ropa), 2; **dry off**
　secarse, 3
dry cleaner tintorería (*f.*), 7
during durante, 4
dust (the furniture) sacudir (los
　muebles), sacar el polvo de (los
　muebles) (*Spain*), 2
dye teñir (i, i)

ear (*outer*) oreja (*f.*), 8; (*inner*)
　oído (*m.*), 8
earring arete (*m.*), 7
earth tierra (*f.*)
earthquake terremoto (m.)
east este (*m.*), 3
eat comer, 2
ecological ecológico/a, 11
economical económico/a, 9
economics economía (*f.*), 1
eight ocho, 1
eighty ochenta, 1
either tampoco, 4; **either . . . or**
　o... o, 4
electrician electricista (*m., f.*), 4
elegance elegancia (*f.*), 5
elephant elefante (*m.*), 11
elevator ascensor (*m.*), elevador
　(*m.*), 5
eleven once, 1
e-mail correo electrónico (*m.*), 9
embrace abrazar, 4
emerald esmeralda (*f.*), 7
emergency room sala de emergen-
　cia (*f.*), 8
empire imperio (*m.*), 12
employment empleo (*m.*), 11
energy energía (*f.*), 11
engineer ingeniero/a (*m., f.*), 4
engineering ingeniería (*f.*), 1
English inglés/inglesa; (*language*)
　inglés (*m.*), 1
enjoy disfrutar, 3; gozar (de), 5;
　enjoy oneself divertirse (ie, i), 3;
　Enjoy your stay! ¡Qué disfrute/n
　de su estadía!, 5
enter entrar, 9
entertain entretener, 3
entertainment entretenimiento
　(*m.*), 9
enthusiastic entusiasmado/a, 2
envious envidioso/a, 1
equipment equipo (*m.*), 6
eraser: chalkboard eraser
　borrador (*m.*), 1
escape huir, 4
essential: it's essential es esencial, 8
ethnic étnico/a, 12
even though, even if a pesar de
　que, 9; **even when, even though,**
　even if aunque, 9
evening noche, (*f.*), P; **Good**
　evening./Good night. Buenas
　noches., P
event acontecimiento (*m.*), 6;
　hecho (*m.*), 10
every day todos los días, 4

everybody, everyone todo el
　mundo, 4
everything todo, 4
evident: it's (not) evident (no) es
　evidente, 8
exam prueba (*f.*), análisis (*m.*), 8;
　physical exam examen físico
　(*m.*), 8
example ejemplo (*m.*)
exceptional excepcional, 1
excited emocionado/a, 2
excursion excursión (*f.*), tour (*f.*), 5
Excuse me. Con permiso.,
　Perdón., P
exercise hacer ejercicio, 2
exhibition exhibición (*f.*), 10
existence existencia (*f.*), 11
expensive caro/a, 2
explain explicar, 4
exploit explotar, 11
exploration exploración (*f.*), 12
extinction extinción (*f.*), 11
eye ojo (*m.*), 8

face cara (*f.*), 3, 8
face up to enfrentar, 11
faculty profesorado (*m.*), 1
fail fracasar, 11
fall caer, 4; **fall asleep** dormirse
　(ue, u), 3; **fall in love (with)**
　enamorarse (de), 4
fall otoño (*m.*), 3
fame fama (*f.*), 6
family member pariente (*m., f.*), 4
fan aficionado/a (*m., f.*), fanático/a
　(*m., f.*), 6
far (from) lejos (de), 4
fare tarifa (*f.*), 5
farewell despedida (*f.*), 5
fascinate fascinar, 4
fascinated fascinado/a, 2
fascinating fascinante, 1
fast rápido/a, 1
fat gordo/a, 1
father padre (*m.*), 1, 4
father-in-law suegro (*m.*), 4
fax fax (*m.*), 9
fear temer, 8
February febrero (*m.*), 1
fed up harto/a, 2
feel sentirse (ie, i), 3; **feel like**
　(*doing something*) tener ganas
　de + (*inf.*), 3
festival festival (*m.*), 10
field cancha (*f.*), 6
fifteen quince, 1
fifty cincuenta, 1

figure figura (*f.*), 10; cifra (*f.*), 12
file archivar, guardar, 9
film filmar, 6; filme (*m.*), 6; **feature film** largometraje (*m.*), 6
finally por fin, 3
find encontrar (ue), 3; **find out** averiguar, 5
fine multa (*f.*), 9
finger dedo (*m.*), 8
finish terminar, acabar, 2
fire (from a job) despedir (i, i)
firefighter bombero/a (*m., f.*), 4
fireworks fuegos artificiales (*m. pl.*), 10
first primero (*m.*), 1; primero/a (*adj.*), 3; **first class** primera clase (*f.*), 5
fish pescar, 5; (*caught*) pescado (*m.*), 3
fit (someone) quedar(le) (a alguien), 7
five cinco, 1
fix up (the bed) arreglar (la cama), 2
flat tire llanta pinchada (*f.*), 9
floor piso (*m.*), 2
florist florería (*f.*), 7
flute flauta (*f.*), 6
folder carpeta (*f.*), 1
folkloric folclórico/a, folklórico/a, 10
follow perseguir (i, i), seguir (i, i), 3
food alimento (*m.*), 8; comida (*f.*), 3; alimentación
foot pie (*m.*), 8
football fútbol americano (*m.*), 6
for a, para, por, 4
foreign extranjero/a, 6
forest bosque (*m.*)
fork tenedor (*m.*), 3
form forma (*f.*), 10
forty cuarenta, 1
found fundar, 12
four cuatro, 1
fourteen catorce, 1
fracture fractura (*f.*), 8
fractured fracturado/a, 8
frame marco (*m.*), 10
free gratis, 7; (*independent*) libre, 5; **free time** tiempo libre (*m.*), 5
freedom libertad (*f.*), 11
French francés/francesa; (*language*) francés (*m.*), 1
Friday viernes (*m.*), 1
fried frito/a, 3
friend amigo/a (*m., f.*), P
friendly amable, simpático/a, 1
friendship amistad (*f.*)
from de, desde, 1, 4; **from time to time** de vez en cuando, 4; **from now on** desde ahora
fruit fruta (*f.*), 3

fry freír (i, i), 5
fuel combustible (*m.*), 11
function función (*f.*), 9
funny cómico/a, 1, 6; chistoso/a

G

game partido (*m.*), 6; juego (*m.*)
garage garaje (*m.*), 2
garbage basura (*f.*); **garbage can** basurero (*m.*), 1
garden jardín (*m.*), 2
gardener jardinero/a (*m., f.*), 4
gas tank tanque de gasolina (*m.*), 9
gasoline gasolina (*f.*), 9
genre género (*m.*), 6
German alemán/alemana; (*language*) alemán (*m.*), 1
get conseguir (i, i), 3; recoger, 5; **get a sunburn** quemarse, 5; **get a tan** broncearse, 5; **get better** aliviarse, 8; mejorar, 8; **get dressed** vestirse (i, i), 3; **get married (to)** casarse (con), 4; **get sick** enfermarse, 8; **get up** levantarse, 3
girl chica (*f.*), P, 4; niña (*f.*), 4
girlfriend novia (*f.*), 4
give dar, 3, 4; (*gifts*) regalar, 4
glass (*drinking*) vaso (*m.*), 3
global warming calentamiento global (*m.*), 11
glove guante (*m.*), 7; **baseball glove** guante (*m.*), 6
go ir, 3; **go (down) (*a street*)** bajar (por), 7; **go away** irse, 3; **go bicycling** montar en bicicleta, 5; **go fishing** ir de pesca, 5; **go horseback riding** montar a caballo, 5; **go on vacation** estar/irse de vacaciones, 5; **go out** salir, 3; **go shopping** ir de compras, 7; **go skindiving, snorkeling** bucear, 5; **go straight** seguir (i, i) derecho, recto, 7; **go surfing** hacer surfing, 5; **go to bed** acostarse (ue), 3; **go up (*a street*)** subir (por), 7; **Let's go!** ¡Vamos!, P
goblet copa (*f.*), 3
godfather padrino (*m.*)
godmother madrina (*f.*)
godson/goddaughter ahijado/a (*m., f.*)
gold oro (*m.*), 7
golden dorado/a, 10
golf golf (*m.*), 6
golf club palo de golf (*m.*), 6
good bueno/a, 1; **it's good** es bueno, 8

Good-bye Adiós., P; **Until we meet again** Hasta la vista., P
good-looking guapo/a, 1
granddaughter nieta (*f.*), 4
grandfather abuelo (*m.*), 4
grandmother abuela (*f.*), 4
grandson nieto (*m.*), 4
grave grave, 8
gray gris, 1
great grandfather bisabuelo (*m.*), 4
great grandmother bisabuela (*f.*), 4
green verde, 1
greenhouse effect efecto invernadero (*m.*), 11
group conjunto (*m.*), grupo (*m.*), 6
growth crecimiento (*m.*), 12
guess adivinar
guest huésped (*m., f.*), 5
guidebook guía (*f.*), 5
guilty culpable
guitar guitarra (*f.*), 6
guitarrist guitarrista (*m., f.*), 6
gym gimnasio (*m.*), 6
gymnastics gimnasia (*f.*), 6
gymwear ropa de gimnasia (*f.*), 6

H

hair pelo (*m.*), 3, 8; **hair dryer** secador/a de pelo (*m., f.*), 2; **hair stylist** peluquero/a (*m., f.*), 4
half medio/a (*adj.*), 7; (*hour*) y media (*f.*), 1
hand mano (*f.*), 3, 8
hand in entregar, 4
handsome guapo/a, 1
hang (up) colgar (ue), 9, 10
happen pasar, 2
happy alegre, contento/a 2; **be happy** alegrarse (de), estar contento/a de, 8;
hard drive disco duro (*m.*), 9
hard-working trabajador/a, 1
hardly apenas
harm dañar, 8
harmonious armonioso/a, 11
harmony armonía (*f.*)
harvest cosecha (*f.*)
hat sombrero (*m.*), 5, 7
have tener, 3; **have a chill** tener escalofríos, 8; **have a cold** estar resfriado/a, tener catarro/resfrío, 8; **have a cough** tener tos, 8; **have a fever** tener fiebre, 8; **have a good time** divertirse (ie, i), 3; **have a solution** tener remedio, 11; **have an appetite** tener apetito, 8; **have breakfast** desayunar, 3; **have dinner** cenar, 3; **have just**

(*done something*) acabar de + (*inf.*), 2; **have lunch** almorzar (ue), 3; **have pain** tener dolor, 8; **have the flu** tener gripe, 8; **have to (*do something*)** tener que + (*inf.*), 3

he él, 1

head cabeza (*f.*), 8

headphones audífonos (*m. pl.*), 6

healer curandero/a (*m., f.*), 8

health insurance seguro médico (*m.*), 11

healthy sano/a, 8

hear oír, 3

heart corazón (*m.*), 8

heavy (*food*) (una comida) fuerte, 3; pesado/a

height apogeo (*m.*), 12

helmet casco (*m.*), 6

help ayuda (*f.*), 9

her ella, 4

here aquí, 3

Hey! ¡Oye!, 5

hieroglyphic jeroglífico/a, 12

high speed alta velocidad (*f.*), 9

highway carretera (*f.*), 9

him él, 4

hip-hop hip-hop (*m.*), 6

historical histórico/a, 10

history historia (*f.*), 1

hockey hockey (*m.*), 6; **hockey stick** palo de hockey (*m.*), 6

homeless people desamparados (*m.*), 11

hope esperar, 8; **I/We/Let's hope so.** Ojalá., 8

horn pito (*m.*), claxon (*m.*), 9

horror de horror, de terror (*adj.*), 6

horse caballo (*m.*), 11

hospital hospital (*m.*), 2

hot (*spicy*) picante, 3; (*temperature*) caliente, 3; **it's hot** hace calor, 3; **be hot/feel hot** tener calor, 3

hotel hotel (*m.*), 2

house casa (*f.*), 2

how? ¿cómo?, P; **How are you?** ¿Cómo está usted?/¿Cómo estás tú?, P; **How can I help you?** ¿En qué le(s) puedo servir?, 5; **How do you say . . . ?** ¿Cómo se dice... ?, P; **How does one get to . . . ?** ¿Cómo se llega a... ?, 7; **How much does . . . cost?** ¿Cuánto cuesta... ?, 5; **How much will you charge me for it/them?** ¿En cuánto me lo(s)/la(s) deja?, 7; **How's it going?** ¿Qué tal?, P

hug abrazar, 4

human being ser humano (*m.*)

humanities humanidades (*f. pl.*), 1

humid húmedo/a, 3

hunger hambre (el) (*f.*), 3; **I am very hungry!** ¡Tengo mucha hambre!, 3; **I'm starving/famished** Estoy muerto/a de hambre., 3

hurricane huracán (*m.*), 3

hurt doler (ue), 8

husband esposo (*m.*), 4

hybrid híbrido/a, 9

I

I yo, 1

ice cream (chocolate, vanilla, strawberry) helado (de chocolate, vainilla, fresa) (*m.*), 3

ice hielo (*m.*); **ice rink** pista de hielo (*f.*), 6; **ice skates** patines para hielo (*m.*), 6

icon icono (*m.*), 9

idea: I haven't got a clue Ni idea., 5

ill, to feel estar mal, P

illness enfermedad (*f.*), 8

illustrate ilustrar, 10

illustration ilustración (*f.*), 10

illustrator dibujante (*m., f.*), 10

image imagen (*f.*), 10

important: it's important es importante, 8

imposing imponente, 12

impossible: it's impossible es imposible, 8

imprison encarcelar, 11

in, on, at en, 1, 3, 4; **in addition to** además de, 12; **in case** en caso de que, 10; **in front of** delante de, 4; **in front of, facing** enfrente de, 4; **in groups** en grupos, P; **in love** enamorado/a, 2; **in order that** a fin de que, 10; **in order to** para, 4; **in pairs** en parejas, P; **in the morning/afternoon/evening** por/de la mañana/tarde/noche, 1; **In whose name?** ¿A nombre de quién?, 5

include incluir, 2

increase aumentar, 11

indigenous autóctono/a, indígena

inexpensive barato/a, 2

infection infección (*f.*), 8

inflammation inflamación (*f.*), 8

inhabited habitado/a, 12

injection inyección (*f.*), 8

injure dañar, 9

inside of dentro de, 4

install instalar, 9

intelligent inteligente, 1

intention propósito (*m.*), 10

interest, be of interest interesar, 4

interpret interpretar, 6

invest invertir (ie, i)

iron (clothes) planchar (la ropa), 2

island isla (*f.*), 5

Italian italiano/a; (*language*) italiano (*m.*), 1

J

jacket saco (*m.*); chaqueta (*f.*), 7

jaguar jaguar (*m.*), 7

jai alai jai alai (*m.*), 6

January enero (*m.*), 1

Japanese japonés/japonesa; (*language*) japonés (*m.*), 1

jazz jazz (*m.*), 6

jealous celoso/a, 2

jewelry joya (*f.*), 7; **jewelry store** joyería (*f.*), 7

journalist periodista (*m., f.*), 4

judge juzgar, 6

juice zumo (*m.*), jugo (*m.*), 3

July julio (*m.*), 1

June junio (*m.*), 1

justice justicia (*f.*), 11

K

keep oneself (healthy) conservarse (sano/a), 8

key llave (*f.*), 1

keyboard teclado (*m.*), 9

kick patear, 6

kill matar, 11

kilometers (per hour) kilómetros (por hora) (*m.*), 3

kitchen cocina (*f.*), 2

knee rodilla (*f.*), 8

knife cuchillo (*m.*), 3

know saber, conocer (zc), 3; **I don't know** No sé., P

L

lack faltar, 4

lake lago (*m.*)

lament lamentar, 8

lamp lámpara (*f.*), 1

language idioma (*m.*), 1

land tierra (*f.*); aterrizar

laptop computadora portátil (*f.*), 9

large grande, 1

later luego, 3

laugh reír (i, i), 5

laundromat lavandería (*f.*), 7

law derecho (*m.*)

lawyer abogado (*m.*, *f.*), 4
lazy flojo/a, perezoso/a,1
learn aprender, 2
leave salir, irse, 3; **leave (*something behind*)** dejar, 3
leg pierna (*f.*), 8
lend prestar, 4
lesson lección (*f.*), 1
library biblioteca (*f.*), 2
lie down acostarse (ue), 3
light ligero/a, 3; claro/a, 10; luz (*f.*), 9; **light and shadow** luz y sombra (*f.*), 10
lightbulb bombillo (*m.*), 11
like (be pleasing) gustar, 2, 8; **I would like (to order) ...** Me gustaría/Quisiera (pedir)..., 3; **like (*a person*)** caer bien, 4; **like very much (love)** encantar, 4
Likewise Igualmente., P
limousine limosina (*f.*), 5
line: to stand in line hacer cola
linguistic lingüístico/a, 12
linguistics lingüística (*f.*), 1
listen escuchar, P, 2; **Listen!** ¡Oye!, 5
listing cartelera (*f.*), 6
literature literatura (*f.*), 1
little poco (*m.*); **a little** un poco, 2
live vivir, 2; **live with** convivir, 10
living room sala (*f.*), 2
loading embarque (*m.*), 5
lodging alojamiento (*m.*), 5
long largo/a, 1
look at mirar, 2; **look for** buscar, 2; **look for shells** buscar conchas, 5
loose (*fitting*) flojo/a, 7; grande, 7
lose perder (ie), 3, 6
lost perdido/a, 12
lot: a lot mucho (*adv.*), 2
lot: a lot of mucho/a (*adj.*), 2
love de amor (*adj.*), 6; **be in love** estar enamorado/a, 4; amar, querer (ie)
lovely lindo/a, 1
lower (*a price*) rebajar, 7
luggage equipaje (*m.*), 5
lunch almuerzo (*m.*), 3; (*in some places*) comida (*f.*), 3
lung pulmón (*m.*), 8
luxurious lujoso/a (de lujo), 5
luxury lujo (*m.*), 5
lyrics letra (*f.*), 6

M

maid criada (*f.*), 4
mailbox buzón (*m.*), 5
mail carrier cartero/a (*m.*, *f.*), 4

maintain mantener, 3
major especialización (*f.*), 1
make arreglar (la cama), 2; hacer, 3; fabricar, 10; **make a (long distance/collect) phone call** hacer una llamada (de larga distancia/ por cobrar), 5; **make an appointment** hacer una cita, 8; **make fun of** burlarse (de), 10; **make sandcastles** hacer castillos de arena, 5; **make sense** tener sentido, 3
makeup maquillaje (*m.*), 7
man hombre (*m.*), 1
manager gerente (*m.*, *f.*), 4
map mapa (*m.*), 1
marble mármol (*m.*), 10
March marzo (*m.*), 1
mariachi musician mariachi (*m.*), 6
married: be married estar casado/a, 4
mask máscara (*f.*), 7
mathematics matemáticas (*f. pl.*), 1
matter importar, 4
May mayo (*m.*), 1
maybe quizás, tal vez, 8
me mí, 4
mean significar, 10
meat carne (*f.*), 3
medical sciences ciencias médicas (*f. s.*), 1
medicine medicina (*f.*), 8
meet (with) (*someone*) encontrarse (ue) (con), reunirse (con), 5
menu carta (*m.*), menú (*m.*), 3
message mensaje (*m.*), 9
meteorologist meteorólogo/a (*m.*, *f.*), 3
midnight medianoche (*f.*), 1
miles (per hour) millas (por hora) (*f.*), 3
mine mío/a(s) (*m.*, *f.*), 7
minivan camioneta (*f.*), 3
minus menos, 1
mirror espejo (*m.*), 2; **rear-view mirror** espejo retrovisor (*m.*), 9
Miss señorita (Srta.) (*f.*), P
mobile ambulante, 7
model modelo (*m.*, *f.*), 10
modem módem (*m.*), 9
modern moderno/a, 2
mom mamá (*f.*), 4
Monday lunes (*m.*), 1
money exchange cambio de dinero/moneda (*m.*), 5
monkey mono (*m.*), 11
morning mañana (*f.*); **Good morning.** Buenos días., P
mother madre (*f.*), 1, 4
mother-in-law suegra (*f.*), 4

motor motor (*m.*), 9
motorcycle motocicleta (*f.*), 3
mouse ratón (*m.*), 9
mouth boca (*f.*), 8
move andar, 2; mover (ue), 9; mudarse (relocate)
movie película (*f.*), 6; **movie theater** cine (*m.*), 2, 6
MP3 player reproductor MP3 (*m.*), 6
Mr. señor (Sr.) (*m.*), P
Mrs. señora (Sra.) (*f.*), P
much, very much mucho (*adv.*), 2
multimedia multimedia (*f.*), 9
mural mural (*m.*), 10
murder asesinar, 11; asesinato (*m.*), 11
murderer asesino/a (*m.*, *f.*), 11
muscle músculo (*m.*), 8
museum museo (*m.*), 2
music música (*f.*), 1; **Mexican-style music** ranchera (*f.*), 6
musician músico/a (*m.*, *f.*), 4, 6
my mi(s), 2
mystery de misterio (*adj.*), 6

N

name nombre (*m.*)
named, to be llamarse, P; **My name is ...** Me llamo..., P
nanny niñero/a (*m.*, *f.*), 11
narration narración (*f.*), 6
natural sciences ciencias naturales (*f. s.*), 1
necessary: it's necessary es necesario/preciso, 8
necklace collar (*m.*), 7
need faltar, 4; necesitar, 2, 8
neighborhood barrio (*m.*), vecindario (m.)
neither tampoco, 4; **neither ... nor** ni... ni, 4
nephew sobrino (*m.*), 4
nervous nervioso/a, 2
network red (*f.*), 9
never nunca, jamás, 4
nevertheless sin embargo, 12
new nuevo/a, 1
next luego, 3; **next to** al lado de, junto a, 4
nice simpático/a, 1
nickname apodo (*m.*)
niece sobrina (*f.*), 4
night noche (*f.*), 1; **Good evening/ Good night** Buenas noches., P; **night stand** mesita de noche (*f.*), 2
nine nueve, 1
ninety noventa, 1
no one, nobody nadie, 4

nominate nominar, 6
nomination nominación (*f.*), 6
none, not any ningún, ninguno/a, 4
noon mediodía (*m.*), 1
north norte (*m.*), 3
northeast/west noreste/oeste (*m.*), 3
nose nariz (*f.*), 8
notes apuntes (*m. pl.*)
notebook cuaderno (*m.*), 1
nothing nada, 4; **Nothing special.** Nada en particular., P
noun sustantivo (*m.*)
novel novela (*f.*), 5
November noviembre (*m.*), 1
now ahora, en este momento, 2
nuclear waste desperdicios nucleares (*m.*), 11
nurse enfermero/a (*m., f.*), 4
nutritious nutritivo/a, 8

O

obtain conseguir (i, i), 3; lograr, obtener, 11
obvious: it's obvious es obvio, 8
occur suceder, 6
October octubre (*m.*), 1
of de, 1, 4; **of the** del, 2; **Of course.** Sí, cómo no., P; por supuesto, 5; ¡Claro que sí!, 7
offer ofrecer (zc), 4
offering ofrenda (*f.*), 10
office oficina (*f.*), 1, 2; **office supply store** papelería (*f.*), 7
OK regular, P
old viejo/a, 1
older mayor, 1; **be older** ser mayor, 4
omelette with potatoes and onions tortilla española (*f.*) (*Spain*), 3
on, on top of en, 3; sobre, encima de, 4; **on board** a bordo, 5; **on foot** a pie, 3; **online** en línea, 9; **on sale** en oferta, 7; **on the right/left (hand side)** a la (mano) derecha/izquierda, 7
one uno, 1
one hundred cien, 1
one hundred ninety-nine ciento noventa y nueve, 1
one hundred one ciento uno, 1
only sólo
open abrir, 2
operation operación (*f.*), 8
optimistic optimista, 1
orange anaranjado/a (*adj.*), 1; naranja

order mandar, 8; pedido (*m.*), 3
organized organizado/a, 1
our nuestro/a(s), 2
ours nuestro/a(s) (*m., f.*), 7
outdoors al aire libre
outside of fuera de, 4
owe deber, 4
owner dueño/a (*m., f.*), 2
ozone layer capa de ozono (*f.*), 11

P

package (tour) paquete (*m.*), 5
paint pintar, 2, 10
paintbrush pincel (*m.*), 10
painter pintor/a (*m., f.*), 4, 10
painting pintura (*f.*), 1, 10; cuadro (*m.*), 10; **oil painting** pintura al óleo (*f.*), 10
pair par (*m.*), 7
palette paleta (*f.*), 10
panda bear oso panda (*m.*), 11
pants pantalones (*m.*), 7
paper papel (*m.*), 1; composición (*f.*)
parade desfile (*m.*), 10
paragraph párrafo (*m.*)
parasol sombrilla (*f.*), 5
Pardon Perdón., P
park estacionar, 7
parking lot estacionamiento (*m.*), 5
pass pasar, 2; **pass by** pasar por, 7
password contraseña (*f.*), 9
patient paciente (*m., f.*), 8
pay pagar, 4
pen bolígrafo (*m.*), pluma (*f.*), 1
pencil lápiz (*m.*), 1
pendant pendiente (*m.*), 7
penguin pingüino (*m.*), 11
people gente (*f. s.*), 2
pepper (*black*) pimienta (*f.*), 3
percent por ciento, 3
percentage porcentaje (*m.*), 3
percussion percusión (*f.*), 6
perfume store perfumería (*f.*), 7
perhaps quizás, tal vez, 8
pessimistic pesimista, 1
pet mascota (*f.*), 4
pharmacy farmacia (*f.*), 7
philosophy filosofía (*f.*), 1
photographer fotógrafo/a (*m., f.*), 4
physical físico/a, 8
physics física (*f.*), 1
physiology fisiología (*f.*), 1
pianist pianista (*m., f.*), 6
piano piano (*m.*), 6
pick up recoger, 5
pickup truck camioneta (*f.*), 3
picnic picnic (*m.*), 5
picture cuadro (*m.*), 10

piece pieza (*f.*), 10
pill píldora (*f.*), pastilla (*f.*), 8
pin prendedor (*m.*), 7
pink rosado/a, 1
place poner, 3
plane avión (*m.*), 3
planet planeta (*m.*), 11
plate plato (*m.*), 3, 7; placa (*f.*), 9
play (*a sport or game*) jugar (ue) (al), 3, 6; **(an instrument)** tocar (un instrumento), 2, 6; **play a role** hacer el papel, 6; **play sports** practicar deportes, 2; **play volleyball** jugar (al) volibol, 2, 5
player jugador/a (*m., f.*), 6
playwright dramaturgo/a (*m., f.*)
plaza plaza (*f.*), 2
plead rogar (ue), 8
pleasant agradable, 1
please por favor, P
Pleased to meet you Mucho gusto., P
pleasure placer (*m.*); **The pleasure is mine.** El gusto/placer es mío., P; **What a pleasure!** ¡Qué gusto!, 5
plot trama (*f.*), argumento (*m.*), 6
plumber plomero/a (*m., f.*), 4
point apuntar, 9
police policía (*m., f.*), 4, 11
political science ciencias políticas (*f. s.*), 1
pollute contaminar, 11
pollution contaminación (*f.*), 11
popular popular, 1
population población (*f.*), 12
porter botones (*m.*), 5
portion porción (*f.*), 8
portrait retrato (*m.*), 10
Portuguese portugués/portuguesa; (*language*) portugués (*m.*), 1
possible: it's possible es posible, 8
post office correo (*m.*), 2
postcard tarjeta postal (*f.*)
poster cartel (*m.*), 1
potato patata (*f.*), papa (*f.*), 3
potter ceramista (*m., f.*), 10
poverty pobreza (*f.*), 11
practice practicar, 2, 6
predict pronosticar, 12
prefer preferir (ie, i), 3, 8
preferable: it's preferable es preferible, 8
pregnancy embarazo (*m.*), 11
premiere estrenar, 6
prepare preparar
prepared preparado/a, 3
prescription receta (*f.*), 8
preserve conservar, 11
president presidente/a (*m., f.*), 4
pretty bonito/a, 1

price   precio (*m.*), 7
priest cura, sacerdote (*m.*)
print   imprimir, 9
printer   impresora (*f.*), 1
prison   cárcel (*m.*), prisión (*f.*), 11
private   privado/a, 2
prize   premio (*m.*), 12
probability   probabilidad (*f.*), 3
probable: it's probable   es probable, 8
problem   lío (*m.*), 11
produce   producir (zc), 3
professor   profesor/a (*m., f.*), P, 4
program   programa (*m.*), 9
protect oneself   protegerse, 5
provided that   con tal (de) que, 10
psychologist   psicólogo/a (*m., f.*), 4
psychology   psicología (*f.*), 1
public   público/a, 10
purchasing power   poder adquisitivo (*m.*), 12
purple   morado/a, 1
purpose   propósito (*m.*), 10
purse   bolsa (*f.*), 7
pursue   perseguir (i, i), 3
push a button   presionar, hacer clic, pulsar, oprimir, 9
put   poner, 3; **put on makeup** maquillarse, 3
pyramid   pirámide (*f.*), 12

Q

quantity   cantidad (*f.*), 8
quarter (*hour*)   cuarto (*m.*), 1

R

rabbit   conejo (*m.*), 4
radio   radio (*m., f.*), 1, 5
rain   lluvia (*f.*), 3; llover, 3
raincoat   impermeable (*m.*), 7
rate   tarifa (*f.*), 5
reach   alcanzar, 3, 11
read   leer, 2; **read books**   leer libros, 2
ready   listo/a, 2
Really?   ¿Verdad?, P
receipt   recibo (*m.*), 7
receive   recibir, 2
reception   recepción (*f.*), 5
receptionist   recepcionista (*m., f.*), 4, 5
recommend   recomendar (ie), 3, 8
record   grabar; disco (*m.*)
recreation   recreo (*m.*), 5
red   rojo/a, 1

red-head   pelirrojo/a, 1
reduce   reducir (zc), 5, 8
refrigerator   refrigerador/a (*m., f.*), 2
register   registrar, 5; registro (*m.*)
regret   lamentar, sentir (ie, i), 8
relative   pariente (*m., f.*), 4
religious   religioso/a, 10
remain   permanecer (zc), 10
remedy   remedio (*m.*), 8
remember   recordar (ue), 3
remote control   control remoto (*m.*), 9
rent   alquilar, 2; **rent videos** alquilar videos, 2; **rent**   alquiler (*m.*), renta (*f.*), 2
repeat   repetir (i, i), P, 3
replica   réplica (*f.*), 10
request   pedir (i, i), 3, 8
research   investigar, 2
reservation   reservación (*f.*), 5
reserve   reservar, 5
resolution   propósito (*m.*), 10
resource   recurso (*m.*), 11
responsibility   responsabilidad (*f.*), 11
rest   descansar, 5
restaurant   restaurante (*m.*), 2
return   volver (ue), 3; (*something*) devolver (ue), 7
reuse   reusar, 11
review   reseña (*f.*), 6; reseñar, 6
rhythm   ritmo (*m.*), 6
rice, meat, and seafood dish (from Valencia)   paella (valenciana) (*f.*), 3
rich   rico/a, 3
ridiculous: it's ridiculous   es ridículo, 8
ring   anillo (*m.*), 7
ripped   roto/a, 7
rite/ritual   rito (*m.*), 10
river   río (*m.*)
robbery   robo (*m.*), 11
robot   robot (*m.*), 9
rock   rock (music)(*m.*), 6; roca (*f.*)
role   papel (*m.*), 6
romantic   romántico/a, 1, 6
room   habitación (*f.*), 5
roommate   compañero/a de cuarto (*m., f.*), P
rooster   gallo (*m.*), 11
rose   rosa (*f.*), 1
route   ruta (*f.*), 3
rug   alfombra (*f.*), 2; tapete (*m.*), 7
ruin   ruina (*f.*) 12
rule   regla (*f.*), P
run   correr, 2
running track   pista (*f.*), 6

S

sad   triste, 2
sail, go sailing   navegar en velero, 5
salad (mixed/potato)   ensalada (mixta/rusa) (*f.*), 3
salesperson   vendedor/a (*m., f.*), 4
salsa (music)   salsa (*f.*), 6
salt   sal (*f.*), 3
sandal   sandalia (*f.*), 5
Saturday   sábado (*m.*), 1
sausage   chorizo (*m.*), 3
save   ahorrar, 11
save   archivar, guardar, 9; **(rescue)** salvar, 11
saxophone   saxofón (*m.*), 6
say   decir (i), 3; **say good-bye** despedirse (i, i), 5
scarce   escaso/a, 11
scarf   bufanda (*f.*), 7
scene   escena (*f.*), 6
schedule   horario (*m.*), 1
school   escuela (*f.*), 1
School (*as in School of Humanities*) facultad (*f.*), 1
science fiction   ciencia ficción, 6; de ciencia ficción (*adj.*), 6
scientific   científico/a
screen   pantalla (*f.*), 6; **flat screen** pantalla plana (*f.*), 9, **plasma screen**   pantalla de plasma (*f.*), 9
script   guión (*m.*), 6
sculptor   escultor/a (*m., f.*), 4, 10
sculpture   escultura (*f.*), 10
search   búsqueda (*f.*); **search engine**   buscador (*m.*), 9
seat   asiento (*m.*), 9
seatbelt   cinturón de seguridad (*m.*), 9
second   segundo/a; **second class** segunda clase (*f.*), 5
secretary   secretario/a (*m., f.*), 4
sedentary   sedentario/a, 8
see   ver, 3; **See you later.**   Hasta luego., P; **See you tomorrow.** Hasta mañana., P
seem   parecer (zc), 4
self-portrait   aurorretrato (*m.*), 10
sell   vender, 4
seller   vendedor/a (*m., f.*), 7
send   mandar, 2; enviar, 4
sense   sentido (*m.*), **to make sense** tener sentido
September   septiembre (*m.*), 1
sequence   secuencia (*f.*), 6
serious   serio/a, 1; grave, 8
servant   criado/a (*m., f.*), 4
serve   servir (i, i), 3
seven   siete, 1

seventy setenta, 1

shadow: light and shadow luz y sombra (*f.*), 10

shame: it's a shame es una lástima, 8

share compartir, 2

shave (i, i) afeitarse, 3

she ella, 1

shellfish marisco (*m.*), 3

shift mover (ue), 9

shine, sparkle brillar

shirt camisa (*f.*), 7

shiver tener escalofríos, 8

shoe zapato (*m.*), 7; **shoe store** zapatería (*f.*), 7

shopping center centro comercial (*m.*), 2

short (*height*) bajo/a, 1; (*length*) corto/a, 1

should deber, 4

show mostrar (ue), 3; **show a movie** presentar (pasar) una película, 6

shower ducha (*f.*), 2

shrimp gamba (*f.*), 3

shut off apagar, 9

shy tímido/a, 1

sick enfermo/a, 2

sickness: altitude sickness soroche (*m.*), 8

side by side al lado de, 4

silk seda (*f.*), 7

silver plata (*f.*), 7

since desde, 4

sing cantar, 2, 6

singer cantante (*m., f.*), 6

single (*room or bed*) sencillo/a, 5; **be single** ser soltero/a, 4

sink: bathroom sink lavabo (*m.*), lavamanos (*m.*), 2

sister hermana (*f.*), 4

sister-in-law cuñada (*f.*), 4

sit down sentarse (ie), 3

six seis, 1

sixty sesenta, 1

size (clothing) talla (*f.*), 7; tamaño (*m.*)

skate patín (*m.*); **inline skates** patines en línea, 6

skating patinaje (*m.*), 6

sketch bosquejo (*m.*), 10

ski esquí (*m.*), 6; esquiar, 6

skiing esquí (*m.*), 6

skilled, skillful hábil, 10, 12

skirt falda (*f.*), 7

skull calavera (*f.*), 10

sky cielo (*m.*), 3

sleep dormir (ue, u), 3

sleepy: be sleepy/tired tener sueño, 3

slow lento/a, 1

slowly despacio, 7; **more slowly** más despacio, P

small pequeño/a, 1; **small serving of food** tapa (*f.*) (*Spain*), 3

smart listo/a, 1

smile sonreír (i, i), 5

snake culebra, serpiente, víbora (*f.*)

sneaker zapato tenis (*m.*), 6

sneeze estornudar, 8

snow nieve (*f.*), 3; nevar, 3

so that para que, 10

soap jabón (*m.*); **soap opera** telenovela (*f.*)

soccer fútbol (*m.*), 6

social program programa social (*m.*), 11

social sciences ciencias sociales (*f. pl.*), 1

social work trabajo social (*m.*), 1

social worker trabajador/a social (*m., f.*), 11

sociology sociología (*f.*), 1

sock calcetín (*m.*), media (*f.*), 7

sofa sofá (*m.*), 2

soldier soldado/a (*m., f.*)

solution solución (*f.*), 11

solve solucionar

some algún, alguno/a/os/as, 4

somebody, someone alguien, 4

something algo, 4

sometimes algunas veces, 4

somewhere else (otro) lado (*m.*), 7

son hijo (*m.*), 4

song canción (*f.*), 6

son-in-law yerno (*m.*), 4

sorry: I'm sorry Lo siento., P, 5

soul alma (el) (*f.*)

sound sonido (*m.*)

soup sopa (*f.*), 3; **cold vegetable soup** gazpacho (*m.*), 3

south sur (*m.*), 3

South American sudamericano/a

southeast/west sureste/oeste (*m.*), 3

spacious amplio/a, 2

Spanish español/a; (*language*) español (*m.*), 1; **Spanish-style music** flamenco (*m.*), 6

Spanish-speaking de habla española, 12

speech discurso (*m.*)

speak hablar, 2, 4

speaker parlante (music) (*m., f.*), 6

species especie (*f.*), 11

spectator espectador/a (*m., f.*), 6

spend (*money*) gastar (dinero), 7

sport deporte (*m.*), 6

sports car coche deportivo (*m.*), 9

sports enthusiast deportista (*m., f.*), 6

sprain (*one's ankle*) torcer(se) (el tobillo), 8

spring primavera (*f.*), 3

stadium estadio (*m.*), 2

stain mancha (*f.*), 7

stained manchado/a, 7

stairs escaleras (*f. pl.*), 2

stand out destacar(se), 12

start comenzar (ie), 3; (*a car, a race*) arrancar, 9

stationery store papelería (*f.*), 7

statue estatua (*f.*), 10

stay quedarse, 3; (*in a hotel*) alojar(se), 5

steak bistec (*m.*), 3

steering wheel volante (*m.*), 9

stemmed glass copa (*f.*), 3

stepbrother hermanastro (*m.*), 4

stepdaughter hijastra (*f.*), 4

stepfather padrastro (*m.*), 4

stepmother madrastra (*f.*), 4

stepsister hermanastra (*f.*), 4

stepson hijastro (*m.*), 4

still life naturaleza muerta (*f.*), 10

stocking media (*f.*), 7

stomach estómago (*m.*), 8

stone piedra (*f.*), 7

stop parar, 7, 9

stoplight semáforo (*m.*), 7

store almacenar, 9; tienda (*f.*), 2; **store window** escaparate (*m.*), 7

storm tormenta (*f.*), tronada (*f.*), 3

stove estufa (*f.*), 2

strange: it's strange es extraño, 8

street calle (*f.*), 2; **street block** cuadra (*f.*), manzana (*f.*), 7

strong fuerte, 3

student alumno/a (*m., f.*), estudiante (*m., f.*), P

study estudiar, 1, 2

subject sujeto (*m.*), 1; **subject matter** materia (*f.*), 1

subway metro (*m.*), 3

succeed triunfar, 11

sugar azúcar (*m.*)

suggest sugerir (ie, i), 5, 8

suit traje (*m.*), 7

suitcase maleta (*f.*), 5

summer verano (*m.*), 3

sun sol (*m.*)

sunbathe tomar el sol, 5

Sunday domingo (*m.*), 1

sunglasses gafas de sol (*f. pl.*), 5

sunscreen protector/bronceador solar (*m.*), 5

support apoyar, 11; apoyo (*m.*)

sure seguro/a, 2; **it's (not) sure** (no) es seguro, 8

surf the Internet (Web) navegar por Internet (la Red/la web), 2

surprise sorprender, 8

sweatsuit, sweatshirt sudadera (*f.*), 7

sweater suéter (*m*.), 7
sweep (the floor) barrer (el piso), 2
sweet dulce, 3
swim nadar, 5; **swim cap** gorro de baño (*m*.), 6; **swim goggles** anteojos (*m. pl*.), 6
swimming natación (*f*.), 6; **swimming pool** piscina (*f*.), alberca (*f*.), 2
swimwear vestido de baño (*m*.), 6
symbolize simbolizar
symptom síntoma (*m*.), 8
synopsis sinopsis (*f*.), 6
syrup jarabe (*m*.), 8
system sistema (*m.*), 1

T

table mesa (*f*.), 1; **coffee table** mesita (*f*.), 2
tablespoon cuchara (*f*.), 3
tactile, pertaining to touch táctil, 9
tail cola (*f.*)
take tomar, 2; llevar, 7; **take a bath** bañarse, 3; **take a shower** ducharse, 3; **take a walk** dar un paseo, 2; **take care of oneself** cuidarse, 8; **take off (one's clothes)** quitarse (la ropa), 3; **take out (the garbage)** sacar (la basura), 2
talk hablar; **talk with friends** hablar con amigos, 2
tall alto/a, 1
tango tango (*m*.), 6
tape grabar, 6
tapestry tapiz (*m*.), 7
tariff tarifa (*f*.), 5
taste probar (ue), 3; **taste like** saber a
tasty sabroso/a, 3
taxi taxi (*m*.), 3
tea té (*m*.), 3
teach enseñar, 4
team equipo (*m*.), 6
teaspoon cucharadita (*f*.), 3
telephone teléfono (*m*.), 1
television televisión (*f*.), 1
tell decir (i), 3; contar (ue)
temperature (minimum/ maximum) temperatura (mínima/máxima) (*f*.), 3
temple templo (*m*.), 12
ten diez, 1
tenant inquilino/a (*m., f.*), 2
tennis tenis (*m*.), 6; **tennis racket** raqueta (de tenis) (*f*.), 6; **tennis shoes** zapatos de tenis (*m*.), 6

terrace terraza (*f*.), 2
terrible: it's terrible es terrible, 8
terrorism terrorismo (*m*.), 11
terrorist terrorista (*m., f*.), 11
test prueba (*f*.), análisis (*m*.), 8
thank agradecer (zc), 4
that (one) ese, esa, eso (éso/a), 3; (*over there*) aquel, aquella (aquél, aquélla), 3
the el, la, los, las 1
theater teatro (*m*.), 1
them ellos/as, 4
theme tema (*m*.), 1
then entonces, luego, 3
therapy terapia (*f*.), 11
there allí, ahí, 3
there, over there allá, 3
there is (not), there are (not) (no) hay, 1
these (ones) estos, estas (éstos/as), 3
they ellos, ellas, 1
thin delgado/a, 1
think creer, pensar (ie), 3, 8; **(have an opinion)** opinar, 8
thirteen trece, 1
thirty treinta, 1
thirsty: be thirsty tener sed, 3
this (one) este, esta, esto (éste, ésta), 3
those (ones) esos, esas (ésos/as), 3; (*over there*) aquellos/as (aquéllos/as), 3
threaten amenazar, 11
three tres, 1
thriller de suspenso (*adj*.), 6
throat garganta (*f*.), 8
Thursday jueves (*m*.), 1
ticket billete (*m*.), entrada (*f*.), 6
tidy (the room) limpiar/ordenar (el cuarto), 2
tie corbata (*f*.), 7
tiger tigre (*m*.), 11
tight estrecho/a, 7; (*clothes*) pequeño/a, 7
tile azulejo (*m.*)
time vez (*f*.); **many times** muchas veces, 4; **at the present time** de la actualidad; **to have a good time** divertirse (ie, i), 3
timid tímido/a, 1
tip propina (*f*.), 3
tire llanta (*f*.), 9
tired cansado/a, 2
title of respect with first name don (D.) (*m*.), doña (Dña.) (*f*.), P
to a, para, 4
today hoy, 1
toe dedo del pie (*m*.), 8
toilet inodoro (*m*.), 2

tomorrow mañana, 1
tongue lengua (*f*.), 8
too también, 4
tooth diente (*m*.), 3, 8
tornado tornado (*m*.), 3
tour excursión (*f*.), tour (*f*.), 5; **tour guide** guía (*m., f.*), 5
tourist turista (*m., f.*), 3
toward hacia, 4
towel toalla (*f*.), 5
toy juguete (*m*.), 7
tradition tradición (*f.*)
train entrenar, 6; tren (*m*.), 3; **train station** estación de tren (*f*.), 2
trainer entrenador/a (*m., f.*), 6
transfer traslado (*m*.), 5
translate traducir (zc), 3
transportation transporte (*m*.), 5
travel viajar, 2, 3; **travel agent** agente de viajes (*m., f.*), 4
traveler viajero/a (*m., f.*)
traveler's check cheque de viajero (*m*.), 5
treat, deal with tratar de, 6
tree árbol (*m.*)
tremble temblar (ie)
trip viaje (*m*.), 3; **Have a nice trip!** ¡Buen viaje!/¡Feliz viaje!, 5
truck camioneta (*f*.), 3; camión (*m*.), 3
true cierto/a; **it's true** es cierto, 8; es verdad, 8; verdadero/a
trumpet trompeta (*f*.), 6
trunk baúl (*m*.), maletero (*m*.), 9
try probar (ue), 3; **try on** probarse, 7
T-shirt camiseta (*f*.), 7
Tuesday martes (*m*.), 1
turn doblar (a), 7; **turn around** dar la vuelta, 7; **turn off** apagar, 9; **turn on** prender, encender (ie), 9
turquoise turquesa (*f*.), 7
turtle tortuga (*f*.), 4
twelve doce, 1
twenty veinte, 1
twist (one's ankle) torcer(se) (el tobillo), 8
two dos, 1

U

ugly feo/a, 1
umbrella paraguas (*m*.), 7
uncertainty incertidumbre (*f*.), 11
uncle tío (*m*.), 4
under bajo, debajo de, 4
understand comprender, 2; entender (ie), 3

underwear ropa interior (*f.*), 7
unemployment desempleo (*m.*), 11
unfriendly antipático/a, 1
uniform uniforme (*m.*), 6
unit unidad (*f.*), P
university universidad (*f.*), 1
unknown desconocido/a
unless a menos que, 10
unloading desembarque (*m.*), 5
unpleasant desagradable, 1
until hasta, 4, 7; hasta que, 9
upset alterado/a, 2
urgent: it's urgent es urgente, 8
us nosotros/as, 4
use usar, 2

V

vacation vacación (*f.*), 5; **be on vacation** estar/irse de vacaciones, 5
vaccine vacuna (*f.*), 8
vacuum cleaner aspiradora (*f.*), 2; **vacuum the rug** aspirar, pasar la aspiradora (por la alfombra), 2
variety variedad (*f.*)
vase vasija (*f.*), 10
vegetable legumbre (*f.*), 3
veterinarian veterinario/a (*m., f.*), 4
videocamera videocámara (*f.*), 9
video game videojuego (*m.*), 9
video recorder videograbadora (*f.*), 9
view vista (*f.*), 5
violin violín (*m.*), 6
virtual reality realidad virtual (*f.*), 9
visit visitar, 2
voice voz (*f.*), 6
volcano volcán (*m.*)
volunteer voluntario/a (*m., f.*), 11
vomit vomitar, 8

W

wait on atender (ie), 5
waiter camarero (*m.*), mesero (*m.*), 3
waitress camarera (*f.*), mesera (*f.*), 3
wake up despertarse (ie), 3
walk caminar, andar, 2; **go for a walk** pasearse/dar un paseo, 5
walking caminata (*f.*), 6
wall pared (*f.*), 1
want querer (ie), 3, 8; desear, 8; **want to (*do something*)** tener ganas de + (*inf.*), 3
war guerra (*f.*), 11

wardrobe ropero (*m.*), armario (*m.*), 2
warehouse almacén (*m.*), 2
warn avisar, 5; advertir (ie, i)
wash lavar, 2; **wash the dishes** lavar los platos, 2
watch reloj (*m.*), 1; **watch a movie** mirar una película, 2; **watch television** ver televisión, 2
water agua (el) (*f.*); **mineral water** agua mineral, 3; **water ski** hacer esquí acuático, 5
watercolor acuarela (*f.*), 10
we nosotros, nosotras, 1
weapon arma (*f.*), 11
wear llevar, 7
weather tiempo (*m.*); **it's good/bad weather** hace buen/mal tiempo, 3; **weather forecast** pronóstico del tiempo (*m.*), 3
weaver tejedor/a (*m., f.*), 12
weaving tejido (*m.*), 7
wedding boda (*f.*)
Wednesday miércoles (*m.*), 1
weight peso (*m.*), 8
Welcome! ¡Bienvenido!, P; **You're welcome.** De nada., P
well bien; **Pretty well, thanks.** Bastante bien, gracias., P; **Very well, thank you** Muy bien, gracias., P
well-being bienestar (*m.*), 8
west oeste (*m.*), 3
western de vaqueros (*adj.*), 6
whale ballena (*f.*), 11
what? ¿qué?, ¿cuál?, P; **What do you recommend?** ¿Qué nos recomienda?, 3; **What does . . . mean?** ¿Qué quiere decir... ?, P; **What is the temperature?** ¿A cuánto está la temperatura?, 3; **What time is it?** ¿Qué hora es?, 1; **What would you like to eat/drink?** ¿Qué desean comer/beber?, 3; **What's new?** ¿Qué hay de nuevo?, P; **What's your name?** ¿Cómo se llama usted?/¿Cómo te llamas?, P
wheel rueda (*f.*), 9
when cuando, 9
when? ¿cuándo?
where? ¿dónde?, P; **Can you tell me where . . . is/are?** ¿Me puede decir dónde está/n... ?, 7; **Where can I exchange money?** ¿Dónde puedo cambiar el dinero?, 5; **where (to)?** ¿adónde?
which ¿cuál?, P
white blanco/a, 1
width ancho (*m.*)

wife esposa (*f.*), 4
win ganar, 6
window ventana (*f.*), 1
windshield parabrisas (*m.*), 9; **windshield wiper** limpiaparabrisas (*m.*), 9
windy: it's windy hace viento, 3
wine (red/white) vino (tinto/blanco) (*m.*), 3
wine, fruit, and soda drink sangría (*f.*), 3
winter invierno (*m.*), 3
wireless inalámbrico/a, 9; **wireless connection (WiFi)** conexión (sin cables) (*f.*), 9
wish for desear, 2
with con, 2, 4; **with an ocean view** con vista al mar, 5; **with breakfast** con desayuno, 5; **with two meals** con media pensión, 5
without sin, 4; sin que, 10
woman mujer (*f.*), 1
wood madera (*f.*), 7, 10
wool lana (*f.*), 7
work trabajar, 2
work of art obra de arte (*f.*), 10
worker trabajador/a (*m., f.*), 4
worried preocupado/a, 2
worry angustia (*f.*), 11; preocuparse, 3, 4, 8
worse: it's worse es peor, 8
write escribir, 2; **write letters** escribir cartas, 2
writing escritura (*f.*), 12

X

X-ray radiografía (*f.*), 8

Y

yard jardín (*m.*), 2
yellow amarillo/a, 1
yesterday ayer
yet todavía, 9
you tú, usted(es), vosotros/as, P, 1
young joven, 1
younger: be younger ser menor, 4
your su(s), tu(s), vuestro/a(s) (*Spain*), 2
yours suyo(s), tuyo/a(s), vuestro/a(s) (*Spain*), 7

Z

zero cero, 1

Index

Text Credits

Artes y Letras : Page 87: Reprinted with permission of the publisher, Children's Book Press, San Francisco, CA, www.childrensbookpress.org Poem from Laughing Tomatoes/Jitomates Risuenos. Poem copyright © 1997 by Francisco Alarcon; page 87: Reprinted with permission of the publisher, Children's Book Press, San Francisco, CA, www.childrensbookpress.org Poem from Laughing Tomatoes/Jitomates Risuenos. Poem copyright © 1997 by Francisco Alarcon; page 87: From Noche Estrellada by Marjorie Agosin. Reprinted by permission of the author.

Artes y Letras : Page 167: Resguardo Personal, by Paloma Pedrero. Reprinted by permission of the author.

Unit 5: Page 201: Copyright © 2001 by Houghton Mifflin Company. Adapted and reproduced by permission from The American Heritage Spanish Dictionary, Second Edition.

Artes y Letras: Page 239: From "Tengo," by Nicolas Guillen, as appeared in Los Dispositivos en la flor, Cuba: Literatura desde la Revolucion, ed. Edmundo Desnoes with Willi Luis, © 1981. Reprinted by permission of Ediciones del Norte; page 239: From La Urdimbre del Silencio, by Norberto James. (c) Norberto James Rawlings, 2005. Reprinted by permission of the author.

Unit 8: Page 297: Reprinted by permission of Editorial América, S.A. from "Contra La Artritis, Piquetes de Abejas," as appeared in GeoMundo, Año 16, Núm. 9, pg. 228; page 297: From Newsweek En Español, July 26, 2000. Copyright © 2000 Newsweek, Inc. All rights reserved. Reprinted by permission; page 298: From Vanidades, Ano 40, no. 5. Copyright © by Editorial Televisa.

Artes y Letras : Page 307: Dos Palabras from *Cuentos de Eva Luna* by Isabel Allende. © Isabel Allende. Reprinted by permission of Agencia Literaria Carmen Balcells, S. A.

Unit 9: Page 310: Reprinted with permission from Quo: El Saber Actual, No. 58, julio 2000, pp. 186-187.

Artes y Letras : Page 373: Como Tu, by Roque Dalton, from Clandestine Poems (Curbstone Press, 1990), reprinted with permission of Curbstone Press. Distributed by Perseus; page 375: By Ernesto Cardenal, fas appeared in Antologia de la poesia amorosa espanola e hispanoamericana, Ed. Victor de Lama. Copyright © 1993.

Unit 11: Page 388: Grupo Interconect © 1998; page 399: From El colombiano, July 7, 1997. Adapted by permission of the author.

Unit 12: Page 408: Reprinted with permission from Mundo Maya Magazine.

Photo Credits

Page. 1: Sylvia Laks; p. 17: Miguel Suárez Pierra; p. 43: Jose Fuste Raga/Corbis; p. 46: (t) Dex Images/Corbis, (m) Alamy/Royalty Free, (b) Alamy/Royalty Free; p. 53: Joan Miró, (*Prades, the Village (prades, el poble*), Summer 1917, (oil on canvas, 65x72.6 cm), Solomon R. Guggenheim Museum, New York; p. 65: University of the Americas; p.

77: Archivo Iconagrafico/Corbis; p. 78: PCL/Alamy; p. 79: (r) Robert Fried, (l) Nick Wheeler/Corbis; p. 84: Deborah Feingold/Corbis (Ramos), Peter Foley/epa/Corbis (Lopez), Mario Anzuoni/Reuters/Corbis (Ferrera), Rune Helestad/Corbis (Rodríguez), Reuters/Corbis (Moreno), Rufus F Folkks/Corbis (Saldaña), Reuters/Corbis (Richardson), Gary Hershorn/Reuters/Corbis (Santoalalla), Nancy Kaszerman/Zuma/Corbis (Rodríguez), Justin Lane/epa/Corbis (Saralegui); p. 85: Carmen Lomas Garza; p. 86: (t) Gary I. Rothstein/epa/Corbis, (b) Francisco Alárcon; p. 87: Marjorie Agosin; p. 89: Archivo Inconografico, S. A./Corbis, (c) Salvador Dali, Gala-Salvador Dali Foundation/Artis Rights Society (ARS), New York; p. 107: Owen Franken/Corbis; p. 121: Nick Dolding/Taxi/Getty Images; p. 122: (t) Alamy/Royalty Free, (b) Craig Lovell/Corbis, p. 123: (m) Peter Wilson/Corbis, (r) K. H. Benser/Zefa/Corbis, (l) Getty Images; p. 129: Giraudon/Art Resource, NY; p. 143: Royalty Free/Corbis; p. 157: Masimo Listri/Corbis; p. 159: (tl) David G. Houser/Corbis, (bl) Travelstock 44/Alamy, (tr) Temp-Sport/Corbis, (br) PictureNet/Corbis; p. 164: Rafael Roa/Corbis (Tomatito), Mike Blake/Corbis (Bebe), Reuters/Corbis (J. Iglesias), Claudio Ornatle/epa/Corbis (E. Iglesias), Peter Foley/epa/Corbis (Sanz), Guadenti Sergio/Sygma/Corbis (Chao); p. 165: José Manuel Merello; p. 166: (t) Stephanie Cardinale/People Avenue/Corbis. (b) public domain, p. 167: Paloma Pedrero; p. 169 Luis Germán Cajiga; p. 170: Bob Krist/Corbis; P. 181: author; p. 183: Nell Rabinowitz/Corbis; p. 197: M. L. Sinibaldi/Corbis; p. 199: (tl) Ulrike Welsch, (tr) Larry Luxner, (b) Robert Frerck/Odyssey; p. 205: "Guajiro Verde" Oils Dania Sierra (c) 2007; p. 206: (t) Hulton-Deutsch Collection/Corbis, (m) AP/Wide World Photos, (b) Mike Segar/Reuters/Cobis; p. 207: (t) Jack Vartoogian, (b) James Sparshatt/Corbis; p. 208: Mark Serota/Reuters/Corbis; p. 221: Wolfgang Kaehler/Alamy; p. 222: (t) Warren Toda/epa/Corbis, (b) AP/Wide World Photos; p. 229: David G. Houser/Corbis; p. 230: Steven Georges/Corbis; p. 231: (tl) AP/Wide World Photos, (tr) Tony Freeman/Photo Edit, (br) Mark Serota/Reuters/Corbis; p. 236: Martine Franck/Magnum Photos (Lam), Stephanie Maze/Corbis (Alicea), Victor Fralle/Reuters/ Corbis (Anthony), Juan Herra/epa/Corbis (Valdez), Reuters/Corbis (Guerra), Getty AFP (Crespo), Chris Pizzello/Reuters/Corbis (Bermudez), Diego Gomez/epa/Corbis (Downs), Fred Prouser/Reuters/Corbis (Lopez), authors (Santiago); p. 237: Aimée García, p. 238: (t) Mike Blake Reuters/Corbis, (b) author; p. 241: Arte Maya/ Rafael González y González; p. 246: (tl) AP/Wide World Photos, (tr) Jose Luis Pelaez/Corbis, (bl) Mark Gamba/Corbis, (br) Simon Plant/Zefa/Corbis; p. 253: Pablo Corral/ Corbis; p. 254: Robert Fried; P. 265: Danny Lehman/Corbis; p. 267: Hermine Dreyfuss; p. 273: Susan Mraz; p. 285: AP/Wide World Photos; p. 295: Danny Lehman/Corbis; p.304: Luis Lemus/Corbis (Neruda), AP/Wide World Photos (Sosa), AP/Wide World Photos (Neruda), Nancy Coste/Corbis (Bachelet), Mario Anzuoni/Reuters/Corbis (Herrera),

Mar Caribe

Barranquilla
Cartagena
Maracaibo
Caracas
San Carlos
La Guaira
TRINIDAD Y TOBAGO
Puerto España
OCÉANO ATLÁNTICO

VENEZUELA
Ciudad Bolívar
Río
Orinoco
Georgetown
Paramaribo

Medellín
Zipaquirá
Bogotá
Salto Ángel
GUYANA
Cayena

Cali
COLOMBIA
SURINAM
GUAYANA FRANCESA

Popayán
San Agustín

Otavalo
Pichincha
Santo Domingo
de los Colorados
Quito
ECUADOR
Chimborazo

Guayaquil

Iquitos

Río Negro

Río Amazonas

Manaos

Belén

Ecuador

CORDILLERA DE LOS ANDES

Río Madeira

Sipán
Trujillo

PERÚ

BRASIL

Recife

Callao
Lima
Machu Picchu

Cuzco
Lago
Titicaca

Puno
La Paz
Cochabamba

Arequipa
Tiahuanaco
Río Paraguay

Arica
Sucre
BOLIVIA

Brasilia

Iquique
Potosí

Bello
Horizonte

Antofagasta
Filadelfia
PARAGUAY
Asunción

Salvador

Trópico de Capricornio

Salta

San Pablo
Río de Janeiro

San Miguel
de Tucumán

Santos

Resistencia

Puerto Iguazú

Río Paraná

OCÉANO
PACÍFICO

Córdoba
Aconcagua
Mendoza

Viña del Mar
Valparaíso
Santiago

Rosario

Puerto Alegre

Río Uruguay

URUGUAY
Buenos Aires
Montevideo
La Plata
Punta del Este

CHILE

ARGENTINA

Concepción

Mar del Plata

Río Colorado
Río de la Plata

Bahía Blanca

Bariloche
Puerto Montt

CORDILLERA DE LOS ANDES

PATAGONIA

Estrecho de
Magallanes

Islas
Malvinas

Punta Arenas
**TIERRA
DEL FUEGO**

Cabo de Hornos

América del Sur

| 0 | 250 | 500 Km. |
| 0 | 250 | 500 Mi. |

ISLAS GALÁPAGOS

San
Salvador
Ecuador

Santa Cruz
San Cristóbal
ECUADOR
Quito
Guayaquil

Isabela

THE ULTIMATE GUIDE

WORLD CUP
2010

THE ULTIMATE GUIDE
WORLD CUP
2010

KEIR RADNEDGE

igloo

igloo

Published in 2010
by Igloo Books Ltd
Cottage Farm
Sywell
NN6 OBJ
www.igloo-books.com

10 9 8 7 6 5 4 3 2 1

ISBN: 978-1-84852-835-2

Produced by BlueRed Press Ltd
World Cup 2010 content author: Michael Heatley
Printed and manufactured in China

CONTENTS

THE ORIGINS OF THE GAME

Modern football is only a century-and-a-half old, but competitive ball-kicking games can be traced back much earlier. FIFA recognizes the ancient Chinese game *tsu-chu* (or *cu-ju*) as modern football's oldest ancestor.

Tsu-chu was popularized around 200–300BC as an exercise in the army. In one variation, players kicked a feather-filled ball into a 12–16 inch (30–40cm) net hung between two 30 foot (9m) high bamboo poles. In AD600, the Japanese game *kemari* was invented. Players passed a small, grain-filled ball between themselves without letting it touch the ground.

Early versions of football in Europe came from the Greek and Roman Empires. These games were more similar to rugby than modern football, with players able to use their hands as well as their feet. The Roman version, known as *harpustum*, grew into *calcio*, a notoriously violent Renaissance game, which gives its name to modern Italian football.

MEDIEVAL FOOTBALL
Records of medieval football (called fute-ball) in France and Britain tell of violent mobs charging through towns, using anything from a pig's bladder

RIGHT Gabriele Bella's painting of a game of football in Venice in the eighteenth century

to the head of a defeated Danish prince as a
ball. Football was so competitive, popular, and
disruptive that it caused riots. Both the Lord
Mayor of London in 1314 and Henry VIII in 1540
attempted to ban the sport, despite Henry having
his own pair of football boots.

RULES AND REGULATIONS

By the 19th century, football—or soccer, as it was
also known from its earliest years—had started to
take a more recognizable shape as part of British
public school curriculums. Two unofficial sets of
rules, one from Cambridge University and another
developed by clubs in the north east of England,
were established to govern the game.

The English Football Association (FA) was formed
in 1863 and published the first consolidated set
of formal laws. Rebel schools, which wanted to
permit running while holding the ball, abandoned
association football and launched rugby football.

AN INTERNATIONAL GAME

Football quickly spread around the world as
sailors, engineers, bankers, soldiers, and miners
introduced it wherever they went. Clubs were
formed in Copenhagen, Vienna, and Genoa, with
British colonial outposts further aiding the spread
of the game. In 1891, Argentina became the first
nation outside the UK to establish a football
league and British sailors helped to popularize
the game in Brazil. Even the United States had
its own "soccer" teams as far back as the 1860s.
By the end of the century, leagues—albeit not
necessarily national ones at this early stage—
were running in England, Scotland, Italy, Holland,
and pre-communist Russia.

The first international match took place the
year after the inaugural FA Cup, when England
played Scotland in 1872, at Hamilton Crescent,
Partick, Glasgow. The British Home Internationals
quickly became a fixture.

THE ORIGINS
OF THE GAME

THE CREATION OF FIFA

By the start of the 20th century, national football associations had been formed in countries across Europe and South America, including Uruguay, Chile, Paraguay, Denmark, Sweden, Italy, Germany, Holland, Belgium, and France.

Carl Anton Wilhelm Hirschman of Holland suggested convening an international meeting of football associations to the English FA's secretary, F. J. Wall. The English FA was initially positive, but left the call unanswered. Robert Guerin from the French Sports Association didn't want to wait indefinitely and, at a match between France and Belgium in 1904, he invited the European associations to join together.

This time the English FA made it clear it was not interested. However, the others agreed and FIFA (Fédération Internationale de Football Associations) came into being on 21 May 1904, in Paris, when representatives agreed a list of regulations, including playing matches according to the English Football Association's law book.

FOOTBALL FACTS

300–200BC *tsu-chu* popularized in China

AD600 *kemari* developed by the Japanese aristocracy

12th century both women and men took part in huge games in England

1314 "football" banned by the Lord Mayor of London

1530 a famous *Calcio* game takes place during the siege of Florence

1848 "Cambridge Rules" published by Cambridge University

1863 English Football Association founded with a set of codified laws for modern football

RIGHT Crowds build at the 1923 FA Cup "White Horse Final" between West Ham United and Bolton Wanderers

Represented at the meeting were France, Belgium, Denmark, Holland, Spain, Sweden, and Switzerland. The seeds were sown for the World Cup, with Article Nine stipulating that FIFA would be the only body with the authority to organize such an international tournament.

Although none of the British nations attended the founding meeting of FIFA, they joined two years later and England's D. B. Woodfall became president.

ENGLAND'S INFLUENCE

The English game remained revered around the world in those days, proof of which is to be found in the English clubs names which survive far and wide. Clubs named after Arsenal are to be found in countries as far apart as Ukraine and Argentina and the famous amateur team, the Corinthians, saw their title adopted by what is now one of Brazil's greatest clubs.

In Italy, the English legacy is still evident in the names of clubs such as Milan and Genoa—not the Italian "Milano" and "Genova"—while the fervent Basque supporters of Athletic Bilbao in northern Spain maintained a private insistence on "Atleti" despite the Franco dictatorship imposing the Spanish-language "Atletico" label.

Students who came to England for an education also took home with them more than the latest developments in engineering, finance, and commerce. One such was Charles Miller, whose Scottish father, a railway engineer in Sao Paulo, had sent his son "home" for an English boarding school education. Young Miller returned to Brazil in 1894 with two footballs in his baggage—and sparked a passion which resulted in a record five World Cup triumphs.

Jimmy Hogan, William Garbutt, and Arthur Pentland were outstanding among English football coaches who taught the finer points of the game on the continent in the first half of the 20th century. Hogan worked in Hungary and then in Austria whose national team he coached in their famously narrow 4-3 defeat by England at Stamford Bridge in 1932.

THE ORIGINAL LAWS OF THE GAME

(as adopted by the Football Association on December 8, 1863)

1. The maximum length of the ground shall be 200 yards, the maximum breadth shall be 100 yards, the length and breadth shall be marked off with flags; and the goal shall be defined by two upright posts, eight yards apart, without any tape or bar across them.

2. A toss for goals shall take place, and the game shall be commenced by a place kick from the center of the ground by the side losing the toss for goals; the other side shall not approach within 10 yards of the ball until it is kicked off.

3. After a goal is won, the losing side shall be entitled to kick off, and the two sides shall change goals after each goal is won.

4. A goal shall be won when the ball passes between the goal-posts or over the space between the goal-posts (at whatever height), not being thrown, knocked on, or carried.

5. When the ball is in touch, the first player who touches it shall throw it from the point on the boundary line where it left the ground in a direction at right angles with the boundary line, and the ball shall not be in play until it has touched the ground.

6. When a player has kicked the ball, any one of the same side who is nearer to the opponent's goal line is out of play, and may not touch the ball himself, nor in any way whatever prevent any other player from doing so, until he is in play; but no player is out of play when the ball is kicked off from behind the goal line.

7. In case the ball goes behind the goal line, if a player on the side to whom the goal belongs first touches the ball, one of his side shall be entitled to a free kick from the goal line at the point opposite the place where the ball shall be touched. If a player of the opposite side first touches the ball, one of his side shall be entitled to a free kick at the goal only from a point 15 yards outside the goal line, opposite the place where the ball is touched, the opposing side standing within their goal line until he has had his kick.

8. If a player makes a fair catch, he shall be entitled to a free kick, providing he claims it by making a mark with his heel at once; and in order to take such kick he may go back as far as he pleases, and no player on the opposite side shall advance beyond his mark until he has kicked.

9. No player shall run with the ball.

10. Neither tripping nor hacking shall be allowed, and no player shall use his hands to hold or push his adversary.

11. A player shall not be allowed to throw the ball or pass it to another with his hands.

12. No player shall be allowed to take the ball from the ground with his hands under any pretence whatever while it is in play.

13. No player shall be allowed to wear projecting nails, iron plates, or gutta-percha on the soles or heels of his boots.

THE WORLD CUP

The World Cup is the planet's greatest sports event.
In terms of competing nations, television viewers,
and finance, it dwarfs every other tournament.
Uruguay were the first hosts—and first winners—in
1930, but the worldwide game is perfectly balanced:
South American nations have won nine cups and so
have Europe's finest. Brazil have carried off the golden
trophies a record five times, followed by Italy (four)
and Germany (three).

THE WORLD CUP
FOUNDATION & 1930s

After a string of false starts, the World Cup was launched in 1930. The inaugural international tournament was the British Home Championship, but FIFA's first attempt to launch a truly international championship in 1906 had fallen flat. Switzerland agreed to host the tournament and even made a trophy, but no-one turned up.

PAGE 10 Italy score the first goal in the 1982 World Cup final

PAGE 11 Italy's Fabio Cannavaro lifts the 2006 trophy

THE RESULT 1930
Location: Montevideo
Final: Uruguay 4 Argentina 2
Shirts: Uruguay white, Argentina light blue-and-white stripes
Scorers: Dorado, Cea, Iriarte, Castro; Peucelle, Stabile

URUGUAY

Ballesteros

Nasazzi   Mascheroni

Andrade Fernandez Gestido

Dorado Scarone Castro Cea Iriarte

M Evaristo Ferreira Stabile Varallo Peucelle

Suarez   Monti   J Evaristo

Paternoster   Della Torre

Botasso

ARGENTINA

England, now a member of FIFA, organized the first large-scale international football tournament as part of the 1908 London Olympic Games.

FIFA became a genuinely international body as countries from North and South America started to join. The Olympic football tournament continued, and from 1914 FIFA took a lead role, officially designating it the "world championship of amateur football."

Yet FIFA still harbored ambitions of launching its own tournament. Not only was the status of football in the Olympics insecure—it was almost dropped entirely from the 1932 Games at Los Angeles—but interest was hampered by the sudden spread of professionalism.

URUGUAY WIN ON HOME TERRITORY
In the 1920s, two Frenchmen, FIFA President Jules Rimet and French Federation Secretary Henri Delaunay, set up a steering committee. In 1928, the FIFA Congress in Amsterdam voted to support a first world championship and Uruguay's bid to host the event easily beat off European competition. As part of the country's centenary celebrations, the event was guaranteed financially by the

RIGHT Czech goalkeeper Planicka punches clear in the 1934 final

government. The Uruguayans boasted an impressive pedigree as double Olympic champions—in 1924 they won in France and four years later they triumphed in Amsterdam—and built the massive Centenario Stadium in Montevideo.

Lucien Laurent of France scored the first-ever World Cup goal in the 4-1 victory over Mexico, but Uruguay's generosity in hosting the tournament was rewarded with ultimate victory, when 80,000 fans packed the Centenario Stadium to witness their 4-2 win over Argentina in the final.

WORLD CUP 1934

Italy were both hosts and winners of the first finals to be staged in Europe. Dictator Benito Mussolini wanted to put on a show to impress his international visitors. But World Cup title holders Uruguay stayed away because they feared their top players would remain in Europe.

Vittorio Pozzo, Italy's manager, included three Argentinian-born players in his squad, while his best home-grown players were forwards Giuseppe Meazza and veteran Angelo Schiavio.

Spain became Italy's most awkward opponents. The heroics of the legendary Spanish goalkeeper Ricardo Zamora held the hosts to a 1-1 draw in the quarter-finals. However, Zamora took such a battering from Italy's over-physical forwards that he was not fit enough to play in the replay.

Italy won 1-0 and then defeated Austria, Europe's other top nation, by the same score. In the final they beat Czechoslovakia 2-1, but only after extra time, with Schiavio scoring the winner.

ABOVE Leonidas (left) leads Brazil to their victory over Sweden in 1938

WORLD CUP 1938

Four years later, Italy won a second time, this time in France. The atmosphere was very different compared to 1934, when Pozzo's team had benefited from home advantage, generous referees, and home support. In France they were jeered by fans angered by Italy's fascist politics.

England, despite being outside FIFA, were invited to compete at the last minute in place of Austria—which had been swallowed up by Adolf Hitler's Germany. However, England's Football Association declined the invitation, even though they had thrashed Germany 6-3 in Berlin shortly before the finals.

The favorites included Brazil, following their astonishing first round match against Poland. Brazil won 6-5 in extra time: Brazil's Leonidas and Poland's Ernst Wilimowski both scored hat-tricks.

Brazil were so confident of beating Italy in the semi-finals that they rested Leonidas to keep him fresh for the final, but their gamble misfired because they lost 2-1. Italy went on to defeat Hungary 4-2 in the final to become the first-ever back-to-back World Cup winners.

THE WORLD CUP
1950s

"All I remember was everyone in tears."

PELÉ RECALLS THE 1950 FINAL

A nation was traumatized when the host, and one of the favorites, Brazil lost to Uruguay in the climax of the first postwar World Cup. The competition ended not with a one-off final but a four-team group, a format not used since.

1950

The closing match, in front of a record crowd of nearly 200,000 in Rio's Maracana Stadium, proved decisive as Uruguay claimed their second title.

Free-scoring Brazil needed only a draw to win their first World Cup, and looked to be on their way when Friaça fired them into the lead. But underdogs Uruguay, captained and marshaled by center half Obdulio Varela, stunned the hosts with late goals by Juan Schiaffino and Alcides Ghiggia. Brazilian fans were furious with their team's failure, with much of the blame heaped on unfortunate goalkeeper Barbosa.

The defeat marked the very last time that Brazil wore an all-white uniform, which was believed to be so unlucky that it was replaced by the now famous yellow shirts. Because of the result, the Uruguay players remained in their dressing room for hours after the final whistle until it was safe to emerge.

The final was not the only shock of the tournament—England had been humbled in the first round by the United States. England lost 1-0 at Belo Horizonte, courtesy of a goal from Haiti-born Joe Gaetjens.

1954

When runaway favorites Hungary thrashed under-strength West Germany 8-3 in their opening round group game, no one expected these sides to meet again in the final—let alone for the West Germans to triumph.

RIGHT 1954 souvenir postcard featuring the Maracana Stadium and views over Rio de Janerio

THE RESULT 1950

Location: Rio
Final: Uruguay 2 Brazil 1
Shirts: Uruguay light blue, Brazil white
Scorers: Schiaffino, Ghiggia; Friaça

URUGUAY

Máspoli

Gambetta   Gonzáles

Andrade   Varela   Tejera

Ghiggia   Julio Pérez   Miguez   Schiaffino   Morán

Chico   Jair   Ademir   Zizinho   Friaça

Danilo   Bauer   Bigode

Juvenal   Augusto

Barbosa

BRAZIL

West Germany's coach Sepp Herberger rested several key players for their first game, while Hungary's captain Ferenc Puskás suffered an ankle injury that was meant to rule him out of the rest of the tournament. Yet Puskás, as the star player, was controversially brought back for the final and even gave his Magical Magyars a sixth-minute lead. Left winger Zoltan Czibor scored again almost immediately, with another rout looking likely.

But the Germans made a spirited comeback. Led by captain Fritz Walter and two-goal hero Helmut Rahn, the Germans battled back for what is known in footballing history as "Das Wunder von Bern"—the miracle of Berne.

Hungary entered the tournament as Olympic champions and overwhelming favorites, but remarkably the final would be their only defeat between 1950 and early 1956.

They thought they had done enough to take the match into extra time, only for an 88th-minute Puskás strike to be controversially disallowed for offside by Welsh linesman Mervyn Griffiths.

The competition produced an amazing 140 goals over 26 matches, including the World Cup's highest-scoring match during Austria's thrilling 7-5 triumph over Switzerland.

1958

Brazil finally ended their wait for their first World Cup crown, with a little help from their latest superstar, Pelé, in Sweden. The 17-year-old Santos prodigy had to wait until Brazil's final group game to make Vicente Feola's starting line-up, with mesmerizing winger Garrincha also given his first opportunity at the finals.

The pair proved irresistible by setting up Vavá for both goals to beat the Soviet Union, before Pelé grabbed a hat-trick in the 5-2 semi-final success over France. Brazil defeated hosts Sweden by the same score in the final, including two goals by Pelé, who broke down in tears at the end.

Yet Brazil were not the only ones to impress. French striker Just Fontaine scored 13 goals, a record for a single World Cup tournament that no one has since come close to emulating. The 1958 finals were also the only time that all four of the UK's Home Nations qualified, although England had lost Duncan Edwards and several other international players in the Munich air disaster.

West Germany lost a bitter and violent semi-final to Sweden. Captain Fritz Walter was fouled out of the game and could not be replaced because substitutes were not allowed at the time.

BELOW Brazil's 17-year-old Pelé shoots for goal in the 1958 final

THE RESULT 1954
Location: Berne
Final: West Germany 3 Hungary 2
Shirts: West Germany white, Hungary cherry red
Scorers: Morlock, Rahn 2; Puskás, Czibor

WEST GERMANY

Turek

Posipal   Liebrich   Kohlmeyer

Eckel   Mai

Rahn   Morlock   O Walter   F Walter   Schäefer

Tóth   Puskás   Hidegkuti   Kocsis   Czibor

Zakarias   Bozsik

Lantos   Lantos   Buzánszki

Grosics

HUNGARY

THE RESULT 1958
Location: Stockholm
Final: Brazil 5 Sweden 2
Shirts: Brazil blue, Sweden yellow
Scorers: Vavá 2, Pelé 2, Zagallo; Liedholm, Simonsson

BRAZIL

Gilmar

D Santos   Bellini   Orlando   N Santos

Zito   Didi

Garrincha   Vavá   Pelé   Zagallo

Skoglund   Liedholm   Simonsson   Gren   Hamrin

Parling   Börjesson

Bergmark   Gustavsson   Axbom

Svensson

SWEDEN

THE WORLD CUP
1960s

Even without Pelé at the helm, Brazil were unstoppable as they comfortably retained their title in South America. Pelé scored in Brazil's first game but was injured in the next match, so he played no further part in the tournament.

RIGHT Garrincha (left) and Amarildo celebrate Brazil's equalizer against Czechoslovakia in the 1962 final

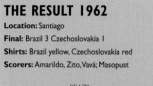

THE RESULT 1962

Location: Santiago
Final: Brazil 3 Czechoslovakia 1
Shirts: Brazil yellow, Czechoslovakia red
Scorers: Amarildo, Zito, Vavá; Masopust

BRAZIL

Gilmar

D Santos   Mauro   Zozimo   N Santos

Zito   Didi   Zagallo

Garrincha   Vavá   Amarildo

Jelinek   Kvasnak   Scherer   Pospíchal

Masopust   Kadraba

Novák   Popluhár   Pluskal   Tichý

Schrojf

CZECHOSLOVAKIA

1962

Pelé's deputy was Amarildo from Botafogo of Rio de Janeiro. Known as "the white Pelé," he made an immediate impact by scoring two goals in the 2-1 win over Spain in their decisive concluding group match. Amarildo also notched an equalizer in the final, but the undisputed star of the tournament was Garrincha, nicknamed "the Little Bird." Garrincha, the world's greatest-ever dribbler, was the two-goal man of the match as Brazil saw off England 3-1. He even overcame the embarrassment of being sent off in the 4-2 semi-final win over hosts Chile.

Brazil managed to persuade the disciplinary panel not to ban their star player, so he played in the final. The defending champions suffered an early shock when midfielder Josef Masopust shot

the Czechoslovakians into an early lead. However, mistakes by goalkeeper Vilem Schroif helped Brazil hit back to register a 3-1 victory. Masopust's consolation, months later, was to be voted as the European Footballer of the Year.

Chile's preparations had been marred by an earthquake two years earlier, yet they surpassed expectations not only off the pitch but on it as they clinched a deserved third place.

The Chileans caused a quarter-final upset by knocking out the highly rated Soviet Union, despite the outstanding efforts of legendary goalkeeper Lev Yashin.

1966

A historic hat-trick hero, a Soviet linesman, and a dog named Pickles were all made famous by the World Cup hosted in England.

West Ham's Geoff Hurst, who started the finals as a reserve striker, became the only man ever to score three goals in a World Cup final as the hosts beat West Germany 4-2 at Wembley Stadium.

But his second strike was one of the most controversial in football history. West Germany leveled through Wolfgang Weber's 89th-minute goal to take the final into extra time. In the first-half of extra time, Hurst produced an angled shot that struck the underside of the crossbar and went down behind the goal line before bouncing back out again for the Germans to clear it to safety.

England claimed they had scored and, despite West Germany's protests, linesman Tofik Bakhramov told Swiss referee Gottfried Dienst that the ball had indeed crossed the line.

Hurst, who fell while shooting at goal, was unsighted. However, fellow striker Roger Hunt was so certain that the ball had crossed the line that he did not bother even following up to put it back into the net. The controversial goal left the Germans deflated and Hurst capped his performance by claiming his hat-trick—and England's greatest footballing triumph—with virtually the last kick of the contest.

Alf Ramsey's hard-working side, nicknamed the "Wingless Wonders," had edged past Uruguay, Mexico, France, Argentina, and Portugal en route to the final. However, there were some complaints that England had been able to play all their matches in their stronghold of Wembley Stadium.

Their quarter-final against Argentina proved to be the most bitter. Visiting captain Antonio Rattin was sent off for dissent by German referee Rudolf Kreitlein but initially refused to leave the pitch and eventually had to be escorted by police.

The tournament had been boycotted by African nations, who were unhappy at their "winner" having to qualify via a play-off with the champions of Asia or Oceania.

For the second successive World Cup finals, Pelé limped out of the tournament early on after being the victim of relentlessly tough tackling. His aging team-mates were unable to raise their game without their star player, and Brazil surprisingly crashed out in the first round.

It was also a story of woe for former champions Italy, whose squad were pelted with rotten vegetables on their return home. They suffered a 1-0 defeat to the minnows of North Korea, whose winner was drilled home by dentist Pak Doo Ik. The Koreans raced into a 3-0 quarter-final lead over Portugal, before Mozambique-born Eusébio inspired the Portuguese to a 5-3 comeback and slotted home four goals.

Eusébio, dubbed the "Black Panther" for his goal scoring prowess, ended the tournament as top scorer with nine goals but was denied a place in the final by Bobby Charlton's two goals, which guided England to a 2-1 semi-final success.

Less than four months before England captain Bobby Moore accepted the Jules Rimet trophy from Queen Elizabeth II, it had been stolen from a London exhibition. Fortunately, a mongrel dog called Pickles dug up the trophy from a South London garden and was promptly rewarded with a lifetime's supply of pet food.

THE RESULT 1966

Location: London
Final: England 4 West Germany 2
Shirts: England red, West Germany white
Scorers: Hurst 3, Peters; Haller, Weber

ENGLAND

Banks

Cohen   J Charlton   Moore   Wilson

Ball   Stiles   B Charlton   Peters

Hurst   Hunt

Emmerich   Held   Seeler

Overath   Beckenbauer   Haller

Schnellinger   Weber   Schulz   Höttges

Tilkowski

WEST GERMANY

ABOVE Pickles, the dog who found the stolen World Cup

LEFT England captain Bobby Moore holds aloft the Jules Rimet trophy

1938   1958   1966

WORLD CUP MOMENTS

ABOVE Just Fontaine parades his top-scoring golden boot

RIGHT France striker Fontaine on the way to his record 13 goals

ABOVE Portugal's Eusébio is floored for a penalty against North Korea

BELOW Geoff Hurst rises above the West German defense at Wembley

ABOVE Czech forward Jan Riha ouwits Brazil's Domingos da Guia

1970

1974

LEFT Romania and England line up in the first round in Mexico

BELOW Brazil's Jairzinho is sent flying by a Uruguayan defender

ABOVE Top-scoring Gerd Müller eludes Yugoslav keeper Enver Maric

BELOW Franz Beckenbauer (white) breaks up a Dutch attack

ABOVE England left back Terry Cooper outwits West German captain Uwe Seeler

LEFT Weary England await extra time in their quarter-final in Leon

THE WORLD CUP
1970s

"Brazil on that day were on a different planet."

ITALY'S GIACINTO FACCHETTI

This was the first World Cup to be broadcast in sun-soaked color around the world. Nothing could match Brazil's famous yellow shirts as Mario Zagallo showcased arguably the most dazzling attacking side in footballing history.

1970

Spearheaded by Pelé, Jairzinho, Rivelino, and Tostão, Brazil were allowed to keep the Jules Rimet trophy after becoming the first country to win three World Cups. Pelé became the only player with a hat-trick of victories, although in 1962 he had been injured very early in the tournament.

Brazil featured in a classic first round contest, when they defeated England 1-0. However, both sides qualified for the quarter-finals. England's title defense came to a dramatic end when West Germany avenged their 1966 final defeat to bounce back from a two-goal deficit to register

an extra time 3-2 win over Sir Alf Ramsey's men. The effort of overcoming England undermined the Germans in their semi-final against Italy, and West Germany ran out of steam and lost another epic, to be edged out 4-3.

Brazil wrapped up the tournament with a 4-1 triumph over Italy in Mexico City. Brazil's fourth goal was the finest of the tournament, and one of the most memorable ever scored in a final. A smooth passing move, the length of the pitch, was finished off by captain Carlos Alberto. Manager Mario Zagallo became the first man to win the World Cup both as a player and a manager.

THE RESULT 1970

Location: Mexico
Final: Brazil 4 Italy 1
Shirts: Brazil yellow, Italy blue
Scorers: Pelé, Gerson, Jairzinho, Carlos Alberto; Boninsegna

BRAZIL

Felix

Alberto Brito Piazza Everaldo

Clodoaldo Gerson Rivelino

Jairzinho Tostao Pelé

Riva Boninsegna
(Rivera)

De Sisti Mazzola Bertini Domenghini
(Juliano)

Facchetti Rosato Cera Burgnich

Albertosi

ITALY

RIGHT Jairzinho scores Brazil's third goal against Italy

1974

Franz Beckenbauer achieved the first half of his own leadership double when he captained hosts West Germany to victory over Holland. The final was played in Munich's Olympic Stadium, the footballing home to Beckenbauer and his FC Bayern team-mates—goalkeeper Sepp Maier, defenders Hans-Georg Schwarzenbeck and Paul Breitner, and strikers Uli Hoeness and Gerd Müller.

Yet the dominant personality of the finals was Holland's center forward Johan Cruyff who, as captain, epitomized their revolutionary style of total football, characterized by a high-speed interchange of playing positions.

Hosts West Germany surprisingly stuttered in the first round but managed to qualify despite suffering a shock defeat to East Germany, who had emerged through the Berlin Wall for the first and last time in World Cup history. Jürgen Sparwasser made a name for himself with an historic strike in the 77th-minute to secure a slender 1-0 success.

West Germany topped their second round group ahead of Poland—qualifying victors over England—while Holland topped the other group ahead of an over-physical Brazil.

English referee Jack Taylor awarded the first World Cup final penalty—Cruyff had been fouled in the opening minute at Munich. Johan Neeskens stepped up to put the Dutch ahead before the hosts had even touched the ball.

West Germany soon leveled matters through a penalty kick and went ahead decisively, courtesy of Müller, just before the half-time interval.

1978

Holland had to settle for second best again, this time without the inspirational Cruyff, who refused to travel to Argentina, amid kidnap fears.

Cruyff's absence was particularly missed in the final as the hosts clinched their inaugural World Cup 3-1 after extra time. Argentina's only European-based player, Mario Kempes, finished as top scorer, with six goals, including two goals in the final.

A ticker-tape assisted storm of home support carried manager César Menotti's Argentina through the first round and to the second group with a tricky meeting against Peru. Needing to win by at least four clear goals, Menotti's men ran out contentious 6-0 winners to deny Brazil a final berth. Instead, Brazil settled for a 2-1 win over Italy in the third place play-off.

In the final, Holland went behind to a Kempes strike before half-time and equalized through substitute striker Dick Nanninga. On the verge of the full-time whistle, Rob Rensenbrink's effort was denied by the post and proved a costly miss as Argentina pulled away in extra time with further goals from Kempes and Daniel Bertoni.

Scotland failed to progress beyond the first round and were shamed by Willie Johnston being kicked out of the tournament after failing a dope test. The dazzling left winger protested his innocence, insisting he was taking Reactivan tablets to treat a cold, but he was banned from internationals and his playing career fizzled out.

LEFT Holland's Johan Cruyff holds off a West German defender

THE RESULT 1974

Location: Munich
Final: West Germany 2 Holland 1
Shirts: West Germany white, Holland orange
Scorers: Breitner (pen), Müller; Neeskens (pen)

WEST GERMANY

Maier

Schwarzenbeck Vogts Beckenbauer Breitner

Hoeness Bonhof Overath

Grabowski Müller Hölzenbein

Rensenbrink Cruyff Rep
(R Van der Kerkhof)

Van Hanegem Neeskens Jansen

Krol Rijsbergen Haan Suurbier
(De Jong)

Jongbloed

HOLLAND

THE RESULT 1978

Location: Buenos Aires
Final: Argentina 3 Holland 1
Shirts: Argentina blue and white, Holland orange
Scorers: Kempes 2, Bertoni; Nanninga

ARGENTINA

Fillol

Tarantini Galván Passarella Olguín

Ardiles Gallego Kempes
(Larrosa)

Bertoni Luqué Ortiz
(Houseman)

Rensenbrink Rep R Van de Kerkhof
(Nanninga)

Haan Neeskens W Van de Kerkhof

Jansen Brandts Krol Poortvliet
(Suurbier)

Jongbloed

HOLLAND

THE WORLD CUP
1980s

The competition swelled to 24 sides in 1982, as Spain played hosts for the first time. Italy ended a 44-year wait for their third title, with captain Dino Zoff becoming the oldest player to win a World Cup at the grand age of 40.

THE RESULT 1982

Location: Madrid
Final: Italy 3 West Germany 1
Shirts: Italy blue, West Germany white
Scorers: Rossi, Tardelli, Altobelli; Breitner

ITALY

Zoff

Scirea Gentile Bergomi Collovati Cabrini

Conti Oriali Tardelli

Rossi Graziani
(Altobelli) (Causio)

Rummenigge Fischer Littbarski
(H Müller)

Dremmler Breitner B Förster
(Hrubesch)

Briegel K Förster Stielike Kaltz

Schumacher

WEST GERMANY

RIGHT Claudio Gentile and skipper Dino Zoff celebrate in Madrid

1982

Toni Schumacher, West Germany's goalkeeper, was fortunate to have been playing in the final. Despite having knocked unconscious France's Patrick Battiston with a brutal foul during a thrilling semi-final in Seville, he somehow escaped punishment.

In the final, Schumacher faced a spot kick from Antonio Cabrini and the Italian left back made history by becoming the first player to miss a penalty in the title decider. In the same match, German Paul Breitner wrote himself into the annals of history when he became the first player to score a penalty in two separate finals.

But second half goals from Paolo Rossi, Marco Tardelli, and Alessandro Altobelli handed Enzo Bearzot's attacking side the trophy. Rossi's hat-trick in a 3-2 win had earlier knocked out a Brazil team that included Falcao, Socrates, and Zico.

Rossi finished up as the tournament's six-goal leading marksman to claim the Golden Boot. This was an astonishing achievement because the Juventus striker had returned to top-class football only six weeks earlier, following a two-year suspension for his role in a match-fixing scandal.

Holders Argentina struggled from the outset and they introduced their new hero, 21-year-old Diego Maradona, who had narrowly missed out on a place in their previous World Cup squad. Yet Maradona was stifled in the opening match, beaten 1-0 by Belgium, and then sent off for retaliation during a second round defeat by Brazil.

Spain were one of the more disappointing World Cup hosts out on the pitch, sensationally beaten by Northern Ireland in their opening match and later eliminated after finishing bottom of a three-nation second round group behind West Germany and England.

A further change of format saw the knockout semi-finals restored. Italy defeated Poland 2-0 in Barcelona to make the final, then West Germany saw off France in Seville, courtesy of the first penalty shoot-out in World Cup history. A magical match swung one way, then the other: Germany opened the scoring but trailed 3-1 before battling back with two goals to force extra time. Schumacher went from villain to hero by stopping the crucial last French penalty from Maxime Bossis.

1986

After his previous World Cup disgrace, Maradona jumped into the spotlight when, virtually single-handedly, he won Argentina their second World Cup by combining audacious skills with equally audacious law-breaking.

The world saw the best and worst of Maradona in a five-minute spell of Argentina's quarter-final contest against England. Although the Argentinian captain punched the ball into the back of the net, Tunisian referee Ali bin Nasser allowed the goal to stand (this was his first and last World Cup game as a referee).

Maradona claimed the goal was "a little bit of Maradona, a little bit the hand of God," a boast that accompanied him for years to the delight of a nation that considered the trick a belated answer to Argentina's military and naval defeat by Britain in the 1982 Falkland Islands conflict.

However, no one could dispute the majesty of Maradona's second strike. A solo slalom took him the full length of the England half, before he swept the ball past embattled goalkeeper Peter Shilton with his left foot, for one of the best-ever goals. Just to prove this had been no accident, maverick Maradona scored a similar solo goal in the 2-0 semi-final victory over Belgium.

Despite being closely marked by West Germany's Lothar Matthäus in the final, Maradona escaped long enough to provide the defense-splitting pass that set up Jorge Burruchaga's late goal to once more clinch World Cup success. The Germans had clawed their way back from a two-goal deficit and looked to be heading toward extra time, before the glittering run and pass from match-winner Maradona.

Franz Beckenbauer, a World Cup winner with West Germany in 1974, was in charge of the national team. Yet even his magic touch off the pitch was simply no match for the genius of Maradona on it.

England's consolation was that striker Gary Lineker went on to win the Golden Boot as the tournament's leading scorer with six goals. His tally included a hat-trick in England's first round defeat of Poland, which sent them to the quarter-finals against Paraguay. England had struggled initially, losing their opening game 1-0 to Portugal, and in the scoreless draw against Morocco they lost key players—Ray Wilkins was sent off and captain Bryan Robson was helped off with an injury.

European champions France sneaked past Brazil on penalties in their quarter-final, but for the second successive World Cup fell in the semi-final to West Germany. The Germans simply cruised into the final against Argentina, courtesy of goals from Andreas Brehme and Rudi Völler.

THE RESULT 1986
Location: Mexico City
Final: Argentina 3 West Germany 2
Shirts: Argentina blue and white, West Germany green
Scorers: Brown, Valdano, Burruchaga; Rummenigge, Völler

ARGENTINA

Pumpido

Cuciuffo Brown Ruggeri

Giusti Burruchaga Batista Olarticoechea Enrique
(Trobbiani)

Valdano Maradona

Rummenigge Allofs
(Völler)

Brehme Eder Magath Matthäus
(Hoeness)

Briegel K Förster Jakobs Berthold

Schumacher

WEST GERMANY

BELOW Diego Maradona sends Peter Shilton the wrong way

THE WORLD CUP
1990

West Germany overcame Diego Maradona and Argentina, gaining revenge for their 1986 final defeat, which meant Franz Beckenbauer joined Brazil's Mario Zagallo as the only other man to win a World Cup as player and coach.

Victory in the Stadio Olimpico saw history made as Franz Beckenbauer became the first man to have won separate World Cups as coach and captain (Zagallo had not captained Brazil), while Argentina saw red and paid the penalty for their negative tactics in the final. Beckenbauer stepped down after the triumphant return home and was promptly succeeded by his former assistant Berti Vogts. However, the Germans have not won a World Cup since.

Unlike four years earlier, the final showdown of Italia '90 was a dull defensive game. Settled by Andreas Brehme's controversial late penalty, it was marred by red cards for Argentina's Pedro Monzon and Gustavo Dezotti. This was the first time that a player had been sent off in a World Cup final.

The 1990 finals were later considered as one of the poorest tournaments in the event's history, partly because of the inferior quality of refereeing. Sepp Blatter, then the general secretary of world governing body FIFA and later its president, decided then and there to launch a campaign to improve refereeing standards.

CAMEROON BRING AN AFRICAN BEAT

Argentina were not a patch on the team who had won the World Cup for the second time in their history just four years earlier. Inspirational captain Diego Maradona was carrying a knee injury and in their showpiece opening match they were pulled apart by nine-man Cameroon, the African surprise package. The Africans, making their debut in the World Cup finals, beat the holders 1-0, thanks to a historic strike from François Omam Biyik.

Cameroon's secret weapon was veteran striker Roger Milla. He provided some of the tournament's highlights but Cameroon were let down by their indiscipline. The Africans led England, managed by Bobby Robson, 2-1 in their quarter-final contest in Naples, but slack defending opened up gaps, which prompted them into conceding two penalties. Both were converted by Gary Lineker, who helped drive England through to their first semi-final appearance for 24 years.

But England's fortune with penalties ran out when they faced West Germany. England finished 1-1 after extra time, but lost the penalty shoot-out 4-3 after Stuart Pearce and Chris Waddle missed their spot-kicks.

England, managed for the last time by Robson, who was moving to PSV Eindhoven, lost to hosts Italy in the third place play-off. By then, the Tottenham midfielder Paul Gascoigne had become a national icon, both for his performances as well as for the tears he shed after being shown a yellow card in the semi-final defeat by the Germans. The card was Gascoigne's second of the tournament, which meant he would have missed the final had England reached that grand stage. Later, Gascoigne returned to Italy to play for Lazio.

THE RESULT 1990
Location: Rome
Final: West Germany 1 Argentina 0
Shirts: West Germany white, Argentina blue
Scorers: Brehme (pen)
Sent Off: Monzón, Dezotti

WEST GERMANY

Illgner
Augenthaler
Berthold (Reuter)   Kohler   Buchwald   Brehme
Hässler   Matthäus
Littbarski   Völler   Klinsmann

Maradona Dezotti

Lorenzo   Basualdo   Troglio   Burruchaga (Calderón)
Sensini   Serrizuela   Ruggeri   Simon (Monzón)
Goycochea

ARGENTINA

England were not the only nation to suffer the pain of penalty punishment. In the second round, Romania fell in the shoot-out to the Irish Republic, who were making an impressive debut under manager Jack Charlton, and Argentina edged past both Yugoslavia in the quarter-finals and hosts Italy in the last four through penalty kicks.

The finest match in the tournament was arguably the second round duel between old rivals Holland and West Germany. Tension surrounding the game was exacerbated in the first half by the expulsions of Holland midfielder Frank Rijkaard and German striker Rudi Völler. Ultimately, West Germany won 2-1, thanks to a sensational performance by striker Jürgen Klinsmann—possibly the best of his career—who scored and made the other goal.

Argentina's new hero, especially in the shoot-outs, was goalkeeper Sergio Goycochea. The first choice, Nery Pumpido, was injured in Argentina's opening group game against the former Soviet Union, so Goycochea played instead.

MARADONA AT HOME IN NAPLES

The duel between Italy and Argentina was staged in Naples, where Maradona was plying his trade at club level. His appeal for Napoli fans to cheer for Argentina backfired, yet they still won.

The downside for Argentina was that their outstanding winger, Claudio Caniggia, received a yellow card for a second time in the tournament and so was suspended from playing in the final.

Maradona had played remarkably throughout Italia '90, considering his injury. But in the final his luck ran out, and he pointed the blame at everyone except himself, including FIFA's Brazilian president João Havelange.

The final straw for Maradona was the controversial award of a late penalty to West Germany for a foul on striker Völler. Lothar Matthäus was the designated German penalty taker. But, citing a muscle strain, the captain handed over the responsibility to Brehme, who made no mistake in shooting past Goycochea.

RIGHT Andy Brehme celebrates his World Cup-winning penalty against Argentina

THE WORLD CUP
1994

After missing out to Mexico in 1986, the United States finally hosted a World Cup and proved better than expected on the pitch by reaching the second round before bowing out to the eventual champions—Brazil.

RIGHT Diana Ross launches the World Cup party in Chicago

The Americans had set themselves a goal of staging the event back in the late 1960s. They had failed with a bid to host the finals in 1986, but won FIFA approval through both their commercial potential and a promise to build a solid professional league.

Bora Milutinovic, a freelance Yugoslav coach, was hired to build a national team on the strength of his work in guiding Mexico, as hosts, to the quarter-finals in 1986. His "Team America" reached the second round before narrowly losing to Brazil, the eventual winners.

The finals proved surprisingly successful, with the average attendance for the tournament reaching its highest-ever figure of 69,000. The total attendance of 3.6 million became the then highest attendance in World Cup history.

The tournament was also the most attended single sport sporting event in US history, and featured the first-ever indoor match in the World Cup finals, when the US hosted Switzerland in the Pontiac Silverdome in Michigan, Detroit.

The competition kicked off at Soldier Field Stadium in Chicago with another penalty miss, when veteran pop star Diana Ross rolled a pretend spot-kick wide during a glitzy opening ceremony in front of US President Bill Clinton.

The opening match saw holders Germany edge past Bolivia 1-0, courtesy of Jürgen Klinsmann's strike on the hour mark. Ultimately, the Germans, playing for the first time as a unified team since the collapse of the Berlin Wall, were dethroned 2-1 by Bulgaria in the quarter-finals.

One of the favorites to win overall had been Colombia, led by their maverick frizzy-haired playmaker Carlos Valderrama, who was dubbed "El Pibe"—the kid. The Colombians had been tipped for great things by no less a judge than Pelé, after an incredible 5-0 win away to Argentina during the qualifying competition, in which winger Faustino Asprilla exploded onto the international scene. Unfortunately, their campaign proved both

THE RESULT 1994
Location: Los Angeles
Final: Brazil 0 Italy 0 (after extra time; Brazil 3-2 on penalties)
Shirts: Brazil yellow, Italy blue

BRAZIL

Taffarel

Jorginho   Aldair Márcio Santos Branco
(Cafu)

Mazinho II Dunga Mauro Silva Zinho
(Paulo Viola)

Romário Bebeto

R Baggio   Massaro

D Baggio Albertini Berti Donadoni
(Evani)

Maldini Baresi Mussi Benarrivo
(Apolloni)

Pagliuca

ITALY

short-lived and tragic. They failed to progress beyond the first group stage, when central defender Andrés Escobar scored an own goal in their 2-1 defeat by the United States.

Colombia's squad returned home to a furious reception from fans and media. The furore was cut short within days, after Escobar was shot dead after an argument near his home. His killer was later jailed for 43 years, but served only 11 years of the sentence before being paroled.

MARADONA MAKES HASTY EXIT

Diego Maradona's final World Cup also proved controversial and short-lived. In 1991 he had fled Italy in disgrace after failing a dope test for cocaine and was banned for 15 months while playing for Napoli. He made a comeback in Spain and then Argentina, playing his way back into the national squad in time for the World Cup finals.

However, after scoring and starring in an opening win against World Cup newcomers Greece, Maradona then failed a further dope test for the stimulant ephedrine, following Argentina's 2-1 win over Nigeria, and was immediately expelled from the tournament. Maradona later blamed the dope test failure on the weight-loss drugs he had been taking prior to the World Cup finals.

His shocked team-mates were not long in following him home to Buenos Aires after their unexpected 3-2 exit at the hands of Romania in the last 16 knockout stage. The Romanian side was built around the creative midfield talents of Gheorghe Hagi, known as the "Maradona of the Carpathians."

For the first time since the four British Home Nations returned to the FIFA fold after World War II, none of them qualified for the finals. However, the Republic of Ireland—largely built around English league players—emerged impressively from a first round group that featured Italy, Mexico, and Norway. They fell at the next hurdle, soundly beaten 2-0 in the last 16 by Holland at the Citrus Bowl Stadium in the midday humidity of Orlando, Florida.

BRAZILIAN BLEND FAITH AND FLAIR

Brazil, despite lacking the flair of some of their previous sides, boasted the most effective strike partnership of the tournament in the European-based pair of Bebeto and Romario.

But a disappointing final against Italy ended scoreless, making it the first in the history of the World Cup to be settled by a penalty shoot-out.

The decisive kick was missed by Italian forward Roberto Baggio, whose goals had been crucial in taking his country all the way to the final at the Rose Bowl Stadium in Los Angeles, California.

Mario Zagallo, the assistant manager of Brazil to Carlos Alberto Parreira, became the first man to be involved in four World Cup winning teams, 20 years after his first attempt at gaining this distinction. Zagallo had been an invaluable outside left in Brazil's victorious teams at Sweden in 1958 and four years later in Chile. He successfully managed Brazil in 1970, but four years later his side crashed out to finish fourth.

ABOVE Consolation for Italy's Roberto Baggio after his decisive penalty miss

THE WORLD CUP
1998

Zinedine Zidane's distinctive balding head won France their first World Cup. The midfielder's headed goals, either side of half-time, was overshadowed by a Brazilian side subdued by striker Ronaldo's pre-match collapse.

THE RESULT 1998

Location: Paris
Final: France 3 Brazil 0
Shirts: France blue, Brazil yellow
Scorers: Zidane 2, Petit
Sent Off: Desailly

FRANCE

Barthez

Thuram   Leboeuf   Desailly   Lizarazu

Petit   Deschamps   Karembeu   Zidane
(Boghossian)

Djorkaeff
(Vieira)

Guivarc'h
(Dugarry)

Ronaldo   Bebeto

Leonardo   Rivaldo   Dunga   César Sampaio
(Denilson)   (Edmundo)

Carlos   Baiano   Aldair   Cafu

Taffarel

BRAZIL

Internazionale striker Ronaldo had been a member of the 1994 Brazil squad, but did not play a game. Yet, by 1998 he was the team's key player and goal scorer. But crucially, on the morning of the World Cup final, he collapsed in the hotel room that he shared with Roberto Carlos, and was taken to hospital for an emergency check-up.

Manager Mario Zagallo, not expecting Ronaldo to be available to play, named an official line-up that featured Edmundo in Ronaldo's place. Surprisingly, Ronaldo appeared in the line-up after being given the medical all clear. Zagallo swiftly obtained FIFA clearance to alter the team line-up and later denied that he had been pressured into including Ronaldo by FIFA officials and/or sponsors. Although Ronaldo did play the entire match, he was never a force in the game and rarely threatened to add to his personal tally of four goals scored during the previous rounds.

Zidane's double and a last-minute third goal from midfielder Emmanuel Petit provided France with a comfortable victory in Saint-Denis, north of Paris. The 3-0 triumph was astonishing because the French side were reduced to ten men after defender Marcel Desailly was sent off.

Desailly's red card cost Thierry Henry an opportunity to make an appearance in the final. The striker had played in all the previous games and as a substitute was expected to play a part. But manager Aimé Jacquet opted to bring on a replacement defender for Desailly instead.

An earlier red card, in England's second round loss to Argentina, had already made David Beckham notorious. England had reached the finals by qualifying from a tough group that included Italy. Under the management of former international midfielder Glenn Hoddle, England had beaten Tunisia and Colombia in their first round group but finished in second spot because of a 2-1 reversal to Romania. It proved a costly slip up because it meant England had to tackle old rivals Argentina in the second round instead of Croatia.

RIGHT Referee Kim Milton Nielsen sends off England's David Beckham

England's Michael Owen, the outstanding new Liverpool striker, scored a superb solo goal, but early in the second half Manchester United midfielder Beckham was sent off by Danish referee Kim Morten Nielsen for flicking a retaliatory foot at the Argentinian midfielder Diego Simeone. England, without the influential Beckham, fought bravely and even had a potential winning "goal" by defender Sol Campbell contentiously disallowed before they eventually succumbed in the lottery of a penalty shoot-out.

Argentina's midfielder Ariel Ortega was given his marching orders during their next game against Holland. Being reduced to ten men meant the same ultimate outcome of defeat. Holland progressed to the finals with a 2-1 win, courtesy of a superb winning goal from Arsenal striker Dennis Bergkamp—later voted the best goal of the finals.

FRANCE FIND WINNING FORMULA

Dutch luck finally ran out. In their semi-final they lost on a penalty shoot-out to Brazil while hosts France, gathering speed and confidence, sneaked past Croatia thanks to the first and second goals of defender Lilian Thuram's international career. France won despite finishing with ten men after Laurent Blanc was sent off after a tussle with Slaven Bilic.

Croatia went on to finish third on their debut at the finals, less than a decade after the country had gained independence out of the wreckage of the former Yugoslavia. Star striker Davor Suker ended up as the tournament's six-goal leading marksman to crown a remarkable season and win the coveted Golden Boot. Less than two months earlier, Suker had became a European club champion with Real Madrid following their slender 1-0 victory over Juventus in the Champions League final.

France went on to defeat Brazil and duly celebrate the triumph for which they had been waiting since fellow countryman Jules Rimet had launched the inaugural World Cup 68 years earlier.

Thousands of delirious fans poured into central Paris to celebrate, and the victorious team undertook an open-top bus parade the following day down the Champs-Elysées. Manager Aimé Jacquet, a former international midfielder, was delighted with the manner of victory because he had been subjected to a barrage of relentless criticism for his tactics and team selection by the daily sports newspaper *L'Equipe*.

Jacquet stepped down after the finals and handed over to assistant Roger Lemerre. The new manager proved that the World Cup triumph had been no fluke by leading France to a further international victory at the subsequent European Championships two years later with a 2-1 success over Italy.

BELOW Team-mates join Zinedine Zidane in celebrating his second goal against Brazil

THE WORLD CUP
2002

Although the trophy went to hot favorites Brazil, the tournament was full of upsets. Holders France made a swift exit, while co-hosts South Korea stunned Portugal, Italy, and Spain to reach the semi-finals.

RIGHT Park Ji-sung of South Korea enjoys that winning feeling against Portugal

South Korea were beaten to third place by Turkey, who had previously never progressed beyond the first round.

This was the first World Cup to be played in Asia. Japan had long been campaigning for the right to stage the finals, and one major step in their bid to impress the world authority FIFA had been the launch of the professional J.League in 1993.

Less than two years before the hosting decision, in 1996, the Japanese were challenged in the bidding race by neighbors South Korea. A major political battle within FIFA ended with a compromise that resulted in both countries being awarded the finals jointly. This decision meant that not only was the 2002 event the inaugural Asian finals but the first, and so far the only, World Cup finals to be co-hosted.

The co-hosting proved highly expensive for FIFA and highly complex in logistical terms. The match schedule for the finals had to be especially organized to ensure that each co-host played all matches in their country. In the end, the tournament organization ran remarkably smoothly.

FRANCE FAIL TO SCORE A GOAL
Out on the pitch, the first of many shocks kicked off with the tournament's grand opening match. Defending champions France were narrowly beaten 1-0 by Senegal, who were making their debut in the finals. Midfielder Papa Bouba Diop

scored the goal for the impressive and organized Senegal side.

France may have been reigning world and European champions but, in a disastrous defense of their World Cup, they were knocked out in the first round without even scoring a goal in their three group games. It was the worst record of any defending nation in the tournament's history, although they were handicapped by the initial absence of Zinedine Zidane. The key midfielder had been injured in a warm-up friendly against South Korea on the eve of the finals. Manager Roger Lemerre, who had guided France, or "Les Bleus," to victory in the European Championship two years earlier, was fired on France's return home, despite having been awarded a contract extension before the finals.

The once-mighty Argentina also failed to make the second round, after finishing third in their group behind England and table-topping Sweden.

THE RESULT 2002
Location: Yokohama
Final: Brazil 2 Germany 0
Scorers: Ronaldo 2
Shirts: Brazil yellow, Germany white

BRAZIL

Marcos

Cafu   Lúcio   Roque Júnior   R Carlos

Ronaldinho   Edmilson   Silva   Kléberson
(Paulista)

Ronaldo   Rivaldo
(Denilson)

Klose   Neuville
(Bierhoff)

Bode   Hamann   Jeremies   Schneider
(Ziege)   (Asamoah)

Metzelder   Ramelow   Linke   Frings

Kahn

GERMANY

With memories of the 1998 World Cup penalty shoot-out still fresh in their memories, Argentina tackled England indoors at Tokyo's Sapporo Dome. England emerged as 1-0 winners courtesy of a penalty converted by David Beckham, who avenged his 1998 World Cup expulsion against the South Americans.

England were guided by Swede Sven-Göran Eriksson, their first foreign manager, and beat Denmark surprisingly easily 3-0 in the second round but then lost 2-1 to Brazil in the quarter-finals. The decisive goal was a long-range fluke shot from Ronaldinho that drifted over the head of helpless England keeper David Seaman. Ronaldinho was sent off in the 57th minute, but Brazil held onto their lead without the influential midfielder for both the rest of this contest and for their semi-final 1-0 victory over Turkey.

SEMI-FINAL SLOTS FILLED BY UNDERDOGS

Japan reached the second round before being eliminated 1-0 by Turkey, while South Korea made the most of their fervent home support to race into the semi-finals and finish fourth overall. South Korea were astutely organized by the Dutch coach Guus Hiddink and inspired by attacking players such as Ahn Jung Hwan, whose extra time goal beat Italy in a dramatic second round tie. Turkey had rarely appeared before in the finals of any major tournament, let alone the World Cup. But they made the most of this opportunity by reaching the semi-final stage. Veteran striker Hakan Sükür scored the fastest-ever goal in the World Cup by taking just 10.8 seconds to give Turkey the lead in a 3-2 win over South Korea in the third place play-off.

The final, played at the International Stadium Yokohama in Japan, belonged to Brazil's prolific striker Ronaldo. He scored twice against a competitive but uninspired German team that clearly missed their key midfielder Michael Ballack, who was suspended after collecting a second yellow card of the tournament in the semi-final.

Ronaldo finished the tournament as its eight-goal leading marksman to not only pick up the Golden Boot but to equal Pelé's Brazilian record of 12 goals overall in World Cup finals.

Oliver Kahn, Germany's captain, became the first goalkeeper to be voted as the best player of the tournament despite making a crucial error to concede the first goal in the final.

Cafu, Brazil's captain, also made history by becoming the first footballer to play in the final of three consecutive World Cups.

BELOW David Seaman is fooled by Ronaldinho's long shot

BELOW Ronaldo scores Brazil's first goal after a mistake by goalkeeper Oliver Kahn

Italy collected their fourth World Cup, although the final shall always be associated with Zinedine Zidane's violent act. The French master was aiming for a fairytale ending to his illustrious career, but instead bowed out disgracefully.

The final pitched France against Italy in Berlin's Olympic Stadium and saw Real Madrid midfielder Zinedine Zidane give France the lead with a cheeky penalty, in what was to be his final game before retiring from the sport.

Italy equalized through a header from rugged central defender Marco Materazzi, which sent the game into extra time. With ten minutes of extra time and the contest still at stalemate, Zidane suddenly launched his head into Materazzi's chest and was sent off for violent conduct by the Argentinian referee Horacio Elizondo.

Subdued France had no Zidane to help them in the penalty shoot-out. Italy, coached by Marcello Lippi, became the second side to win the World Cup on penalties after the French striker David Trezeguet hit the bar with his attempt.

Despite such a disgraceful end to his career, Zidane was voted player of the tournament because of his efforts in masterminding victories over Spain, Brazil, and Portugal to reach the final.

Italy proved to be the tournament's most consistent team, largely thanks to the contributions of the outstanding goalkeeper Gianluigi Buffon, center back and captain Fabio Cannavaro, and influential midfielder Andrea Pirlo.

Their success was all the more dramatic since it occurred at the same time as a trial in Italy, in which senior figures in club football were being accused and found guilty of systemic match-fixing. Juventus official, Luciano Moggi, was the controversial central figure in the corruption scandal. Five of Italy's successful squad and seven other World Cup players returned to Italy after the tournament to find that their club had been relegated to Serie B as punishment. The once mighty trio of Juventus, Lazio, and Fiorentina were demoted.

Italy had beaten Germany 2-0 during extra time at the semi-final stage. The hosts had been one of the most exciting teams to watch under the guidance of former striker Jürgen Klinsmann.

KLINSMANN LEADS GERMAN REVIVAL

The German federation had appointed Klinsmann, a World Cup winner in 1990, as coach in the summer of 2004, following their nation's disappointing showing at the UEFA European Championship. Klinsmann demanded a free hand, which included the right to continue to live in California and bring in his choice of new staff—coaches, assistants, and fitness experts. His approach drew initial skepticism among other coaches and fans. By the time the World Cup finals started, it became clear that Klinsmann was winning fans with his tactics and approach to matches.

Germany made an adventurous—and, crucially, winning—start, by defeating Costa Rica 4-2 in the opening game. New heroes included young striker Lukas Podolski and defender Philipp Lahm. Ultimately, the German effort was halted in a semi-final in Dortmund by Italy in what was

THE RESULT 2006
Location: Berlin
Final: Italy 1 France 1 (after extra time, Italy 5-3 penalties)
Shirts: Italy blue, France white
Scorers: Materazzi; Zidane (pen)
Sent Off: Zidane

ITALY

Buffon

Grosso Cannavaro Materazzi Zambrotta

Camoranesi Gattuso Pirlo Perrotta
(Del Piero)   (De Rossi)

Totti Toni
(Iaquinta)

Henry Zidane
(Wiltord)

Malouda Vieira Makélélé Ribéry
(Diarra)   (Trezeguet)

Abidal Gallas Thuram Sagnol

Barthez

FRANCE

arguably the finest game of the tournament. Italy snatched victory through last-gasp goals in extra time from Fabio Grosso and Alessandro Del Piero.

The Germans scored a 3-1 third place play-off win over Portugal, resulting in a far better finish to their campaign than many home fans had feared.

DULL ENGLAND SUFFER ON SPOT-KICKS

In contrast to the Germans, England's World Cup performances were dreary, in Sven-Göran Eriksson's third and last tournament as national coach. The quarter-finals were once again the end of the road as England lost on penalties for the second time in three World Cups, beaten by Portugal in a shoot-out for the second time in a row—after a similar finish in the 2004 UEFA European Championship held in Portugal.

England's hopes had been hindered by a pre-tournament foot injury to star striker Wayne Rooney, which delayed his arrival. Then fellow striker Michael Owen was seriously injured during a freak accident in a group game against Sweden.

Rooney was sent off for stamping on defender Ricardo Carvalho during the quarter-final contest. Cristiano Ronaldo, Rooney's Manchester United team-mate, endured a hate campaign on his return to English football after having been caught smiling and winking at the Portuguese bench following Rooney's expulsion.

Portugal's progress was ended by France, who inflicted a 1-0 semi-final defeat in a lackluster match through Zidane's 33rd-minute penalty.

South America's challenge ended in the quarter-finals. In the group stage, a surprisingly adventurous Argentina had contributed the goal of the tournament against Serbia & Montenegro, a 24-pass move finished by Esteban Cambiasso. But they lost to Germany on penalties in the quarter-finals while Brazil lost their hold on the trophy at the same stage by a 1-0 reversal to France.

German striker Miroslav Klose finished top scorer with five goals, the lowest tally since 1962, for the winner of the Golden Boot.

BELOW Italy's Marco Materazzi acclaims his equalizer in the final

BOTTOM Zinedine Zidane beats Gigi Buffon to open the score for France

1978

1986

WORLD CUP MOMENTS

ABOVE Keeper Jan Jongbloed comes to Holland's rescue

RIGHT Dutch defender Ruud Krol foils Scotland's Asa Hartford

BELOW Argentina's fans hail Daniel Passarella

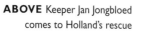

ABOVE Diego Maradona celebrates victory over England

BELOW Gary Lineker pulls one goal back for England

1990   1994   1998   2002   2006

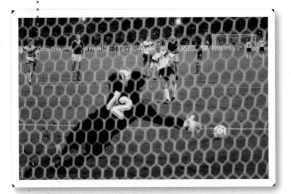

ABOVE Andy Brehme converts
Germany's penalty winner in the final

ABOVE David Beckham scores
England's winner against Argentina

BELOW Sent-off Zinedine
Zidane makes an exit

ABOVE Romario celebrates a
quarter-final goal against Holland

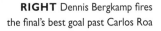

RIGHT Dennis Bergkamp fires
the final's best goal past Carlos Roa

THE WORLD CUP 2010

Football fans all over the world have one ultimate goal: to watch their country's team qualify, compete and win the Jules Rimet trophy – the symbol of football supremacy. The grueling hours of practice, the hard-fought matches, the injuries and the disappointments are all forgotten when teams secure that place to compete. Hopes ride high. With stats, stunning photographs, details on players, managers and teams' history, this is the place to follow that dream.

ARGENTINA

Argentina began their qualification marathon with some degree of fear as veteran coach Alfio Basile returned to lead the side.

PAGE 36 Jackson Martinez of Columbia celebrates his team's first goal during their qualifying match against Chile in October 2009.

PAGE 37 Reneilwe Letsholonyane (right), of World Cup 2010 hosts South Africa in action during a pre-tournament friendly match.

BELOW Head coach Diego Armando Maradona celebrates the victory over Uruguay that qualified Argentina for World Cup 2010.

Basile had guided the team to the 1994 World Cup where they finished third in their group, barely scraping through to the knockout stages when Romania immediately eliminated them. A repeat performance would not be tolerated, but they had to make it there first.

Basile had been invited back after José Pekerman resigned following the quarter-final defeat to host nation Germany in 2006. Having lost stalwarts such as Ayala and Crespo, it was down to the new breed of players like Carlos Tevez and Lionel Messi to make their mark, having both won trophies at club level.

Argentina got off to a good start in Buenos Aires, a disciplined performance that saw off Chile with two first-half goals from Juan Román Riquelme. Another 2-0 win with goals from Gabriel Milito and Lionel Messi away to Venezuela meant that Argentina topped the group and memories of USA '94 were beginning to fade. Riquelme hit another brace against Bolivia the following month, after Sergio Agüero had put them one-up in a 3-0 victory. Argentina were flying, having not yet conceded one goal, and scoring seven.

Despite Carlos Tevez receiving a red card early on in the match, Messi's goal after half an hour made it seem like another romp was probable against Colombia. But, when the home side hit two in the final 30 minutes, it handed the group leaders a shock defeat despite ending 2007 ranked number one in the world. Another defeat looked certain when the team returned to action in June against Ecuador. But substitute Rodrigo Palacio equalized with the last kick of the game.

Having suffered heavy losses in their last two matches, Argentina were desperate for a positive result against Brazil, and could have sealed the match had Messi not squandered two late chances. The 0-0 draw left them within touching distance of Paraguay at the top of the group, and they were up next.

The opportunity to lead the group was dashed after Gabriel Heinze scored an own goal after 13 minutes. The task was made harder when Tevez received his second red card of the campaign. It took a goal from substitute Sergio Agüero to salvage a point and keep Paraguay from running away with the group.

September 2008 proved frustrating as the team threw away two points with the last kick of the game in Peru. Esteban Cambiasso put the visitors ahead with just eight minutes left, but Johan Fano's last-gasp leveler left Argentina third. Nothing less than victory against Uruguay at home would be acceptable for coach Basile, and the team delivered; goals from Messi and Agüero in the first 15 minutes were enough to withstand a second-half goal from Fenerbahçe defender Diego Lugano.

But it was the calm before the storm. A 1-0 loss away to Chile four days later would see Basile hand in his resignation. Javier Mascherano slammed his teammates for the form that led to Basile leaving his job. "It has to do with the players that the coach has resigned; it has to do with the weak level we showed. We are all responsible."

Though former Boca Juniors coach Carlos Bianchi was the bookie's favorite, the AFA decided to take a chance on Argentina's favorite son, one Diego Maradona—but the jury was out on his abilities. He was certainly set up for success; Basile had left the team third in the table and in an automatic qualification spot. Maradona had eight games to keep them there.

An inspired 4-0 thrashing of Venezuela in March 2009 got his competitive reign off to the best possible start, but the next result shocked the world. Minnows Bolivia inflicted Argentina's equal heaviest defeat, wiping them out 6-1 in La Paz, with Maradona claiming, "Every Bolivia goal was a stab in my heart." Riquelme declared he would never again play while Maradona was in charge—it appeared his reign was already falling apart.

Victory over Columbia in June was followed by another defeat to Ecuador. Despite the team's patchy form, Maradona signed a one-year contract extension, and issued a rallying cry ahead of the Brazil clash: "We're going to win because we have better players."

They went down 3-1, Napoli winger Jesús Dátolo grabbing their only goal. Another defeat to Paraguay days later left Argentina facing the real possibility of missing out on qualification.

Two games remained for them to save themselves. Gonzalo Higuaín and a last-minute Martín Palermo goal gave Argentina a dramatic 2-1 victory over Peru and set up a make-or-break game against Uruguay; the winner would proceed

ABOVE Argentina's Carlos Tevez (left) battles for the ball with Bolivia's Rivero Kuhn (right).

to South Africa automatically, while the loser would have to settle for the playoffs.

After Mario Bolatti became a national hero as he came off the bench to hit a late winner, Maradona launched an expletive-laden tirade at the world's press, saying "I want to say that all the people that criticized me and treated me as garbage can eat their words!" The tournament would certainly be more interesting for Argentina's inclusion.

ROAD TO WORLD CUP 2010

Argentina	2-0	Chile
Venezuela	0-2	Argentina
Argentina	3-0	Bolivia
Columbia	2-1	Argentina
Argentina	1-1	Ecuador
Brazil	0-0	Argentina
Argentina	1-1	Paraguay
Peru	1-1	Argentina
Argentina	2-1	Uruguay
Chile	1-0	Argentina
Argentina	4-0	Venezuela
Bolivia	6-1	Argentina
Argentina	1-0	Columbia
Ecuador	2-0	Argentina
Argentina	1-3	Brazil
Paraguay	1-0	Argentina
Argentina	2-1	Peru
Uruguay	0-1	Argentina

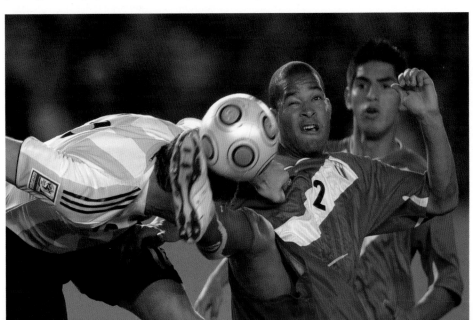

LEFT Argentina's Martin Palermo (left) heads the ball next to Peru's defender Alberto Rodriguez (middle).

BRAZIL

With governing body CONMEBOL placing South American teams in a group of 10, former champions Brazil faced a demanding 18-game campaign, starting a year before other confederations.

ROAD TO WORLD CUP 2010

Columbia	0-0	Brazil
Brazil	5-0	Ecuador
Peru	1-1	Brazil
Brazil	2-1	Uruguay
Paraguay	2-0	Brazil
Brazil	0-0	Argentina
Chile	0-3	Brazil
Brazil	0-0	Bolivia
Venezuela	0-4	Brazil
Brazil	0-0	Columbia
Ecuador	1-1	Brazil
Brazil	3-0	Peru
Uruguay	0-4	Brazil
Brazil	2-1	Paraguay
Argentina	1-3	Brazil
Brazil	4-2	Chile
Bolivia	2-1	Brazil
Brazil	0-0	Venezuela

RIGHT Brazil's Kaká (left) controls the ball in front of Venezuela's Gerzon Chacon (right).

Under ex-player Dunga Brazil were going back to basics rather than relying on the reputation of their larger stars.

This strategy saw the emergence of players such as Juventus midfielder Felipe Melo, with strikers Nilmar and Luís Fabiano returning after years out of the side.

After victory in the 2007 Copa América, the most successful team in World Cup history were expected to qualify with ease. The team got off to a poor start, 0-0 away to Columbia, before returning to Rio to thump Ecuador 5-0. Vágner Love scored the first goal, Ronaldinho the second, and Elano squeezed a goal in between a brace from Kaká.

The hot-and-cold form continued in November 2007 when Brazil let a one-goal lead slip against

Peru; Kaká's third in two games just before half time was canceled out by Juan Vargas. Three days later, there were concerns as Uruguay took an early lead in São Paolo before a Fabiano double salvaged Brazil's unbeaten start.

It would be seven months before Brazil resumed play in the group but it was not a happy restart; goals from Roque Santa Cruz and Salvador Cabañas ensured Paraguay replaced Brazil at the summit. Another 0-0 three days later, this time against archrivals Argentina, proved frustrating for Dunga.

There was an improved performance in September 2008 as Brazil cruised to a 3-0 victory over Chile; another brace from Fabiano and a first for new Manchester City signing Robinho secured the away win. But, once more plagued by inconsistency, Brazil failed to find the net again against Bolivia; another two points lost.

Ronaldinho was dropped for the October matches against Venezuela and Columbia, but Dunga stressed it was not irreversible: "He needs more practice time, more rhythm. He will improve."

Brazil coped without him, hammering four past Venezuela in San Cristóbal. Kaká marked his return from injury with a goal, and Robinho continued his fine form for club and country. Adriano made it three in the first 20 minutes before Robinho sent Brazil home with the points. In what was becoming the theme of their campaign, Brazil once again failed to win the following match, playing out another 0-0 draw against Columbia.

As 2008 ended, Dunga was under pressure for his side's inability to string two wins together. Brazil were joint second in the group with Argentina behind leaders Paraguay. With seven games left, it was time to cut out the mistakes.

Roma midfielder Julio Baptista struck against Ecuador with just 20 minutes left, but Christian Noboa equalized with one minute left to ensure Brazilian frustration continued. Peru at home was earmarked a must-win game, and Fabiano eased any early fears with an 18th-minute penalty. He followed up with a second and, when Melo scored a third in the second half, fans were hoping the inconsistency had ended.

Goals were again no problem against Uruguay, as Brazil recorded a four-goal haul. Dani Alves and Juan netted the first two, before Luis Fabiano got his seventh goal in 13 games and Kaká capped an emphatic victory.

When Paraguay struck first four days later, fans would be forgiven for fearing another draw, but a Robinho volley and a scrappy winner from Nilmar made it three victories in a row. Now top of the group, a win against Argentina in September 2009 would secure a place in South Africa.

However, the Confederations Cup was just four days away. Victory in South Africa strengthened Dunga's position and meant confidence in the camp was again high, particularly for tournament top scorer Fabiano. He added another two to his tally in a 3-1 victory over Argentina after Benfica captain Luisão put Brazil one-up.

The win sent them to the World Cup but fans would argue the party should have begun far earlier. The samba celebrations began with a 4-2 win against Chile in their next game, Nilmar scoring a hat trick and Baptista adding a fourth.

As the final two fixtures approached, the team's desire to win seemed to trail off. They were 2-0 down to second-bottom Bolivia, and not even a Nilmar goal in the second half could spark a comeback. It was Brazil's first loss in 19 matches. The defeat was followed by yet another 0-0 draw, against Venezuela. Brazil still managed to hold on to top spot, just one point in front of Chile and Paraguay.

ABOVE Gilberto Silva (left) of Brazil jumps above Matias Fernandez of Chile to win the ball.

Top scorer Luis Fabiano insisted, "This is a group that can win, that breaks records. Brazil are on the right path and we have to maintain this unity. Of course we will have to correct some things, but we are following the right path." They certainly needed Fabiano firing if they were to win their sixth World Cup.

LEFT Luis Fabiano (left) scores the first goal against Argentina during Brazil's 3-1 victory.

WORLD CUP 2010, TEAMS
ENGLAND

England kicked off their qualifying campaign for South Africa with a point to prove after failing to reach Euro 2008. The taste of defeat to Croatia was still fresh as the team traveled to Barcelona to face minnows Andorra.

The venue was switched to Spain in order to accommodate a large crowd, as was the case when the two teams met in 2006. England had become a better side under former Real Madrid and Juventus manager Fabio Capello; the Italian, appointed in December 2007, was known for his discipline and tactical mind, and it appeared to be paying off.

England had lost only once with Capello at the helm—a 1-0 friendly defeat to France in his second game. No such mistake was repeated as, with John Terry once again leading, Chelsea teammate Joe Cole bagged both goals as Andorra were soundly beaten.

All thoughts were already on the next game. After England were drawn with Croatia in their qualifying group, David Beckham revealed his wounds from their last encounter had not yet fully healed: "All players like to get their own back on a team who've beaten them and we'll be no different…we have to go there and perform better than we did in the Euros."

The battle lines were drawn as the team arrived in Zagreb. Croatia's home record was very impressive—they had lost just one competitive fixture at the Maksimir Stadium in nearly two decades—so heads were turned when Theo Walcott blasted England ahead within half an hour. It was the beginning of a rout, the Arsenal winger going on to grab a hat trick, with Wayne Rooney compounding the Croats' misery.

While Croatia would regain some measure of pride, thrashing Andorra in their next game, it just got better for England. As the new Wembley hosted its first World Cup qualifier, the Three Lions turned on the style against Kazakhstan, crushing them 5-1 in front of nearly 90,000. Kuchma scored an own goal while Ferdinand and Defoe grabbed their first goals of the campaign. Rooney struck twice, sending out a message to the rest of Group Six—England had won three out of three, scoring an impressive 11 and conceding just two.

Four days later, Rooney bagged another brace against Belarus in Minsk. Gerrard put England one-up before Pavel Sitko equalized on 28 minutes. With Capello's men bulldozing the group, and Wayne Rooney unstoppable, it was unfortunate there was a five-month break between qualifiers.

England picked up where they left off in April 2009, defeating Ukraine 2-1. Crouch had put the whites ahead, before Andriy Shevchenko equalized with 15 minutes left. It was left to captain John Terry to score a rare goal with his feet on 85 minutes to send Ukraine home empty-handed.

As the midway point of qualifying approached, England hit their peak, hitting an incredible 10 goals in two games with no reply. First to be put to the sword were the Kazakhs, falling to a 4-0 home defeat with Gareth Barry, Emile Heskey, and Rooney putting England three-up before a

BELOW Wayne Rooney (left) and Fabio Capello (right) in discussion during England's 1-0 loss to Ukraine.

Lampard penalty completed the victory.

A return to home turf saw Andorra hit for six; Rooney and Defoe notched a brace apiece, with Lampard and Crouch also getting in on the action. Rooney, lauded as England's talisman in the run-up to Euro 2004, was now living up to the title.

The final stretch beckoned and England had a 100% record in the group. It was equally fitting and inevitable that qualification for the World Cup would be secured with a result over Croatia at Wembley. It was a businesslike performance, Lampard netting a penalty within 10 minutes and Gerrard sending England in 2-0 up. The style was turned on in the second half as the Chelsea and Liverpool midfielders bagged a second goal each. Arsenal striker Eduardo hit back but it was Rooney who ended the display with an incredible ninth goal of the campaign.

England were on the plane to South Africa with three games still to play. Their 100% record had finally put to bed the events of two years earlier.

Capello insisted the team would not rest on their laurels as they prepared to face Ukraine, who still had it all to play for. But England put in an uninspiring performance, compounded by Robert Green's sending-off in the first half. A second-half Nazarenko goal handed England their first defeat, and marked the first time they had failed to score.

The team prepared to end the campaign on a high in front of the Wembley faithful against

Belarus. With Capello inviting all current England representatives to the game there was a real sense of occasion as Peter Crouch put the hosts in front in just four minutes. Shaun Wright-Phillips added the second and Crouch completed a personal double 15 minutes from time to stake his claim for a place in the squad for the finals.

With only one blot on their qualifying copybook, England accepted that the expectations of the nation had once again been considerably raised as they prepared to try to win the World Cup for the second time in their history.

ROAD TO WORLD CUP 2010

Andorra	0-2	England
Croatia	1-4	England
England	5-1	Kazakhstan
Belarus	1-3	England
England	2-1	Ukraine
Kazakhstan	0-4	England
England	6-0	Andorra
England	5-1	Croatia
Ukraine	1-0	England
England	3-0	Belarus

ABOVE Danijel Pranjic of Croatia (left) is unable to stop Theo Walcott of England (right) scoring.

LEFT Peter Crouch (right) scores his second goal against Belarus during England's 3-0 victory.

FRANCE

"Les Bleus" had a World Cup qualifying campaign peppered with controversy and criticism, and one which came just 20 minutes from, possibly, being derailed.

ABOVE Bacary Sagna beats Serbia forward Nikola Zigic during their 1-1 draw in Belgrade.

The 1998 champions still had a team considered one of the best in the world, and would certainly be among the favorites in South Africa. But qualifying was not to prove a straightforward task.

Coach Raymond Domenech had been in charge of France since 2004. His predecessor Jacques Santini had resigned, unable to emulate the success of World Cup and European Championship winners Aimé Jacquet and Roger Lemerre respectively.

A stuttering qualifying campaign for the 2006 World Cup put Domenech under immediate scrutiny. But a run to the final, including victories over Spain, Brazil, and Portugal, won some doubters over, even though France eventually lost to Italy.

Domenech's team selection frequently baffled fans and media alike, although the recall of previously retired players such as Lilian Thuram and Claude Makelele appeared to pay off, as both were instrumental in Germany.

The team had a disastrous Euro 2008, exiting at the group stages despite a team that was strong in all departments. The international experience of William Gallas in defense complemented the tenacity of young full-backs Bacary Sagna and Patrice Evra. The team had attacking flair in the form of wingers Florent Malouda and Sidney Govou and goal-scoring potential in strikers Nicolas Anelka and Thierry Henry.

The pressure was on for the players and manager to succeed. But their first qualifying game in Vienna was nothing less than a disaster as France lost 3-1 to Austria, Govou hitting their

only goal. Domenech attacked the world's media after the match: "I'm happy the guillotine no longer exists, otherwise some of you would have been delighted to send me there."

A 2-1 victory over Serbia days later did little to appease the doubters, Henry and Anelka notching two goals in 10 minutes at the beginning of the second half. The year ended on a worrying note for France as Romania held them to a 2-2 draw in Constanta. The hosts raced to a 2-0 lead after 20 minutes and it took Franck Ribery and Bordeaux midfielder Yoann Gourcuff to spare French blushes.

Successive 1-0 victories against Lithuania were anything but convincing, but nevertheless gave France a much-needed six-point boost. Franck Ribery grabbed the only goal in both matches, contributing to his rising stock.

The trend of narrow victories over smaller countries continued as they edged past the Faroe Islands in August 2009, a first international goal from André-Pierre Gignac collecting the points. But 1-1 draws against Romania and Serbia meant France had to face up to the possibility of the playoffs instead of automatic qualification. Serbia were four points ahead after their draw, with just two games left to play.

France showed their desire to qualify automatically with a 5-0 thumping of the Faroe Islands—Gallas, Anelka, and Real Madrid striker Karim Benzema among the scorers. Unfortunately, Serbia recorded the same scoreline against Romania; participation in the playoffs was now reality.

LEFT William Gallas is mobbed after his controversial playoff winner against the Republic of Ireland.

There was controversy, however, as replays showed Thierry Henry had handled the ball before crossing it to Gallas, an incident likened to Maradona's "Hand of God" goal against England at the 1986 World Cup. "I didn't deliberately do it," said Henry, "but it was handball. The ball bounced off my hand, the referee did not see it and I played on... I'm happy we have qualified."

A clearly relieved Domenech echoed his captain's sentiments. "I am very happy for the players and the staff and the people here. The only word we need to say tonight is that we are very happy at the qualification."

France had stumbled over the line to qualify for the World Cup. But they had reached their fourth consecutive World Cup finals, and hope was running high for a repeat, or better, of their 2006 performance.

ROAD TO WORLD CUP 2010

Austria	3-1	France
France	2-1	Serbia
Romania	2-2	France
Lithuania	0-1	France
France	1-0	Lithuania
Faroe Islands	0-1	France
France	1-1	Romania
Serbia	1-1	France
France	5-0	Faroe Islands
France	3-1	Austria
Republic of Ireland	0-1	France
France	1-1	Republic of Ireland (AET)

BELOW Nicolas Anelka hits the winner in the first leg of France's playoff against the Republic of Ireland.

A 3-1 victory at home to Austria coupled with a Serbian defeat meant France only finished one point below the leaders, but still had to beat the Republic of Ireland in the playoffs to secure a place at the tournament. France had at least avoided meeting "stronger" opponents in Portugal, Russia or Greece thanks to FIFA controversially seeding the draw.

Domenech was bullish ahead of the tie. "The advantage is that we all know the Irish team, it's like another England. All the (French) players know them. We even have some players who play alongside them, so there won't be too many surprises."

The first leg in Dublin was a close affair, a deflected goal from Nicolas Anelka deciding the tie. But confidence was shattered 30 minutes into the second leg in Paris when Ireland leveled the tie on aggregate. The game looked set for penalties before William Gallas headed in from a yard out.

GERMANY

Germany began their qualifying schedule with only one aim—to target their first World Cup triumph in nearly two decades.

ROAD TO WORLD CUP 2010

Liechtenstein	0-6	Germany
Finland	3-3	Germany
Germany	2-1	Russia
Germany	1-0	Wales
Germany	4-0	Liechtenstein
Wales	0-2	Germany
Azerbaijan	0-2	Germany
Germany	4-0	Azerbaijan
Russia	0-1	Germany
Germany	1-1	Finland

The progression started under Jürgen Klinsmann, who had taken the national team to third place in the 2006 World Cup and was very popular with fans after his exploits as a player. Despite Germany's commendable finish he resigned immediately afterward, with assistant Joachim Löw promoted to the top job.

Löw decided to stay at the helm after defeat to Spain in the final of Euro 2008. He was buoyed by the prospect of a winnable qualification group, Russia being the only rival with any real international pedigree.

Germany made the short trip to Liechtenstein for their opening fixture and cruised to a 6-0 victory. Two Lucas Podolski goals either side of half time were followed up by a blitz in the final 30 minutes, Rolfes, Schweinsteiger, Hitzlsperger, and Westermann's first international strike completing the rout.

The next game would not prove so easy. Germany had to fight back three times to take a point against Finland in Helsinki, thanks to Miroslav Klose, who completed his hat trick with just seven minutes remaining. It was a wake-up call, but Löw was happy with his side's spirit. "If you draw 3-3 then you can't say that everything went really well, but we can say that it was a point gained."

Germany continued rotating their games around the stadia built for the 2006 World Cup as they took on Russia in Dortmund. The game was a straightforward affair, Podolski and captain Michael Ballack ensuring they were two-up before half time, before a strike from Andrei Arshavin for the Russians.

A 1-0 defeat of Wales four days later ensured Germany were on course for the finals as 2008 ended. Hamburg midfielder Piotr Trochowski scored the only goal in Mönchengladbach against

RIGHT Michael Ballack of Germany scores past goalkeeper Wayne Hennessey of Wales during Germany's 2-0 victory.

a Welsh side that had won two of their previous three games.

However, all was not well in the camp. Michael Ballack, an outspoken critic of previous administrations, turned his attention to Löw, blasting the coach for dropping Werder Bremen midfielder Torsten Frings to the bench, claiming it showed a lack of respect to the 31 year-old who had amassed 78 caps for his country.

Although the player later said sorry, the in-fighting had exposed Germany as seemingly ripe for the picking. This proved not to be the case as 2009 began in Leipzig, Germany blowing away Liechtenstein with four goals in less than an hour. They went two-up through Ballack and Marcell Jansen, while Schweinsteiger and Podolski grabbed a further brace within five minutes of the restart. The victory strengthened Germany's position at the top spot of Group Four with five games to play.

A professional performance against Wales at the Millennium Stadium in April brought a 2-0 victory, thanks to Ballack and Wales defender Ashley Williams who scored an own goal. Although it seemed Ballack had put his recent troubles behind him, a bust-up with teammate Podolski in the second half once again showed German frailties.

Off the pitch wasn't proving any easier. The international retirement of Oliver Kahn and Jens Lehmann, who held the monopoly on the position for years, left Löw with little international experience to call upon. Lehmann announced his desire to return, but Werder Bremen keeper Tim Wiese blasted. "He is absolutely over-rated and out of touch with reality. It is a real pity."

Despite the continued sniping, Germany rolled over Azerbaijan in August 2009. Schweinsteiger maintained Germany's penchant for early goals with an 11th-minute strike, while Klose returned to the score sheet in the second half. More had been expected against the minnows, especially with former Germany coach Berti Vogts at the helm.

A stronger message was sent to their old boss a month later with the return game in Hannover. An early Ballack penalty set the tone as Klose

added two more in 10 minutes in the second half. Ballack's sparring partner Podolski completed the 4-0 romp, leaving just Germany and Russia to battle it out for top spot in the group.

The game in Moscow was tense, the only goal arriving after 35 minutes when Klose got his seventh of the campaign. The disciplined display ensured Germany qualified for the World Cup with one game to spare. Löw was overjoyed with his side after their calm display. "We came here with no intention of playing for a draw. We only wanted to win."

Germany's chances looked good; the flair of Schweinsteiger and Lahm coupled with the experience and quality of veterans Ballack and Klose seemed to provide the perfect balance for a strong campaign in South Africa.

First, however, the team that gathered in Hamburg for their final match against Finland was inexperienced and it required a Podolski goal in the final minute to deny the Finns victory.

It didn't take the gloss off a solid, unbeaten campaign for the Germans, who were already looking to South Africa and the possibility of a fourth World Cup win.

ABOVE Miroslav Klose (right) celebrates scoring the winning goal with midfielder Mesut Oezil (left) during Germany's 1-0 victory over Russia.

BELOW German midfielder Piotr Trochowski (right) tackles Finland's Kasper Haemaelaeinen (left) during the 1-1 draw in Hamburg.

ITALY

Current holders Italy found themselves in the peculiar position of having to qualify for the World Cup in South Africa. A FIFA ruling in 2002 denied them a guaranteed place, even though the host nation were spared the task of qualifying.

After high expectations were dashed in Euro 2008 under former player Roberto Donadoni, Marcelo Lippi, the architect of Italy's success in Germany, was re-appointed. The chance to retain the trophy in 2010 proved too tempting for the 61-year-old tactician, as he took charge for a second time in June 2008.

The core of Lippi's champions was still intact, but players such as Gianluigi Buffon and Gennaro Gattuso were now into their 30s. But with striker Alberto Gilardino and midfielder Daniele De

BELOW Alberto Gilardino (center) slides in to score Italy's dramatic, late equalizer against the Republic of Ireland.

Rossi hitting their peak, many hoped Italy could find the right mix.

The team got off to a winning start, though were lucky to leave Cyprus with three points; Antonio Di Natale scored his second of the game two minutes into injury time. Success against Georgia later that week was more convincing. De Rossi bagged both goals at Udinese's Stadio Friuli, and the Azzurri had a 100% record after their opening fixtures. Lippi was content with his side's start to the campaign. "We finished with two good results and now we can go home and get five or six [domestic] games under our belts before the next matches."

The return to domestic action did not appear to sharpen the strikers' instincts as Italy drew a blank against Bulgaria with the likes of Buffon and Andrea Pirlo missing. With winless Montenegro up next, Lippi demanded improvement. "If we win, then the draw in Sofia will become a good result but, if we don't, then they will become two bad matches."

The 2-1 victory with two goals from midfielder Alberto Aquilani ensured Italy topped Group Eight as 2009 beckoned, but fans were hoping the new year would bring more goals.

Lippi's first squad of the year was hampered by injury and age, with veterans Alessandro Del Piero and Filippo Inzaghi again left out, as well as first-team regulars Gilardino and Gattuso. Despite this, they were too much for Montenegro; a Pirlo penalty and

a Giampaolo Pazzini header ensured the minnows were glad to see the back of the world champions.

A showdown with second-place Ireland beckoned in Bari. Disaster struck when Italy were reduced to 10 men within five minutes; Pazzini received his marching orders after an elbow on John O'Shea. But it was the home side that took the lead just six minutes later; Fabio Grosso threaded a ball to Vicenzo Iaquinta who finished coolly. The one-man deficit proved costly, however, as Ireland bossed the game and grabbed a deserved equalizer three minutes from time.

The team had five months until their next qualifier, and the Confederations Cup in South Africa offered some respite from the pressure. After a disappointing tournament saw them finish third in their group, including a shock 1-0 defeat to Egypt, confidence was low in the Italian camp. Following a 2-0 victory over Georgia, a return to the Stadio Olimpico in Turin spelt trouble for visitors Bulgaria; Italy were going back to basics.

A thoroughly professional performance saw Italy break away from Ireland at the top, four points ahead with two to play. Grosso struck early with a volley after 10 minutes, and Iaquinta set up a comfortable second half by grabbing the second goal just before the half-time whistle. Only one point was needed against Ireland in October to ensure the holders were able to defend their crown.

Seventy thousand crammed into Croke Park,

most hoping Ireland could pull off the victory. And it was the home side that took the lead early on, before Mauro Camoranesi leveled the score 15 minutes later.

Ireland looked to have sealed victory with just three minutes left to play; Sean St. Ledger wheeled away to celebrate the goal that left Italy's automatic qualification far from guaranteed. But it was not to be, as Gilardino secured the point needed in the last minute.

With just a game against Cyprus left, Italy had booked their place in the finals, but it was far from convincing. The victories were never comprehensive, and the lack of goals was cause for concern with free-scoring sides such as Brazil and England having already qualified.

An under-strength side started out in Parma with their place in South Africa secured, and it looked like the minds of the players were already there as the Cypriots took a shock 2-0 lead. Quality shone through in the second half, though, as Gilardino struck three times in 14 minutes to secure the three points.

Though unbeaten in the group, Lippi issued a rallying call to his team: "We want to defend our title and that means doing a lot better. If we want to win the World Cup again, we have to step up the tempo now. Italy, like all the big nations, never goes to these tournaments just to take part."

ROAD TO WORLD CUP 2010

Cyprus	1-2	Italy
Italy	2-0	Georgia
Bulgaria	0-0	Italy
Italy	2-1	Montenegro
Montenegro	0-2	Italy
Italy	1-1	Republic of Ireland
Georgia	0-2	Italy
Italy	2-0	Bulgaria
Republic of Ireland	2-2	Italy
Italy	3-2	Cyprus

NETHERLANDS

The Netherlands were placed in the smallest of the UEFA qualifying groups. Playing against some perceived minnows, they were out to make a statement.

The Netherlands' record in World Cups had been less than satisfactory, despite two final appearances in the 1970s.

Like Spain coach Luis Aragonés, Marco Van Basten chose the end of Euro 2008 to announce his resignation, deciding instead to manage Ajax. He was replaced by Feyenoord manager Bert Van Marwijk, who had a high standard to maintainI; Van Basten was revered for his illustrious playing career.

Hopes were high the new crop of Dutch players could match expectations. Players such as Arjen Robben, Klaas-Jan Huntelaar, and Rafael Van Der Vaart were all mid-20s and playing at Europe's top clubs.

The team kicked off solidly with a 2-1 away victory at Macedonia through Atletico Madrid defender John Heitinga and Van Der Vaart. There was controversy surrounding the match as striker

Dirk Kuyt hit out at Van Marwijk's decision to leave him on the bench for the game, opting instead to bring him on for the final 20 minutes in place of Van Persie. "I will never accept my role as 12th man. Being a substitute is unacceptable to me."

His coach defused the situation, claiming, "Dirk just looks in the mirror and wants to get more out of his career. He demands a starting place from himself, not from me. That only means that he is a good sportsman."

Kuyt was restored to the starting XI for the October 2008 match against Iceland in Rotterdam, as was record cap holder Edwin Van Der Sar. Injuries to both first-choice goalkeepers Maarten Stekelenburg and Henk Timmer caused Van Der Sar to come out of retirement.

Hamburg center-back Joris Mathijsen opened the scoring for the hosts after just 15 minutes before Huntelaar grabbed his first of the campaign. It was two wins out of two for the Netherlands as they headed to Oslo to face Norway. Mark Van Bommel struck after an hour to ensure the points and Van Der Sar got the send-off he hoped, keeping two clean sheets during his brief return.

Stekelenburg returned between the sticks for Holland's first game of 2009 when Scotland visited the Amsterdam Arena, despite Van Marwijk's best efforts to coax Van Der Sar back permanently; Huntelaar and Van Persie put them two-up by half time before Kuyt hit a late third.

Another four goals without reply crushed Macedonia, and the coach chose to express his confidence in his keeper amid all the talk of

BELOW Nigel de Jong of The Netherlands (left) scores while compatriot Robin van Persie (center) and Gretar Steinsson of Iceland (right) look on.

nostalgia. "I will stick by Stekelenburg. He has the most potential of all [my goalkeepers] and is the best available." Kuyt continued where he left off with a first-half double either side of a 25th-minute Huntelaar strike, and Van Der Vaart wrapped up proceedings with two minutes to go.

The Dutch were flying, and needed a victory against Iceland to become the first UEFA team to qualify for the finals. Another goal avalanche looked on the cards as a header from Nigel De Jong and Van Bommel's strike put them 2-0 up within 15 minutes, but it stayed that way until defender Kristján Sigurðsson pulled one back with three minutes to go.

Six wins out of six meant Holland were unchallenged, but the coach would not allow thoughts to wander until the campaign was over. This was proved with a 2-0 defeat of Norway, André Ooijer and Arjen Robben ensured the perfect sequence continued in Rotterdam ahead of their last game against Scotland.

On the eve of the game and the Oranje still without an established number one, Van Der Sar started the next chapter of his "will he won't

ABOVE Dutch forward Klaas-Jan Huntelaar slots the ball past Macedonian goalkeeper Tome Pacovski.

he" saga while recovering from a broken hand: "The rehabilitation of my injury is the most important thing right now. After that, I will focus on [Manchester] United and then we will see what is happening with the national team."

Meanwhile Van Marwijk was quick to play down any thoughts of complacency, instead keen to be the first manager to lead the Dutch through qualifying with a 100% record. "Winning all eight games is an extra motivation for me. The players also have that extra motivation."

There was less than 10 minutes on the clock when Hamburg winger Eljero Elia came off the bench to secure the perfect qualifying campaign. It was only Elia's second international appearance, showing the future was bright for the team as the tournament approached.

With the likelihood that Group Nine would not receive a playoff place, most of the media attention turned elsewhere, leaving a certain understated orange team to conduct their business and hope that it would be third time lucky in South Africa.

ROAD TO WORLD CUP 2010

Macedonia	1-2	Netherlands
Netherlands	2-0	Iceland
Norway	0-1	Netherlands
Netherlands	3-0	Scotland
Netherlands	4-0	Macedonia
Iceland	1-2	Netherlands
Netherlands	2-0	Norway
Scotland	0-1	Netherlands

LEFT Dirk Kuyt (number 9) of the Netherlands wins the ball against Steven Naismith of Scotland.

PORTUGAL

Portugal had long been seen as underachievers on the world footballing stage.

Despite improved performances at Euro 2004 and World Cup 2006, it was widely believed that nothing short of a trophy for Portugal would do, given their current crop of players.

The Portuguese FA brought in a man who knew all about nurturing player potential; Carlos Queiroz was appointed manager in July 2008, despite a less than successful spell in the early 1990s where Portugal failed to qualify for both Euro 1992 and the 1994 World Cup.

He was, however, in charge of the Portuguese side that won the 1989 and 1991 FIFA Youth Championships, with teams that included

BELOW José Bosingwa keeps Sweden striker Kim Kallstroem at arm's length.

future stars Paulo Sousa and, latterly, Luis Figo and Rui Costa.

That, coupled with a stint as Real Madrid manager, and two spells as assistant to Alex Ferguson at Manchester United, meant hopes were high Queiroz could get the best out of the national team and inspire them to their first ever World Cup win.

The new generation of Portuguese stars was promising. In Bruno Alves, Pepe, and José Bosingwa they had three defenders at their peak, while players such as Deco and Simão had a wealth of European experience as well as killer instinct in front of goal.

But the jewel in the crown was undoubtedly Cristiano Ronaldo. The player named the world's best was both captain and inspiration for the team. Many thought the World Cup would be diminished without him, so the pressure was on for Portugal to top a group containing tough opposition in both Sweden and Denmark.

A 4-0 hammering of Malta gave them a dream start; an own goal in the first half was followed up by three second-half goals from Werder Bremen striker Hugo Almeida, Simão, and Manchester United's Nani.

Portugal were devastated in Lisbon days later when they thought victory was assured after Deco scored against Denmark with four minutes remaining, but two late goals from the visitors left Portugal with nothing.

It would be the start of a barren run that would threaten Portugal's chances of making it past the group stage. Three successive 0-0 draws—two against Sweden and another against Albania—

would leave them in critical condition. They only had six points from five matches.

They were heading for another draw against Albania until Bruno Alves snatched victory with a header in injury time. Many were hoping it would kick-start Portugal's qualification challenge, but it was not to be as, days later, they drew 1-1 with group leaders Denmark, leaving it late again, with Sporting Lisbon striker Liédson scoring with four minutes left.

As teams entered the final stretch, things did not bode well for Portugal, and failure to qualify looked a real possibility. They had to win their last three games and hope Sweden slipped up along the way. It was no longer in their own hands. A Pepe goal in the 10th minute won the game against Hungary in Budapest—a vital away win but, with Sweden winning as well, games were fast running out.

Hungary visited Lisbon days later in the second match of their double-header. This time Portugal were far more comfortable, running out 3-0 winners with a Simão brace either side of a Liédson goal. With Denmark toppling Sweden, Portugal's playoff place was theirs to lose, with just Malta left to play.

The downside to the victory was Ronaldo's substitution after just 27 minutes. A later scan showed he would be out for a month, missing Portugal's final group match and the playoffs—if they reached them.

But the team showed they could cope without their talisman as they crushed Malta 4-0 in Lisbon, their desire to reach the finals showing just in time.

Portugal were seeded in the playoff draw and were paired with Bosnia & Herzegovina, who had impressed in a group that included Spain.

Striker Simão called on his teammates to perform in the absence of Ronaldo. "It would have been important to have him, but we have top-quality players who will do their best. The perfect Saturday would be a win for Portugal without conceding goals."

He got his wish; a Bruno Alves header gave them a narrow victory in the Estadio da Luz, despite the visitors hitting the woodwork a number of times. The second leg in Zenica was equally tense, but the tie was put beyond doubt after 56 minutes when Porto midfielder Raul Meireles struck from a Nani cross.

Portugal had come into form at precisely the right time. Despite only losing once in qualification, their inability to find the goal caused too many draws but, when it mattered, they had players all over the pitch who hit the goals to send them through, even without Cristiano Ronaldo. That would be enough to worry other teams, if and when they reached their top level in South Africa.

ABOVE It was a frustrating qualifying campaign for the Portuguese, and Cristiano Ronaldo in particular.

ROAD TO WORLD CUP 2010

Malta	0-4	Portugal
Portugal	2-3	Denmark
Sweden	0-0	Portugal
Portugal	0-0	Albania
Portugal	0-0	Sweden
Albania	1-2	Portugal
Denmark	1-1	Portugal
Hungary	0-1	Portugal
Portugal	3-0	Hungary
Portugal	4-0	Malta
Portugal	1-0	Bosnia & Herzegovina
Bosnia & Herzegovina	0-1	Portugal

LEFT Raul Meireles celebrates his goal against Bosnia that confirmed Portugal's passage to South Africa.

SPAIN

Spain began the qualifying process as perhaps the most feared team on the planet. Victory at Euro 2008 placed them as kings of Europe, and they began their road to South Africa ranked number one in the world by FIFA, despite never having won a World Cup.

ABOVE David Villa celebrates after scoring his second goal in Spain's 5-0 win against Belgium.

RIGHT Gerard Piqué of Spain (center) climbs high to win the ball from Bosnia's Miralem Pjanic (right).

Manager Luis Aragonés left his post after the summer's triumph to return to club management. Former Real Madrid boss Vincente Del Bosque was charged with carrying the expectations of an ambitious nation.

The form of strikers David Villa and Fernando Torres led many in Spain and beyond to believe qualification would be a foregone conclusion. The pressure was on for Del Bosque to deliver.

The squad was largely the same as 2006, but youngsters such as Torres and Cesc Fabregas had matured. The campaign got off to a low-key start in Murcia; a solid performance saw them squeeze past Bosnia & Herzegovina, Villa getting the only goal of the game just before the hour. With Bosnia & Herzegovina going on to thrash Estonia 7-0 in their next game, it would be seen as a good result.

Spain made the short trip to Albacete for their second fixture against Armenia. This time, the goals rained as Joan Capdevila opened the scoring after seven minutes, before Villa grabbed a brace either side of the break. Villarreal midfielder Marcos Senna topped off a magnificent performance with a fourth on 83 minutes.

October 2008 saw Spain travel to Estonia where they achieved their third win out of three under Del Bosque. Real Betis defender Juanito opened the scoring with a header with 34 minutes played, before Torres was felled in the box and Villa put away the resulting penalty just

four minutes later. Carlos Puyol made it three in the second half and ensured Spain continued their 100 percent record in style.

Wesley Sonck shocked the Spanish with an early strike for Belgium in their next match, a lead that would last just half an hour before Andrés Iniesta leveled the scores. Villa ensured the three points with his fifth goal in four games.

Spain began the New Year at the Bernabéu where they welcomed unbeaten Turkey in the first

of a double-header over just five days. Barcelona defender Gerard Piqué settled the game on the hour mark in a low-key affair. The return fixture in Istanbul was not as easy, as Fenerbahçe striker Semih put the home side ahead in the first half. It was left to Liverpool pair Xabi Alonso and Albert Riera to salvage the three points, the latter scoring two minutes into injury time. Spain were proving they could win ugly—albeit with a bit of luck.

As summer approached. the Confederations Cup beckoned; Spain continued their incredible form, including breaking the world record of 15 consecutive victories. A shock defeat in the semi-finals to the United States meant they had to settle for third place after victory over the hosts South Africa, though they still had four players in FIFA's team of the tournament.

The defeat in South Africa only served as inspiration for further success as they returned to action in September 2009, scoring eight goals in two games without reply. The first team they defeated was Belgium at the Estadio Riazor. David Silva and Villa nabbed a brace apiece while Piqué also got on the scoresheet in a 5-0 crushing.

"It seems incredible that we are not yet qualified" said an exasperated Torres after the game. Indeed, it was the team's seventh victory in a row in the group, but victory against Estonia in Mérida would seal the deal. Cesc Fabregas got the ball rolling before young wingers Santi Cazorla and Juan Mata added a goal each later on to ensure the celebrations began in earnest.

Spain had brushed aside all before them in qualifying, with two games left to play. They could be forgiven for not concentrating fully when they journeyed to Armenia four days later but Del Bosque insisted there would be none of that. "We only have five games before the tournament—we have to profit from them to the max."

Playing for their World Cup futures, the players impressed. Despite an equalizer from Arzumanyan after Fabregas had put the visitors ahead, Mata continued his fine start to his international career with the winner from the penalty spot.

Spain's campaign came full circle as they lined up against Bosnia in Zenica for their final game, their hosts already guaranteed a playoff place. Piqué and Silva put the table-toppers two-up within 15 minutes before a second-half brace from Alvaro Negredo in his first international start made it four. A last-minute fifth from Mata made it 5-2.

The result was the perfect finish to the perfect qualifying campaign; 10 wins from 10 games, with 28 scored and only five conceded meant every team was looking over their shoulders at Spain, who were looking to justify their place at the top of the world rankings.

BELOW The ball on its way to the net as Cesc Fabregas scores for Spain against Estonia.

ROAD TO WORLD CUP 2010

Spain	1-0	Bosnia & Herzegovina
Spain	4-0	Armenia
Estonia	0-3	Spain
Belgium	1-2	Spain
Spain	1-0	Turkey
Turkey	1-2	Spain
Spain	5-0	Belgium
Spain	3-0	Estonia
Armenia	1-2	Spain
Bosnia & Herzegovina	2-5	Spain

USA

The United States had to play an incredible seven games just to contest the final CONCACAF qualifying group. After crushing Barbados 9-0 over two legs in June 2008, they entered a third-round group consisting of Trinidad & Tobago, Guatemala, and Cuba.

It was the beginning of a tough schedule for coach Bob Bradley, who had moved up from assistant to Bruce Arena following a disastrous World Cup in Germany.

The US national team had long been considered a force for the future, with football rising in popularity. Tim Howard was a worthy successor to Kasey Keller in goal, while Landon Donovan had experience far beyond his 27 years, racking up over 100 caps. The emergence of young striker Jozy Altidore and form of attacking midfielder Clint Dempsey meant hopes were high.

A 69th-minute Bocanegra goal was enough to ensure a winning start away to Guatemala. The following month Dempsey made it two from two in Havana against Cuba. Eleven thousand at Toyota Park, Illinois, saw Bradley's son Michael score the first against Trinidad & Tobago before Dempsey continued his form with a second. Houston Dynamo striker Brian Ching scored the third.

It rained goals in Washington as the US destroyed Cuba 6-1 in October. DeMarcus Beasley struck twice in the first 30 minutes before the visitors replied. Any disappointment was quickly dispelled as Donovan, Ching, Altidore, and Oguchi Onyewu sent Cuba packing.

The win meant the team had qualified for the fourth and final round of qualifying, but there were still two games to go. Defeat to Trinidad & Tobago followed; 40-year-old Russell Latapy hit the first for the home side, before Charlie Davies equalized. But a penalty from Dwight Yorke just four minutes later ended matters. A 2-0 US victory over Guatemala ended the round on a high with Kenny and Freddy Adu grabbing the goals.

The United States kicked off 2009 and their final qualifying group with victory over Mexico in Columbus. The 2-0 success came courtesy of a brace from Michael Bradley. It was the first of 10 matches in a group of six, the top three heading to the World Cup automatically.

BELOW Clint Dempsey (right) of the United States vies for the ball with Salvadorean Alfredo Pacheco (left).

In March, late goals from Altidore and Columbus Crew captain Frankie Hejduk ensured a share of the spoils against El Salvador. The team bounced back with victory over Trinidad & Tobago in Nashville. Altidore grabbed a hat trick in front of 30,000 fans.

June was a busy month. A 3-1 away defeat to Costa Rica was not the best preparation, with only a Donovan penalty in the 92nd minute preventing a heavier loss. He scored from the spot again against Honduras en route to a 2-1 victory as the team headed to their summer tournament.

The US surprised fans and critics alike by reaching the Confederations Cup final, even leading Brazil by two goals before losing 3-2. The hangover was evident as they lost to Mexico on their return to qualifying action; Davies helped them start brightly with a goal on nine minutes,

but it was canceled out by Israel Castro before Miguel Sabah wrapped up the points at the Estadio Azteca.

Not a team to lose two in a row, the US took their frustrations out on El Salvador in Utah, Dempsey and Altidore scoring in the last five minutes of the first half after the visitors had taken the lead.

Ricardo Clark scored the only goal of the game four days later as they overcame Trinidad & Tobago in Port of Spain, their first away victory of the fourth round.

The team traveled to Honduras knowing victory would secure qualification. Julio de León put the home side ahead before Donovan and a Conor Casey double seemed to put the game out of sight. De León's second produced a nervy last 10 minutes but the US hung on to clinch a spot at the finals.

The team's homecoming looked set to be spoiled when Costa Rica's Bryan Ruiz hit a quick-fire double. Michael Bradley's second-half goal made it a nervy finish for the visitors. It was the 94th minute when left-back Jonathan Bornstein headed in from a corner to leave the US top of the group with the last move of the campaign.

ABOVE United States goalkeeper Tim Howard (right) and midfielder Michael Bradley (left) celebrate after drawing 2-2 with Costa Rica.

ABOVE Jozy Altidore of the United States runs with the ball during the United States 3-0 win against Trinidad & Tobago.

ROAD TO WORLD CUP 2010

USA	2-0	Mexico
El Salvador	2-2	USA
USA	3-0	Trinidad & Tobago
USA	2-1	Honduras
Costa Rica	3-1	USA
Mexico	2-1	USA
USA	2-1	El Salvador
Trinidad & Tobago	0-1	USA
Honduras	2-3	USA
USA	2-2	Costa Rica

Algeria wanted to qualify for their first World Cup in 24 years to right the injustice suffered in Spain in 1982.

ABOVE Nadir Belhadj leads the array of Algerian stars in Europe.

In 1982 Algeria were controversially eliminated when Germany played out a 1-0 victory over Austria to ensure both teams progressed at Algeria's expense.

The wounds were still raw for a country that had only had its own recognized international side since 1962. They turned to Rabah Saadane, the man who led them in the last World Cup finals they had reached in 1986. Saadane was appointed in 2007 for his fifth spell as Algeria manager.

He had, arguably, the strongest group of internationals since Algeria's 1990 African Cup of Nations' triumph. Players with top-flight European experience included defenders Madjid Bougherra and Nadir Belhadj, who played for Glasgow Rangers and Portsmouth respectively. And goals were never far away with attacking players such as Wolfsburg's Karim Ziani and striker Rafik Saifi.

Algeria eased to the third round of CAF qualifying, finishing top of a group including Gambia, Senegal, and Liberia. Algeria then stumbled with a surprising 0-0 draw away to Rwanda, but quickly compensated with a 3-1 success over rivals Egypt in Blida. A 2-0 victory over Zambia two weeks later ensured they topped their group.

After a narrow 1-0 win in the return match against Zambia, they cruised past Rwanda 3-1, with Ziani and Belhadj among the scorers. With just Egypt left to play, Algeria were in the position of knowing anything better than a 2-0 defeat would guarantee them a place in South Africa.

If Algeria lost by two it would leave them equal on points, goal difference and head-to-head results

with Eqypt, meaning that a one-off playoff match would be required to determine the winner.

Algerians were ready to celebrate qualification with Egypt leading by one goal, but their opponents scored again with the last kick of the game to force a playoff. The momentum was firmly with Egypt. Sudan was chosen as the neutral venue and a volley from Vfl Bochum defender Antar Yahia just before half time proved decisive in a tense and scrappy affair.

Despite the last-minute slip-up, Algeria had managed to progress in a high-pressure atmosphere, and looked forward to a possible revenge match with Germany in South Africa.

ROAD TO WORLD CUP 2010

Senegal	1-0	Algeria
Algeria	3-0	Liberia
Gambia	1-0	Algeria
Algeria	1-0	Gambia
Algeria	3-2	Senegal
Liberia	0-0	Algeria
Rwanda	0-0	Algeria
Algeria	3-1	Egypt
Zambia	0-2	Algeria
Algeria	1-0	Zambia
Algeria	3-1	Rwanda
Egypt	2-0	Algeria
Algeria	1-0	Egypt

AUSTRALIA

Australia were finally realizing their potential as a national team and had their sights set on a third World Cup finals appearance.

Since switching confederations to AFC in 2005 had eased Australia's task of qualifying, and they were keen to make their mark on the world stage.

A last-minute penalty had seen them eliminated by eventual-winners Italy in 2006, and the Australians were determined to take this second chance. Coach Pim Verbeek continued the trend of Dutch managers after fellow countryman Guus Hiddink's success at the last tournament.

The squad was strong, with key players in veteran goalkeeper Mark Schwarzer and midfielders Harry Kewell and Tim Cahill. The latter was an important source of goals, with prolific strikers John Aloisi and Archie Thompson both winding down their careers.

Australia topped their group when they entered the third round of qualifying, despite suffering defeats

to Iraq and the People's Republic of China. Scott Chipperfield got the only goal against Uzbekistan to ensure a winning start in round four. A 4-0 crushing of Qatar in Brisbane meant this continued.

A win over Bahrain in November 2008, courtesy of a last-minute Mark Bresciano goal showed resilience and, with Japan up next, they would need to show their dominance. The two teams drew a blank in Yokohama, but Australia were still well placed to win the group.

Another victory over the Uzbeks in Sydney—goals from Kewell and Joshua Kennedy sealing Australia's fourth win in five qualification games so far—meant only one point was needed to become one of the first teams to qualify for the tournament behind the hosts. This was secured after an uneventful match in Qatar. Verbeek had been criticized for his brand of football, but the results spoke for themselves. Australia had qualified after only six matches.

The team returned home to Sydney four days later to continue the celebrations, victory over Bahrain securing first place in the group. Wingers Mile Sterjovski and David Carney provided the goals in front of 39,000 jubilant fans. The party continued a week later, victory over second-place Japan ensuring that Australia had beaten all their rivals at least once. Two second-half goals from Cahill settled the match after the visitors had gone ahead through Tulio.

Australia went into their third World Cup finals with belief they could defeat anyone, and hopes of bringing home the trophy for the first time.

ROAD TO WORLD CUP 2010

Australia	3-0	Qatar
China PR	0-0	Australia
Australia	1-0	Iraq
Iraq	1-0	Australia
Qatar	1-3	Australia
Australia	0-1	China PR
Uzbekistan	0-1	Australia
Australia	4-0	Qatar
Bahrain	0-1	Australia
Japan	0-0	Australia
Australia	2-0	Uzbekistan
Qatar	0-0	Australia
Australia	2-0	Bahrain
Australia	2-1	Japan

LEFT Harry Kewell is first to the ball against Uzbekistan's Timur Kapadze.

WORLD CUP 2010, TEAMS
CAMEROON

Cameroon aimed to continue their run as Africa's most successful World Cup nation by qualifying for their sixth finals.

Otto Pfister, Cameroon's seasoned coach, had good international experience. He also had a lot of talent to work with: record cap holder Rigobert Song, now with Trabzonspor, Tottenham's Benoît Assou-Ekotto at the back, and Barcelona striker and national captain Samuel Eto'o.

The Indomitable Lions entered CAF qualification at the second round stage, and eased to the top of their group, winning five games and drawing one in a group containing minnows Cape Verde, Tanzania, and Mauritius.

The next stage started off disastrously for Cameroon. They lost their first match to Togo before drawing 0-0 at home with Morocco. This led to Pfister being sacked and replaced by former Glasgow Rangers and Paris Saint-Germain coach Paul Le Guen.

Le Guen's impact was instant, with Cameroon picking up two victories over Gabon in four days; the first was a 2-0 win away from home. In the return match, the home side came out on top with a 2-1 win. Eto'o furthered his impressive international goal tally with a strike in both games.

Revenge over Togo was secured via a 3-0 drubbing in October 2009. But, despite their fast-improving fortunes, Cameroon had to win on the final matchday away against Morocco and hope that Gabon failed to secure victory in Togo.

They came out 2-0 winners in Morocco. Then wild celebrations began as news came through that Togo had beaten Gabon 1-0.

The country that became the first ever African nation to reach the World Cup quarter-finals and took England to extra time in Italia 1990, was dreaming of a repeat performance in South Africa.

RIGHT Midfielder Achille Emana, (center), of Cameroon fights for the ball against Morocco.

ABOVE Benoît Assou-Ekotto shields the ball from Gabon's Roguy Meye during a 2-0 victory.

ROAD TO WORLD CUP 2010

Cameroon	2-0	Cape Verde
Mauritius	0-3	Cameroon
Tanzania	0-0	Cameroon
Cameroon	2-1	Tanzania
Cape Verde	1-2	Cameroon
Cameroon	5-0	Mauritius
Togo	1-0	Cameroon
Cameroon	0-0	Morocco
Gabon	0-2	Cameroon
Cameroon	2-1	Gabon
Cameroon	3-0	Togo
Morocco	0-2	Cameroon

CHILE

Chile have a checkered World Cup history; they were banned in 1990 and 1994 and have failed to win a match in the finals since their third-place finish in 1964.

Drawing on the experience of former Argentina coach Marcelo Bielsa, Chile had a tough task in a group requiring 18 games, and including Brazil and Argentina. A first-match defeat against Argentina was proof of the task ahead.

After a 2-0 victory over Peru, Chile had a 2-2 draw against Uruguay where top scorer Marcelo Salas scored the last goals of his international career before retirement.

Defeat to group leaders Paraguay in November 2007 was followed up by successive victories against Bolivia and Venezuela.

Bielsa had a young team; the first XI that were in their 20s. The veteran was goalkeeper Claudio Bravo, who had gathered 40 caps. But goals were coming from attacking midfielder Matías Fernández and striker Humberto Suazo.

They were taught a footballing lesson in September 2008 when Brazil cruised to a 3-0 victory, but hammered Colombia a few days later.

The win-loss pattern continued into October, where defeat to Ecuador preceded their most famous result of the campaign—a 1-0 victory over Argentina. The win had an impact on both teams, with Argentina coach Alfio Basile sacked after the defeat.

For Chile, it sparked a five-game unbeaten streak that saw victories registered against Peru, Paraguay, and Bolivia. Brazil ended it with a 4-2 victory, 11 months after Chile's run began, but now Chile required only three points to qualify. They got six; a 4-2 triumph away to Colombia and a 1-0 success over Ecuador.

It was a job well done for the team, now in its first World Cup finals in 12 years.

ROAD TO WORLD CUP 2010

Argentina	2-0	Chile
Chile	2-0	Peru
Uruguay	2-2	Chile
Chile	0-3	Paraguay
Bolivia	0-2	Chile
Venezuela	2-3	Chile
Chile	0-3	Brazil
Chile	4-0	Colombia
Ecuador	1-0	Chile
Chile	1-0	Argentina
Peru	1-3	Chile
Chile	0-0	Uruguay
Paraguay	0-2	Chile
Chile	4-0	Bolivia
Chile	2-2	Venezuela
Brazil	4-2	Chile
Colombia	2-4	Chile
Chile	1-0	Ecuador

LEFT Chile's Jorge Valdivia (center) celebrates after scoring against Colombia at the Atanasio Girardot stadium in Medellin, Colombia.

DENMARK

When Denmark were drawn with Portugal and Sweden, their prospects did not look good, but they went on to surprise everyone.

Success had proved hard to come by for the Danes, since they shocked the football world in 1992 by capturing the European Championship.

Manager Morten Olsen, in his ninth year with the national side, was hoping to spring another surprise by qualifying for the World Cup. An opening stalemate against Hungary preceded a famous 3-2 victory over favorites Portugal in Lisbon.

After Nani ensured Portugal led at half time, Nicklas Bendtner looked to have secured a point with a strike six minutes from time. Deco then slotted home a penalty, but injury-time goals from Christian Poulsen and Werder Bremen's Daniel Jensen snatched victory for Denmark.

Three successive 3-0 victories over Malta (twice) and Albania ensured the Danes topped their group at the beginning of 2009. A 22nd-minute strike from Wolfsburg midfielder Thomas Kahlenberg ensured victory over Sweden before they cemented their position with a draw against Portugal.

Only a goal from substitute Liédson denied Denmark another famous victory over Portugal, but they were still keeping competitors at arm's length after their blistering start. A 1-1 draw with Albania did little to derail their qualification charge, and victory over Sweden would secure their passage to South Africa.

A goal from Jakob Poulsen with just 12 minutes to go confirmed this in front of 38,000 fans in Copenhagen and condemned once-fancied Portugal to the lottery of the playoffs. Not even defeat to Hungary in their final match could detract from Danish celebrations, Buzáky hitting

the only goal of a game that had no bearing on the group.

Though a surprise, Danish success was testament to the players who were regularly performing in the top leagues. Experienced Premier League goalkeeper Thomas Sorensen provided the foundation for a stable defense that included Liverpool's Daniel Agger, while creative players such as Dennis Rommedahl and Arsenal's Nicklas Bendtner meant that goals were never far away.

LEFT Nicklas Bendtner proves he's as good with his head as with his feet.

ABOVE Daniel Jensen (left) shows his elation at hitting the winner against Portugal.

ROAD TO WORLD CUP 2010

Hungary	0-0	Denmark
Portugal	2-3	Denmark
Denmark	3-0	Malta
Malta	0-3	Denmark
Denmark	3-0	Albania
Sweden	0-1	Denmark
Denmark	1-1	Portugal
Albania	1-1	Denmark
Denmark	1-0	Sweden
Denmark	0-1	Hungary

Ghana were hoping to continue their rapid ascent as a global footballing force by qualifying for their second World Cup in a row.

The CAF qualification groups required teams to compete also for a place at the 2010 African Cup of Nations, so there was all to play for.

Many were surprised when Ghana appointed Serbian Milovan Rajevac in August 2008—limited top-level experience had made him an outsider for the position, but the success of predecessor and countryman Ratomir Dujkovic, who'd left in 2006 to manage China, convinced the Ghanaian FA he could lead them to South Africa.

Rajevac had a wealth of talent at his disposal, with many of the national team plying their trade at the highest level in Europe. Lyon center-back John Mensah and Fulham right-back John Pantsil were stars of the back-four, while midfielders Michael Essien and Sulley Muntari had plenty of European experience despite being only 25 and 26 respectively.

Although not playing for a club side, captain Stephen Appiah still featured regularly, with stints at Juventus and Fenerbahçe proof of his quality. There were also high hopes for young Rennes forward Asamoah Gyan.

It was Prince Tagoe who got Ghana's campaign off to a winning start, however, with the only goal of the game against Benin. Strike partner Matthew Amoah got three goals in two games as they defeated Mali and Sudan by the same 2-0 scoreline. It was a blistering start for the team known as the Black Stars.

When the team reconvened after a summer break, Ghana needed just one more victory to qualify after playing just four games. It was midfield duo Muntari and Essien who combined once again to put Sudan to the sword and ensure Ghana's participation in the World Cup, less than six months after they began their group.

Perhaps understandably, the campaign tailed off in the last two games; with qualification assured, a mid-strength team lost 1-0 to Benin before a 2-2 home draw with Mali ended proceedings on a subdued note. Nevertheless, Ghana were just the eighth team to reach the World Cup finals, a blistering (for the most part) campaign having deservedly sent them racing up the football world rankings.

ABOVE Prince Tagoe pictured on the ball during a match with Sudan, against whom Ghana clinched qualification.

ROAD TO WORLD CUP 2010

Ghana	1-0	Benin
Mali	0-2	Ghana
Sudan	0-2	Ghana
Ghana	2-0	Sudan
Benin	1-0	Ghana
Ghana	2-2	Mali

WORLD CUP 2010, TEAMS
GREECE

In recent years, Greece have shown how stability and hard work can bring success to a small footballing nation.

ROAD TO WORLD CUP 2010

Luxembourg	0-3	Greece
Latvia	0-2	Greece
Greece	3-0	Moldova
Greece	1-2	Switzerland
Israel	1-1	Greece
Greece	2-1	Israel
Switzerland	2-0	Greece
Moldova	1-1	Greece
Greece	5-2	Latvia
Greece	2-1	Luxembourg
Greece	0-0	Ukraine
Ukraine	0-1	Greece

Since manager Otto Rehhagel took the reins in 2001 Greece have become European champions. They had their sights on their second World Cup finals.

The famous victory over Portugal in the Euro 2004 final saw Greece's stock rise dramatically and, despite failing to qualify for the 2006 World Cup and a disastrous Euro title defense in 2008, they were still considered well-placed to top their group.

Greece still had in their team Angelos Basinas, Giorgos Karagounis, and Angelos Charisteas, who scored in the final in 2004. With fellow strikers Georgios Samaras and Theofanis Gekas, goals were guaranteed.

Three wins against Luxembourg, Latvia, and Moldova displayed their credentials, with Gekas and Charisteas grabbing three goals apiece. The team had scored eight and had yet to lose one.

The run halted against Switzerland in October 2008 when Greece lost 2-1 at home. A 1-1 draw in Israel followed. Four days later, a Samaras penalty secured a 2-1 win.

Defeat to Switzerland in the last 10 minutes meant Greece had to contemplate the playoffs. A last-minute goal from Moldova in their next match meant the spoils were shared, and Greece's chances of automatic qualification were slim.

Gekas grabbed four goals in a 5-2 victory over Latvia. That, coupled with a Swiss win against Luxembourg, meant Greece had to win on the final day and hope that Switzerland lost.

Despite Greece beating Luxembourg 2-1, Switzerland got the point they needed to qualify, and a two-legged playoff match versus the Ukraine awaited.

The first leg ended goalless in Athens, setting up a winner-take-all showdown in Donetsk. It was settled with one goal from Panathinaikos striker Dimitris Salpingidis after half an hour, sending Greece to South Africa.

RIGHT The Greek players celebrate qualifying for the World Cup after their playoff match against Ukraine.

HONDURAS

Honduras were desperate to reach only their second ever finals under former Colombia coach Reinaldo Rueda.

LEFT Wilson Palacios shoots for goal against the United States.

A number of players had broken into Europe's top sides in recent years, most notably David Suazo at Inter Milan, while Wigan Athletic had taken Maynor Figueroa, Hendry Thomas, and Wilson Palacios, before the latter secured a big-money transfer to Tottenham Hotspur.

Veteran striker Carlos Pavon provided the goals, with record cap-holder Amando Guevara the team leader. Pavon scored his first of the campaign in a draw against Trinidad & Tobago. It was a welcome point after a defeat in their opener against Costa Rica.

Pavon added another alongside Carlo Costly as they picked up their first three points against Mexico. Defeat against the United States days later inspired the team to a run of three consecutive victories against El Salvador, Costa Rica, and Trinidad & Tobago. They were halted 1-0 by Mexico, but were in a strong position with two games to go.

A brace from Torino midfielder Julio César de León was not enough to beat the Americans, whose victory secured their own qualification. Costa Rica were in pole position for the final qualification spot as the teams approached the last matchday, with Honduras two points behind.

Honduras had to win and hope that Costa Rica lost or drew against the US. Pavon came through once again, with the only goal of the game and, as Costa Rica drew, Honduras narrowly qualified for the finals on goal difference.

Pavon was the group's top scorer with seven.

ROAD TO WORLD CUP 2010

Costa Rica	2-0	Honduras
Trinidad & Tobago	1-1	Honduras
Honduras	3-1	Mexico
USA	2-1	Honduras
Honduras	1-0	El Salvador
Honduras	4-0	Costa Rica
Honduras	4-1	Trinidad & Tobago
Mexico	1-0	Honduras
Honduras	2-3	USA
El Salvador	0-1	Honduras

IVORY COAST

The Ivory Coast were determined to qualify for a second successive World Cup after their first appearance in the finals in 2006 had ended in swift elimination.

ROAD TO WORLD CUP 2010

Ivory Coast	5-0	Malawi
Guinea	1-2	Ivory Coast
Burkina Faso	2-3	Ivory Coast
Ivory Coast	5-0	Burkina Faso
Malawi	1-1	Ivory Coast
Ivory Coast	3-0	Guinea

ABOVE Kolo Touré (left) and Souleymane Bamba pile on the pressure during a 5-0 victory over Burkina Faso.

But the Elephants were one of a number of African teams on the rise, having entered FIFA's top 20 rankings for the first time in 2006.

Vahid Halilhodžic was charged with emulating former manager Henri Michel and ensuring the Ivorians once again graced the world stage. The team were certainly well equipped to do it, with many players regularly competing with the world's elite. Didier Drogba and Kolo Touré were stars of the Premier League, while Kolo's brother Yaya was a key player for Spanish giants Barcelona.

With results also counting towards 2010 African Cup of Nations qualification, a good start was imperative. The players were well aware of this as they eased to a 5-0 home success over Malawi, Drogba grabbing a brace. The match was overshadowed, however, by a stampede before kick-off, in which 19 people lost their lives.

June 2009 saw two crucial away victories and the Ivory Coast were beginning to impose themselves on the group. A 2-1 triumph in Conakry against Guinea was followed up by a 3-2 success in Burkina Faso. A close affair was settled by a Drogba strike on 70 minutes after the sides went in level at half time.

The two countries met again in September; this time the Ivory Coast breezed by with another five-goal haul in a not-so-close encounter and Drogba grabbed yet another double. The 100 percent record meant only one point was needed in Malawi to progress to the finals.

When defender Jacob Ngwira put the hosts ahead just after the hour, it looked like the Ivory

ABOVE Ivorian players conduct muted celebrations against Malawi after the stampede that killed 19 Ivory Coast fans.

Coast might have to wait until the final matchday for qualification. Enter Didier Drogba, who came off the bench to score in under two minutes and clinch the solitary point required. A brace from Lille striker Gervinho helped the Ivorians to a 3-0 thumping of Guinea in their final game, wrapping up a campaign that saw only two points dropped.

The Ivory Coast qualified with ease, proof of their dominance in CAF. But they would be hoping for a kind draw in South Africa, where all eyes would be on the mercurial yet enigmatic Drogba to fire his country to glory.

JAPAN

Japan's emergence as a footballing force in the last decade had raised expectations as they began qualification.

But Brazilian legend Zico resigned as manager in 2006 and, after his replacement, Yugoslavian Ivica Osim, had his reign cut short due to ill health, Takeshi Okada was given the task of driving his national team toward South Africa.

Okada was no stranger to the task, having taken Japan to their first World Cup in 1998. There was a sense of both nostalgia and optimism in the air as Japan kicked off their campaign against Bahrain. But it turned to horror as they nearly squandered a three-goal lead, conceding two in the last five minutes.

Boasting a squad that played mainly in Japan, Okada had carried on the work of his predecessors, forging a hard-working unit of players. He preferred Seigo Narazaki to veteran goalkeeper Yoshikatsu Kawaguchi, while the tenacity of Celtic's Shunsuke Nakamura made Japan a force to be reckoned with in midfield.

Japan topped their third-round group, despite succumbing twice to Bahrain. They had their revenge in the next round, winning 3-2, but they couldn't overcome a stubborn Uzbekistan team in Saitama. They recovered with a 3-0 away drubbing of Qatar. Tatsuya Tanaka scored the first before second-half goals from Tamada and Tulio clinched victory.

2009 brought a showdown with Australia; both teams were vying for top spot and the honors were even after a goalless draw in Yokohama. Shunsuke Nakamura scored the only goal of the game in March to ensure that Bahrain would again come away with nothing and put Japan on the brink of qualification.

They became only the second team to qualify after hosts South Africa, by overcoming a potential tricky tie away to Uzbekistan. A Shinji Okazaki header in the ninth minute was enough to take the points. With two games left to play, Japan appeared to suffer from complacency against Qatar in Saitama, but a 1-1 draw did not dampen the celebrations of a fourth successive qualification.

Japan's final fixture was a showpiece match with also-qualified Australia. It took two second-half goals from Tim Cahill to win the match after Tulio had put Japan ahead. But the result was largely irrelevant. Fans were hoping Okada, the man who led them to their finest hour, could do so again in South Africa.

BELOW Shunsuke Nakamura (right) beats Qatar's Hamed Shami Zaher in Yokohama.

ROAD TO WORLD CUP 2010		
Japan	4-1	Thailand
Bahrain	1-0	Japan
Japan	3-0	Oman
Oman	1-1	Japan
Thailand	0-3	Japan
Japan	1-0	Bahrain
Bahrain	2-3	Japan
Japan	1-1	Uzbekistan
Qatar	0-3	Japan
Japan	0-0	Australia
Japan	1-0	Bahrain
Uzbekistan	0-1	Japan
Japan	1-1	Qatar
Australia	2-1	Japan

KOREA DPR

Despite only ever having qualified for one World Cup, Korea DPR—North Korea, as they were known on their sole finals appearance in 1966—had been the first Asian team to progress beyond the first round.

ROAD TO WORLD CUP 2010

Jordan	0-1	Korea DPR
Korea DPR	1-1	South Korea
Turkmenistan	0-0	Korea DPR
Korea DPR	1-0	Turkmenistan
Korea DPR	2-0	Jordan
South Korea	0-0	Korea DPR
United Arab Emirates	1-2	Korea DPR
Korea DPR	1-1	South Korea
Iran	2-1	Korea DPR
Korea DPR	1-0	Saudi Arabia
Korea DPR	2-0	United Arab Emirates
South Korea	1-0	Korea DPR
Korea DPR	0-0	Iran
Saudi Arabia	0-0	Korea DPR

Living in the shadow of their more successful neighbors, South Korea, only served as further inspiration for the team and for manager Kim Jong-Hun. His team had an uphill struggle ahead, with a lack of top-level experience; the majority of the squad played domestically in Asia, with only Hong Yong-Jo playing in Europe for Russian side FC Rostov.

They advanced from the third round level on points with South Korea, but their inexperience was highlighted in their first match of round four as none of their starting XI had amassed more than 50 caps. Despite this handicap, they grabbed the three points courtesy of second-half goals from Choe Kum-Chol and An Chol-Hyok.

A 1-1 draw against South Korea preceded a 2-1 reverse to Iran, leaving Korea DPR with just four points from their first three games as 2009 approached. Man In-Guk ensured their play picked up in the New Year, with the only goal of the game against Saudi Arabia in February; another win would mean qualification was back on track.

That win duly arrived the next month against United Arab Emirates in Pyongyang. Man In-Guk struck again in injury time to add to Pak Nam-Chol's earlier effort in a 2-0 victory.

Their run was brought to a halt after a late winner for South Korea in their second encounter, but they were still well placed to qualify with playoff rivals Iran and Saudi Arabia to face in their last two games. A goalless draw against the former set up a tense final day in which any one from three teams could secure a place.

Korea DPR could qualify with a point, providing archrivals South Korea prevented Iran from winning. They secured their point and Iran could not emerge victorious either, meaning the standings in the group table stayed as they were. Korea DPR had qualified on goal difference to their first tournament in over four decades.

BELOW Captain Hong Yong-Jo leads the charge on goal against Saudi Arabia.

MEXICO

Mexico began the CONCACAF fourth round of World Cup qualification with former England manager Sven-Göran Eriksson in charge, despite unrest among the fans.

The Swedish manager was charged with continuing the team's solid record for qualifying for the tournament; Mexico had only missed one finals in nearly three decades, and that because of a FIFA ban.

Eriksson had inherited a promising youthful team, inspired by the experience of ageing forward Cuauhtémoc Blanco—and, with stars such as Arsenal's Carlos Vela and Giovanni Dos Santos, goals were always likely. But the team

suffered from inconsistency both on and off the pitch, a fact that threatened to derail their hopes of qualification.

A 2-0 reverse to the United States was quickly canceled out by a 2-0 victory over Costa Rica. But defeat to Honduras in April 2009 would bring an abrupt end to Eriksson's reign of only 11 months. The timing was not ideal, but Mexico were hoping for an upturn in fortunes with the swift re-appointment of former manager Javier Aguirre.

There was no immediate impact, however, as the frustration continued. A late winner from El Salvador resulted in a 2-1 scoreline, leaving Mexico adrift of the pack. Goals from Guillermo Franco and Oscar Rojas secured victory over Trinidad & Tobago and, when Miguel Sabah hit a late winner to defeat the United States in August, qualification was once again being talked about.

Victories against Costa Rica and Honduras put Mexico in the surprising position of needing just one more win to qualify. The three points were secured in style with a 4-1 blasting of El Salvador, Blanco and Vela among the scorers.

In a stop-start campaign, Eriksson and Aguirre had used over 60 players, and the patchy sequence of results fully reflected that fact. Mexico came back twice to share the spoils in their last match with Trinidad & Tobago—their first and only draw of the group, offering proof of their inconsistency. Fans and manager alike would be hoping for greater stability if they were to challenge in South Africa.

ABOVE Striker Carlos Vela (right) bests El Salvador's Marvin Gonzalez during Mexico's 4-1 victory.

LEFT Sven-Göran Eriksson instructs Mexico veteran Cuauhtémoc Blanco.

ROAD TO WORLD CUP 2010

USA	2-0	Mexico
Mexico	2-0	Costa Rica
Honduras	3-1	Mexico
El Salvador	2-1	Mexico
Mexico	2-1	Trinidad & Tobago
Mexico	2-1	USA
Costa Rica	0-3	Mexico
Mexico	1-0	Honduras
Mexico	4-1	El Salvador
Trinidad & Tobago	2-2	Mexico

NEW ZEALAND

New Zealand saw a golden opportunity to qualify for the World Cup after Australia switched to the AFC confederation in 2005.

ROAD TO WORLD CUP 2010

Fiji	0-2	New Zealand
Vanuatu	1-2	New Zealand
New Zealand	4-1	Vanuatu
New Caledonia	1-3	New Zealand
New Zealand	3-0	New Caledonia
New Zealand	0-2	Fiji
Bahrain	0-0	New Zealand
New Zealand	1-0	Bahrain

This left New Zealand as the only seeded side in a qualification group with very poor opposition. This increased the pressure on coach Ricki Herbert and his side.

New Zealand were granted entry directly to the final stage of qualification, the OFC Nations Cup. The four teams would be placed in a table, with the winner advancing to the playoffs.

Herbert's team lacked top-level football experience; only captain Ryan Nelsen played in the European top flight with Blackburn Rovers, while striker Rory Fallon played with Plymouth Argyle in the Coca-Cola Championship.

The All Whites kicked off with two away victories, 2-0 against Fiji and 2-1 against Vanuatu. Gold Coast United striker Shane Smeltz bagged a goal in each game.

Smeltz continued with a run of six goals in three games. He hit a first-half brace in the return against Vanuatu and scored another double in a 3-1 victory against New Caledonia. He once again hit two, as New Zealand cruised to a 3-0 win at home against New Caledonia.

Defeat in the final match against Fiji was inconsequential: New Zealand had set up a qualification playoff against a nation yet to be decided, but would have to wait 12 months.

They appeared at the 2009 Confederations Cup in South Africa but were eliminated in the group stage, failing to score a single goal, not good preparation for their World Cup decider against Bahrain.

The two-legged affair began with a 0-0 stalemate in Riffa. A goal in first-half injury time from Fallon decided the tie at the Westpac Stadium in Wellington, and sent New Zealand to only their second World Cup finals.

LEFT Rory Fallon secures New Zealand's first World Cup finals appearance in nearly three decades.

WORLD CUP 2010, TEAMS
NIGERIA

Nigeria began qualification with a point to prove. The team missed out on a place at the World Cup in 2006 on head-to-head encounters with Angola, despite having a better goal difference.

Coach Shaibu Amodu was brought in for a fourth time, having managed the side in 2002. The team had spent many years in the shadow of Cameroon, and had a strong team.

Established goalkeeper Vincent Enyeama was shielded by Joseph Yobo at center-back and Mikel John Obi in midfield, making up a strong spine. With attack-minded players such as Nwankwo Kanu, Obafemi Martins and Yakubu, they had a side with experience and style.

Nigeria proved this by topping their group in the second round of qualification, having had a bye through the first. They had a 100 percent record. Results also counted toward qualification for the 2010 African Cup of Nations.

Nigeria progressed to a four-team group, the winner qualifying automatically for the finals. A 0-0 draw against Mozambique was cause for concern and, while a 2-0 home victory against Kenya allayed those fears, there was a lot to do—especially with Tunisia winning two from two.

Two draws against Tunisia helped but, with two games left, Nigeria were still trailing by two points. Another goalless draw with Mozambique looked likely to end their hopes, but a last-minute winner by Malaga striker Victor Obinna set up a tense final day.

Nigeria had to win against Kenya in Nairobi and hope Mozambique won against Tunisia. Late goals in both matches altered the landscape of the group. Mozambique beat Tunisia, and an Obafemi Martins strike in the 83rd minute secured a 3-2 victory over Kenya, sending Nigeria fans into dreamland.

ROAD TO WORLD CUP 2010

Nigeria	2-0	South Africa
Sierra Leone	0-1	Nigeria
Equatorial Guinea	0-1	Nigeria
Nigeria	2-0	Equatorial Guinea
South Africa	0-1	Nigeria
Nigeria	4-1	Sierra Leone
Mozambique	0-0	Nigeria
Nigeria	2-0	Kenya
Tunisia	0-0	Nigeria
Nigeria	2-2	Tunisia
Nigeria	1-0	Mozambique
Kenya	2-3	Nigeria

LEFT Obafemi Martins takes on all comers against Mozambique.

NIGERIA **71**

PARAGUAY

Paraguay set about qualifying, hoping continuity would see them through.

Argentinean coach Gerardo Martino was appointed in 2007 and intended to lead his settled team to a fourth successive World Cup finals.

Several key players retired, including goalkeeper José Luis Chilavert. New keeper and captain Justo Villar inspired a team built from the back, but Salvador Cabañas and Roque Santa Cruz promised goals up front.

Paraguay picked up four points from their first two matches—a goalless draw at Peru and a 1-0 victory at home to Uruguay. They then thrashed Ecuador 5-1, with Nelson Valdez and Santa Cruz among the scorers. A 3-0 victory over Chile ended 2007 on a high before Paraguay vanquished Brazil 2-0.

Defeat away to Bolivia and a draw against Argentina weakened Paraguay's grip on the top spot, but victories over Venezuela and Colombia ensured they still led the pack. Paraguay beat Peru by one goal to nil.

2009 started badly as Paraguay picked up just one point from four games; defeats to Uruguay, Chile, and Brazil meant they slipped to third. In September they got back on the winning trail, defeating Bolivia 1-0 courtesy of a Cabañas penalty in first-half injury time. Results elsewhere meant they could still guarantee qualification with victory over Argentina.

Valdez settled the game inside the first half-hour and Paraguay had made it. They eventually finished third in the group after a 2-1 victory away to Venezuela was followed by defeat against Colombia.

RIGHT Paulo Cesar da Silva (left) and Dario Veron (right) of Paraguay battle for the ball with Nicolas Fedor (center) of Venezuela.

SERBIA

Serbia were competing as an independent nation. No longer part of Yugoslavia or aligned with Montenegro, they appointed Radomir Antic to lead them to the World Cup.

LEFT Dejan Stankovic of Serbia holds his national flag after his team beat Romania in October 2009.

Antic had the pedigree for the job, one of only two men to manage both Real Madrid and Barcelona. His team included a wealth of top European experience. With Manchester United center-back Nemanja Vidic and Chelsea's Branislav Invanovic, and captain Dejan Stankovic from Inter Milan.

The team kicked off in Belgrade with a 2-0 win over the Faroe Islands. An own goal from the visitors got the ball rolling and Valencia forward Nikola Žigic hit a late second. Despite defeat against France in Paris days later, Serbia still believed in a playoff spot.

A 3-0 demolition of Lithuania in October 2008 helped. Three goals in nine first-half minutes sent Serbia on their way to another victory against Austria.

Another three-goal haul was enough for Serbia to take the points in Romania despite conceding two themselves. A 1-0 victory over Austria in June 2009 and two goals without reply against the Faroe Islands four days later, gave them their fifth consecutive victory.

France held them to a 1-1 draw in Belgrade. It was a crucial point, because Serbia only had to beat Romania at home to guarantee participation in the World Cup finals.

This they did, thumping Romania 5-0 in front of nearly 40,000 fans. A surprise loss to Lithuania in their final match was only their second of the campaign.

ROAD TO WORLD CUP 2010

Serbia	2-0	Faroe Islands
France	2-1	Serbia
Serbia	3-0	Lithuania
Austria	1-3	Serbia
Romania	2-3	Serbia
Serbia	1-0	Austria
Faroe Islands	0-2	Serbia
Serbia	1-1	France
Serbia	5-0	Romania
Lithuania	2-1	Serbia

SLOVAKIA

Slovakia reached their first finals as an independent nation and finally emerged from the shadow of the Czech Republic.

ROAD TO WORLD CUP 2010

Slovakia	2-1	Northern Ireland
Slovenia	2-1	Slovakia
San Marino	1-3	Slovakia
Slovakia	2-1	Poland
Czech Republic	1-2	Slovakia
Slovakia	7-0	San Marino
Slovakia	2-2	Czech Republic
Northern Ireland	0-2	Slovakia
Slovakia	0-2	Slovenia
Poland	0-1	Slovakia

BELOW Erik Jendrišek is pictured after hitting a late winner against the Czech Republic.

Despite the majority of Czechoslovakia's 1976 European Championship winning team being Slovaks, recent success had been considerably more difficult.

The two were paired in a group that also included Poland, Slovenia, and Northern Ireland. Slovakia got off to a solid start in a 2-1 defeat of Northern Ireland in Bratislava.

Defeat to Slovenia was followed by a 3-1 victory away to San Marino. A late home brace from Stanislav Šesták then snatched three points from Poland.

2009 brought the first long-awaited showdown with the Czech Republic, FC Kaiserslautern striker Erik Jendrišek's 82nd-minute winner ensuring a 2-1 victory.

Despite their position outside FIFA's top 20 teams, the Slovaks boasted names such as

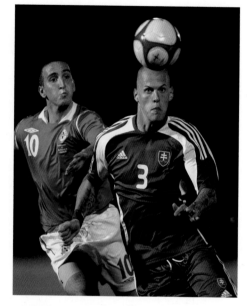

ABOVE Defender Martin Škrtel outruns Martin Paterson of Northern Ireland during a 2-0 away win.

Liverpool defender Martin Škrtel and West Bromwich Albion's Marek Cech. Coach Vladamir Weiss's disciplined approach ensured they remained on course for qualification.

Slovakia beat San Marino 7-0—but this could not inspire a second win against their rivals. Despite going ahead twice, Slovakia had to settle for a point.

A 2-0 defeat of Northern Ireland in Belfast put Slovakia's qualification back on track, but another loss to Slovenia meant a nail-biting final match. A tense game was settled by an own goal after three minutes, Polish defender Seweryn Gancarczyk the guilty party.

Slovakia were going to the World Cup.

SLOVENIA

Slovenia have made a habit of surprising everyone by qualifying for international tournaments since their split from Yugoslavia in the early 1990s.

They were hoping to cause another upset in their quest to reach their second ever World Cup.

Manager Matjaž Kek was a low-profile appointment, having worked his way up from managing Slovenia's Under 15 and 16 sides after an undistinguished playing career that saw him pick up just one cap for his country.

Kek had a side that relied on hard work. They had a solid goalkeeper in Udinese's Samir Handanovic who, at 25 years old, had established himself as number one for both club and country. In midfield Robert Koren had success in the Premier League with West Bromwich Albion, and FC Köln striker Milivoje Novakovic had scored regularly since his international debut in 2006.

Slovenia had a tough group that included Slovakia and the Czech Republic. They faced Poland in Wroclaw first, and a point was rescued in the first half.

Slovenia's solid start continued with a 2-1 victory over Slovakia. Slovenia topped their group after the first two rounds of games.

October 2008 saw Northen Ireland sent home with nothing after two late goals from Novakovic and Zlatan Ljubijankic.

One point from two meetings with the Czech Republic was followed by a 1-0 defeat to Northern Ireland in Belfast. Slovenia now had four games left to make a push for qualification.

A 5-0 home win over minnows San Marino helped, with Koren grabbing a brace, and, when Slovenia beat Poland, 3-0 a place in the playoffs was looking like a reality.

ABOVE The Slovenian players celebrate after beating Slovakia 2:0 during their World Cup 2010 qualifying campaign.

A 2-0 win against Slovakia confirmed that, while a 3-0 triumph over San Marino ended an impressive campaign. Russia in the playoffs was the reward for their efforts.

As the first leg was ending in Moscow, Slovenia were 2-0 down, but a late goal from C.D. Nacional midfielder Nejc Pecnik gave Slovenia a crucial away goal.

Striker Zlatko Dedic scored just before half time in Maribor to give Slovenia a shock victory on away goals and sent Russia out of the tournament. It was a remarkable achievement.

ROAD TO WORLD CUP 2010

Poland	1-1	Slovenia
Slovenia	2-1	Slovakia
Slovenia	2-0	Northern Ireland
Czech Republic	1-0	Slovenia
Slovenia	0-0	Czech Republic
Northern Ireland	1-0	Slovenia
Slovenia	5-0	San Marino
Slovenia	3-0	Poland
Slovakia	0-2	Slovenia
San Marino	0-3	Slovenia
Russia	2-1	Slovenia
Slovenia	1-0	Russia

SOUTH AFRICA

Host nation South Africa were granted automatic qualification to their third World Cup. They did, however, enter the second phase of CAF qualification in an attempt to qualify for the African Cup of Nations.

It was a stern test for new coach Joel Santana, who had replaced fellow Brazilian Carlos Alberto Parreira who was forced to vacate the position for personal reasons. Many were hoping Santana's extensive experience in South America, where he had managed several teams including Fluminese and Vasco da Gama, would translate to the international stage. Unfortunately, his new team finished second to Nigeria in the first qualifying round.

After being banned by FIFA for nearly three decades due to apartheid, South Africa had not been past the World Cup group stages in two attempts in the 1990s. Now, expectation was at an all-time high, as the team prepared to do battle on home soil. Players such as Everton's Steven Pienaar and Blackburn's Aaron Mokoena offered experience at the highest level, while the emerging talents of young goalkeeper Itumeleng Khune gave South Africa stability at the back.

The Confederations Cup of 2009 was regarded as the dress rehearsal for the World Cup for both team and country as Santana could assess his squad in a competitive setting. The team got off to an uninspiring start, drawing 0-0 with Iraq before defeating New Zealand 2-0 with a brace from Red Star Belgrade striker Bernard Parker.

Despite losing 2-0 to Spain, the hosts joined Spain in the semi-finals where they faced Brazil. It was a spirited performance, and extra time beckoned before a late strike from Dani Alves meant that South Africa had to fight for third place. This meant a rematch with Spain, who had suffered a surprise loss to the United States.

It took an extra-time winner from Xabi Alonso to settle the game when it ended 2-2 after 90 minutes, three of the four goals coming in a frantic final five minutes.

It was a respectable fourth place for South Africa but, after the team endured a poor run of eight defeats in nine games, Santana was sacked and Parreira reinstated. With a World Cup winner at the helm the South Africans were hopeful of a good tournament.

BELOW Captain Aaron Mokoena leads by example, tackling the threat of Brazil's Robinho.

SOUTH KOREA

South Korea surprised everyone with a fourth-place World Cup finish in 2002.

Despite faltering since, they were determined to put in a repeat performance in 2010.

After experimenting with Dutch coaches, countryman Huh Jung-Moo was appointed for a third time. The former midfielder had been intermittently involved with South Korea since 1989 as coach and manager, and was assistant to Dutchman Jo Bonfrere in 2004.

His side had European experience, none more than captain Park Ji-Sung, the first Asian to play in a Champions League final with Manchester United in 2009. The goals came from strikers Seol Ki-Hyeon and Lee Dong-Gook, who had experience in England's top flight with Fulham and Middlesbrough.

After progressing through round three in a group with rivals Korea DPR, they faced their neighbors again in round four. Teenage midfielder Ki Sung-Yong who got their opening goal in a 1-1 draw against rivals Korea DPR, his strike equalizing a penalty.

South Korea's first win came against the United Arab Emirates in Seoul, a brace from winger Lee Keun-Ho and goals from Ji-Sung and Kwak

Tae-Hwi sealing a 4-1 victory. 2008 ended with a 2-0 triumph over Saudi Arabia, a last-minute goal coming from Monaco striker Park Chu-Young.

A free kick from Spanish-based midfielder Javad Nekounam looked like it had secured Iran victory over the South Koreans in February 2009, but Park Ji-Sung rescued a point with another late strike.

Three points against Korea DPR were then secured courtesy of a late goal from Kim Chi-Woo, leaving South Korea on the brink of qualification. A victory over United Arab Emirates in Dubai would send them to their seventh consecutive finals.

They wrapped up the game—and qualification—in the first half with goals from Park Chu-Young and Ki Sung-Yueng. The team played out two draws in their final fixtures against Saudi Arabia and Iran.

The team with the best World Cup qualifying record were back, having failed to suffer a single defeat in qualifying.

ROAD TO WORLD CUP 2010

South Korea	4-0	Turkmenistan
Korea DPR	0-0	South Korea
South Korea	2-2	Jordan
Jordan	0-1	South Korea
Turkmenistan	1-3	South Korea
South Korea	0-0	Korea DPR
Korea DPR	1-1	South Korea
South Korea	4-1	United Arab Emirates
Saudi Arabia	0-2	South Korea
Iran	1-1	South Korea
South Korea	1-0	Korea DPR
United Arab Emirates	0-2	South Korea
South Korea	0-0	Saudi Arabia
South Korea	1-1	Iran

LEFT South Korea's Kwak Tae-Hwi (right) heads a goal against United Arab Emirates in October 2008.

SWITZERLAND

Switzerland enlisted the best to ensure they reached South Africa. Seasoned manager Ottmar Hitzfeld arrived, having left Bayern Munich for a second time.

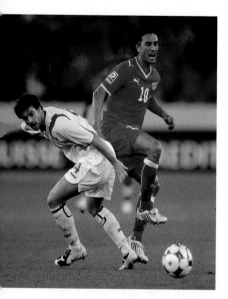

ABOVE Midfielder Hakan Yakin (right) chases a loose ball with a Luxembourg defender.

ROAD TO WORLD CUP 2010		
Israel	2-2	Switzerland
Switzerland	1-2	Luxembourg
Switzerland	2-1	Latvia
Greece	1-2	Switzerland
Moldova	0-2	Switzerland
Switzerland	2-0	Moldova
Switzerland	2-0	Greece
Latvia	2-2	Switzerland
Luxembourg	0-3	Switzerland
Switzerland	0-0	Israel

Hitzfeld's track record was formidable, winning the European Cup with both Bayern and Borussia Dortmund. But it was his early coaching success in Switzerland that convinced the FA he was right for the job.

The Swiss were hoping to avenge their last World Cup finals appearance when they were eliminated without conceding a goal after defeat to Ukraine on penalties. Switzerland nearly kicked off with a win in Tel Aviv, but let a 2-0 lead slip.

Switzerland found themselves with just one point after two games when Luxembourg struck late to win in Zurich four days later. Victory over Latvia was their first, goals from Sebastian Frei and Blaise Nkufo—his third in three games—sealing the win.

The two strikers struck again to beat group favorites Greece in October 2008. Successive 2-0 victories over Moldova re-established the Swiss as a force and qualification was a real possibility. They went some way to realizing that dream by defeating Greece a second time, in Basel, to top the group.

After rescuing a point against Latvia, the Swiss defeated Luxembourg 3-0, Philippe Senderos firing two in two minutes before Basel's Benjamin Huggel added a third. It meant only one point was needed in the final match against Israel to qualify. While uninspiring, the drab 0-0 draw in front of their home support secured the necessary point. Switzerland had qualified for their eighth World Cup finals.

It was a deserved achievement. Johan Djourou and Philippe Senderos had been schooled at

Arsenal, while Wolfsburg's Bundesliga-winning Diego Benaglio was consistent between the posts.

With relative veterans Alexander Frei and Hakan Yakin, and new players Gelson Fernandes and Johan Vonlan, this blend of youth and experience gave high hopes in Zurich.

BELOW Stephane Grichting hit his first international goal against Greece.

URUGUAY

Uruguay's passage to the World Cup finals was a 20-match marathon that began three years before the tournament.

The country credited with being the first-ever World Cup hosts and winners were hoping to put recent barren years behind them and recapture the trophy.

Head coach Oscar Tabárez had been brought back in after leading Uruguay to the World Cup in 1990, where they progressed to the last 16. Uruguay had only qualified once since—in 2002.

There had been a number of successful Uruguayan exports in Europe, none more than striker Diego Forlan. He was charged with delivering the goals alongside young Ajax man Luis Suárez. At the back, defensive duo Diego Lugano and Maxi Pereira were key players for Fenerbahçe and Benfica, respectively.

Uruguay's campaign got off to a great start with a 5-0 victory over Bolivia before a single-goal reverse against Paraguay. November 2007 saw Uruguay pick up just one point from two games as they drew with Chile and lost 2-1 to Brazil in Sao Paulo.

A 1-1 draw with Venezuela was followed by a 6-0 thrashing of Peru, with Forlan bagging a hat trick. Victory over Colombia and a frustrating 0-0 draw with Ecuador did little to move Uruguay ahead of the pack.

A loss to Argentina preceded a scrappy draw with Bolivia, meaning Uruguay ended 2008 with much to do. The following year started with a 2-0 win over Paraguay, then came a 0-0 draw against Chile. The team's inability to string wins together was threatening to cost Uruguay dearly.

Uruguay were thumped 4-0 by Brazil at the Estadio Centenario. It looked like they had recovered, leading Venezuela 2-1 days later, only to be held at the final whistle.

LEFT Sebastian Abreu heads the goal against Costa Rica that sent Uruguay to South Africa.

ROAD TO WORLD CUP 2010

Uruguay	5-0	Bolivia
Paraguay	1-0	Uruguay
Uruguay	2-2	Chile
Brazil	2-1	Uruguay
Uruguay	1-1	Venezuela
Uruguay	6-0	Peru
Colombia	0-1	Uruguay
Uruguay	0-0	Ecuador
Argentina	2-1	Uruguay
Bolivia	2-2	Uruguay
Uruguay	2-0	Paraguay
Chile	0-0	Uruguay
Uruguay	0-4	Brazil
Venezuela	2-2	Uruguay
Uruguay	3-1	Colombia
Ecuador	1-2	Uruguay
Uruguay	0-1	Argentina
Costa Rica	0-1	Uruguay
Uruguay	1-1	Costa Rica

Two wins from their final three games secured a playoff place for Uruguay, despite losing to Argentina in their final match. Uruguay were then set to face Costa Rica, who finished fourth in their CONCACAF qualifying group.

Uruguay journeyed to San Jose first, where defender Lugano grabbed his fourth and most important goal of the qualifying fixtures. Uruguay headed back to Montevideo with a crucial away goal.

A 1-1 draw followed days later, confirming Uruguay's progression to the finals.

EUROPE

CONMEBOL

ABOVE Republic of Ireland players protest the controversial France winner that sent them to South Africa.

RIGHT Spain celebrate victory over Belgium, qualifying with a perfect record.

ABOVE Diego Maradona cuts a lonely figure as his Argentina side are humbled 6-1 by Bolivia.

BELOW Luis Fabiano celebrates scoring against Argentina. Only six points separated group winners Brazil from fourth place.

ABOVE England secure qualification with a 5-1 drubbing of Croatia, Frank Lampard a scorer.

CONCACAF

CAF

ASIA

ABOVE A nation rejoices as Honduras reach only their second World Cup finals.

BELOW Algeria's Khaled Lemmouchia (right) challenges Egypt's Ahmed Hassan (2nd right) during the second leg of the qualification playoffs.

LEFT Lucas Neill salutes fans as Australia become the third team to earn qualification.

BELOW Political issues forced rivals South Korea and Korea DPR to play their qualifier in neutral China.

ABOVE Fans show their delight at the United States reaching their ninth World Cup finals.

RIGHT Ivory Coast made it through both stages of CAF qualification without losing a match.

CRISTIANO RONALDO

Cristiano Ronaldo burst onto the football scene in 2001. Now renowned as one of the planet's best player, there appears to be no stopping him.

RIGHT Cristiano Ronaldo (right) shields the ball from Sweden's Daniel Majstorovic (left) during an October 2008 match.

ABOVE Portugal's prodigiously talented Cristiano Ronaldo.

After signing with Sporting Lisbon at the age of 12, Ronaldo soared through the ranks and quickly made it to the first team, scoring a brace on his debut. It was a dazzling performance against Manchester United that inspired United manager Alex Ferguson to pay more than $US 20 million (£12 million) for him in 2003.

Less than a week after his United debut Ronaldo made his first appearance for Portugal. He was later included in their squad for Euro 2004. He scored in their opening match, a shock 2-1 defeat by eventual winners Greece, and again in the semi-final success against the Netherlands, but Portugal went on to lose in the final.

Despite this disappointment, Ronaldo went on to fire seven goals in Portugal's qualifying campaign for the 2006 World Cup. He scored once at the finals, as his country finished in fourth place, but major footballing honors were yet to come. In 2007 he won his first Premier League title, and was named Portugal's player of the year.

The following year, Ronaldo picked up another Premier League winner's medal, as well as scoring eight goals to help Manchester United lift the European Cup. He was crowned the world's greatest player by picking up the treble of FIFPro World Player of the Year, the Ballon d'Or, and the European Golden Shoe.

These awards made Ronaldo one of the most feared players in the game. Despite scoring eight goals in qualification, Ronaldo and Portugal could not progress past the quarter-finals of Euro 2008, losing 3-2 to Germany.

After a second successive Champions League final and third Premier League title in a row, Ronaldo became the most expensive player in the world when he signed for Spanish giants Real Madrid in 2009. He endured an indifferent World Cup qualifying campaign, however, Portugal scraping through the playoffs against Bosnia and Herzegovina.

FACTFILE

Full Name:
Cristiano Ronaldo dos Santos Aveiro
Date of Birth: February 5 1985
Place of Birth:
Funchal, Madeira, Portugal
Height: 6 ft 1 in (1.86 m)
Playing Position: Forward
National Team: Portugal
1st Appearance: 2003

DIDIER DROGBA

Didier Drogba is the danger man of the Ivory Coast team. The striker's instincts in front of goal have made him a success both domestically and on the international stage, and he fired his teammates to their second successive World Cup finals in 2010.

Born in March 1978, Drogba started at French club Le Mans in Ligue 2, signing his first professional contract aged 21. Though starting his career somewhat late, he managed to score seven goals in his first full season with the team.

In 2002, Drogba moved to Guingamp. It was during his stint there, that he made his debut for the Ivory Coast, against South Africa in September.

He scored his first goal for the national side in January 2003, beginning a phenomenal run that would see him score more than 40 goals by the time he received his 60th cap.

Domestically, Drogba left Guingamp for a season at French giants Marseille before his exploits attracted interest from cash-rich Chelsea. He signed for the London team for $US 40 million (£24 million) in 2004 and captured the Premier League championship with his new team in his first season.

It was no coincidence that Drogba's free scoring coincided with the Ivory Coast's most successful period. They finished second in the 2006 African Cup of Nations, the powerful striker hitting three goals including the winner in the semi-final.

Either side of that tournament, Drogba scored the goals to send his national side to their first-ever World Cup finals in Germany. He hit nine goals in qualifying as they topped their group. However, Drogba only scored one at the tournament as Ivory Coast were swiftly eliminated, finishing third behind Argentina and Netherlands in what was known as the "group of death."

This disappointment didn't stop Drogba, however, as he netted three more times in the 2008 African Cup of Nations. He also provided the firepower to secure a second World Cup appearance for the Ivory Coast. Drogba's six goals included the equalizer against Malawi that confirmed qualification.

FACTFILE

Full Name:
Didier Yves Drogba Tébily
Date of Birth: March 11 1978
Place of Birth:
Abidjan, Côte d'Ivoire
Height: 6 ft 2 in (1.88 m)
Playing Position: Striker
National Team: Ivory Coast
1st Appearance: 2002

LEFT Didier Drogba is the Ivory Coast's all-time leading goal-scorer.

DIEGO FORLÁN

Diego Forlán is a player with a strong football pedigree. His father and grandfather were both professional footballers and Diego set out to be the most successful of the trio.

Winning the European Golden Shoe on two separate occasions has certainly confirmed that.

He made his professional debut at Argentinean side Independiente at the age of 19, and impressed after maintaining a ratio of nearly a goal every two games. He was rewarded with a transfer to English giants Manchester United.

FACTFILE

Full Name:
Diego Martín Forlán Corazo
Date of Birth: May 19 1979
Place of Birth:
Montevideo, Uruguay
Height: 5 ft 10 ½ in (1.79 m)
Playing Position: Striker
National Team: Uruguay
1st Appearance: 2002

RIGHT Diego Forlan's seven goals fired Uruguay to their 11th World Cup.

It was while with United in 2002 that Forlán made his debut for his country; he grabbed his first goal after just four minutes in a 3-2 defeat to Saudi Arabia to announce his arrival on the international stage. Forlán was included in Uruguay's squad for the 2002 World Cup, and scored against Senegal in his only appearance of the tournament.

His goal tally at Manchester United was not as high as many had expected, despite helping the club win the Premier League and FA Cup double and, in 2004, Forlán moved to Villarreal. It was in Spain that his career began to take off both domestically and internationally.

Forlán helped Uruguay reach third place at the 2004 Copa America, and scored six times in their qualification campaign for the 2006 World Cup. However, Uruguay lost to Australia on penalties in the CONMEBOL versus OFC playoff.

In 2005 Forlán won his first European Golden Shoe after hitting 25 league goals for Villarreal. His three goals for Uruguay in the 2007 Copa America were not enough to help them to a 15th title, as they had to settle for fourth place.

Forlán's best campaign for Uruguay came during qualification for the 2010 World Cup, where he hit seven goals en route to their playoff victory over Costa Rica. In 2009 he won the Golden Shoe for the second time.

Diego Forlán has proved himself vital to both his clubs and his country during his career.

FERNANDO TORRES

Already an important player for his club and country before he had reached his 20th birthday, the responsibility didn't seem to faze Fernando Torres, who has thrived on pressure throughout his career.

The Spanish player signed his first professional contract with Atletico Madrid in 1999 at age 15, and made his club debut two years later. Once promoted to La Liga, Torres was noticed by national manager Iñaki Sáez, who gave him his first cap in 2003 against Portugal.

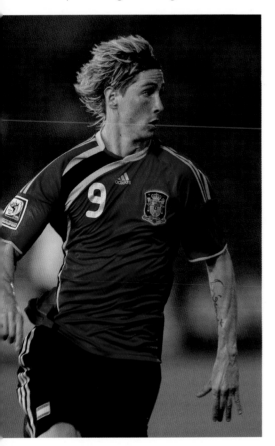

It was not Torres' first appearance in a Spain jersey, however, having come up through the youth ranks. His later teenage years were spent scoring for club and country at the top level.

An appearance at Euro 2004 yielded no goals, but Torres hit six to help Spain qualify for the World Cup in 2006. Five of his haul came in Spain's last two matches, keeping them in second qualifying spot ahead of Bosnia and Herzegovina. Torres scored a further three in the finals, but Spain could not progress beyond the second round.

Torres left Atletico in 2007 for five-time European champions, Liverpool, where he continued his goal-scoring, hitting more than 20 in his first season for the Reds.

Both Torres' and Spain's finest hour came at Euro 2008 as Spain captured the crown. Torres only scored two during the tournament, the first against Sweden in a group match. But his winner in the final against Germany gave Spain only the second trophy in their international history.

Torres went on to score three times at the 2009 Confederations Cup, courtesy of a hat trick against New Zealand, before Spain suffered a shock defeat to the United States. An injury-ravaged qualifying campaign for the World Cup left Torres without any goals, though his country still reached South Africa.

In 2009 Fernando Torres became the youngest Spanish international to reach 60 caps.

FACTFILE

Full Name:
Fernando José Torres Sanz
Date of Birth: March 20 1984
Place of Birth: Madrid, Spain
Height: 6 ft 1 in (1.85 m)
Playing Position: Striker
National Team: Spain
1st Appearance: 2003

LEFT Fernando Torres was named man of the match in the Euro 2008 final when he helped Spain capture the trophy.

FRANCK RIBÉRY

Franck Ribéry is a rising star in French football, despite only emerging in the national side at the relatively late age of 23.

FACTFILE

Full Name: Franck Bilal Ribéry
Date of Birth: April 7 1983
Place of Birth:
Boulogne-sur-Mer, France
Height: 5 ft 7 in (1.70 m)
Playing Position: Winger
National Team: France
1st Appearance: 2006

RIGHT Franck Ribéry has become a key part of France's team in just three years.

Ribéry's attacking instinct and eye for a killer pass has made him an integral part of France's mission to regain international silverware.

He spent his early career plying his trade in the lower leagues in France before getting his break in Ligue 1 with FC Metz in 2004. He only stayed at each club for one season, however.

Ribéry arrived at Turkish giants Galatasaray in 2005 and, although it was to prove another brief stay, he captured the Türkiye Kupası—the equivalent of the FA Cup—scoring his only goal in the final.

From there, Ribéry moved to French club Olympique Marseille amid controversy, Galatasaray having allegedly not paid him for an extended period. He immediately won the Intertoto Cup and his performances, both domestically and in Europe, finally brought Ribéry to the attention of France manager Raymond Domenech.

Ribéry made his national debut in May 2006 and he was quickly included in France's squad for the World Cup in Germany a month later. His first international goal came against Spain in the last 16. He played from the start in the final but could not help his country overcome Italy.

Ribéry quickly became a mainstay in the national team, with recently retired legend Zinedine Zidane naming him "the jewel of French football." Bayern Munich clearly agreed, and paid US$ 40 million (25 million euros) for Ribéry's services in 2007, testament to his rising stock after languishing in France's lower leagues just a few years before.

Ribéry was selected for Euro 2008 where, after reaching the World Cup final, expectations were again high. After a disastrous group stage, the misery was compounded for Ribéry as he ruptured his ankle ligaments, leaving him sidelined.

He returned to score some crucial goals as France eventually qualified for the 2010 World Cup. His two in two games against Lithuania secured a vital six points for "Les Bleus," though injury forced Ribéry out of the playoff victory over the Republic of Ireland.

WORLD CUP 2010, STAR PLAYERS
GIANLUIGI BUFFON

Gianluigi Buffon made his professional debut at just 17. Since then, he has established himself as one of the great goalkeepers of his generation.

Two years after his first appearance for Serie A side Parma, he was picked for his country during a World Cup qualifier in Russia. Buffon acquitted himself well and made the squad for the 1998 tournament in France at just 20 years of age.

He was part of a Parma team including Hernan Crespo and Fabio Cannavaro that won the UEFA Cup and the Copa Italia in 1999, but he missed out on a spot at Euro 2000 due to a broken finger. Buffon had to watch established number one Francesco Toldo help Italy to second place.

In 2001 Buffon signed for Italian giants Juventus for a world record fee (for a goalkeeper) of more than US$ 80 million (50 million euros). It was here that his career would reach new levels; multiple Scudetto wins saw him recognized as the best goalkeeper in the world and helped him succeed Toldo as Italy's number one.

Buffon traveled to the World Cup in 2002 as Italy's first-choice goalkeeper, but the team could not progress beyond the second round, losing to hosts South Korea.

Buffon would go on to experience some troubled years, but still maintained his world-class standards. Italy exited Euro 2004 at the group stage despite not losing a game, and in 2006 Juventus were found guilty of match-fixing and relegated to Serie B. Buffon pledged allegiance to his club, claiming he had not yet won that league and wished to do so, testament to his loyalty and competitive nature.

That summer Buffon helped his country capture their fourth World Cup, keeping an incredible five

LEFT Gianluigi Buffon has earned more than 100 caps for Italy in a career that has already seen him lift the World Cup.

FACTFILE

Full Name: Gianluigi Buffon
Date of Birth: January 2 1978
Place of Birth: Carrara, Italy
Height: 6 ft 3 in (1.91 m)
Playing Position: Goalkeeper
National Team: Italy
1st Appearance: 1997

clean sheets, and he was named in the team of the tournament. It was Buffon's finest hour—the world's best keeper helped Italy win the world's biggest prize.

Another inclusion for team of the tournament at Euro 2008 underlined Buffon's dominance as he passed 30.

WORLD CUP 2010, STAR PLAYERS
IKER CASILLAS

Iker Casillas is captain of his country with more than 100 international caps.

ABOVE Iker Casillas leads from the back as Spain's captain.

With goalkeepers usually playing until their mid-30s, Casillas has many years ahead of him and is already considered one of the greatest goalkeepers in the world.

He began his career aged just nine at Real Madrid, playing in the youth system before moving through their "C" and "B" teams. Casillas made his professional debut for the senior side in 1999 and quickly established himself as first choice. Success followed almost immediately, with Madrid capturing the Champions League in 2000. At just 19 years old, Casillas had already won the biggest prize in European club football, keeping a clean sheet in the final.

It was also in 2000 that Casillas debuted for Spain, after playing at almost every youth level in previous years. It took him longer to dislodge Santiago Cañizares from the first team, however; Casillas was included in the Euro 2000 squad, but failed to make an appearance.

By the 2002 World Cup, he had earned a second Champions League medal and was first choice for his country. Despite Casillas saving two penalties against the Republic of Ireland in the round of 16, Spain still exited the competition at the quarter-final stage to South Korea.

A two-time La Liga winner by Euro 2004, Casillas played in all of Spain's matches, conceding just two goals, though these were crucial enough to see his country eliminated at the group stage.

A quarter-final exit to France in the 2006 World Cup did not hint at the success to come for both Casillas and Spain. He entered Euro 2008 wearing the captain's armband, and kept clean sheets throughout the knockout stages as Spain stormed to the championship.

Casillas helped his country last nearly three years without losing an international match from November 2006 to June 2009. During this period, he and his deputy, Liverpool's Pepe Reina, played more than seven games without conceding a goal.

Spain went through their entire 2010 World Cup qualifying campaign without losing a game. Casillas played in all but one match, and conceded just four times.

By the time he reached his century of international caps, more than half of those appearances had resulted in clean sheets, proof of his skill and consistency.

FACTFILE

Full Name:
Iker Casillas Fernández
Date of Birth: May 20 1981
Place of Birth:
Mostoles, Madrid, Spain
Height: 5 ft 11 ½ in (1.82 m)
Playing Position: Goalkeeper
National Team: Spain
1st Appearance: 2000

WORLD CUP 2010, STAR PLAYERS
KAKÁ

Brazilian Kaká is regarded around the world as a footballing superstar. His goals and flair have seen him win nearly every trophy on the world and European stage with club and country.

Kaká began his career in the youth ranks at Sao Paulo and, on making his debut in the senior side, was noticed by national coach Luiz Felipe Scolari.

Despite only having two caps to his name, Kaká was included in the 2002 World Cup squad. Aged 20, he was the youngest player, and only appeared once in a 5-2 romp over Costa Rica, replacing Rivaldo. But Kaká still picked up a winner's medal as Brazil triumphed in Japan and South Korea.

Kaká was soon signed by Serie A giants AC Milan in 2003. He made a good start, scoring 10 goals in his first season and capturing the Scudetto, the first of many domestic trophies.

In 2005, Kaká triumphed again with the national team, this time at the Confederations Cup. He was much more influential than in 2002, scoring in the final against archrivals Argentina. However, Kaká scored only once at the 2006 World Cup, where Brazil could not get past the quarter-final stage.

He returned to Milan and 2007 proved to be a phenomenal year at club level. Kaká scooped the Champions League, UEFA Super Cup, and FIFA World Club Cup and, in the process, he was named European and World player of the year. Kaká was the hottest property in football, and continued to perform consistently.

2009 was a season of transition. After six years, Kaká left Milan for Real Madrid for a reported fee of $US 92 million (£56 million), a new world record. There was to be no rest, however, as he went straight into the 2009 Confederations Cup,

scoring a brace in Brazil's opening fixture against Egypt, before going on to win the tournament for a second time.

Kaká fired five goals in Brazil's World Cup qualifying campaign. This gave him the opportunity to secure his second World Cup before his 30th birthday, and cement his position as one of the world's best players.

BELOW Kaká is considered one of the best players in the world, with a transfer value to match.

FACTFILE

Full Name:
Ricardo Izecson dos Santos Leite
Date of Birth: April 22 1982
Place of Birth: Brasilia, Brazil
Height: 6 ft 1 in (1.86 m)
Playing Position:
Attacking Midfielder
National Team: Brazil
1st Appearance: 2002

WORLD CUP 2010, STAR PLAYERS
LANDON DONOVAN

Landon Donovan is the crown jewel of modern American soccer. In a nation where football is trying to establish itself as a popular sport, Donovan's success for both club and country has gone some way to achieving that aim.

ABOVE Landon Donovan holds the record for goals and caps for the United States.

After coming through soccer academy, Donovan was noticed in Germany after a strike rate of nearly a goal a game for the US Under-17 side. He became the youngest American player to go abroad when he was signed by Bundesliga club Bayer Leverkusen in 1999.

Donovan made his senior debut for the national side in 2000 against Mexico and scored on his debut. It was the perfect start to a career that would see him become his country's all-time leading goal-scorer.

Unhappy with his opportunities in Germany, Donovan was loaned to San Jose Earthquakes in 2001 in a deal that would last three years and establish him as a force in the US league.

Donovan traveled with the national squad to Japan and South Korea for the 2002 World Cup, and immediately hit the headlines. He scored twice en route to the quarter-finals, being named FIFA's best young player in the process.

The United States reached the finals for the eighth time in 2006, thanks in no small part to Donovan's seven goals in qualification. It was during this period that he arrived at LA Galaxy, following a brief return to Leverkusen.

Donovan had a poor World Cup in Germany, where the US failed to win a single game. They recovered quickly, storming to the 2007 CONCACAF Gold Cup, with four goals from Donovan, including the first in the final.

He briefly returned to Germany for a loan

spell at Bayern Munich in January 2009 during the MLS close season. Donovan was handed the US captain's armband for the first time competitively that summer in the group stages of the Confederations Cup. The States made it to the final, losing to Brazil, despite a Donovan goal that put them 2-0 up in the first half.

Donovan's five goals in qualifying brought the US a ninth World Cup appearance, including the goal against Honduras that confirmed their place. It was yet another achievement for Donovan, the most successful player in US football history.

FACTFILE

Full Name:
Landon Timothy Donovan
Date of Birth: March 4 1982
Place of Birth: Ontario, California
Height: 5 ft 8 in (1.73 m)
Playing Position:
Attacking Midfielder
National Team: United States
1st Appearance: 2000

WORLD CUP 2010, STAR PLAYERS
LIONEL MESSI

Announced by Diego Maradona as his "successor," Lionel Messi has been making headlines on the pitch ever since his breakthrough in 2004.

Messi became the youngest player to appear for Barcelona upon his debut, and added "youngest scorer in La Liga" to his accolades with his first career goal in 2005.

He gained further recognition that same year as the Argentina Under-20 side stormed the FIFA World Youth Championship, Messi picking up best player and top scorer accolades with six goals.

The following month he was called up to the senior side, but was sent off on his debut for an alleged elbow. Messi did enough to earn a spot at the 2006 World Cup finals, scoring in a 6-0 rout of Serbia and Montenegro and having a strike ruled offside against Mexico.

Messi nearly didn't make the tournament, however. An injury sustained for Barcelona against Chelsea in the Champions League threatened to sideline him. He watched his side pick up the European Cup while he was nursed back to health.

Messi's fine form continued as he scored two goals to help Argentina to the final of the 2007 Copa America, before they lost 3-0 to Brazil. At the end of the year, Messi came third in the voting for European Footballer of the Year.

His finest international moment so far came in China at the 2008 Olympic Games. Once Barcelona relented after initially refusing to let him go, he helped his country to football gold with the winner in the final against Nigeria—his third goal of the tournament.

Messi enjoyed a successful year in 2009 when he captured the Champions League with Barcelona, playing and scoring in the final. His goal was the second of the game and sealed a 2-0 triumph over Manchester United.

FACTFILE

Full Name:
Lionel Andrés Messi
Date of Birth: June 24 1987
Place of Birth: Rosario, Argentina
Height: 5 ft 7 in (1.69 m)
Playing Position: Winger
National Team: Argentina
1st Appearance: 2005

LEFT Lionel Messi (left) vies for the ball with Colombian defender Pablo Armero (right) during a June 2009 World Cup qualification match.

WORLD CUP 2010, STAR PLAYERS
MICHAEL BALLACK

Despite winning a number of domestic trophies, the goal-scoring midfielder has yet to taste glory with the country he captains.

ABOVE Ballack has captained his country since 2004.

FACTFILE

Full Name: Michael Ballack
Date of Birth: September 26 1976
Place of Birth: Görlitz, Germany
Height: 6 ft 2 ½ in (1.89 m)
Playing Position: Midfielder
National Team: Germany
1st Appearance: 1999

After solid performances in the lower leagues for local side Chemnitzer FC, Ballack was transferred to FC Kaiserslautern in 1997, immediately capturing the Bundesliga in his first season. It was here he got his break for the German national side; coach Berti Vogts noticed the qualities of the player known as "Little Kaiser" for his Beckenbauer-esque qualities.

Ballack debuted in April 1999 against Scotland and soon forced his way into the Euro 2000 squad. Though he only played one match at the tournament, he went on to help Germany reach the 2002 World Cup finals.

Ballack's first three goals for his country were not enough to help them qualify automatically, but he was instrumental in the playoff success over Ukraine, hitting three more in two games for a 5-2 aggregate victory.

2002 was a year of disappointment for Ballack, who narrowly missed out on the Champions League and Bundesliga with Bayer Leverkusen. And it got worse at the World Cup where, though he scored three times including the only goal of the semi-final victory over South Korea, a yellow card forced him out of the final. Germany compounded Ballack's misery by losing to Brazil.

Despite these setbacks, Ballack—by now at Bayern Munich—hit four goals in qualifying to send Germany to Euro 2004. However, they failed to progress from their group. It was after the tournament that new manager Jürgen Klinsmann awarded Ballack the national captaincy.

Ballack led his team to third place in the 2005 Confederations Cup with a four-goal haul, before leading them to another third-place finish in the following year's World Cup. More pain followed in Euro 2008 as Germany lost to Spain in the final.

Despite the upturn in German fortunes since Ballack's appointment as captain, he has yet to experience glory with his country.

ABOVE Michael Ballack has scored more than 40 goals from midfield in a 10-year career with Germany.

MICHAEL ESSIEN

Michael Essien has emerged as one of Africa's best players of recent years. He consistently turns in powerful performances in midfield, proving himself a key player for both Chelsea and Ghana.

Essien signed his first professional contract at French side Bastia at 18 years old, and was originally a defender. However, after impressing in midfield while covering an injury, it was quickly agreed it was his best position.

Essien made his debut for Ghana in January 2002 in a warm-up match for the African Cup of Nations. He also played in the tournament, where Ghana lost to Nigeria in the quarter-finals.

In 2003, French giants Olympique Lyonnais recognized Essien's talents and signed him for more than US$ 11.5 million (7 million euros). Here, he quickly established himself in a defensive midfield role, winning the Ligue 1 championship two years in a row.

This brought him to the attention of Premier League champions Chelsea, who signed him for US$ 40 million (£24.4 million) in 2005. Essien promptly helped them to their second successive title, his third in three seasons. His commitment and classy style of play made him a lynchpin for both club and country.

Essien was selected in Ghana's 2006 World Cup squad, and played in all three of their group matches. He was suspended for the round of 16 against Brazil, however, when his country were eliminated.

Essien assisted Ghana to third place at the 2008 African Cup of Nations, scoring twice, including a strike against Nigeria in the quarter-finals.

Injury during World Cup qualification sidelined Essien for nearly the entire 2008/09 season

for Chelsea. However, due to the break in play between the second and third rounds of CAF qualification, he only missed one match, helping his country reach the 2010 finals.

Chelsea manager Carlo Ancelotti summed up Essien's versatility and importance: "I think Essien is one of the most important players in midfield in the world. He can play everywhere in midfield with the same result."

Essien leads the new crop of Ghanaian footballers that helped Ghana to their highest FIFA ranking in 2008.

FACTFILE

Full Name: Michael Kojo Essien
Date of Birth: December 2 1982
Place of Birth: Accra, Ghana
Height: 5 ft 10 in (1.78 m)
Playing Position: Midfielder
National Team: Ghana
1st Appearance: 2002

LEFT Michael Essien is widely regarded as one of the best midfield players in world football.

WORLD CUP 2010, STAR PLAYERS
MIROSLAV KLOSE

Miroslav Klose was born in Poland, but he qualified for the German national team through his grandfather.

ABOVE Miroslav Klose is head over heels after scoring the goal that sent Germany to South Africa.

Since his debut, Klose has become one of his adopted country's most successful strikers.

Klose made his professional debut at the late age of 19, at FC Kaiserslautern. After playing for the reserve side, he broke into the first team and impressed Germany coach Rudi Völler. Klose made his debut for Germany in March 2001.

His choice paid off when, in his first World Cup in 2002, Germany topped their group. Klose became Germany's top scorer in the competition with five goals, including a hat trick against Saudi Arabia; Germany made it to the final but lost to Brazil.

A poor Euro 2004 preceded a move from Kaiserslautern to Werder Bremen, where Klose was valued as much for his assists to other players as for his goals.

He made Germany's 2006 World Cup squad, and again scored five as Germany attempted to regain the trophy on home soil.. Though he finished as the tournament's top marksman, and was voted best player, Germany lost to eventual winners Italy in the semi-final.

In 2007, Klose moved to German champions Bayern Munich, and he helped them win the Bundesliga and DFB-Pokal double in his first season.

Klose scored five times while helping Germany qualify for Euro 2008, going on to score in both the quarter-finals and semi-finals of the tournament. Unfortunately for Klose, his wait for an international trophy continued as Germany failed to overcome Spain in the final.

Germany finished top of their qualifying group for the 2010 World Cup and Klose netted an impressive seven goals on the way, the most important condemning Russia to the playoffs and ensuring Germany's passage to South Africa.

FACTFILE

Full Name: Miroslav Marian Klose
Date of Birth: June 9 1978
Place of Birth: Opole, Poland
Height: 5 ft 11 ½ in (1.82 m)
Playing Position: Striker
National Team: Germany
1st Appearance: 2001

LEFT Klose finds the net against Azerbaijan, one of his seven goals during World Cup qualifying.

ROBIN VAN PERSIE

Robin Van Persie is a striker of both amazing talent and volatile temperament.

While Van Persie's potential is unquestionable, off-field incidents have threatened to curtail the development one of the most promising young players in world football.

Van Persie began his club career, aged 14, with Erste Divisie side SBV Excelsior. His pace and natural eye for goal soon got him noticed by other clubs. But disagreements with coaching staff led to a move to Feyenoord, the two clubs having an agreement allowing the fast transfer of players.

It was the beginning of a turbulent period at the Rotterdam club, where more arguments—this time with coach Bert Van Marwijk—reduced his playing time. He eventually moved to Arsenal for less than £4 million in 2004.

A year later, Van Persie finally got the call from his country, debuting in a World Cup qualifier in 2005. He scored in only his second game and played his way into manager Marco Van Basten's squad for the finals.

Van Persie started every match at the tournament. He scored against Ivory Coast as the Netherlands progressed past the group stage, but they lost to Portugal in the last 16.

Van Persie was instrumental in Netherlands reaching Euro 2008, topping his country's scoring charts with four goals, only for them to lose to Russia in the quarter-finals.

Many onlookers may have believed Van Persie's international career was in doubt after the tournament, because old adversary Van Marwijk was appointed national manager. But the two showed there were no hard feelings and the forward found himself in his new coach's squads.

It appeared Van Persie was coming into his own for the Netherlands, as well as making good progress at Arsenal, but he suffered a bad ankle injury in November 2009.

LEFT Van Persie has the potential to make a big impact on the 2010 World Cup.

FACTFILE

Full Name: Robin Van Persie
Date of Birth: August 6 1983
Place of Birth:
Rotterdam, Netherlands
Height: 6 ft 2 in (1.88 m)
Playing Position: Striker
National Team: Netherlands
1st Appearance: 2005

SAMUEL ETO'O

Samuel Eto'o is one of the most successful African footballers in history. His speed, skill, and eye for goal have made him a deadly force both in Europe and internationally over the last decade.

FACTFILE

Full Name: Samuel Eto'o Fils
Date of Birth: March 10 1981
Place of Birth: Douala, Cameroon
Height: 5 ft 11 in (1.80 m)
Playing Position: Striker
National Team: Cameroon
1st Appearance: 1996

RIGHT Samuel Eto'o proudly captains Cameroon to their sixth World Cup finals appearance.

Though his early career in European football was characterized by uncertainty, Eto'o's country recognized his skill immediately; he won his first international cap at 16 in 1996. He was included in Cameroon's 1998 World Cup squad, but only made one appearance, a 3-0 group-stage loss to Italy.

Meanwhile, Eto'o was successively loaned out to Spanish trio Leganés, Espanyol, and Mallorca by Real Madrid before settling on a permanent move to Mallorca in 2000.

His successful spell on the Spanish island coincided with many international triumphs. At just 19, Eto'o won a gold medal at the 2000 Olympic Games in Sydney; he hit the equalizer for Cameroon against Spain to take the final to extra time and, eventually, penalties.

Five goals in Cameroon's two successive African Cup of Nations wins in 2000 and 2002 sent Eto'o on his way to becoming both the tournament's, and his country's, top scorer. He netted his first World Cup goal in 2002, the winner against Saudi Arabia in the group stages. But Cameroon failed to qualify for the finals in 2006, despite Eto'o's four goals.

By this point, Eto'o had signed for Barcelona and had already picked up his first La Liga title. Despite missing out on Germany in 2006, he made up for it by helping his club win the Champions League, scoring in the final against Arsenal. Three years later, he became only the second player to score in two Champions League finals when he struck after just 10 minutes against Manchester United to help secure a second European Cup in 2009.

Eto'o scored nine goals to help Cameroon reach the 2010 World Cup, including the winner in their final match against Morocco.

With an international strike rate of nearly one goal every two games, Eto'o is every part as important to Cameroon as Roger Milla was in the nation's 1990 journey to the quarter-finals.

WORLD CUP 2010, STAR PLAYERS
THIERRY HENRY

In a career spanning nearly two decades, Thierry Henry has become one of the most decorated players in the game.

ABOVE Thierry Henry's pace is too much for Serbia goalkeeper Vladimir Stojkovic.

His instinct in the penalty area has seen Henry register more than 300 goals, and pick up every major honor in world football.

Henry graduated from the prestigious French football academy at Clairefontaine and made his first professional appearance for Monaco under Arsène Wenger. Success came in the form of the Ligue 1 championship and an appearance in a Champions League semi-final.

This brought Henry to the attention of France manager Aimé Jacquet, who gave him his debut in October 1997. He was a surprise inclusion in the 1998 World Cup squad, but ended the tournament with three goals and a winner's medal.

A brief spell at Juventus preceded a move to Arsenal, where Henry would establish himself as one of the world's deadliest strikers. He picked up another international trophy in 2000, when

France won the European Championship, three more goals making him his country's top scorer in successive tournaments.

After missing out on France's 2001 Confederations Cup win, Henry had a disastrous 2002 World Cup, being red-carded against Uruguay; his country crashed out without him contributing a goal. The pain was eased slightly by Arsenal picking up the Premier League and FA Cup double, Henry scoring 32 goals in all competitions.

He hit four goals, including the winner, in the final as France retained the Confederations Cup in 2003, completing a treble of international victories. A surprise exit in Euro 2004 to Greece soured Henry's enjoyment of a second Premier League title, though he scored two goals at the tournament.

Losses to Barcelona and Italy in the Champions League and World Cup finals, respectively, were low points in an otherwise successful 2006 for Henry. He became Arsenal's all-time leading goal-scorer that year and achieved the same milestone for France in 2007.

Following a move to Barcelona from Arsenal, he was France's only scorer in another below-par performance at Euro 2008, but in 2009 he would finally capture the Champions League.

Henry scored four times as France qualified for the 2010 World Cup finals, though he attracted rare criticism by controversially handling the ball while creating France's winner in the playoffs against the Republic of Ireland.

RIGHT It took Henry just 10 years to surpass Michel Platini as France's all-time top scorer.

FACTFILE

Full Name: Thierry Daniel Henry
Date of Birth: August 17 1977
Place of Birth:
Les Ulis, Essonne, France
Height: 6 ft 2 in (1.88 m)
Playing Position: Striker
National Team: France
1st Appearance: 1997

TIM CAHILL

Tim Cahill has become perhaps the most recognizable face in Australian football, but it could have been so different.

FACTFILE

Full Name: Timothy Joel Cahill
Date of Birth: December 6 1979
Place of Birth:
Sydney, Australia
Height: 5 ft 10 in (1.78 m)
Playing Position: Midfielder
National Team: Australia
1st Appearance: 2004

Two substitute appearances for Western Samoa in an Under-20 tournament when he was just 14 threatened to derail Cahill's international ambitions.

FIFA would initially not let him play for another country but, since the ruling was overturned, Cahill has never looked back, becoming an integral cog in the Australian national team. His career skyrocketed after one goal in particular brought him to the attention of the football world.

Cahill arrived in England in 1997 after Millwall snapped him up from Sydney United. He made his debut the following year, but it wasn't until he scored the only goal in an FA Cup semi-final against Premier League Sunderland that his career took off. Though Millwall lost the final to Manchester United, interest in Cahill was high and he signed for Everton two months later.

He finally made his debut for Australia in March 2004, while still at Millwall, four years after the Australian FA originally called him up for the 2000 Olympic Games. Cahill participated in the 2004 Games, but Australia finished second to eventual winners Argentina in the group stage.

Cahill scored seven goals in qualification for the 2006 World Cup, helping Australia reach the finals for only the second time in their history. And it was in Germany that he had his proudest moment to date for the national team.

Australia were trailing 1-0 to Japan in their opening group match when Cahill was brought on. He scored twice in the last six minutes to turn the game on its head, before John Aloisi hit a third in injury time. These heroics counted for little, however, as the Australians were knocked out by Italy via a controversial 95th-minute penalty.

Cahill struck four goals as Australia reached their second consecutive finals in South Africa.

LEFT Tim Cahill displays his trademark goal celebration against Qatar.

WORLD CUP 2010, STAR PLAYERS
WAYNE ROONEY

Wayne Rooney has often been hailed as the great hope of English football, and has already proven vital to the national team's success.

Rooney's burst onto the scene at just 16 years of age, and his pace and power soon made him one of the world's best strikers.

He came off Everton's bench to score the winner against then League champions Arsenal in 2002, and was immediately hailed as Britain's best young player. The hype did not faze him and he made his debut for England a year later, aged just 17.

Rooney's debut against Australia made him the team's youngest-ever player. He added youngest scorer to his list of personal accolades when he netted against Macedonia in September 2003. Rooney had his breakthrough tournament for England at Euro 2004, scoring twice against Switzerland and again against Croatia.

The weight of the nation was on his shoulders as fans hoped for their first trophy since 1966. However, disaster struck against Portugal in the quarter-finals when Rooney was injured, and his team went on to lose on penalties.

Rooney gained interest from a host of other clubs and signed for Manchester United in August 2004 for a fee of more than US$ 40 million (£25 million)—a record figure for a player less than 20.

Panic struck when Rooney was injured in the run-up to the World Cup in 2006. He made the tournament after intense rehabilitation, but it was a case of history repeating against the Portuguese in the quarter-final stage as he again exited the game early, this time sent off for a foul on Ricardo Carvalho.

The quick-tempered forward returned to competitive action after suspension, scoring twice in a disappointing Euro 2008 qualifying campaign, where England failed to qualify.

England's path to South Africa saw Rooney hit an incredible nine goals, including braces against Andorra, Belarus, and Kazakhstan, on the way to them finishing top of their group.

His goal tally cemented his importance to the team and his country's hopes, a fact recognized when he was made captain for a friendly against Brazil in late 2009.

LEFT Rooney scores his ninth qualifying goal in a 5-1 win over Croatia at Wembley Stadium.

ABOVE Despite being only 24 years old, Wayne Rooney has already scored more than 100 career goals.

FACTFILE

Full Name: Wayne Mark Rooney
Date of Birth: October 24 1985
Place of Birth:
Croxteth, Liverpool, England
Height: 5 ft 10 in (1.78 m)
Playing Position: Striker
National Team: England
1st Appearance: 2003

EUROPEAN CHAMPIONSHIP

The creation of the European Championship and UEFA, the governing body of football in Europe, went hand in hand. FIFA had existed since 1904 and it ruled the world, but half a century later the European countries opted to register their own identity. By the end of the 1950s, not only was the European Championship a reality but the European Champion Clubs' Cup had sparked a revolution.

EUROPEAN CHAMPIONSHIP
FOUNDATION & 1960s

The idea of a rival competition to the World Cup was nothing new. Frenchman Henri Delaunay, who lent his name to the tournament, discussed the concept before World War II but never saw his dream become reality.

PAGE 36 Miroslav Klose scores for Germany against Turkey, 2008

PAGE 37 Euro 2004 winners Greece celebrate

FIFA feared such a tournament for the elite might undermine the status of its own World Cup but finally, in 1958, the European Championship took shape under its original name of the European Nations Cup. Sadly, Delaunay, Secretary General of the French Football Federation, died in 1954 and was unable to witness the creation of his dream. So his colleagues ensured that his name lived on by giving the tournament the alternative title of Coupe Henri Delaunay.

The inaugural competition comprised 17 countries playing on a two-leg knockout basis followed by the semi-finals, a third place play-off and then the final in one host country—appropriately enough in France.

Spain withdrew from their quarter-final against the Soviet Union because of political pressure by dictator Francisco Franco while England, Italy and West Germany failed to enter for fear of fixture congestion. The Soviets, inspired by legendary goalkeeper Lev Yashin, went on to become the first winners. They recovered from a one-goal deficit to overcome Yugoslavia 2-1 in a tense final in the old Parc des Princes in Paris.

The next competition, in 1964, was also marred by political interference. This time, Greece withdrew, after being told to face Albania in an early round though the nations were officially at war.

At least by now Cold War tension between the Soviet Union and Spain had eased, which was fortunate because the Soviets qualified for the finals

that were hosted by Spain. In the semi-finals, the Soviet Union defeated Denmark 3-0 in Barcelona, while Spain scrambled past Hungary, courtesy of a 2-1 in extra time win in Madrid.

Spain soon went a goal behind in the final at Real Madrid's Santiago Bernabéu Stadium, much to the distress of most of the 79,115 spectators. Fortunately for the hosts, Barcelona's Jesus María Pereda equalized and Zaragoza's Marcelino Martínez wrote himself into Spanish sporting history by heading in a late winner. England had entered for the first time, but had not progessed beyond the first round. New manager Alf Ramsey saw his men held 1-1 by France at Sheffield Wednesday's Hillsborough stadium, to then collapse 5-2 four months later in Paris.

CHALLENGE OF COMPETITION CHANGES

The tournament's name was now altered to the European Championship for the 1968 event and along with it came a change of format. For this event, eight groups of teams faced each other twice, with the top nation from each group progressing to two-legged quarter finals. Italy were hosts and for the first and only time a match was decided on the toss of a coin.

England, as the reigning World Champions, qualified for the inaugural European Championship finals with largely the same squad that had won the 1966 World Cup. So hopes were high that the Three Lions could roar to

THE RESULT 1960
Location: Paris
Final: Soviet Union 2 Yugoslavia 1 (after extra time)
Shirts: Soviets red, Yugoslavia blue
Scorers: Metreveli, Ponedelnik; Galic

SOVIET UNION

Yashin

Tchekeli · Maslenkin · Kroutikov

Voinov · Netto

Metreveli · Ivanov · Ponedelnik · Bubukin · Meshki

Kostic · Galic · Jerkovic · Matus · Sekularac

Perusic · Zanetic

Jusufi · Miladinovic · Durkovic

Vidinic

YUGOSLAVIA

a second successive major championship. But England fell 1-0 to a late goal by Yugoslavia in a match littered with fouls and marred by Alan Müllery's sending-off one minute from the final whistle with Dragan Dzajic scoring the decisive strike.

Italy beat the Soviets in the other semi-final on an infamous coin toss after a scoreless stalemate and no time to organize a replay.

Yugoslavia dominated in the final at Rome, but were punished for not being able to beat Dino Zoff more than once. Italy equalized nine minutes from time, made five changes for the replay and strolled past the exhausted Yugoslavs 2-0.

RIGHT The Henri Delaunay Cup

BELOW Spain vs USSR in the 1964 final, Madrid

THE RESULT 1964

Location: Madrid
Final: Spain 2 Soviet Union 1
Shirts: Spain blue; Soviets red
Scorers: Pereda, Martínez; Khusainov

SPAIN

Iribar

Rivilla Zoco Olivella Calleja

Pereda Fusté Suárez

Amaro Martínez Lapetra

Khusainov Ponedelnik Chislenko

Korneev Ivanov Voronin

Mudrik Anichkine Shesternev Chustikov

Yashin

SOVIET UNION

THE RESULT 1968

Location: Rome
Final: Italy 1 Yugoslavia 1 (after extra time)
Shirts: Italy blue, Yugoslavia white
Scorers: Domenghini; Dzajic

ITALY

Zoff

Burgnich Castano Guarneri Facchetti

Domenghini Ferrini Juliano Lodetti

Anastasi Prati

Dzajic Musemic Petkovic

Holcer Acimovic Trivic

Damjanovic Paunovic Pavlovic Fazlagic

Pantelic

YUGOSLAVIA

EUROPEAN CHAMPIONSHIP
1970s

"I don't think we could have played any better."

HELMUT SCHÖB

West Germany produced the finest football yet seen in the competition en route to a 1972 victory in Belgium, seeing off the Soviet Union at the Heysel Stadium. But both Italy and England failed to reach the finals.

THE RESULT 1972

Location: Brussels
Final: West Germany 3 Soviet Union 0
Shirts: Germany white, Soviets red
Scorers: Müller 2, Wimmer

WEST GERMANY

Maier

Höttges Beckenbauer Schwarzenbeck Breitner

Hoeness Wimmer Netzer Heynckes

Müller Kremers

Kozinkevich Banischevsky Baidachny
(Onishenko)

Konkov Kolotov Troshkine
(Dolmatov)

Kaplichny Istomine Khurtsilava Dzodzuaschvili

Rudakov

SOVIET UNION

1972

Belgium had delighted their fans by sending home holders Italy along the way, while England were ousted by the in-form West Germans in the two-leg knock-out quarter-finals.

West German manager Helmut Schön rebuilt his team after reaching the 1970 World Cup semi-finals in Mexico. Veteran striker Uwe Seeler had retired, so Schön looked to fast-rising Bayern Munich for the foundation of his new team.

The key man was Franz Beckenbauer, already a World Cup hero in 1966 and 1970, who was moved back from midfield to his personally favored role of attacking sweeper.

Striker Gerd Müller was another of the 1970 heroes alongside the new stars from Bayern Munich, namely attacking left back Paul Breitner and striker Uli Hoeness. Furthermore, Schön replaced Wolfgang Overath in midfield with the Borussia Mönchengladbach playmaker general Gunter Netzer.

Beckenbauer and Netzer commanded the first leg of the quarter-final at England's Wembley Stadium guiding the Germans to their inaugural victory with a 3-1 success. They had little difficulty securing a scoreless draw in the return leg against Sir Alf Ramsey's surprisingly unadventurous England side in West Berlin.

Belgium hosted the four-team finals but faced favorites West Germany at the semi-final stage. The Germans edged through 2-1 with two goals

from the prolific Müller. In the other semi-final, the Soviet Union maintained their record of reaching the last four of every final since the tournament's inception and overcame Hungary—which missed a late penalty—via Anatoli Konkov's deflected shot.

In the final, West Germany were in control, with the Soviets psychologically beaten by their recent 4-1 thrashing at the hands of West Germany. Müller, who had scored all four in the recent friendly, was on fire in the final and notched a goal in each half in the 3-0 triumph. Midfielder Herbert Wimmer added the third to claim Germany's first European Championship in front of 50,000 fans.

RIGHT Captains Bobby Moore of England and Franz Beckenbauer of West Germany, 1972

1976

The tournament, in Yugoslavia, was the last in which the hosts were chosen at a late stage after the qualifying rounds. The finals went on to be expanded to eight nations, with the hosts granted automatic exemption for the qualifying rounds.

Czechoslovakia emerged as surprise winners—launching their outsiders' campaign in the semifinals by stunning Holland. Two years earlier, the Dutch had come close to being crowned world champions and, with many of their outstanding players peaking, had been expected to reach the final at the very least.

It was a sad occasion for Johan Cruyff because it was to be his last shot at glory as an international player. This became his final major tournament in a Dutch national team shirt.

West Germany, as World Cup holders, had good reason to assume that they were well-placed to win, but that complacency meant they found themselves trailing 2-0 at halftime against

hosts Yugoslavia. Gerd Müller had retired from national team football but another Müller, Köln center forward Dieter, (no relation), came to the Germans' rescue on his international debut. He scored twice in the second half with his 82nd-minute equalizer forcing extra-time. Müller went on to complete a hat-trick in a famous 4-2 victory.

The final offered yet more drama, with Czechoslovakia taking an early two-goal lead against the West Germans. Manager Helmut Schön was kept waiting until the last minute of normal time before he could celebrate an equalizer from Bernd Holzenbein. Extra time failed to produce a winner, so penalties were necessary to decide the title for the first time in the history of the championship. West Germany's Uli Hoeness was the first to crack when he kicked the ball over keeper Ivo Viktor's bar and Czechoslovakia took the title after their midfield general Antonin Panenka kept his cool and scored with a chip past the West German keeper Sepp Maier.

LEFT Herbert Wimmer scores West Germany's second goal in the 1972 final against the Soviet Union

THE RESULT 1976

Location: Belgrade
Final: Czechoslovakia 2 West Germany 2 (Czechoslovakia 5-3 on penalties after extra time)
Shirts: Czechs red, Germany white
Scorers: Svehlík, Dobiás; Müller, Hölzenbein

CZECHOSLOVAKIA

Viktor

Pivarnik · Ondrus · Capkovic · Gogh

Dobiás (Vesely) · Móder · Panenka · Masny

Svehlík (Jurkemik) · Neboda

Hölzenbein · Müller

Hoeness · Beer (Bongartz) · Bonhof · Wimmer (Flohe)

Vogts · Schwarzenbeck · Beckenbauer · Dietz

Maier

WEST GERMANY

EUROPEAN CHAMPIONSHIP
1980s

UEFA responded to the fast-increasing popularity of the European Championship in 1980 by opting to widen out the qualifying potential and make the finals tournament itself more of a spectacle.

THE RESULT 1980

Location: Rome
Final: West Germany 2 Belgium 1
Shirts: Germany white, Belgium red
Scorers: Hruebsch 2; Vandereycken

WEST GERMANY

Schumacher

Kaltz   Förster   Stielike   Dietz

Briegel   Schuster   Müller   Rummenige

Hrubesch   Allofs

Ceulemans   Van der Elst

Vandereycken   Cools   Mommens   Van Moer

Renquin   Meeuws   Millecamps   Gerets

Pfaff

BELGIUM

1980

This time, seven countries progressed out of a solely group-based qualifying system to contest the title in Italy along with the host nation, staging the event for the second time in four tournaments. Two groups of four were contested, the winners of each progressing directly to the final in the Stadio Olimpico in Rome.

Hosts Italy had fully expected to be there for the climax after being drawn in the easier of the two groups. The formidable West Germans, holders Czechoslovakia, and two-times World Cup runners-up Holland had all wound up in the other pool. Instead Italy scored a single goal and missed out on top spot, underdogs Belgium taking their place instead. England failed to progress beyond the group, their concentration disturbed by hooligan violence at their tie against hosts Italy in Turin.

RIGHT West Germany's Horst Hrubesch hails his last-minute winning goal

TOP RIGHT Holland's captain Ruud Gullit in triumph in 1988

1984

Michel Platini dominated the finals from start to finish, scoring a record nine goals and captaining hosts France to their first major international trophy. On his way to winning the European Player of the Year three times, Platini scored the lone winning goal against Denmark in the opening match, hat-tricks against Belgium and Yugoslavia, one against Portugal in the semis and the opener against Spain in the final.

Manager Michel Hidalgo used Platini in a free attacking role at the apex of a superbly balanced midfield featuring Luis Fernandez, Jean Tigana, and Alain Giresse. They topped their group with three wins in three games, nine goals scored and only two conceded by keeper Joel Bats.

Holders West Germany failed to progress even beyond the group stage. They finished third behind Spain and Portugal and ahead of only Romania, and sacked manager Jupp Derwall, their winning boss in 1980, on their return home.

1988

Holland landed their one and only major prize in the 1988 finals in West Germany to complete a continental double, PSV Eindhoven having carried off the European Champions' Cup only weeks earlier. As ever, the Dutch had internal problems to resolve along the way. Striker Marco Van Basten had to be persuaded to play by friend and mentor Johan Cruyff. Manager Rinus Michels left Van Basten out of the line-up for the Dutch players opening group defeat by the Soviet Union, but Van Basten started next time out against England and hit a hat-trick. England, already beaten by the Irish Republic, then lost 3-1 to the Soviets and finished bottom of the group.

Confident hosts West Germany topped the other group ahead of Italy, Spain, and Denmark, but were knocked out in the semi-finals proved the end of their road. Holland hit back from one-down to beat their hosts 2-1 in extra time and followed this up by beating an injury and suspension-weakened Soviet Union in the final. Van Basten's volleyed second goal was hailed as one of the finest of all time.

The decisive match in the other group was played out in Naples between West Germany and Holland. Playing their best football since the 1974 World Cup, West Germany seized the initiative and carved out a 3-0 lead with a hat-trick by Klaus Allofs before a Johnny Rep penalty and Rene Van de Kerkhof's long-distance effort gave Holland late but vain hope. Man of the match for the Germans was young blond midfielder Bernd Schuster.

West Germany were clear favorites to beat Belgium in the final and snatched an early lead through giant center forward Horst Hrubesch. Belgium came out fighting at the start of the second half, however, and equalized through a penalty converted by Rene Vandereycken, though the Germans claimed that sweeper Uli Stielike's foul had been committed just outside the box. In the final minutes, Hrubesch scored again, heading home a corner from another outstanding newcomer in Karl-Heinz Rummenigge.

THE RESULT 1984
Location: Paris
Final: France 2 Spain 0
Shirts: France blue, Spain red
Scorers: Platini, Bellone

FRANCE

Bats

Domergue (Amoros) — Battiston — Le Roux — Bossis

Tigana — Fernandez — Platini — Giresse

Lacombe (Genghini) — Bellone

Carrasco — Santillana

Casas (Sarabia) — Manrique — Gomez — Javier

Urquiaga — Puig (Bonillo) — Redondo — Camacho

Echarri

SPAIN

THE RESULT 1988
Location: Munich
Final: Holland 2 Soviet Union 0
Shirts: Holland orange, Soviet white
Scorers: Gullit, Van Basten

HOLLAND

Van Breukelen

Van Aerle — Rijkaard — R Koeman — Van Tiggelen

Vanenburg — E Koeman — Wouters — Muhren

Gullit — Van Basten

Protassov (Pasulko) — Belanov

Mikhailichenko — Zavarov — Litovchenko — Aleinikov

Rats — Demanyenko — Khidiyatulline — Gotsmanov (Baltacha)

Dassaev

SOVIET UNION

1960s

1980s

EUROPEAN CHAMPIONSHIP **MOMENTS**

LEFT Slav goal keeper Blagoje Vidinic halts a Soviet attack

BELOW England fall to hosts Italy in Turin in the first round

RIGHT Eusébio's Portugal crashed out early in the 1964 event

BELOW Spain celebrate their 1964 success

BELOW Michel Platini was France's nine-goal top scorer in 1986

1980s

BELOW Kevin Keegan is sent crashing by a Spanish defender

RIGHT Denmark's Kim Vilfort holds the 1992 trophy

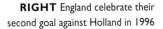

ABOVE Iain Giresse of France controls the ball during the 1984 European Championship final

RIGHT England celebrate their second goal against Holland in 1996

1990s

2000s

BELOW Spanish reserve goalkeeper Pepe Reina (right) and teammate David Villa celebrate victory in 2008

ABOVE England prepare to take the three Lions to the 2000 finals

EUROPEAN CHAMPIONSHIP
1990s

The dynamic Danish team surprised Europe in Sweden in 1992. This was also the first time a unified Germany took part in international competition and the first time that players' names were printed on their backs.

FAR RIGHT Paul Gascoigne volleys England's second goal against Scotland at Euro 96

THE RESULT 1992
Location: Gothenburg, Germany
Final: Denmark 2 Germany 0
Shirts: Denmark red, Germany white
Scorers: Jensen, Vilfort

DENMARK

Schmeichel

Sivebæk   Nielsen   Olsen   Piechnik
(Christiansen)

Christofte   Jensen   Vilfort   Larsen

Povlsen   Laudrup

Riedle   Klinsmann

Brehme   Hässler   Sammer   Effenberg
(Doll)   (Thom)

Helmer   Reuter   Kohler   Buchwald

Illgner

GERMANY

1992

Denmark's remarkable feat was as unexpected as their very participation. The Danes joined the tournament only after Yugoslavia were barred for security reasons on the eve of the finals—and when the Yugoslav squad was already in Sweden—after political instability in the Balkans had erupted into armed conflict.

Richard Moller Nielsen, the Danish team's manager, was at home redecorating his kitchen when he took the call instructing him to recall his players from their family holidays in the sun.

Not surprisingly, the Danes failed initially to impress before managing to finally string their game together for the last group match against France. The French, managed by Michel Platini, disappointed despite having been unbeaten in the qualifiers and fielding an attack that featured Jean-Pierre Papin and Eric Cantona.

UEFA had changed the tournament format once more, inserting knock-out semi-finals between the group stage and the final.

Denmark, defying numerous injuries, took the lead twice in their semi-final against a complacent Holland, both goals scored by Henrik Larsen. In the resultant penalty shoot-out, Marco Van Basten—Holland's match-winner from the 1988 final—saw his penalty saved by Peter Schmeichel.

In the other semi-final, holders Germany never needed to get out of second gear on their way to a 3-2 victory over hosts Sweden. The unified German side included the likes of Karlheinz Riedle, Thomas Hässler, and Jürgen Klinsmann, and few believed Denmark could test them in the final in the Ullevi stadium in Gothenburg.

Instead, they showed skill, cunning, and determination in abundance. Schmeichel laid claim to being the best goalkeeper in the world, while Lars Olsen was a rock in the center of defense and Brian Laudrup—young brother of Michael—proved a danger on the counterattack.

Against the Germans, midfielder John Jensen put Denmark ahead and Kim Vilfort capped a fairytale fortnight with a second goal 12 minutes from the end of the game.

1996

In 1966, the number of finalists doubled to 16 for the first major tournament staged in England since the World Cup 30 years earlier. Germany clinched their third crown when Oliver Bierhoff scored the first ever "golden goal" in the competition's history.

The golden goal was a short-lived attempt to find a better solution to deciding drawn matches. Instead of using penalties, a match was halted the moment a breakthrough goal was scored during extra time.

England, who had lost in the semi-finals, at least had the satisfaction of seeing Germany, their competition, re-establish their position on the footballing map after their failure to qualify for the previous World Cup and a decade of disaster.

Granting hosting rights to England had been an important signal from UEFA that it considered the English game had at last got on top of the problem of hooliganism. England boasted the finest stadia in Europe because of the massive rebuilding necessitated by the imposition of all-seater requirements.

Paul Gascoigne's wonder goal against Scotland set the tournament alight, but even better was to come when England swept Holland aside 4-1 at Wembley with a display rarely matched in their modern footballing history.

In the semi-finals, however, Germany broke English hearts by holding their nerve in a penalty shoot-out. Gareth Southgate saw his penalty saved by German keeper Andy Köpke, and midfielder Andreas Möller made no mistake with his subsequent penalty shot. The Germans thus progressed to a final back at Wembley against the technically adroit Czechs, who had ousted Aimé Jacquet's France in yet another shoot-out in the other semi-final.

The Germans, under the management of former title-winner Berti Vogts, were typically well-organized, with Matthias Sammer an excellent sweeper. But they failed initially to break down a counterattacking Czech side, who took the lead though a penalty from Patrik Berger.

The Czechs were 30 minutes from victory at that point. But then German manager Vogts sent on center forward Bierhoff as a substitute. First he equalized and then, five minutes into extra time, wrote himself into the record books with the first-ever golden goal in a major tournament.

THE RESULT 1996
Location: Wembley, London
Final: Germany 2 Czech Republic 1
(Germany on golden goal in extra time)
Shirts: Germany white, Czechs red
Scorers: Bierhoff 2; Berger

GERMANY

Köpke

Babbel   Helmer   Sammer   Ziege

Hässler   Strunz   Eilts   Scholl
         (Bode)   (Bierhoff)

         Klinsmann   Kuntz

              Kuka

Berger   Bejbl   Nedved   Poborsky
                                (Smicer)

Nemec Suchoparek Kadlec Rada Hornak

              Kouba

CZECH REPUBLIC

EUROPEAN CHAMPIONSHIP
2000s

"At last we have proved Spain can be winners."

MANAGER LUIS ARAGONES

France, the reigning world champions, beat Dino Zoff's Italy at the first European Championship final to be co-hosted—by Belgium and Holland—in 2000. Greece won the 2004 contest and resurgent Spain the 2008 finals.

FAR RIGHT Cristiano Ronaldo of Portugal in action during the 2004 quarter-final match between Portugal and England

RIGHT France enjoy their second title win in Rotterdam in 2000

2000

France squeezed past bitter rivals Italy in the final of the 2000 European Championship. Sylvain Wiltord equalized in the final seconds of the 90 minutes, allowing David Trezeguet to score 13 minutes into extra time with a thunderous volley. France thus became the first reigning World Cup Champions to add the European crown to their list of achievements.

Italy had come so close to winning the title, but manager Dino Zoff resigned in anger after the defeat, upset by the public criticism of his tactics and team selection by Prime Minister Silvio Berlusconi.

For England, the event proved a huge disappointment. Under the management of former player Kevin Keegan, they failed to progress beyond the group stage.

THE RESULT 2000

Location: Rotterdam
Final: France 2 Italy 1
(France on golden goal in extra time)
Shirts: France blue, Italy white
Scorers: Wiltord, Trezeguet; Delvecchio

FRANCE

Barthez

Thuram Desailly Blanc Lizarazu
(Pires)

Djorkaeff Deschamps Vieira Zidane
(Trezeguet)

Henry Dugarry
(Wiltord)

Delvecchio Totti
(Montella)

Fiore Iuliano Di Biagio Albertini
(Del Piero) (Ambrosini)

Maldini Cannavaro Nesta Pessotto

Toldo

ITALY

2004

The 2004 finals produced an upset few had predicted. Greece, who had qualified previously for only one World Cup (1994) and one European championship (1980), shocked hosts Portugal 1-0 by beating them in a dramatic final.

The Greeks, who had begun the tournament as 150-1 outsiders, also eliminated holders France as well as the Czech Republic, in this case with a silver goal, a rule that replaced the previous golden goal in 2003 before being abolished shortly afterwards. The silver goal meant that teams played on to the next formal stoppage (half-time or full-time) in extra time after a goal had been scored.

Greece's victory over Portugal in the final in Lisbon came courtesy of a solid defense, great goalkeeping, and an opportunist goal by Angelos Charisteas. The result stunned European football. However, it was not the only surprise of the tournament—Germany, Italy, and Spain had all been knocked out in the group stage.

Portugal's defeat in the final in Lisbon—in front of their own fans, denied manager Luiz Felipe Scolari a unique feat. Scolari would have become the first non-European manager to have won the continental crown.

2008

Spain ended a 44-year losing spell by winning the finals in Austria and Switzerland. Neither of the co-hosts made it through the opening group stage, but that did not affect the party atmosphere in Vienna after Spain, winners in 1964 and runners-up in 1984, defeated Germany 1-0 in the final. Liverpool's Fernando Torres scored the winning goal after 33 minutes.

Veteran manager Luis Aragones, a reserve to the winners of 1964, said afterwards: "At last we have proved that Spain can win the big prizes." After years of underachievement in major tournaments. Spain won all six of their matches, albeit they needed two fine saves from goalkeeper-captain Iker Casillas to defeat World

Cup-holders Italy on penalties in the quarter-finals. Xavi Hernandez, the Barcelona midfielder who laid on Torres's goal in the final, was hailed as UEFA's official player of the tournament.

Portugal, Croatia, Holland, and Spain were decisive winners of the groups. All were certain of qualifying after two of their three matches and rested key players in their concluding matches. That break in competitive momentum proved fatal for all but Spain, however, since the other three all lost in the quarter-finals.

Portugal blamed their quarter-final exit to Germany partly on the distractions raised by manager Luiz Felipe Scolari's imminent move to Chelsea, and partly on a media frenzy over the uncertain future of Cristiano Ronaldo.

Germany struggled to get the better of Austria in their concluding group match before defeating Portugal and then Turkey 3-2 in a dramatic semi-final. Major disappointments were World Cup runners-up France, who were first-round failures.

THE RESULT 2004

Location: Lisbon, Portugal
Final: Greece 1 Portugal 0
Shirts: Greece white, Portugal red
Scorers: Charisteas

PORTUGAL

Ricardo

Miguel (Paulo Ferreira)   Andrade   Ricardo Carvalho   Nuno Valente

Ronaldo   Maniche (Rui Costa)   Costinha   Deco

Figo   Pauleta (Nuno Gomes)

Charisteas   Vryzas (Papadopoulos)

Giannakopoulos   Basinas (Venetidis)   Katsouranis   Zagorakis

Fyssas   Dellas   Kapsis   Seitaridis

Nikopolidis

GREECE

THE RESULT 2008

Location: Vienna, Austria
Final: Spain 1 Germany 0
Shirts: Spain red, Germany white
Scorers: Torres

SPAIN

Casillas

Ramos   Puyol   Marchena   Capdevila

Senna

Iniesta   Xavi   Fabregas (Alonso)   Silva (Cazorla)

Torres

Klose (Gomez)

Podolski   Ballack   Schweinsteiger

Hitzlsperger (Kuranyi)   Frings

Lahm (Jansen)   Metzelder   Mertesacker   Friedrich

Lehmann

GERMANY

REGIONAL CUPS

The speed with which football encircled the globe as well as the rapid-fire popularity of the World Cup inspired players, officials, and fans from Chile to China. Each region soon created its own governing body, which ultimately launched its own "copycat" competitions for national teams. The Copa America was the first, launched in 1916, and this was eventually copied in Africa, Asia, Europe, and Oceania, plus Central and North America.

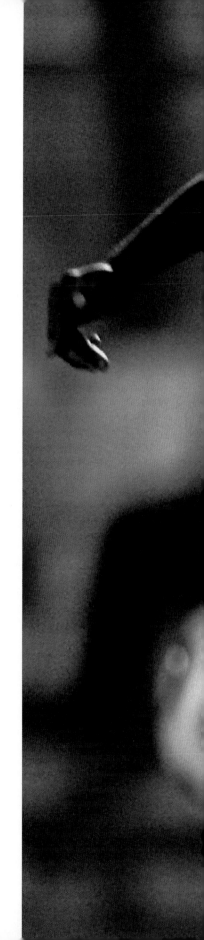

REGIONAL CUPS
COPA AMERICA

The Copa America boasts the unique distinction of being the world's longest-running international football tournament. It began in July 1916 as part of Argentina's centenary independence celebrations.

ABOVE Argentina's midfielder Juan Roman Riquelme takes on Coloia in 2007

PAGE 50 The Uruguay team which won the 1917 Copa America

PAGE 51 Samuel Eto'o scores against Angola in the 2006 African Nations Cup

The competition was originally called the Campeonato Sudamericano de Selecciones (South American Championship of National Teams). Participation was limited initially to member nations of CONMEBOL, the South American football confederation. However, because the organization comprises only ten nations, the competition was expanded in 1993 to include invited participants from the Caribbean and North and Central America.

Usually two or three teams receive such an invitation, invariably one of them being Mexico, partly because of the geographical proximity and partly because of the lucrative television rights.

The United States have also been invited regularly since 1997, but have turned down the offer several times because of scheduling conflicts with Major League Soccer. However, they did accept an invitation for the 2007 tournament, ending a 12-year absence.

Until recently, the tournament used to take place every two years, but in 2007, CONMEBOL decided that it should be held every four years but in an odd-numbered year so that it did not clash with the World Cup and European Championship. The 2007 event took place in Venezuela, so a second rotation will begin in 2011, starting with Argentina. Uruguay and Argentina have each won the championship 14 times, followed by Brazil with eight. These totals exclude unofficial, early 20th-century competitions.

SOUTH AMERICAN CHAMPIONSHIP

In its early years, when it was known as the South American Championship, the tournament did much to popularize the game and raise standards of play across the continent.

The 1940s are regarded as its heyday, but a generation later it fell into neglect, because South America's military governments looked disparagingly at their neighbors. The national federations of major countries such as Brazil, Argentina, and Uruguay also began to question the wisdom of competing after scouts from Italy and Spain began to converge on the event and, almost before the final whistle had been blown, lured their star players away to Europe.

Most painfully hit were Argentina. They won the 1957 tournament on the inspiration of an outstanding inside-forward trio of Humberto Maschio, Antonio Valentin Angelillo, and Omar Enrique Sivori. The manner of their triumph prompted predictions of World Cup glory the following year. However, within months, all three had been spirited away to Italy; all three were even playing for Italy within three years.

The gradual return of democracy in the mid-1980s—coupled with the growing power of television—sparked a resurgence of interest in the competition, with the event played in a single country, rather than on a home-and-away basis.

Problems remain for South American administrators to resolve. The most important is the fact that the Copa is staged in the middle of the South American winter—which is also the close-season in Europe, where all the most glamorous players operate. Not only are European clubs reluctant to release their players, but the stars themselves are wary of the risk of burn-out. Thus Barcelona's Ronaldinho and Milan's Kaka both withdrew from the Brazilian squad heading for the 2007 event in Venezuela. As it happened, even without them, Brazil won the trophy. In the final they defeated Argentina for the second time in a row.

EXPLOSIVE FINAL

In 2004, in Lima, Brazil won on penalties after Argentina had twice taken the lead, the second time through substitute Cesar Delgado, with three minutes of normal time remaining. Adriano equalized in the third minute of stoppage-time with his seventh goal of the competition.

That goal sparked a brawl as Brazil's players celebrated in front of the Argentina bench. Argentina responded by squirting water at their opponents and referee Carlos Amarilla summoned riot-police to stop the trouble. Adriano was booked for removing his shirt.

Argentina seemed more unsettled by the incident and missed their first two penalties: Andres D'Alessandro fired his effort at goalkeeper Julio Cesar and Gabriel Heinze fired wildly over the bar. Brazil converted all their penalties, just as they had in their semi-final win over Uruguay.

In 2007, Brazil found it much easier. Argentina were favorites but never justified their status and subsided to one early spectacular goal from Julio Baptista, an unfortunate own goal by their own captain Roberto Ayala, and then a superb counterattacking strike from Dani Alves.

LEFT Brazilian players celebrate their victory against Argentina in 2007

REGIONAL CUPS
AFRICAN NATIONS CUP

Africa has become a magnet for cash-rich European clubs who are seeking an apparently unending source of talents. The biennial tournament has been played since 1957.

Players such as Didier Drogba, Samuel Eto'o, Michael Essien, and Jay-Jay Okocha have moved into superstardom within the European club system, using their experience and talents to inspire youngsters back home to follow in their footsteps. But it was not always the case. In the colonial era of much of the last century, European national teams brought African players such as Just Fontaine and Eusébio onboard for their own use.

Fontaine, born and brought up in Morocco, set a World Cup record of 13 goals in 1958 while representing France. Eusébio, born and brought up in Mozambique, finished as top scorer with nine goals for Portugal in the 1966 World Cup finals. But a move for change was already underway. Ten years earlier, in 1956, the Confederation of

RIGHT Jay-Jay Okocha on the attack for Nigeria in the 2004 finals

BELOW South Africa's "Bafana Bafana" line up before their 2002 clash with Burkina Faso

African Football had been organized in Lisbon and plotted a first Cup of Nations the following year in Khartoum, the capital city of Sudan. It has since been staged virtually every two years, which makes it international football's African regional championship.

EGYPT CROWNED AS SIX OF THE BEST

Only three nations competed that first time. There should have been four but South Africa were barred because its own government, wedded to the segregationist apartheid system, refused to approve the selection of a multi-racial team.

Ironically, 39 years later—after the downfall of apartheid—South Africa returned to rescue the Confederation by staging the event after Kenya's late withdrawal as hosts.

Egypt, Ethiopia, and Sudan became the pioneer nations of a tournament that grew steadily down the years to encompass four, six, eight, 12, and eventually 16 finalists. In the early days, north African countries were the sides to beat, a trend that has also been the case half a century later, judging by the last three competitions.

Holders Egypt, the very first African champions, have a poor World Cup record. However, they have won the African title a record six times, most recently in Ghana in 2008.

A team inspired by the goalkeeping of Essam El-Hadary, the creative talent of Hosny Abd Rabou, and the penetration of Amr Zaky opened up with a 4-2 win over Cameroon. Egypt beat Sudan 3-0 and drew 1-1 with Zambia when they were already assured of topping their group. Egypt went on to beat Angola 2-1 in the quarter-finals, Ivory Coast 4-1 in the semis, and Cameroon 1-0 in the final at the Ohene Djan Stadium, Accra.

Mohamed Aboutrika became the individual hero after grabbing the winning strike in the 77th minute, his fourth goal of the finals. Cameroon's consolation was that Barcelona's Eto'o pipped Aboutrika as top scorer with five goals.

THE EARLY YEARS

Eto'o and Aboutrika follow in a tournament tradition for showcasing gifted individuals including heroes of yesteryear, such as the Ghanaian dribbling wizard Osei Kofi, Ethiopian captain Luciano Vassallo, and Egypt's captain Rafaat Ateya. In that inaugural tournament he scored the very first goal in a 2-1 win over Sudan then scored all four in Egypt's 4-0 thrashing of Ethiopia in the final.

The organization of the second tournament was granted to Egypt with the same three nations. A last-minute goal saw Egypt retain the trophy with a breathtaking 2-1 win over Sudan.

Four teams met in Addis Ababa for the third edition, with hosts Ethiopia seeing off the challenge of Egypt 4-2 in an exciting final. Ethiopia's last Emperor, Haile Selassie, handed over the Cup to skipper Vassallo. Eight nations took

part in Ghana in 1963, with a new format of an elimination round, semi-finals, and final. This format remained until 1976, when a second round league system was introduced.

Morocco took advantage, although the new formula proved unpopular and, in 1978, knockout semi-finals and a final were restored, along with penalty shoot-outs. Further alterations were made for the 1992 event in Senegal, when a dozen sites competed. By now the qualifying rounds were organized into mini-leagues rather than a straightforward knockout system.

A more recent expansion raised the number of entrants in the finals to 16, which proved popular with Africa's own nations but unpopular in Western Europe, where clubs resented being forced to relinquish their key players in the middle of their own league campaigns.

The most notable trend over the last two generations has been a significant shift of power. Ethiopia versus Sudan (both former champions) would have been a classic in the 1960s, whereas Cameroon against Nigeria brings excitement now.

BELOW Didier Drogba enjoys Ivory Coast's progress to the 2006 semi-finals

REGIONAL CUPS
OTHER NATIONAL TEAM COMPETITIONS

The history of national team competitions and their status as the ultimate peak of football achievement goes all the way back to the first official Scotland v England match on November 30, 1872. That goalless draw at Hamilton Crescent in Partick led to the creation of the British Home Championship.

Association football's first national team competition was staged annually until 1984, when it was killed off by dwindling crowds and the fixture congestion engendered by qualifying matches for the World Cup and European Championship.

At one stage, the British Home Championship also served as the World Cup qualifying section. That was after the World War II, when the British associations—England, Scotland, Wales,

and Northern Ireland—had rejoined FIFA after a gap of more than 25 years. FIFA designated two seasons of the British championship as the qualifying group. England finished top and went to Brazil. The runners-up were also granted a place in the finals, but the Scottish association said it would only send a team if they finished top of the group. They finished runners-up to England and duly stayed at home.

The British championship was put to the same use before the 1954 World Cup, but for the last time. Other nations objected that this gave the British a guaranteed place at the finals and the smaller British nations—Wales and Northern Ireland—objected that they were always going to be at a qualifying disadvantage against England and Scotland. Ironically, for the next World Cup, "open" qualifying saw all four home nations go on to the finals, for the first and last time.

The awkward nature of international travel in football's early years was a significant factor in the creation of regional competitions. Small, impoverished federations in days long before the advent of television and sponsorship could barely afford–or manage–to send a squad of players and handful of officials to a neighboring country for a tournament. Criss-crossing the world's oceans

RIGHT Ante Milicic strikes for Australia against the Solomon Islands in 2004

BELOW Harry Kewell leads the "Socceroos" to an easy win

in an era when passenger flights were merely the stuff of science fiction would have been virtually impossible. Thus the South Americans set up their own tournament in the early 1900s, but it was not until the late 1950s that Europe and Africa dared go fully international.

THE GROWTH OF COMPETITIONS

A European nation teams' competition had been organized in the 1920s and 1930s. This was the brainchild of Austrian and Hungarian football administrators, among them the Austrian Hugo Meisl, who also dreamed up the Mitropa Cup for the clubs of central Europe. The Gerö Cup was organized under the auspices of the world federation, FIFA, since a formal European federation was not brought into existence until the mid-1950s.

Elsewhere around the world, the desire for national team competition saw the fledgling central American confederation launch its own event in 1941; the first winners were Costa Rica. Further championships were staged only irregularly, even after the formal creation in 1963 of CONCACAF, which finally bonded into one organization the various nations, large but mainly small, who made up the football world of central America (including some northern South American countries), the Caribbean and, of course, North America (which meant the United States and Canada).

The regional competition was eventually reorganized and stabilized, in 1991, as the Gold Cup. It takes place in spring, every two years. Mexico and the United States, the two major powers of the region, have dominated the modern era with four wins apiece. Canada have won once, while none of the central American nations have won it at all.

Oceania remains the world game's poor relation in all senses, including competitive status. The region is FIFA's smallest, with only 11 members, and its standing within the world game was further reduced by Australia's departure in 2006 to join the Asian confederation.

An Oceania Nations Cup was begun in 1973 but its diminished entry has placed its long-term future in doubt.

ASIAN CUP
RECENT WINNERS
1972 Iran
1976 Iran
1980 Kuwait
1984 Saudi Arabia
1988 Saudi Arabia
1992 Japan
1996 Saudi Arabia
2000 Japan
2004 Japan

ALL-TIME WINNERS:
Iran, Japan, Saudi Arabia 3 each; South Korea 2; Iraq, Israel, Kuwait 1 each

CONCACAF GOLD CUP
(North, Central American, and Caribbean Nations)

RECENT WINNERS
1991 United States
1993 Mexico
1996 Mexico
1998 Mexico
2000 Canada
2002 United States
2003 Mexico
2005 United States
2007 United States

ALL-TIME WINNERS
Mexico, United States 4 each; Canada 1

OCEANIA NATIONS CUP
RECENT WINNERS
1973 New Zealand
1980 Australia
1996 Australia
1998 New Zealand
2000 Australia
2002 New Zealand
2004 Australia

ALL-TIME WINNERS
Australia 4; New Zealand 3

CLUB WORLD CHAMPIONSHIPS

RIGHT Milan's Pippo Inzaghi
(Number 9) scores for Milan
against Boca Juniors in 2007

AC Milan have been crowned champions four times in the event's various guises. The competitions are now reformed after early years were marred by scandal and violence.

The Intercontinental Cup kicked off in 1960 as a home and away meeting between the champions of Europe and South America. The idea had sprung from South American officials, who had launched their own Copa Libertadores for the purpose of challenging Europe at club level.

Real Madrid were crowned the first winners. Their legendary team, inspired by the greats of Alfredo Di Stefano and Ferenc Puskás, drew 0-0 with Peñarol of Uruguay in the torrential rain at Montevideo, then stormed to a 5-1 victory back in their Santiago Bernabéu fortress in Spain. Within a matter of a few years, the competition

almost ground to a halt, following a string of brutal matches involving Argentinian sides. Celtic were furious at their treatment by Racing Club in 1967. A year later, Manchester United's maverick George Best lost his temper after incessant provocation by his marker José Hugo Medina of Estudiantes de La Plata and both were sent off.

Estudiantes, under coach Osvaldo Zubeldia, were notorious for their cynical tactics. In 1969, the Estudiantes players bombarded their Milan opponents with practice balls as they tried to warm up before the game in Argentina. Milan won 4-2 on aggregate, but three Estudiantes players—goalkeeper

Alberto José Poletti, plus defenders Ramón Alberto Aguirre Suárez and Raúl Horacio Madero—received lengthy bans for their bad behavior.

Several European champions, such as Bayern Munich, Liverpool, and Nottingham Forest, declined to compete. The teams usually cited fixture congestion, because they feared losing key players to tough South American tackling. The 1975 and 1978 contests were not held.

EIGHTIES REVIVAL

The competition was rescued in 1980, when the Japanese Football Federation, keen to promote the sport in the Far East, found sponsorship support from car manufacturer Toyota to host the final as a one-off game. The inaugural showpiece was played in Tokyo until 2001, with neighboring Yokohama hosting the 2002 and 2004 finals.

The competition always mattered more to the South Americans than the Europeans. Even the wealthiest South American clubs could not match their European rivals in financial terms, so the Intercontinental Cup gave them a chance to underline a belief in their superior skill and talent.

The last final in Tokyo's National Stadium saw Bayern Munich edge past Boca Juniors 1-0 in extra time. The final moved to Yokohama's new National Stadium the following year.

CLUB WORLD CHAMPIONSHIP

Meanwhile, FIFA had become directly involved in football at international club level. FIFA staged a Club World Championship in 2000 at Brazil's Maracanã Stadium. Noisily impatient clubs from outside Europe and South America were invited. European champions Manchester United even withdrew from the FA Cup in England to play at the urging of the FA, who were bidding in vain to host the 2006 World Cup. Corinthians beat Vasco da Gama 4-3 on penalties after the goalless all-Brazilian affair.

FIFA set a precedent and, in 2004, it swallowed up the original match into its expanded mini-tournament. Japan remained, initially at least, as host nation. But no longer was the competition the preserve of the Europeans and South Americans.

In 2005, FIFA followed up its 2000 experiment. The competition would still be played in Japan, but now it was global. The top teams from all over the world would play off. Brazil's São Paulo won the first of the revised events, beating European champions Liverpool 1-0 in the final.

They now had rivals in hosting, which included Al-Ahly (Egypt), Al-Ittihad (Saudi Arabia), Deportivo Saprissa (Costa Rica), and Sydney (Australia). Internacional of Porto Alegre maintained Brazilian domination in 2006, beating Barcelona 1-0. Coach Abel Braga said: "Our club's history will now come under two headings, before and after Japan 2006. We're world champions!"

Al-Ahly were there again in 2006, along with some new challengers: Auckland (New Zealand), Club America (Mexico), and Jeonbuk Hyundai (South Korea).

AC Milan's 4-2 victory over Boca Juniors in 2007 was Europe's first triumph since Porto's in 2004. Perhaps more significantly for the future, Japan's Urawa Reds took third place and African champions Etoile du Sahel were fourth.

ABOVE Skipper Paolo Maldini and his Milan team-mates celebrate world domination

REGIONAL CUPS **MOMENTS**

1960s

1970s

ABOVE Liverpool's Steve Heighway on target against Servette

ABOVE The UEFA Cup is second in status to the Champions League

RIGHT Archie Gemmell scores Celtic's second goal during the 1970 European Cup final

ABOVE Colin Bell scores for Manchester City against Lierse

ABOVE Tottenham knock Milan out of the UEFA Cup in 1972

1970s

2000s

ABOVE Fans cheer Liverpool on to final victory over Borussia Mönchengladbach

ABOVE Corinthians celebrate their Club World Cup triumph in 2000

LEFT Liverpool in triumph after their golden goal win over Alaves in 2001

ABOVE A consolation goal for Wolves against Porto in 1974

RIGHT Alan Thompson's goal for Celtic knocks out Barcelona

INTERNATIONAL CLUB COMPETITIONS

The **UEFA** Champions League is the most lucrative international club competition ever to be played. It has evolved over the last 80 years, and there are further exciting changes planned for the future that will make matches more entertaining for fans. The original tournament was the **Mitropa Cup**—also known as the **La Coupe de l'Europe Centrale**. This was held among the leading clubs of central Europe during the late 1920s and 1930s. The European Champions' Club Cup was launched in the mid-1950s, along with the now renamed **UEFA Cup** and the defunct **UEFA Cup Winners' Cup**. Each contest has provided a flood of memorable goals, unforgettable moments, and great drama.

COUPE
CHAMPIONS
EUROPÉENS
Finale
1956

INTERNATIONAL CLUB COMPETITIONS
FOUNDATION & 1950s

"The Champions League is where every player wants to be."

KAKA OF MILAN

UEFA has come a long way since it was founded in Basel on 15 June 1954. It currently stands as the richest and most important of the six continental confederations of world governing body FIFA. UEFA oversees the numerous competitions from its headquarters in Nyon, a town on the shores of Lake Geneva in Switzerland.

EUROPEAN CUP

1950s FINALS
1956 Real Madrid 4 Reims 3
1957 Real Madrid 2 Fiorentina 0
1958 Real Madrid 3 Milan 2 (after extra time)
1959 Real Madrid 2 Reims 0

All the world's greatest players—from South America to southern Africa to south-east Asia —have a strong desire to play for European clubs, tempted by both the lucrative contracts and the chance of winning high-profile titles and medals.

UEFA was formed as a result of talks between the respective Football Federations of Belgium France and Italy. It was set up during the 1954 World Cup.

France's Henri Delaunay was the driving force. and immediately tackled the role of general secretary; Denmark's Ebbe Schwartz was voted in as the inaugural president.

UEFA grew hand in hand with the European Champions' Club Cup. This tournament was dreamed up by the then editor of the French sports daily newspaper *L'Equipe*, Gabriel Hanot, who became irritated by the claims of a

ABOVE The FIFA president, Sir Stanley Rous

RIGHT Red Star goalkeeper Beara foils a Manchester United attack

PAGE 62 Arie Haan is carried off the pitch by Ajax fans in 1971

PAGE 63 The victorious 1956 Real Madrid team celebrates

national English newspaper that Wolverhampton Wanderers—after beating Hungary's Kispest Honvéd in a friendly—were the champions of the world. Hungary had recently humiliated England 6-3 and 7-1.

So Hanot proposed a formal annual competition, but the concept proved so popular with the top clubs that the organisational work exceeded the newspaper's organising capacity.

In April 1955, UEFA agreed to take over the running of the European Champions' Club Cup. That decision laid the foundation for its power base, just in time. Later that month, three leading officials—Ernst Thommen (Switzerland), Dr Ottorino Barassi (Italy) and Sir Stanley Rous (England)—conceived the idea of the International Inter-Cities' Industrial Fairs Cup, the forerunner to today's UEFA Cup.

Three years later, UEFA introduced the European Nations' Cup and in 1960 the UEFA Cup Winners' Cup became a reality, running parallel with the European Champions' Clubs Cup.

The Champions' Club Cup, based on a two-leg knock-out system, grew from strength to strength despite severe problems with hooliganism, political turmoil, and stadium disasters. Lennart Johansson, the UEFA president between 1990 and 2007, was the man responsible for converting the Champions' Club Cup into the Champions League.

UEFA became a political player too, clashing with the European Union over television rights. Then came the Bosman Judgement, which established the primacy of EU labor law over football's own regulations and sparked the mass migration of leading players to Western Europe. In January 2008 Johansson was replaced as president by Michel Platini, the former France star who had won the Champions' Cup.

Real Madrid dominated the early European Champions' Club Cup, crowned winners at the first five successive wins. Santiago Bernabéu was the president who oversaw their phenomenal rise. He had the vision to raise Madrid's 20,000 capacity Chamartín ground and create a giant stadium that would house a great team. Bernabeu

and his secretary Raimundo Saporta built that team. Their best signing was the Argentinian forward Alfredo Di Stefano. Madrid beat Barcelona to sign him from Colombian club Millonarios, aided by some help from the Spanish sports ministry.

Di Stefano was the pivotal figure in Madrid's success. He was the team's leader and finished league top scorer every season between 1955 and 1959. Madrid scaled the heights with a 7-3 victory over Eintracht Frankfurt in the 1960 final at Hampden Park, Glasgow. Di Stefano netted three, Puskas four.

BELOW Joseito, one of Real Madrid's home-grown Spanish heroes

INTERNATIONAL CLUB COMPETITIONS
EUROPE 1960s

Real Madrid launched a new European competitive decade in glory. Their 7-3 thrashing of Eintracht Frankfurt—West Germany's first finalists—in Glasgow in 1960 was hailed by experts as the greatest match of all time.

The inspirational Alfredo Di Stefano hit a hat-trick but was out-scored by Hungarian Ferenc Puskas who scored four goals. Madrid's five-year reign ended the next season, when they were beaten by Spanish rivals Barcelona. The Catalans had long envied Madrid their headline status in Europe; their success had been limited to a couple of victories in the lesser Inter-Cities' Fairs Cup.

They signed some of the world's finest players and coaches and believed their hour had come when, with the help of refereeing errors, they defeated Madrid in the opening rounds of the 1960–61 Champions' Cup.

Barcelona were then clear favorites to win the final but they were surprisingly beaten by Benfica from Lisbon. Two of Barcelona's stars, the Hungarian forwards Sandor Kocsis and Zoltan Czibor, had finished on the favorites' losing side at the same stadium in Bern, Switzerland, seven years earlier in the World Cup final against West Germany. Then, as now, the score was 3-2.

Benfica, unlike cosmopolitan Barcelona, relied solely on Portuguese players but this gave them the option of plucking many outstanding players from Portugal's African colonies. The most important was Eusebio da Silva Ferreira, from Mozambique, who scored two goals the following year when Benfica thrashed the aging maestros of Real Madrid 5-3 in Amsterdam. The Hungarian veteran Puskas ended up on the losing side despite scoring another Champions' final hat-trick.

A hat-trick of titles proved beyond Benfica, however, as the balance of power in Europe swung towards Italy and the city of Milan.

AC Milan overthrew Benfica in 1963, in the first European final at Wembley. Eusebio struck early for Benfica but was then played out of the game by Milan winghalf Giovanni Trapattoni as the Italians hit back twice through their Brazilian center-forward Jose Altafini. He thus finished with 14 goals in the campaign, then a record. Milan's creative inspiration came from their "Golden Boy" inside forward Gianni Rivera, supported by other Italian internationals such as captain and sweeper Cesare Maldini and winger Bruno Mora.

Milan's reign lasted only one season, however. They fell in the quarter-finals the next term to Real Madrid, who were, in turn, beaten 3-1 in the final in Vienna by Internazionale, Milan's city neighbors.

Inter were managed by master coach Helenio Herrera. In the spring of 1960 Herrera had been sacked by Barcelona after a European defeat at Madrid's hands. Now he enjoyed taking his belated revenge. Herrera was born in Morocco but brought up in Argentina. He became a professional footballer in France and had worked hard on the tactics, science, and psychology of football. At Inter he imposed a ruthless tactical system based on a rugged sweeper in Armando Picchi, man-marking

defenders such as Tarcisio Burgnich and Giacinto Facchetti, a perceptive playmaker in Luis Suarez and lightning counterattackers such as Sandro Mazzola and Jair da Costa.

Inter secured two cups—against Real Madrid in 1964 and Benfica in 1965—before Celtic and Manchester United struck the first blows for British football. In 1967 Scotland's Celtic, under the shrewd management of Jock Stein, carried all before them at home and abroad. Their brand of thrilling football swept aside even iron-clad Inter in the final in Lisbon. Not surprisingly, Celtic's team earned the nickname of the "Lisbon Lions."

One year later Manchester United marked the tenth anniversary of the Munich air disaster by seizing the trophy for the first time themselves. Matt Busby had built a remarkable new team, built around the inspiration of another Munich

ABOVE George Best celebrates United's second goal against Benfica

RIGHT Celtic's Billy McNeill takes delivery of the European Cup

survivor Bobby Charlton. Charlton was partnered in attack by George Best and Denis Law. Injury meant Law missed the final in which United beat Benfica 4-1 in extra time at Wembley, thanks to two goals from Charlton, now United's captain.

Their reign, however, lasted only one year. United were dethroned in the 1969 semi-finals by Milan—still led by Rivera—who then beat Holland's emerging Ajax Amsterdam in the final in Madrid's Estadio Bernabeu. Ajax were the first Dutch club to have reached the Champions' final. Their coach Rinus Michels was building a team and a style which would earn worldwide admiration. But their day had yet to dawn.

The 1970s was a European Cup decade which could be split into three reigns—those of Ajax Amsterdam, Bayern Munich, then the English. First though, in 1970, came Feyenoord of Rotterdam, Ajax's long-time rivals.

ABOVE Ajax Amsterdam, hat-trick winners in the early 1970s

Feyenoord, managed by the former Austrian international defender Ernst Happel, became the first Dutch team to win the trophy, beating 1967 winners Celtic 2-1. Sweden striker Ove Kindvall scored the winner four minutes from the end of extra time.

Ajax followed, with a vengeance. Their center forward Johan Cruyff was one of the all-time greats. His touch and vision inspired Ajax to three European titles and Holland to reach the 1974 World Cup Final.

Johan Neeskens was a tough-tackling, driving midfielder, Gerrit Muhren added craft, while Ruud Krol was a marauding leftback. In addition, coach Rinus Michels's players could switch positions in

bewildering style in the formation known as "total football." They won three finals, all comfortably. They defeated Panathinaikos of Greece 2-0 at Wembley put together their best performance of the three to defeat Internazionale 2-0 in Rotterdam, and then finished off with a 1-0 win over Juventus in Belgrade. Cruyff scored both goals against Internazionale.

It had been clear, however, that he would be lured away at some stage to Spanish football and that ultimately occurred in the summer of 1973 when Ajax reluctantly sold him to Barcelona for a then world record £922,000.

The departure of Cruyff left Ajax vulnerable to a challenge from German champions Bayern Munich, led by Franz Beckenbauer, a great creative midfielder who had perfected the role of attacking sweeper. Sepp Maier was a brilliant goalkeeper and Gerd Muller the greatest striker of his age. Muller scored 365 times in 427 Bundesliga appearances and 68 times in 62 games for West Germany.

Georg Schwarzenbeck was a defensive rock beside Beckenbauer, Paul Breitner was a gifted attacking full back, and Uli Hoeness was a clever forward. But Bayern had to battle for their three successive final wins. First opponents were Atletico Madrid in Brussels in 1974. Only a last-minute goal by Schwarzenbeck at the end of extra time earned a replay—the only one in the history of the competition—which Bayern won easily by 4-0. Leeds had a seemingly good goal disallowed before Franz Roth and Muller netted in the 1975 final; then Dominque Rocheteau hit the woodwork for Saint-Etienne ahead of Roth's winner a year later at Hampden Park, Glasgow.

Bayern grew old together—and the English succeeded them. The quiet, thoughtful Bob Paisley at Liverpool and the charismatic, and outspoken, Brian Clough at Nottingham Forest both built winning teams.

Liverpool's revival had been masterminded by Scottish manager Bill Shankly and Paisley, his assistant, was comparatively unknown when he took over in the summer of 1975. Very soon, however, it became clear that Paisley was a managerial giant. It was under his guidance that Liverpool won their first European Champions' Cup by defeating Borussia Monchengladbach 3-1 in the 1977 final in Rome.

At the time, Borussia were one of Europe's outstanding football teams under the guidance of meticulous coach Hennes Weisweiler and with an attack inspired by Denmark's first European Footballer of the Year, Allan Simonsen.

In Rome, however, Weisweiler's planning and Simonsen's energy proved no match for a Liverpool side, who had found a style pitched midway between the demands of frenetic English league football and the more thoughtful version demanded by European competition.

The match was a personal triumph for Liverpool's England right-winger Kevin Keegan, who memorably outwitted the Germans' terrier-like defender Berti Vogts.

It was Keegan's last game for Liverpool. Within weeks he had been sold to Hamburg and Liverpool used the fee to replace him with an even more outstanding player in Scotland forward Kenny Dalglish, bought from Celtic.

Dalglish emulated Keegan's success when, a year later, he scored the lone winning goal for Liverpool in their second Champions' final victory over Brugge of Belgium. Liverpool's reign ended early the next season with the success of the English team Nottingham Forest. Under the idiosyncratic management of the controversial Brian Clough, Forest went all the way to defeat Sweden's Malmo in the 1979 final. The decisive goal was scored by the England forward Trevor Francis.

Months earlier Francis had become Britain's first $2 million (£1 million) footballer when Clough bought him from Birmingham City. The Malmo game was his Champions' Cup debut.

LEFT John Robertson flies the flag for Nottingham Forest

EUROPE 1980s

One event overshadowed the European Cup in the 1980s: the Heysel disaster of 1985. Thirty-nine fans, Italian and Belgian, were crushed to death as Liverpool fans attacked Juventus fans before a European Cup final in Brussels.

ABOVE The wrecked terracing at Heysel in 1985

It was Juventus' first Champions' Cup victory but that went almost unnoticed amid the carnage. Michel Platini, now UEFA president, and their star forward, said: "I'm physically and emotionally incapable of going back to Heysel. It's a wound that cannot be healed."

UEFA blamed Liverpool and their supporters. English fans had long been associated with hooliganism. UEFA banned all English teams indefinitely. That was later reduced to a five-year ban with an extra year for Liverpool.

UEFA and other officials were also punished by the Belgian legal system for a series of blunders, which extended from choosing an inadequate venue in the first place, to failure to ensure sufficient security controls. For instance, the wire fence which separated Liverpool and Juventus fans at the Heysel stadium was little more than chicken wire and easily breached.

In due course the Heysel—which had hosted previous Champions' Cup finals in 1958, 1966, and 1974—was razed. The King Baudouin Stadium was built in its place, in the shadow of the Atomium (this had been constructed for the world exhibition of 1958, which had been hosted by Brussels).

The tragedy was all the more shocking for English football since it took place only 18 days after 56 people had died in a fire at the Bradford City stadium. Not until after the 1989 Hillsborough disaster, however, were draconian measures finally put in place to improve security and safety at sports stadia. These were adopted across English sport and were just in time to avert the threatened introduction of a restrictive and potentially ruinous membership-card system.

English clubs had extended their domination of the European Champions' Cup throughout the early 1980s, in a series of low-key finals. First Nottingham Forest extended their successful run to two years by defeating Kevin Keegan's

Hamburg on a lone goal from Scotland winger Jimmy Robertson in 1980. Then Liverpool were equally cautious in beating Real Madrid the following year on a late goal from fullback Alan Kennedy. In 1982, Aston Villa pipped Bayern Munich also by 1-0, despite losing their keeper, Jimmy Rimmer, to injury early in the match. Center-forward Peter Withe scored the goal from close range, almost falling over the ball as he did so.

The only interruption to English command came from Hamburg who, inspired now by midfielder Felix Magath, beat Juventus 1-0 in 1983. It was a second win with a different club for Hamburg's Austrian coach, Ernst Happel. He had previously guided Feyenoord to victory in 1970.

Hamburg's reign did not last long however. In 2004, Liverpool returned to lift the trophy again; this time with a penalty shoot-out win over Roma on the Italians' home ground. The game marked the end of the love affair between Roma's fans and their Brazilian midfielder Paulo Roberto Falcao after his apparent reluctance to take one of the spot kicks.

The expulsion of English clubs from European competition in the second half of the 1980s left a gap which no one other European club could fill. Romania's Steaua Bucharest became the first eastern European winners on penalties against favorites Barcelona—coached by Englishman Terry Venables—in 1986. Porto beat Bayern 2-1 the following season; a result Uli Hoeness described as among the worst in Bayern's history. Holland's PSV Eindhoven shaded Benfica on penalties again in 1988.

Soon afterwards, real champions soon emerged in Italy's revived club Milan. The club had been refinanced in the mid-1980s by media magnate and future prime minister Silvo Berlusconi. He paid off the club's debts, invested heavily in Dutch stars such as Ruud Gullit, Frank Rijkaard, and Marco Van Basten. All three men had been instrumental in their country's 1988 European Championship victory.

ABOVE Marco Van Basten raises the reward for his two goals against Steaua

Milan won the Italian league in 1988, then thrashed Steaua Bucharest in the following season's Champions' Cup final. The final was staged in Barcelona amid a TV blackout after local technicians went on strike. Berlusconi flew in staff from his own Italian TV channels to ensure that no-one in Europe should miss his team's achievement.

Already, however, the talismanic Van Basten was starting to become more vulnerable to a series of ever-more damaging injuries which would ultimately force him into premature retirement—he played his last game in 1993.

FOOTBALL FACTS

THE FINALS
1980 Nottingham Forest 1 Hamburg 0
1981 Liverpool 1 Real Madrid 0
1982 Aston Villa 1 Bayern Munich 0
1983 Hamburg 1 Juventus 0
1984 Liverpool 1 Roma 1 (Liverpool 4-2 on penalties after extra time)
1985 Juventus 1 Liverpool 0
1986 Steaua Bucharest 0 Barcelona 0 (Steaua 3-0 on penalties after extra time)
1987 FC Porto 2 Bayern Munich 1
1988 PSV Elindhoven 0 Benfica 0 (PSV 6-5 on penalties after extra time)
1989 Milan 4 Steaua Bucharest 0

1950s 1960s 1970s

ABOVE A derby goal for Alfredo Di Stefano (left) of Real Madrid against Atletico

BELOW Ferenc Puskas scores Real Madrid's first goal in the 1962 Champions' final against Benfica

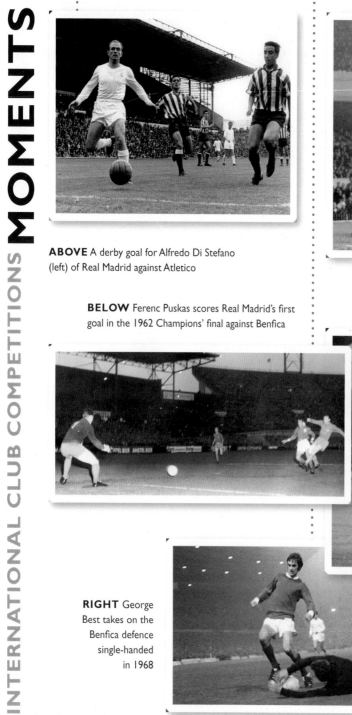

RIGHT George Best takes on the Benfica defence single-handed in 1968

ABOVE Ray Kennedy strikes for Arsenal in the 1979 Fairs Cup final

ABOVE Chelsea's David Webb heads past Brugge keeper Luc Sanders

1980s

1990s

2000s

ABOVE Liverpool manager Joe Fagan relaxes with the European Cup

ABOVE Arsenal easily see off FK Austria in 1991

RIGHT Celtic's Lubomir Moravcik outwits the Juventus defense

BELOW Sol Campbell heads Arsenal in front against Barcelona in the 2006 Champions League final

BOTTOM
Pippo Inzaghi grabs Milan's second against Liverpool in 2007

RIGHT Paolo Maldini in triumph after Milan's thrashing of Barcelona in 1994

INTERNATIONAL CLUB COMPETITIONS
EUROPE 1990s

The late 1990s marked the biggest change in the format of the European Cup since the competition was established more than 40 years earlier. No longer would it be a knockout competition for league champions.

From 1956 onward, the structure had been simple. The holders and the champions of each European county had met in a series of two-leg ties, leading to a one-match final. The team who scored most goals in the matches, home and away, progressed. It was a copy of the formula devised for the Mitropa Cup, which had proved hugely popular in central Europe in the 1930s.

BELOW Ole Gunnar Solskjaer wins the 1999 final for Manchester United

Initially, if scores were level after two matches a replay on neutral territory was organized. When it became more difficult to find neutral zones the clubs tossed to decide who would stage the replay. Eventually, however, the pressures of time led to the play-offs being scrapped—with the second leg of a balanced tie being extended into 30 minutes of extra time and then, if necessary, to a penalty shoot-out.

In 1991–92 this format was radically altered under pressure from wealthy clubs, including Real Madrid, Barcelona, Milan, Internazionale, Manchester United, Liverpool, and Bayern Munich. Extra clubs were admitted from the major nations and experiments began with a mini-league formula, until the present system—eight groups, then three knockout rounds before the final—was perfected.

These changes, which also raised the clubs' income through TV and sponsorship, were matched by another crucial development—the Bosman Judgement which, in December 1995, ruled that restrictions on the number of foreign players in any team and playing squad were illegal. The world's best players inevitably gravitated to a handful of rich European clubs, largely in England, Italy, and Spain.

These changes were presided over by a Swedish president of UEFA, Lennart Johansson, who managed efficiently the difficult jobs of maintaining UEFA's control over the European competitions,

while simultaneously keeping the big clubs happy, largely thanks to the share of the revenue generated by the European competitions.

The drama of the European finals continued. One of the most dramatic moments came in 1999, when Teddy Sheringham and Ole Gunnar Solskjaer scored in the last seconds of stoppage time to lead Manchester United to an astonishing victory over Bayern Munich in Barcelona. Bayern had led by a single goal from Mario Basler for most of the match. United's victory secured them a historic treble of European Cup plus domestic league and FA Cup success, a unique achievement by an English club.

Johan Cruyff's "Dream Team" earned Barcelona's first Champions' Cup in 1992, when Ronald Koeman's rocket settled the contest against Sampdoria in extra time at Wembley. Fabio Capello's Milan then produced the finest performance of the 1990 finals when they unexpectedly came out in attack to rout Cruyff's Barcelona in 1994.

Surprisingly, Milan were beaten themselves a year later by a revived Ajax Amsterdam. Coincidentally, Ajax were guided to victory out on the pitch by the experienced string-pulling in midfield of Frank Rijkaard, a European Cup-winning hero with the Italian club in 1989 and 1990.

Ottmar Hitzfeld, a winning coach with Borussia Dortmund and Bayern, oversaw Dortmund's 3-1 success against Juventus in 1997 when Karlheinz Riedle scored twice, then fellow German Jupp. Heynckes guided Real Madrid to victory in 1998. Pedja Mijatovic scored Madrid's winner to secure their seventh Champions' Cup at the expense of favorites Juventus and their French midfield star, Zinedine Zidane.

Surprisingly, Heynckes was sacked by Madrid's impatient president Lorenzo Sanz on the grounds that the team had not, in addition, won the Spanish league. Sanz's unpredictable direction of the club backfired when impatient fans voted him out of a job and voted in millionaire builder Florentino Perez.

ABOVE Red Star Belgrade, first and last Yugoslav winners, in 1991

The decade was not without its scandal. Olympique de Marseille became the first French champions of Europe in 1993. They beat Milan 1-0 in what would prove the last final in Munich's Olympic stadium. But their victory was tarnished by revelations that they had fixed matches to help secure their domestic dominance in France.

In particular, several Marseille players had been approached to fix a match the previous weekend, because a draw would secure the French league title for Marseille while also keeping their opponents, Valenciennes, within sight of safety at the other end of the table. Jacques Glassmann, one of the Valenciennes players who had been approached, informed his club's directors. A process was launched, which ended in a jail term for, among others, the Marseille president Bernard Tapie. Glassman, booed by French crowds in the aftermath, was awarded a FIFA Fair Play award in 1995 in recognition of his actions.

FOOTBALL FACTS

THE FINALS
1990 Milan 1 Benfica 0
1991 Red Star Belgrade 0 Marseille 0 (Red Star 5-3 on penalties after extra time)
1992 Barcelona 1 Sampdoria Genoa 0 (after extra time)
1993 Marseille 1 Milan 0
1994 Milan 4 Barcelona 0
1995 Ajax Amsterdam 1 Milan 0
1996 Juventus 1 Ajax 1 (Juventus 4-2 on penalties after extra time)
1997 Borussia Dortmund 3 Juventus 1
1998 Real Madrid 1 Juventus 0
1999 Manchester United 2 Bayern Munich 1

INTERNATIONAL CLUB COMPETITIONS
EUROPE 2000s

By 2000, the European Cup had become the Champions League, though not a league of champions. The format had been swayed heavily in favor of the elite clubs that made up the G-14 group from the major western leagues.

The G-14 group could enter three or four teams each season and dominated the competition. But it was not the teams which towered over their domestic leagues who lifted the Champions' Cup. Only three winners—Bayern Munich in 2001, Barcelona in 2006, and Manchester United in 2008—also won their domestic championships in the same season.

It was as if chasing a domestic championship and the Champions League was a task too far. But a few clubs adapted ideally to the last 16 knock-out system. Liverpool, under Rafa Benitez, were the prime example. They won the Champions' Cup in 2005, despite finishing 37 points behind Chelsea in the Premiership.

In 2007, when they lost to Milan, they ended up 21 points behind Manchester United. English critics claimed that Benitez knew Liverpool could not match the consistency of Chelsea or Manchester United; his season's strategy revolved around the latter stages of the Champions League.

Chelsea twice fell to Liverpool in Champions League semi-finals, much to coach Jose Mourinho's disgust. Revenge was sweet in 2008 after the

RIGHT Delight for Milan's Kaka means despair for Liverpool

high-profile Portuguese "Special One" had been replaced by Israeli Avram Grant who subsequently led Chelsea to victory in the semi-final.

Milan, meanwhile, also put all their eggs in the Champions League basket. The 2007 winners finished 36 points behind Serie A champions and local rivals Internazionale. Both Liverpool and Milan rested and rotated players with the European Cup in mind, a pragmatic possibility often denied to their championship-chasing rivals.

Only once was the cycle of big clubs winning broken, when the favorites all went down in the 2004 quarter-finals. That left Mourinho to guide Porto to an easy victory over Monaco.

The most dramatic final of the decade was staged in 2005 in Istanbul. Milan led Liverpool 3-0 at half time through Paolo Maldini's early goal and two strikes by Hernan Crespo. Steven Gerrard inspired Liverpool's fight back as he, Vladimir Smicer, and Xavi Alonso scored within seven minutes of each other to force extra time. The tie was settled on penalties. Andriy Shevchenko, Milan's winning penalty taker in 2003 against Juventus, had his shot saved by Jerzy Dudek.

Madrid, playing with pace and power, had swarmed over Valencia in the all-Spanish final of 2000. Fernando Morientes, Steve McManaman, and Raul swept aside Hector Cuper's team. Caretaker boss Vicente Del Bosque had quelled the competing egos in the Madrid dressing room. He guided them to victory again in 2002, when Zinedine Zidane volleyed a magical winner against Bayer Leverkusen at Hampden Park, Glasgow. Leverkusen thus finished the season as runners-up not only in the Champions League but also in the German league and cup.

Barcelona won again for Spain in 2006 in the Stade de France after teetering on the verge of defeat against Arsenal who went ahead through center-back Sol Campbell and held out until an unlucky 13 minutes from time. Arsenal, ultimately, suffered for having to play much of the game with ten men after the early expulsion of their German goalkeeper, Jens Lehmann.

One factor in this decade had been a demonstration of the power of the big leagues. After an all-Spanish final in 2000 (Real Madrid beating Valencia) came an all-Italian final in 2003 (Milan beating Juventus) and then an all-English final in 2008.

The latter saw Manchester United win the crown for the third time after defeating Chelsea, also runners-up to United in the Premier League, on penalties. It was the first Champions final to have been staged in Moscow and the prospect of an invasion of English fans prompted the Russian authorities to make the unique concession of converting match tickets into visas.

Just to prove that football is no respecter of personalities, the three failures in the shoot-out were committed by United's Cristiano Ronaldo and by Chelsea's John Terry and Nicolas Anelka. Ronaldo's miss was particularly surprising—he had scored a career-best 42 goals for United over the course of the season and he would go on to lead Portugal into the quarter-finals of the European Championship.

United's success was perfectly timed in the year which marked the 50th anniversary of the Munich air disaster.

ABOVE Zinedine Zidane strikes his magnificent volleyed goal for Real Madrid in the 2002 final

UEFA CUP & CUP WINNERS' CUP

The UEFA Cup and the now-defunct Cup Winners' Cup have always been poor relations of the Champions League.

ABOVE Tottenham's John White, Bill Brown, Cliff Jones, Ron Henry, and Terry Dyson enjoy a happy homecoming to the UK in 1963

These were competitions for the "nearly" clubs who had fallen short of winning the major domestic trophy. Originally, the UEFA Cup was known as the Fairs Cup. It was founded in 1955 —a fortnight after the Champions' Cup—by future FIFA president Sir Stanley Rous and vice-presidents Ottorino Barrasi of Italy and Ernst Thommen of Switzerland.

With one eye on post-war rapprochement between Europe's former enemy nations, it was originally confined to representative teams whose cities staged trade fairs. Since the games were organized to coincide with the trade fairs, the first

tournament lasted three years. The final was held in 1958, when a team made up entirely of FC Barcelona players beat a London representative side 8-2 on aggregate over two legs.

Club teams were admitted to the next competition, and Barcelona beat Birmingham City 2-0 on aggregate in the 1960 final. Barcelona's heroes were the Hungarian Ladislav Kubala and Spain's own Luis Suarez. The competition was played annually after that. Initially, southern European clubs dominated, but Leeds' win in 1968 heralded a change. English teams (Newcastle, Arsenal, Leeds, Tottenham, and Liverpool) won the trophy for the next five years.

In 1971, the tournament was re-named after the European federation took formal control. The Fairs label was scrapped and the competition was called the UEFA Cup. Initially it continued as a two-leg knockout competition and the closing stages sometimes boasted a more glamorous mixture of clubs than the Champions' Cup. Winners down succeeding years included the likes of Real Madrid, Internazionale, Juventus, and Roma.

Everything changed, however, with the development of the Champions League. The quality threshold dropped significantly with the departure from the UEFA Cup of the bigger second, third, and fourth-placed clubs and the massive influx of clubs from the newly independent nations thrown up by the fragmentation of the Soviet Union and Yugoslavia.

UEFA also bowed to pressure from the clubs to produce a group stage which guaranteed three home matches for each club, while then allowing some teams that were knocked out of the Champions League entry into the UEFA Cup at the halfway stage for the knockout rounds. However, the system of five-team groups was unsatisfactory for fans and fixture patterns and is being reorganized again from 2009.

Sevilla, under coach Juande Ramos, proved masters of the competition in 2006 and 2007, though they had to thank a spectacular shoot-out performance from goalkeeper Andres Palop for the second of their two victories, over fellow Spanish opposition in Espanyol.

An intriguing factor in the UEFA Cup has been evidence of the revival of Russian club football after the chaos that followed the collapse of the Soviet Union. CSKA Moscow won the UEFA Cup in 2005, beating Sporting of Libson in front of their own fans, and then Zenit St Petersburg beat Rangers in 2008. Zenit also provided the

nucleus of the Russian national side which proved outstanding six weeks later in reaching the semi-finals of the European Championship.

From 1999 onward, entrance into the UEFA Cup was also the formal reward for clubs who had won their national cups. This followed UEFA's decision to scrap the Cup Winners' Cup which had been running since 1960. The Cup Winners' Cup was always a poor relation because, while popular in Britain, the domestic knockout event had barely caught on in many other countries.

Italy's Fiorentina won the first final, beating Rangers of Scotland. Tottenham became the first British winners of a European competition when they defeated Atletico Madrid 5-1 in the final in 1963. The last final, in 1999, saw Italy's Lazio, coached by Sven-Goran Eriksson, beat Mallorca at Villa Park, Birmingham.

BELOW Andres Palop wins the 2007 UEFA Cup for Sevilla by saving Marc Torrejon's penalty

1963

2000s

INTERNATIONAL CLUB COMPETITIONS MOMENTS

ABOVE Eusébio thunders Benfica ahead against Milan in the 1963 Champions' final

ABOVE Real Madrid stars enjoy their 2000 Champions League triumph over Valencia

LEFT Oliver Kahn hails his own vital penalty stop against Valencia in 2001

ABOVE Jimmy Greaves takes Atletico Madrid apart to make history in 1963 Champions' final against Benfica

RIGHT Juan Riquelme (right) leads Boca Juniors to Libertadores glory against Cruz Azul

2000s

ABOVE Boca coach Carlos Bianchi leads the celebrations after victory over Santos

ABOVE Pepe Reina of Liverpool celebrates beating Chelsea in the 2007 semi-final

ABOVE Ever Alfaro of Deportivo Saprissa takes Mexico's Pachuca by surprise

BELOW Liverpool players hail their victory over Milan in 2005

RIGHT Ronaldo heads Manchester United ahead against Chelsea

BELOW David Beckham on MLS duty for Galaxy against Chivas

INTERNATIONAL CLUB COMPETITIONS
SOUTH AMERICA

"For me, penalties

are a lottery."

COACH RENATO GAUTO

The Copa Libertadores is the South American equivalent of the European Champions' Cup. The winners tackle their European counterparts for the prestigious honor of becoming the world's greatest club.

ABOVE Boca captain Diego Cagna strikes a cup-winning pose in 2003

The Copa Libertadores grew out of a tournament of seven south American champions, played in Santiago de Chile in 1948 and won by the Brazilian club Vasco da Gama—a side that were named after the great Portuguese explorer.

A dozen years later the Copa Libertadores was launched as an annual tournament. The reasoning was that South American club directors, notably those of Peñarol from Uruguay, had seen the success of the European Champions' Cup and wanted a version of their own.

Once the Copa Libertadores was established, then the vision was to eventually introduce an annual series matching the champions from Europe and South America to tackle each other for the coveted world club crown.

The Copa Libertadores kicked off in 1960 with the participation of the champions from Argentina, Bolivia, Brazil, Chile, Colombia, Ecuador, Paraguay, Peru, and Uruguay.

Much to the delight of many South American club directors, Peñarol from Uruguay were crowned champions after defeating Paraguay's Olimpia 2-1 on aggregate.

Pedro Spencer, the free-scoring Ecuadorian striker, was Peñarol's inspiration and went on to become the most prolific marksman in the history of the Copa Libertadores.

Peñarol, happily fulfiling their original ambition, went on to arrange a world club showdown with their European counterparts Real Madrid.

However, the Spanish side steamrolled past Peñarol to the tune of 5-0.

Peñarol bounced back to be crowned South American champions the following season, but then they were toppled by Brazilian outfit Santos. The legendary Pelé proved to be the inspiration for Santos, who also won two years in a row and saw off the first serious Argentinian challenge from Boca Juniors.

Although Peñarol and Montevideo rivals Nacional would both win the Copa Libertadores again, Uruguay's pre-eminence faded and the tournament is currently dominated by clubs from Argentina and Brazil. Their supremacy has been interrupted only by a trio of wins for Olimpia, two successes apiece from Colombia's Atlético Nacional and Once Caldas, and a single triumph by Chile's Colo Colo.

Over the years the Copa Libertadores has featured a string of dramas—from crowd pitch invasions to 20-plus penalty shoot-outs and some of the most cynical football imaginable. Culprits for the latter were the Argentinian club Estudiantes de La Plata in the late 1960s. Under influential coach Osvaldo Zubeldía, they took anti-football to a vicious new art and a new low for the sport.

Originally the competition involved only the champions from each country. Since the knock-out formula failed to grip the imagination of the fans, most countries stage two league championships in a single year. Opening up the Copa Libertadores

to two teams proved a successful solution. The simultaneous introduction of a first-round group stage also assisted with travel costs, as the two clubs from whichever country would be drawn in the same group as the two clubs from another country. This meant teams could travel together and, for convenience, play their matches on successive days,

The tournament expanded in the 1970s, allowing Argentina and Brazil five clubs each along with three teams each from other countries— including new participants, Venezuela and Mexico.

Mexico does not belong to the South American confederation and are guests in the competition, their best ever showing was Cruz Azul losing to Boca Juniors in the 2001 final.

Boca Juniors, winners of the Copa Libertadores in 2000, 2001, 2003, and 2007, can lay claim to

being the dominant club of South American soccer's new century. Brazilian clubs are their only real challenge, often led by three-time winners São Paulo. However, Liga de Quito pulled off a major surprise in the 2008 final after they became the first Ecuadorian winners and earned a place in FIFA's 2008 Club World Cup in Japan.

Opponents, Brazil's Fluminense were also in the final for the first time and were red-hot favorites. Liga de Quito won the first leg of the final with surprising ease, 4-2, at high altitude in Quito. Fluminense fought back to square the final on aggregate with a 3-1 success, winning the return match 3-I in Rio de Janerio's Maracanã Stadium, but paid a literal penalty for complacency. The contest was decided by penalty kicks, which Liga de Quito won 3-I, courtesy of the heroics of three saves by veteran goalkeeper José Cevallos.

INTERNATIONAL CLUB COMPETITIONS
REST OF THE WORLD

The contest between national champions is not confined to Europe and South America. Central and North America started its own championship in 1962. Africa followed two years later. Asia began its continent-wide challenge in 1967.

AFRICAN CHAMPIONS LEAGUE

RECENT WINNERS
2003 Enyimba (Nigeria)
2004 Enyimba (Nigeria)
2005 Al-Ahly (Egypt)
2006 Al-Ahly (Egypt)
2007 Etoile Sahel (Tunisia)

LEADING ALL-TIME WINNERS
Al-Ahly (Eg), Zamalek (Eg) 5 each; Canon (Cameroon), Hafia Conakry (Guinea), Raja Casablanca (Morocco) 3 each

ASIAN CLUB CUP

RECENT WINNERS
2003 Al-Ain (United Arab Emirates)
2004 Al-Ittihad (S Arabia)
2005 Al-Ittihad (S Arabia)
2006 Jeonbuk Motors (S Korea)
2007 Urawa Red Diamonds (Japan)

LEADING ALL-TIME WINNERS
Esteghlal (Iran), Al-Hilal (S Arabia), Al-Ittihad (S Arabia), Maccabi Tel-Aviv (Israel), Pohang Steelers (S Korea), Thai Farmers Bank (Thailand) 2 each

Only the Oceania confederation held back, until 2004–05. But the defection of Australia to the Asian confederation has robbed the tournament of its strongest teams.

The central American competition has long been dominated by Mexican clubs. Teams from North America have yet to make an impact, despite the emergence of the NASL and David Beckham's move to LA Galaxy. The biggest challenge to Mexican supremacy has come from Costa Rica. LD Alajualense and Deportivo Saprissa have both proved recent powers in the tournament.

Interest in the CONCACAF club competitions was enhanced by the creation first of the Copa Interamericana and then by the expansion of the Club World Championship. The Copa Interamericana pitched the winners of the CONCACAF Champions' Cup against the champions of South Americans, the winners of the Copa Libertadores.

Early in the 21st century FIFA scrapped the old World Club Cup, contested by the champions of "only" Europe and South America, and replaced it with the Club World Championship into which the winners of all the regional club competitions were guaranteed entry.

Clubs from the Arab north have historically dominated the African Club Championship. Egypt's Al-Ahly from Cairo have been the team to beat. Their toughest opponents have been the Tunisian side Etoile du Sahel.

Other major rivals have come from west Africa, a prominent recent recruiting ground for Western European clubs. Perhaps this is one reason for the North African clubs' success: they do not lose as many players to Europe as their southern neighbors.

Southern Africa has yet to make its mark, despite boasting some of the richest and most passionately supported clubs on the continent, such as the Kaizer Chiefs and Orlando Pirates, South Africa's only winners in 1995. Ahead of the country's staging of the 2010 World Cup, a major disappointment for South African fans has been that its clubs have not made a greater impression at international competitive level.

Israeli teams dominated the opening days of the Asian competition. Maccabi Tel-Aviv won twice and Hapoel once, before the Israelis were forced out for political reasons. The Arab-dominated Asian confederation expelled Israel, whose clubs remained absent from international competition for almost 30 years. Israel joined UEFA in the 1990s after which its clubs entered the European competitions.

In the meantime, middle-eastern sides had taken command of the Asian club tournaments until the development of the ambitious, rich new leagues in both Japan and South Korea. The J.League side Urawa Red Diamonds underlined the power of the J.League when they became Asian champions in 2007 after beating Sepahan from Iran. They succeeded Jeonbuk Hyundai Motors, who ended the Arab supremacy in 2006.

The Japanese and Koreans gained in power thanks both their importing of European and South American coaches but also from the experience the best of their players had gained playing in Europe. The Middle East countries largely missed that international exchange, partly because their clubs could pay the players so well there was no financial incentive for them to seek a move to Europe.

Africa, Asia—now strengthened by Australia—and central/North American have already shown they can challenge the traditional powers. But Oceania seems destined to remain a backwater. The departure of Australia to join the Asian confederation was a serious blow to the status of Oceania and the champions of the region—always now the champions of New Zealand—are not certain to retain their place in the Club World Championship.

The FIFA president, Sepp Blatter, has said: "We want everyone to take their place in the greatest competitions but we also have to protect the status and value of those competitions."

LEFT Etoile de Sahel guard the African Super Cup

BELOW LEFT Pachuca players celebrate after beating Los Angeles Galaxy in a shoot-out in 2007

OCEANIA CLUB CHAMPIONSHIP

RECENT WINNERS
2005 Sydney FC (Australia)
2006 Auckland City (New Zealand)
2007 Waitakere United (New Zealand)

CENTRAL/NORTH AMERICAN CLUB CUP

RECENT WINNERS
2003 Toluca (Mexico)
2004 LD Alajuelense (Costa Rica)
2005 Deportivo Saprissa (Costa Rica)
2006 America (Mexico)
2007 Pachuca (Mexico)

LEADING ALL-TIME WINNERS
America (Mexico), Cruz Azul (Mexico) 5 each; Deportivo Saprissa (Costa Rica), UNAM (Mexico) 3 each

GREAT NATIONS

International power in football is defined by
a mixture of achievement and history. Success
or failure at the World Cup finals is what counts
to today's modern critic, followed by titles in the
various regional championships. Brazil boast five
World Cup victories, one more than mighty Italy.
Germany have scored a hat-trick of successes on
the world stage, with Argentina and Uruguay twice
crowned as world champions, while England and
France have each triumphed once. The role of the four
British Home Nations is acknowledged worldwide,
especially as England are major crowd pullers.

GREAT NATIONS
BRAZIL

England may have invented the modern game, but Brazil —and Edison Pelé in particular—have perfected it to such an extent that they can now boast a record-breaking five World Cup wins.

ABOVE Brazil team in 1970

PAGE 86 Brazil star Garrincha skips past Wales defender Terry Hennessey in 1962

PAGE 87 The 1986 France team before their match against Canada

Few dare argue with the Brazilian pre-eminence in modern football—especially after watching the timeless re-runs of Garrincha and Pelé swaggering their way to Brazil's first World Cup win in 1958 or, 12 years later, witnessing the color-soaked TV scenes from Brazil's third World Cup triumph in the Mexican sunshine.

Since then, successive new generations of Brazilians have consistently lived up to Pelé's romantic notion of "the beautiful game." But the

original link was an English one. In 1894, Brazilian Charles Miller, whose father was originally from England, brought over the first footballs to be seen in Brazil, after a study trip in Southampton where he was taught the game. Miller envisaged a game for expatriates and their families, but its popularity swiftly spread and Brazil can now boast the proud achievement of being the only nation to have competed in every World Cup final.

The country's first footballing hero was Arthur Friedenreich, who, in the early part of the 20th century, was also popularly supposed to have been the first senior player to have scored over 1,000 goals. Emulating him was Leonidas, who spearheaded Brazil's attack at the 1938 World Cup finals in France. Unwisely, the team's directors decided to rest Leonidas from the semi-final against World Cup title holders Italy in order to be fresh for the final—which, of course, they never reached.

Brazil were awarded hosting rights to the next World Cup finals, but its realization had to wait until after World War II. It was originally due to be played in 1949, but a mixture of European uncertainty and slow preparation work put the staging back to 1950. Brazil reached the final only to suffer a shock 2-1 defeat to Uruguay in front of almost 200,000 disbelieving fans. As Brazil had lost the final while dressed in all-white, they superstitiously decided to make the switch to their current strip of yellow shirts and blue shorts—arguably today's most famous football uniform.

Brazil reached the quarter-final stage at the 1954 World Cup finals in Switzerland, returning to Europe to take the world title in Sweden four years later with almost an entirely new team. Coach Vicente Feola had brought in the mercurial outside right Garrincha and a 17-year-old inside left called Pelé.

As a teenage sensation, Pelé shared top billing for Brazil with wizard dribbler Garrincha, nicknamed "the Little Bird," and the midfield duo of Didi and Zito. In 1970, Pelé was complemented by the likes of Gerson, Roberto Rivelino, Tostao, and explosive Jairzinho—the last of whom was the only winner to score in every match per round at the World Cup finals. When Pelé retired in 1977, he boasted over 1,000 goals in a career with Brazil, Santos and New York Cosmos.

Brazil had to wait for 24 years to claim their fourth World Cup, edging past Italy on penalty kicks at the 1994 finals in the United States. Brazil's Bebeto and Romario were the deadliest strike pairing at the tournament going into the match against Italy, yet the match finished goalless.

Ronaldo was a member of the 1994 squad without playing and, in 1998, he was hampered by injury and illness as Brazil surrendered their crown to France. Yet Ronaldo was the two-goal hero in the 2002 final victory over Germany and in 2006 became the World Cup's all-time leading scorer.

Brazil's immense size long hindered the development of a national league until 1971, and the traditional old regional championships still generate fierce rivalry. Flamengo and Fluminense insist that they are the best-supported clubs, although São Paulo have a record five league titles.

The wealth of Brazilian football has always rested on the Rio-São Paulo axis, with the South American country now the world's greatest exporter of players. Most members of Brazil's recent World Cup squads have been European-based, a stark contrast to 1958 and 1962, when their entire squads played for Brazilian clubs.

ABOVE Pelé in action against Italy in the 1970 World Cup final

Santos have been the most internationally acclaimed club in Brazilian football history. This is largely due to their perpetual global touring in the 1960s, when they cashed in on the fame and drawing power of Pelé. Despite the touring, Santos—even at their peak—were an extremely fine team that in 1962 and 1963 won both the Copa Libertadores and the World Club Cup.

Outstanding Brazilian coaches over the years have included World Cup-winning managers Feola, Aimoré Moreira, Mario Zagallo, Carlos Alberto Parreira, and Luiz Felipe Scolari, as well as Claudio Coutinho, Sebastião Lazaroni, and Tele Santana.

Heroes down the years have included Kaka, the 2007 World Player of the Year, and Cafu—the only player to have featured in the final of three consecutive World Cups (1994, 1998, and 2002).

FOOTBALL FACTS

CHAMPIONS—LAST TEN YEARS

1998 Corinthians
1999 Corinthians
2000 Vasco da Gama
2001 Atlético Paranaense
2002 Santos
2003 Cruzeiro
2004 Santos
2005 Corinthians
2006 São Paulo
2007 São Paulo

ARGENTINA

Argentina took until 1978 to lift the World Cup despite producing legendary coaches, players, and teams. Their greatest player was the controversial Diego Maradona, who inspired them to a second world title in 1986.

Argentina has been producing great coaches, players, and teams for so long that it was remarkable that it took until 1978 before the talented men in the distinctive blue-and-white stripes won their first World Cup.

Argentina had come close to the title before, but finished as runner-up in the inaugural 1930 finals to hosts Uruguay. In 1978, it took home advantage, with brilliant goals from Mario Kempes, the midfield promptings of Ossie Ardiles, and shrewd managerial guidance by César Luis Menotti to fire them to victory.

They added a second crown at the 1986 World Cup finals in Mexico. This time they were inspired by Diego Maradona, who had failed to make the successful 1978 squad due to a lack of experience.

Argentina then finished as the runner-up to West Germany at the 1990 World Cup finals, despite Maradona's talents being restricted by his knee injury.

Maradona's slide from glory continued at the 1994 World Cup finals in the United States, when he failed a dope test and was immediately sent home in disgrace. In his absence, Argentina bowed out to Romania in the second round. They reached the quarter-final stage four years later, crashed out in the first round in 2002 and made it to the quarter-finals in 2006.

Despite a controversial career, Maradona remains an idol for his outrageous talent and the sheer nerve with which he scored a remarkable two goals against England in the 1986 World Cup finals. These goals are legendary. One was helped in with his hand, the other one after a solo run from the halfway line.

Argentina have played a major role in the history of the Copa Libertadores, the South American equivalent of Europe's Champions League, which has been dominated by six clubs —Argentinos Juniors, Boca Juniors, Estudiantes, Independiente, Racing Club, and River Plate. Argentina's Boca Juniors and River Plate are among the world's greatest clubs, with the

BELOW Alfredo Di Stefano scores for Real Madrid

majority of the country's finest players having used them as a springboard to lucrative careers in Europe. Boca Juniors' uniform is blue and yellow, River Plate famously play in white shirts with a red sash.

In the late 1940s, River carried all before them with a forward line nicknamed "The Machine" for its goal-scoring efficiency. They fielded two inside forwards, Juan Manuel Moreno and Angel Labruna, while in reserve was a young Alfredo Di Stefano. The side broke up in the early 1950s, when Argentinian league players went on strike in a demand for improved contracts and wages. Many players, including Di Stefano, were lured away to a "pirate" league in Colombia and never returned.

Boca became the first Argentinian club to reach a South American club final in 1962, but narrowly lost to Pelé's Santos in the Copa Libertadores. Independiente, from neighboring city Avellaneda, became Argentina's first Continental champions in 1964 and Racing Club were crowned as the country's first Intercontinental Cup champions in 1967.

Argentina have won the Copa America 11 times, most notably in 1957 when the inspirational performances of inside forward Humberto Maschio, Antonio Valentín Angelillo, and Omar Sivori established them as early favorites to win the following year's World Cup. By the 1958 World Cup finals, the trio had been sold to Italian clubs and Argentina's hopes went with them.

From then on there was a steady stream of Argentinian players heading for the riches on offer in Europe. By the mid-1990s, as most Western European countries eased their restrictions on foreign players, a minor industry grew up in "finding" European forebears—and European Union passports—for many Argentinian players.

The national game has been split down the years between a clash of styles. In the 1960s and 1970s, coaches such as Juan Carlos Lorenzo (Boca), Manuel Giudice (Independiente) and Osvaldo Zubeldía (Estudiantes de La Plata), ruthlessly put the achievement of results above the quality of play and entertainment. Yet the

country's football federation deserved enormous credit for appointing the more positive Menotti as coach. Under Menotti, Argentina's triumph and style of play at the 1978 World Cup finals inspired a significant shift in opinion.

There has, however, been a failure to deal with hooligan violence in domestic Argentinian football. In fact, many club directors have preferred to provide complementary match tickets and transport for the more notorious hooligans, known as "Barras Bravas," to avoid major disruption in the stadiums and around the grounds.

BELOW Maradona's "hand of God" goal against England in 1986

GREAT NATIONS
ITALY

"We play to win, otherwise what's the point?"

PAOLO ROSSI

Italy has tasted glory on the world stage with four World Cup crowns. A dramatic penalty shoot-out won them the final against France in 2006—12 years after they lost the World Cup to Brazil on penalties.

ABOVE Luigi Riva outpaces Brazil defender Brito in the 1970 World Cup final

Italy is second only to Brazil in terms of World Cup wins, having lifted the Jules Rimet trophy four times. Known as "the Azzurri," or "Blues," the national side also triumphed at the 1968 European Championship, but this has been their lone triumph at confederation level. They came close, however, in 2000. Under the management of former World Cup-winning goalkeeper Dino Zoff, they had a 2-1 defeat to France on the "golden goal" rule in Rotterdam, Holland.

A combination of English and Swiss students and teachers introduced the sport to Italy in the second half of the 19th century, with the English influence still evident in the anglicized style of club names such as AC Milan and Genoa (rather than Milano and Genova).

Their national league was founded in the late 1920s, and top Italian clubs took part with limited success in the Mitropa Cup—an inter-war predecessor of the modern-day competition known as the Champions League.

Turin-based Juventus proved to be the outstanding side of the 1930s, winning the league title five years in a row and providing the backbone of the national team that won the World Cup in 1934.

Italy had refused to play in the 1930 World Cup finals in Uruguay, but won the next two world crowns thanks to the managerial wisdom of Vittorio Pozzo and the genius of inside forward Giuseppe Meazza. Pozzo played three Argentinians

in the team that beat Czechoslovakia in the 1934 final. Pozzo responded to criticism by pointing out their eligibility to national service, saying: "If they can die for Italy, then I'm sure they can play football for Italy!"

Torino also won five consecutive titles in the 1940s with an outstanding squad that was so strong the national team used ten of their players in one match. However, the Torino squad was destroyed by a 1949 plane crash returning from playing a testimonial match in Lisbon.

The Torino disaster wrecked the national team's prospects ahead of their World Cup defence in Brazil in 1950. Also, many clubs invested financial strength in foreign players, which did nothing to help rebuild the national team. In 1958, Italy failed for the first time to progress through the qualifying system and into the World Cup finals.

During the early 1960s, clubs such as AC Milan and their bitter rivals Inter Milan ruled the European scene, even though the national team were unable to follow suit. Italy's participation in the 1966 World Cup finals remains notorious for their 1-0 defeat at the hands of North Korea, one of football's biggest upsets.

Adversity turned to glory when Italy captured the 1968 European Nations Cup after a replay. And two years later, inspired by the legendary figures of Giacinto Facchetti, Sandro Mazzola, Gigi Riva, and Gianni Rivera, Italy took part in one of the greatest games ever played. They edged past

ABOVE Dino Zoff defies
Brazil's Roberto and Oscar

RIGHT Paolo Rossi hails
Alessandro Altobelli's third goal
in the 1982 World Cup Final

West Germany 4-3 in extra time to secure a
place in the final of the World Cup. But they were
so exhausted after the victory in the altitude of
Mexico that they surrendered 4-1 to Brazil.

Italy arrived at the 1982 World Cup finals in
the wake of a match-fixing scandal. Coach Enzo
Bearzot and veteran captain Dino Zoff imposed
a press blackout. Paolo Rossi had just returned
from a two-year ban for his alleged role in the
scandal and proved to be their inspiration, with six
goals—including a hat-trick against Brazil—guiding
his nation to overall victory.

For the next 24 years, the leading league clubs
kept the Italian flag flying at international level with
a string of European trophies.

Pride was finally restored at national team level
in 2006 when, after Zinedine Zidane's infamous
head butt, Italy became world champions again
by beating France in a penalty shoot-out in Berlin.
Yet this triumph was partially overshadowed

by another match-fixing scandal that saw a
number of teams, including Juventus, relegated
as punishment to Serie B. Juventus had been
under investigation for the illegal administration
of unspecified stimulants to their players when
telephone-tap investigators uncovered a match
manipulation system created by Juventus' "transfer
king" Luciano Moggi.

Evidence produced at a variety of hearings
suggested that Moggi had used his influence with
referees to generate yellow and red cards and
suspensions for opposing players before they
were due to play against Juventus and that he had
also put pressure on players and coaches over
transfers and even national team selection.

FOOTBALL FACTS

CHAMPIONS—LAST TEN YEARS
1999 AC Milan
2000 Lazio
2001 Roma
2002 Juventus
2003 Juventus
2004 AC Milan
2005 (not awarded: Juventus title
revoked)
2006 Internazionale
2007 Internazionale
2008 Internazionale

GREAT NATIONS
NETHERLANDS

Dutch football is synonymous with "total football"—the all-action strategy pioneered by Ajax Amsterdam under the inspiration of center forward Johan Cruyff in the early 1970s.

FOOTBALL FACTS

CHAMPIONS—LAST TEN YEARS

1999	Feyenoord
2000	PSV Eindhoven
2001	PSV Eindhoven
2002	Ajax Amsterdam
2003	PSV Eindhoven
2004	Ajax Amsterdam
2005	PSV Eindhoven
2006	PSV Eindhoven
2007	PSV Eindhoven
2008	PSV Eindhoven

Yet while Cruyff provided the brains and leadership out on the pitch, it was Ajax Amsterdam's coach Rinus Michels who masterminded the strategy. With two fabulous feet and mesmeric ball skills, Cruyff was at the heart of the Holland team—all of their goals in the 1974 World Cup finals either started or ended with a contribution by their captain.

Cruyff was supported by Johan Neeskens out of midfield, Ruud Krol from full back, and the duo of Johnny Rep and Rob Rensenbrink in attack. At the peak of their success, the team were nicknamed "Clockwork Orange," after the color of their shirts as well as their precision passing. They again finished as runner-up at the World Cup finals, even without Cruyff at the helm in 1978.

Yet in terms of international status, Holland had been late developers. A crucial reason was the fact that it was not until the the mid-1950s that domestic clubs such as Feyenoord, Sparta and Excelsior—notably all from Rotterdam—forced the recognition of professionalism, even initially part-time. The amateur status that ruled the Dutch game previously meant that star players, such as Faas Wilkes, had been forced abroad to the likes of Italy and Spain to earn a living from their talent.

Feyenoord became the first Dutch club to reach the semi-final stage of the European Champions' Cup in 1963, when they lost narrowly to Benfica. This was the start of a remarkable era, during which Feyenoord won the domestic double—league and cup—in both 1965 and 1969.

They then became the first Dutch club to win a European crown in 1970, edging past Celtic in extra time with a team that included outside left Coen Moulijn—one of the finest of Dutch players before the Ajax era.

Later Feyenoord, while largely playing second fiddle to Amsterdam Ajax at home, won the UEFA Cup twice. In recent years, PSV Eindhoven have also been regular group stage contenders in the Champions League.

Holland's national team had not qualified for the World Cup finals since the inter-war period but this, and the entire international status of Dutch football, was about to change with the explosive eruption of Amsterdam Ajax, which had reached the 1969 Champions' Cup final and then won it in 1971, 1972, and 1973, before Cruyff was sold to Barcelona.

Cruyff stepped out of national team football at the end of 1977 but Dutch football continued to produce an apparently endless stream of talented players and coaches.

PSV Eindhoven won the 1988 European Champions' Cup under the wily management of Guus Hiddink, while Holland won the European Championship in West Germany six weeks later. The Dutch national hero at that time was AC Milan—and former Amsterdam Ajax—striker Marco van Basten, who scored a group stage hat-trick against England, a semi-final winner against West Germany and a magnificent volleyed winning goal against the Soviet Union in the final at Munich's Olympic Stadium.

Controversy was never far away whenever the Dutch faced their German arch rivals. A spitting incident involving Holland midfielder Frank Rijkaard and German striker Rudi Völler marred a dramatic clash in the second round of the 1990 World Cup finals in Italy, which Holland lost 2-1.

Too often at major tournaments, Holland's potential has been undermined by squabbling between players and coaching staff over tactics and team selection. Inspirational forward Ruud Gullit, a former World and European Player of the Year, refused to put on the shirt and play for Holland at the 1990 World Cup finals. Manager Hiddink sent midfielder Edgar Davids home during Holland's continued involvement in the 1996 European Championship after internal squabbling among the squad.

The unpredictability of the Dutch game's biggest names was evident up to the spring of 2008. Van Basten, by now manager of Holland, agreed to return as coach to Amsterdam Ajax after the European Championship in Austria and Switzerland, with Cruyff as a senior consultant. However, Cruyff had barely been confirmed in the role before he withdrew in an apparent disagreement with Van Basten—his one-time protégé—over youth strategy.

This is a sector that has become more crucial than ever to the Dutch game. The Ajax youth set-up is famed worldwide, with its players coached in a style and tactical system imposed on all the teams right through to the senior professionals. The club raises significant income selling players to the big leagues in England, Italy, and Spain to supplement its income from regular annual participation in European competitions.

RIGHT Johan Cruyff, captain and center forward of Holland and Ajax Amsterdam in the early 1970s

1960s

1970s

RIGHT Pelé celebrates Brazil's first in the 1970 World Cup final victory

BELOW Fabio Capello (front, left) lines up for Italy against England in 1973

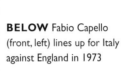

ABOVE North Korea and Portugal emerge for their sensational 1966 World Cup tie

BELOW The Soviet Union greet their English host fans in 1966

RIGHT Franz Beckenbauer betters rival captain Johan Cruyff in the 1974 World Cup final

GREAT NATIONS MOMENTS

1970s 1980s 1990s 2000s

ABOVE Argentina poised to win their first World Cup, in 1978

RIGHT England line up, optimistically, ahead of their 1982 World Cup assault

BELOW Holland in 1978 —about to finish World Cup runners-up once more

ABOVE Didier Six opens up for France against Czechoslovakia in 1982

ABOVE Mexico head for a 2-1 defeat by Portugal in Germany in 2006

LEFT Gary Lineker's penalty goal against West Germany in 1990 is not enough for England

GREAT NATIONS
ENGLAND

England lays justifiable claim to be the home and birthplace of football—the game itself is thought to originate in the Middle Ages, but its rules weren't formalized until the mid-19th century.

The formation of the Football League in 1863, the first FA Cup Final in 1872, and the introduction of a revolutionary league system in 1888 were major events in the game's development in England.

But the country has only one World Cup triumph to date; the 1966 glory at London's Wembley Stadium. This victory was founded upon Alf Ramsey's coaching, Bobby Moore's captaincy, Bobby Charlton's long-range shooting, and Geoff Hurst's famous hat-trick. Bobby Robson's team, inspired by Paul Gascoigne and Gary Lineker, came close to tasting success by reaching the 1990 World Cup semi-final in Italy.

Despite international disappointment, England has some of the world's richest and most watched domestic teams. The national game's image was marred by hooliganism and tragedy in the 1980s and only booming television revenues and the lucrative FA Premier League's 1992 launch have helped tempt over some of the world's top talents.

FOOTBALL FACTS

CHAMPIONS—LAST TEN YEARS

1999 Manchester United
2000 Manchester United
2001 Manchester United
2002 Arsenal
2003 Manchester United
2004 Arsenal
2005 Chelsea
2006 Chelsea
2007 Manchester United
2008 Manchester United

RIGHT England Captain Bobby Moore plants a winning kiss on the World Cup in 1966

Manchester United, the world's best supported club, have dominated this in recent years, with big-spending Chelsea now wanting a slice of glory.

Manchester United claimed England's first European Champions' Cup by beating Lisbon's Benfica in 1968, some five years after Bill Nicholson's Tottenham had become the first English winners of a European trophy in the Cup Winners' Cup. Under the management of Sir Alex Ferguson, Manchester United won an unique hat-trick for an English club in 1999, with victory in the Premier League, FA Cup, and the Champions League to complete a unique hat-trick for an English club.

A third Champions League triumph followed in 2008, when United defeated Chelsea in a penalty shoot-out in Moscow in the first all-English final in the competition's history.

English clubs dominated Europe, with the European Cup won by an English side for five successive years in the late 1970s and early 1980s.

The dark side of the English passion for football has been a long history of hooliganism. Trouble began to be noted in English League grounds in the early 1970s, but English fans' passion for traveling to away matches meant that hooliganism was exported and earned clubs a bad name. Leeds United were barred from European football in the mid-1970s after their fans, angered by controversial refereeing in the 1975 Champions' Cup final against Bayern Munich, ripped out seats in the Parc des Princes in Paris.

A string of incidents occurred over the next decade and it was only after the Heysel disaster of 1985, when 39 Juventus fans died in Brussels after being charged by Liverpool followers, that both football and the law took action. The process was expanded after a crowd crush disaster at Hillsborough, Sheffield, in 1989. All-seater demands were imposed on all major sports venues, leading to the building of new grounds and total redevelopment of others. The pace of the stadia and security revolution persuaded UEFA to grant England hosting rights to the European Championship finals in 1996, which proved to be a huge success on and off the pitch.

English football has led the world game in many ways. In the late 1920s and early 1930s it was Arsenal, thanks to manager Herbert Chapman and forward Charlie Buchan, that conceived the "WM" system, a formation, that dominated the sport for four decades. In the early 1990s, England opened the way for foreign investors and owners, also creating the FA Premier League at a crucial time when satellite television was booming and clubs were turning to the London Stock Exchange.

Enormous controversy was generated by the purchase of Manchester United by the American Glazer family, although concerns about the club's debt and any loans were soon completely overshadowed by their remarkable continuing success on the pitch.

Chelsea emerged as United's major rivals after the remarkable takeover in 2003 by Russian oligarch Roman Abramovich, who invested seemingly limitless sums in paying off the club's debts and buying in some of the world's finest players. Abramovich's early rewards included Premier League titles in 2005 and 2006.

ABOVE David Beckham lines up England's winning penalty against Argentina in 2002

GREAT NATIONS
FRANCE

France's contribution to football goes far beyond its national team's significant achievements on the pitch. French administrator Jules Rimet was the brains behind the creation of the World Cup finals.

Another French administrator, Henri Delaunay, paved the way for the European Championship. Gabriel Hanot, editor of the daily sports newspaper *L'Equipe*, was the creative force behind the European Champions Clubs' Cup.

France's greatest achievement on the field was their World Cup victory, on home soil, in 1998. Inspired by midfielder Zinedine Zidane, they saw off Paraguay, Italy and Croatia in the knock-out stage before crushing Brazil 4-0 in the final.

Two years later, David Trezeguet scored the "golden goal" that beat Italy 2-1 in the 2000 European Championship final. Sylvain Wiltord had forced extra time with a last-gasp equalizer.

Zidane, who retired from international football after the 2004 European Championship, made an impressive comeback as France reached the final of the 2006 World Cup, but was sent off for head butting an opponent during defeat by Italy.

One of the greatest personalities in the modern French game has been Michel Platini. In 1984, he towered over the Euro finals—in France—scoring nine goals as the home team went on to beat Spain 2-0 in the final. Later, Platini progressed to become the country's national manager, President of the Organizing Committee of the 1998 World Cup and then a Counsellor to the FIFA President before being elected UEFA President in 2007.

French club football is often overshadowed by the national team, as so many home-grown players have moved abroad. One of the persisting

problems for the league has been the lack of an established, successful club in the French capital, Paris. The power of the French game has resided largely in the provinces—the comparatively new team Paris Saint-Germain once reached the final

RIGHT Raymond Kopa, the first French footballer to be hailed European Player of the Year

of the now-defunct European Cup Winners' Cup, but are better known for a long series of boardroom and ownership battles.

The first French club to make an international impression were Reims. Prompted by creative center forward Raymond Kopa, they reached the first European Champions' Cup final in 1956 and were losing finalists again three years later. Kopa was the playmaker for the France side that finished third in the 1958 World Cup finals and helped set up most of Just Fontaine's record tally of 13 goals. Fontaine had been brought into the team only at the last minute because of injury to Reims team-mate René Bliard.

No French club managed to reach the European Champions' Cup final again until the eruption of Olympique Marseille in the late 1980s and early 1990s. The team were bankrolled by the flamboyant businessman-turned-politician Bernard Tapie.

A team starring top-scoring French player Jean-Pierre Papin and England winger Chris Waddle finished as runner-up in the 1991 European Champions' Cup, losing on penalties to Red Stade Belgrade. Two years later, Olympique Marseille defeated AC Milan 1-0 with Papin playing for the Italian club. But that triumph was tarnished almost immediately as Marseilles were thrown out of European competition over a domestic match-fixing scandal that saw Tapie imprisoned.

Other French football clubs and their directors were punished, with sentences ranging from suspensions to fines for financial irregularities.

Lyon President Jean-Michel Aulas said: "What we need in the French game is greater financial freedom to run our own affairs. Then maybe we wouldn't have these other problems. Fans demand success and directors want to give that to them, for their own reasons."

Software millionaire Aulas knew his subject well. He had taken over Lyon when the club were in the second division, and supplied both financial and administrative resources to secure promotion and then a record run of seven successive league titles from 2002 to 2008.

Aulas even pressed successfully for a relaxation of laws barring sports clubs from obtaining outside, foreign investment. He claimed that, without new revenue streams, French clubs could not afford to buy the best players nor could they develop stadia to such an extent that the country could ever hope to host the finals of the World Cup or European Championship.

The factor that has continued to elude Aulas has been success in European competitions. Lyon have regularly reached the knock-out stage of the European Champions League without ever reaching even the semi-finals. Saint-Etienne (1976) and AS Monaco (2004) remain the only other French clubs aside from Reims and Marseille to have reached a European Champions League final. Saint-Etienne lost narrowly to Bayern Munich while AS Monaco crashed 3-0 to Porto.

BELOW Zinedine Zidane outplays Italy's Gennaro Gattuso in the 2006 World Cup final

GREAT NATIONS
GERMANY

"After the game is always before the next game."

SEPP HERBERGER

Germany have long been one of the most powerful countries in international football and their leading club, Bayern Munich, are one of the most famous, thanks to four European Champions' Cup victories.

FOOTBALL FACTS

CHAMPIONS—LAST TEN YEARS

1999	Bayern Munich
2000	Bayern Munich
2001	Bayern Munich
2002	Borussia Dortmund
2003	Bayern Munich
2004	Werder Bremen
2005	Bayern Munich
2006	Bayern Munich
2007	Stuttgart
2008	Bayern Munich

Football had difficulty establishing itself initially in Germany because of the social strength of the gymnastic movement. Attitudes changed gradually partly because of football's popularity among young people and, partly because toward the end of World War I, the Kaiser ascribed British strength of character on the battlefield to the morale and physical qualities developed through the team sports played at schools and universities.

Football clubs thrived in the inter-war years even though the domestic game was riven with tension over the issue of professionalism. Even under Hitler's National Socialist government in the 1930s, football was considered a recreation with payments to players prohibited. This did not prevent many clubs from bending the rules.

The leading club in the 1930s were FC Schalke, which came from the mining town of Gelsenkirchen in the Ruhr. All their players were paid as miners. Their star winger Ernst Kuzorra revealed years later: "The nearest we saw of a mine was the pithead in the distance."

The German game was organized in a regional championship, topped off by a play-off series to decide the national champions. The play-off final regularly drew crowds of 70,000–80,000. FC Schalke were crowned champions six times and won the domestic cup once in the 1930s. Their inside forward, Fritz Szepan, led Germany to third place in the 1934 World Cup. Kuzorra

and Szepan both have roads named in their honor around the present FC Schalke stadium.

After the war, political reality saw Germany divided into west and east sectors. Ultimately, Soviet-supported East Germany, known as the German Democratic Republic, developed its own football federation and league. Although East Germany became a force in international swimming and athletics, it did not replicate this success in football. East Germany only ever qualified for the World Cup finals in 1974, and in the same year, Magdeburg won the nation's only European club trophy by taking the Cup Winners' Cup.

In contrast, football in West Germany went from strength to strength. Wily coach Sepp Herberger and captain Fritz Walter guided the West German team to a shock victory over hot favorites Hungary in the final of the 1954 World Cup. The victory was known as the "miracle of Berne." Hungary—as Olympic champions—had not been beaten for four years. Further World Cup triumphs followed in 1974 and in 1990.

In 1990, the collapse of the Berlin Wall led to the reunification of Germany and the integration of East German football into the German football federation, which had always styled itself as the "overall" Deutscher Fussball Bund.

Germany, whether West or unified, have also finished as World Cup runner-up four times (1966, 1982, 1986, and 2002) and third three times

(1976, 1992, and 2008). They have also won the European Championship three times (1972, 1980, and 1996) and three times finished as runner-up (1976, 1992, and 2008).

A significant factor in the national team's success was the creation of the unified, fully professional Bundesliga in 1963. Bayern Munich, who have won 20 modern championships to add to their success in 1932, hold the record for the greatest number of domestic titles. The greatest personality to emerge from within Bayern Munich was Franz Beckenbauer, known as "Der Kaiser," who netted 68 goals in 62 games for his country, including the winning goal in the 1974 World Cup final against Holland.

As captain and sweeper, Beckenbauer led Bayern Munich to a European Champions' League hat-trick (1974, 1975, and 1976). He was ably supported by a host of stars that included goalkeeper "Sepp" Maier, full-back Paul Breitner, midfielder Uli Hoeness, and the greatest goal scorer of the modern era, Gerd Müller.

Beckenbauer later coached West Germany to 1990 World Cup victory over Argentina in Italy, having guided them to the final four years earlier. In the meantime, he coached Bayern Munich to UEFA Cup success in 1996 and became their club president in time to oversee their fourth European Champions' League victory in 2001.

Moving on up the political ladder, Beckenbauer led the German bid to win hosting rights to the 2006 World Cup finals for Germany and was then president of the FIFA Organizing Committee. As a vice-president of the German Football Federation he was also voted onto the executive committees of both FIFA and UEFA.

TOP RIGHT Hosts West Germany await kick-off in the 1974 World Cup finals

RIGHT Bayern's Gerd Müller pounces on a defensive slip

GREAT NATIONS
PORTUGAL

The Portuguese team are often known as the "Brazilians of Europe," thanks to the flamboyance of Eusébio in the 1960s, the "golden generation" of Luis Figo, João Pinto, and Rui Costa in the 1990s, and the country's latest idol, Cristiano Ronaldo.

FOOTBALL FACTS

CHAMPIONS—LAST TEN YEARS
1999 Porto
2000 Sporting Lisbon
2001 Boavista
2002 Sporting Lisbon
2003 Porto
2004 Porto
2005 Benfica
2006 Porto
2007 Porto
2008 Porto

FAR RIGHT Eusébio floors Hungary's defence in the 1966 World Cup finals

RIGHT Cristiano Ronaldo escapes Germany's Philipp Lahm at Euro 2008.

Traditionally the power of the Portuguese game has been dominated by the three leading clubs of Benfica, Porto, and Sporting Lisbon. Only Belenenses in 1948 and Boavista in 2001 have broken their monopoly of the league since its formation in 1934. Benfica lead the way with 31 championships, with Porto picking up 16 of their 23 titles in the past 24 years.

Football was introduced to Portugal through the ports in the 19th century, but the relatively small size of the country meant the national team had little or no impact internationally. However, Portugal had a source of playing talent in their African territories, such as Angola and Mozambique. An increasing number of African players were imported by the clubs and, from the late 1950s, also selected for the national team. Such players included Benfica's goalkeeper Jose Alberto Costa Pereira, striker Jose Aguas, and the two inside forwards Joaquin Santana and Mario Coluna.

All four were members of Benfica's Champions' Cup-winning side that, in 1961, defeated favorites Barcelona 3-2 in Berne, Switzerland. Simultaneously, Benfica had also acquired the greatest African discovery of all in young striker Eusébio da Silva Ferreira. One year later he scored two thundering goals as Benfica defeated Real Madrid 5-3 to win their second Champions' Cup. Eusébio would also lead Benfica to three more finals, albeit finishing on the losers' side against AC Milan (1963), Inter Milan (1965), and Manchester United (1968).

A mixture of Sporting Lisbon's defense, along with Benfica's midfield and attack, provided the backbone for the Portuguese national side that finished third in their first ever World Cup finals,

Eusébio a nine-goal top scorer in England.

Like the country itself, Portuguese football suffered from economic decline in the following decades but a new era dawned with triumphs in the 1989 and 1991 World Youth Cups. Ever since the emergence of the so-called "golden generation," Portugal became a potential threat at major tournaments.

Porto emerged as the dominant club under the controversial presidency of Jorge Nuno Pinto da Costa. He hired an equally controversial coach in Jose Mourinho and was rewarded with victory in the 2003 UEFA Cup and then, more impressively, in the European Champions League a year later —before Mourinho was lured away to Chelsea.

Portugal reached the semi-final stage of the 2000 European Championship in Belgium and Holland. The inability to compete in wages with the giants of England, Italy, and Spain meant the departure of stars such as Figo (Barcelona, Real Madrid, and Inter Milan), Simao Sabrosa (Barcelona and Atletico Madrid), Deco (Barcelona), and Cristiano Ronaldo (Manchester United). The national team gained from these players—technically and tactically—competing in better-quality leagues.

From 2003–08, the Portuguese Football Federation hired Luiz Felipe Scolari, Brazil's 2002 World Cup-winning coach, to bring the competitive best out of the country's depth of talent. Scolari succeeded to a qualified degree. Portugal finished as runner-up on home territory in the 2004 European Championship—losing to outsiders Greece in the final—and were fourth at the 2006 World Cup finals in Germany. Scolari conceded on leaving in 2008 to return to club football with Chelsea: "I did not win something big which is what I came to do."

Scolari's final game with Portugal was at the 2008 European Championship finals, when Portugal fell 3-2 to Germany in the quarter-finals. Critics in Libson claimed the team had been distracted by the mid-event announcement of Scolari's new job and by uncertainty over whether Ronaldo would be leaving Manchester United for Real Madrid.

GREAT NATIONS
SPAIN

No talented national side has underachieved quite as badly as Spain, who surprisingly have yet to win the World Cup. Yet their recent triumph at the 2008 European Championship could kick-off a new era.

Spain have a history rich in great players and their 2008 European Championship victory means that their best players—goalkeeper and captain Iker Casillas, the midfielder trio of Cesc Fabregas, Xavi Hernandez and Andres Iniesta, and the strikeforce of Fernando Torres and David Villa—can claim equality of star billing in the hall of fame with older heroes. These included legends of the 1920s and 1930s, when goalkeeper Ricardo Zamora, defender Jacinto Quincoces, and inside forward Luis Regueiro helped Spain become the first foreign nation to beat England 4-3 in Madrid in 1929.

At the end of the 1950s, a team packed with stars such as Alfredo Di Stefano, Ladislav Kubala, and Luis Suarez saw Spain ranked as favorites to win the inaugural Nations Cup. However, when the 1960 quarter-final draw matched Spain against the Soviet Union, dictator Francisco Franco ordered the team to withdraw on political grounds.

Even so long after the Spanish Civil War, Spain still had no diplomatic relations with countries from the Communist Block. In 1964, on home soil, Spain won its first title success. Relations with the East had thawed significantly enough for the USSR squad to be allowed entry into Spain for the European Championship finals. Strikers Jesus Pereda and Marcelino each scored in Spain's 2-1 victory over the Soviets.

Spain's failure to achieve national team success in the succeeding four decades remains one of football's mysteries. The football federation has long run one of the most successful international youth sections and Juan Santisteban, once a European Cup-winning halfback with Real Madrid, has been perhaps the most respected age level coach in the world. But the best the seniors could point to was a runner-up spot at the 1984 European Championship finals and a stunning 5-1 win over Denmark in the second round of the 1986 World Cup finals, when

RIGHT Captain Fernando Olivella and coach Jose Villalonga, European winners in 1964

ABOVE Fernando Torres heads
for glory against Germany in 2008

Emilio Butragueno, nicknamed "the vulture," scored four goals.

However, at club level the story could not be more different. Real Madrid were Europe's first club champions in 1956 and retained the trophy for the next four years, during a period of total domination in which the team enthralled with their victories in an entertaining manner. With nine European Champions' Cups, two UEFA Cups, and 31 domestic league titles, Real Madrid have their own special place in the history books.

They also led the way in European stadium development, which they owed to the vision of Santiago Bernabeu—a former player and coach, who became president in 1943. Bernabeu issued bonds to finance the building of a new stadium that was opened in 1947, and named the Bernabeu Stadium. Its capacity was increased in the late 1950s to 125,000, as fans flocked to watch their heroes and superstars at work.

In terms of power and ambition, however, the Catalan institution stands not far behind. With its motto of "More than a Club," Barcelona claims a unique loyalty on and off the field. Yet the club has never dominated the European Champions League Cup in the manner of their bitter rivals, Real Madrid. Barcelona were finalists in 1961 and 1986. But they have won twice, beating Sampdoria at Wembley Stadium in 1992 and seeing off Arsenal at the Stade de France in 2006.

GREAT NATIONS
RUSSIA

Europe's most populous nation has rarely punched its weight in international football. So far, its greatest days came in the early 1960s, while it was a part of the Soviet Union.

Moscow, the capital of the USSR, was the central force in its national football. It boasted all the major clubs—Dynamo, Spartak, Torpedo, Lokomotiv, and CSKA—and had all the finest players. The size of the country made it difficult for any other clubs to compete effectively until air travel was possible. Even that was a risk, with the entire first team squad of Pakhtakor Tashkent killed when their plane crashed in 1979.

By the mid-1960s, however, major powers were emerging in the club game in Georgia and Ukraine especially, and also in Armenia and Belarus.

Dynamo Tbilisi, Dynamo Kiev, Dynamo Minsk, and Ararat Yerevan may have owed their creation to the Soviet model but all developed a style of football very different to the physical Moscow style. Tbilisi and Kiev played football with a Latin-style touch of flair. Kiev twice won in the European Cup Winners' Cup and Tbilisi won it once but their officials and coaches and players never co-exited happily with the Moscow factions.

The Soviet Communist attitude to sport brought other complications. The USSR ignored FIFA and would not compete internationally until after World War II. A tour of Britain by Moscow Dynamo in the winter of 1945 marked a slight thaw. Two years later the Soviet Union joined FIFA on condition that it could have a permanent vice-president.

By definition, Soviet footballers were amateurs, not paid for playing football though they were

paid for their nominal roles in the armed services or other professions. The Soviet Union felt free to send its strongest possible team to the Olympics, while Western European rivals were weakened by the transparency of their own players' professional status. The Soviet national team competed internationally for the first time at the 1952 Olympic Games, which they duly won four years later in Melbourne, Australia. Their heroes were world-class footballers, goalkeeper Lev Yashin, and left-half skipper Igor Netto.

Yashin was a hero again when the Soviets won the inaugural 1960 European Championship. Milan Galic had given Yugoslavia the lead, right winger Slava Metreveli leveled, and journalist turned-center forward Viktor Ponedelnik wrote his own page in history by scoring the extra time winner.

RIGHT Russia prepare for their Euro 2008 adventure

The Soviet Union lost the 1964 final 2-1 to Spain and finished fourth in the 1966 World Cup finals.

The change in the balance of power is reflected in the league honors list when the Soviet Union was finally wiped off the map after the experiment with perestroika undermined the entire system. Kiev won 13 league titles in the Soviet era, Spartak Moscow 12, Dynamo Moscow 11, CSKA Moscow seven, and Lokomotiv Moscow three.

Yet not once in the Soviet era did a club from the Russian Republic win a European cup. That feat had to wait until 2005 when CSKA Moscow beat Sporting Lisbon 3-1 in the UEFA Cup final. Zenit St. Petersburg followed their example in 2008, when they also won the UEFA Cup, beating Rangers. Those achievements demonstrated how far Russian clubs have come since the break up of

the Soviet Union and the formation of a Russian league—then virtually bankrupt—in 1992.

The collapse of central funding for football clubs from the various state organizations threw the domestic game into turmoil. Within a decade, only Lokomotiv were still in the controlling, supporting hands of the railway unions. All the other clubs had long since been cast adrift by the secret police (Dynamo), army (CSKA), and farms (Spartak).

The domestic game was rescued by the oligarchs who had taken massive financial advantage of the collapse of Communism and the bargain-basement sell-offs of the major utilities. Roman Abramovich's oil company Sibneft originally supported CSKA and the Russian energy giant Gazprom funded the 2007 champions Zenit. The outcome has been that Russian clubs now import star players from all over the world.

ABOVE Legendary goalkeeper Lev Yashin defies Portugal's Eusébio at the 1966 World Cup

GREAT NATIONS
REST OF THE WORLD

From small nations such as Luxembourg and San Marino to the array of African sides and former Soviet states, the status and power of world football is forever changing.

BELOW Bulgaria's Hristo Stoichkov (left) celebrates another goal for Barcelona

ALBANIA (Europe): Despite being among UEFA's founder members in 1954, Albanian football has been hampered by the country's poverty and isolation. They beat newly-crowned European champions Greece in the 2006 World Cup qualifiers, but are still waiting to reach their first tournament—though Albania's star midfielder Lorik Cana has proved outstanding at Marseille.

ALGERIA (Africa): Having broken away from France in 1958, Algeria's footballers beat eventual finalists West Germany at the 1982 World Cup thanks to Lakhdar Belloumi's goal but were eliminated in a convenient draw between the West Germans and Austria. Their finest moment came when Moussa Saïb captained the hosts to success at the 1990 African Cup of Nations. JS Kabylie are dominant at home, having won 13 league titles.

ANDORRA (Europe): Not too much can be expected of a country with a population of 72,000, squeezed between Spain and France. Andorra's team, largely made up of part-timers, only began playing international football in 1997. Ce Principat and FC Santa Coloma have won three league titles apiece since 1995.

ANGOLA (Africa): On the rise after years of being constrained by civil war and having their finest players poached by Portugal, Angola made an encouraging World Cup finals debut in 2006. Petro Atlético have been crowned as Angolan champions 13 times.

AUSTRALIA (Asia): After achieving nothing at the 1974 World Cup, the "Socceroos" did not bounce back until 2006, when Dutch manager Guus Hiddink made effective use of such talents as Tim Cahill, Harry Kewell, and Mark Viduka. The nation left the uncompetitive Oceania Football Federation for Asia later that year. The A-League kicked off in 2005–06, with one grand final triumph apiece for Melbourne Victory, Newcastle Jets, and Sydney FC.

AUSTRIA (Europe): The so-called "Wunderteam" of the 1930s, inspired by playmaker Matthias Sindelar and coach Hugo Meisl, finished fourth at the 1934 World Cup. Austrian coach Ernst Happel took Holland to the 1978 World Cup final; the Ernst Happel Stadium in Vienna is named after him. The stadium was also the venue for the Euro 2008 final. Rapid Vienna lead the way in home games, with an astonishing 31 league titles.

AZERBAIJAN (Europe): This former Soviet state has struggled since independence despite a spell in charge by World Cup-winning Brazil captain Carlos Alberto. The main stadium in Baku is named after linesman Tofik Bakhmarov, who decided England's third goal in the 1966 World Cup final really did cross the line. Neftchi Baku have won five league titles.

BELARUS (Europe): Midfielder Alexander Hleb put Belarus on the map with his club displays in Germany and England, but the former Soviet state narrowly missed out on a place at the 2002 World Cup finals after a last-gasp defeat to Wales. Dinamo Minsk have been the dominant side, with seven league crowns to their credit.

BELGIUM (Europe): Despite its small size, Belgium reached the 1980 European Championship final, beat holders Argentina in the opening game of the 1982 World Cup, and finished fourth in 1986 under Guy Thys. Goalkeeper Jean-Marie Pfaff, defender Eric Gerets, midfielder Jan Ceulemans, and forward Enzo Scifo formed the side's spine. Anderlecht have won not only a record 29 league titles but one UEFA Cup, a pair of European Super Cups, twice been crowned European Champions, and twice won the Cup Winners' Cup.

BOLIVIA (South America): The Hernando Siles Stadium in the capital of La Paz is one of the world's highest playing surfaces, at 3,637 meters above sea level. The national side have struggled, although they did win the 1963 Copa America courtesy of a 5-4 win over Brazil. Bolívar FC have won the domestic league 15 times.

BOSNIA-HERZEGOVINA (Europe): This former Yugoslav republic was accepted by UEFA in 1991, but promising players such as midfield schemer Zvjezdan Misimovic have not yet been able to reach a major tournament. Their football association has been under fire for its problems.

BULGARIA (Europe): This is one of Eastern Europe's most consistent producers of quality players. The national team's finest achievement was in reaching the World Cup semi-finals in

1994 with a team starring the legendary Hristo Stoichkov and Emil Kostadinov. The record domestic champions are CSKA Sofia with 31 league titles to their credit.

CAMEROON (Africa): Known as the "Indomitable Lions," they were the surprise package at the 1990 World Cup. They upset holders Argentina and pushed England hard in the quarter-finals, spearheaded by veteran striker Roger Milla. Barcelona's Samuel Eto'o holds the scoring record for the African Cup of Nations, a competition that Cameroon have won four times. Canon Yaoundé have won the African Championship three times to match their 11 domestic league titles.

CANADA (North America): Often over-shadowed by CONCACAF rivals such as Mexico and the US, Canada failed to win the CONCACAF Gold Cup in 1990. This was despite spectacular saves from their former Premiership goalkeeper Craig Forrest and the goalscoring talents of Carlo Corazzin.

ABOVE Samuel Eto'o acknowledges the cheers greeting another of his goals for Cameroon

GREAT NATIONS
REST OF THE WORLD

CHILE (South America): Strike duo Marcelo Salas and Iván Zamorano helped guide Chile to the 1998 World Cup quarter-finals. But Chile's best run came when hosting the 1962 tournament, when they eventually lost to Brazil in a fiery semi-final. Colo-Colo have won 27 Chilean league titles, more than double the tally of their main rivals.

CHINA (Asia): The national team faced Manila in Asia's first international match in 1913, but made their World Cup finals debut only in 2002 when they lost all three matches. Versatile midfielder Zheng Zhi captained the side that hosted but lost the 2004 Asian Cup final to Japan.

COLOMBIA (South America): Carlos Valderrama, Faustino Asprilla and goalkeeper Rene Higuita (famous for his "scorpion kick") made Colombia one of the world's most entertaining sides in the 1990s. Iván Córdoba's goal beat Mexico in the 2001 Copa America final. Club Deportivo Los Millonarios, whose riches lured stars such as Alfredo Di Stefano in the 1940s and 1950s, have picked up 13 league titles.

CONGO DR (Africa): Under their former name of Zaire, they became the first black African side to reach the World Cup finals. But at the 1974 competition they were humiliated by eventual champions West Germany. They were crowned African champions in 1968 and 1974, but government support for the sport has dwindled since then, despite striker Lomana LuaLua's recent Premiership experience. AS Vita Club and DC Motema Pembe each have 11 league titles.

ABOVE Colombia's Carlos Valderrama has earned more than 100 caps playing for his country

COSTA RICA (Central America): Consistent performers who reached their first World Cup in 1990 under charismatic coach Bora Milutinovic. They also appeared at the 2002 and 2006 tournaments. with striker Paolo Wanchope as the figurehead. They have won nine CONCACAF championships, though surprisingly none since 1989. Former CONCACAF club champions Deportivo Saprissa have a record 26 domestic league titles.

CROATIA (Europe): This Balkan country taught England a footballing lesson in qualifiers for the 2008 European Championship—just as they did to Germany on their way to third place at the 1998 World Cup. Back then they were inspired by the likes of Robert Prosinecki, Golden Boot winner Davor Šuker, and future national coach Slaven Bilic. More recently, Brazilian-born striker Eduardo and nimble midfielders Luka Modric and Ivan Rakitic have caught the eye. Dinamo Zagred have won the league 11 times since Croatia achieved independence from the former Yugoslavia.

CYPRUS (Europe): Small fry who were thrilled to pull off 1-1 draws against Italy, Czechoslovakia, and France in the 1990s. APOEL Nicosia and Omonia Nicosia have won the Cypriot league 19 times each.

CZECH REPUBLIC (Europe): The Czechs formed the larger part of the old Czechoslovakia, which reached the World Cup Final in 1934 and 1962—when Czech wing half Josef Masopust was voted European Footballer of the Year. Czechoslovakia won the European Championship in 1976. The "new" Czech Republic side lost the

Euro 1996 final to Germany on a "golden goal." They also reached the semi-finals of Euro 2004. Sparta Prague have dominated domestic football, winning 11 championships since the Czechs and Slovaks split in 1993. But the best Czech players inevitably move to the big clubs in the West. Pavel Nedved of Juventus was voted European Footballer of the Year in 2003. Other stars have included Petr Cech (Chelsea), Tomas Rosicky (Dortmund and Arsenal), and Champions' Cup-winner Vladimir Smicer (Lens and Liverpool).

DENMARK (Europe): The Danes' greatest triumph came in 1992, when a goal by John Jensen beat Germany 1-0 to win the European Championship final. The Danes also reached the semi-finals of Euro 1984 and the last 16 of the 1986 World Cup. Denmark has produced many stars for rich Western clubs, such as the Laudrup brothers (Michael and Brian), Morten Olsen, and Manchester United great Peter Schmeichel.

ECUADOR (South America): Qualified for the last two World Cup finals tournaments and reached the last 16 in 2006.

EGYPT (Africa): Won the African Cup of Nations for a record sixth time in 2008, beating Cameroon 1-0 in the final.

EL SALVADOR (Central America): Reached the 1970 World Cup finals by beating local rivals Honduras. This stoked up an already tense situation between the two countries, culminating in a six-day conflict that became known as "the football war."

ESTONIA (Europe): Flora Tallinn have dominated the domestic championship since Estonia became a republic in 1992.

FAROE ISLANDS (Europe): The Faroes' best results have been a 1-0 win over Austria and a 2-2 draw with Scotland, both in European Championship qualifiers.

FINLAND (Europe): Noted for producing players for Europe's big clubs, such as Jari Litmanen (Ajax) and Sami Hyypia (Liverpool). The domestic championship has been dominated by HJK Helsinki, United Tampere, and Haka Valkeakoski.

GEORGIA (Europe): Their greatest moment came in 1981, when Dinamo Tbilisi, inspired by midfielder David Kipiani, beat Carl Zeiss Jena 2-1 in the European Cup Winners' Cup final.

GHANA (Africa): Ghana reached the last 16 of the 2006 World Cup finals with a team featuring Premier League stars such as Michael Essien and Sulley Muntari. They have won the African Cup of Nations four times.

ABOVE Theo Zagorakis, a European title-winning hero for Greece

GREAT NATIONS
REST OF THE WORLD

GREECE (Europe): Shock winners of the 2004 European Championship when Otto Rehhagel's side beat hosts Portugal 1-0 in the final with a goal from Angelos Charisteas. They then failed to qualify for the 2006 World Cup finals. Panathinaikos reached the 1971 European Cup final, losing to Ajax at Wembley. Olympiakos have dominated the domestic game, winning 11 of the last 12 championships. In 2008, they became the first Greek side to play in the last 16 of the Champions League.

HAITI (Central/North America): Haiti reached the World Cup finals in 1974 when Emmanuel Sanon scored a historic goal against Italy but have not been back since. They were CONCACAF champions in 1957 and 1973.

HONDURAS (Central/North America): Reaching the World Cup finals for the only time in 1982, they had been CONCACAF champions the previous year.

HUNGARY (Europe): The "Magnificent Magyars" were the finest team in the world in the early 1950s. Led by Ferenc Puskas, they included greats such as striker Sandor Kocsis, playmaker Nandor Hidegkuti, flying winger Zoltan Czibor, goalkeeper Gyula Grocis, and wing half Jozsef Boszik. But they were shocked by West Germany in the 1954 World Cup Final and the team broke up two years later after the Budapest uprising against Soviet control. A new side finished third in the 1964 European Championship and reached the 1966 World Cup quarter-finals after beating Brazil 3-1. Hungary have struggled at international level ever since.

ICELAND (Europe): Yet to make an impact in major competitions, they are, however, well known for exporting star players, such as former Chelsea and Barcelona forward Eidur Gudjohnsen.

INDIA (Asia): The team reached the World Cup finals once, in 1950, but withdrew after FIFA barred them from playing in bare feet.

IRAN (Asia): Although they have reached the World Cup finals three times, they have yet to reach the last 16. They have won the Asian Cup three times. Iran's best player Ali Daei has won 149 caps.

IRAQ (Asia): Iraq are the current Asian Cup holders after beating favorites Saudi Arabia 1-0 in the 2007 final.

ISRAEL (Asia): Israeli clubs dominated the early years of the Asian Club Championship, before political problems forced the country out into the cold and then into UEFA. The national team were World Cup finalists in 1970.

BELOW Haiti's Sanon runs with the ball in a 1974 World Cup match against Italy

LEFT The Ivory Coast team before their game against Ghana in the 2008

IVORY COAST (Africa): Winners of the African Cup of Nations in 1992, the national team reached the World Cup finals for the first time in 2006. The country is most famous for exporting star players such as Didier Drogba and Salomon Kalou (Chelsea), Kolo Toure (Arsenal), and Toure Yaya (Barcelona).

JAMAICA (Central America): Their best performance was reaching the 1998 World Cup finals with a team that included many England-based players.

JAPAN (Asia): Reaching the World Cup finals in 1998, Japan advanced to a best-yet place in the last 16 on home soil in 2002. They have won the Asian Cup three times.

KAZAKHSTAN (Europe): After gaining independence from the Soviet Union, the country switched from the Asian Confederation to UEFA in 2002. Arguably their greatest player was Oleg Litvinenko, who died tragically in November 2007, just four days short of his 34th birthday.

KUWAIT (Asia): The national team had one appearance in the World Cup finals in 1982. They managed a draw with Czechoslovakia but lost to both England and France. During the last of these, France famously "scored" while some of the Kuwaiti players had stopped playing, having heard a whistle. They walked off the pitch in protest and resumed only after the goal was disallowed.

LATVIA (Europe): Having regained their independence in 1991, they are the only Baltic team to have qualified for the European Championship finals when they upset Turkey in the qualifiers.

LIECHTENSTEIN (Europe): One of the whipping boys of European football, comprising mainly part-timers, the tiny principality improved in the Euro 2008 qualifiers when they upset Latvia 1-0 and followed that up with a 3-0 win over Iceland.

LITHUANIA (Europe): They came third in their group in both the Euro 96 and 1998 World Cup qualifying campaigns. Since then they have managed away draws with both Germany and Italy but, like many former Soviet states, they lack depth of quality as yet.

LUXEMBOURG (Europe): Historically one of Europe's minor teams, they once went 12 years without winning a competitive fixture.

GREAT NATIONS
REST OF THE WORLD

ABOVE Mexico's Rafael Marquez and keeper Oswaldo Sanchez clear their lines at the 2006 World Cup

MACEDONIA (Europe): Only since the breakup of Yugoslavia have they had their own officially recognized team. The inaugural Macedonian side featured Darko Pancev, who won the Champions League with Red Star Belgrade in 1991. Away draws with England and Holland represent two of the country's modest high spots.

MALTA (Europe): With one of the oldest national associations in Europe, Malta owes much of its football fanaticism to the island's former British occupation. With a population of under 400,000, however, the national team draws from one of the smallest on the European continent.

MEXICO (Central and North America): Having qualified for no fewer than 13 World Cup finals, Mexico are hugely experienced. They reached the quarter-finals in 1970 and 1986, both times on home soil. Their 2-1 defeat by Argentina in the 2006 World Cup was regarded as one of the finest technical matches of recent tournaments.

MOLDOVA (Europe): Their two best-ever results came within a month of each other in the mid-1990s during the qualifiers for Euro 96, beating Georgia and Wales.

MONTENEGRO (Europe): Came into existence only after the 2006 World Cup after being politically tied to Serbia. The 2010 tournament is their first competitive opportunity.

MOROCCO (Africa): The first African team to win a group at the World Cup (1986), finishing ahead of Portugal, Poland, and England. Although always a contender, they have won the African Nations Cup only once, in 1976. Mustapha

Hadji is arguably their best-known player having starred with both Benfica and Deportivo de La Coruna.

NEW ZEALAND (Oceania): In a country where rugby union is king, the New Zealand football league is semi-professional. They have reached the World Cup finals only once, in 1982, but lost all three games.

NIGERIA (Africa): With a rich footballing pedigree, Nigeria has exported a string of exceptional players to Europe. Current squad members include Obefemi Martins and Mikel John Obi. The "Super Eagles" usually reach the World Cup finals though they missed out in 2006 when Angola qualified instead.

NORTHERN IRELAND (Europe): Fans still talk nostalgically about their heyday when they qualified for the 1982 World Cup, reaching the quarter-finals, having beaten hosts Spain. Norman Whiteside became the youngest-ever player in the finals, at 17 years 41 days. Billy Bingham, a player in the team who had also reached the quarter-finals in 1958, was the manager and led his country to the finals again in 1986, the smallest European nation to qualify twice.

NORTH KOREA (Asia): The North Koreans' shining moment came in the 1966 World Cup when they upset Italy 1-0 to gain a spot in the quarter-finals. There, they went 3-0 up against Portugal, but the brilliance of Eusébio and his four goals stopped the fairytale and the match ended with the Koreans down 5-3. They have never threatened a repeat; political isolation has cost their football dear.

NORWAY (Europe): The greatest moment in Norwegian football, a 2-1 win over Brazil in the 1998 World Cup, sparked wild scenes back home. Rosenborg, the country's leading club, have perennially competed in the Champions League but almost all of Norway's top players go abroad even though the domestic league is now professional.

PARAGUAY (South America): Although they reached the second round of the World Cup in 1986, 1998, and 2002, they have never advanced beyond that stage. They Won the Copa América 1953 and 1979.

PERU (South America): Peru's "golden generation" in the 1970s and early 1980s was highlighted by the skills of Teofilo Cubillas, who scored five goals in two different World Cup finals. Defender Hector Chumputaz was one of the first South American players to have one hundred international appearances.

POLAND (Europe): They have twice finished third in the World Cup in 1974 and 1982, thanks to talents of outstanding players such as Zbigniew Boniek and Grzegorz Lato. Goalkeeper Jan Tomaszewski, whose performance at Wembley in 1973 prevented England reaching the World Cup finals in West Germany, remains an icon..

QATAR (Asia): Opening up the domestic league to foreign players turned Qatar into an attractive and lucrative new destination for veteran stars. But Qatar's wealth has also been invested in a sports academy to help develop home-grown talent.

REPUBLIC OF IRELAND (Europe): The Irish enjoyed their most euphoric era under the guidance of Jack Charlton and his successor Mick McCarthy. They qualified for Euro 88, reaching the quarter-finals of the 1990 World Cup and making the last 16 at both the 1994 and 2002 World Cups. The side gets its strength from the fact that most of the squad star in the English Premier League.

ROMANIA (Europe): The national side contested the first World Cup in 1930, and their "golden generation," led by Gheorghe Hagi, reached the 1994 World Cup quarter-finals. Steaua Bucharest became the first Eastern European side to win the European Champions Cup in 1985. The domestic scene is dominated by the clubs from Bucharest, with Steaua and Dinamo holding 41 titles between them.

SAUDI ARABIA (Asia): Three-time Asian Cup champions, their former goalkeeper Mohamed Al-Deayea is the most capped international male footballer, with 181 appearances. Al-Hilal have won the league title 11 times since it began in 1972.

SCOTLAND (Europe): The first-ever international game took place between Scotland and England in 1872. The fixture remains one of football's fiercest rivalries. Scotland have never reached the second stage of an international tournament, despite a famous victory over the Netherlands in 1978. The "Old Firm," Celtic and Rangers, enjoy a near-monopoly on the Scottish Premier League Championship. In 1967, Celtic became the first British team to win the European Champions Cup. Scottish players and managers have contributed enormously to the English League, including Kenny Daglish and Graeme Sounness at Liverpool and Sir Alex Ferguson at Manchester United.

SENEGAL (Africa): This nation's team stunned the world by beating defending title-holders France in the 2002 World Cup on their way to becoming only the second African team to reach the tournament's quarter-finals.

SERBIA (Europe): They became a single footballing nation in 2006 after Montenegro gained independence. Serbia's most powerful clubs remain the ones that dominated within the original Yugoslavia—Partizan and Red Star, both from Belgrade.

ABOVE Kenny Dalglish, hero of Scotland and Celtic

GREAT NATIONS
REST OF THE WORLD

SLOVAKIA (Europe): Originally a member of FIFA in 1907, Slovakia rejoined in 1994 after the break-up of Czechoslovakia. But they have yet to qualify for an international tournament's final stages.

SLOVENIA (Europe): A decade after gaining independence from Yugoslavia, Slovenia reached its first finals in the 2000 European Championship and the 2002 World Cup. NK Maribor, which beat Villarreal to win the 2006 Intertoto Cup, hold the most Slovenian league titles, with seven.

SOUTH AFRICA (Africa): They will become the first African nation to host the World Cup finals in 2010. Re-admitted to world footballing bodies in 1990 after the end of apartheid, the national team won the African Cup of Nations in 1996 after stepping in at the last minute as hosts. South African players Benni McCarthy, Mark Fish, Lucas Radebe, and Quinton Fortune have been successful at European club level.

BELOW Trinidad's Dwight Yorke strikes for goal against Paraguay

SOUTH KOREA (Asia): With their semi-final appearance in 2002, South Korea recorded the best-ever performance by an Asian team in the World Cup. Traditionally strong in Asia, they won the first two Asian Cups. Manchester United's Park Ji-Sung is the most famous South Korean player in the world. Seongnam Ilhwa Chunma are the K-League's most successful team with seven championship trophies. Korean clubs have won the Asian Champions Cup seven times since 1985.

SWEDEN (Europe): World Cup runners-up as hosts in 1958, Sweden have also reached three other semi-finals, the most recent being third place in 1994. Swedish players have been successful across Europe, and Swede Sven-Göran Eriksson won the Italian title at Lazio before managing England to three successive quarter-finals. IFK Gothenburg are the leading domestic title-winners with 18, just ahead of Malmö on 15. IFK are also the only Swedish club to have won a European trophy, twice landing the UEFA Cup.

SWITZERLAND (Europe): One of Switzerland's major roles in the world game is off the pitch—hosting FIFA headquarters in Zurich and UEFA's headquarters near Geneva. Switzerland holds the dubious honor of being the only team to be eliminated from the World Cup (in 2006) in a penalty shoot-out without netting a single spot-kick. The domestic league is dominated by Grasshopper Club (27 titles) and the recently resurgent FC Zurich and FC Basel.

TOGO (Africa): Togo's first-ever appearance in the World Cup in 2006 was blighted by a dispute over player bonuses. The federation was subsequently fined by FIFA for "behavior unworthy of a participant in the World Cup."

Tragedy struck in 2007, when 20 members of their delegation to the African Cup of Nations qualifier, including the Sports Minister but not any players, were killed in a helicopter crash. They have never gone past the first stage of the African Cup of Nations.

TRINIDAD AND TOBAGO (Central and North America): Ex-Manchester United striker Dwight Yorke is such a hero in Tobago that the national stadium bears his name. Other notable players to have succeeded in England include goalkeeper Shaka Hislop, Stern John, and Kenwyne Jones. Trinidad and Tobago qualified for their first World Cup in 2006, where they were eliminated without scoring a goal.

TURKEY (Europe): Turkey's biggest footballing success came in the 2002 World Cup, where they finished third. Turkish teams have proved fearsome opposition in the UEFA Champions League, especially in their home legs, where an intimidating atmosphere is guaranteed. Hakan Sukur, scorer of the fastest-ever World Cup goal in 11 seconds in 2006, is Turkish football's top scorer. Only four clubs have won the Turkish top flight since 1959—Fenerbahce and Galatasaray (17 each), Besiktas (11), and Trabzonspor (six).

TUNISIA (Africa): Tunisia were the first African team to win a World Cup finals match, beating Mexico 3-1. They won the African Cup of Nations as host in 2004.

UKRAINE (Europe): Having provided some of the finest players to the Soviet Union national team for years, Ukraine reached the quarter-finals in their first World Cup as an independent nation, in 2006. Dynamo Kiev, the most successful Ukrainian team with 12 championships, were often the only challenger to Moscow clubs' domination during the Soviet era. Andriy Shevchenko and Sergei Rebrov spearheaded their European campaigns in the mid–late 1990s before the latter moved on to great success in Italy with AC Milan.

UNITED ARAB EMIRATES (Asia): The UAE has a lively and popular domestic league, dominated by Al-Ain FC, the first UAE winners of the Asian Champions Cup, in 2003. The national team's only appearance at a World Cup in 1990 ended in three defeats. Their one major international success was in winning the 2007 Gulf Cup of Nations.

UNITED STATES OF AMERICA (Central and North America): Though football struggles to compete with other American sports, the game is hugely popular with both young men and women. The US women's team are one of the most successful in the world, having won the inaugural Women's World Cup in 1991 and repeated the feat in 1999, thanks to key players such as Brandi Chastain and Mia Hamm. The men's professional domestic league, the MLS, has attracted European stars such as David Beckham.

URUGUAY (South America): The first hosts and first winners of the World Cup in 1930, Uruguay won the tournament again in 1950, but are no longer the international force they once were. Peñarol (36) and Nacional (30) have won the most national championships.

VENEZUELA (South America): Venezuela are the only member of the South American federation never to have qualified for the World Cup finals. Their best performance in the Copa America came when they reached the quarter-finals as hosts in 2007.

WALES (Europe): Few Welsh teams play in the English Football League. Cardiff City are the only non-English side to ever win the English FA Cup (in 1927) and they were runners-up to Portsmouth in 2008. Wales reached their only World Cup finals in 1958, with "Gentle Giant" John Carles, leading them to a quarter-final defeat against Brazil. Despite producing word-famous players in the 1980s and 1990s, they have failed to qualify for an international tournament since then.

ABOVE David Beckham turns on the style in the US for LA Galaxy

GREAT CLUBS

Club football provides the power base that keeps
supporters mesmerized across the world, week-in
and week-out. Initially, domestic leagues and cup
competitions provided the staple diet for fans, but
then the glamor of international competition provided
icing on the cake from the 1950s onwards. Nowadays,
international competition is crucial to the financial
health of many clubs, and provides the funds that keep
fans entertained with high-profile new signings.

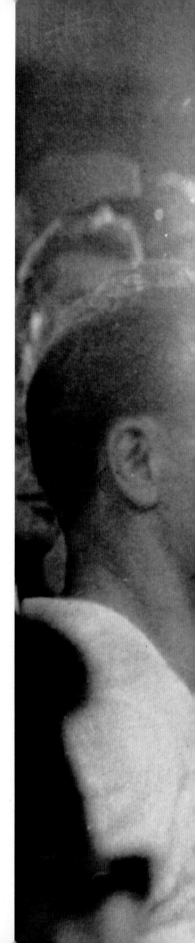

GREAT CLUBS
EUROPE

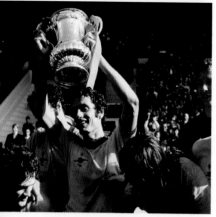

TOP Johan Cruyff, three times a European champion with Ajax

ABOVE Arsenal celebrate their 1971 FA Cup final victory

PAGE 120 Liverpool celebrate a goal in 2005

PAGE 121 Zarrago, Real Madrid's captain, holds aloft the European cup

AJAX AMSTERDAM (Holland)

Ajax reached their peak in the early 1970s, when they pioneered the style known as "Total Football" and won the European Champion Clubs' Cup three times in a row. Coach Rinus Michels painstakingly built the side, led by the legendary Johann Cruyff, for five years before their victories from 1971 to 1973. Cruyff was the coach when Ajax lifted their next European trophy, the Cup Winners' Cup, in 1987. The club's renowned youth system cultured another European Cup-winning side in 1995, which finished as runner-up the following season. But the effects of the "Bosman Rule" have diminished Ajax's power, and now their stars inevitably move to richer clubs abroad.
Titles: World Club Cup 1972, 1995; European Champions League 1971, 1972, 1973, 1995; UEFA Cup 1992; Cup Winners' Club Cup 1987; Dutch champions 29 times; Dutch cup 17

ARSENAL (England)

Arsenal became the dominant force in England in the 1930s. Manager Herbert Chapman created their first truly great side, which won four league titles in five seasons, including three in a row between 1933 and 1935. After two post-war titles, Arsenal went through a barren spell. Victory over Anderlecht in the 1970 Fairs Cup final brought their first trophy for 17 years. They won the domestic "double" the following season and star player George Graham later delivered two more titles as coach with a host of home-grown players. Long-serving manager Arsène Wenger imported a host of foreign players with a French connection. His rewards include two league and cup "doubles."
Titles: UEFA/Fairs Cup 1970; Cup Winners' Cup 1994; English champions 13 times; FA Cup 10; League Cup 2

ASTON VILLA (England)

Aston Villa were one of the 12 founding members of the Football League in 1888. They were a major force in its early years, winning five championships between 1894 and 1900 and the "double" in 1897. But after lifting the FA Cup in 1920, they went 37 years before gaining another major honor, beating Manchester United in the FA Cup final. Their most remarkable success was winning the European Cup in 1982. A quarter-final defeat by Juventus in 1983 signaled the start of a decline, and they were relegated in 1987. Aston Villa regained their elite status a season later. They finished league runner-up in both the 1988–89 and 1992–93 seasons.
Titles: European Cup 1982; English champions 7 times; FA Cup 7; League Cup 5

ATHLETIC MADRID (Spain)

Athletic Madrid have spent years playing second fiddle to neighbors Real Madrid, although they overshadowed their bitter rivals in the early 1950s, when master coach Helenio Herrera guided them to successive titles. Spanish champions in 1973, they came within a minute of winning the European Champion Clubs' Cup a year later. But were denied glory by a late equalizer that forced a replay, which Bayern Munich won 4-0. Athletic Madrid won the 1974 World Club Cup after Bayern Munich declined to compete. The club became synonymous with instability during the reign of president Jesus Gil, who hired and fired 23 different coaches between 1987 and 2003. They revived under Mexican coach Javier Aguirre, and in 2008 secured entry into the European Champions League for the first time in over a decade.
Titles: Intercontinental Cup 1974; Cup Winner's Cup 1962; Spanish champions 9 times; Spanish cup 9

BARCELONA (Spain)

Barcelona's motto is *"mas que un Clube,"* meaning "More than a Club," and they have long been a symbol for Catalonia's regional pride. Their bitter rivalry with Real Madrid is a key feature of Spanish football. Ronald Koeman's European Champion Clubs' Cup final winner against Sampdoria in 1992 healed Barcelona's wounded pride after so many disappointments in the competition, including defeats in the final to Benfica and Steaua Bucharest. Coach Johann Cruyff created the winning "Dream Team," featuring Koeman, Pep Guardiola, Hristo Stoichkov, and Michael Laudrup—which many regard as Barcelona's best-ever team. Frank Rijkaard, Cruyff's protege, later crafted the 2005–06 side that beat Arsenal 2-1 in the UEFA Champions League final and won La Liga. Ronaldinho and Samuel Eto'o were the stars. Rijkaard failed to win a trophy for two years, which cost him his job at the end of the 2007–08 season. Such are Barcelona's high expectations.

Titles: European Champions' Club Cup 1992, 2006; UEFA/Fairs Cup 1958, 1960, 1966; Cup Winner's Cup 1979, 1982, 1989, 1997; Spanish champions 18 times; Spanish cup 24

BAYERN MUNICH (Germany)

Bayern Munich succeeded Ajax as the dominant team in Europe in the mid-1970s, winning the UEFA Champions Club Cup three times in a row. The great Franz Beckenbauer was their conductor, supported by prolific striker Gerd Müller, and goalkeeper Sepp Maier. But Bayern came within a minute of losing the 1974 final to Athletic Madrid, before Georg Schwarzenbeck leveled. They won the replay 4-0. A year later they beat Leeds United 2-0 in the final and they completed their trio with a 1-0 win over Saint-Etienne. Bayern added a fourth Champions Club Cup triumph in 2001, when goalkeeper Oliver Kahn defied Valencia in a penalty shoot-out. Bayern have dominated the Bundesliga for nearly 40 years, winning 20 championships to add to their all-German title of 1932.

Titles: Intercontinental Cup 1976, 2001; European Champions League 1974, 1975, 1976, 2001; UEFA Cup Winners' Cup 1967; UEFA Cup 1996; German champions 21 times; German cup 14

BENFICA (Portugal)

Benfica fans look back on the 1960s as their club's golden years. They succeeded Real Madrid as European champions by beating Barcelona 3-2 in the 1961 final, then retained the European Champion Clubs' Cup with a 5-3 win over Real Madrid. Benfica also reached the final in 1963, 1965, and 1968 and supplied the bulk of the Portugal side that finished third in the 1966 World Cup finals. Benfica's hero was the great striker Eusébio. The team was packed with internationals, with Mario Coluna pulling the strings in midfield. Benfica lost in recent finals to PSV Eindhoven, on penalties in 1988, and AC Milan in 1990. They have since faded as a European power and been eclipsed at home by Porto and Sporting Lisbon.

Titles: European Champion Clubs' Cup 1961, 1962; Portuguese champions 31 times; Portuguese cup 24

BELOW Henrik Larsson, Carles Puyol and Ronaldinho take the Champions League Cup by tickertape storm in 2006

GREAT CLUBS
EUROPE

BORUSSIA DORTMUND (Germany)

Borussia Dortmund became the first West German team to lift a European trophy after they beat Liverpool in the 1966 Cup Winners' Cup final. But their greatest day came in 1997, when Ottmar Hitzfeld's side stunned Juventus 3-1 in the UEFA Champions League final. Hitzfeld had brought back Matthias Sammer, Andy Möller, Jürgen Koller, and Stefan Reuter from Italy to form the core of the team. Five years later, Borussia Dortmund won the Bundesliga and reached the UEFA Cup final, losing to Feyenoord Rotterdam. They came perilously close to bankruptcy in 2005.

Titles: Intercontinental Cup 1997; UEFA Champions League 1997; UEFA Cup Winners' Cup 1966; German champions 6 times; German cup 2

CELTIC (Scotland)

Celtic were the first British club to win the European Champion Clubs' Cup when they beat Internazionale 2-1 in the 1967 final at Lisbon. The team were then known as the "Lisbon Lions," and were all born within a 30-mile radius of Glasgow. Celtic also reached the final in 1970. They were managed by Jock Stein, and included outstanding figures such as Tommy Gemmell, Billy McNeill, Bobby Murdoch, and Jimmy Johnstone. That team began to break up after losing the 1974 European Cup semi-final to Athletic Madrid. But they still set a domestic record of nine consecutive championships. Celtic revived memories of those glory days with a run to the 2003 UEFA Cup final. Their fierce rivalry with Rangers dominates.

Titles: European Champions Clubs' Cup 1967; Scottish champions 41 times; Scottish Cup 31; League Cup 13

CHELSEA (England)

Chelsea's recent transformation into a European power has been bankrolled by Russian oil billionaire Roman Abramovich, the club's owner since 2003. His appointment of Portugal's Jose Mourinho as manager a year later galvanized the club. Mourinho spent heavily to win the Premier League and the League Cup, and delivered another league title in 2006. He left Chelsea in September 2007, despite guiding them to FA Cup and League Cup victories, after falling out with Abramovich. Israeli Avram Grant then took Chelsea to their first UEFA Champions League final, but was sacked after their shoot-out defeat by Manchester United. Chelsea, as 1955 league champions, had been the first English team invited to play in the European Cup but declined, following pressure from the Football League.

Titles: UEFA Cup Winners' Cup 1971, 1998; English champions 3 times; FA Cup 4; League Cup 4

DYNAMO KIEV (Ukraine)

Dynamo Kiev were the first club from the former Soviet Union to win a European trophy when they beat Hungary's Ferencváros in the 1975 European Cup Winners' Cup final. They saw off Athletic Madrid 3-0 to win the same competition 11 years later. The Ukrainians led non-Russian opposition to the Moscow clubs during the Soviet era, winning 13 championships and nine cup finals. They are seasoned UEFA Champions League competitors, despite normally needing to start in the qualifying stages, and reached the semi-final stage in 1999. Andriy Shevchenko was their inspiration with eight goals, earning him a lucrative move to AC Milan.

Titles: European Cup Winners Cup 1975, 1986; Soviet champions 13 times; Ukrainian champions 12 times; Soviet cup 9; Ukrainian cup 9

BELOW Barcelona's Thierry Henry fails to breach Celtic's defense

EVERTON (England)

Everton, formed in 1878, were founder members of the Football League, and one of its most successful clubs for many years. They reached their peak under Howard Kendall in the mid-1980s. They won the FA Cup in 1984, the league title (ahead of their great rivals, Liverpool) and the UEFA Cup Winners' Cup a year later, and added another title in 1987. In between, they finished as runner-up to Liverpool in the league and FA Cup. However, the ban on English clubs after the Heysel Stadium disaster denied Everton the chance to build on their European success, and eventually the team broke up. A string of managers struggled to rebuild the club in the years that followed, before David Moyes steered Everton to a UEFA Champions League qualifying place in 2005. The 2-0 win over Manchester United in the 1995 FA Cup remains their last major honor.
Titles: UEFA Cup Winners' Cup 1985; English champions 9 times; FA Cup 5

FEYENOORD ROTTERDAM (Holland)

Feyenoord Rotterdam became the first Dutch team to win the European Champions Club Cup when they beat Celtic 2-1 after extra time in 1970 in Milan. Four years later, they lifted the UEFA Cup after drawing with Tottenham in the first leg in London and winning the return 2-0. Three of that victorious side, Wim Rijsbergen, Wim Jansen, and Wim Van Hanegem, played for Holland in the 1974 World Cup final. Following almost 20 years without further European success, Feyenoord Rotterdam were surprise UEFA Cup winners in 2002, beating Borussia Dortmund 3-2. They have failed to make any impact in Europe since, and have not won the Dutch title since 1999. Instead, they have become a supplier of stars, including talents such as Robin van Persie, Dirk Kuyt, Salomon Kalou, and Royston Drenthe to clubs in richer leagues.
Titles: Intercontinental Cup 1970; European Champion Clubs' Cup 1970; UEFA Cup 1974, 2002; Dutch champions 14 times; Dutch cup 11

INTERNAZIONALE (Italy)

Internazionale were a dominant world power in the mid-1960s. They defeated Real Madrid 3-1 in the 1964 European Champion Clubs' Cup final and beat Benfica 1-0 a year later. But they lost the 1967 final against Celtic. However, coach Helenio Herrera was criticized for his defensive tactics and they were an unpopular side with neutral spectators, despite fielding greats such as full back Giacinto Facchetti, midfielder Luis Suarez, and attacker Sandro Mazzola. Internazionale reached another UEFA Champions Club Cup final in 1972, when they were swept aside by Ajax. They won only two domestic championships between 1972 and 2005. Internazionale have collected the past three Serie A titles, but have yet to reach the semi-final stage of the UEFA Champions League.
Titles: Intercontinental Cup 1964, 1965; European Champion Clubs' Cup 1964, 1965; UEFA Cup 1991, 1994, 1998; Italian champions 16 times; Italian cup 5

JUVENTUS (Italy)

Juventus boast an enviable record of appearing in the final of seven UEFA Champions League. The tragedy of the Heysel Stadium disaster dwarfed their first success, when Michel Platini's goal edged out Liverpool in the 1985 final. They won again in 1996, when Marcello Lippi's team beat Ajax Amsterdam on penalty kicks. Juventus have also lost finals to Ajax, Hamburg SV, Borussia Dortmund, Real Madrid, and AC Milan. They have amassed a record number of Italian titles, but recent successes have been dogged by controversy. Their three title wins between 1995 and 1998 were the subject of a doping enquiry. In 2006, Juventus were stripped of their 2005 and 2006 Serie A titles following a match-fixing scandal. The punishment included relegation, sending them to Serie B for the first time. Despite a 30-point deduction, they won promotion.
Titles: Intercontinental Cup 1985, 1996; European Champions Clubs' Cup 1985, 1996; Cup Winners' Cup 1984; UEFA/Fairs Cup 1977, 1990, 1993; Italian champions 27 times; Italian cup 9

ABOVE Alessandro Del Piero of Juventus celebrates a goal against Celtic in 2001

GREAT CLUBS
EUROPE

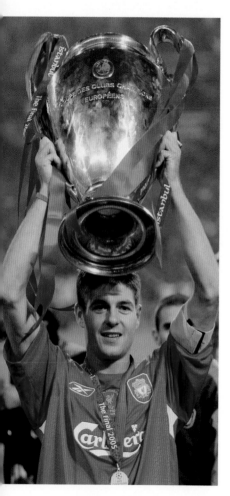

ABOVE Liverpool captain Steven Gerrard lifts the 2005 European Cup in Istanbul

LIVERPOOL (England)

Liverpool are the most successful English club in European competitions. They have won the European Cup Winners' Cup five times, the UEFA Cup three times, and have a hat-trick of European Super Cup prizes. Liverpool reached two other European Cup finals and may well have added more appearances to the list, but for the ban imposed on English clubs after the Heysel Stadium disaster. Liverpool changed their style in Europe after a home defeat by Red Star Belgrade and swiftly reaped the rewards from a more patient approach. Bob Paisley, who succeeded Bill Shankly, was the architect of their success. He steered Liverpool to a hat-trick of triumphs in the European Cup Winners' Cup—1977, 1978, and 1981—before handing over to Joe Fagan for their 1984 triumph. The Steven Gerrard-inspired comeback known as "the Miracle of Istanbul" brought Liverpool their fifth European Cup Winners' Cup in 2005. Paisley's team dominated in England as well as Europe. Such stars as Kenny Dalglish, Alan Hansen, Ian Rush, Graeme Souness, and Phil Thompson helped Liverpool to win a total of 18 championships—an English record. They have not won the league since 1990, and ending that run has become the club's priority.
Titles: European Champion Clubs' Cup 1977, 1978, 1981, 1984, 2005; UEFA Cup 1973, 1976, 2001; European Super Cup 1977, 2001, 2005; English champions 18 times; FA Cup 7; League Cup 7

LYON (France)

Lyon have monopolized French football since 2002. They have won the past seven championships, a domestic record. In 2008, they completed a league and cup "double." The 2002 title was Lyon's first, and a realization of the dreams of Jean-Michel Aulas, club president since 1987. Now Aulas, a computer software millionaire, is chasing an even bigger prize: the European Champions League. He has employed a succession of top French coaches—Jacques Santini, Paul Le Guen, Gerard Houllier, and Alain Perrin—who have all delivered championships. But Lyon have yet to advance beyond the quarter-final stage in European competitions except in the 1997 Intertoto Cup, which they won. One of their biggest problems is that they keep losing key players to UEFA Champions League rivals, such as Michael Essien to Chelsea and Mohamadou Diarra to Real Madrid. Striker Karim Benzema is the latest outstanding player off their production line.
Titles: Intertoto Cup 1997; French champions 7 times; French cup 4

MANCHESTER CITY (England)

Life has rarely been dull for fans at Maine Road or the new City of Manchester Stadium. Manchester City's recent history has seen them suffer the indignity of dropping into the second division before climbing back to the Premier League. They were relegated again, only for Kevin Keegan to lead them up again in 2002. Keegan, Stuart Pearce, Sven-Göran Eriksson, and Mark Hughes have each been in charge since their return to the big time. In the 1980s, they had seven bosses in ten years but Manchester City were at their best in the late 1960s. Manager Joe Mercer and assistant Malcolm Allison guided them to the championship in 1968, the FA Cup in 1969 and the European Cup Winners' Cup and League Cup the next season.
Titles: European Cup Winner's Cup 1970; English champions 2; FA Cup 4; League Cup 2

MANCHESTER UNITED (England)

Scottish managers have crafted Manchester United's post-war achievements. Sir Matt Busby built the team known as "the Busby Babes" who won two championships and reached the European Champion Clubs' Cup semi-finals twice, before being torn apart by the Munich air disaster in 1958. Busby went on to create another great side—featuring Bobby Charlton, Denis Law, and George Best—that won two more championships. They became the first English team to lift the European Champions' Club Cup, ten years after Munich. Sir Alex Ferguson then achieved greatness in his own style after delivering Manchester United's first league title for 26 years in 1993. His sides have dominated the lucrative Premier League era, claiming 10 of the 16 titles. They have added two UEFA Champions League triumphs—in 1999 and 2008. Manchester United's astonishing late rally, capped by Ole Gunnar Solskjaer's winner, pipped Bayern Munich in the 1999 final and gave the club a unique "treble", adding to the prizes of the Premier League and FA Cup. Nine years later, United keeper Edwin van der Sar held his nerve in the final shoot-out against Chelsea after Cristiano Ronaldo's goals had propelled Manchester United to another domestic league title.

Titles: Intercontinental Cup 1999; European Champion Clubs' Cup 1968, 1999, 2008; UEFA Cup Winners' Cup 1991; English champions 17 times; FA Cup 11; League Cup 2

AC MILAN (Italy)

AC Milan come second only to Real Madrid in terms of UEFA Champions League success, having captured the prize seven times and appeared in four other finals. They first lifted it in 1963 by deposing holders Benfica 2-1, and six years later crushed Ajax Amsterdam 4-1. They had to wait 20 years for their next victory, when the Dutch trio of Ruud Gullit, Frank Rijkaard, and Marco Van Basten inspired Arrigo Sacchi's cultured side to a 4-0 win over Steaua Bucharest. AC Milan triumphed again in 1994, tearing Barcelona apart 4-0. Defeat by Ajax Amsterdam the following

year signaled the end of an era. The Dutchmen had already gone, but two defenders remained who would star in the next decade—Alessandro Costacurta and Paolo Maldini. AC Milan edged past Juventus on penalty kicks in 2003, then lost one of the most dramatic finals in 2005, after leading Liverpool 3-0 but were defeated on penalty kicks. They gained revenge on Liverpool two years later, when they won 2-1 and Maldini collected his fifth winners medal in the UEFA Champions League.

Titles: Intercontinental Cup 1969, 1989, 1990, 2007; European Champion Clubs' Cup 1963, 1969, 1989, 1990, 1994, 2003, 2007; European Cup Winners' Cup 1968, 1973; Italian champions 17 times; Italian cup 5

OLYMPIQUE MARSEILLE (France)

Olympique Marseille's greatest achievement also led to their greatest crisis. They became the only French team to have won the UEFA Champions League, when they saw off AC Milan in the 1993 final. But Valenciennes defender Jacques Glassmann alleged that Marseille's Jean-Jacques Eydelie had tried to bribe him and two other players to "go easy on them" in Marseille's last game before the final. The bribe attempt was

ABOVE Andrea Pirlo of AC Milan takes a free kick against Atalanta in 2008

GREAT CLUBS MOMENTS

1960s

ABOVE Tottenham's Jimmy Greaves shoots for goal against Burnley

BELOW Celtic keeper Ronnie Simpson defies Internazionale in Lisbon

1970s

ABOVE Zico (left) is a legendary figure for Flamengo and Brazil

LEFT Benfica's Portugal hero Eusébio bears down on goal

BELOW Manchester United parade the Champions Cup in 1968

1980s   2000s

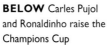

ABOVE Hugo Sanchez top-scored for Mexico, Real and Atletico Madrid

BELOW Alex (Santos) tackles Boca's Carlos Tevez

BELOW Carles Pujol and Ronaldinho raise the Champions Cup

RIGHT David Beckham takes to the wing for LA Galaxy

ABOVE Milan forward Kaka eludes Inter's Nelson Rivas

ABOVE RIGHT Etoile Sahel carry off the African Super Cup

GREAT CLUBS
EUROPE

traced back to Marseille's managing director Jean-Pierre Bernes and then to club president Bernard Tapie, who was jailed for his involvement. Olympique Marseille, who had won the previous five championships, were stripped of their 1993 crown and relegated to the second division. UEFA disqualified them from competing for a short period. The club reached the UEFA Cup final in 1999 and 2004, but the bribe scandal ended their recent glory days.
Titles: UEFA Champions League 1993; French champions 9 times; French cup 10

PORTO (Portugal)
Porto tasted glory under Jose Mourinho, as the new century unfolded. He steered them to the championship and a 2003 UEFA Cup final victory over Celtic. A year later, they were crowned champions of both Portugal and Europe. Mourinho's team destroyed AS Monaco 3-0 in the UEFA Champions League final, to deliver Porto's second such triumph. Mourinho then left for big-spending Chelsea, taking defensive duo Paulo Ferreira and Ricardo Carvalho with him. Porto have not advanced beyond the last 16 since. Their 2008 league title was their fifth in six seasons.
Titles: Intercontinental Cup 1987, 2004; European Champion Clubs' Cup 1987, 2004; UEFA Cup 2003; Portuguese champions 23 times; Portuguese cup 17

PSV EINDHOVEN (Holland)
PSV have overtaken Holland's former elite, Ajax Amsterdam and Feyenoord Rotterdam. They broke the dominance of the "Big Two" in the 1970s, when they won three championships in four seasons. They also snatched the UEFA/Fairs Cup in 1978 with a 3-0 aggregate win over Bastia. PSV Eindhoven's greatest moment came ten years later, when they beat Benfica on penalties in the European Champion Clubs' Cup final. The side have continued to challenge in the UEFA Champions League despite losing stars to England (Arjen Robben and Park Ji-Sung), Germany (Mark Van Bommel), and Spain (Arouna Kone). They lost on away goals to AC Milan in the 2005 semi-finals and reached the quarter-finals two years later.
Titles: European Champion Clubs' Cup 1988; UEFA Cup 1978; Dutch champions 21 times; Dutch cup 8

RANGERS (Scotland)
Rangers' run to the 2008 UEFA Cup final, which they lost 2-0 to Zenit St. Petersburg, marked the end of a 36-year gap since their last appearance in a European showpiece. In the previous final, they

BELOW Jorge Costa and Vitor Baia lead Porto's European victory parade in 2004

beat Dynamo Moscow 3-2 to lift the European Cup Winners' Cup—their only European prize. In 1961, Rangers had lost the first European Cup Winners' Cup final to Fiorentina. A year earlier, Rangers reached the UEFA Champions League semi-finals, but crashed 12-4 on aggregate to Eintracht Frankfurt. They made their biggest impact on the UEFA Champions League in 1993, when they finished a point behind winners Marseille in the last eight group stage. Rangers have won a record 51 Scottish League titles.

Titles: European Cup Winners' Cup 1972; Scottish champions 51 times; Scottish Cup 32; League Cup 25

REAL MADRID (Spain)

Real Madrid are the best known club in the world. They won each of the first five finals of the European Cup—defeating Reims twice, Fiorentina, AC Milan, and Eintracht Frankfurt—before the competition became known as the UEFA Champions League. The club was guided by visionary president Santiago Bernabeu, with the team ably led by the legendary Argentinian center forward Alfredo Di Stefano—who played in all five finals. The most renowned final was the 7-3 victory over Frankfurt in 1960, when Di Stefano hit a hat-trick and Hungary great Ferenc Puskás netted four goals. Winger Paco Gento was the only attacking link with that golden past when Real Madrid's new-look team edged Partizan Belgrade 2-1 to win the trophy again, six years later. They had to wait until 1998 for their next success, when Predrag Mijatovic scored the clincher against Juventus. Vicente Del Bosque revived past glories, steering Real Madrid to victories in 2000 and 2002. He was sacked after their 2003 semi-final, and club president Florentino Perez put together a star-studded side with the top players known as "Galacticos." Since Del Bosque's departure, Real Madrid reached the quarter-final stage just once.

Titles: Intercontinental Cup 1960, 1998, 2002; European Champion Clubs' Cup 1956, 1957, 1958, 1959, 1960, 1966, 1998, 2000, 2002; UEFA Cup 1985, 1986; Spanish champions 32 times; cup 17

AS ROMA (Italy)

AS Roma have enjoyed their most successful decade recently. They won Serie A in 2001 and have finished runner-up five times in the past seven years. They have also reached the UEFA Champions League quarter-finals in each of the past two campaigns. The fulcrum of AS Roma's success has been Francesco Totti, who holds the records for games and goals.

Titles: UEFA/Fairs Cup 1961; Italian champions 3 times; Italian cup 9

TOTTENHAM HOTSPUR (England)

Tottenham Hotspur became the first English club to win a European trophy when they beat Athletic Madrid 5-1 in the 1963 European Cup Winners' Cup final. The team, built by Bill Nicholson and skippered by Danny Blanchflower, are considered Tottenham's best ever. They won the first league and cup "double" of the 20th century in 1961, collecting the FA Cup again the following season, and reaching the European Champion Clubs' Cup semi-final Tottenham have added two UEFA Cup victories to their European honors.

Titles: European Cup Winner's Cup 1963; UEFA Cup 1972, 1984; English champions 2 times; FA Cup 8; League Cup 4

BELOW Tottenham Hotspurs' double-winning players enjoy their open-top bus parade in 1961

GREAT CLUBS
SOUTH AMERICA

ABOVE Juan Román Riquelme, a latter-day hero for Boca Juniors

BOCA JUNIORS (Argentina)

No South American club has won more international titles than the Argentinian club from La Bombonera, the Buenos Aires stadium whose affectionate nickname translates as "The Chocolate Box." Their "*Superclásico*" rivalry with River Plate is one of the fiercest in the world, with Boca Juniors' supporters considering themselves as the city's working-class underdogs. Diego Maradona spent a title-winning season with the club before leaving for Spain in 1982, before coming back 13 years later. Juan Román Riquelme, was a modern-day heir whose return for a second spell led to Copa Libertadores glory in 2007.
Titles: World Club Cup 1977, 2000, 2003; Copa Libertadores 1977, 1978, 2000, 2001, 2003, 2007; Copa Sudamericana 2004, 2005; Argentine league 23 times

COLO COLO (Chile)

The "Snow Whites" of Santiago became the first, and so far only, Chilean club to win the Copa Libertadores—the South American equivalent of the UEFA Champions League—in 1991 when they beat Paraguay's Olimpia Asuncion 3-0 on aggregate. They are Chile's most successful club, with 41 domestic trophies and the only club to have contested every season without relegation since the league was founded in 1933.
Titles: Copa Libertadores 1991; Chilean league 24 times; cup 14

FLAMENGO (Brazil)

Flamengo began life in 1895 as a rowing club but embraced football 16 years later, after a breakaway by aggrieved members of neighboring Fluminense. They have since become Brazil's best-loved club, with an estimated fanbase of 40 million. Though, it was not until the late 1970s and early 1980s that they extended their domestic brilliance to the international arena. Zico was voted Man of the Match as Flamengo trounced Liverpool 3-0 in the 1981 Intercontinental Cup.
Titles: Intercontinental Cup 1981; Copa Libertadores 1981; Brazilian league 4 times, cup 2

INDEPENDIENTE (Argentina)

Years of decline and debts forced Independiente to sell wonder-kid Sergio Agüero to Athletic Madrid for $34m (£17m) in 2006, yet the club's history is perhaps as glorious as any in Argentina—including a record seven Copa Libertadores titles. These include four in a row between 1972 and 1975 that were inspired by midfielder Ricardo Bochini, who played for 20 years with the club. They have also been home to the World Cup-winning trio of Daniel Bertoni, Jorge Burruchaga and Oscar Ortiz.
Titles: Intercontinental Cup 1973, 1984; Copa Libertadores 1964, 1965, 1972, 1973, 1974, 1975, 1984; Argentine league 14 times

PENAROL (Uruguay)

Uruguay's most prestigious club provided the two scorers when Brazil were amazingly beaten in the 1950 World Cup finals, namely Alcides Ghigghia and Juan Schiaffino. At times in the 1960s, Peñarol could even outshine Pelé and Santos, including a 5-0 win in 1963, featuring a hat-trick by Alberto Spencer. He remains the all-time top scorer in the Copa Libertadores, leading the Montevideo club to three of their five triumphs. Peñarol have been crowned World Club champions three times.
Titles: Intercontinental Cup 1961, 1966, 1982; Copa Libertadores 1960, 1961, 1966, 1982, 1987; Uruguayan league 36 times

RIVER PLATE (Argentina)

Along with Buenos Aires arch rivals Boca Juniors, River Plate remain one of Argentina's biggest, best-supported teams. Their formidable five-man forward line of the early 1940s was dubbed "*La Máquina*" (The Machine) but a sixth striker that decade was perhaps their greatest of all, Alfredo Di Stefano. Argentina's 1978 World Cup-winning captain Daniel Passarella spearheaded a club revival in the 1970s, before boyhood fan Hernan Crespo shot to fame at the Estadio Monumental in the 1990s. 1986 was a perfect year for River hinchas, not only were Argentina crowned World Champions, but River captured the league, the Copa Libertadores and the World Club Cup, beating Steaua Bucharest.

Titles: World Club Cup 1986; Copa Libertadores 1986, 1996; Supercopa Sudamericana 1997; Copa Interamericana 1987; Argentine league 32 times

SANTOS (Brazil)

For much of the 1960s, Santos were the side the whole world wanted to see—largely thanks to their iconic No10, Pelé. As well as clinching two world club titles beating Benfica and AC Milan, and several state championships, the Brazilian entertainers toured the world almost non-stop to play money-making exhibition matches for huge crowds. Pelé's departure in 1972 inevitably signaled an end to the glory days, and they had to wait until 2002 for their next Brazilian league title. In recent years the club has produced such young stars as Robinho, Elano, and Diego.

Titles: World Club Cup 1962, 1963; Copa Libertadores 1962, 1963; Copa CONMEBOL 1998; Brazilian champions 2 times

SÃO PAULO (Brazil)

Brasilia is the country's capital, Rio's clubs have the most fervent support, and neighbors Santos boasted Pelé, but São Paulo can claim to be Brazil's most successful club. Leonidas da Silva in the 1940s, Gerson in the 1970s, Careca in the 1980s and more recently Kaka have contributed to their collection of domestic and world titles.

Their Copa Libertadores win in 2005 made them the first Brazilian club to claim a hat trick of titles, and the first team to beat a side from the same country in the final, Atletico Paranaense.

Titles: World Club Cup 1992, 1993, 2005; Copa Libertadores 1992, 1993, 2005; Copa CONMEBOL 1994; Recopa Sudamericana 1993, 1994; Supercopa Sudamericana 1993; Brazilian champions 5 times

VASCO DA GAMA (Brazil)

Vasco da Gama was founded in 1898 by Portuguese immigrants, they take their name from the revered Portuguese explorer of the 14th and 15th centuries, and call for much of their support on Rio's Portuguese communities. World Cup-winning striker Romario started his career at Vasco in 1985 and retired in 2008 after his fourth term at the club, which included the goal he claimed was the 1,000th of his career. But his 316 goals for Vasco da Gama were less than half the tally of their leading goalscorer, Roberto Dinamite. He scored 698 in 1,110 games between 1971 and 1993. Vasco has not won the league since 2000.

Titles: Copa Libertadores 1998; Brazilian champions 4 times

BELOW Pelé takes aim for Santos in 1973

GREAT CLUBS
REST OF THE WORLD

ABOVE Jaime Moreno of DC United looks for an opening against the New York Red Bulls

AL-AHLY (Egypt)

Little wonder the Cairo side were named in 2000 as the Confederation of African Football's club of the century. Egypt's so-called "People's Club" has won a record five African club championships, and a major haul of domestic titles. They even managed to remain unbeaten from 1974 to 1977. The "Red Devils," whose former players include Egypt's record scorer Hossam Hassan, have a ferocious rivalry with city rivals Zamalek. Foreign referees are often asked to handle their turbulent derby games.

Titles: African Champions League 1982, 1987, 2001, 2005, 2006; African Cup Winners' Cup 1984, 1985, 1986, 1993; African Super Cup 2005; Arab Champions Cup 1996; Arab Cup Winners' Cup 1994; Arab Super Cup 1997, 1998; Egyptian league 33 times, Egyptian cup 35

CLUB AMERICA (Mexico)

Club America have been Mexico's big spenders since a 1959 takeover by television giant Televisa. Until recent years at least, such power guaranteed success, including a record five crowns as CONCACAF Champions (the same number won by rivals Cruz Azul) and ten league titles (Chivas have won 11 championships). Big-name foreign imports have included Argentina's Oscar Ruggeri, Chilean Ivan Zamorano, and Romania's Ilie Dumitrescu. But they have also developed home-grown talent such as Mexican playmaker Cuauhtemoc Blanco. Club America play at the 114,465-capacity Azteca in Mexico City, the only stadium to have hosted two World Cup finals.

Titles: CONCACAF Champions Cup 1978, 1987, 1991, 1993, 2006; CONCACAF Cup Winners' Cup 2001; Copa Interamericana 1978, 1991; Mexican league 10 times, Mexican cup 5

DC UNITED (United States)

Captain John Harkes, returning home from the English Premier League, and coach Bruce Arena led the Washington DC-based club to the first two MLS titles in 1996 and 1997. They also became the first US club to win the CONCACAF Champions' Cup in 1998. But trophies have proved harder to come by since Arena left to become national coach in 1998, despite high-profile signings such as iconic Hristo Stoichkov and Freddy Adu—who made his debut aged 14.

Titles: CONCACAF Champions Cup 1998; Copa Interamericana 1998; US MLS Cup four times; US Open Cup 1

ETOILE SAHEL (Tunisia)

Tunisia may have underachieved internationally, with only one African Cup of Nations triumph. But their oldest club has proved the pride of a nation, with impressive performances in all CAF competitions. Dynamic young striker Armine Chermiti helped them achieve surprise Champions League glory in 2007. Victory over holders Al-Ahly, made them the first club to have, won each of the African Federation's Club trophies.

Titles: African Champions League 2007; CAF Cup 2006; African Cup Winners' Cup 1997, 2003; African Super Cup 1998, 2008; Tunisian league 8; President's Cup 7; League Cup 1

LOS ANGELES GALAXY (United States)

LA Galaxy pulled off the most high-profile signing in MLS history when world superstar and England's iconic David Beckham joined from Real Madrid in 2007. Another great, Holland's Ruud Gullit, was then appointed LA Galaxy coach after a disappointing first season for Beckham. The midfielder's arrival helped the club sell 700 times

as many replica shirts as before, and inspire hope among directors and fans that they might win the CONCACAF Champions League Cup for a second time. Long-serving Cobi Jones was among the scorers when they won in 2000.
Titles: CONCACAF Champions Cup 2000; US Open Cup 2

KAIZER CHIEFS (South Africa)
Kaizer Chiefs, one of South Africa's first professional clubs, take their name from the former international midfielder, Kaizer Motaung. He co-founded the club in 1970 after returning from a spell in the US. He has since served them as a player, in three separate stints as coach, and now as club president. The Chiefs passionately contest the Soweto derby with Orlando Pirates, another of Motaung's old teams. Their home at Johannesburg's FNB Stadium is being rebuilt as Soccer City to host the 2010 World Cup final.
Titles: African Cup Winners' Cup 2001; South African league 2

POHANG STEELERS (South Korea)
Pohang Steelers dominated in the 1970s and 1980s, then suffered a 15-year barren spell in the K-League until their 2007 title triumph. In 1997, they became the third South Korean team to win the Asian Champions League by beating compatriots and defending champions Seongham Ilhwa Chunma. They retained the trophy the following year against China's Dalian Wanda. Crucial to their success in the 1990s was reliable center back Hong-Myung Bo, who went on to become his country's most-capped player.
Titles: Asian Champions League 1997, 1998; South Korean league 3; South Korean cup 1

UNAM PUMAS (Mexico)
UNAM Pumas, the club affiliated to Latin America's largest university, has long put a useful emphasis on youth and proudly produced Mexican legends such as Luis Garcia, Jorge Campos, and Hugo Sanchez. The inspirational striker scored 96 goals for UNAM Pumas from

1976 to 1981, then returned as coach 19 years later, guiding the club to four trophies in 2004. Characterful goalkeeper Campos loved to roam upfield but also occasionally played in attack with 35 goals to his credit in 199 games. UNAM Pumas' home in Mexico City was the main venue for the 1968 Olympics Games.
Titles: CONCACAF Champions Cup 1980, 1982, 1989; Copa Interamericana 1981; Mexican league 5, Mexican cup 1

URAWA RED DIAMONDS (Japan)
Urawa Red Diamonds, won four league titles and four Emperor's Cups before the Japanese game turned professional in 1993. They made a bad start in the J.League, finishing bottom in the first two seasons. The team nicknamed "The Nearly Men" lived up to their image by just missing out on the 2004 and 2005 titles. But they finally sparkled, to become J.League champions in 2006 and win the Asian Champions League in 2007. Star players have included Japanese midfielder Shinji Ono and Brazilian striker Edmundo.
Titles: Asian Champions League 2007; Japanese league 5; Emperor's Cup 6; J.League Cup 1

BELOW Urawa Reds Diamonds take the glory after their Asian Champions League triumph in 2007

GREAT PLAYERS & MANAGERS

Match and trophy-winning performances depend on a combination of teamwork and spirit from both the players and their managers. Even the stars that shine like no other—such as Stanley Matthews, Diego Maradona, Ronaldo, Pelé, and Zinedine Zidane—would have been unable to express their genius without a manager to guide them. Nowadays, players are not only chasing the ball but also the opportunities to earn fame, fortune, and even notoriety for their successes and failures, goals and gaffes.

MANAGERS

TOP Sir Matt Busby (right) admires George Best's European footballer prize

ABOVE Fabio Capello, star midfielder turned star manager

PAGE 136 Guus Hiddink trains his team in preparation for the 2008 UEFA European Championship.

PAGE 137 Thierry Henry playing for Arsenal against PSV Eindhoven

SIR MATT BUSBY (born 26 May 1909, died 20 January 1994)

Greatest success: European Champion Clubs' Cup 1968 (Manchester Utd)

Busby managed Manchester United between 1945 and 1969 and again for the 1970–71 season. He was responsible for creating the "Busby Babes" who won the league in both 1956 and 1957. After the 1958 Munich air crash in which 23 people died, including eight players, he built a new side with the survivors and new players such as George Best. Busby's crowning glory was the emphatic 4-1 defeat of Benfica in the European Champion Clubs' Cup final at Wembley in 1968.

FABIO CAPELLO (born 18 June 1946)

Greatest success: 1994 European Champions League (AC Milan)

The Italian was appointed England's coach in December 2007. He had previously won the league title with every club he had managed: AC Milan, Real Madrid, Roma, and Juventus. He also coached AC Milan to their masterful 4-0 thrashing of Johan Cruyff's Barcelona in the 1994 Champions League final.

BRIAN CLOUGH (born 21 March 1935, died 20 September 2004)

Greatest successes: 1979 and 1980 European Champion Clubs' Cups (Nottingham Forest)

Clough was the first manager since Herbert Chapman to win the Championship in England with two different clubs (Derby County and Nottingham Forest). He was an iconic if idiosyncratic manager who could draw the best out of problematic players. His outspoken manner did not always endear himself to players—he lasted only 44 days at Leeds United in 1974.

HERBERT CHAPMAN (born 19 January 1878, died 6 January 1934)

Greatest successes: 1924, 1925, 1931, and 1933 English league titles (Huddersfield Town and Arsenal)

Chapman is associated indelibly with Arsenal in the 1930s, but he made his name as a manager of Huddersfield Town in the 1920s. He laid out a five-year plan for success for Arsenal, which came to fruition exactly on schedule when his team won the 1930 FA Cup at the expense of his former club, Huddersfield Town. The victory laid the foundations for a decade in which Arsenal dominated English football.

VINCENTE FEOLA (born 1 November 1909, died 6 November 1975)

Greatest success: 1958 World Cup (Brazil)

Feola famously guided Brazil to their first World Cup triumph in Sweden, although he took some persuading from senior players to pick both Garrincha and Pelé in the middle of the tournament when they appeared to be floundering. Because of illness, Feola missed their successful defense of the World Cup in 1962. He returned for the luckless 1966 finals in England, when his side went out in the group stage. Feola finished with an outstanding career record of only losing six matches out of the 74 his team played.

SIR ALEX FERGUSON (born 31 December 1941)

Greatest successes: 1999 and 2008 European Champions League Club Cups (Manchester Utd)

Ferguson has become the most successful manager in the history of English football since he succeeded Ron Atkinson at Manchester United in 1986. Ferguson was lured south from Aberdeen, which he had famously guided to victory at the expense of Real Madrid in the European Cup Winners' Cup final. His success at United began with an FA Cup win in 1990, and included an incredible treble of winning the Champions League, Premier League, and FA Cup in 1999. Ferguson came close to a repeat of this feat in 2008, winning the Premier League title and the Champions League in the 50th anniversary year of the Munich air crash.

JOSEF "SEPP" HERBERGER (born 28 March 1897, died 20 April 1977)
Greatest success: 1954 World Cup (West Germany)
Herberger became manager of Germany in 1938 and used all his sports and political influence to try to keep his players away from the battle fronts during World War II. He returned as national manager after the war and won West Germany's first World Cup in 1954. The final was aptly labeled the "Miracle of Berne" after his team beat hot favorites Hungary 3-2.

HELENIO HERRERA (born 17 April 1910, died 9 November 1997)
Greatest successes: 1964 World and European Champion Clubs' Cups (Internazionale)
Herrera, known widely in his heyday simply as "HH," managed a number of top clubs and national teams (including Italy and Spain), winning 16 major trophies. Born in Morocco but brought up in Argentina, he played in France before concentrating on coaching in France, Spain, and Italy. Herrera pioneered the use of psychological motivational ploys and, more controversially, artificial substances.

GUUS HIDDINK (born 8 November 1946)
Greatest success: 1988 European Champion Clubs' Cup (PSV Eindhoven)
Hiddink, a former central defender who wound down his career in the North American Soccer League, sprang to prominence at PSV in the late 1980s as a manager. He enjoyed success in Spain with Real Madrid and Valencia before leading

South Korea to a fourth place finish in the 2002 World Cup. Hiddink had previously managed the Dutch national team at Euro '96 and led Australia to the finals of the 2006 World Cup for their first appearance in the tournament for 32 years. He then revitalized the Russian national team, guiding them to the semi-final stage of Euro 2008.

VALERI LOBANOVSKI (born 6 January 1939, died 13 May 2002)
Greatest successes: 1975 and 1986 European Cup Winners' Cups (Dynamo Kiev)
Lobanovski was a hero in the Ukraine before the collapse of the Soviet Union. He was the Dynamo Kiev manager for 15 years, twice winning the Cup Winners' Cup and also beating Bayern Munich to take the 1975 European Supercup. Lobanovski spent three spells managing the Soviet Union and also managed the Ukraine.

CÉSAR LUIS MENOTTI (born 5 November 1938)
Greatest success: 1978 World Cup (Argentina)
In 1978, the left-leaning César Luis Menotti made himself immune from action by the ruling military junta because he was busy leading Argentina to their first-ever World Cup success. Menotti believed in positive, attacking football, which set him at odds with other top Argentinian coaches of the era such as Juan Carlos Lorenzo and Osvaldo Zubeldía. Menotti quit after Argentina's shock second round group exit at the 1982 finals in Spain, suffering defeat at the hands of Brazil and Italy.

BOB PAISLEY (born 23 January 1919, died 14 February 1996)
Greatest successes: 1977, 1978, and 1980 European Champion Clubs' Cups (Liverpool)
Paisley stepped up, virtually unknown outside Anfield, from the role of assistant when Bill Shankly retired unexpectedly in 1974. During his nine years in charge, Paisley guided Liverpool to six league titles. Paisley remains the only man to have managed one club to three European Cups. He won 19 major titles in all.

ABOVE Sepp Herberger plots the "Miracle of Bern"

BELOW Sir Alex Ferguson makes a winning point in training

MANAGERS

VITTORIO POZZO (born 12 March 1886, died 21 December 1968)

Greatest successes: 1934 and 1938 World Cups, 1936 Olympic Games (Italy)

Pozzo, who was also a journalist, learned to love football during a period of study in England. In 1934 he had no doubts about using former Argentina internationals, such as Luis Monti and Raimundo Orsi, to strengthen his first World Cup-winning side. Ruthlessly, he then scrapped almost the entire team to build a new side for the 1938 competition. In between these triumphs, Pozzo guided Italy to gold medal success at the 1936 Olympic Games. Sadly, Pozzo retired in 1949 after the Superga air disaster wiped out the entire playing staff of Torino, around whom he was planning to build a team for the 1950 World Cup.

SIR ALF RAMSEY (born 22 January 1920, died 28 April 1999)

Greatest success: 1966 World Cup (England)

Ramsey shall always hold a special place in the hearts of England fans as the only manager to have brought the country success in a major competition. A year after his achievement, he was knighted. However, Ramsey was forced out in early 1974 because of England's unexpected failure to qualify for the World Cup finals in West Germany.

SIR BOBBY ROBSON (born 18 February 1933)

Greatest successes: 1978 FA Cup, 1981 UEFA Cup (Ipswich Town)

Robson was a managerial legend at Ipswich Town, where he remained for 13 years before his England call-up. At club level, Robson's side twice finished as runner-up in the league, but made amends by capturing the FA Cup in 1978 and lifting the UEFA Cup in 1981. Robson moved abroad to win league championships in both Holland and Portugal. He later took England to the brink of the 1990 World Cup final—they fell only in a penalty shoot-out to West Germany—before returning to club management.

ARRIGO SACCHI (born 1 April 1946)

Greatest successes: 1989 and 1990 European Champions League (AC Milan)

Sacchi never played football professionally but more than made up for that as a coach. "You don't need to have been a horse to become a successful jockey" was arguably one of his best quotes. He had been plucked from Serie B obscurity by Silvio Berlusconi, the new AC Milan owner, in the mid 1980s, and swiftly introduced a new, positive, and—most importantly—winning approach to the Italian game. AC Milan's squad was bursting with talent, including the trio of Dutchmen Ruud Gullit, Marco Van Basten, and Frank Rijkaard. His AC Milan successes led to an appointment as coach of Italy, who finished as runner-up to Brazil in the 1994 World Cup.

HELMUT SCHÖN (born 15 September 1915, died 23 February 1996)

Greatest success: 1974 World Cup (West Germany)

Under Schön's 14-year-leadership, West Germany won the World Cup on home territory in 1974, after finishing third at Mexico in 1970 and runner-up to England in 1966. West Germany hosted the World Cup finals as worthy winners of the 1972 European Championship under Schön. He is the only manager to have won both the World Cup and European Championship and the sole manager to hold the titles simultaneously.

BELOW Sir Alf Ramsey in training in 1974

BILL SHANKLY (born 2 September 1913, died 29 September 1981)
Greatest success: 1966 and 1973 English league titles, 1973 UEFA Cup (Liverpool)
Shankly is remembered by Liverpool fans as their greatest ever manager, his legend embellished by a string of witty one-liners such as: "some people believe football is a matter of life and death. I'm very disappointed with that attitude. I can assure you it is much, much more important than that." Liverpool had been a club stuck in the second division doldrums when Shankly took over in 1959, but he soon transformed it on and off the field, and developed a unique team spirit and identity that lives on to this day. He secured Liverpool's inaugural European trophy in 1973, courtesy of a UEFA Cup final victory over Borussia Mönchengladbach.

JOCK STEIN (born 5 October 1922, died 10 September 1985)
Greatest success: 1967 European Champion Clubs' Cup (Celtic)
Jock Stein was one of the most successful Scottish managers ever. Between 1965 and 1978, his Celtic side lifted the European Champion Clubs' Cup, ten Scottish League titles, eight Scottish Cups, and six Scottish League Cups. Stein's Celtic became the first British club to win the European Champion Clubs' Cup as a result of his "Lisbon Lions" defeating Internazionale in 1967 in Portugal. He took over the position of Scotland's manager in 1978, where he remained until he died of a heart attack just after his Scottish side had equalized against Wales and earned a place in the 1986 World Cup finals.

GIOVANNI TRAPATTONI
(born 17 March 1939)
Greatest success: 1985 European Champion Clubs' Cup (Juventus)
Giovanni Trapattoni is Italy's most successful club manager, winning seven Serie A titles and the European Cup. He and Germany's Udo Lattek are the only managers to have won all three major European club titles. He had a glittering career as an AC Milan defender, where he twice won the European Cup. Trapattoni has a wealth of experience, having coached both Milan clubs, Fiorentina, Juventus, Bayern Munich (twice), Benfica, Stuttgart, and Red Bull Salzburg, with an impressive record of ten domestic titles in four countries. He was also in charge of the Azzurri from 2000 to 2004, but his side struggled in both the 2002 World Cup finals and 2004 European Championship. In May 2008, he took over the reins of the Republic of Ireland.

ARSÈNE WENGER (born 22 October 1949)
Greatest successes: 1998 and 2002 English league and FA Cup doubles (Arsenal)
Arsène Wenger made a major contribution in transforming the English game after being brought in by Arsenal in 1996. He was comparatively unknown in England when he first arrived, despite being both successful and respected in France and Japan. Since then, Wenger has guided Arsenal to three league titles and four FA Cup triumphs, including league and cup doubles in 1998 and 2002. Remarkably, the 2003–04 season saw Wenger became the first manager in the English league to complete an entire league campaign unbeaten. He is the club's most successful and long-serving manager.

MARIO ZAGALLO (born 9 August 1931)
Greatest success: 1970 World Cup (Brazil)
Mario Zagallo is a Brazilian icon, having enjoyed a magnificent career in football, both as a player and a coach. He played as an industrious left winger in the World Cup-winning sides in 1958 and 1962, then graduated to manage the side in 1970, winning the 1970 finals in Mexico. With this victory, he became the first person to win the World Cup as both a player and a coach. His career with Brazil has continued in various roles, including the post of technical director at the 2006 World Cup finals. His Brazilian team won the World Cup in 1994 but finished as runner-up to France in the 1998 World Cup finals.

ABOVE Bill Shankly laid the foundations for the Liverpool revival

BELOW Arsène Wenger guided Arsenal to two domestic doubles

EUROPEAN PLAYERS

MARCO VAN BASTEN

(born 31 October 1964)

Holland: 58 games, 24 goals

Marco Van Basten scored one of the finest goals in international history when he volleyed home Holland's second in their victory over the Soviet Union in the final of the 1988 European Championship. The goal sealed Van Basten's reputation as one of the finest center forwards to grace European football, not only with Holland but also with top club sides Ajax Amsterdam and Milan. Injury forced his premature retirement.

FRANZ BECKENBAUER (born 11 September 1945)

West Germany: 103 games, 14 goals

Franz Beckenbauer is one of the few defenders guaranteed a place in any football hall of fame. Initially a playmaker, "The Kaiser" was converted into a creative sweeper by Yugolaslavian coach Tschik Cajkovski at Bayern Munich in the 1960s. He won every honor at domestic level and lifted the World Cup as the West German captain in 1974 and again as national coach in 1990. In recent years he has served as president of Bayern, as a member of the FIFA executive, and has chaired the organizing committee for the 2006 World Cup.

DAVID BECKHAM (born 2 May 1975)

England: 102 games, 17 goals

A boyhood Manchester United fan, David Beckham went on to win a historic treble with the club in 1999. He was subsequently sold to Real Madrid in 2003, winning the Spanish league in the last of his four seasons with the club, then joined LA Galaxy. Beckham played in three World Cup finals for England, which included a controversial sending off against Argentina in 1998.

GEORGE BEST (born 22 May 1946, died 25 November 2005)

Northern Ireland: 37 games, 9 goals

Best was arguably the greatest player never to have made an appearance in the World Cup finals. A magical talent, one of the most exciting to grace English football, he made his Manchester United debut as a winger aged 17 in 1963 and went on to win the European Champion Clubs' Cup in 1968 and two league titles, before being driven out of the British game by the pressures of his own fame. His greatest exploit was in United's 5-1 thrashing of Benfica in Lisbon in a European Champion Clubs Cup quarter-final in 1966. He was voted European Footballer of the Year in 1968.

LIAM BRADY (born 13 February 1956)

Republic of Ireland: 72 games, 9 goals.

Liam Brady was the commanding heart of Arsenal's midfield in the 1970s and won the

RIGHT George Best, both European Champion and European Footballer of the Year in 1968

FA Cup three times in a row. Regularly voted as Footballer of the Year in both England and the Republic of Ireland, he emigrated to Italy for a much-admired league title-winning stint with Juventus and further spells with Ascoli, Internazionale, and Sampdoria. He returned to England with West Ham United before retiring and later rejoining Arsenal as youth boss. Brady has joined his former boss at Juventus, Giovani Trapattoni, on the backroom staff of the rejuvenated Republic of Ireland squad.

SIR BOBBY CHARLTON

(born 11 October 1937)

England: 106 games, 49 goals

Bobby Charlton had just established himself in the Manchester United side when the squad was tragically torn apart by the 1958 Munich air crash—eight players died in the disaster. Charlton survived and helped lead the reconstruction of the devastated Manchester United side. Ten years later, he captained them to victory in the European Champion Clubs' Cup. He scored two goals in the 4-1 victory over Benfica in the final at Wembley Stadium. Two years earlier, Charlton's unerring shooting had helped fire England to their sole success as World Cup champions. He was briefly manager of Preston but returned to his beloved Manchester United as a director. He was knighted in 1994.

JOHAN CRUYFF (born 25 April 1947)

Holland: 48 games, 33 goals

Johan Cruyff, son of a cleaner at the Ajax Amsterdam offices, grew up to be the epitome of Holland's "Total Football" revolution, as well as being voted European Footballer of the Year three times in the 1970s. Ajax's unique style of play brought the club—and Cruyff—three successive victories in the European Champion Clubs' Cup. Cruyff, despite being the club's captain, was sold to Barcelona for the then world record of $1.85 million (£922,000) prior to the 1974 World Cup finals, where hosts West Germany edged past the Dutch 2-1 in the final. Cruyff controversially

refused to play in the 1978 World Cup finals in Argentina, because of the kidnap threats made to him and his family. Holland reached the semi-final stage, but critics believe that with his presence they could have returned from South America with the coveted Jules Rimet trophy. When he returned to Ajax as technical director, the side went on to win the 1987 European Cup Winners' Cup. He later managed Barcelona, who he guided to victory in the 1992 European Cup.

KENNY DALGLISH (born 4 March 1951)

Scotland: 102 games, 30 goals

Kenny Dalglish achieved a remarkable feat by winning league titles as both a player and a manager in England with Liverpool and in Scotland with Celtic. A nimble, quick-thinking forward, Dalglish moved from Glasgow to Anfield in 1978 as replacement at Liverpool for the legendary Kevin Keegan. He duly proved that he could fill the boots of the Kop hero—he was the club's leading scorer in his first season. After a glittering playing career for Liverpool, he successfully made the transition to managing the club in 1985, and became the only player-manager in modern times to steer his club to a domestic double in both league and FA Cup. His glittering career saw him equal the scoring record with Denis Law for Scotland, but he stands alone with the record for most appearances.

DIXIE DEAN (born 22 January 1907, died 1 March 1980)

England: 16 games, 18 goals

Dixie Dean remains the most prolific striker of English football after rattling home 60 goals in just 39 matches for Everton in the 1927–28 season. His record is virtually untouchable, but the center forward was merely taking advantage of a recent change to the offside law. Dean's incredible career total of 349 goals in 399 games helped Everton collect two league titles and one FA Cup. However, Dean only played 16 times for England, despite scoring 18 goals in those games.

BELOW Johan Cruyff, a club champion of Europe as both player and coach

GREAT PLAYERS & MANAGERS
EUROPEAN PLAYERS

ABOVE Just Fontaine in triumph after scoring four goals against West Germany in the 1958 World Cup

JUST FONTAINE (born 18 August 1933)
France: 21 games, 30 goals

Just Fontaine was a fast, brave center forward who wrote his name into World Cup history by scoring 13 goals for third-placed France in the 1958 finals—Fontaine scored in all six games. Fontaine, born in Morocco, was brought to France to play for Nice, with whom he won the French League title in 1956. He was then sold to the great Reims side that dominated French football at the time. In the 1957–58 season, his goals helped secure the double of the French League and cup for Reims. Fontaine only got his chance in the 1958 World Cup finals because Reims team-mate Rene Bliard was ruled out with an ankle injury. Fontaine's career was ended prematurely in 1961, because of two serious leg fractures. He won the domestic league four times and the French Cup twice.

FRANCISCO GENTO
(born 21 October 1933)
Spain: 43 games, 5 goals

"Paco" Gento set a record in 1966 when, as captain of Real Madrid, he collected a sixth European Champion Clubs' Cup Winner's medal. Gento, from Santander in northern Spain, was nicknamed "El Supersonico" for his electric pace on the left wing. His distracting effect created valuable extra space to assist the goal-scoring exploits of team-mates such as Alfredo Di Stefano and Ferenc Puskás. Gento was a key figure in Real Madrid's triumphs of the 1950s and 1960s, scoring 126 goals in 428 games over 18 years. He won the domestic league title 12 times, represented Spain in the 1962 and 1966 World Cup finals, and played a key role in the side that dominated the first five European Champion Clubs' Cup finals with successive victories in the late 1950s.

EUSÉBIO (born 25 January 1942)
Portugal: 64 games, 41 goals

Eusébio da Silva Ferreira, a Mozambican-born Portugese striker, was nicknamed the "Black Panther" for his valuable goals. He inspired Benifica to a 5-3 victory over Real Madrid in the Champion Clubs' Cup with Benfica in 1962, although his team could only finish as the runner-up in the same competition in 1963, 1965, and 1968. Over the 15 years Eusébio spent at Benfica, he won the Portuguese league title ten times. In the 1966 World Cup finals in England, he guided Portugal to third place and won the Golden Boot as top scorer in the competition with nine goals. His finest performance was in the memorable quarter-final against North Korea. The Koreans raced to a 3-0 lead before Eusébio came on and scored four goals to give his country a 5-3 victory.

RUUD GULLIT (born 1 September 1962)
Holland: 66 games, 17 goals
Ruud Gullit was hailed as Europe's finest player in the late 1980s, when he moved from Dutch football to help inspire a revival at AC Milan. Gullit, World Player of the Year in 1987 and 1989, was a favorite of AC Milan owner Silvio Berlusconi, winning two European Champion Clubs' Cups and three Italian league titles. He captained Holland in the 1988 European Championship, heading home the opening goal in the 2-0 victory over Russia in the final. He moved to Chelsea as a player and later became their coach—he was the first non-British manager to win the FA Cup. He subsequently had brief spells as manager of Newcastle United and Dutch giants Feyenoord.

GHEORGHE HAGI (born 5 February 1965)
Romania: 125 games, 35 goals
Gheorghe Hagi was nicknamed the "Maradona of the Carpathians" during the late 1980s because of his cultured left foot and silky skills. His huge self-confidence helped him to push forward from midfield to score goals, but his main strength lay in his skill and vision as a playmaker. Such outstanding talent earned special permission, in a restrictive political era, to move abroad to ply his trade. He played for Real Madrid, moved to Brescia in Italy, and then on to Barcelona before ending his career at Turkish side Galatasaray. Hagi was the fulcrum of the Romanian side that reached the quarter-final stage of the 1994 World Cup.

THIERRY HENRY (born 17 August 1977)
France: 100 games, 44 goals
Thierry Henry set a scoring record for Arsenal over eight seasons, proving to be a bargain signing even at $21 million (£10.5 million) when he was bought from Juventus in 1999. At Arsenal he was converted from a winger to a striker, and went on to win a slew of honors, with the club. He also won World Cup and European Championship medals with France and was named in the 2006 FIFPro World XI team. In 2007 he was sold to Barcelona.

GEOFF HURST (born 8 December 1941)
England: 49 games, 24 goals
Sir Geoff Hurst remains the only player to have scored a hat-trick in a World Cup Final, an achievement which ultimately earned him a belated knighthood. Hurst only came into the England side because Jimmy Greaves was injured. As well as his match-winning performance in the final, Hurst scored what proved to be the decisive goal in the quarter-final against Argentina.

RAYMOND KOPA (born 13 October 1931),
France: 45 games, 18 goals
Raymond Kopa was the son of a Polish mining family from northern France. His talent was first spotted by Angers, who then sold him on to Reims in 1950. He was sold to Real Madrid after the Spanish club defeated Reims in the European Champion Clubs' Cup final in 1956. At Real Madrid he won the European Champion Clubs Cup three times and was crowned 1958 European Footballer of the Year. Kopa won four French and two Spanish league titles.

ABOVE Thierry Henry, a record marksman with both Arsenal and France

GREAT PLAYERS & MANAGERS MOMENTS

1930s

1940s

1960s

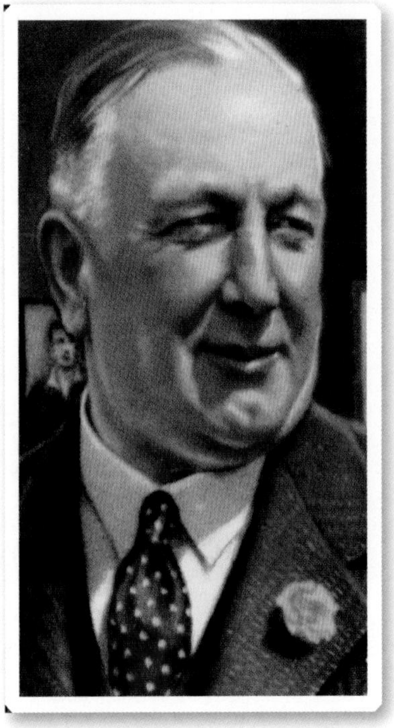

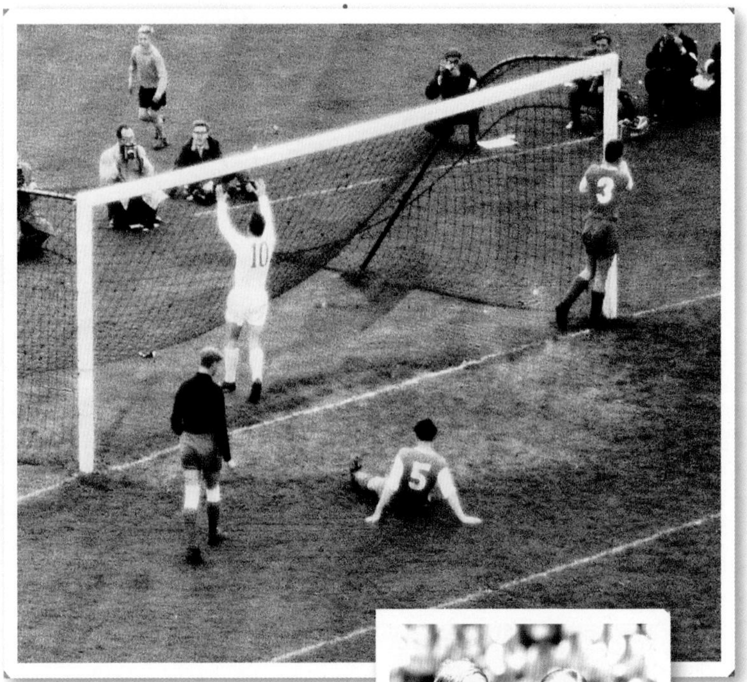

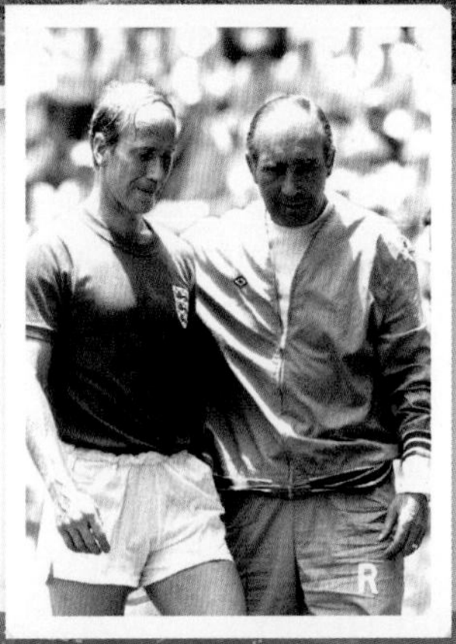

ABOVE Herbert Chapman, Arsenal's first great manager

BELOW Jimmy Hogan staging a coaching lesson for troops

ABOVE Alfredo Di Stefano scores for Real Madrid against Eintracht

RIGHT England boss Sir Alf Ramsey (right) with Bobby Charlton

BELOW Bobby Charlton shoots for goal against France at Wembley

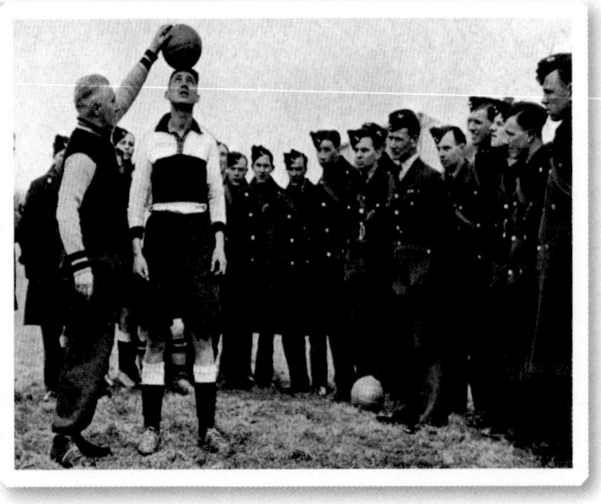

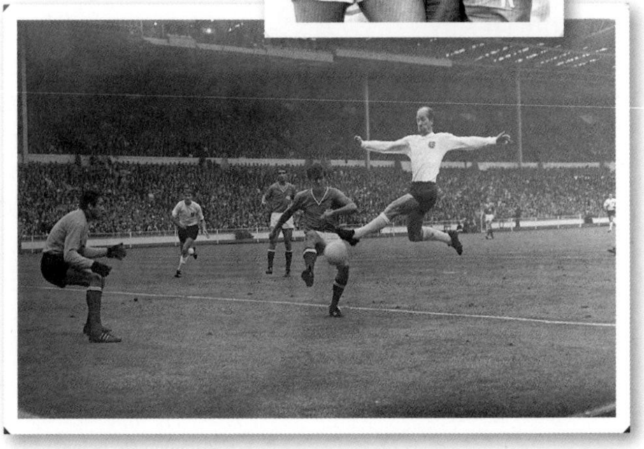

1970s

1990s

2000s

ABOVE Nottingham Forest's Brian Clough in trademark green jumper

ABOVE Sir Bobby Robson points the way for Newcastle

ABOVE Giovanni Trapattoni brings the winning touch to Ireland

ABOVE Mario Zagallo, a World Cup winner as player and manager

ABOVE Arsène Wenger took Arsenal to the double in his first full season

LEFT Sir Alex Ferguson lifted Manchester United to new glory

EUROPEAN PLAYERS

HANS KRANKL (born 14 February 1953)
Austria: 69 games, 34 goals
Hans Krankl was one of the great Austrian center forwards. In 1978 he scored 41 goals for Rapid Vienna, winning the Golden Boot as Europe's leading league scorer. He starred for Austria at the World Cup finals in Argentina, where he netted the winning goal against West Germany—Austria's first victory over their neighbors for 37 years. He went on to play for Barcelona, where he won the 1979 European Cup Winners' Cup.

MICHAEL LAUDRUP (born 15 June 1964)
Denmark: 104 games, 37 goals
Michael Laudrup stood out in Denmark's outstanding team that reached the semi-finals of the 1984 European Championship and the second round at the 1986 World Cup finals. He achieved club success with Juventus before moving to Lazio, and he was part of Johan Cryuff's "Dream Team" at Barcelona where he won four league titles. He also played for for Real Madrid and Ajax.

DENIS LAW (born 24 February 1940)
Scotland: 55 games, 30 goals
Denis Law, whatever the competing talents of Bobby Charlton and George Best, was the king of Old Trafford in the 1960s. His ebullient personality, and his ability to create chances and goals out of nothing, earned him the adulation of Manchester United fans. Law started at Huddersfield Town, and had brief spells at Manchester City and Torino before being brought to Manchester United in 1962. He repaid the club's financial investment with 171 goals in 309 league games. He won the European Footballer of the Year prize in 1964.

GARY LINEKER (born 30 November 1960)
England: 80 games, 48 goals
Gary Lineker made his name with home town Leicester City, but his career took off after his transfer to Everton in 1985. Lineker moved on to Barcelona, winning the European Cup Winners' Cup, and in the 1986 World Cup finals Lineker won the Golden Boot as the leading scorer with six goals. The prolific striker returned to England for a successful spell with Tottenham before ending his career in Japan.

JOSEF MASOPUST (born 9 February 1931)
Czechoslovakia: 63 games, 10 goals
Josef Masopust was a midfield heir in the 1950s and early 1960s to the great pre-war traditions of Czechoslovak football. An attacking midfielder, he played the majority of his career with the army club Dukla Prague before moving to Belgium

BELOW Denis Law takes the high road for Manchester United at Old Trafford

and turning out for Crossing Molenbeek. He reached his peak at the 1962 World Cup in Chile, where he helped to inspire his side all the way to the final. Although he opened the scoring against Brazil for an unexpected lead, the holders fought back to triumph 3-1. Masopust won the 1962 Footballer of the Year award following his outstanding displays in Chile, where he was nicknamed "the Czech Knight."

STANLEY MATTHEWS (born 1 February 1915, died 23 February 2000)
England: 54 games, 11 goals

Sir Stanley Matthews was the first active player to be knighted as reward for extraordinary service to the game both before and after World War II. He was an outside right whose mesmerizing talent earned him the nickname the "Wizard of Dribble." Matthews achieved his ambition to win the FA Cup with Blackpool in 1953, when, aged 38 he famously rescued his side from a 3-1 deficit by setting up three goals. In 1956, he received the inaugural European Player of the Year. His fitness and enthusiasm saw him play at the 1954 World Cup finals and then lead his original club, Stoke City, to promotion back into the old first division in 1962.

GIUSEPPE MEAZZA
(born 23 August 1910, died 21 August 1979)
Italy: 53 game, 33 goals

Giuseppe Meazza was one of only two Italian players—Giovanni Ferrari was the other—to have won the World Cup for the Azzurri both at home and also away from Italy. Meazza was a powerful, goal-scoring inside forward with Internazionale in the 1930s, scoring 287 goals in 408 games for the club. He was a World Cup winner at home in 1934 and was the captain in France when Italy triumphed in 1938. He won three league titles and finished as top scorer in Serie A three times. He played briefly for AC Milan and guested for Juventus and Varese during World War II. He finished his playing career at Atalanta before managing Internazionale.

BOBBY MOORE (born 12 April 1941, died 24 February 1993)
England: 108 games, 2 goals

Bobby Moore proved to be an ideal captain for England, leading them to glory at the 1966 World Cup and also during their unsuccessful defense of the trophy in 1970. He played for the majority of his career with West Ham United, initially as an attacking wing half before moving to the heart of defense. Respected by his team-mates for his tough tackling and silky skills, Moore achieved a remarkable hat-trick at Wembley Stadium by winning the FA Cup in 1964, the European Cup Winners' Cup in 1965, and the World Cup in 1966. A bronze statue of Moore stands outside the new Wembley Stadium. He finished his career with Fulham, San Antonio, and finally Seattle.

ABOVE Stanley Matthews teasing Manchester United's Roger Byrne in an international training session

EUROPEAN PLAYERS

ABOVE Ferenc Puskás, legendary No 10 for Honved and Real Madrid

GERD MÜLLER (born 3 November 1945)

West Germany: 62 games, 68 goals

Gerd Müller was the most prolific goal scorer in modern German football and the all-time top scorer at the World Cup finals. He was voted European Player of the Year in 1970, having scored ten times at that year's World Cup finals in Mexico—he hit successive hat-tricks against Bulgaria and Peru—to finish as the highest scorer and win the Golden Boot. He notched an incredible 398 goals for Bayern Munich, where he was a key figure during the mid-1970s, when they won the European Champion Clubs' Cup three times in succession. He also scored the winning goal for West Germany in the 1974 World Cup final victory over Holland.

FERENC PUSKÁS (born 2 April 1927, died 17 November 2006)

Hungary: 85 games, 84 goals
Spain: 4 games, no goals

Ferenc Puskás is one of the game's all-time greats, famed for his goals, his leadership, and the way that he reconstructed his career after the 1956 Hungarian Revolution. Puskás and Hungary were unbeaten for four years, going into the 1954 World Cup finals as Olympic champions, but fell 3-2 to West Germany in the final. He defected to the West, where he rebuilt his career with Real Madrid and won the league title five times and the European Cup three times.

CRISTIANO RONALDO
(born 5 February 1985)

Portugal: 55 games, 20 goals

Cristiano Ronaldo became Britain's most expensive teenager when, aged 18, he cost Manchester United the remarkable sum of $25 million (£12.4 million) in 2003. At first, the self-indulgence of his trickery on the right wing frustrated fans and team-mates alike, but once he adapted to the difficult demands of the English game, he proved to be equally dangerous on the left wing and a real handful to deal with in the air. In the 2007–08 season, he scored 42 goals in all competitions, which helped guide Manchester United to a double of the English league title and the Champions League.

PAOLO ROSSI (born 23 September 1956)

Italy: 48 games, 20 goals

Paolo Rossi looked a great prospect after the 1978 World Cup finals, but he was banned for two years over a match-fixing scandal. The striker only returned to top-class action weeks before the 1982 World Cup finals kicked off, yet he finished as the top scorer with six goals to his credit. These strikes included a hat-trick to deliver the knock-out blow to Brazil in the quarter-final. Rossi continued to score, helping guide Italy to world champions and himself to the coveted Golden Boot.

MATTHIAS SINDELAR (born 10 February 1903, died 23 January 1939)

Austria: 43 games, 27 goals

Matthias Sindelar was the inspirational center forward of the Austrian "Wunderteam" that ruled European football in the late 1920s and early 1930s. Sindelar, nicknamed the "Man of Paper" because of his delicate build, won a league title, twice triumphed in the Mitropa Cup, and scored five Austrian Cup successes with Austria Vienna. A World Cup semi-finalist in 1934, five years later he died of carbon monoxide poisoning in his Viennese apartment in unexplained circumstances.

HRISTO STOICHKOV

(born 8 February 1966)

Bulgaria: 83 games, 37 goals

Hristo Stoichkov, once banned for life from the sport but reinstated on appeal, was a huge success at club and national team level. In 1994, Stoichkov picked up the European Player of the Year prize and won the Golden Boot as joint highest scorer at the World Cup finals as he inspired Bulgaria to reach the semi-finals. His move to Barcelona in 1990 saw him collect four Spanish league titles and the Spanish cup once.

FRITZ WALTER (born 31 October 1920, died 17 June 2002)

West Germany: 61 games, 33 goals

Fritz Walter owed his life to national manager Sepp Herberger and repaid him in glory. Walter, an inside forward from Kaiserslautern who made his international debut just before World War II, was kept away from the front by Herberger's string-pulling before finally being drafted in 1942. He was captured and eventually repatriated by the Soviet army. He relaunched his football career and captained Herberger's West Germany to their unexpected World Cup final victory over the mighty Hungary in 1954.

LEV YASHIN (born 22 October 1929, died 20 March 1990)

Soviet Union: 78 games, no goals.

Lev Yashin, nicknamed the "Black Spider," ranks as arguably the greatest ever goalkeeper. Originally an ice hockey star, he succeeded "Tiger" Khomich between the posts at Dynamo Moscow in the early 1950s. Yashin won a gold medal in the 1956 Olympics, followed by victory at the 1960 European Championship. In 1963 he became the first goalkeeper to capture the European Player of the Year prize. Yashin played in three World Cup finals, reaching the semi-finals in his last appearance in 1966. He was awarded the Order of Lenin in 1967 and he retired in 1971. He is immortalized in the form of a statue at the entrance to the Dynamo Stadium in Moscow.

ZINEDINE ZIDANE (born June 23, 1972)

France: 108 games, 31 goals

Zidane was the outstanding French playmaker of the late 1990s and early 2000s. He was making headlines until the very last moment of his career—he was sent off in extra time in the 2006 World Cup Final, his last game, for headbutting Italy's Marco Materazzi. He scored twice in France's 1998 World Cup final win over Brazil and also starred for Bordeaux, Juventus, and Real Madrid.

DINO ZOFF (born 28 February 1942)

Italy: 112 games, no goals

Dino Zoff made his name with Udinese and Mantova before making the big time, first with Napoli and later with Juventus. He set numerous records at Juventus and picked up almost every title possible—initially as player and then as coach. Zoff was Italy's goalkeeper captain when they swept past all opponents at the 1982 World Cup finals. Aged 40, Zoff was the oldest player to win the World Cup after the Azzurri thumped West Germany 3-1 in the final. After retiring as Italy's most capped player, he coached Juventus, Lazio, and Fiorentina, as well as the national team, which he guided to the final of the 2000 European Championship.

BELOW Dino Zoff saves against Brazil in the 1978 World Cup

AMERICAS' PLAYERS

ABOVE Alfredo Di Stefano scores for Real Madrid against Manchester United

ANTONIO CARBAJAL (born 7 June 1929)
Mexico: 48 games, no goals
Antonio Carbajal became the first player to appear in the finals of five World Cup competitions, but ended up on the winning side only once. The Leon goalkeeper's debut in the finals was against Brazil in 1950, when he conceded four goals. He played in the 1954, 1958, and 1962 World Cup finals before bowing out after a scoreless draw against Uruguay in the 1966 finals. Carbajal kicked off his career at Mexico City, but played at Leon for the majority of his career.

JOSÉ LUIS CHILAVERT (born 27 July 1965)
Paraguay: 74 games, eight goals
José Luis Chilavert was renowned for his scoring achievements despite being a goalkeeper. He claimed 62 goals from penalties and free kicks in a 22-year career with clubs in Argentina, France, Paraguay, Spain, and Uruguay (Spain was the only country where he did not win at least one league title.) Chilavert's ultimate ambition was to score a goal in the World Cup finals, but he failed, despite having scored four in qualifying matches for the 2002 tournament. He was voted the world's top goalkeeper three times.

ROBERTO CARLOS (born 10 April 1973)
Brazil: 125 games, 11 goals
Roberto Carlos da Silva Rocha proved to be one of Brazil's most popular exports to Europe because of the power of his shooting and the exuberance of his attacking play from left back. In 2002, he won the World Cup with Brazil and the European Champions League with Real Madrid. Roberto Carlos played more games for Real Madrid than any other foreigner, before moving to Turkey with Fenerbahce.

TEÓFILO CUBILLAS (born 8 March 1949)
Peru: 81 games, 26 goals
Teófilo Cubillas shot to stardom as an inside forward in the outstanding Peru team that reached the 1970 World Cup quarter-finals and the second round at the 1978 World Cup finals. Cubillas was voted South American Player of the Year in 1972, and won the Copa America with Peru in 1975. He began his career with Alianza of Lima, then played in Switzerland, Portugal, and the United States.

DIDI (born 8 October 1929, died 12 May 2001)
Brazil: 68 games, 20 goals
Didi, full name Valdir Pereira, won the World Cup twice with Brazil in 1958 and 1962. Brazil might not have even been at the finals in 1958 at all, but for a remarkable free-kick from Didi that bent in the air and flew into the net against Peru in a qualifying tie. The "Falling Leaf" became Didi's trademark and has been copied by players all over the world ever since. He played most of his career with Botafogo of Rio de Janeiro either side of a short, unhappy spell in 1959–60 with Real Madrid.

ALFREDO DI STEFANO
(born 4 July 1926)
Argentina: six games, six goals
Spain: 31 games, 23 goals
Alfredo Di Stefano remains, for many experts, the greatest ever player because of his all-action performances as a pitch-roaming, high-scoring center forward. He starred for Argentina's River Plate and Colombia's Millonarios, before inspiring Real Madrid to victory in the first five European Champion Clubs' Cup competitions. Di Stefano scored in all five finals, and totalled 216 league goals for Real Madrid over 11 years.

LANDON DONOVAN (born 4 March 1982)
United States: 100 games, 35 goals
Landon Donovan promises to be the long-serving, outstanding international that US football has long been waiting for. By the age of 26 the midfielder had already reached a century of international appearances and starred in two World Cup finals. Donovan had two spells with Bayer Leverkusen, but has preferred to play in the United States, latterly for Los Angeles Galaxy.

ENZO FRANCESCOLI
(born 12 November 1961)
Uruguay: 72 games, 15 goals
Enzo Francescoli, nicknamed "The Prince", is arguably the last great Uruguayan player. However, he played the majority of his club career in Argentina, France, and Italy. He played the 1989–90 season with Olympique Marseille, where he was the footballing hero and inspiration for the teenage Zinedine Zidane. A tall, graceful inside forward, Francescoli was a three-times winner of the Copa America with Uruguay and played twice at the World Cup finals. He was voted South American Player of the Year in both 1984 and 1995.

GARRINCHA (born 28 October 1933, died 20 January 1983)
Brazil: 50 games, 12 goals
Garrincha, full name Manoel dos Santos Francisco, lived a life that was a tale of triumph and tragedy. Nicknamed "the Little Bird," he won the World Cup in 1958 and 1962, with his goals proving to be decisive. He was at Rio's Botafogo for 12 years, scoring 232 goals in 581 games. Yet his love of the good life meant he was also his own worst enemy and a nightmare for coaches. He tragically died of alcohol poisoning.

JAIRZINHO (born 25 December 1944)
Brazil: 81 games, 33 goals
Jairzinho, full name Jair Ventura Filho, was the free-scoring successor to the Brazilian tradition of great outside rights, from Julinho in the mid-1950s to Garrincha in the late 1950s and 1960s. He played, like his hero Garrincha, for Rio's Botafogo. In 1970, he recovered twice from a broken right leg and became the only player to score in every round of the World Cup finals in Mexico, scoring seven goals overall. Jairzinho, nicknamed "God," also played in the World Cup finals of 1966 and 1974. He famously discovered an outstanding 12-year-old in Rio de Janerio, a talent called Ronaldo.

KAKÁ (born 22 April 1982)
Brazil: 59 games, 22 goals
Kaká, full name Ricardo Izecson dos Santos Leite, was generally hailed as having established himself as the world's top player in 2007. During 2007, he set up AC Milan's victory in the European Champions League and was voted both FIFA Player of the Year and European Player of the Year. The supremely gifted Brazilian forward originally made his name with São Paulo, following a remarkable recovery from a swimming pool accident that left him temporarily paralysed. AC Milan paid a comparatively low $10 million (£5 million) for him in 2003.

MARIO KEMPES (born 15 July 1954)
Argentina: 43 games, 20 goals
Mario Kempes emerged with Rosario Central in the early 1970s and was one of the finest prospects on view when he played for Argentina at the 1974 World Cup finals. Valencia snapped up Kempes, who twice finished leading scorer in Spain and was one of only two foreign-based players called up by Argentina boss César Luis Menotti for the 1978 World Cup. Kempes was an inspiration, scoring six goals for the hosts, including two in the extra time victory over Holland.

DIEGO MARADONA
(born 30 October 1960)
Argentina: 91 games, 34 goals
Diego Maradona ranks among the greatest ever players, despite controversy over his off-the-pitch antics and the "Hand of God" goal against England in the 1986 World Cup quarter-finals.

BELOW Argentina captain Diego Maradona had a big hand in winning the 1986 World Cup

ABOVE Bobby Moore with Pelé at the 1970 World Cup

Discovered by Argentinos Juniors, he starred for Boca Juniors before moving for world record fees to Barcelona and then Napoli. Captain and inspiration in the 1986 World Cup finals, his second strike against England is considered to be one of the greatest ever goals. A runner-up in the 1990 World Cup, he was suspended from the sport in 1991 after failing a drugs test, and three years later failed a World Cup finals' doping test.

PELÉ (born 23 October 1940)
Brazil: 92 games, 77 goals
Pelé, full name Edson Arantes do Nascimento, made his league debut for Santos aged 15. One of only a few who could realistically claim to be the greatest footballer who ever played, he was a World Cup winner at 17—scoring twice in the 5-2 victory over Sweden in the 1958 final. Injury prevented Pelé playing in the 1962 World Cup final and he endured an unhappy tournament in 1966, but he was back at his best for the 1970 final and scored in the 4-1 win over Italy. He came out of retirement in 1975 to help New York Cosmos spearhead the North American Soccer League revolution before hanging up his boots in 1977, having amassed over 1,000 goals.

RONALDINHO (born 21 March 1980)
Brazil: 80 games, 32 goals
Ronaldinho, full name Ronaldo de Assis Moreira, was the attacking midfielder who inspired Barcelona to two league titles and also victory in the 2006 Champions League. He joined Barcelona after spells with Grêmio in Brazil and Paris Saint-Germain. A key figure in Brazil's 2002 World Cup win, Ronaldinho was voted FIFA World Player of the Year in 2004 and 2005.

RONALDO (born 22 September 1976)
Brazil: 97 games, 62 goals
Ronaldo Luis Nazário de Lima was discovered as a 12-year-old by World Cup-winning hero Jairzinho. Five years later, he was at the 1994 World Cup, albeit a non-playing member of the Brazilian squad. In 1998, he was a runner-up amid controversy—playing despite having been taken ill shortly before Brazil's listless final defeat by France. Ronaldo made amends by scoring twice in the 2002 World Cup final win over Germany and scored a record 15th goal at the 2006 World Cup finals. Knee injuries have marred much of his senior career with PSV Eindoven, Barcelona, Internazionale, Real Madrid, and AC Milan.

HUGO SÁNCHEZ (born 11 July 1958)
Mexico: 58 games, 29 goals
Hugo Sánchez numbers among the most prolific scorers in the history of Mexican football and as one of its greatest personalities. He led the attack in three World Cup finals, and ranks as the second-highest overall scorer in Spain's La Liga, with 234 goals amassed at Athletic Madrid and Real Madrid. He was the international manager of Mexico for 16 months until March 2008.

HECTOR SCARONE (born 1 January 1900, died 4 April 1967)
Uruguay: 51 games, 31 goals
Héctor Scarone, nicknamed "the Magician," was the original star of the World Cup after leading Uruguay to victory over Argentina in the inaugural finals in 1930. He played briefly in Europe with Barcelona and Internazionale, and for two seasons with Palermo. He won eight Uruguayan league titles and scored 301 goals in 369 games with Nacional Montevideo.

ALBERTO PEDRO SPENCER

(born 6 December 1937, died 3 November 2006)

Ecuador: 11 games, four goals (four games, one goal for Uruguay)

Alberto Pedro Spencer is record scorer in the history of the Copa Libertadores. He scored 54 goals in 12 years, mostly for Uruguay's Peñarol, and was the first world-famous Ecuadorian player. Spencer had been recommended to Peñarol, with whom he went on to win two World Club Cups and eight league titles, by Juan Lopez—Uruguay's manager for the 1950 World Cup win in Brazil.

CARLOS VALDERRAMA

(born 2 September 1961)

Colombia: 111 games, 11 goals

Carlos Valderrama, nicknamed "The Kid," was a colorful character who led Colombia from midfield at the World Cup finals of 1990, 1994, and 1998. He was renowned almost as much for his outrageous, long blond hair as for his supreme talent. He was voted South American Player of the Year and represented Colombia a record 111 times. Valderrama spent most of his 22-year career in Colombia, although he played for Montpellier in France and Real Valladolid in Spain before a six-year career in the United States' MLS.

OBDULIO VARELA (born 20 September 1917, died 2 August 1996)

Uruguay: 49 games, 10 goals

Obdulio Varela was the attacking center half who captained Uruguay to World Cup victory in 1950. Varela apparently told the team to ignore their manager's talk and follow his orders—they bounced back with two goals to spring one of the World Cup's greatest shocks: a 2-1 win over Brazil.

IVAN ZAMORANO (born 18 January 1967)

Chile: 69 games, 34 goals

Ivan Zamorano was Chile's iconic hero in the 1990s, when he led the national team's World Cup attack and starred in European football. Zamorano was brought to Europe by the Swiss club Saint Gallen. After three terms he moved to

the Spanish La Liga for six seasons. In 1995 he was the league's top scorer, with 27 goals for Real Madrid. He went on to win the 1998 UEFA Cup with Internazionale before returning to Chile with Colo Colo via a two-year stint in Mexico.

ZICO (born 3 March 1953)

Brazil: 88 games, 66 goals

Zico, full name Artur Antunes Coimbra, shot to stardom with Rio de Janerio's Flamengo in the mid-1970s. He followed his 16-year career in Brazil with a two-year spell with Udinese in Italy before returning to Flamengo. However, despite being a legendary Brazil forward, he failed to win a World Cup and missed a crucial World Cup quarter-final penalty against France in 1986. He won the 1990 World Club Cup, inspiring Flamengo's victory over Liverpool, then coached with success in Japan and Turkey.

ABOVE Zico takes on Argentina's Jorge Olguín in the 1982 World Cup finals

1970s

ABOVE Gerd Müller, triple European champion with Bayern Munich

ABOVE Sepp Maier in training in Munich's Olympic stadium

LEFT Franz Beckenbauer hoists aloft the World Cup in 1974

BELOW Uli Hoeness finds space in the World Cup final

BELOW Franz Beckenbauer (left) closes in on England's Colin Bell

1980s

1990s

2000s

ABOVE France winger Didier Six (right) takes on the Czech defense

BELOW Ossie Ardiles in English action for Tottenham

ABOVE David Beckham strikes a winning penalty against Argentina

ABOVE Eric Cantona making his debut for Manchester United

ABOVE Steve Gerrard celebrates another of his England goals

LEFT Cristiano Ronaldo top-scored with 31 goals in the 2008 Premier League

REST OF THE WORLD

ABOVE Hong Myung-Bo is challenged by Mexican forward Cuauhtemoc Blanco in 1998

DIDIER DROGBA (born 11 March 1978)
Ivory Coast: 52 games, 33 goals
Didier Drogba was a late starter, not making his professional breakthrough until he was 20 with French club Le Mans. He moved on to Guingamp in the French first division at the age of 24 before being bought by Marseille, who he led to the 2004 UEFA Cup final. His next step was a transfer to newly-enriched Chelsea for a then club record $48 million (£24 million). He has scored over 70 goals in four seasons for the club and has won the Premier League, FA Cup, and League Cup. He was named African Player of the Year in 2007.

SAMUEL ETO'O (born 10 March 1981)
Cameroon: 76 games, 31 goals
Samuel Eto'o is an explosive Cameroon striker who was brought to Europe by Real Madrid.

However, he failed to impress the club and was sold. He has made them regret it with four wonderful seasons each at Mallorca and then Barcelona. In 2006, Eto'o won the Golden Boot as Europe's leading league scorer with 26 goals, helping to fire Barcelona to their Champions League success over Arsenal as well as winning the Spanish Super Cup.

HONG MYUNG-BO
(born 12 February 1969)
South Korea: 135 games, nine goals
Hong Myung-Bo was the first Asian player to appear in four World Cup finals tournaments. Originally a powerful defensive midfielder, he was soon switched to central defense. He made his international debut in 1990 and was chosen to be part of the South Korean World Cup squad in Italy later that year. He earned international admiration for his displays in the 1994 and 1998 World Cup finals, despite the first round exits. He was a national hero long before he captained South Korea to the final four on home territory at the 2002 World Cup finals.

HOSSAM HASSAN (born 10 August 1966)
Egypt: 170 games, 69 goals
Hossam Hassan is the world's second most capped player with 170 appearances for the Pharaohs, just behind Mohammed Al Deayea's 181 games for Saudi Arabia. He has yet to announce retirement and continues to break Egyptian records: winning 41 titles as a player, playing 21 matches over seven African Nations' Cup competitions, and being the oldest scorer in an Egyptian national shirt. Hossam has also played for Paok Saloniki in Greece, Neuchatel Xamax in Switzerland, and El-Ain in the UAE.

ROGER MILLA (born 20 May 1952)

Cameroon: 102 games, 28 goals

Roger Milla had long been an African hero before his goal-celebrating dance around the corner flags brought him global fame at the 1990 World Cup. Milla scored four times at those finals, making him the oldest ever World Cup goal scorer at the age of 38. He returned to the World Cup finals four years later, before retiring with an impressive career record: he twice picked up the African Player of the Year award (1976 and 1990), and in 2007 was voted the best African Player of the last 50 years by the Confederation of Africa (CAF).

HIDETOSHI NAKATA

(born 22 January 1977)

Japan: 77 games, 11 goals

Hidetoshi Nakata was the first Japanese player to make a major impact in Europe. Nakata had been hailed Asian Player of the Year before his 1998 World Cup finals debut. He played in the next two World Cup finals, announcing his shock retirement immediately after the 2006 World Cup match against Brazil in Germany. Nakata played seven seasons for various sides in Italy's Serie A and had a short spell in England's Premier League with Bolton Wanderers.

JAY-JAY OKOCHA (born 14 August 1973)

Nigeria: 74 games, 14 goals

Augustine "Jay-Jay" Okocha provided the midfield command that lifted Nigeria's "Super Eagles" out of the nearly-rans of Africa to near-regular appearances at the World Cup finals. He played in the 1994, 1998, and 2002 finals, but the "Super Eagles" somehow failed to qualify for the 2006 World Cup finals. Okocha helped Nigeria win the 1996 Olympic gold medal and was a recipient of the African Player of the Year award. He played for a variety of clubs in Germany, Turkey, France, and England. At the end of the 2007–08 season, after helping Hull City to attain Premier League status, he was released from his contract.

SAEED AL-OWAIRAN

(born 19 August 1967)

Saudi Arabia: 50 games, 24 goals

Saeed Al-Owairan won the accolade of the Asian Player of the Year in 1994, largely thanks to his memorable solo strike against Belgium in that year's World Cup finals. His goal for Saudi Arabia was comparable with Diego Maradona's sensational strike against England in 1986. Saeed Al-Owairan had only played as a professional for two years before his famous goal.

LEFT Samuel Eto'o celebrates yet another goal for Barcelona in 2008

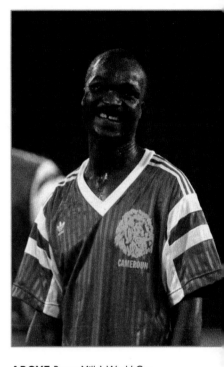

ABOVE Roger Milla's World Cup exploits earned him a string of international awards

INDEX